Judicial Dis-Appointments

Judicial Dis-Appointments

Judicial Appointments Reform and the Rise of European Judicial Independence

MITCHEL DE S.-O.-L'E. LASSER
Jack G. Clarke Professor of Law, Cornell Law School

OXFORD
UNIVERSITY PRESS

OXFORD
UNIVERSITY PRESS

Great Clarendon Street, Oxford, OX2 6DP,
United Kingdom

Oxford University Press is a department of the University of Oxford.
It furthers the University's objective of excellence in research, scholarship,
and education by publishing worldwide. Oxford is a registered trade mark of
Oxford University Press in the UK and in certain other countries

First Edition published in 2020

Impression: 1

Published in the United States of America by Oxford University Press
198 Madison Avenue, New York, NY 10016, United States of America

British Library Cataloguing in Publication Data

Data available

Library of Congress Control Number: 2020937007

ISBN 978–0–19–886885–9

Printed and bound by
CPI Group (UK) Ltd, Croydon, CR0 4YY

For
Liz, Sacha and Zoe

Acknowledgments

This book has been years in the making. It began in a thoroughly enjoyable manner, over an intimate meal among friends in Cornell Law School's Peace Tower. I had prepared a simple dinner for a scholar visiting from abroad, a good friend who had come to Ithaca for a couple of weeks with his wife and son to deliver a few lectures. Catching up on friends and colleagues we had in common, he described the tragicomic professional disappointment that one of them had recently endured. I knew right away that I had just been gifted my next major research project. I would never have imagined that it would take so much time and work to bring it to fruition. But it has been a delight at (almost) every stage.

As should become apparent over the course of the ensuing pages, the research not only raised challenging theoretical problems, but also posed tremendous practical difficulties. In order to write knowledgeably about the realities of highly opaque judicial appointments processes and about the puzzling European efforts to reform them, I needed to engage in private conversations with a host of key figures. This required extensive travel not only to Luxembourg and Strasbourg, but also to a long list of European capitals in order to engage in discreet *tête-à-têtes* with knowledgeable judicial, academic, and political insiders at both the national and the supranational levels. For me, such research is candy. For my interlocutors, I am not so sure!

I must therefore give my heartfelt thanks to a list of contacts far too long to enumerate here. Among the most important, I must include especially Matej Acetto, John Bell, Isabelle Berro-Lefèvre, Michal Bobek, Tamara Ćapeta, Jean-Paul Costa, Andrew Drzemczewski, Anna Falk, Stéphanie Francq, Olivier Fuchs, Daniele Gallo, Janneke Gerards, Michele Graziadei, Dieter Grimm, Helen Keller, Charlotte Hellner Kirstein, Renate Jaeger, Christophe Jamin, Irène Kitsou-Milonas, Zdenek Kuhn, Koen Lenaerts, Carl Otto Lenz, Rob Linham, Miguel Maduro, Mikael Madsen, Jonathan Mance, Thomas Markert, Roberto Mastroianni, Peter Mueller-Graff, Fernanda Nicola, Peter Paczolay, Ana de Palacio, Jan Passer, Robert Pelikán, Tamara Perišin, André Potocki, Gonçalo Ribeiro, Siniša Rodin, Jean-Marc Sauvé, Wojciech Sawicki, Kim Lane Scheppele, Evelyne Serverin, Bernard Stirn, Giuseppe Tesauro, Patrick Titiun, Alan Uzelac, Fredrik Wersäll, Jim Whitman, and Luzius Wildhaber. I have listed their names alphabetically in order to avoid assorted complications; and I have omitted the names of those who asked that I do so.

I also need to express enormous gratitude to my home institution. Cornell Law School has been my intellectual and professional home for almost fifteen years. It has offered unparalleled institutional and scholarly support. More importantly, it has given me lifelong friends and colleagues whose intellectual and personal engagement continues to be the source of daily joy. I can think of no more bright, fun and challenging a set of dinner companions than the colleagues from the Law School and around campus that Liz and I have routinely welcomed on short notice to our home in Ellis Hollow: Diane Brown, Wendy Brown, Cynthia Chase, Sherry Colb, Jonathan Culler, Mike Dorf, Paul Fleming, Jason Frank, Sital Kalantry, Caroline Levine, Odette Lienau, Andre Marmor, Jens and Nancy Ohlin, Liz Peck, Eduardo Peñalver, Aziz Rana, Camille Robcis, Nelson Tebbe, Chantal Thomas, Gerald Torres, Brad Wendel, and many more. Writing these lines in the midst of the Covid-19 crisis, I miss them all a great deal.

In addition to creating such a rewarding personal and intellectual life, Cornell Law School has offered a level of sustained research support without which this book could never have gotten off the ground. Though not a quantitative analysis, this project nonetheless required gathering a great deal of data. I needed to find out not only what was going on in the fantastically opaque realm of supranational and domestic judicial politics, but why? Who were the prime movers behind (or against) this or that reform? How were they thinking about the reforms and their potential effects? More generally, how did they conceive of the evolving judicial role and of its relation to the greater legal, economic, political and social universe? And how did the assorted judicial reforms fit into these conceptions? Quite simply: what was on their minds?

To make headway required getting on planes to travel from Ithaca to destinations all over Europe, taking the time to talk to whomever was willing to see me and whomever they then suggested I go see. I did this for years. And Cornell Law School made it possible. In addition to our Dean, Eduardo Peñalver, and his predecessor, Stewart Schwab, special thanks need to be conveyed to the family of Jack Clarke. Jack supported comparative and international legal research at Cornell Law School to an astonishing degree, leaving a lasting mark on legal academics everywhere.

Finally, work on this project coincides almost exactly with the life I have shared with my wife, Liz Anker. Liz is a fiercely committed intellectual who has pushed me throughout to broaden my analytic perspectives and to take more intellectual risks. I cannot thank her enough for doing so: writing the book was much more fun as a result. I hope it is a little more insightful as well. I therefore dedicate the book to her, to our Sacha and Zoe, and to our phlegmatic companion, Louie.

Ithaca
Paris
Lisboa

Table of Contents

PART III: JUDICIAL INDEPENDENCE? AGAIN?

PART IV: A QUALITY DISCUSSION

PART V: SCANDAL!

1
Introduction

To seek social change, without due consideration of the manifest and latent functions performed by the social organization undergoing change, is to indulge in social ritual rather than social engineering.

Robert Merton[1]

In 2009 and 2010, the European Court of Justice (ECJ) and the European Court of Human Rights (ECtHR) underwent separate reforms to their respective judicial appointments processes. Though very different institutions, with very different remits and very different modes of judicial appointment, they adopted very similar—and rather remarkable—reforms: each would now make use of an expert panel of judicial notables to vet the candidates proposed to sit in Luxembourg or Strasbourg. Once established, these two vetting panels then followed with actions no less extraordinary: they each immediately took to rejecting a sizable percentage of the judicial candidates proposed by the Member State governments.

What had happened? Why would the Member States of the European Union and of the Council of Europe, which had established judicial appointments processes that all but ensured themselves the unfettered power to designate their preferred judges to the European courts, and who had zealously maintained and exercised that power over the course of some fifty years, suddenly decide to undermine their own capacity to continue to do so?

This book sets out to solve this mystery. Its point of departure is that it would be a mistake to view the 2009–10 establishment of the two vetting panels in isolation from other European judicial developments. Though these acts of institutional creation are certainly the most notable recent developments, they actually represent but the crowning achievement of a process of European judicial appointments reform that has been running unremittingly since the 1990s. This longstanding and tenacious movement has actually triggered a broad set of interrelated debates and reforms, encompassing not only judicial appointments per se, but also a much wider set of issues, including judicial independence, judicial quality, judicial councils, the separation of powers, judicial gender equity, and more.

[1] Robert Merton, *Manifest and Latent Functions*, *republished in* Social Theory and Social Structure 73, 135 (1968).

Taken together, this broad set of reforms offers an increasingly settled and coherent picture of what European judges and the European courts should be. This new portrait, so fundamentally different from the received depiction of international courts and judges, reproduces in important respects several of the institutional features that characterize the judiciary in most contemporary Civilian jurisdictions; and yet, it fundamentally challenges the conceptual parameters of the classic Civilian judiciary. What is this new portrait and where does it come from? What people and institutions produced it and why did they do so?

As we shall see, both (1) the felt need to engage in such reforms and (2) the eventual substance of those reforms demonstrate a new understanding of what the European courts are and what their place in the European political/constitutional order should be. They evince a rising consciousness of the immense power of the European courts and of their leading role in the European order. The ongoing European judicial appointments reforms crystalize this growing awareness, address the apparent implications of this rise to power, and offer conflicted and conflicting responses to it. On the one hand, the judicial reform debates recognize the European courts' rise in status and power as a necessary feature of the new European order. And on the other, they fear that rise as a potential deformation of, and threat to, proper institutional, political, and constitutional arrangements. This fundamental tension drives the tortured European reform efforts and the fractured manner in which they have played out.

The supporters of the European judicial appointments reforms present them as the necessary entailments of a settled and pre-existing understanding of liberal democracy and of its institutional, conceptual, legal, and constitutional requirements. But frankly, if this were so, then there would have been no need to engage in such reforms in the first place; nor would the substance of the reforms, nor the institutions they created, nor those institutions' norms, procedures, and decisions have provoked such resistance. There is perhaps no better indication of the novelty of this European judicial construction than the felt need to institute these reforms, the long and arduous attempts to establish them, and the assorted forms of opposition that they have encountered. The threat that these new arrangements pose for pre-existing institutional, legal, political, constitutional, and conceptual structures could hardly be more plain, notwithstanding the concerted attempts of reformers to present them as little more than the necessary entailments of pre-existing and generally held understandings.

I believe that it is utterly essential to recognize these tensions and to account for them. This book therefore makes a key methodological assumption that I think best to state clearly from the start. It is impossible to understand these assorted European judicial reforms without grasping that they mean different things to different people, that they are pursued for different reasons by different actors with different interests, that their meaning and supposed entailments vary accordingly, and, furthermore, that these meanings and associated entailments change significantly over time. As a result, these reforms should be studied in a number of different ways and viewed through a number of different lenses.

To address fruitfully the seemingly straightforward questions—"Why have these reforms been undertaken?," "What do these reforms do?," and "What do these reforms mean?"—therefore requires a flexible and layered methodological approach. This book constructs one through the sequence of its chapters. To design such a methodology, the first step is to recognize that although the book's subject matter is judicial reform, many of the central characters in this reform are national governments, supranational institutions, and important legal influencers. As a result, the book widens its judicial focus by making good use of existing international relations (IR) theory.

Its second methodological step, however, is to refuse to be drawn into the endless methodological quarrels that have so divided IR theory over the last few decades. To the contrary, the book leverages the diversity of IR theory to bring to light the diversity of different types of actors and interests in play and to underline the substantive, procedural, institutional, political, and conceptual richness of European judicial reforms that might, on first reading, appear relatively straightforward (not to say mundane).

In order to accomplish this analytic task, the book aims to bring together at least three important methodological traditions that are usually treated as competing, if not downright antagonistic. The first is intergovernmentalist theory, whose coldly realist worldview sees international relations as the product of national governments acting selfishly on behalf of their respective State interests. This perspective does in fact generate extremely important insights into the European judicial appointments reforms. As we shall see, these judicial developments actually function as cleverly veiled mechanisms for protecting dominant national interests: they empower some European Member States to exercise control over others.

But that is not the end of the story. The book therefore layers this intergovernmentalist perspective with a "neo-functionalist" and "neo-institutionalist" one.[2] Viewed through this lens, the key players are not so much the Member States and their governments, but the European institutions that they have created over the last fifty plus years (such as the ECJ and the ECtHR, the two judicial vetting panels, the Council of Europe's Committee of Ministers and its subsidiary bodies, and so on). These institutions have gradually developed their own independent interests and agendas; and they have increasingly come to exercise power in a manner that

[2] IR and political science theorists have spilled endless ink on the potential distinctions between these closely associated terms. *See, e.g.*, James Caporaso & Alec Stone Sweet, *Conclusion: Institutional Logics of European Integration*, *in* THE INSTITUTIONALIZATION OF EUROPE 221(ALEC STONE SWEET, WAYNE SANDHOLTZ & NEIL FLIGSTEIN eds.,2001); Paul Colomy, *Neofunctionalism and Neoinstitutionalism: Human Agency and Interest in Institutional Change*, 13 SOCIOLOGICAL FORUM 265 (1998); Neil Fligstein & Alec Stone Sweet, *Constructing Markets and Polities: An Institutionalist Account of European Integration*, 107 AM. J. SOCIOLOGY 1206 (2002).

their Member State creators could not reasonably have foreseen, would likely not have wished, and can now only poorly control.

Finally, constructivist theory cautions us against treating European judicial independence, judicial authority, or judicial quality as fixed ideas or stable values whose meaning and consequences predate their elaboration by the assorted players involved in the judicial appointments reforms. Indeed, we should not even treat the identity and alignments of these players as fixed or foreordained: they are elaborated over the course of their interaction with the judicial issues, whose own meanings and significance shift over time. These issues are sites for debate and contention, not settled and predetermined values; and the players who engage in these contentious debates come together, align themselves, splinter, realign, and so on as the debates develop over time under real world conditions.

These three methodologies, combined and deployed together to make sense of the European judicial appointments reforms, lead to a series of conclusions that I state right now so that they can be kept in mind as we work through this book's detailed account of the many procedural and institutional developments of the last twenty-five years. The first, and by far the most important point, is that the 2009–10 dates associated with the establishment of the two European judicial vetting panels are misleading. The reforms actually date back to the mid-1990s and have continued doggedly ever since.

Historicizing the panels in this manner leads to the book's primary and inescapable conclusion: when one cuts through all of the accompanying verbiage, it becomes increasingly clear that the triggering event for all these reforms was actually the fall of the Berlin Wall and the immediately ensuing push for the mass and speedy accession of Central and Eastern European States of the former Soviet Bloc into the EU and the Council of Europe. This tectonic political shift—which has been almost completely ignored in the academic literature on judicial appointments—generated massive instability and uncertainty, to which the panoply of ensuing European judicial reforms represents a concerted response. These measures were above all an insurance policy against the wildly disruptive potential of doubling the size of the European high courts virtually overnight with judges hailing from as yet unreconstructed "transitional states" from Sofia, to Warsaw, to Moscow.

Viewed from an intergovernmentalist perspective, the judicial reform packages emerge chiefly as a mechanism for the long-established European Member States to control the governments of Europe's newest Member States. After all, each of the new Central and Eastern European judges—whose voting power would match that of their French, German, or British colleagues—would now be joining immensely powerful courts that routinely exercise constitutional authority over all the European Member States. Faced with this stark and impending juridico-political reality, the longstanding Member States of Western Europe made a clear-eyed judgment: they chose to trade some measure of control over their own judges in exchange for the capacity to exert some measure of control over the behavior of the governments of the new accession States, governments whose nature, capacities, and inclinations could not—in the immediate wake of socialist rule—be confidently predicted.

At the same time, the solutions developed to contain these looming risks both reflected and generated important institutional dynamics. In other words, the European judicial reforms also offer a tale of incremental but persistent institutional self-aggrandizement, leading to unanticipated, unintended, and often undesired consequences. To study these reforms is to witness a parade of European and governmental institutions formulating, acquiring, and exercising ever-increasing capacities—or at least doing their level best to do so. These institutions include, at a minimum, the high European courts; the two new judicial vetting panels; assorted European political institutions, such as the specialized committees of the Parliamentary Assembly of the Council of Europe (PACE); expert and academic groupings, such as the Venice Commission and assorted blue ribbon panels convened under European institutional auspices; and even sub-formations of such intergovernmental institutions as the Committee of Ministers of the Council of Europe, which nominally represent the interests of the Member States themselves. Each of these institutional players has taken a very active role in debating, promoting, and managing judicial reforms of assorted kinds, and doing so precisely when mass accession raised intergovernmental anxieties to new heights.

As we shall see, the range and number of such expert legal entities point to the emergence of a highly influential caste of high-grade, politically and institutionally savvy judges and jurists operating simultaneously at three distinct nodes: (1) at the intersection of the domestic and supranational spheres, (2) at the intersection of the judicial and the political (usually civil service) domains, as well as (3) at the intersection of the judicial and the academic fields.

The best example of this increasingly recognizable and important institutional archetype is the Panel established under Article 255 of the EU's Treaty of Lisbon to vet judicial candidates put forward by the Member States to sit on the ECJ in Luxembourg. Once established, this Article 255 Panel quickly took upon itself not only to reject a surprisingly large percentage of candidates to the EU courts, but also to define almost *ex nihilo* the criteria for a proper European judge. Indeed, the 255 Panel has gone so far as to pressure Member State governments to establish—and then dutifully report on—national institutions and processes instituted to select and propose judicial candidates to sit in Luxembourg.

This emergent cast of players and their budding institutional strongholds have had a mixed degree of success in exerting their will over the political entities that initially created them. Unlike the well-positioned and brilliantly managed 255 Panel, the Council of Europe's "Advisory Panel of Experts," established to vet candidates to sit on the ECtHR in Strasbourg, has engaged in public and unseemly struggles with assorted Member State governments and Council of Europe political institutions, leading to repeated scrapes and embarrassments. The 255 Panel, on the other hand, has had a relatively smooth transition to power. Yet even there, one can hardly claim that the overall picture has been an unmitigated success: the 255 Panel appears to have had little success in quelling the increasingly blunt and shrill legitimacy challenges that national sovereigntists (especially Brexiteers) have leveled against the European judiciary in general, and the ECJ in particular.

What this book stresses over and over again, however, is that the current state of the European judicial reforms is by no means the inevitable outcome of some mechanical set of developments. It is not as if the European judicial institutions, their features, their roles, or their relationships with political and other players were somehow preordained by some pre-existing logic of the nature of the judicial role, by some settled concept of judicial independence, by the self-evident requirements of the judicial profession at the supranational level, and so on. This book demonstrates the full extent to which this is simply not the case. The assorted developments have been gradual, piecemeal, and contested at every turn.

Indeed, the current state of the European judicial debates and reforms is the result of the gradual construction of a whole constellation of meanings, interests, alliances, and so on. The notion of judicial independence that is currently dominant within the European judicial institutions has little to do with prior understandings. Similarly, the portrait of the international or European judge, of the qualities she must possess, and of the means to assess, recognize, and value those qualities, has shifted dramatically over the last twenty-five years. Furthermore, although the current procedures and institutions that characterize the European judicial appointments process do possess parallels at the domestic level, they nonetheless represent a major shift from pre-existing practice.

Finally, this complex package of institutional, procedural, legal, political, and conceptual features has been gradually constructed in the context of wildly fluctuating circumstances, ranging from the Cold War, to the fall of the Berlin Wall and the ensuing mass accession of former Eastern Bloc nations into the EU and the Council of Europe, to the financial crisis of 2007–08, to the immigration crisis of 2015, to the ongoing Brexit debates. These pressing events have posed immense and capricious pressures on the European judicial and political institutions, presenting them with vast and evolving legitimacy challenges. The institutional, procedural, and conceptual solutions elaborated in each phase then set the parameters for ensuing developments and crises, posing new challenges to ever evolving judicial institutions. The current phase, characterized by the development of the judicial appointments panels and by the ongoing and associated elaboration of the European doctrines of judicial independence and judicial quality, and by the sometimes dogged resistance to these very developments by governmental and other actors, is no different.

The book concludes relatively pessimistically. It argues that the current solutions—if taken at their word as mechanisms for promoting European judicial authority and legitimacy—are fundamentally myopic. They are professionally conceived, professionally driven, and professionally oriented solutions that are poorly suited to address the shrill, large-scale, populist, and sovereigntist legitimacy challenges that Brexit-style critiques now pose to the European courts. These new challenges, for all of their crass nationalism, do strike at fundamental assumptions and do make increasingly clear not only that the European courts have broken into popular consciousness, but also that they are now rightly understood to be major regulatory players on both the domestic and the European stages. Gone are the days of the European courts' toiling in blessed anonymity: everyone understands that the ECJ and ECtHR are constitutional actors and policymakers of the very first rank. But with this awareness comes the obligation to legitimize the courts, their remits, their methodologies, and their actions to the general public.

For all that the ongoing judicial appointments, judicial independence, and judicial quality reforms may perhaps help to professionalize the European courts before their primary professional interlocutors (including most importantly the domestic supreme and constitutional courts), and for all that these reforms have helped to strengthen the institutional position of the European courts and of assorted associated entities (such as the 255 Panel, the Advisory Panel of Experts, and assorted European committees), and for all that they have enabled the established Western Member State governments to increase the likelihood of appointing acceptable European judges from the new Member States of Central and Eastern Europe, none of this has had much positive effect at all on the large-scale legitimation crisis that the European courts now suffer before the virulent critiques of Brexiteers and their ilk. The reforms are far too modest for that: they represent mere fiddling around the edges of intra-professional relations, rather than addressing the truly massive identity-based representational challenges that those critiques represent.

There is one silver lining, although the need for it is depressing in its own right. As this book's historical analysis clearly demonstrates, it would be an anachronism to think that the assorted European judicial independence and judicial appointments reforms, including the eventual establishment of the vetting panels in 2009–10, were triggered by and directed toward the authoritarian developments currently well underway in Central and Eastern Europe, most prominently in Hungary and Poland: those authoritarian developments post-date almost all of the important European judicial debates and reforms. But this does not mean that the norms, institutions, and procedures that have been established cannot in fact serve to place some restraints on these increasingly authoritarian regimes.

Indeed, it is no accident that Fidesz in Hungary and PiS (Law and Justice) in Poland have each targeted the judiciary in such a concerted manner. Like everyone else, they have come to understand just how central a constitutional player the judiciary has become at both the domestic and the European levels. As is well known, both parties have engaged in programmatic efforts to hamstring their constitutional and other courts, pack them with candidates of their own choice, constitutionalize these changes, and so on. Their judicial (or anti-judicial) efforts have quite logically been directed primarily at domestic judges, and especially at the constitutional courts and judges best positioned to oppose their authoritarian projects.

But for coolly calculating regimes such as Fidesz or Law and Justice, the next logical step is obviously to place judicial allies onto the European courts. Indeed, they would be particularly keen to fill the Strasbourg position. As we shall see, the "national judge" always sits on the panel deciding a case in which his/her country is involved; and in such cases, that country is effectively always defending itself against the charge that it has violated the human rights of the plaintiff. One must therefore presume that any competently authoritarian regime will to seek to immunize itself against such challenges by making tactical decisions regarding the staffing of those institutions tasked to review its problematic behavior.[3] The European judicial reforms will certainly prove useful in combatting such predictable and crude attempts to stack the judicial deck.

The European judicial reforms can therefore play a meaningful role in safeguarding the integrity of the European courts from tactical governmental subversion via judicial appointments. Perhaps such basic protection is all one can reasonably demand. The professionalism required by those reforms can certainly stand in the way of crude attempts at court stacking; and they may help at the margins to boost the authority of the ECJ and the ECtHR before their domestic judicial interlocutors. But such rearguard actions are highly unlikely to generate the positive social legitimacy gains that the judicial reforms were designed to promote for Europe and its increasingly embattled courts.

I. Chapter Summary

The book organized as follows. Part I focuses on the European Union's Court of Justice. Chapter 2 historicizes EU judicial developments by going all the way back to the original 1950s negotiations hammering out the institutional framework of the EU (then the European Coal and Steel Community). The historical record demonstrates that, from the very beginning, the European Member States possessed a strong impulse to have the ECJ protect their interests in the face of the threats posed by the new European institutions. This self-protective impulse went hand in hand with a corresponding desire of the Member State governments to reserve to themselves virtually unchallenged power to appoint judges of their

[3] Needless to say, such a regime can obviously not be as effective at controlling the staffing of international courts as it would be at doing so domestically: as a general rule, it can only hope to control the appointment of one judge—rather than of all the judges—on the court in question.

own choosing. The net result was the adoption of a judicial appointments mechanism that, contrary to appearances, secured national governmental prerogatives as strongly as possible: the requirement of unanimous governmental consent for all judicial appointments actually empowered Member State governments to pick their judges unilaterally, lest they play tit-for-tat with any other government that might stand in the way of their preferred judicial appointment. And thanks to short and renewable judicial terms, their judicial appointees would remain that much more dependent on governmental good will back home.

Given this background, the institution of the 255 Panel represents a truly major development. It establishes a blue-ribbon panel, composed overwhelmingly of leading national supreme court and constitutional judges, to vet judicial candidates put forward by Member State governments to sit in Luxembourg. This new institutional framework fundamentally transformed the unanimity requirement. Instead of shielding national governments from potential opposition to their judicial nominees, unanimity would now shield the 255 Panel from potential governmental overrides: all national governments would have to decide in concert to override a negative judgment made by this newly created blue-ribbon vetting panel. In the post-1989 period, the working assumption that governments could unilaterally appoint their preferred judges had been overturned.

Chapter 3 explains how the 255 Panel, empowered by this institutional and procedural set-up and led by its formidable President, Jean-Marc Sauvé of the French Conseil d'Etat, quickly took a pair of remarkable positions. First, it immediately began to reject a very substantial percentage of the judicial candidates put forward by the Member States to sit in Luxembourg. Second, it decided unilaterally to publish an Activity Report, in which it chose to elaborate in detail its own understanding of the professional characteristics that would serve as the basis for its review of all newly proposed judicial candidates. Published in this manner, and backed up by the Panel's effective enforcement powers, this description became *ipso facto* a binding set of professional requirements that the Panel imposed on all Member State governments and their judicial candidates.

Finally, the 255 Panel has not been content to define and exercise its vetting power in these already impressive ways. In professional and academic writings published under their own names, President Sauvé and his Panel colleague Lord Mance have lobbied openly for the 255 Panel to exercise a broader range of powers. Envisioning the Panel as the "germ of a council of the judiciary within the European Union,"[4] they have pushed for the Panel to exercise an active role in the

[4] Jean-Marc Sauvé, *Selecting the European Union's Judges: The Practice of the Article 255 Panel*, *in* SELECTING EUROPE'S JUDGES: A CRITICAL REVIEW OF THE APPOINTMENT PROCEDURES TO THE EUROPEAN COURTS 78, 84 (MICHAL BOBEK ed., 2015) ["Bobek (2015)"]. Though he does not specifically address such potential expansion of the Panel's remit, Lord Mance does pay a great deal of attention to judicial appointment commissions (especially at the domestic level), whose "scope and diversity" he openly favors expanding. The framing of his analysis suggest that his views are quite consonant with those of his colleague Sauvé. *See* Lord Mance, "The Composition of the European Court of Justice" (The

selection—and not merely in the vetting—of candidates for European judicial office. In so doing, they have effectively sought to regularize the EU courts and the 255 Panel as a proper judicial structure designed along classic domestic lines.

Part II turns its attention to the ECtHR. Mirroring Chapter 2's approach to the ECJ, Chapter 4 historicizes the Court all the way back to the period of its initial creation. This exercise demonstrates just how suspicious the Contracting Parties to the European Convention on Human Rights were of the proposed ECtHR. Though the newly formed Council of Europe had drafted the Convention in 1950, the Court was not established until 1959: the entire decade of the 1950s had somehow slipped by without creating the court that might actually apply the Convention. As if this lack of judicial enforcement machinery were not sufficient to protect the States, the Convention itself included two notoriously "optional" opt-in provisions. Every Contracting State could choose (1) whether to accept the jurisdiction of the Court and (2) whether to accept that individuals could petition under the Convention for redress against violations that the State may have committed. Finally, the Convention established an institutional structure that all but sidelined the Court as a potentially influential actor: it created a powerful Commission that would filter most complaints as "inadmissible" and resolve almost all the rest by diplomatic compromise.

But the ECtHR was abruptly and completely transformed in 1998, when Protocol 11 abolished the Commission and the "new" Court was granted original and compulsory jurisdiction over individual complaints brought to Strasbourg under the Convention. Chapter 3 explains that the sudden transformation of the Court was, as in the case of the reforms to the ECJ, largely a product of the fall of the Berlin Wall: the number of Contracting Parties, which had grown modestly from fourteen in 1950 to twenty-one in 1987, would balloon to forty-one by 2000. Equally important, those new accession States hailed overwhelmingly from the former Soviet sphere. With this sudden and dramatic change in the membership of the Council of Europe, the remit of the Court and of the Convention was radically transformed: instead of a subsidiary and largely symbolic means of human rights protection, the Court would now be tasked with actively and directly applying the Convention in such a manner as to promote "the building-up of fundamental rights, democracy and the rule of law."[5]

This impending transformation, which would expand both the Court's composition and its remit, immediately triggered a wave of debates and reforms regarding judicial appointments, judicial independence, and judicial quality. Council

text of a talk given to the United Kingdom Association for European Law, October 19, 2011) 6–7, available at https://www.supremecourt.uk/docs/speech_111019.pdf.

[5] PACE, Recommendation 1194 (1992) on Reform of the control mechanism of the European Convention on Human Rights, para. 3 (emphasis added).

of Europe institutions passed a long list of measures, such as the Committee of Ministers' Recommendation "On the Independence, Efficiency and Role of Judges," which bluntly demanded that "decisions concerning the professional career of judges should be based on objective criteria, and the selection and career of judges should be based on merit, having regard to qualifications, integrity, ability and efficiency."[6] This demand was then extended to the national process used to select candidates for European judicial appointment.[7] And the demands from Strasbourg kept on coming: the domestic institution tasked with managing the judicial profession (from hiring, to promotion, to discipline) should be a formally established "independent authority with substantial judicial representation," and should apply formal norms via "formal procedures."[8] When seeking to fill a judicial position in Strasbourg, national authorities would have to issue a formal call for candidates in the specialized press, establish and apply formal and transparent procedures for the selection of candidates, and include at least one woman in their slate of three nominated candidates.[9]

At the European level, reforms were instituted to ensure that the procedure for examining and selecting judicial candidates would demonstrate "more efficiency and professionalism."[10] Candidates would now "fill in a model curriculum vitae, so that the Assembly [would] have comparable information at its disposal" when selecting among candidates. Member State governments would have to transmit these three CVs in alphabetical order, rather than in their order of preference.[11] Finally, the candidates would "be interviewed by a sub-committee of the Assembly, for their qualities to be assessed"; this would lead to a formal recommendation to the Assembly.[12] The establishment of the Advisory Panel of Experts in 2010 was thus but the crowning procedural and institutional achievement of a very long line of reforms to the judicial appointments process—and to the adjacent issues of judicial independence, judicial councils, and judicial quality—that dated back to the fall of the Berlin Wall some twenty years before.

[6] Committee of Ministers, Recommendation Rec R (94) 12 on Independence, efficiency and role of judges (October 13, 1994), 6 ["1994 Recommendation on the Independence of Judges"].

[7] *See, e.g.*, PACE Committee on Legal Affairs and Human Rights (Rapporteur: Lord Kirkhill), Report on the procedure for examining candidatures for the election of judges to the European Court of Human Rights 1, Doc 7439, 1403-15/12/95-1-E (1995) ["PACE Report for Examining ECtHR Judicial Candidatures"]; Council of Europe, The European Charter on the Statute for Judges, DAJ/DOC (98)23, available at https://rm.coe.int/16807473ef.

[8] Consultative Council of European Judges, "Opinion No. 1 on Standards Concerning the Independence of the Judiciary and the Irremovability of Judges," CCJE (2001) OP No. 1 ["CCJE Opinion No. 1 on the Independence of the Judiciary"], available at https://rm.coe.int/1680747830.

[9] *See id.*

[10] *Id.*

[11] *See* PACE Recommendation 1429 (1999) on National procedures for nominating judges to the ECHR, PACE Recommendation 1649 (2004) on Candidates for the ECHR, and PACE Resolution 1432 (2005) on Procedure for elections held by the Parliamentary Assembly other than those of its President and Vice-Presidents.

[12] PACE Report for Examining ECtHR Judicial Candidatures.

Chapter 5 explains, however, that once established, the Advisory Panel (APE) suffered a very different fate than its EU counterpart. Like the 255 Panel, the Advisory Panel has objected to a very significant percentage of proposed judicial candidates. Located, however, in a far less institutionally protected and tactically advantageous position and often begrudged by both the PACE and an increasingly obstreperous cohort of Member State governments, the Advisory Panel has faced a series of embarrassing snubs from all directions. On several occasions, national governments intent on naming their preferred judges to a court before which they must defend themselves have effectively ignored the Panel's assessments; and the PACE, treating the Panel as an institutional competitor, has refused repeatedly to back it up. Incensed at such slights, the Panel has made a rather public row, calling—fairly unsuccessfully—for a strengthening of its procedural and institutional position.[13] These conflicts clearly reveal tensions, not to say fissures, between the European judiciary, European political institutions, and domestic political actors. As the ensuing chapters will explain, however, we should not think of these conflicts merely as reflecting existing tensions; they also represent important and sometimes novel legal, political, institutional, and ideological interventions, undertaken by specific actors operating at the intersection of the European and domestic domains, as well as of the legal, judicial, political, and academic fields.

In these confrontations, one can begin to make out the broad outlines of interesting cleavages and alignments, ranging from national and regional divisions (e.g., East vs. West or new vs. established Member States) to institutional ones (e.g., the Advisory Panel vs. the PACE and its committees). To these should be added increasingly evident struggles between political institutions (such as the national governments and the PACE), on the one hand, and judicial and academics players (such as the APE, the ECtHR's presidents, and influential authors), on the other, and the Committee of Ministers teetering somewhere in between.

Parts III and IV begin the process of trying to make sense out of the judicial appointments reforms detailed in the previous chapters. They do so by examining the two themes that have come to dominate the judicial appointments debates: judicial independence and judicial quality. Part IV addresses the issue of judicial independence. Chapter 6 presents the primary literature, which consists of a stunningly long list of judicial independence measures adopted on an ongoing basis by assorted Council of Europe institutions over the last twenty plus years. A 1994 Committee of Ministers Recommendation "On the Independence, Efficiency and Role of Judges," passed during the heyday of mass accession of the new Member States from Eastern and Central Europe, is couched explicitly in terms of "the defence of democracy and the rule of law." The 1998 "European Charter on the Statute for Judges" focuses on the establishment of independent judicial councils

[13] As we shall see, these institutional relationships continue to evolve over time.

as a means to promote "the competence, independence and impartiality" of the judiciary. The Opinion No. 1 on "Standards Concerning the Independence of the Judiciary and the Irremovability of Judges," adopted in 2001 by the Consultative Council of European Judges, reveals a growing frustration with Eastern European judicial developments and advances an increasingly aggressive position on the requisite stature of the judiciary at both the domestic and the supranational levels. And the list of oft-repetitious measures goes on.

Chapter 7 then turns to the secondary literature on judicial independence. Relatively little time will be spent on the classic notion of the term, which, to cite Lewis Kornhauser's devastating critique, has proven "not useful": "judicial independence" simply cannot be isolated from other closely associated analytic terms, such as the separation of powers or the rule of law; and it inevitably hinges on fundamentally contested notions of adjudication.[14]

The chapter focuses instead on more tactical accounts of judicial independence, such as those put forward by Martin Shapiro; by Lee Epstein, Jack Knight, and Olga Shvetsova; by Nuno Garoupa and Tom Ginsberg; and, to return to the sources, by William Landes and Richard Posner. For all their differences, these tactical accounts hold in common the idea that judicial independence should not be treated as a self-evident virtue in its own right, nor just as a mechanism to help promote other rule of law values, but as a tool to advance the interests of particular institutional players in their struggles against others. This analytic perspective thus calls attention to the particular players and interests involved and stresses how judicial independence (and/or judicial accountability) can be tactically deployed as weapon or shield, as the case may be. Above all, judicial independence emerges in these works as a mechanism for entrenching a desired state of affairs, and thus as a tool for savvy institutional players to protect their interests and prerogatives in periods of large-scale political, institutional, ideological, or other uncertainty.

The chapter concludes by launching the book's in-depth analysis of the European judicial appointments reforms. It leverages the tactical accounts to generate a predominantly intergovernmentalist account of the ongoing judicial independence and judicial appointments debates/reforms. It explains that the European judicial appointments puzzle possesses two key features. First, these European judicial independence and appointments debates/reforms function in a multi-level environment. The ECJ and the ECtHR are of course European courts: they operate at the European level. But they also interact quite directly with domestic-level institutions, including not only the domestic courts, but also the national political authorities that proposed their judicial candidates in the first place. The underlying difficulty that drives so much of the judicial independence and judicial

[14] *See* Lewis Kornhauser, *Is Judicial Independence a Useful Concept*, *in* JUDICIAL INDEPENDENCE AT THE CROSSROADS: AN INTERDISCIPLINARY APPROACH 45 (STEPHEN B. BURBANK AND BARRY FRIEDMAN eds.,2002).

appointments debates in this multi-level context is that European judges and judicial candidates can simultaneously be extremely weak relative to domestic political players (e.g., relative to executive branch actors at the judicial appointment or reappointment phase) and yet colossally powerful at the European level (e.g., as ECJ or ECtHR judges at the judicial decision-making phase). This combination carries self-evident dangers: the very same judges who can exert tremendous European legal power can be terrifically professionally vulnerable back home. No wonder judicial independence and appointments issues are proving so volatile and important.

What this does not really explain is why these issues suddenly burst onto the scene as pressing matters in 2009–10. The first answer, already suggested, is that the 2009–10 date associated with the establishment of the two judicial vetting panels is misleading. The reforms actually date back to the mid-1990s and have continued unrelentingly ever since. When placed in appropriate historical perspective, these reforms emerge as a clever response to the tremendous instability threatened by the rapid mass accession of former Eastern Bloc countries to the EU and the European Convention on Human Rights (ECHR). Faced with the sudden doubling of judges at the ECJ and the ECtHR, and fully cognizant of the immense power wielded by those European courts, including in such charged contexts as the global financial crisis of 2008 and the impending European migration crisis, the established Member States were abruptly willing to accept what they had been unwilling to countenance since the very creation of those courts in the 1950s: the establishment of norms, procedures, and institutions that could impinge on their own ability to select "their" judges effectively at will.

Viewed through a tactical lens, the European judicial independence measures appear not so much as mechanisms to ensure the independence of European judges and courts from European political authority, but as devices to ensure the independence of individual judges from their national governments. This in turn suggests that the judicial independence measures are first and foremost judicial accountability mechanisms, if by this we mean devices for ensuring that the new accession States from Central and Eastern Europe can be held accountable to their more established Western European counterparts for their choice of judicial candidates. This governmental accountability for judicial appointments might provide some stability in the face of the disruption that might be caused not only by adding new and large-scale political uncertainty, but also by diluting established judicial votes by half virtually overnight.

Part IV pursues this tactical analysis. Once we understand that established and new Member States hold different interests with respect to judicial independence, and that judicial independence for some actually means governmental accountability toward the others, a new tactical puzzle emerges. Given the ever increasing power of the ECJ and ECtHR, it would not have been attractive for the established Member States to trade away the judicial appointment powers that they had long guarded so zealously. Might there be some way to maintain as much of these powers as possible while simultaneously holding the governments of the newly acceded States to account for their choice of judicial candidates?

Chapter 8 describes the two-pronged solution to this dilemma. The first part was the elaboration of a laundry list of norms, procedures, and institutions formalizing the process of European judicial appointments. In order to satisfy Council of Europe requirements, for example, Member States must make formal and public calls for candidates to fill judicial positions on the European courts; they should formally adopt and apply formal procedures for examining these candidates, and so on. The same holds true at the European level, where the assorted institutions involved in judicial appointments—including the elaborate committee and subcommittee structures instituted by the Council of Europe, the PACE, the APE, the EU's Council, and Article 255 Panel, and so on—must now do the same. But this formalization goes well beyond the procedural realm, as is demonstrated, for example, by the PACE's adoption of carefully elaborated norms about the required gender breakdown of candidate lists, the linguistic proficiency of candidates, and so on. Indeed, this tendency has even manifested itself on the institutional front, as the establishment of such formal and dedicated institutional mechanisms as the Article 255 Panel, the APE, domestic judicial councils, etc. demonstrates so clearly.

The second, and deeply related, part of the solution has been the increasingly strident focus on the theme of judicial "quality." This theme, which emerged on the eve of the great 2004 accession of twelve new Member States to the EU and which intensified on the eve of the 2009–10 establishment of the 255 Panel and of the APE, has continued to flourish in European institutional and academic debates ever since. The two European judicial vetting panels, for example, have gone to significant lengths to define the attributes of properly qualified candidates for appointment to the ECJ and the ECtHR.

Chapter 9 explains that the combination of these two solutions has yielded a regime of "formalized quality" (to coin an inelegant—if descriptively faithful—term) that operates quite differently for the established and the new accession States of Europe. Endowed with relatively large populations and with legal institutions (including educational ones) that have coevolved with Europe over decades, the longstanding Western Member States were not meaningfully challenged by the formal quality demands placed on their judicial selections. The same cannot be said for almost all of the new accession States from the former Eastern Bloc. With relatively small populations, few jurists versed in European law, and a legal profession largely compromised by its associations with the fallen socialist political regimes, the governments of the new Member States felt the full brunt of the quality demands now formalized into European norms and procedures: they were poorly positioned to play favorites between, and thus demand fealty from, qualified judicial candidates. In short, the formalized quality regime could generate a good deal of judicial independence of Eastern judicial figures from their governments, while subjecting those governments to a good deal of accountability to the West for their judicial nominations. Better yet, thanks to the demographic and historical asymmetries between Eastern and Western Europe, this regime effectively permitted the Western European governments to purchase this accountability at low cost, that is, with a minimum of disruption to their own traditional appointment prerogatives. This regime has therefore served as an inexpensive but effective insurance policy that protects the established European "acquis" from major political and/or judicial disruption originating from the East.

Part V adds another layer to the loosely intergovernmentalist approach deployed in the two preceding chapters. Rather than focus exclusively on the varied interests of different national governments in European judicial appointments reform, it turns its attention toward a wide assortment of institutional players, ranging from the two high European courts, to the domestic supreme courts, to particular classes of judges on those courts, to the two European appointments panels and the PACE Committee on the Election of Judges, to assorted academic and administrative players.

In order to reorient its analysis toward these other players, this Part deploys a methodology that is a loose hybrid of two others. The first is fundamentally neo-functionalist and neo-institutionalist in orientation. It recognizes the full extent to which such institutions have gone their own way, despite their initial creation by national governmental actors. It examines how these institutions have developed and advanced their own agendas and interests, sometimes in ways that stray quite far from what the national governments might have predicted and wished *ex ante* (and often *ex post*). Surely, none of the European Member States imagined, never mind expected and desired, that the 255 Panel would take it upon itself unilaterally to require that each Member State explain and justify the process by which it had selected the particular candidate it was proposing to sit in Luxembourg. Rare indeed would be the Member State government that would welcome such meddlesome oversight over how it makes its own decisions about how to staff high-level positions.

The second perspective is more constructivist in orientation:[15] it resists treating European judicial independence, judicial authority, or judicial quality—or even the judicial maintenance of European legal stability (such as the *acquis communautaire*)—as values that are self-evident, fixed, and foreordained. To the contrary, it suggests that these issues and values can only be properly understood by examining them as sites for debate and contention, indeed, as interventions that not only

[15] For classic statements of constructivist theory in the political science and international relations literature, *see, e.g.*, Emanuel Adler, *Seizing the Middle Ground: Constructivism in World Politics*, 3 Eur. J. Int. Relat. 319 (1997); Peter J. Katzenstein ed., The Culture of National Security: Norms and Identity in World Politics (1996); John G. Ruggie, *What Makes the World Hang Together? Neo-utilitarianism and the Social Constructivist Challenge*, 52 Int. Org. 855 (1998); Alexander Wendt, *Anarchy is What States Make of It*, 46 Int. Org. 391 (1992).

shape the contours and content of those values, but that also reformulate the interests, identities, and alignments of all the players involved.

In order to add this institutional and ideological perspective to the state-centered approach of the previous two chapters, Part V focuses its attention on a persistent feature of the European judicial appointment debates over the last fifteen to twenty years: *scandal*. These debates have disclosed a series of unsavory episodes, especially regarding appointments to the ECtHR. Member States have retaliated against judges who have crossed them in sensitive cases. They have attempted—sometimes successfully—to place seemingly unqualified or unsuitable judicial candidates in Strasbourg for patently self-serving and inappropriate reasons. The PACE's Committee on Elections has at times played along with such governments by favoring less qualified candidates. And the PACE itself has repeatedly permitted these governments to ignore the APE; indeed, it has even elected judges the APE and/or the Committee on Elections had branded as unqualified or otherwise unsuitable. These scandals, which helped to provoke European judicial appointments reform (including the establishment of the two European vetting panels), have nonetheless failed to vanish once those reforms were instituted. To the contrary, the APE has itself reported repeatedly and publicly on such scandals in pointed and ongoing exchanges with other institutions of the Council of Europe.

Leading with a series of such scandals, Chapter 10 describes the privileged information that has been made more or less publicly available by these unpleasant controversies. It examines who has disclosed such information and what they have done with it. It uses this set of disclosures as a means to study the perspectives and interests of classes of players who cannot be easily assimilated to State governments, such as particular groupings of academics, civil servants, judges, and institutions. It elaborates explanations by adopting a dynamic understanding of the relationship between these players and the normative, institutional, and ultimately conceptual structures within which—and on which—they operate.

In order to make the most of such disclosures, Chapter 11 puts to use the existing theoretical literature on scandal. This literature, elaborated primarily in the fields of sociology, anthropology, and political science, proves immensely useful for teasing out and making sense of the European judicial appointments debates. In all its variations, this literature insists that scandal ought not be treated as a simple and pre-existing event. Scandal is instead an unpredictable struggle over norms and values that unfolds dynamically over time. It is a process of making public revelations in an attempt to mobilize forces to challenge and eventually change an existing state of normative, institutional, and/or political affairs.

The chapter concludes by re-examining the European judicial appointments debates and scandals through the analytic prism provided by scandal theory. As we shall see, these scandals reveal a good deal about the pre-existing state of legal, judicial, and political affairs. In particular, they expose tensions and fissures not only between longstanding and newly acceded Member States, between European and other institutions, and between professional and other interest groups, but also between competing visions of the judicial role and its relation to politics, governmental interests, and so on.

But the scandals also *do* something. They forge—or at the very least seek to forge—a novel set of alignments. They seek to create a sense of outrage and to mobilize the ensuing reaction, pointing it in particular directions in order to arrive at new ends. The scandals are therefore a form of political engagement that aims to reorganize and reconstruct existing institutions, interests, and ideologies into new constellations. As a result, they offer a privileged perspective on the dynamic transformation that the European judicial landscape is currently undergoing.

The great advantage of making use of scandal theory is that it prompts us to recognize the full extent to which the judicial appointments debates and their associated themes, such as judicial independence and quality, have been works in progress. As so often tends to be the case, scandals do not merely demonstrate that there has been a transgression of pre-existing norms, though they do tend to present themselves in this guise. Instead, they use their revelations as a means to argue in favor of particular procedural, institutional, normative, and/or ideological positions in an otherwise contested field.

In the judicial appointments context, the scandals are interventions in charged debates over the proper relation between the political and the judicial, over the proper understanding of the separation of powers, over the very meaning of judicial independence, over the proper role of the judiciary, over the proper way of theorizing and legitimizing (or delegitimizing) the European courts and "Europe" in general, and so on. And they have been an important mechanism for waging inter-institutional and professional battles over leadership at the intersection of the judicial, political, and academic domains.

To take those scandals at their word, one might imagine that the executive branches of the established Western European Member States had never played a predominant role in judicial appointments and judicial affairs, that liberal democracy worthy of the name could never exist—never mind thrive—should not elaborate formal firewalls exist between the branches of government, that only a college of elite figures at the intersection of the judicial and academic domains and of the domestic and supranational spheres could possibly manage the rigors and complexities facing the high European courts. For all the kernels of truth in such propositions, we shall see that most are—as a historical, never mind a theoretical, matter—demonstrably and self-servingly false. What scandal theory helps us to see a little more clearly is that such propositions are loaded arguments, not reliable statements of fact; and that they have been put forward by particular players in particular fights designed to arrive at particular conclusions under particular historical conditions.

What the scandals almost always hold in common is that they stress the democratic *bona fides*—or, more accurately, the lack of democratic *bona fides*—of the

Member State governments involved. They are object lessons about what *not* to do in a democratic State. And it is no accident that these lessons emerged precisely at the era of the accession of such a large and destabilizing group of new Member States from the former Eastern Bloc. This major geopolitical—never mind legal—upheaval prompted a reconsideration of the borders demarcating the judicial from the political sectors in Europe, at both the domestic and the supranational levels. The key point is that this elaborate set of debates and reforms was really a *reconsideration* of such borders, not a *reiteration* of settled understandings about them.

The scandals effectively claim that the imputed governments do not understand, or care about, or live up to, the procedural, institutional, political, and conceptual requirements that lie at the very heart of a proper liberal democratic order. But in order to make such claims, the scandals have had to propound a series of novel positions that had never in fact been widely shared before in the established Member States of Western Europe. These were novel positions on the utter centrality of judges in a proper liberal democratic order, on the coequal status of the judiciary in the separation of powers, on the place of fundamental rights in such regimes, and—on a more granular level—on the procedural and institutional firewalls that must protect the judicial appointments process from heavy-handed governmental interference.

In other words, the judicial appointments debates, scandals, and reforms represent a *redefinition* of basic democratic tenets, institutions, and procedures occasioned primarily by mass Eastern accession. This redefinition was therefore overtly (and conveniently) directed eastward. But the reality is that its effects would require—however discretely—significant adjustments in the established Western Member States as well. The endless judicial appointments, judicial independence, and judicial quality reforms of the last twenty plus years indicate quite clearly that, far from operating in a settled conceptual environment, these debated reforms have been taking place on actively contested turf from London to Paris to Rome to Stockholm, never mind from Prague to Chişinău to Moscow.

Part VI endeavors to make sense of the European judicial appointments reforms. Chapter 12 presents seven separate interpretations of these debates and reforms that should be added to the one that this book consistently puts forward as the predominant explanation for the ongoing reforms: the relatively sudden accession of a large number of new Member States from the former Eastern Bloc. On the one hand, the idea is to recognize that there is no one way to make sense out of the complex web of issues, players, interests, positions, arguments, proposals, etc. that have been put into play. To the contrary, it is only to be expected that such highly contested debates and reforms would give rise to contested understandings, conflicted motivations, inconsistent and at times counterproductive claims, and so on. On the other hand, I believe that there exists in fact a relatively small number of dominant takes on these issues and on how they connect with each other, and that by examining them closely, we can see, as through a kaleidoscope, what the European judiciary and European judicial politics are becoming.

Viewed from one angle, the reforms can be understood as the supranational transplantation of institutional forms. In particular, they reflect the rise and spread of judicial councils tasked with overseeing a wide panoply of judicial matters, ranging from appointments, to training, to discipline, to organization. These judicial councils have become utterly standard fare at the national level, to such an extent that the World Bank and others have come to treat them as "part of the standard package of institutions associated with judicial reform and rule of law programming."[16] The establishment of the APE and of the 255 Panel represents the gradual transplantation of this institutional form from the domestic to the supranational realms, starting with the supranational support for the further adoption of national judicial councils, leading to the use of such national judicial councils to help select European and international judges, leading to the establishment of quasi-judicial councils at the European level in the form of the 255 Panel and the APE to vet candidates to the Luxembourg and Strasbourg Courts, leading to the proposed use of the 255 Panel to rank (and thus effectively to select) the judicial candidates applying to serve as judges of the General Court or the ECtHR.

At the same time, the transplantation of the domestic institutional form of the judicial council to the supranational level demonstrates a second impulse: to normalize the European courts, that is, to treat them increasingly as recognizable and routine legal and judicial fora that happen to function at the supranational level. This represents a significant conceptual shift both for the European courts and for the judges who serve on them. From their inception, the ECJ and ECtHR had never appointed their judges via a process of professional training and promotion akin to the processes traditionally operating for "ordinary" judges at the domestic level. Not only had the national governments made sure to institute appointment mechanisms that effectively empowered them to appoint and reappoint (and thus remove) judges more or less as they wished, but they had also originally devised procedural rules that guaranteed that "their" judges would sit on the bench in any important case in which that country was party. Clearly, these judges were understood to play some sort of ambassadorial—or at least representational—role on behalf of their countries' legal and political orders.

By treating European judges increasingly as ordinary judges akin to those appointed by bureaucratic and examination-based means, the reforms demonstrate an impulse to legalize the European courts, to turn them increasingly into professional law appliers as opposed to legal quasi-ambassadors, and thus to turn the European systems into more traditional and positivist legal orders, rather

[16] Nuno Garoupa & Tom Ginsberg, *Guarding the Guardians: Judicial Councils and Judicial Independence*, 57 Am. J. Comp. L. 103, 109 (2009). Needless to say, cause and effect blurs: the World Bank not only reflects but promotes such a rise in judicial councils.

than policy-based systems of intergovernmental negotiation and accommodation. Similarly, they drive against a constitutional understanding of the European courts: they evoke the institutional procedures and professional trappings that traditionally characterize the national civil service judiciaries, rather than the overtly political appointments process that authorizes "neo-Kelsenian" constitutional courts to tackle large-scale political/constitutional controversies. The reforms suggest that the European courts are being (or at least should be) de-constitutionalized and de-internationalized, which is to say, depoliticized.

Third, this judicial legalization/normalization/professionalization represents a key strategy in negotiating the relationship between the European courts and their domestic counterparts. It offers assurances not only to the domestic legal elites, but also, and more importantly, to the domestic high courts, that the processes used to fill European judicial vacancies will be appropriately transparent, standardized, independent, professionalized, and quality-based. It is therefore a means of establishing the all-important authority of the European courts and of enlisting support from their most crucial interlocutors: the domestic high courts.

But the inter-judicial dynamics also run in the opposite direction. For all that the reforms betray a nearly obsessive European fixation on maintaining the authority of the European courts and of their judgments, the central institutional mechanism that has been deployed to do so—an elite vetting panel—has been self-evidently populated by particularly prominent judicial figures recruited from the most eminent domestic high courts. The 255 Panel, particularly effective in this regard, has been presided from its inception by the commanding leader of the French Conseil d'Etat, Jean-Marc Sauvé, and has included such eminent figures as Lord Mance of the UK's Supreme Court, Peter Paczolay, President of the groundbreaking Hungarian Constitutional Court, and most recently and probably most importantly, Andreas Vosskuhle, President of the most influential national court in Europe: the German Federal Constitutional Court. In some very important sense, it is this corps of leading national judicial figures that has coopted the 255 Panel: they have not only taken over quite personally the task of vetting all candidates for EU judicial office, but have also granted themselves the power to define the standards by which such candidacies shall be measured. In so doing, they have effectively become the arbiters of what sorts of judges should fill European judicial positions and thus what the European judiciary in general should look like.

Fourth, this two-way power negotiation not only operates vertically between the domestic and European courts, but also functions horizontally as separation of powers disputes. After all, when the European panels oversee the judicial candidates proposed by the Member State governments for the European bench and the processes by which they were selected, the panels are quite explicitly reinforcing the judicial independence of the European judiciary against interference by the national governments. One can of course visualize such interactions in vertical terms: the *European* courts are being protected from the *national* governments;

but they must clearly be understood in horizontal terms as well: the European *courts* are being protected from the national *governments*. Indeed, this horizontal dimension only becomes more apparent when one recognizes, for example, that the "European" vetting panels are composed overwhelmingly of national supreme or constitutional court judges. As a result, it is the domestic judicial leadership that is currently guarding the boundary between (national) governmental and (European) judicial authority: leading national judges are now controlling how their own national governments are appointing judges to the European Courts. When this new institutional dynamic is added to the long list of normative measures adopted to promote European judicial independence and judicial quality via the judicial appointments process, it is hard not to read these developments as fundamentally reordering the constitutional relationship between the judiciary and the political branches of political authority.

The fifth conclusion is that this constitutional restructuring has generated a set of governing propositions that would likely not have been maintained in *any* European country when, in 1950, national delegates engaged in the foundational debates that eventually led to the creation of the ECJ and the ECtHR. The new orthodoxy was utterly typical of the "rule of law" and "law and development" literatures of the post-1989 period. It held not only that courts should move into the heartland of the national and supranational constitutional orders, ideally as a coequal branch of government, but also that judges and courts must be *the* central institution for defending individual rights and freedoms, safeguarding democracy and the rule of law, guaranteeing the separation of powers, and protecting against oppression by an overweening State.[17]

Although this "neoliberal" civics lesson was clearly addressed in the first instance to the acceding "transitional democracies" of Central and Eastern Europe, one should not lose sight of the fact that this judge-centered focus was as novel in Paris as it was in Prague. Suddenly, the age-old fear of a *gouvernement des juges* was history: one need no longer fret obsessively over the dangers that a retrograde judiciary might pose to a properly representative/republican political order. Not only should public authority be shared more symmetrically between three "coequal" branches of government, but one might even argue in favor of the dispassionate judicial enforcement of vested rights over the oft-misguided regulatory whims of fleeting political majorities.

Viewed through this new intellectual prism, however, judicial power existed on the horns of a dilemma. On the one hand, the judiciary must be empowered to make major rights-based decisions and must be protected to do so free from arbitrary and/or self-serving governmental interference. On the other hand, placing such power in the hands of such judges created obvious risks, as judges

[17] *See, e.g.*, CCJE Opinion No. 1 on the Independence of the Judiciary.

demonstrated a recurring tendency to engage in naïve and misguided "activism," leading to destabilizing jurisprudential interventions on a wide range of important issues. The aggressive judicial elaboration of imaginative doctrines, such as the jurisprudence of fundamental rights and freedoms, could all too often disrupt settled expectations, leading to everything from abusive levels of social benefits, to out of control immigration, to economic and jurisprudential uncertainty, to governmental liability, to emasculated policing, to voting rights for convicts, and so on.[18]

From this neoliberal vantage point, the solution to the dilemma posed by such judicial activism was the very same solution devised to constrain the flood of unpredictable new judges descending from the East: the establishment of judicial screening panels (i.e., the 255 Panel and the APE) that would insist on appropriately stringent judicial quality standards.[19] This solution might of course reflect the crude positivism that often shined through neoliberal theory of the period, ranging from Courts to the World Bank's Doing Business reports, which appeared to suggest that judges could mechanically deduce required judicial outcomes in specific cases from broad statements of rights.[20] But in its more Europe-specific vein, it tended instead to reflect a strong if inchoate deontological conviction that professionalism and quality usually lead in practice to a deliberate and shrewd judicial modesty. As a result, the appointments panels could simultaneously (1) protect the judiciary from the capricious domination of executive branch actors and (2) save the judiciary from the lowbrow attraction of judicial activism.

The sixth conclusion is that these Panels, once constituted, went off on their own paths in a manner that would very likely not have been anticipated or desired by the governmental entities that created them. Far from limiting itself to vetting (more or less seriously) national candidates for European judicial office, the 255 Panel, for example, took upon itself (1) to fashion and impose on the Member States detailed criteria for office that reflected its own idea of a proper European judge; (2) to "invite" each national government to explain and justify the procedure by which it had selected its judicial candidate for Luxembourg, thereby inducing—if not quite ordering—Member States to adopt a selection procedure that included "a public call for applications," an appropriately established and composed "national selection committee" whose recommendations would be followed by the Member State governments themselves, etc.; (3) to reject a remarkably high percentage of judicial candidates put forward by the Member States, including from countries such as Sweden and France (never mind newly acceded countries from the East); and (4)

[18] *See, e.g.*, CJEU judgment of 03.07.1986, C-66/77 Lawrie-Blum; CJEU judgment of 20.09.2001, C-184/99 Grzelczyk; Francovich v. Italy, Joined Cases C-6/90 & C-9/90, 1991 E.C.R. I-05357; Ireland v. UK, Application (5310/71) [1978] Eur. Ct. H.R. 1; Dudgeon v. UK, 45 Eur. Ct. H.R. (ser. A), 14 (1981); Hirst v. UK (No. 2) [2005] Eur. Ct. H.R. 681; Al-Jedda v. UK (27021/08) [2011] Eur. Ct. H.R. 1092.

[19] Djankov, La Porta, Lopez-di-Silanes, and Shleifer did attempt (however crudely) to define what judicial "quality" might mean. *See* Simeon Djankov, Rafael La Porta, Florencio Lopez-di-Silanes, & Andrei Shleifer, *Courts*, 118 QUARTERLY JOURNAL OF ECONOMICS 453 (2003).

[20] *See supra* note 18.

to propose running on its own the selection processes for judicial candidates to an enlarged General Court and to the ECtHR. Although ultimately less effective, the APE has done all in its power to play as powerful a role as possible in the ECtHR appointments process, skirmishing openly with the PACE and its Committees and with the numerous Member States that have publicly thumbed their noses at the upstart Panel.

Finally, Chapter 12 recognizes and describes how the emergence of the APE and 255 Panels offers the clearest evidence of the gradual construction and emergence of a leading professional elite that straddles simultaneously the judicial and academic spheres and the national and supranational divides. This influential grouping brings together jurists based in a hodgepodge of different professional spheres. Many were originally national judges housed within the powerful national civil service judiciaries. Though based in those domestic judicial structures, they have frequently demonstrated a strong interest in European legal or judicial issues by taking part, for example, in assorted pan-European judicial organizations. Many more, however, were originally full-time academics, typically teaching in university law faculties and focusing on European and/or constitutional law. Indeed, some were university professors who then became national judges and then became European judges.

What these jurists have had in common is an abiding scholarly interest in managing the complex relationships between the European and national legal orders. And as this book describes in detail, these academic judges and judicial academics have converged on a common intellectual prism. Reflected in the official work of the Panels, recounted in the published scholarly work of their members, and reiterated in the leading academic analyses of the European judicial reforms, this prism takes for granted the rightful place of the judiciary in the separation of powers, the necessary centrality of the judiciary at the intersection of the domestic and supranational spheres, the fundamental importance of guaranteeing the quality and independence of the European judiciary, and so on. In other words, the elaboration of this cast of professional leaders has gone hand in hand with the elaboration of the intellectual framework that has come to dominate the European judicial appointments reforms.

Chapter 13 concludes the analysis by examining whether the procedural, substantive, institutional, and conceptual framework of the European judicial appointments reforms successfully addresses the legitimacy challenges confronting the ECJ and the ECtHR. As the book explains, the dominant position on European judicial appointments reform insists (1) that European judicial authority and legitimacy need urgently to be shored up and (2) that this should be accomplished largely through judicial appointments mechanisms, including not only proper judicial selection procedures at the national level, but especially proper judicial vetting panels at the European level. The clear assumption is that if judicial quality, competence, and independence were properly assured in the appointments process, then the legitimacy of the European courts would surely follow suit.[21] This chapter challenges this dominant assessment and its associated prescriptions. It argues that they represent for the most part myopic, self-referential, and likely ineffectual professional responses to legitimacy problems that are not only of a greater dimension, but also of a different kind.

The chapter begins by laying out the orthodox analysis and prescription put forward by the major judicial figures, institutional players, and academics involved in the European judicial appointments debates. Then ECtHR President Jean-Paul Costa forcefully voiced this dominant perspective in the urgent letter he sent in 2010 to the Ambassadors of the Council of Europe's Member States, proposing the establishment of a panel of experts to vet judicial appointments to the Strasbourg Court:

> In terms of the future of the Court and therefore the Convention system, one of the decisive factors will be the quality of its Judges. Whatever reforms are undertaken, the system will fail if judges do not have the necessary experience and authority.
>
> The quality of the Judges is important not only to guarantee the high standard of the decisions delivered and the jurisprudence developed. It is also essential because, in a subsidiary system where human rights protection falls primarily to the national courts, the European Court as the ultimate arbiter of human rights issues must be composed of persons of sufficient standing and authority to command the respect of national judges, including senior national judges. If this is not the case, the Court itself will suffer from a deficit of authority and the system will lose credibility and effectiveness.[22]

A long list of judicial, institutional, and academic figures has reiterated this increasingly orthodox set of thematic and programmatic associations. In a more self-congratulatory tone, President Jean-Marc Sauvé of the 255 Panel intoned, "there has therefore gradually emerged, within the European Union, a veritable 'judicial power,' whose independence and legitimacy have been further reinforced by the creation of the Article 255 Panel."[23] Similarly, Professor Michal Bobek (now

[21] *See, e.g.*, Bobek (2015).

[22] Jean-Paul Costa, Letter from the President of the European Court of Human Rights, addressed to member states' Permanent Representatives (Ambassadors) on June 9, 2010 ["Costa Letter"], in PACE Committee on Legal Affairs and Human Rights (Rapporteur: Wohlwend), Report on National procedures for the selection of candidates for the European Court of Human Rights, PACE document 12391 (October 6, 2010) Appendix, available at http://assembly.coe.int/nw/xml/XRef/X2H-Xref-ViewPDF.asp?FileID=12764&lang=en.

[23] Jean-Marc Sauvé, "Le rôle du comité 255 dans la séparation des pouvoirs au sein de l'Union européenne" 9, intervention lors du colloque pour le 130ème anniversaire du Conseil supérieur de la magistrature le 24 octobre 2013, http://www.conseil-etat.fr/fr/discours-et-interventions/la-separation-des-pouvoirs-l-union-europeenne-et-le-comite-255-.html at 3. Sauvé has further argued that the development of this full-fledged European judicial power manifests as the ECJ's emergence as "a veritable

ECJ Advocate General Bobek) states in the Prologue to his leading volume on the European judicial appointments reforms: "A consensus appears to exist on the fact that the expert panels have been put in place in order to guarantee greater professional quality of the judicial appointees, and thusly enhance the legitimacy of both European courts."[24] Current orthodoxy thus consistently underlines the seemingly intimate connection between judicial appointments, judicial authority, and judicial legitimacy.

The chapter opens its critique of this orthodoxy by turning to the important 2013 study published by Başak Çali, Anne Koch, and Nicola Bruch, "The Social Legitimacy of Human Rights Courts: A Social Interpretivist Theory of the Legitimacy of the European Court of Human Rights."[25] As these authors convincingly show, domestic political, judicial, and legal elites do not regard the ECtHR in isolation as a standalone institution. Instead, they always assess its legitimacy by relating it to domestic institutions. Indeed, it is these elites' perception of their own domestic setting that, more than anything else, drives their perception of the Strasbourg Court. Thus, for example, "a politician from the United Kingdom who believes that parliamentary sovereignty is vital to the democratic culture and that the United Kingdom is faring well in terms of domestic human rights protections" is likely to come to a "more reluctant assessment" of the legitimacy of the ECtHR and of its interventions.[26] That politician's perception of the British "human rights situation" and "commitment to domestic institutions" are likely to militate against viewing the legitimacy of the European courts in a positive light.

These findings strongly suggest that the domestic assessment of the European courts is primarily a function of domestic factors over which those courts have relatively little influence or control. If this is true, then tinkering with European judicial appointments reform might conceivably help a little on the margins; but it appears unlikely to alter negative domestic legitimacy assessments in a truly significant manner.

The virulent British critiques of the European courts provide a penetrating, if unpleasant, example of such negative assessments. In stark contrast to the relative obscurity in which they laboured until the 1980s, the European courts have risen to such a level of public prominence that British politicians and the British tabloid press have made escaping the jurisdiction of the ECJ (and perhaps the ECtHR) a central plank of the Brexit agenda. As Theresa May declared emphatically in her May 2016 speech to the Tory Conference:

supreme court, playing the role of motor of European integration and promoter of fundamental rights." *See id.* at 6.

[24] Bobek (2015) at 22.

[25] 35 Hum. Rts. Q. 955 (2013).

[26] *Id.* at 977.

> But let's state one thing loud and clear: we are not leaving the European Union only to give up control of immigration all over again. And we are not leaving only to return to the jurisdiction of the European Court of Justice. That's not going to happen.
>
> We are leaving to become, once more, a fully sovereign and independent country—and the deal is going to have to work for Britain.[27]

As this revealing passage demonstrates all too clearly, escaping ECJ jurisdiction has somehow become a hot button political issue comparable to controlling unwanted immigration.

Chapter 13 examines this astonishing state of affairs in order to draw conclusions about the legitimacy challenges currently facing the European courts. It begins by recognizing the recurring tendency of pro-European commentators to dismiss the virulent critiques of the European courts by harping on their (self-evident) factual and legal inaccuracies. Over and over, ECJ insiders and supporters drive home the same seemingly sensible, but ultimately pedantic, point: misinformation leads to misunderstandings and, ultimately, to misguided hostility.

The chapter argues that this dogged insistence on taking the virulent critiques at their word and focusing on their inaccuracies fundamentally misapprehends the nature of the challenges they pose to European judicial legitimacy. This facile approach leads the supporters of European judicial authority down fruitless analytic and programmatic paths. It allows them to engage in unthreatening policy debates (e.g., over judicial independence and quality) and to promote procedural and institutional reforms that do little if anything to address the core of the challenges they face.

This condescending professional approach represents in effect a useful evasion. It shifts the debate into a register that is comfortably recognizable to high-grade functionaries of the European institutions and their associated academic commentators. Once displaced to that register, the debates can focus on professional qualifications, linguistic proficiency, institutional and procedural reform, and the like: worthy subjects of reform to be sure, but ones highly unlikely to have a meaningful effect on nationalist angst of a very different sort. These are but the debates of professionals, by professionals, for professionals; and as a bonus, they offer excellent windows of professional and institutional opportunity for the high-ranking judicial, academic, and civil service players who engage in them. But these intra-professional debates and solutions misapprehend, and perhaps simply ignore, the large-scale political identity issues that motivate the virulence of the current critiques.

[27] Theresa May, "Britain after Brexit: A Vision of a Global Britain," available at http://www.independent.co.uk/news/uk/politics/theresa-may-speech-tory-conference-2016-in-full-transcript-a7346171.html.

In order to elucidate these issues of political community, the chapter returns to the devastating critique that Joseph Weiler once leveled against the orthodox solutions put forward to handle the EU's notorious "democratic deficit." Those classic solutions had rested on the insight that the EU (then the European Community) had effectively substituted executive for parliamentary authority by transferring domestic parliamentary powers to domestic executives now operating at the European level as the Council of Ministers. Indeed, they argued, this structural deficiency was compounded by the Luxembourg Accord, which effectively permitted national executives to wield unilateral veto power (or threaten to do so) in Council in the name of "very important national interests." The vertical shift of power from the national to the European level had therefore concealed a horizontal shift from parliamentary to executive authority, which had only been magnified via the Luxembourg veto. The proffered solution—which was perfectly logical as a matter of formal democratic theory—was to reverse the parliamentary loss both by increasing the legislative authority of the European Parliament and by doing away with the Luxembourg Accord and its attendant veto. European regulatory power would then be wielded by an appropriately parliamentary body, which would solve Europe's legitimacy crisis.

Weiler's devastating response was that Europe's legitimacy shortage was not a problem of formal democratic theory. The problem was a straightforward matter of political community and social legitimacy: European citizens did not really understand themselves as European in the first place. As a result, European regulatory power was experienced as a foreign imposition, regardless of which branch of government actually wielded it. Empowering the EU to act (regardless of whether it did so via the European Parliament) would therefore only aggravate Europe's legitimacy problem; and all the more so if one also did away with the comforting notion that national executives could as a last resort "protect" their countries' vital interests by deploying the Luxembourg veto.[28]

Chapter 13 argues that twenty-five years on, the same basic logic unfortunately continues to apply, this time in the judicial context. There can be no doubt regarding the formal legitimacy of the European courts. The ECJ and the ECtHR have been established by formally legitimate Treaty means; their judges are appointed via legally established mechanisms, and so on. It is misguided, therefore, to attempt to address the much decried legitimacy deficit of the high European courts by focusing reform efforts on such formal bases of European judicial authority as the judicial appointments process.

To state the point directly: the core of the legitimacy challenges of the high European courts does not really lie in those courts' composition; in their particular modes of judicial selection, appointment, or election; or in the status, experience,

[28] *See* Joseph Weiler, *The Transformation of Europe*, 100 Yale L.J. 2403, 2428–30, 2473–74 (1991).

or linguistic capacities of their judges. It lies above all in the simple fact that they are European and that they are therefore understood to threaten legitimate (read: national) authority, culture, and customs, that is, the supposed seats of true political and social community.

Viewed from this perspective, it becomes all too clear that today's virulent tabloid critiques and their political counterparts—for all of their periodic vitriol regarding the insufficient qualifications and independence of European judges—are thus not truly directed at the European courts *as courts* or at European judges *as judges*. To take them at their word is to miss the point; and to respond to them on the merits is to get caught down a blind alley that leads only to technical and theoretical debates and to procedural and institutional reforms that, while interesting and potentially productive for professional insiders and to their own institutional and professional interests, do little or nothing to address the deeper (nationalist) crisis of legitimacy that these critiques actually represent. Such professional debates are accordingly no more likely to give a significant boost to European judicial legitimacy than were the old attempts to boost European political legitimacy by debunking the persistent myths that "Brussels" was dead-set on banning curved cucumbers, standardizing coffin and condom dimensions, and the like.[29] Nor are the comparatively modest and obscure judicial appointment reforms of today likely to be more legitimacy enhancing than were the far more visible and ambitious democratic deficit reforms of yesteryear.

This book therefore concludes that the legitimacy challenges facing the ECJ and ECtHR are primarily about Europe *tout court* and about the threat that Europe represents to domestic authority, culture, and customs, i.e., to what continues to be experienced as rooted political community. On this view, there is nothing specifically *judicial* about the critiques. The populist claims about a supposed lack of European judicial qualifications or independence are largely pretextual: the real legitimacy challenge to the ECJ and the ECtHR is quite simply that these courts are clearly not national and accordingly threaten what legitimately is.

That said, this finding should not obscure another, seemingly contradictory, conclusion. True, the current fights over, for example, the ECJ represent for the most part but a variation on the old critiques of the Commission and are thus not really about the Court *qua* court. Nevertheless, the mere fact that the ECJ would now be considered comparable to the Commission is in itself a significant development: it suggests that the Court is in fact increasingly (and correctly) understood as a front-line policymaking institution, regardless of whether that understanding jives with traditional Civilian (or, for that matter, British common law) conceptions of the judicial role. As a result, the critiques *are* about the Court, but *qua*

[29] The European Commission maintains to this day an online index of such "Euromyths." *See* http://blogs.ec.europa.eu/ECintheUK/euromyths-a-z-index.

political institution; and this is indeed an important development concerning the nature of the Court *qua* court.

This recognition of the Court as a front-line, policymaking political institution is of course not news for European academics, who have long recognized—and generally celebrated—the central role that the ECJ has played in the construction of Europe. Nor is it news for knowledgeable European political insiders, who, for example, designed the 1992 Maastricht Treaty's "three pillar system" in large part to shield entire categories of European political judgments from the recognized threat of ECJ intervention.[30]

But it does represent a rather new phase in the popular understanding of the European courts. And once matters have moved into that register, it is wishful thinking to imagine that mere tinkering over judicial qualifications and judicial appointments procedure might suddenly establish or ground the legitimacy of European judicial authority. Such professional, procedural, and institutional reforms might perhaps improve—if only on the margins—the standing of the European courts in the eyes of domestic legal elites; but that is not where the real challenges now lie. For once the European courts are *generally* recognized as major policymaking political institutions, then there is no escaping the issues of political community, political representation, and affective allegiance that have so bedeviled Europe as a whole.

If, then, the European judicial appointment reforms and their satellite measures on judicial independence, judicial quality, and judicial councils are designed to promote the overall social authority and legitimacy of the ECJ and the ECtHR, one cannot but conclude that these reforms—including the establishment and operation of the two vetting panels—are bound to be disappointing. They sidestep the truly pressing issues of European judicial authority and legitimacy, choosing instead to tinker around the edges of such matters as judicial experience, linguistic competence, institutional procedure, and the like. Although such secondary matters probably could give a little boost to the standing of the European judiciary in certain limited professional quarters, their real work takes place in other registers.

As our intergovernmentalist analysis suggests, these reforms function first and foremost as a means of protecting the interests of the longstanding Member States in preserving the European status quo against the tremendous uncertainties posed by the sudden and mass accession of new entrants from the former Eastern Bloc. They are in effect a backhanded manner to control the exercise by the new Member States of governmental prerogatives long cherished by governments in the West.

As our neo-institutionalist and neo-functionalist analysis suggests, they represent the means by which existing and newly established European institutions have

[30] Martin Shapiro has sharply critiqued this design decision. *See* Martin Shapiro, *The European Court of Justice*, *in* Judicial Independence in the Age of Democracy: Critical Perspectives from Around the World 273, 297–98 (Peter H. Russell & David M. O'Brien eds.,2001).

been able to go their own way in a manner unpredicted and undesired by the governments that created them. They are an inter-institutional power grab in which the vetting panels and their academic and institutional allies (such as certain subcomponents of the Committee of Ministers) have struggled to wrest control over judicial appointments from the governments that traditionally dominated them.

As our constructivist analysis suggests, these struggles have actually redefined what counts as judicial and political authority in the European context. The very notions of judicial independence, judicial quality, and judicial power, including their connotations and implications, have been utterly transformed by these debates. This reconstruction of who European judges are and should be, of the appropriate contours of governmental will, of the separation of powers, of the nature of supranational judicial and political authority, indeed of the very meaning of each of these terms, of the relations between them, and of the substantive, procedural, and institutional entailments they all supposedly demand: *these* have been the true stakes of the debates.

When viewed in this broad and multifaceted manner that layers intergovernmental, neo-institutionalist, constructivist analytic prisms, we can appreciate that the European judicial appointments debates represent a major reconstitution of the substantive, procedural, and institutional and conceptual foundations of European judicial and political authority. The bad news is that this reconstruction shows no sign of significantly promoting its manifest purpose: boosting the authority and legitimacy of European judicial power. The good news is that, should there exist sufficient political will and professional savvy, this reconstruction can nonetheless prove at least somewhat useful in curbing some of the egregious governmental abuses of judicial authority that countries like Hungary and Poland are currently wont to produce. Whether such political will and professional savvy can be effectively mustered in particular instances is of course forever open to debate and contestation. But if they are, at least the procedural, institutional, and normative tools are now in place and can in fact be put to some productive use. The really bad news, of course, is that current events demand that this be done. But one should not be fooled: engaging in such a rearguard action, however pressing it may indeed be, is extremely unlikely to do much at all to elevate the social authority and legitimacy of the European courts, never mind of Europe as a whole.

PART I

THE NEW APPOINTMENT PROCESSES OF THE ECJ: THE 255 PANEL

I start the analysis of the new appointment processes at the European courts with the modifications made to the European Union's system. I do this first for chronological reasons: it was the EU that initially added a screening mechanism to its judicial appointments process, adopting its new "Article 255" procedure with the Treaty of Lisbon, which came into force on December 1, 2009. But there is also an issue of sequencing and influence: the EU's formal adoption of these new procedures undoubtedly affected the Council of Europe and its European Court of Human Rights (ECtHR), which, after repeatedly referring to the new EU measures, followed suit shortly thereafter.[1]

This Part begins to lay the factual and conceptual foundation for much of the book's ensuing analysis. Chapter 2 offers a moderately detailed history of the developments that gradually led to the adoption of the EU's current 255 process. The story starts very early, in the summer and fall of 1950, when national delegates for the original six members of the proposed European Coal and Steel Community (ECSC) debated mechanisms for reviewing decisions taken by the ECSC's key supranational decision-making institution: the High Authority (which eventually morphed into the EU's primary "executive branch" institution, the European Commission).

This prehistory demonstrates that the current judicial appointment debates are hardly novel. From the very beginning, thoughtful jurists and national representatives fully grasped the conundrums posed by any system of appointment to international or supranational "judicial" institutions. I use the term "judicial" in quotation marks for good reason: in the early stages of the 1950 debates, it was by no means evident that an ECSC reviewing mechanism would or should be judicial in nature. To the contrary, debates took place in a fascinatingly inchoate

[1] As we shall see in Chapter 4, however, the first important steps toward the establishment of a European-level judicial screening mechanism were actually taken by the institutions of the Council of Europe, not by those of the EU.

institutional environment—a sort of institutional primordial soup in which no one knew what might eventually be the nature (never mind the composition or competences) of each of the new institutions of the proposed ECSC.[2] In this context, in which fundamental institutional forms and functions were truly up for grabs, the composition of—and appointment to—such potential institutions were heatedly debated in a manner that really does shed light on current developments.

Chapter 2's history then briefly highlights the three main moments leading to the more recent Article 255 developments: the European Court of Justice's (ECJ) 1995 Report to the Study Group preparing the 1996 Intergovernmental Conference (which eventually led to the Treaty of Amsterdam), the 2000 Ole Due Report on the Future of the European Communities' Court System (which first proposed a judicial selection panel), and the 2003 European Constitutional Convention's Discussion Circle on the Court of Justice (which yielded the Treaty of Lisbon and its Article 255 process). All three generated important developments for the eventual establishment of the Article 255 selection panel.

After this historical survey, Chapter 3 turns to the operation of the 255 Panel. It begins by explaining the Panel's basic rules and procedures. It then examines the Panel's initial composition and its shifting membership, drawing particular attention to the fact that the Panel is quite clearly dominated by high-ranking national judicial figures.

The chapter then offers a detailed study of the 255 Panel's actions. These actions can be divided into two main categories: (1) the Panel's review of candidates proposed by Member States to fill positions on the Court of Justice and the General Court and (2) the Panel's publication of its Activity Report. The Panel's review—and especially its rejection—of candidates proposed by Member States has been a landmark development: the new Article 255 system has refused entry to a very healthy percentage of judicial candidates put forward by the national governments. But as we shall see, the further import of these refusals has been to magnify the interest and influence of the Panel's Activity Reports. These highly significant Reports, which have been composed entirely on the Panel's own independent initiative under the leadership of the redoubtable Jean-Marc Sauvé, have all but dictated the ground rules for the EU's judicial appointment process: not only have they elaborated quite detailed criteria for the examination of proposed judicial candidates, but they have also strongly motivated the establishment of national procedures for those candidates' initial selection.

The chapter's examination of the 255 Panel's Activity Reports, when combined with the Chapter 2's earlier historical survey, leads to a series of interim conclusions. They suggest that the Article 255 system has transformed European judicial

[2] For the most important and insightful analysis of the development of the European Communities as a fundamentally legal institution, *see* Antoine Vauchez, Brokering Europe: Euro-Lawyers and the Making of a Transnational Polity (2015) ["Vauchez (2015)"].

politics. The reforms have changed EU judicial appointments from a system governed by unilateral national governmental fiat to one governed by aggressive professional review performed by a college of high-ranking national judicial figures operating at the European level as the 255 Panel. This new procedural and institutional reality clearly reflects and establishes a new relationship not only to judicial appointments, but also—as this book's ensuing chapters will explain—to the separation of powers, to the judicial role, and to judicial competence and independence.

2
The Prehistory and History of the 255 Panel

I begin our examination of European judicial appointment processes by turning all the way back to the pre-history of the EU. I do so not only because that early history is truly fascinating, but also because it is so enlightening: it serves to remind us of the complex political, institutional, and ideological conundrums that have always permeated the European project. Current institutional developments are in some sense only the latest mutation of an ongoing set of dilemmas and debates.

I. The ECSC Negotiations

On May 9, 1950, French foreign minister Robert Schuman presented his famous Schuman Declaration, which proposed the creation of a European Coal and Steel Community (the precursor to what has since become the European Union). The six prospective Member States (France, Germany, Italy, and the Benelux countries) would pool coal and steel production, which would make war between France and Germany "not merely unthinkable, but materially impossible," "lay a true foundation for their economic unification," and realize "the first concrete foundation of a European federation."[3] The Declaration set the stage for intensive negotiations between the six prospective Member States. For our purposes, the key debates are those that focused on how to review decisions taken by the ECSC's vital supranational decision-making institution: the High Authority (the precursor to the European Commission).

The interest in this early episode of institutional design lies in the relatively freeform nature of the participants' early proposals. Although the point of these discussions was to elaborate a mechanism for reviewing the High Authority's decisions, there was little agreement about what this really meant. Firstly, the participants disagreed on whether the High Authority's decisions ought to be reviewable at all. One camp, dominated by the French and their formidable leader Jean Monnet, was fundamentally suspicious of any review at all: they were zealously protective of the powers of the High Authority, which was the transformative supranational institutional innovation of the ECSC project.[4] At the other end of the

[3] https://europa.eu/european-union/about-eu/symbols/europe-day/schuman-declaration_en.

[4] *See* Anne Boerger-De Smedt, *La Cour de justice dans les négociations du traité de Paris instituant la CECA*, 14(2) J. of Eur. Integration Hist. 7 (2008) ["Boerger-De Smedt (2008)"].

spectrum was a camp composed primarily of representatives of the small Benelux countries, who were deeply concerned about the High Authority's potentially vast and centralized powers, powers that might well be deployed in a utilitarian manner that could all too easily override the interests of their small countries.[5]

This conflict between the French and Benelux positions quickly spilled over into jurisdictional issues. The question was not merely whether, but also which types of, High Authority decisions should be reviewable. Unsurprisingly, the Benelux countries favored a broad understanding of reviewable acts, arguing in favor of extending review beyond merely scrutinizing the legality of the High Authority's decisions under the ECSC Treaty. In particular, they explicitly fought to defend vital state interests by permitting review of the economic and political advisability ("*opportunité*") of High Authority decisions. Predictably, Monnet and the French were ardently opposed to this position, as such broad reviewability might paralyze the High Authority by encouraging the second-guessing of all its policy judgments.

This jurisdictional debate then spilled over into institutional ones. In particular, what institution might review the High Authority's decisions? All kinds of ideas were floated early on. Perhaps the Member States—and perhaps even directly and individually concerned firms—could be empowered to call upon the High Authority to reconsider one of its decisions and demand that the decision be confirmed by a supermajority vote of two thirds.[6] Maybe an "organism of conciliation and arbitration" or a "litigation court" could quickly intervene when a High Authority decision threatened "vital interests" of a Member State or was "incompatible with its sovereignty."[7] Perhaps an ad hoc three- or five-member college of arbitration or mediation might review the High Authority's economic judgments, while the International Court of Justice might engage in review of the legality of its decisions. The Dutch argued that an Economic Ministerial Committee could serve as such a first-level appellate body, which would have to garner a two-thirds or even a three-quarters supermajority to sustain a challenged High Authority decision. Maybe government commissioners should be attached to the High Authority to introduce appeals to some kind of judicial organ. In short, a great deal of time, effort, and imagination went into the seemingly straightforward question of how to design a review mechanism for decisions taken by the High Authority.

Tellingly, the key development in this debate was Monnet's eventual recognition that what was driving these suggestions was the failure of the early French working proposals to include an institutional mechanism for expressing national interests. Gradually accepting the need to fill this lacuna, Monnet and the French eventually acceded to the strong Benelux misgivings and a new institutional solution was found: a special Council of Ministers of the Member States. The supranational

[5] *See id.* at 13.
[6] *See id.* at 14.
[7] *See id.* at 13.

High Authority (eventually, the Commission) had found its institutional counterpower: the intergovernmentalist Council of Ministers.[8]

This episode demonstrates the tremendous institutional and theoretical flux that permeated the ESCS negotiations. The Member State representatives had no fixed institutional organization in mind, to such an extent that they did not make a series of distinctions that now seem reasonably clear, such as the distinctions between the executive and the judicial, between the political and the legal, between the European and the international, and so on. Even when the institutional framework of the European Communities was eventually settled, it was decidedly byzantine. Antoine Vauchez writes:

> The baroque features of these institutional arrangements could make the specialists almost dizzy. Could one really talk of 'political oversight' in the case of an essentially consultative European Parliamentary Assembly? Could an institution lacking any legislative function be called a parliament? Further still, how could the Commission truly be an 'executive branch' of the Communities when at the same time it shared a 'legislative function' with the Council? What sort of Court could have the attributions of an administrative jurisdiction to oversee the legality of Community acts, those of a Constitutional Court to ensure the balance of power between institutions, and those of an arbitrage tribunal to resolve conflicts arising from the creation of the Common Market?[9]

For our purposes, this lack of differentiation is especially important because it reveals the tenuousness of these seemingly self-evident distinctions. In particular, it reveals (1) the *very intimate* connection between the creation of a mechanism to review European institutional decisions and the protection of the national interests of Member States, as opposed to (2) the *comparatively weak* connection between such a protective review mechanism and the judiciary. Indeed, the fascinating twist to the story is that the big breakthrough in the debates over reviewing High Authority decisions lay *not* in the creation of a court,[10] but in the creation of the Council of Ministers, an institution explicitly composed of ministerial-level representatives of the Member State governments who could be counted on to protect vital national interests. In other words, what might have led self-evidently to a legal/judicial solution morphed quite easily into a political/executive one.

[8] *See id.* at 15.

[9] Vauchez (2015) at 20. *See also* Piers Ludlow, *Value, Flexibility and Openness. The Treaty of Rome's Success in Historical Perspective*, *in* EUROPEAN INTEGRATION IN HISTORICAL PERSPECTIVE FROM ROME TO BERLIN: 1957–2007, 17–39 (JULIO BAQUERO CRUZ & CARLOS CLOSA MONTERO eds., 2009).

[10] As Antoine Vauchez states with regard to the Treaty of Rome, which only came into being almost a decade later, "legal experts … left no trace of a European 'Constitutional Charter' or of a 'Supreme Court' [in the Rome Treaties]." *See* Vauchez (2015) at 5.

Only after this major breakthrough did an ex-post review mechanism take shape and do so in a recognizably judicial form. After all, the establishment of the Council of Ministers provided a strong mechanism for the expression of national interests in the ECSC system, thereby counterbalancing the supranational tendencies of the powerful High Authority; but it did not offer a procedural mechanism for reviewing specific decisions eventually taken. How, then, to conceive of—and then design—the judicial institution that would engage in such ex-post review of ECSC actions? With the Council now established, the negotiators finally began to speak explicitly of a "Court of Justice." But, what would be its jurisdiction and composition? And how would its members be selected? The debates began anew.

To some extent, the terms of these debates simply repeated those that led to the creation of the Council. Belgium, Luxembourg, and even Germany continued to push for review of decisions that might threaten the vital interests of a Member State; and Luxembourg continued to insist on the capacity to trigger review of the economic or political advisability of High Authority decisions. Meanwhile, the French, and especially Monnet and his legal advisor Paul Reuter, continued to resist extensive review, invoking the traditional French fear of a "*gouvernement des juges*" that might operate at the expense of the supranational High Authority.[11]

Although the French eventually succeeded for the most part in limiting the Court's jurisdiction to overtly legal challenges, this hardly settled two other questions: (1) How should the Court be composed? and (2) What should (or should not) be the nature of the relationship between national governments and the Court's judges? The positions taken on such questions were not only widely divergent, but also highly internally inconsistent.

Take the French position. Thanks in part to the limitation of its jurisdiction, the French came to accept that this reviewing institution might be composed of a permanent court rather than of ad hoc judicial or arbitral panels. Moreover, they gradually came to imagine that this court might, like the High Authority, function as a supranational and even federal institution. Committed as they were to the supranational dimension of the ECSC, the French therefore sought to promote this potential feature of the proposed court by insisting that its judges—like the members of the High Authority—remain completely independent from Member State governments. "The High Authority and the Court of Justice," argued Reuter, must "be composed of *absolutely independent figures who must maintain no link whatever to the States*. In this respect, they would constitute an extremely advanced, and one might almost say perfect, fulfillment of the supranational community."[12] In accordance with this new perspective, the French proposed that the judges be

[11] Boerger-De Smedt (2008) at 12; Paul Reuter, *La conception du pouvoir politique dans le Plan Schuman*, 1 Revue française de Science politique 256, 274 (1951).

[12] ANL/AE, dos.11384, Mémorandum sur les institutions (annexe 1 du Rapport sur les travaux poursuivis à Paris ... du 20 juin au 10 août 1950), *quoted in* Boerger-De Smedt (2008) at 16 (emphasis added).

selected from a group of "figures offering every guaranty of independence and competence."[13]

Yet, when it came time to design a method for selecting these "absolutely independent" judges, the French specified that they be appointed by common accord of the governments for renewable six-year terms, which is to say, by a process that guaranteed maximum possible national control! After all, appointment by common accord of the governments effectively meant that each government would be able to select its own judge without serious threat of being challenged: the unanimity arrangement empowered each individual government not so much because it could exercise veto powers over the judges proposed by others, but because it could appoint its own judges with impunity, lest it play tit-for-tat with any potential challenging government's own judicial candidate. Furthermore, a relatively short and renewable term would allow a government to replace a judge who earned its displeasure, an eventuality far too obvious for any competent judge to miss.

The Germans, for their part, were also committed to the federal possibilities of the ECSC. But they put more stock in the federal potential of the Assembly than did the French.[14] This was reflected in their early proposal that the Court's judges be elected by the Assembly,[15] a proposal that they eventually abandoned in favor of the French intergovernmentalist appointment plan.

This French plan created a grave tension—if not a complete contradiction—between the French promotion of (1) "absolutely independent [judicial] figures" as a means to bolster the supranational potential of the Court and (2) judicial appointment by common accord of the governments for renewable six-year terms, which placed judicial candidates at the mercy of their national governments. Not to be outdone, the Belgians offered an almost diametrically opposed tension/contradiction of their own. The Benelux camp had been strenuously arguing in favor of designing the judicial review mechanism in such a manner as to ensure effective judicial protection of vital national interests. Yet the Belgians now resisted the government-friendly French judicial appointment process: the Belgian diplomat Fernand Muûls explicitly argued that the French proposal would leave the judges at the mercy of their governments' good will at both the appointment and the reappointment stages, which would unacceptably threaten those judges' independence.[16]

The French would not be moved. On the one hand, they insisted on "absolutely independent [judicial] figures." But on the other, they defended a

[13] This language appeared in the French draft treaty of November 8, 1950. *See* Boerger-De Smedt (2008) at 19. Article 32(1) of the ECSC Treaty of Paris reads "The Court shall be composed of seven judges, appointed for six years by agreement among the governments of the member States from among persons of recognized independence and competence."

[14] Boerger-De Smedt (2008) at 18, note 51.

[15] *Id.* at 19.

[16] Fernand Muûls, "Note concernant le projet de traité relatif au charbon et à l'acier, 16.11.1950," AMAElB, Dos.gen. CECA 5216, *cited in* Boerger-De Smedt (2008) at 20.

government-empowering process of judicial appointment. The French legal advisor Paul Reuters offered two justifications for this government-empowering process. First, it reserved to the governments "their rightful role" ("*le rôle qui leur revenait*"). Second, group discussions about appointments to the Court and to the High Authority would permit "satisfactory [outcomes] to be negotiated in favor of all the Member States." Clearly, neither of these justifications squares easily with the "absolute independence" of prospective judicial candidates.

In her fine historical account of these debates, Anne Boerger-De Smedt offers a blunt assessment:

> Reuter did not specify what exactly was this "[rightful] role" that was reserved to the governments. Was it that the governments would keep the upper hand over the Court by controlling [its membership] and by ensuring themselves that any judge who became undesirable could be tossed aside after his first term? Probably. The appointment process for the judges and the temporary nature of their employment offered reassuring guarantees for the governments. Regardless, the chosen procedures responded more to political preoccupations than to legal preferences ... As a result, the independence of the European judges was simply stipulated by the Treaty without being truly guaranteed.[17]

This stipulation was eventually codified in Article 32(1) of the ECSC Treaty of Paris, which specified that the Court's judges would be chosen "among persons of recognized independence and competence." This standard was then modestly amended a few years later in Article 167 of the Treaty of Rome (establishing the European Economic Community), which adopted language cut and pasted from the Statute of the International Court of Justice:

> The judges and the advocates-general shall be chosen from among persons of indisputable independence who fulfil the conditions required for the holding of the highest judicial office in their respective countries or who are jurists of a recognised competence; they shall be appointed for a term of six years by the Governments of Member States acting in common agreement.[18]

[17] Boerger-De Smedt (2008) at 21.

[18] Article 2 of the ICJ Statute states: "The Court shall be composed of a body of independent judges, elected regardless of their nationality from among persons of high moral character, who possess the qualifications required in their respective countries for appointment to the highest judicial offices, or are jurisconsults of recognized competence in international law." *See* Pierre Pescatore, *Les travaux du "groupe juridique" dans les négociations des traités de Rome*, 2 REVUE D'HISTOIRE LUXEMBOURGEOISE 34 (1982), available at http://www.cvce.eu/obj/pierre_pescatore_les_travaux_du_"groupe_juridique"_dans_la_negociation_des_traites_de_rome-fr-1d333821-00f1-495a-ba5b-305a2a2536d3.html. It should be noted that even this standard of competence was a shift for the purposes of the Rome Treaty.

As a result, the tensions and contradictions of the early ECSC Treaty negotiations have been hardwired into the EU's institutional architecture ever since.[19]

I have dedicated a certain amount of space to the negotiations over the ECSC's eventually judicial mechanism of review because they are deeply revealing. These negotiations demonstrate quite clearly the fundamental tension between the supranational and intergovernmentalist impulses of the original six Member States. Although these six were divided into fairly readily identifiable camps, each was itself divided, albeit in characteristic ways, between the two impulses. As a result, the tensions—and perhaps even the contradictions—that came to be embedded in the judicial appointment provisions of the Treaties do not represent a straightforward flaw or failure. To the contrary, they render rather faithfully the competing interests and impulses that animated the European project from the very start. Each of the original six was torn in its own way between a vague supranational vision and rather specific national interests, and between faith in and suspicion toward judicial and other European institutions.

The early ECSC negotiations allow us to see how an institutional, political, and conceptual primordial soup gradually congealed into more clearly differentiated European institutions, roles, and competences. But the elaboration of this increasingly settled institutional landscape did not permanently settle the vexing tensions that underlay the European project. The protection of national interests, for example, which was so important to the initial debates about how to review the High Authority's decisions, drove the creation of the Council of Ministers. But this major institutional development hardly put an end to governmental desires to protect those vital national interests. The issue of national governmental prerogatives therefore reemerged once again when negotiations then turned to the nature, jurisdiction, and composition of the Court of Justice and to the appointment of its judges. The net result was that the Member States, for all of their stated desire for "absolutely independent" judges, ended up signing quite consciously onto a system of judicial appointment that left a great deal of control in the hands of the national governments.

As Antoine Vauchez explains, "coal and steel judges" were largely substantive specialists, including a "trade-unionist-judge" and an "economist-judge," and so on. The shift to a standard based oriented toward "jurists of a recognised competence" represented a shift in "perspective that considerably reinforced the juridical capital of the collective Community judiciary." *See* Vauchez (2015) at 51–54.

[19] With the exception of the Treaty of Lisbon's reference to the new Article 255 procedure, the language of this provision is essentially unchanged. Article 253 of the Treaty of Lisbon states: "The Judges and Advocates-General of the Court of Justice shall be chosen from persons whose independence is beyond doubt and who possess the qualifications required for appointment to the highest judicial offices in their respective countries or who are jurisconsults of recognised competence; they shall be appointed by common accord of the governments of the Member States for a term of six years, after consultation of the panel provided for in Article 255."

II. The ECJ's 1995 Report

The issue of judicial appointments then lay all but dormant for decades until the mid-1990s, when it began to be raised periodically in EU institutional debates. Interestingly and perhaps tellingly, no explicit reason was overtly given for the rather sudden surge in interest in the topic. Although a full discussion of such considerations will be elaborated throughout the course of this book, we need to recognize one pivotal historical fact right away: the fall of the Berlin Wall and the rapid dissolution of the Soviet Union and of its traditional sphere of influence. In 1994, 1995, and 1996, no fewer than ten former Eastern Bloc countries formally applied for accession to an EU that was then comprised of only twelve Member States.[20] Indeed, Europe agreements or Association agreements by these applicant countries had actually been signed several years earlier, beginning with Hungary and Poland in 1991. As of the mid-1990s, EU enlargement was therefore on the immediate horizon.[21] And although the accession of Austria, Finland, and Sweden on January 1, 1995 took the EU from twelve to fifteen Members States, the expansion eastward was obviously going to be very different in scope and in kind: by 2004, the EU would suddenly be comprised of twenty-seven Member States.

In May 1995, i.e., at the height of this accession period, the ECJ submitted a report on the operation of the Maastricht Treaty in anticipation of potential revisions by the impending 1996 Intergovernmental Conference. The twelve-page Report addressed a fairly broad list of issues, ranging from the role of the courts in the EU, to the application of the Treaty of Maastricht, to the possible revision of provisions relating to the judicial system. It was in connection with such potential revisions that the Court authored the following paragraphs, which are worth quoting at some length:

> 17. The Court does not intend to express any opinion with regard to the procedure for the appointment of its members or the term of their appointment, beyond those aspects which concern the preservation of its independence and its functional efficiency.
>
> The Court stresses that the procedure for appointment laid down by the Treaties and the practice generally followed in renewing the terms of office of its members have satisfactorily ensured its independence and the continuity of its case-law.
>
> The Court would not, however, object to a reform which would involve an extension of the term of office with a concomitant condition that the appointment

[20] Those countries were, in chronological order, Hungary, Poland, Slovakia, Romania, Latvia, Estonia, Lithuania, Bulgaria, the Czech Republic, and Slovenia. *See* http://europa.eu/legislation_summaries/enlargement/2004_and_2007_enlargement/e50017_en.htm.

[21] *See id.* Formal accession negotiations began as of 1998; and the great enlargement to twenty-five Member States eventually took place in 2004.

> be non-renewable. Such a reform would provide an even firmer basis for the independence of its members and would strengthen the continuity of its case-law.
>
> Provided that the fixed term of appointment of each member were calculated from the time of taking office, such a solution would also have the advantage, over time, of limiting the operational inconveniences regularly suffered by the Court's activities as a result of the partial replacement rule. However, without needing to express an opinion at this stage on the other proposals which have been put forward, the Court considers that a reform involving a hearing of each nominee by a parliamentary committee would be unacceptable. Prospective appointees would be unable adequately to answer the questions put to them without betraying the discretion incumbent upon persons whose independence must, in the words of the Treaties, be beyond doubt and without prejudging positions they might have to adopt with regard to contentious issues which they would have to decide in the exercise of their judicial function.[22]

This passage is notable in several regards. First, and most obviously, it demonstrates the Court's intense preoccupation with its own independence and with that of its members. Each of the four paragraphs includes its own specific reference to such independence. Second, it associates that independence not only to the appointments process, but also to the "continuity" and effectiveness of the court's case-law, hence the numerous references to "the continuity of its case-law" (twice), the Court's "functional efficiency" and so on. Indeed, earlier in the Report, the ECJ summarized its position quite clearly: "Any decision affecting the structure of the judicial system must therefore ensure that the [European] courts remain independent and their judgments binding. Were that not to be the case, the very foundations of the Community legal order would be undermined."[23] Third, it reopens issues that were already discussed almost fifty years before during the ECSC negotiations: the relatively short and renewable six-year terms for ECJ judges, and the role that the Parliament (then the Assembly) might potentially play in the appointment process.

The ECJ's 1995 Report thus offers a richly tantalizing, if somewhat opaque, set of associations. Probably its most important feature is simply its date (1995), coinciding perfectly with the flurry of hopeful applications from would-be EU Member States from the East. This temporal association is hardly fortuitous. After all, the long passage quoted above is excerpted from Paragraph 17 of the Report. What, then, does the Court address in Paragraph 16? Nothing other than EU enlargement. On the one hand, the ECJ warns that maintaining the system of one judge

[22] Report of the Court of Justice on certain aspects of the application of the Treaty on European Union, published in the Court's 1995 Activity Report 19, at 28, para. 17 (emphasis added), available at https://www.cvce.eu/content/publication/2003/4/2/3644862f-2e8f-4170-9616-e573a41b61c5/publishable_en.pdf ["1995 Annual ECJ Report"].

[23] *Id.* at 21, para. 4 (emphasis added).

per country would so increase the size of the Court that this "might mean that the plenary session of the Court would cross the invisible boundary between a collegiate court and a deliberative assembly." Furthermore, the increase in the number of Chambers "could pose a threat to the consistency of the [ECJ's] case-law." "On the other hand," argues the Court, "the presence of members from all the national legal systems on the Court is undoubtedly conducive to harmonious development of Community case-law, taking into account concepts regarded as fundamental in the various Member States and thus enhancing the acceptability of the solutions arrived at. It may also be considered that the presence of a Judge from each Member State enhances the legitimacy of the Court." The prospect of the EU's Eastern enlargement thus fed directly into the ECJ's thinking about appointments procedure, with concerns ranging from the Court's size and internal consistency, to developing and promoting the Court's case-law, to enhancing the Court's legitimacy. These concerns then fed into Paragraph 17 of the Report, which foregrounds the Court's preoccupation with the independence and appointment of its judges and the continuity and effectiveness of its case-law.

The ensuing chapters will devote a great deal of attention to this fascinating if rather tangled set of associations. What matters at this stage of the analysis is simply to recognize and reconstruct the gradual establishment of this field of associated issues. In this spirit, let us move on to the next important step in the development of the ECJ's appointments debates: the 2000 Ole Due Report on the Future of the European Communities' Court System.

III. The 2000 Ole Due Report

The Ole Due Report was a product of the Intergovernmental Conference leading to the Nice Treaty of 2001, whose primary task was to reform EU institutions in preparation for the pending eastward expansion.[24] Although the focus of such institutional reform was directed primarily at the EU's political institutions (viz., the powers of Parliament, composition of the Commission, and voting in Council), all knowledgeable observers understood perfectly well that the European Courts were increasingly crushed by an unmanageable caseload that would only get geometrically worse with the EU's pending enlargement. The Community Courts had recently produced a self-study of the problems facing the EU judicial system, but offered no clear set of proposals.[25] In an attempt to make some tangible progress,

[24] *See* Liz Heffernan, *A European Certiorari Revisited, in* THE TREATY OF NICE AND BEYOND: ENLARGEMENT AND CONSTITUTIONAL REFORM 355 (MADS ADENAS & JOHN USHER eds., 2003) ["Heffernan (2003)"]. The 1999 Treaty of Amsterdam had ultimately failed to perform this task.

[25] *See* Court of Justice and Court of First Instance, *The Future of the Judicial System of the European Union (Proposals and Reflections), republished in* THE FUTURE OF THE JUDICIAL SYSTEM OF THE EUROPEAN UNION 111 (ALAN DASHWOOD & ANGUS JOHNSTON eds., 2001).

the Commission set up an independent working group, chaired by former ECJ President Ole Due.

The Ole Due Report was therefore overwhelmingly concerned with addressing the institutional effects of Eastern enlargement: "The biggest challenge to the Community court system will flow from the enlargement of the Union envisaged for the coming years," when the "number of Member States will in all likelihood virtually double," aggravating not only the Court's already terrible caseload and backlog, but also the linguistic difficulties inherent in doubling the number of languages in which the Court must operate.[26] The Report offered a broad range of proposals, ranging from modifying the Article 234 referral procedures to changing the Court's jurisdiction in certain classes of cases. Nonetheless, its proposed reforms were ultimately quite conservative.[27] On the institutional front, the Report assumed that the Court would continue to have the same number of judges as Member States. This would require that plenary sessions be modified to limit the number of judges to a manageable size, likely thirteen (i.e., about half the number of Member States); and the importance of five-judge Chambers would increase accordingly.[28] All of this was reasonable enough, if decidedly unexciting.

And so went the Report for some fifty workmanlike pages, until it arrived at its final two substantive paragraphs. Then the Report suddenly stated, almost out of the blue and without any supporting explanation:

> The Working Party would suggest that, to ensure the smooth working of both courts, the term of office of their Members should be increased to twelve years as from the date of actual appointment and that this term should not be renewable.
>
> The Working Party would also suggest that the appointment of all Members of the Court of Justice and the CFI should be scrutinised on the basis of a comprehensive file submitted by each Member State. To assist the Member States in their deliberations, an advisory committee consisting of highly-qualified independent lawyers should be set up to verify the legal competence of candidates.[29]

Eight concluding lines later, the Report signed off without further ado.

The final substantive paragraph of the Ole Due Report thus effectively gave birth to what was to become the Article 255 Panel. But what had motivated this potentially major proposal? And what did it have to do with the Court's unmanageable caseload and/or with EU enlargement? The Report said not a word. Similarly, what lay behind the proposal that the length of judicial office be changed from renewable six-year terms to unrenewable twelve-year terms? Again, the Report ventured

[26] Ole Due Report at 9–10.
[27] *See* Heffernan (2003) at 356.
[28] Ole Due Report at 47.
[29] *Id.* at 51.

no meaningful explanation, offering nothing more than the vacuous phrase "to ensure the smooth working of both courts . . . ."

At this point in the analysis, we can only guess at what drove this pair of proposals. But it is worth noting the obvious: the key historical development that framed and motivated the entire Ole Due Report was the pending accession of ten countries from the former Soviet sphere. This enlargement would almost double the number of EU Member States and accordingly almost double the number of judges sitting in Luxembourg. Surely, the numeric importance and the geopolitical provenance of the expansion must have been crucial factors motivating both the front-end proposal to vet candidates proposed by the national governments and the back-end proposal to do away with reappointments by moving to a longer and nonrenewable term of judicial office. As the Ole Due Report gave no further justifications, however, our brief historical survey can for now venture no more specific explanations.

However tantalizing the last two paragraphs of the Ole Due Report may be, they led nowhere, at least for the time being. The Treaty of Nice did implement modest changes to the jurisdiction and organization of the Court of Justice and the Court of First Instance (CFI).[30] But the Treaty did absolutely nothing with regards to judicial appointments: neither the appointments process nor the length of the terms of judicial office was changed in any way.

IV. The 2003 Constitutional Convention's Discussion Circle on the ECJ

The appointment issues were instead taken up a couple of years later during the discussions that took place under the framework of the European Constitutional Convention. The Convention process not only included Plenary Sessions, but also established a series of eleven "Working Groups" on major issues and three "Discussion Circles" for more technical matters.[31] One of these three Discussion Circles focused on the Court of Justice.

The first notable feature of the Convention's Discussion Circle on the Court of Justice is its composition, which differs strikingly from the Ole Due Working Party. The Ole Due committee consisted of an extremely high-powered group of seven jurists, five of whom were former ECJ Justices or Advocates General, one of whom was about to be, and one high-powered antitrust professor/lawyer.[32] The

[30] For a contemporaneous account of the potential significance of the Nice modifications of the European judicial provisions, *see* Joseph Weiler, *The judicial Après-Nice*, *in* The European Court of Justice 215 (Gráinne de Búrca & J.H.H. Weiler eds., 2002) [trying to make the best of the seemingly modest changes made by the Nice Treaty].

[31] *See* http://european-convention.europa.eu/EN/organisation/organisation2352.html?lang=EN.

[32] The group consisted of former ECJ President Ole Due (Chair), former ECJ Justices Yves Galmot, Ulrich Everling, former ECJ Justice and Advocate General Lord Slynn of Hadley, former ECJ Advocate

Discussion Circle, however, was composed almost entirely of Member State diplomats, national political figures, and European Parliamentarians. Of its twenty members, only two had ever been judges (both at the national level).

In one key respect, however, the two groups were rather similar: they all but shut out contributions from the soon-to-be Member States from the East. The seven members of the 2000 Ole Due Working Party were drawn exclusively from established EU Member States. And of the twenty members of the 2003 Discussion Circle, only two were Eastern European, despite the fact that ten new Member States from the East were scheduled to accede to the EU the ensuing year! In short, the Ole Due Working Party was essentially a small group of ex ECJ judges; the Discussion Circle consisted of a large group of national political/diplomatic figures and MEPs; and neither—to put it mildly—made a meaningful effort to include voices from Eastern Europe.

The second notable aspect of the Discussion Circle is that it really did focus heavily on judicial appointment issues. That discussion started with a studiously passive presentation made by ECJ President Gil Carlos Rodríguez Iglesias, who did little more than endorse the Court's 1995 Report (which, as we have seen, had indicated that "the procedure for appointment laid down by the Treaties and the practice generally followed in renewing the terms of office of its members have satisfactorily ensured its independence and the continuity of its case-law.")[33] Hewing to that Report, Iglesias reiterated that "The Court would not, however, object to a reform which would involve an extension of the term of office with a concomitant condition that the appointment be non-renewable," specifying that were such an option taken, the term should be of twelve, rather than nine, years, lest experienced judges be replaced too quickly.[34]

Despite this bland beginning, the Discussion Circle's debates quickly heated up. Three issues came to the fore in rapid succession. The first signals that major concerns must have been brewing. The Record of the meeting pithily states: "On the procedure for appointing judges and advocates-general: some members wanted to retain appointment 'by common accord' of the governments, but more wanted them to be appointed by Council act."[35] This seemingly technical statement is actually deeply meaningful. As we have seen, the existing process of appointment

General José Luis da Cruz Vilaça, soon-to-be ECJ Justice Rosario Silva de Lapuerta, and the antitrust specialist professor/lawyer/former General Director of Competition at the Commission Aurelio Pappalardo.

[33] *See* Oral presentation by M. Gil Carlos Rodríguez Iglesias, President of the Court of Justice of the European Communities, to the "discussion circle" on the Court of Justice on February 17, 2003, CONV 572/03, available at http://european-convention.europa.eu/pdf/reg/en/03/cv00/cv00572.en03.pdf, quoting 1995 ECJ Report.

[34] *Id.*

[35] Record of the meeting on February 17, 2003 of the discussion circle on the Court of Justice, CONV 573/03, available at http://european-convention.europa.eu/pdf/reg/en/03/cv00/cv00573.en03.pdf.

"by common accord" of the governments amounts to an inverted veto system: each government effectively selects its own judge without the threat of being challenged, lest it play tit for tat with the challenging government's own judicial candidate.

Appointment "by Council act," however, could radically change this state of affairs, especially if the Council were to act by qualified majority (as would likely be the case, or there would be no need to change from the existing unanimity system). Such a novel approach would remove a challenged state's capacity to play a simple game of tit for tat: if its own candidate were challenged, this Member State would now need to rally a coalition in order to retaliate. And since the initial challenge would by definition have had to come from a coalition (i.e., a blocking minority), responsibility would thereby be diffused. Against whom would the challenged state and its allies retaliate? All of the blocking minority's component states? The rules of the game would be utterly transformed.

Needless to say, we can only guess at the precise game theoretic implications of such a procedural shift in the appointment process, especially insofar as there is no clear indication of exactly what procedures might have been proposed for such a "council act." What can be inferred, however, is that the Discussion Circle was prepared to countenance potentially major changes in the appointment process; indeed, it appears that a majority of the Circle was actually in favor of them. And it is hard to see how such changes would not have gone in the direction of undermining the longstanding capacity of each EU Member State to appoint with impunity its own favored judicial candidate. The suggestion, in other words, is that Member States were suddenly interested in policing the judicial candidates proposed by other Member States.

The second issue was clearly related to the first. The Report states:

> The idea of setting up a panel to assess the candidates was well received, although some members preferred to keep the present system; some members proposed that governments should put forward more than one candidate while others preferred a single candidate; the importance of establishing criteria which would guarantee the professional quality, independence and impartiality of the candidates was stressed; the Council would decide on the composition of the panel (it could include a former President of the Court, Presidents of Constitutional or Supreme Courts of the Member States; it was also suggested that the European Parliament might designate a member of the panel); some members opposed the idea that the panel could interview the candidates.[36]

Here the Discussion Circle takes up in earnest the suggestion first proposed by the Ole Due Working Party. Although the discussion appears to have been at least

[36] *Id.*

somewhat fractured, a few points appear to have garnered clear support and thereby established the fundamental architecture of the ensuing reforms. There should be a panel. The core of its membership should probably lie in prominent Member State supreme court justices, with subsidiary contributions from the ECJ and the European Parliament. And the establishment of such a panel was apparently motivated by the recognized "importance" of "guarantee[ing] the professional quality, independence and impartiality of the candidates." But why these goals might be best advanced by a panel composed in such a way was never explained.

Although these agreements were reached and eventually bore fruit, it is worth pausing for a moment to flag one point that failed to generate much consensus and another that did, but nonetheless failed in the end to yield tangible results. The former was the suggestion that the process of EU judicial appointments move in the direction of the procedures used for appointment to the ECtHR, in which the Parliamentary Assembly of the Council of Europe ["PACE"] plays a central role. Traces of this longstanding suggestion can be seen as far back as the 1995 ECJ Report, which had expressly stated:

> [T]he Court considers that a reform involving a hearing of each nominee by a parliamentary committee would be unacceptable. Prospective appointees would be unable adequately to answer the questions put to them without betraying the discretion incumbent upon persons whose independence must, in the words of the Treaties, be beyond doubt and without prejudging positions they might have to adopt with regard to contentious issues which they would have to decide in the exercise of their judicial function.[37]

Traces can also be seen in the Discussion Circle's debates, in which "some members proposed that governments should put forward more than one candidate." This also echoes the Strasbourg process, in which the Parliamentary Assembly elects each judge from among three candidates put forward by the national governments.[38] The attempt to empower the European Parliament in the appointments process thus never really got much traction. In the end, it yielded no more than the relatively modest proposal—wrested after all by a Discussion Circle that included a significant number of MEPs—that the European Parliament be entitled to designate one of the members of the proposed vetting panel.

But one important issue did get a lot of attention and did garner large-scale support: changing the ground rules concerning the length and renewal of judicial tenure. Time and again, the debates over judicial appointments returned to the vexing issue of the relatively short and renewable six-year terms that had been put into effect way back in 1950. Ever since the issue of judicial appointments started

[37] 1995 ECJ Activity Report.
[38] *See infra* Chapter 4.

being actively discussed in the mid-1990s, almost no one spoke openly in favor of maintaining the old approach: as was already perfectly clear in 1950, these short renewable terms left every sitting ECJ judge vulnerable to sanction by his/her own government, which could simply refuse to put that judge forward for renewal.

The remedy was all too obvious: to change judicial appointments to a single unrenewable term of longer duration. The Court's 1995 Report addressed the issue tactfully: although the current system was satisfactory, the ECJ "would not, however, object to a reform which would involve an extension of the term of office with a concomitant condition that the appointment be non-renewable. Such a reform would provide an even firmer basis for the independence of its members and would strengthen the continuity of its case-law." The Ole Due Report bluntly concluded that "the term of office of their Members should be increased to twelve years as from the date of actual appointment and that this term should not be renewable." In his remarks to the Discussion Circle, ECJ President Iglesias maintained a detached position reminiscent of 1995 ECJ Report, but nonetheless added: "But if it were decided to opt for a longer non-renewable term of office, I must tell you that a nine-year term does not seem long enough to us and that a twelve-year term would be preferable." Bo Vesterdorf, the President of the EU's CFI, while agreeing with President Iglesias "that it is not essential to alter the current system," nonetheless specified that if "a decision were taken to change the current system, the CFI would prefer its Members to be appointed for a single non-renewable term of at least twelve years. A nine-year term would, in our opinion, be clearly too short and would not allow the CFI to take sufficient advantage of the valuable judicial experience of its Members, which maintains the continuity and consistency of its case-law."[39] And a majority of the members of the Discussion Circle itself were in favor of single unrenewable terms of judicial office whose length should be extended to nine, and perhaps twelve, years: "As regards the judges' term of office, most members favoured a non-renewable nine-year term, although some could also accept a longer, non-renewable term of 12 years."[40]

In the end, the conclusions of the Discussion Panel therefore led to two important proposals regarding judicial appointments. The first, which addressed the vetting panel, was stated with significant conviction and precision:

> 6. The circle also felt it was appropriate to set up an "advisory panel", which would have the task of giving the Member States an opinion on whether a candidate's profile was suited to the performance of his/her duties, particularly on the basis of

[39] Bo Vesterdorf, President of the Court of First Instance of the European Communities, Oral presentation to the "Discussion Circle" on the Court of Justice on February 24, 2003, CONV 575/03, available at http://european-convention.europa.eu/pdf/reg/en/03/cv00/cv00575.en03.pdf.

[40] Record of the meeting on February 17, 2003 of the discussion circle on the Court of Justice, CONV 573/03, available at http://european-convention.europa.eu/pdf/reg/en/03/cv00/cv00573.en03.pdf.

> objective criteria relating to professional qualifications. The panel—whose deliberations would not be public and which would not hold any hearings—might be made up of former members of the Court and representatives of national supreme courts, while the European Parliament might also appoint a legal expert. However, one member was opposed to the idea of the European Parliament's involvement because he saw in it a danger that the appointment process would become politicised. The circle emphasised that setting up a panel of this kind might make Member States more demanding in the choice of candidates they put forward. The circle also felt that Member States should continue to put forward only one candidate.[41]

The second proposal, which addressed terms of judicial office, was more equivocal. Presenting the ECJ and CFI Presidents as "preferring the current system" though "open to the possibility of introducing a longer and non-renewable term" (ideally of twelve-years' duration), the Circle concluded:

> 8. The circle felt that the Constitution might make a distinction between the system of terms of office for the Court and the CFI. Most members of the circle were in favour of prolonging the term of office of members of the Court and making it non-renewable. However, other members pointed out that the current system had worked well and that it was preferable to keep it. In any event, the circle proposed in this context that the Treaty should explicitly mention the independence and impartiality of judges. The circle agreed to retain the current system for judges at the CFI (renewable six-year term).[42]

As for the procedure for formally appointing the judges, the Circle proposed maintaining the existing system, although it did register meaningful dissent:

> 5. On the procedure for appointing judges and Advocates-General to the Court of Justice . . . and the Court of First Instance . . . , most members of the circle were in favour of maintaining the status quo (appointment by common accord of the governments of the Member States). However, some members felt that appointment should be by act of the Council and, of these, several felt that the Council should act by a qualified majority.[43]

The Circle had apparently changed its stance: what on February 17, 2003 had been a majority in favor of shifting to appointment by Council act[44] had by March 25

[41] Final report of the discussion circle on the Court of Justice, CONV 636/03, available at http://european-convention.europa.eu/pdf/reg/en/03/cv00/cv00636.en03.pdf.

[42] *Id.*

[43] *Id.* (emphasis in original).

[44] *See supra* note 35 and accompanying text.

turned into a majority in favor of "maintaining the status quo (appointment by common accord of the governments of the Member States)." Member States would apparently continue to be shielded by the threat of playing tit for tat when proposing their judicial candidates.

Now that we are on the verge of concluding our background history of the development of the current EU judicial appointments scheme, let us simply pause to note the constellation of issues, features, and solutions that have gradually coalesced since the initial ECSC debates in 1950, and especially since the re-emergence of the appointments debates in the mid-1990s. As those debates have progressed, the major procedural and institutional issues came to be identified as follows: (1) the process of formal appointment (by common accord or by Council act (perhaps by qualified majority voting)); (2) the number of candidates proposed by the Member State governments (one or three); (3) the length of the judicial term (six, nine, or twelve years); (4) the possibility of reappointment; (5) the potential role of the European Parliament; and finally (6) the establishment of an advisory panel for the assessment of judicial candidates, including (7) the panel's composition and (8) the panel's powers and processes (advisory or more binding role, its capacity to hold interviews and to engage in public hearings or deliberations, etc.). To these material considerations must be added key concerns that permeate the terms of the debates: (9) judicial independence; (10) the professional quality of the candidates; (11) the stability and effectiveness of the ECJ's case-law; and (12) the potential politicization of the judicial selection process. With this constellation of twelve issues clearly in view, we can now turn to the modifications actually undertaken in the wake of the Treaty of Lisbon.

V. The Treaty of Lisbon

The Treaty Establishing a Constitution for Europe, signed on October 29, 2004 failed to be ratified after its rejection by French and Dutch voters in the spring of 2005. The substance of the Treaty was instead passed as the more palatably titled Treaty of Lisbon, which entered into force at the end of 2009. In practice, this meant that the substance of the Constitutional Treaty's provisions concerning judicial appointments, based on the Discussion Circle's debates, was effectively enacted by the Treaty of Lisbon. For the sake of completeness, I set out the key provisions here:

TEU ARTICLE 19

1. The Court of Justice of the European Union shall include the Court of Justice, the General Court and specialised courts....

2. The Court of Justice shall consist of one judge from each Member State. It shall be assisted by Advocates-General. The General Court shall include at least one judge per Member State. The Judges and the Advocates-General of the Court of Justice and the Judges of the General Court shall be chosen from persons whose independence is beyond doubt and who satisfy the conditions set out in Articles 253 and 254 of the Treaty on the Functioning of the European Union. They shall be appointed by common accord of the governments of the Member States for six years. Retiring Judges and Advocates-General may be reappointed.

...

TFEU ARTICLE 253

The Judges and Advocates-General of the Court of Justice shall be chosen from persons whose independence is beyond doubt and who possess the qualifications required for appointment to the highest judicial offices in their respective countries or who are jurisconsults of recognised competence; they shall be appointed by common accord of the governments of the Member States for a term of six years, after consultation of the panel provided for in Article 255. . . .

Retiring Judges and Advocates-General may be reappointed. . . .

TFEU ARTICLE 254

. . . The members of the General Court shall be chosen from persons whose independence is beyond doubt and who possess the ability required for appointment to high judicial office. They shall be appointed by common accord of the governments of the Member States for a term of six years, after consultation of the panel provided for in Article 255 . . . Retiring members shall be eligible for reappointment.

TFEU ARTICLE 255

A panel shall be set up in order to give an opinion on candidates' suitability to perform the duties of Judge and Advocate-General of the Court of Justice and the General Court before the governments of the Member States make the appointments referred to in Articles 253 and 254.

The panel shall comprise seven persons chosen from among former members of the Court of Justice and the General Court, members of national supreme courts and lawyers of recognised competence, one of whom shall be proposed by the European Parliament. The Council shall adopt a decision establishing the

> panel's operating rules and a decision appointing its members. It shall act on the initiative of the President of the Court of Justice.[45]

It had taken some nine years, but the Ole Due Report's proposal that "an advisory committee consisting of highly-qualified independent lawyers should be set up to verify the legal competence of candidates"[46] had eventually resulted in the birth of the Article 255 Panel. But it is important to recognize that the Treaty's judicial appointments provisions had in all other respects refused to modify the status quo ante. Appointments continued to be made by common accord of the governments of the Member States. The length of judicial office was not changed from the short six-year terms; and the terms remained renewable. The 255 Panel was the only significant change. As we shall see, however, it would prove major.

[45] Consolidated versions of the Treaty on European Union and the Treaty on the functioning of the European Union [The Treaty of Lisbon], available at http://register.consilium.europa.eu/doc/srv?l=EN&f=ST%206655%202008%20INIT.

[46] Ole Due Report at 51.

3
The 255 Panel in Operation

I. The Establishment of the Panel

In accordance with the terms of Article 255, and on the initiative of European Court of Justice (ECJ) President Vassilios Skouris, the Council passed a pair of decisions establishing the Panel's Operating Rules and appointing its members.[1] The Operating Rules are minimalist, fitting comfortably on a single page; but they do include a few key provisions. Other than specifying that Panel members serve four-year terms and can be reappointed once, the most significant establish the Panel's working methods. Of particular importance is that the Rules appear to impose a veil of secrecy over the Panel's work. Thus, "The deliberations of the panel shall take place *in camera*." Similarly, although the rules specify that new judicial candidates shall be given a hearing before the Panel, "the hearing shall take place in private." Finally, although the Panel is to generate a "statement of reasons" that sets out "the principal grounds on which the panel's opinion is based," that statement/opinion "shall be forwarded to the Representatives of the Governments of the Member States," which suggest that it would *not* to be published.[2]

However important the Operating Rules and their imposed secrecy may be, the decision appointing the members of the first 255 Panel may well prove to have been far more consequential. Working off a list initially provided by ECJ President Skouris,[3] the Council decision appointed the following seven: Jean-Marc Sauvé ("Vice-President"—effectively the Head—of the French Conseil d'Etat[4]), Peter Jann

[1] Council Decision 2010/124/EU of February 25, 2010 relating to the operating rules of the panel provided for in Article 255 of the Treaty on the Functioning of the European Union [2010] OJ L50/18; Council Decision 2010/125/EU of February 25, 2010 appointing the members of the panel provided for in Article 255 of the Treaty on the Functioning of the European Union [2010] OJ L50/20. *See* Vassilio Skouris, Recommendation relating to the operating rules of the panel provided for in Article 255 TFEU, Brussels, January 11, 2010, 5195/10, JUR 5 INST 2 COUR 1; Vassilio Skouris, Recommendation concerning the composition of the panel provided for in Article 255 TFEU, Brussels, February 2, 2010, 5932/10 JUR 57 INST 26 COUR 13.

[2] *See* Council Decision 2010/ 124/ EU of February 25, 2010 relating to the operating rules of the panel provided for in Article 255 of the Treaty on the Functioning of the European Union [2010] OJ L50/ 18.

[3] *See* Tomas Dumbrovsky, Bilyana Petkova, & Marijn van der Sluis, *Judicial Appointments: The Article 255 TFEU Advisory Panel and Selection Procedures in the Member States*, 51 CML Rev. 455, 460 (2014) ["Dumbrovsky et al. (2014)"]; Vassilios Skouris, President of the ECJ, Recommendation concerning the composition of the panel provided for in Article 255 TFEU, Brussels, February 2, 2010, 5932/10 JUR 57 INST 26 COUR 13.

[4] The titular head of the Conseil d'Etat is the sitting Prime Minister of France. But the French Administrative Code explicitly confers the effective presidency on the Vice-President. *See* Article L. 121-1 du Code de justice administrative.

(former Justice of the Austrian Constitutional Court and of the ECJ), Lord Mance (Justice of the UK Supreme Court), Torben Melchior (President of the Danish Supreme Court), Peter Paczolay (President of the Hungarian Constitutional Court), Ana de Palacio (former Spanish Minister of Foreign Affairs and MEP), and Virpi Tiili (former Finnish Judge of the Court of First Instance (CFI)).

What are the key characteristics of this inaugural 255 Panel? First, and most obvious, the seven consisted overwhelmingly of judicial figures: other than the member proposed by the European Parliament (Ana de Palacio), it was composed entirely of high-level judges. Second, these judges are predominantly national: only two of the six (Jann and Tiili) had been European judges (ECJ and CFI, respectively), one of whom (Jann) had also been a national constitutional court judge. One might say, therefore, that four and a half of the six judges (or some three fourths) were national, as opposed to European, judges.

Third, although the composition of the Panel leans distinctly toward national supreme court judges, such national judges tended to have strong European ties. Lord Mance had served as Chairman of the Consultative Council of European Judges and as a Trustee of the European Law Academy.[5] Torben Melchior had been the President of the Network of European Supreme Court Presidents.[6] And Peter Paczolay was a longtime member—and eventually honorary President—of the Venice Commission of the Council of Europe.[7]

Finally, the geographic distribution of the seven might raise an eyebrow. In the decision appointing the Panel, the Council had stated that "Account should be taken of a balanced membership of the panel, both in geographical terms and in terms of representation of the legal systems of the Member States."[8] Yet the Panel's composition tilts tremendously toward established and wealthy Member States from Northern and Western Europe. Of the seven members, only one hailed from Eastern Europe (Peter Paczolay of Hungary) and only one from Southern Europe (Ana de Palacio of Spain). This could surely not have escaped the notice of everyone involved, from ECJ President Skouris (who first proposed the names) to the Council members, who voted to adopt the list.

Lest anyone imagine that the professional and geographic characteristics of the inaugural 255 Panel were accidental, one need only examine those of its successor, which began its work at the expiration of the initial four-year term. Three of the original seven members stayed on for a second term: President Jean-Marc Sauvé (French Conseil d'Etat), Lord Mance (UK Supreme Court), and Peter

[5] https://www.jcpc.uk/about/biographies-of-the-justices.html; https://www.canterbury.ac.uk/social-and-applied-sciences/law-criminal-justice-and-computing/mediation-clinic/advisory-board.aspx.

[6] *See* http://reseau-presidents.eu/news/news-february-2010.

[7] http://www.venice.coe.int/WebForms/pages/?p=cv_191.

[8] Council Decision 2010/125/EU of February 25, 2010 appointing the members of the panel provided for in Article 255 of the Treaty on the Functioning of the European Union [2010] OJ L50/20.

Paczolay (Hungarian Constitutional Court). To these were added Pauliine Koskelo (President of the Supreme Court of Finland), Christiaan Timmermans (Dutch former Justice of the ECJ), Andreas Vosskuhle (President of the German Federal Constitutional Court), and the European Parliament's choice, Luigi Berlinguer (former Italian Minister of Education and MEP). As even the most cursory analysis immediately reveals, the defining characteristics of the 255 Panel were rather studiously maintained and even reinforced. Once again, the Panel consists of six high-level judges, plus the European Parliament's choice. The national character of the judges is further strengthened: the three outgoing judicial members—one ECJ, one CFI, and one national supreme court judge—were replaced by one ECJ and two national judges, which means that the former CFI judge was effectively replaced by yet another national supreme court justice. The net result is that the balance between the judicial members of the Panel has shifted from four national and two European judges to five national and a single European judge. The strong European ties of the domestic judges have also been maintained: Pauliine Koskelo, for example, had been a Director at the European Investment Bank (and furthermore, has recently been appointed as the Finnish Judge on the European Court of Human Rights (ECtHR)).

Finally, the geographic distribution of the Panel membership could hardly have been more faithfully preserved, with absolutely no shift whatever toward better representation of Eastern or Southern Europe, or, for that matter, of less established or wealthy Member States. An Austrian judge had been replaced with a German; a Dane with a Dutchman; and a Finn with ... a Finn! Even the Parliament's choice stayed regional, as a Spaniard was replaced with an Italian. It is difficult to imagine that such rigidly consistent patterns could be the result of chance or oversight.[9]

In short, the inaugural 255 Panel was composed with a rather distinct profile. It was above all a very high-end judicial panel composed of elite Member States supreme court justices with relatively strong European connections, hailing overwhelmingly from established and wealthy Member States from Northern and Western Europe. This profile was then entrenched and even further reinforced with the appointment of the second Panel. There are of course many ways to interpret the decisions that led to this state of affairs, each of which posits a different understanding of the complex tensions and relationships that characterize the European project, such as the vexing relations between the Member States and Europe, and more specifically between the national and European courts, between assorted national political, cultural and economic interests, and those national and European courts, etc. Before we address such issues head on, however, we need to continue

[9] Allow me to note in passing an issue that has become far more controversial in the ECtHR context, and which we will therefore address squarely in Chapter 4: gender equity. The gender balance of the 255 Panel is patently deficient; and oddly, it has only deteriorated with the new appointments. What had been a 5:2 male to female ratio has now become 6:1.

to lay the factual groundwork by examining the actions actually taken by the 255 Panel over the course of its few years of activity.

II. The 255 Panel's Work

The Article 255 Panel has engaged in two primary modes of activity. In accordance with its Treaty-defined mandate, it has "give[n] opinions on candidates' suitability to perform the duties of Judge and Advocate-General of the Court of Justice and the General Court before the governments of the Member States make the appointments."[10] This has obviously been the core of its work and has taken up the great majority of its time. But the Panel has also performed another kind of labor, which, though seemingly banal and technocratic, has arguably been every bit as important as the Panel's actual review of judicial candidates: for the first few years of its existence, it published Reports of its activity on an annual basis.[11] These Reports, which have been composed entirely on the Panel's own independent initiative, have effectively dictated the ground rules for the EU's judicial appointment process: they have defined the criteria by which judicial candidates are to be examined, and in so doing, they have exerted significant pressure on the national processes for selecting proposed European judges.

A. The Panel's Decisions

1. Introduction: the lack of transparency

In discussing the Article 255 Panel's work, it is important to recognize from the start a fundamental feature of the Panel: as suggested by its Operating Rules, the Panel functions largely behind closed doors. Although it is no secret *when* a Member State must propose a judicial candidate to one of the EU courts (the dates for each opening are regularly published) or *who* the Member State has eventually proposed (the Member State forwards the name and c.v. of the candidate to the European authorities), from that point forward, the process takes place out of public view. The Panel's meetings are held *in camera*; its interviews of judicial candidates take place in private; and its opinion on those candidates is forwarded only

[10] Article 255 of the Lisbon Treaty.

[11] It published a report annually for the first three years and after a hiatus, has since published a fourth and fifth on an annual basis. *See* Article 255 Panel, Activity Report of the panel provided for by Article 255 of the Treaty on the Functioning of the European Union, First Report of February 17, 2011 (No. 6509/11); Second Report of January 22, 2013 (No. 5091/13); Third Report of December 13, 2013 (No. SN 1118/2014); Fourth Report of February 10, 2017; Fifth Activity Report of February 22, 2018 ["Activity Report"]. All of these Activity Reports are available at https://curia.europa.eu/jcms/jcms/P_64268/en/.

to the governments of the Member States. As a result, analysis of the Panel's work can only proceed on the basis of information gleaned from alternative sources.

The Panel has even reinforced this secrecy. Most importantly, the Panel has interpreted EU law to forbid the public disclosure of the Panel's opinions regarding judicial candidates. In the words of the Panel's President, Jean-Marc Sauvé, "EU law in the area of protection of personal data as interpreted by the Court of Justice have led the Panel to the conclusion that its opinions cannot be disclosed to the public, be it directly or indirectly. The same applies with respect to Panel's hearings."[12] Furthermore, "the Panel concluded that the tenor of the opinions rendered, favourable or not, cannot be disclosed to the public, be it directly or, by the fiat of detailed statistics, indirectly."[13]

The first effect of this opacity is a much recognized lack of transparency in EU judicial appointments. Why did the 255 Panel give or withhold its seal of approval to this or that judicial candidate? No reason is ever publicly given. In fact, notice is never officially given about the threshold question of whether the Panel gave or refused its approval in the first place! The external observer must instead make certain inferences. If a given candidate has just been appointed to the Court "by common accord of the governments," one might reasonably assume that the 255 Panel gave its blessing. In theory, however, even this is not technically necessary: nothing in the Treaty or the Panel's Operating Rules says that the Panel's assessment of a candidate is in any way binding on the governments. Similarly, if judicial candidate Dupont, put forward by the Belgian government, somehow never gets appointed and Belgium is suddenly going through a new search process to fill a vacancy on the EU courts, one might reasonably assume that Dupont did not fare well in the 255 process. But without inside information, the outside observer can never know for sure: maybe Dupont is instead facing health problems.

Parts IV and V will study the effects of this lack of transparency in depth. For now, it is enough to note that this intentional opacity provides enviable cover for all the players immediately involved in the judicial appointments process at the EU level. The 255 Panel is never at risk of a public reckoning for its assessment of a particular judicial candidate. Meanwhile, the particular candidate and proposing national government are provided fig leaves should the 255 assessment go badly.

[12] Jean-Marc Sauvé, *Selecting the European Union's Judges: The Practice of the Article 255 Panel*, *in* SELECTING EUROPE'S JUDGES: A CRITICAL REVIEW OF THE APPOINTMENT PROCEDURES TO THE EUROPEAN COURTS 78, 81 (footnote omitted) (MICHAL BOBEK ed., 2015) ["Bobek (2015)"].

[13] *Id.* at note 7. Although the Panel can obviously decide for itself whether to publish its opinions, the Member States could theoretically decide not to abide by that decision. In practice, the interpretive decision made by the Panel would have tremendous sway, given the Panel's eminent judicial composition. Indeed, if push came to shove and resulted in litigation, it is hard to imagine that the ECJ would not back up the Panel's interpretation.

And even the governments as a group (i.e., acting "by common accord") are spared the need to defend (and perhaps even to make) certain appointments decisions.[14]

But the lack of transparency also creates a premium on information about what is going on inside the 255 process. And because the only truly reliable source of such information is the Article 255 Panel itself, the Panel exercises an empowering monopoly on this information, the content and flow of which it effectively controls. The 255 Panel has therefore been very clever about the need to maintain secrecy: it has exercised mastery over its own information, simultaneously limiting and monopolizing its dissemination.

Having explained the reasons for the paucity of publicly available information about the 255 Panel's work, it is therefore symptomatic that we must now turn to the Panel for much of the information that follows. This information comes from two sets of sources. The first, which we will soon discuss in significant detail, are the "Activity Reports" that the Panel saw fit to publish annually in the first three years of its operation. The second are speeches and published articles by two members of the 255 Panel, President Jean-Marc Sauvé and the influential Lord Mance, which the Panel has effectively adopted by listing them in Annexes to its Activity Reports.[15]

2. The numbers

As the Panel's own Activity Reports make quite plain, over the first four years of its work (2010–13), the Article 255 Panel delivered sixty-seven opinions on candidatures to the EU courts.[16] Of these, seven have been unfavorable.[17] This is not a trivial number: fully 10% of the candidates put forward by the national governments to fill judicial positions on the EU courts have been formally deemed unfit to exercise such positions.

The numbers are even more striking than this would suggest. The next important piece of information, which the 255 Panel underlines in its Report and which President Sauvé is all too happy to stress in his published work, is that less than half of the sixty-seven candidacies were for first-term judicial candidates: thirty-two were first-time candidacies and thirty-five were for renewals of sitting EU judges. Furthermore, no candidate for renewal has ever been issued an unfavorable assessment by the 255 Panel.[18] As the Panel and Sauvé thus make sure to point out, this means that the Panel rejected 22%—almost a quarter—of all new judicial candidates.[19] This, I think it is fair to say, is a rather astonishing number, especially given

[14] In theory, the opacity of the process might make it easier for the 255 Panel to make a prudentially difficult decision to reject a given candidate, thereby sparing the Council the need to work through a thorny case.

[15] *See* Annex 4 of the Second and Third Activity Reports and Annex 7 of the Fourth and Fifth Activity Reports.

[16] Third Activity Report at 9.

[17] *Id.*

[18] *Id.*

[19] *See id.*; Sauvé in Bobek (2015) at 83.

that until the Treaty of Lisbon came into effect, "no nominee was ever officially rejected in the fifty plus years since the creation of the ECSC, although the governments of the Member States theoretically possessed the power to refuse to grant their 'accord' to any nomination."[20]

Things get even more interesting when one pieces together further information. This requires drawing inferences from the discrepancy between which candidates were initially proposed by Member States and the judges eventually appointed to the judicial positions. Upon doing so, one ends up with revealing statistics. In particular, all seven of the Panel's unfavorable opinions were for candidates to the EU's General Court. Two things follow. First, the Panel has issued unfavorable opinions for a whopping 33% (seven of twenty-one) of the new candidacies to the General Court. Second, no candidate to the ECJ has ever been the subject of an unfavorable opinion.

Interestingly, the geographic distribution of the unhappy candidacies is open to some question. This is where the opacity of the Panel's work generates analytic difficulties: the lack of straightforwardly available information has led to somewhat divergent conclusions about exactly which candidates failed to measure up to the Panel's standards. For his part, Henri de Waele concludes that the failed candidates hailed from Greece, Italy, Belgium (2010); Malta and Sweden (2011); Lithuania (2012); and the Czech Republic (2013).[21] Dumbrovsky, Petkova, and van der Sluis agree on five of de Waele's list of seven, but replace the candidates from Belgium and Malta with those from Romania and Cyprus.[22] Norbert Engel and Bo Vesterdorf back up de Waele's claim on the Belgian and Maltese candidates; yet de Waele relies on Dumbrovski et al. for the Lithuanian and Czech ones.[23]

If one relies on de Waele, this list would mean that three of the failed candidates came from Southern Europe (Greece, Italy, and Malta), two from Eastern Europe (Lithuania and the Czech Republic), and two from Northern Europe (Belgium and Sweden). The profile suggested by Dumbrovski et al. is somewhat different, with again three from Southern Europe (Greece, Italy, and Cyprus), but with three from Eastern Europe (Romania, Lithuania, and the Czech Republic) and only one from Northern Europe (Sweden). Either way, the geographic diversity of the unhappy group cannot be missed. But with such a relatively small group, the shift of a single data point (i.e., Belgium or Romania) significantly changes matters. If Dumbrovski et al. are correct, then condemnation is directed overwhelmingly toward Eastern

[20] Dumbrovsky et al. (2014) at 458. As we shall see below, the Member States have never gone against a Panel decision, whether favorable or unfavorable. *See infra* text accompanying notes 24–26.

[21] Henri de Waele, "Not Quite the Bed that Procrustes Built: Dissecting the System for Selecting Judges at the Court of Justice of the European Union," in Bobek 24, 45–46 (2015).

[22] Dumbrovsky et al. (2014) at 459.

[23] *See* N.P. Engel, *More Transparency and Governmental Loyalty for Maintaining Professional Quality in the Election of Judges to the European Court of Human Rights*, 32 HUMAN RIGHTS L.J. 448 (2008) ["Engel (2008)"]; Bo Vesterdorf, *La nomination des juges de la Cour de Justice de l'Union européenne*, 47(3) CAHIERS DE DROIT EUROPÉEN 610 (2012); de Waele at 45, note 98 and 46, note 100.

and Southern Europe; but if de Waele is right, then condemnation appears rather meticulously balanced between Eastern, Southern, and Northern Europe.

In principle, the unfavorable opinion issued by the Article 255 Panel merely serves to "to give an opinion on candidates' suitability to perform the duties of Judge and Advocate-General … before the governments of the Member States make the appointments." In practice, however, the 255 Panel's judgments have proven to be completely determinative. Indeed, the 255 Panel has effectively said as much in its reports, going to the bother of proclaiming about the "*Outcome of [its] opinions*":

> 4. The panel's opinions, whether favourable or otherwise, *have always been followed* by the governments of the Member States.[24]

This amusingly prideful statement reveals a great deal. On one level, it simply states that the Panel is batting 1000, which, as we shall see in Chapters 4 and 5, is by no means to be taken for granted: Luzius Wildhaber's Advisory Panel of Experts at the ECtHR could hardly say the same.[25] But the passage also suggests that the Panel plays a very significant role in the appointments process, despite Article 255's relatively restrained language. Far from merely giving an *opinion* on candidates' suitability, the Panel appears to be handing down *judgments*: the Panel's opinions are always followed. Furthermore, the Panel strongly suggests that it is not simply playing the role of policeman, denying unqualified candidates access to the EU bench: the passage cunningly states that "the panel's opinions, *whether favourable or otherwise*, have always been followed by the governments." In other words, the Panel's wording indicates not only that the governments have refused to appoint candidates deemed unsuitable, but also that the governments have not failed to appoint those candidates that the Panel has deemed suitable. In this passage, the Panel therefore publicly announces that it is playing the role of both positive and negative gatekeeper to the EU bench. The Panel means to be taken very seriously indeed.

President Sauvé has explicitly proffered a procedural explanation for the Panel's otherwise surprising authority. In a recent piece, he states:

> [T]he absence of … binding force [of the Panel's opinions] is to a large extent offset by the mechanism of the appointment procedure. With the appointment by the common accord, i.e. by a unanimous decision of all Member States, being the principle, the disagreement of one single Member State suffices for there being no

[24] *See* Fourth Activity Report at 13 (emphasis in original). *See also* Second Activity Report at 6; Third Activity Report at 10; Fifth Activity Report at 15.

[25] *See infra* Chapters 4 and 5.

> appointment. Thus, the accord of all Member States is in fact needed for overruling an unfavourable opinion of the Panel.
>
> There has never been this kind of unanimity amongst the Member States in the past that would lead to a decision opposing the direction suggested by the Panel. . . .
>
> In all [the Panel's unfavourable appointments] cases, after the unfavourable opinion issued by the Panel, no appointment ensued, which is certainly unprecedented in international courts. One might speculate that any other result would be very difficult: the appointment procedure *de facto* endows the Panel's opinion with the force comparable to that of an assent procedure, in particular once the opinion issued is negative.
>
> The system of appointment of Union's judges gives therefore a special weight to Panel's opinions.[26]

Sauvé's explanation complements our analysis of the veto system effectively established by the process of appointment "by general accord of the governments."[27] At first blush, his explanation might suggest that the EU judicial appointments process functions *de facto* as a double veto system, as the 255 Panel can effectively veto an appointment before each of the Member States has a chance to do so. But the reality on the ground is that the Panel has become the final arbiter of the suitability of judicial candidates. First, the power of Member States to play tit for tat effectively means that no Member State can take the risk of vetoing another's proposed judicial candidate, especially once the Panel has given that candidate its blessing: this would just invite a retaliatory veto. This means that the Panel effectively exercises a monopoly power to veto candidates, as its approval of a candidate is ultimately determinative.

Second, when the Panel exercises this veto, it is effectively impossible for it to be overruled, as this would require unanimous action by the Member States. Although a Member State did once attempt, in the early days of the Panel, to enlist the others to override an unfavorable Panel opinion against its proposed candidate, the effort was thwarted by a single Member State's refusal to play along (and thereby cripple the Panel); and once this precedent had been set, no Member State has ever seriously attempted such a maneuver again.[28]

The net result is that the Panel wields the final say on European judicial appointments. The longstanding capacity of each Member State to appoint its own judicial candidate with impunity has thus been changed into the unilateral power of the Panel to veto (or approve) proposed candidates. The 255 Panel has effectively

[26] Sauvé in Bobek (2015) at 82–83.
[27] *See supra* Chapter 2, text accompanying note 35.
[28] With apologies, confidentiality stands in the way of providing more in the way of details.

become *the* central institutional player in the judicial appointments process at the EU level.

B. The Activity Reports

At the end of its first year of operation, the Article 255 Panel instituted an extremely shrewd practice: publishing an "Activity Report." The Panel offered the following explanation:

> At the end of its first calendar year of existence the panel deemed it appropriate to draw up the present report, the purpose of which is to retrace its activities and enable the Union's institutions, the Member States' governments and, if appropriate, future candidates for the posts of Judge or Advocate-General of the Court of Justice and the General Court to gain a better understanding of the procedures in place for examining candidatures and the panel's interpretation of the provisions which it is charged with applying.[29]

With this explanation and the corresponding Report, the 255 Panel has taken full advantage of the information gap which it had itself contributed to creating.[30] Having forbidden the publication of its own opinions, the Panel has effectively established a monopoly on almost all relevant information regarding EU judicial appointments. When the Panel then turned around and started publishing its Activity Reports, those Reports therefore took on all the greater importance.

The influence of the Activity Reports became even more pronounced thanks to their composition and content. Rather than limiting itself to a statistical account of the Panel's annual work (which it did in fact produce in a pithy one-page Section I), the first Activity Report saw fit to offer an extended four-page explanation of the process by which the Panel assesses candidacies for judicial positions ("II. Consideration and examination of candidatures") and a detailed three-page exposition of the substantive criteria by which such assessment is made ("III. Assessment of candidates' suitability to perform the duties of Judge of the Court of Justice and the General Court"). As a result, some seven of the eight pages of the Panel's first Activity Report consisted *not* of a report of the Panel's specific activity, but of general discussion of procedural and substantive norms that the Panel had elaborated and adopted to govern its own decision-making. As a practical matter, the Report thus establishes (and then publishes and expounds upon) the rules governing the Panel's assessment of all candidates to the EU bench.

29 First Activity Report.
30 *See supra* Part III(II)(A)(1).

What, then, are those rules? The Panel begins with procedural matters. It first establishes a few "general principles" regarding its examination of candidates. The Member States bear primary responsibility for putting forward the best possible candidates. The Panel cannot select among candidates, nor can it try to influence the overall composition or professional profile of the EU courts. It limits itself to the documents put forward by the Member States and the candidates, as well as to the candidate's publications, and so on.

The Panel then explains that it utilizes a somewhat different procedure for new candidates than for reappointment candidates. In practice, reappointment candidates are subject to relatively peremptory review. But new candidates are not. Part of the Panel's assessment process for such new candidates is directed specifically at the proposing government. The Report explains:

> [T]he panel, pursuant to point 6 of its operating rules, asks the government proposing the application to pass on the essential reasons why it chose the proposed candidate and a letter explaining the reasons for the application and a bibliographic list of the candidate's publications. The panel also asks for information on the national procedure that led to the candidate being selected, inviting the government to say inter alia whether there was a public call for applications, whether a national selection committee was set up and if so how the national selection committee was made up and what it recommended.[31]

In this tremendously important passage, the Panel imposes a *burden of justification* on the Member States. Contrary to what the crafty language of the passage would seem to imply ("pursuant to point 6 of its operating rules ... "), this burden is *not* a product of the Panel's Operating Rules, which merely state that "The panel may ask the government making the proposal to send additional information or other material which the panel considers necessary for its deliberations." With this burden, the Panel therefore establishes a set of new demands on the Member State governments, which must now proffer the "essential reasons why it chose the proposed candidate" and must provide "information on the national procedure that led to the candidate being selected," including "whether there was a public call for applications, whether a national selection committee was set up and if so how the national selection committee was made up and what it recommended." With this pivotal passage, the Panel effectively announces that it has taken on the task of assessing not only each proposed candidate, but also the national procedures by which the Member State has selected and proposed that candidate.

[31] First Activity Report at 6.

Part of the Panel's assessment process is also directed at the candidates themselves. In accordance with point 7 of the Panel's Operating Rules, new candidates are to be called in for an hour-long interview before the Panel. The Report explains:

> The reason for the hearing of the candidate is to supplement the examination of the content of the dossier. It enables the panel to assess, in particular, the candidate's professional experience, legal expertise, aptitude for working in an environment in which a number of legal traditions are represented, language skills, reasons why the candidate considers that he or she is suited for the performing the duties of a Judge at the Court of Justice or General Court and how the candidate envisages doing so. The hearing, which lasts an hour, begins with an introductory presentation in which the candidate briefly introduces himself/herself. The candidate may speak in English, French or any other official language of the European Union. Next, the members of the panel put questions to the candidate, in English or French, for 50 minutes, on the various aspects of the candidature (skills/expertise, experience, motivation, etc.). The candidate is asked to respond in the language in which the question was asked. If the candidate considers his or her mastery of both English and French inadequate, he or she may respond in any other official language of the European Union.[32]

In this paragraph, the Panel begins what will turn out to be an extensive, detailed, and conspicuously repetitious explanation of the key substantive criteria for its judicial assessment. As we are about to examine those criteria in some detail, let us simply pause for a moment to note the seriousness of the interview: it represents a full hour before a panel of prominent judicial figures that cannot help but take on the character of an examination. And to make matters interesting, that examination is meant to be conducted in both English and French. Only if the candidate publicly confesses that his "mastery of both English and French [is] inadequate" is another language to be used. The logic is self-evident: French is, after all, the ECJ's working language; and English is, well, English.[33]

What, then, are the substantive criteria that the Panel uses to assess candidates to the EU courts? The answer is thoroughly foreshadowed in the block quote immediately above.[34] As if this first foreshadowing were not enough, the Panel gives a second in the very next paragraph: "To support its assessment of the candidate's legal expertise, experience, suitability for the office of Judge, independence and impartiality, the panel may take into account …"[35] Still not satisfied,

[32] *Id.*

[33] Given its overall thoroughness, it is odd that the Report does not to bother to explain the English language component of the interview. For more on the practical implications of these language standards, *see infra* text accompanying note 59.

[34] *See supra* note 32.

[35] First Activity Report at 6–7.

the Report anticipates yet a third time in the paragraph after that: "[T]he panel's opinions … set out the reasons underlying their tenor, favourable or otherwise, and concerning the candidate's legal capabilities, professional experience, ability to perform the duties of a Judge with independence and impartiality, knowledge of languages and aptitude for working in an international environment."[36] Having thrice repeated variations on this list of attributes required of judicial candidates, the Panel Report finally arrives at the long and important section that lays out these requirements in greater detail.

The Panel begins by recounting the demands of Articles 253 and 254 of the Treaty of Lisbon, which establish that the members of the ECJ and General Court "shall be chosen from persons whose independence is beyond doubt" and "who possess the qualifications required for appointment to the highest judicial offices in their respective countries or who are jurisconsults of recognised competence" (for the ECJ) or "who possess the ability required for appointment to high judicial office" (for the General Court). The Panel then prepares what will turn out to be three full pages expounding upon what these requirements really mean for the purposes of its assessment of proposed judicial candidates. It explains:

> Although the criteria established by the Treaty on the Functioning of the European Union are exhaustive, the panel nevertheless considers that they could be more clearly and precisely explained. The panel's assessment … is therefore made on the basis of six considerations: the candidate's legal expertise, professional experience, ability to perform the duties of a Judge, assurance of independence and impartiality, language skills and aptitude for working as part of a team in an international environment in which several legal systems are represented.[37]

As is perhaps all too obvious, the Panel uses the vague language of Articles 253 and 254 as a springboard for imposing a series of requirements that the Panel itself delineates. Generating familiarity, normativity, and authority by repeating these requirements four times in some two pages, the Panel effectively defines and inculcates those characteristics that it will demand of all judicial candidates. Although it "stresses that its assessment of the candidature is an overall assessment," the Panel nonetheless warns that "if a candidature is clearly lacking in one of these areas, this could be grounds for an unfavourable opinion."[38] Having defined the required criteria, the Panel is prepared to enforce them.

How, then, does the Panel elaborate upon these criteria? The Panel begins with the first requirement, legal expertise, which it assesses firstly on the basis of "the candidates' career history, and, where relevant, on the basis of [her] published

36 *See id.* at 7.
37 *Id.* at 8–9.
38 *Id.* at 9.

works." The Panel considers her "discharge of high-level judicial, administrative or academic duties, university degrees (such as a doctorate) and experience of teaching or training, as well as experience as a legal expert or consultant to supreme courts or very important institutions, or participation in scientific associations devoted to the study of law."[39] This description evinces a decidedly Civilian understanding of appropriate career preparation for elite judicial or quasi-judicial posts. Legal expertise is correlated with university degrees, teaching and research, and with government work, be it in the judicial or administrative realms. Private practice does not even begin to appear on the Panel's radar screen.

Having thus elaborated on career paths and training, the Panel then specifies the type of legal expertise that it values. It "seeks to determine the breadth and solidity of the candidates' knowledge of the major judicial issues, the challenges involved in the rule of law, and the key aspects of the Union's legal system and EU law, as well as the candidate's ability to reflect on the application of this law by Member States' legal systems, and on the relationships between these systems and European law."[40] Clearly, the Panel is interested in candidates who possess a certain reflective capacity, who demonstrate a penchant for thinking about the large-scale, systemic, and pragmatic legal issues that emerge from the interaction of the EU and Member State systems. Although the Panel readily acknowledges that knowledge of EU law is a "factor" in its assessment of a candidate, it is "less important" than capable reflection on the application of EU law within the Member States and on the primary stakes currently involved.[41] Once again, it is difficult to imagine who would fit such a description other than someone who considered or confronted such issues on a consistent basis, such as European legal scholars, high-level national judges (whether in the judicial or administrative branch), or high-ranking government administrators or advisors of one kind or another. The same holds for "knowledge" concerning "the challenges involved in the rule of law": this too suggests high-level candidates who are used to handling delicate (and potentially explosive) legal and policy issues.[42]

The Panel thus gives every indication that it is seeking highly professionalized candidates. It confirms this in the next section of the Report, which addresses the second criteria, "professional experience." This section focuses on both the time period and the nature of legal experience that the Panel expects of the candidates

[39] *Id.*

[40] *Id.*

[41] *See id.* The translation of the French word "enjeu" is difficult. The French version of the Report speaks of "ses principaux enjeux actuels." The English version speaks of "the major ongoing challenges involved." While this translation is certainly acceptable, I believe that it would be more faithful to the resonance of the French to translate the phrase as "the primary stakes currently involved (or in play)." Given that the Panel's Chair was Jean-Marc Sauvé, one must assume that the text was originally written in French.

[42] As I will discuss further below, this "rule of law" reference is historically and geographically significant: it is undoubtedly directed primarily eastward toward the new accession States of the former Eastern Bloc. For more on this issue, *see infra* Parts III–VI.

for judicial office. On the first point (time), the Panel makes one of its most glaring executive decisions: it unilaterally decides, on no basis other than its "analogy" to "staff of an equivalent level in the European Civil Service, and with reference to the national practices of which it is aware," that ECJ candidates must—absent "exceptional" cases—have at least "twenty years' experience of high level duties" (and General Court candidates, "twelve or even fifteen years") for their experience "to be deemed sufficient."[43]

These new seniority rules are of course notable for having effectively been constructed out of whole cloth. But they are also deeply revealing for substantive and practical reasons as well. The issue turns once again on the new accession states from the East, most of which had long labored under deeply problematic—not to say authoritarian—political regimes. As is well known, transition from these regimes left a gaping hole within the professional ranks of the state: senior civil servants, including judges, were almost necessarily compromised figures.[44] Transition thus called for renewal, which would have to come primarily in the form of youth. This led to the problem of so-called "baby judges": relatively youthful (some argued, overly youthful) candidates put forward primarily by new Member States from the East to fill positions on the European courts.

Not surprisingly, the problem of very youthful judges manifested earlier and more acutely in Strasbourg than in Luxembourg: the European Convention system includes forty-seven signatory states. That is, it includes some twenty more signatory states than the EU, most of which hail from Eastern Europe (and beyond) and signed onto the European Convention on Human Rights (ECHR) some ten years before the large-scale accession of new EU Member States in 2004 (even Russia and the Ukraine had signed onto the ECHR by 1996).[45] This led to the appointment of some eight ECtHR judges thirty-six years old or younger between 1998 and 2011.[46] As we shall see in the next chapter, ECtHR President Jean-Paul Costa responded by addressing a letter to the Committee of Ministers of the Council of Europe on July 9, 2010 that cried out: "The system will fail if judges do not have the necessary experience and authority."[47]

[43] *See* First Activity Report at 6–7.

[44] *See, e.g.*, Jiří Malenovský, *L'INDÉPENDANCE DES JUGES INTERNATIONAUX*, 349 RECUEIL DES COURS DE L'ACADÉMIE DE DROIT INTERNATIONAL DE LA HAYE 187 (2011); Mikael Rask Madsen, "The Legitimization Strategies of International Judges: The Case of the European Court of Human Rights," in Bobek (2015) at 259, 277.

[45] It was, after all, infinitely easier to sign onto a relatively straightforward human rights convention than to work through the brutally complex economic and regulatory thicket required to join the EU.

[46] *See* David Kosař, *Selecting Strasbourg' Judges: A Critique*, *in* SELECTING EUROPE'S JUDGES: A CRITICAL REVIEW OF THE APPOINTMENT PROCEDURES TO THE EUROPEAN COURTS 120, 141 (MICHAL BOBEK ed., 2015).

[47] *See* Engel (2008) at 448–49, 451; Letter from Jean-Paul Costa, President of the European Court of Human Rights, addressed to member states' Permanent Representatives (Ambassadors) on June 9, 2010 ["Costa Letter"], in Committee on Legal Affairs and Human Rights (Rapporteur: Wohlwend), Report on National procedures for the selection of candidates for the European Court of Human Rights, PACE document 12391 (October 6, 2010), Appendix, available at http://assembly.coe.int/nw/xml/XRef/X2H-Xref-ViewPDF.asp?FileID=12764&lang=en.

The 255 Panel responded to the problem with a straightforward solution: to establish explicit norms about minimum years of experience, thereby effectively establishing age minimums by another name. After all, it is hard to imagine how someone could have a minimum of "twenty years' experience of high level duties" under their belt and not be some forty-five to fifty years old. Of course, however well this approach may address the youth/inexperience issue, it only aggravates the problem that led to young and inexperienced candidates in the first place: the paucity of older candidates from new accession states who were qualified yet possessed sufficiently clean hands.

Other than these notable fiats regarding the required length of experience, the Panel had little interesting to offer regarding the type of experience required. Noting that it "does not give preference to any particular type of professional path," the Panel explained that the ability to perform judicial duties on the EU courts "could result from professional experience in judicial office, for example, or alternatively from employment as a lawyer, academic or senior official, or from a career path that successively or simultaneously combines several of these types of experience."[48] This time, the Panel at least opens the door to the possibility of a practitioner joining the EU bench.[49]

On the third and fourth criteria—the candidate's "ability to perform the duties of Judge" and "assurance of independence and impartiality"—the Report has relatively little to say. It does offer a general statement about "the candidate's ability to offer analyses that are appropriate both in principle and in terms of their practical implications," thereby expressing once again a pragmatic turn of mind reminiscent of its concern that a candidate be capable of reflecting upon the major stakes involved in the interaction between the EU and domestic legal systems. And it does warn that the Panel must determine "whether there is evidence of any kind that could engender the slightest reservation regarding the candidate's ability to perform the duties of Judge with independence and impartiality." But it has no further insights to offer.

Finally, the Panel lumps together its final two criteria under the rubric, "Language skills and aptitude for working in an international environment in which several legal systems are represented." As to the language component, the Panel explains that it considers it "an advantage, although not a determining factor," that a candidate be proficient in "several" of the EU's official languages; and it is a "factor" that the candidate be "at least potentially able to become proficient in the working language of the [EU] courts" (i.e., French). In addition to its language testing at the interview, the Panel "may take into consideration published texts written by the candidates in a language other than their mother tongue and,

[48] First Activity Report at 10.
[49] *Cf.* text accompanying note 39.

for example, their participation in the work of international organisations or in international meetings, seminars or conferences."[50]

Finally, the Panel does more than simply look for language proficiency when assessing the candidate's "aptitude for working in an international environment." It demands a certain level of comparative legal awareness:

> Aptitude for working in an international environment in which several legal systems are represented is also assessed in terms of ability to comprehend the broad categories and principles of the legal systems of the Member States of the European Union, in addition to the legal system of the country proposing the candidature, as well as ability to appreciate the issues that may arise from applying Union law there.[51]

Having laid out this final criterion, the Panel closes its First Activity Report with a concluding paragraph expressing its hope that the Report provides "a better understanding of the examination requirements for candidates ... as well as the factors that it takes into consideration in its assessment of candidates' suitability for these offices."

Having now worked through the Panel's First Activity Report is some detail, what are the key take-away points? By far the single most important feature of the Report is, quite simply, its very existence. By producing such a Report, and by using it to articulate and publicize its procedures and criteria for assessing judicial candidates, the 255 Panel unilaterally establishes the procedural and substantive rules that effectively structure much of the judicial appointments process to the EU courts.

Of course, and as the Panel's subsequent Reports make clear, those rules govern the 255 Panel itself: the Panel not only repeats those criteria multiple times within its very first Report, but it reiterates them over and over again from one Report to the next, effectively treating them as ruling norms. But those rules govern much more than the Panel's own actions. By establishing and publicizing the criteria by which the Panel assesses candidates, the Report effectively imposes those criteria on the Member States and on their potential candidates. After all, the Panel has proven itself quite willing to issue unfavorable opinions: although it did not so specify in its Report, the Panel had, in its very first year of activity, gone so far as to reject three of the five new candidates to the General Court. As a result, only very foolish or recalcitrant governments would bother putting forward candidates who did not reasonably fulfill the requirements publicly pronounced by the Panel in its Activity Report.[52]

[50] First Activity Report at 11.
[51] *Id.*
[52] Indeed, one would expect that publication of, and thus familiarity with, the Panel's norms would result in increasingly rare Panel rejection of candidates: in theory, Member States should respond by

But the Report's procedural rules did more still: by requiring that each Member State government explain the procedures by which, and justify the reasons for which, it had selected a given candidate, the Panel was quite clearly incentivizing—and arguably dictating—preferred, if not exactly required, judicial selection mechanisms *at the national level,* i.e., the process by which Member State *x* selected candidate *y*. This effect is all the more remarkable in that the Lisbon Treaty made no mention whatsoever of regulating such domestic selection mechanisms. Indeed, none of the *debates* about judicial selection going back to 1950 left any trace of having so much as considered such a proposal.

To illustrate this point, one need only mention that the 255 Panel was even more pointed and specific on these domestic procedural issues than we have already seen.[53] The Panel declares:

> To support its assessment of the candidate's legal expertise, experience, suitability for the office of Judge, independence and impartiality, the panel may take into account the conditions under which the Member State concerned selected the candidate and, in particular, whether there is a national merit-based selection procedure and, if so, how it is organised (transparency and objectivity of the procedure, involvement of a national selection committee, composition of that committee, and so on). The panel may also take into account other selection procedures offering at least equivalent guarantees, such as choice of the candidate by a Member State's highest court. It may also check whether the candidate proposed by the Member State government was adopted at the conclusion of the national procedure.[54]

Only very thick-headed government advisors could fail to grasp that the Panel was defining "best practices" for the national selection procedure, best practices that the government would be wise to institute and follow. For even though the Panel demurely states that the existence and actual operation of such a procedure are but "parts of a comprehensive assessment of the candidature ... along with the other criteria the panel applies," the Panel does bother to mention that they "are indeed factors [the Panel] may take into account." The existence and publication of the Panel's Report thus establishes procedural and substantive rules that have come to structure much of the judicial appointments process to the EU courts, including at the national level.

proposing candidates capable of passing muster under those norms. Interestingly, it is not entirely clear that this has truly happened: the Panel's Fourth Report indicates that "16.6% (six out of 36) of the opinions on candidatures for a first term of office were unfavourable." Fourth Report at 11. This rate is not markedly different from the 22% figure listed in the Panel's Third Report.

[53] *See supra* text accompanying notes 31–51.

[54] First Activity Report at 7.

The other key feature of the Report is the overall profile that it effectively constructs for successful candidates to the EU bench. While there are certainly plenty of specifics to fill in and significant room for variation, the Panel's explanations of its six criteria undoubtedly combine to yield the broad outlines of a proper judicial candidate. Just as important, perhaps, is the converse: combining the six criteria appears to rule out—if not formally disqualify—certain types of potential candidates.

What, then, would a proper ECJ candidate tend to look like under the 255 Panel's criteria? She would very likely be at or near the peak period of her professional career. Given the minimum twenty years of experience, she would be at least forty-five. And given six-year renewable terms, and assuming at least twelve years of desired service before reaching a typical retirement age, one would reasonably expect the typical first-time candidate to be roughly between the ages of forty-five and sixty, and most likely between fifty and fifty-five.[55]

The candidate would ideally be a highly professionalized state actor (either a high-ranking judge or executive branch actor) or seasoned academic. After all, who else would have both the capacity and occasion to engage in the kind of broad reflection on the interface between the European and domestic legal regimes that the Panel overtly values? Who else would have twenty plus years of experience in such matters? And who else would publish on these issues in a manner that would put the Panel in a position to consult their publication record, as the Report repeatedly discusses?

This combination of seniority, experience, and publication record also suggests that if the candidate were an executive branch actor, she would likely be of a more technocratic than overtly political bent. This would only be reinforced by the requirement of independence placed on the candidate: a personal advisor to a political figure or someone who were a significant legal/political figure in her own right and who would thus be sensitive—never mind beholden—to political calculations and patronage would be poorly positioned to withstand Panel scrutiny.

This high-level technocratic, judicial, or academic profile is strengthened by the linguistic and comparative law demands instituted by the 255 Panel. The Panel values candidates proficient in "several" of the EU's official languages; and it seriously tests French and English language proficiency by embedding it into the very structure of its interview process, in which questions—and hopefully answers—are conducted in those two languages. Indeed, the Panel goes so far as to speak of

[55] Mikael Madsen has done some solid number crunching on the age of ECJ judges and has concluded that the average age of sitting ECJ judges is now indeed in this range: "the average age of the members of the bench is now around 51–52 years (compared to mid-60s of the 1959 Court), including a number of judges—mainly from eastern Europe but not only—in their 30s." Madsen in Bobek (2015) at 277 (footnote omitted). Note that the youth of Eastern candidates, recognized by Madsen, lowers the average age to slightly below what one might otherwise expect from the 255 Panel's criteria. Of course, those criteria have only been in place for a few years. One might reasonably expect, therefore, that the average age would slowly increase to expected levels over the next ten or so years.

taking "into consideration published texts written by the candidates in a language other than their mother tongue."[56] But who, frankly, publishes in foreign languages other than people with a rather high-level technocratic, judicial, or academic profile? In practice, one might reasonably expect a great deal of overlap between such jurists and those who "participat[e] in the work of international organisations or in international meetings, seminars or conferences."[57] Similarly, who might have the comparative legal training sufficient "to comprehend the broad categories and principles of the legal systems of the Member States of the European Union" and "to appreciate the issues that may arise from applying Union law there," other than jurists who have acquired foreign law degrees (such as Masters/LLM degrees from abroad) and/or who function at the heart of a highly international legal environment?

In sum, although the Panel's set of six criteria may not yield a single, precise, and required profile for judicial candidates, it does yield the broad outlines of what a prototypical version of such a candidate is likely to look like: a fifty-year old judge, academic, or high-level civil servant with significant experience in European legal issues, very good language skills (especially in French and English), and comparative legal training (likely gained through some combination of legal education and international legal work). Perhaps not terribly surprisingly, this set of characteristics would appear to fit most high-level EU civil servants.[58]

At least as important, however, is the type of candidate who is effectively foreclosed by the Panel's six criteria. To some extent, one need only think of the inverse version of the ideal profile to visualize the undesirable candidate. But I think it more useful to focus on a couple of the key criteria. Take the language requirements. In this day and age, and especially in Europe, it is increasingly rare for a serious jurist with international interests not to speak several languages, and in particular, to speak quite good English. The flip side of this reality is sufficiently important to stress. *Failure* to speak several languages, and especially English, now functions as a marker. As a result, the 255 Panel's language requirements effectively exclude the parochial, inward looking, national candidate.

In fact, the use of French as the Court's official working language has a fascinating—and arguably paradoxical—practical effect. French has, of course, long been the language of international diplomacy.[59] In theory, therefore, the use of

[56] First Activity Report at 11.

[57] *See id.*

[58] For anthropological examinations of Europe and its institutional milieus, *see, e.g.*, IRÈNE BELLIER & THOMAS M. WILSON eds., AN ANTHROPOLOGY OF THE EUROPEAN UNION: BUILDING, IMAGINING AND EXPERIENCING THE NEW EUROPE (2000); CRIS SHORE, VICTORIA A. GODDARD, & JOSEP R. LLOBERA eds., THE ANTHROPOLOGY OF EUROPE: IDENTITIES AND BOUNDARIES IN CONFLICT (1994); KARIN GEUIJEN, PAUL'T HART, SEBASTIAAN PRINCEN, & KUTSAL YESILKAG eds., THE NEW EUROCRATS: NATIONAL CIVIL SERVANTS IN EU POLICYMAKING (2008), available at https://www.jstor.org/stable/j.ctt46mvpw.

[59] French superseded Latin as the dominant language of European diplomacy in the late seventeenth century. See SIMEON POTTER, OUR LANGUAGE 180 (1964).

French as the Court's working language only simplifies transnational interchange by reverting to the commonly recognized diplomatic language. The twist, of course, is that French has declined precipitously in favor of English as the *de facto lingua franca* of international discourse, diplomatic convention notwithstanding. As the divide between diplomatic convention and linguistic realities becomes ever more pronounced, the insistence on using French as the Court's working language therefore functions not to *lower* linguistic barriers in/to the Court, but to *raise* them: in truth, fewer and fewer jurists are capable of working effectively in French. The French language requirement thus operates to raise the bar for judicial candidates, and to do so in a manner that operates selectively. It effectively skews the applicant pool, devaluing candidates who have failed to demonstrate a tangible and pre-existing commitment to international culture.

This anti-parochial tilt is further reinforced by the 255 Panel's demand that candidates possess a demonstrable "aptitude for working in an international environment in which several legal systems are represented," which is "assessed in terms of ability to comprehend the broad categories and principles of the legal systems of the Member States of the European Union ... as well as ability to appreciate the issues that may arise from applying Union law there."[60] Indeed, these international *bona fides* are even supported by the otherwise seemingly gratuitous specification that candidates possess the "ability ... to debate within a collegial judicial environment": When combined with the independence criteria, the Panel appears to be ruling out the possibility of appointing obstructionist judicial candidates who might subvert the European project from inside the EU judiciary in a manner that Eurosceptics have deployed with a modicum of success in other European institutions, such as the European Parliament.

In sum, although the criteria established by the 255 Panel in its First Activity Report do not dictate the precise profile of judicial candidate that Member States must put forward to fill positions on the EU courts, they nonetheless go a long way toward ruling out certain profiles and privileging others. If nothing else, anyone who (1) has studied EU/Member State interactions sufficiently to be meaningfully reflective about the modes and stakes of those interactions, who (2) has sufficiently polished French and English language skills to engage in oral debates concerning such matters and perhaps to have published on them, who (3) has twenty or more years of high-level experience under their belt, and who (4) knows enough about foreign legal systems to be able to grasp something of the complexities involved in applying EU law in such jurisdictions is *extremely* unlikely to be something other than a highly professionalized and good-faith supporter (of one variant or another) of the European project.

[60] First Activity Report at 11.

C. "Personal" Publications

To conclude our initial introduction to the work of the Article 255 Panel, I would like to linger briefly over speeches and articles published by two of the most prominent members of the original 255 Panel, President Jean-Marc Sauvé and Lord Mance of the UK Supreme Court. Although these publications are not made in the name of the Article 255 Panel, it is fair to say that the line between the personal and the institutional could hardly be more blurred. The first reason for this intermingling is obvious: as both were eminent (and two-term) members of the Panel, their publications regarding European judicial appointments and especially the Panel cannot help but be considered highly probative information and perhaps even semi-official pronouncements. This is all the more so given the fact that Sauvé was, after all, the President of the Panel (indeed, the only one it had in its first eight years of existence). The second reason is that the Panel has actively promoted such a blurring of lines: in its Second, Third, and Fourth Activity Reports, the Panel has listed relevant publications by both President Sauvé and Lord Mance in an Annex—entitled "List of publications by members of the panel on the subject of its activities" and "List of publications by members of the panel relating to its work." In the Second and Third, these constituted Annex 4 to the Panel's Report. What were Annexes 1–3? Nothing less than (1) a reprinting of Treaty Articles 253–255 (establishing the qualifications and appointment processes to the EU courts), (2) the Council decision setting the operating rules of the 255 Panel, and (3) the Council Decision appointing the Members of the Panel. In short, the Panel could hardly have done more to cast the "personal" publications of President Sauvé and Lord Mance in a quasi-institutional and even quasi-official light.

In the writings of these two most prominent members of the 255 Panel, the key and recurring theme is that the judicial appointments process had previously been characterized by the unrestrained exercise of political whim. Under the guise of "mutual trust" and appointment "by common accord," each Member State government was utterly free to nominate whomever it chose without any fear of second-guessing, never mind refusal.[61] This could not help but expose the EU judicial order to risks and critique. President Sauvé writes:

> The preexisting situation was vulnerable in effect to critique regarding the capacities of certain candidates or regarding the real motives for their nomination, as they were all called upon to become judges without any system of filtering or any impartial evaluation, at least at the European level. This risk, even if only virtual, was of a nature to cast a shadow over the EU judicial system.[62]

[61] *See* Sauvé in Bobek (2015) at 78–79.

[62] J.-M. Sauvé, "Le rôle du comité 255 dans la séparation des pouvoirs au sein de l'Union européenne" 9, intervention lors du colloque pour le 130ème anniversaire du Conseil supérieur de la magistrature

Lord Mance describes this prior state of affairs as a "primitive situation" in which there was no scrutiny whatsoever of the nominations made by Member State governments. He quotes Gilbert Guillaume, former President of the International Court of Justice, to the effect that "the nominees presented by each Government are in fact endorsed by the Council of Ministers without any real discussion." As a result, "[a]ppointment was for Governments alone, and it is not clear that any nominee was ever refused."[63]

The Article 255 Panel was thus a means of putting an end to such unchecked governmental control and to the political dynamics that went along with it. Sauvé explains:

> In other words, the Treaty of Lisbon inserted into the space between the Member States and the judicial system of the European Union an element of independent and impartial evaluation of candidates' ability. What is being sought is to:
>
>> put the mechanism of judicial appointments at a proper distance from the political heat and power games;
>>
>> make sure that the judges appointed possess the qualities that are necessary for the holding of their future office.
>>
>> The aim of the Panel is thus to contribute, commensurably with its powers, to the safeguard and to the increase of an independent, well-qualified, and legitimate judicial power within the European Union.[64]

This passage, which lumps together a great many distinct themes in a manner that this book will disentangle in the ensuing chapters, makes the key association: governmental control of judicial appointments by the Member States leads to "political heat and power games," which, given the court's powers, damages the legitimacy of the European judiciary.

As Lord Mance goes to some pains to stress, this link between judicial appointments and politics is neither new nor reserved to the international sphere. Recounting in some detail the British tradition of appointing the Attorney General as Lord Chief Justice of England as a reward for political services, Mance speaks approvingly of the rise of such appointments mechanisms as judicial councils, which increasingly take judicial appointments out of this politically dominated realm.[65]

le 24 octobre 2013, available at http://www.conseil-etat.fr/fr/discours-et-interventions/la-separation-des-pouvoirs-l-union-europeenne-et-le-comite-255-.html ["Sauvé (2013)"].

[63] Lord Mance, "The Composition of the European Court of Justice" (The text of a talk given to the United Kingdom Association for European Law, October 19, 2011) 9, available at https://www.supremecourt.uk/docs/speech_111019.pdf ["Mance (2011)"].

[64] Sauvé in Bobek (2015) at 79.

[65] Mance (2011) at 5–7.

On the international front, Mance explains, even more than on the British domestic one, the politics of judicial appointments have continued to operate until quite recently. Mance thus quotes at length from Paul Mahoney, former Registrar of the ECtHR and then President of the EU's Civil Service Tribunal: "The selection procedures (domestic and international) are described as 'ad hoc and often politicised processes', 'scattered and haphazard', 'in many ways flawed' and 'shrouded in mystery', being 'neither open nor accountable', with 'some countries [being] accused of seeing their judge as a 'legal ambassador' on the court [in question]'."[66] Because most treaties are "silent on the national selection procedures for international courts ... , the Governments [are] free to do more or less what they want. Nominees are generally chosen by the same Governments which are thereafter parties in the judicial proceedings."[67]

Unfortunately, the alternatives to the ECJ's appointment procedures are hardly better. As Mahoney noted regarding elections for international judges: "If there is an election of judges, Governments have been seen to indulge in political lobbying and bargaining in favour of their (preferred) national candidate, with increasing recourse to professional marketing methods."[68] Mance thus quotes from an Interights Report of May 2003 about the ECtHR appointment process, which had bluntly stated: "States have absolute discretion with respect to the nomination system they adopt... In practice, even in the most established democracies, nomination often involves a 'tap on the shoulder' from the Minister of Justice or Foreign Affairs, and frequently rewards political loyalty more than merit." Furthermore, the "Committee of Ministers, while on paper the body that should be empowered to engage with governments on their nomination procedures and reject unacceptable lists, is concerned more with safeguarding state sovereignty than with ensuring the quality of nominated candidates."[69]

As Sauvé makes sure to stress, however, suggestions for electoral modifications to the EU's appointments process were misguided. They only invited further political machinations:

> The system of appointment of Union's judges [now] gives therefore a special weight to Panel's opinions. The weight of the opinions would carry much less if, by contrast, after the opinion of the Panel was issued, the judges of the Union would be appointed or elected by the majority in the Council or in the European Parliament. Even if the election of judges by a parliamentary assembly has its advantages in terms of the publicity of debates and votes, it can hardly be substantiated in terms of properly evaluating the relevant criteria and the ability for

[66] *Id.* at 10.
[67] *Id.*
[68] *Id.*
[69] *Id.* at 8, quoting Interights (Dr. Jutta Limbach, Chair), "Judicial Independence: Law and Practice of Appointments to the European Court of Human Rights" 9 (May 2003) ["Interights Report"].

> holding a judicial office … The procedure does not necessarily contribute, to put it euphemistically, to prioritizing the consideration of qualifications necessary for the judicial office. It leaves in fact open door to purely political mechanisms such as creation of majorities that may, in some cases, give only little importance to those qualifications. Unfortunately, experience demonstrates that such risk is not just imaginary. Moreover, the domination of political authority in the process of judicial appointments may also be questionable in terms of the requirement of the separation of powers.[70]

As this passage argues, the issue involves not only dubious political machinations, but also a more fundamental structural principle: the separation of powers.

President Sauvé could hardly make this distinction between political chicanery and the separation of powers more explicit, entitling one of his major speeches: "The Role of the Article 255 Panel in the Separation of Powers within the European Union."[71] The real problem, he explains, is the link that remains between the judicial candidates and their Member State governments. On the one hand, "the independence of the European courts is in all respects assured." But on the other, "in a context in which the judges 'are appointed by common accord of the governments of the Member States,' which is to say in which the 'umbilical cord' remains between the judges and the States, certain questions nonetheless remained to be resolved." "It is to these [questions]," explains Sauvé, "that the Panel created by Article 255 [of the Treaty of Lisbon] seeks to respond."[72] As a result of the Panel's work to ensure the independence and competence of the judicial candidates, "there has therefore gradually emerged, within the European Union, a veritable 'judicial power,' whose independence and legitimacy have been further reinforced by the creation of the Article 255 Panel."[73]

To Sauvé, the best evidence of the gradual establishment of this full-fledged European judicial power can be seen above all in the ECJ's emergence as "a veritable supreme court, playing the role of motor of European integration and promoter of fundamental rights."[74] To Mance, "The Court of Justice has been a central achievement of the European Union—a court with unparalleled transnational power. It has cemented European development in fields expanding far beyond the original common market concept."[75] In fact, "The Court of Justice has been concerned to develop a significant fundamental rights jurisprudence. A famous example is [*Kadi*]."[76]

70 Sauvé in Bobek (2015) at 83–84.
71 *See supra* note 62.
72 *See id.* at 3.
73 *Id.*
74 *See id.* at 6.
75 Mance (2011) at 1.
76 *Id.* at 3, citing Cases C-402/05 P and C-415/05 Kadi and Al Barakaat v. Council and Commission.

For Sauvé, it is precisely because of this rise in importance of the Court, of its development of a fundamental rights jurisprudence, and thus of its establishment as a full-fledged judicial power that the judicial appointment process raises fundamental separation of powers concerns. He pithily explains:

> In this context, one blind spot remained: the appointment of EU judges by common accord of the Member States. The Article 255 Panel was conceived as a means to respond and, as a consequence, to contribute to securing the position of an independent and impartial judicial power in the European Union.[77]

In short, the quasi-official writings of President Sauvé and Lord Mance explicitly claim that the true stakes of the judicial appointment process debates is nothing less than the establishment of a true judicial power in a system characterized by a proper separation of powers.

To both Sauvé and Mance, however, the possibility of judicial reappointment represents the clearest indicator of the problematic "umbilical cord" that remains between EU judges and the Member States that nominate them. Sauvé explains: "Undoubtedly, another risk has certainly not completely disappeared: that a Member State may oppose the renewal of the mandate of a [sitting] judge for purely political reasons or for reasons of pure political convenience, reasons which, furthermore, need not be disclosed. This real problem cannot be overcome by the Panel ... "[78] As a result, states Mance, it is "unavoidable that some judges may feel or at least appear to feel under stress as to whether they may or may not be appointed,"[79] which may, as the 2003 Interights report suggested, have a conscious or unconscious effect on their decision-making.[80] Indeed, some Member States, "even among the old founder members" (such as Germany), do not have "a healthy tradition of reappointing [their] judges and advocates general" because they "regard[] the post as politically significant."[81] Of course, the solution to this problem is straightforward: changing the current six-year renewable judicial terms into a single non-renewable term of longer duration.[82] Under the existing Treaty framework, however, "the panel can do nothing about the question of non-renewal of a judge's mandate."[83]

What the Panel has been able to do, writes Sauvé, has been to deny appointments to unqualified candidates, especially those with insufficient "length of high-level professional experience" or with "inadequate" "legal expertise."[84] Indeed, some

77 Sauvé (2013) at 10.
78 *Id.* at 9.
79 Mance (2011) at 12.
80 *See* Interights Report.
81 Mance (2011) at 17.
82 *See* Sauvé (2013) at 9.
83 Mance (2011) at 17.
84 Sauvé in Bobek (2015) at 83.

"wholly lacked knowledge of EU law and had insufficient expertise concerning basic notions of EU law and the relationship between legal systems."[85] Even more, by specifying the content of the criteria explicitly or implicitly established by the Lisbon Treaty, the Panel has, Sauvé proudly reports, "taken on the task, by discreet brush strokes, of trying to compose the portrait of what makes a good judge and, in particular, a good EU judge."[86]

This important definitional task also compliments the burden that the Panel has imposed on Member States to justify the selection of the candidates they propose for the EU bench. Writes Sauvé: "Primarily, the Panel asks the [Member State] government[] to transmit explanations both as to the national selection procedures and as to its reasons motivating its proposed candidate."[87] As Mance explains:

> An important feature of the panel's practice is, in my view, that it enquires of each nominating state whether any national selection committee was constituted, and, if it was, of whom it consisted and what its recommendations were. There is increasing evidence of formal selection processes being instituted in a number of European countries.[88]

Sauvé and Mance thus make no bones about the Panel's establishment of criteria for the EU bench; nor do they minimize the importance of the Panel's imposition of the requirement that Member State governments justify not only their particular judicial selection but also their judicial selection procedures—a requirement that has in fact led to the recent establishment of "formal selection processes ... in a number of European countries."[89]

Finally, President Sauvé and Lord Mance are hardly shy in expressing their hopes regarding further tasks and powers that the 255 Panel might soon take on. In concluding his "Separation of Powers" article, President Sauvé addresses these issues in a final section, entitled "Is the Role of the Panel to Evolve?" The 255 Panel might, he suggests, play a key role in two different contexts. First, it could help to resolve the vexing issue of staffing the EU's lower court, the General Court, whose caseload has proven to be far greater than its capacities. As it appeared unlikely at the time that the Court would be literally doubled in size (permitting each Member State to appoint another judge), some mechanism would eventually have to be

[85] *Id.*

[86] Sauvé (2013) at 8. *See also* Sauvé in Bobek (2015) at 82 ("The opinions carry, first of all, a certain moral authority that keeps growing over the years. The gradual emergence and fine-tuning of Panel's consistent views as to what makes a 'good European judge' contribute to this authority. These views, which are disseminated in particular through the activity reports and, as far as the Member States are concerned, can also be inferred from the study of the individual opinions rendered, are one of the chief contributions of the Panel.")

[87] Sauvé (2013) at 7.

[88] Mance (2011) at 18.

[89] *See id.*

devised for selecting the judges who might fill a smaller number of new positions.[90] The 255 Panel, writes Sauvé, might evaluate and rank—on the basis of "their competences and capacities"—those candidates who might respond to a public call for applications.[91]

Second, should the EU formally accede to the ECHR, the EU would have to select a judge to sit on the ECtHR. The 255 Panel might once again evaluate and rank—on a basis "founded essentially on merit"—those candidates who might respond to a public call for applications, which would permit the EU to compose the traditional list of three candidates to put forward to the Council of Europe for selection and appointment by the Parliamentary Assembly of the Council of Europe. Sauvé concludes: "These two developments would ultimately serve to reinforce the role played by the 255 Panel in strengthening the independence and legitimacy of the judicial power within the European Union."[92] In fact, President Sauvé and Lord Mance almost never miss an opportunity to suggest that the 255 Panel play such a ranking role in such new contexts.[93]

It is in this hypothetical context of the potential expansion of the Panel's powers that one can perhaps best perceive the conception that the 255 Panel, and especially its powerful President, Jean-Marc Sauvé, hold of the Panel's essential nature. In concluding his article on the separation of powers in the EU, Sauvé thus portrays the 255 Panel as "a sort of minimalist judicial council or judicial council *light*."[94] Similarly, in his article in Michal Bobek's book on SELECTING EUROPE'S JUDGES, Sauvé states that the 255 Panel "could perhaps be seen ... as a germ of a council of the judiciary within the European Union."[95] Viewed as such, the Panel "exercises its full responsibilities and contributes, within the limits of its charge, to strengthening the independence and legitimacy of the European courts within the European Union's horizontal and vertical separation of powers. The Panel's field

[90] What then seemed unlikely has now come to pass: the decision has been taken to double the size of the General Court. *See* Regulation 2016/1192, available at https://eur-lex.europa.eu/eli/reg/2016/1192/oj.

[91] *See* Sauvé (2013) at 9.

[92] *Id.*

[93] *See, e.g.*, Sauvé in Bobek (2015) at 84–85 ("Further improvements of the system put in place within the EU could certainly be envisaged or desired. They could follow in particular from further evolution of the role of the Panel, be it in relation to the potential increase of the number of judges at the General Court or, once it becomes relevant, the appointment of the EU Judge to the European Court of Human Rights. In both of these cases, a public call for applications could be envisaged and the Panel might in particular be asked to evaluate and rank the candidates according to their merit, a task which would be certainly attainable."); Mance (2011) at 27; Jean-Marc Sauvé, "The future of the European Union courts; Increased workload: organisation, appointment and training of judges," Conference organized by the Council of Bars and Law Societies of Europe, Monday April 28, 2014, available at http://www.conseil-etat.fr/content/download/4032/12124/version/1/file/28_04_2014_discours_president_sauve_en.pdf.

[94] Sauvé (2013) at 10.

[95] Sauvé in Bobek (2015) at 84. Though he does not specifically address such potential expansion of the Panel's remit, Lord Mance does pay a great deal of attention to judicial appointment commissions (especially at the domestic level), whose "scope and diversity" he openly favors expanding. The framing of his analysis suggest that his views are quite consonant with those of his colleague Sauvé. See Mance (2011) at 6–7.

of action therefore carries much further than the apparent modesty of its powers might suggest."[96]

III. Conclusion

This chapter has described the truly remarkable transformations in the judicial appointments process to the ECJ. That process has gradually shifted quite radically from one that—under the guise of communal action through "common accord"—all but guaranteed unilateral governmental power to appoint and reappoint judges to Luxembourg at will. The Treaty of Lisbon and subsequent developments have effectively subjected ECJ appointments to the veto power of the newly established 255 Panel. This dramatic shift has been compounded by the Panel's savvy use of its Activity Reports not only to define, and thereby to impose its vision of "what," to use the words of its President Jean-Marc Sauvé, "makes a good judge and, in particular, a good EU judge,"[97] but also to induce Member States to adopt appropriate selection mechanisms at the domestic level.

These important procedural and institutional reforms also reflect and produce significant conceptual developments. On the one hand, the reforms clearly reflect a new willingness to subject the Member State's judicial appointments decisions to second-guessing on the grounds of judicial competence and independence. This new willingness necessarily reflects and establishes a new relationship not only to judicial appointments, but also to the separation of powers, to the judicial role, and to judicial competence and independence. This book's ensuing chapters will address each of these issues, giving them the dedicated treatment they deserve. For now, it is enough to recognize that the vetting panel established by Article 255 of the Treaty of Lisbon represents a fundamental shift in European judicial politics.

[96] Sauvé (2013) at 10.
[97] *Id.* at 8.

PART II

THE NEW APPOINTMENT PROCESSES OF THE ECtHR

The Advisory Panel of Experts

In many key respects, the developments in the European Court of Human Rights' (ECtHR) judicial appointments processes offer deep parallels to those we just studied at the European Court of Justice (ECJ). Established in roughly the same post-War period of the 1950s, each represented bold super-national European interventions that simultaneously sought to minimize the threat they posed to classic domestic political arrangements. Each self-consciously developed multidimensional institutional designs that, to contemporary eyes, appear opaque, cumbersome, and arguably confused. But these clever design solutions sought to finesse the complexities and tensions that existed not only between the assorted States that signed onto them, but also the ambivalences that lurked within them.

The ECtHR and the ECJ have been shaped by fundamentally similar historical, political, and intellectual forces. Many of those pressures, such as the fall of the Berlin Wall and the large-scale accession of new States from the East, though often prompting broadly similar reforms, have nonetheless generated quite different results. The ECtHR, for example, has taken a much slower path to institutional relevance and power. Some of this is a function of its more limited jurisdictional remit: unlike the ECJ, it is only a fundamental rights court, with none of the trade-based, free-movement jurisdiction that, while distinctly less substantively flashy, has nonetheless proven to generate more far-reaching effects on domestic and European constitutional structures. Some of this is also a function of the ECtHR's far more cumbersome institutional machinery: the Council of Europe's original tri-partite institutional structure (the Parliamentary Assembly (PACE), the Court, and the Committee of Ministers) was hardly conducive to swift or dramatic action—nor, frankly, was it meant to be.

The judicial appointments reforms of the two European high courts therefore reveal both similarities and differences. On the one hand, both courts were deeply affected by the post-1989 accession of Eastern European states. On the other hand, this wave of accessions combined with distinctive institutional arrangements to generate significantly different results. For example, the ECtHR actually faced a significantly larger number of applicant states and did so somewhat sooner than the ECJ. This made sense: accession to a relatively simple human rights convention was far more straightforward (and somewhat less politically fraught) than accession to the EU's complex and integrated economic, political, and arguably constitutional order. As we shall see, however, this larger and earlier wave interacted with the Council of Europe's complex institutional and procedural forms in a distinctive manner: reforms that could be relatively easily and straightforwardly undertaken by the EU needed to work through a far more convoluted procedural and institutional structure in Strasbourg. This chapter therefore offers a demonstration of the significant effects produced by variations in background conditions: the peculiarities of institutional forms, the specific personalities in play, the different jurisdictional and geographical environments, and so on have eventually led to widely divergent experiences between the ECJ's 255 Panel and the ECtHR's Advisory Panel of Experts (APE).

This Part is organized as follows. Chapter 4 offers a historical reconstruction of the ECtHR's judicial appointment reforms. Once again, I push this historical analysis significantly farther back than other scholars, who almost uniformly trace their analyses no earlier than 1998. Their chosen date makes superficial sense, as it points to Protocol 11 to the Convention, which profoundly modified the Council of Europe's existing institutional architecture by establishing a "new," permanent, full-time and single Court, thereby abolishing the Commission and granting individuals direct access to the newly reorganized Court.[1] But to use Protocol 11 as the effective birthdate of the Court as we know it today is of course to minimize quite drastically the first forty years of the Court's existence, badly obscuring important and ongoing structural tensions that were hardwired into the Convention system.

Our historical analysis will therefore pay just enough attention to the formative debates during the foundational period of the European Convention on Human Rights (ECHR) to recognize some of the complexities, tensions, and ambivalences that shaped the establishment of the Convention system in its original form, so that we might grasp their persistence and ongoing relevance to today's institutional, procedural, and substantive debates concerning judicial appointments.

My working thesis underlines once again the point implicit in Chapter 2's early historical reconstruction: it is a mistake to take as our starting point that the ECJ and the ECtHR are (and always have been) courts, *tout court*. Of course they are both courts. But the history of their formation, institutional forms, jurisdictional remits, and procedural approaches all tends to complicate what it has meant to be

[1] *See* Protocol No. 11 to the Convention for the Protection of Human Rights and Fundamental Freedoms, Restructuring the Control Machinery Established Thereby, available at https://www.echr.coe.int/Documents/Library_Collection_P11_ETS155E_ENG.pdf; Andrew Drzemczewski, *The European Human Rights Convention: Protocol No. 11 Entry Into Force and First Year of Application*, Documentação e Direito Comparado, nos 79/80 (1999), available at http://www.gddc.pt/actividade-editorial/pdfs-publicacoes/7980-a.pdf.

"a court." Just as an examination of the early European Coal and Steel Community (ECSC) debates reveals the desire of the original six Member States to protect themselves and their national interests against High Authority decisions (which they did by establishing an institution that eventually became the Council of Ministers, and which only secondarily led to the formation of the ECJ), so does an examination of Convention history demonstrate that the Convention's Contracting Parties wished very much to protect themselves against the "control machinery" that they were themselves creating. They did so by designing a remarkably complex procedural and institutional structure that not only manifested their ambivalence, but which has profoundly affected the developmental path of the Court ever since.

Once we have briefly paused over these early formative debates, we can turn our attention to the emergence of Protocol 11, which undoubtedly altered the Convention system in fundamental ways. As of 1998, the Court suddenly became *the* key institution of the Council of Europe: the Commission was abolished, the role of the Committee of Ministers was significantly reduced, and individuals gained direct access to the Strasbourg Court. What motivated these major changes, which so profoundly altered the nature of this judicial institution, and what were to be their likely effects? As we shall see, Protocol 11 transformed the ECtHR, dramatically changing its nature as a court. It is for this reason that we cannot truly examine the judicial appointments debates without contextualizing them: what appears in the literature to be freestanding, post-1998 reforms to the Strasbourg judicial appointments process is actually the continuation of an ongoing process of transformation of the institutional machinery of the Convention system and, accordingly, the continuation of longstanding debates about what such a court was and ought to be. To omit this contextualizing history is to drive from view much that has proven important and enduring in these transformations.

The judicial appointments reforms therefore turn out to be part of much broader debates about the "courtliness" of the ECtHR. This analysis reinforces what we observed in Chapter 2's examination of the ECJ's formation: in some important sense, the ECtHR's original structure was much more interesting and flexible than what it has turned into. In comparison to the rather imaginative institutional design solutions and intellectual frameworks of the 1950s, it almost appears as if the European legal and political environments have become—for better or worse—increasingly simplistic, inflexible, and doctrinaire about what exactly a court must be.

Once we have thus set the table, the chapter will turn to the judicial appointment reforms per se, almost all of which date from the post-accession period. These reforms have addressed a few substantive issues and a series of procedural ones. The substantive reforms sought primarily to guarantee a measure of gender balance and language proficiency on the Court. The procedural ones aimed to rationalize the judicial appointments process at both the domestic and the European levels. These procedural reforms ranged from insisting that domestic authorities advertise the search for judicial candidates, submit their candidates to the European authorities in an alphabetical list, and use a model CV format (so as not to try to game the selection process at the European level), to requiring that a committee of the PACE interview the list of candidates proposed by the national authorities and that the PACE reject lists that fail to provide a "real choice" between three legitimate candidates, to empowering the PACE to reject lists if the national selection process has not been sufficiently fair, transparent, and consistent. Finally, the 2010 Protocol 14 to the Convention changed the length of judicial office from six-year renewable terms to a single nine-year term.[2]

Following the example of the ECJ, the ECtHR then quickly took the important step in 2010 of establishing a panel of eminent jurists to review the suitability of the judicial candidates proposed by the States to fill vacancies on the Court. As we shall see, this Advisory Panel of Experts (APE), originally headed by former ECtHR President Luzius Wildhaber, has—in stark contrast to the ECJ's Article 255 Panel—had a decidedly difficult time in the performance of its task.

Chapter 5 will present the difficulties increasingly encountered by the APE. These include tensions between the APE and the PACE (and especially with the PACE's committee tasked with running judicial elections) and those between the APE and State governments uninterested in heeding the APE's recommendations. These difficulties have given rise to a series of increasingly well-known scandals or "incidents," in which both the States and the PACE have thumbed their noses at an increasingly frustrated APE, whose prickly Chair, Luzius Wildhaber, did not fail to voice his displeasure in public and in increasingly sharp tones.[3]

This chapter therefore helps to prepare the analyses of Part V, which argue that these unseemly (if rather juicy!) conflicts simultaneously *reveal* existing tensions in the complex field of European judicial politics and represent important and telling *interventions* within it. These conflicts obviously expose deep fissures between domestic political actors and the European judiciary. But they also represent institutional, professional, and ideological battles between assorted players operating at the intersection of the European and domestic domains, including PACE administrative insiders, ECtHR judges, domestic judges, legal academics, Eastern and Western European legal players, and so on. A more comprehensive theory of these conflicts will have to await Parts V and VI; but this Part combines with the last to set the stage for the ensuing analysis.

[2] Protocol 15 increases the age limit for ECtHR judges to seventy-four.
[3] These scandals will be discussed in Part V.

4
The Prehistory and History of the APE

I. History: Back to the Beginning

As in Chapter 2, I propose that we spend at least a little time looking back to the formative era of the Court in order to develop a better sense of the deep and long-standing tensions that have marked the establishment and operation of such a supranational judicial institution. The key point is painfully obvious; but it is nonetheless routinely left entirely out of the picture of scholarly analysis of the European judicial appointment debates. The point is quite simply that even before the ECtHR was formally established, the Contracting Parties to the ECHR were *extremely* wary of an international human rights court that might interfere with national authorities, legal systems, and traditions. For all of the post-War commitment to fundamental rights values, and for all of the Cold War propaganda value of signing onto such an international fundamental rights oriented organization as the Council of Europe, the Contracting Parties had little intention of putting themselves at the mercy of a readily accessible international fundamental rights court.

In fact, the Contracting Parties put a great deal of effort into constructing an institutional structure for the Convention system that would minimize their direct exposure to unwanted rulings. From today's vantage point, one cannot help but grin knowingly at the byzantine nature of their creation. To begin with, the sheer amount of time between the drafting of the European Convention by the newly formed Council of Europe in 1950, its entry into force in 1953, and the establishment of the Court in 1959 is indicative of just how keen the Contracting States were (*not*) to subject themselves to judicial supervision.

As if this were not enough, the Convention included two notoriously "optional" opt-in provisions. First, a Contracting State did not have to accept the jurisdiction of the Court at all! Article 46 of the original Convention stated that "[a]ny of the High Contracting Parties may at any time declare that it recognises as compulsory ... the jurisdiction of the Court,"[4] which of course meant that *without* such an affirmative declaration, any State could refuse such jurisdiction. And indeed, few accepted: when the Convention finally came into force in 1953, only *two* of the then fourteen signatory States (Denmark and Ireland) accepted the

[4] Article 46 of the 1950 ECHR, available at http://www.echr.coe.int/Documents/Collection_Convention_1950_ENG.pdf.

Court's jurisdiction;[5] and these two were hardly international leaders. Even worse, the Court only came into existence in 1959. The reason for this was painfully simple: for the Court to come into existence, Article 56 of the original Convention required that eight States agree to the (future) Court's jurisdiction under Article 46. This baseline requirement was not fulfilled for some nine years (by which point the Council of Europe possessed fifteen Member States).

Second, a Contracting State did not have to accept that individuals could petition under the Convention for redress against violations that the State may have committed. And once again, few did: when the Convention finally came into force in 1953, only *three* of the fourteen signatory States (Denmark, Ireland, and Sweden) accepted the right of individual petition.[6] One need hardly stress the implications that these two optional aspects of the Convention had for the (lack of) teeth of the Convention and of the Court . . .

Finally, the Convention established an institutional structure that can only be considered obstructionist. For starters, it created a tremendously powerful Commission that filtered those complaints that could be brought to Strasbourg. The Commission's job was, frankly, to dismiss the great majority of cases as "inadmissible" and to resolve the rest by diplomatic compromise. Second, the Convention also created an intergovernmental Committee of Ministers that handled all interstate cases. Due to these two institutions and their respective remits, the Court could not be directly petitioned at all. It could only hear those few cases that (1) the Commission had declared admissible and (2) had failed to bring to negotiated settlement, and furthermore (3) the Commission or—in exceptionally rare cases—one of the State parties had decided to bring before the Court.

Needless to say, the construction of such elaborate barriers to the Court was hardly accidental. In August 1950, for example, the British Lord Chancellor William Allen Jowitt declared that almost all in the government "came to the conclusion that we were not prepared to encourage our European friends to jeopardise our whole system of law, which we have laboriously built up over the centuries, in favour of some half-baked scheme to be administered by some unknown court."[7] Candidly demonstrating a categorical rejection of an enforceable Convention, he wrote:

> It completely passes the wit of man to guess what results would be arrived at by a tribunal composed of elected persons who need not even be lawyers, drawn

[5] Ed Bates, *The Birth of the European Convention on Human Rights—And the European Court of Human Rights*, The European Court of Human Rights between Law and Politics 17, 40 (Jonas Christoffersen & Mikael Rask Madsen eds., 2011) ["Bates (2011)"].

[6] *Id.*

[7] Henry G. Schermers, Protocol 11 to the European Convention on Human Rights, at 2 available at https://europainstitut.de/fileadmin/schriften/317.pdf, quoting Anthony Lester, *Fundamental Rights: The United Kingdom Isolated?*, Public Law 46 Spring, 46–72 (1984).

> from various European States possessing completely different systems of law, and whose deliberations take place behind closed doors ... Any student of our legal institutions ... must recoil from this document with a feeling of horror ... I cannot view with equanimity a still further appeal to a secret court, composed of persons with no legal training, possessing the unfettered right to expound the meaning of 17 Articles which may mean anything, or—as I hope—nothing.[8]

Indeed, the governments understood perfectly well the risks that a truly enforceable Convention might represent. In the post-War period, their greatest fears were of an explicitly political nature, such as the unwelcome (!) possibility that opponents to colonial policies might try to use the Convention as a means to undermine colonial authority. As the British Colonial Secretary bluntly stated:

> The introduction of such a system of appeal to an international authority is likely to cause considerable misunderstanding and political unsettlement in many Colonial territories. The bulk of the people in most Colonies are still politically immature and the essence of good government among such people is respect for one single undivided authority which they are taught to recognise as responsible for their affairs. The right of petition to an international body would obscure this principle and would suggest to Colonial peoples either that the ultimate authority in the affairs of their territory is not the Crown or that there is more than one ultimate authority. This confusion would undoubtedly be exploited by extremist politicians in the Colonies in order to undermine the authority of the Colonial Government concerned. Loyalty would be shaken: administration would be made more difficult and agitation more easy.[9]

No less threatening was the possibility that oppositional political parties, such as the German communist party, might avail themselves of the Convention as a means to combat oppressive governmental measures.[10]

The Convention's (obstructionist) jurisdictional and institutional structure worked all too well. The Commission unceremoniously rejected 178 of the first 195 complaints, including those by the German communists.[11] These results undoubtedly helped to put national governments at ease, which would eventually help their gradual acceptance not only of the Convention, but also of the jurisdiction of the Court and of the right of individual petition. But in the meantime, as Ed Bates concludes in his reconstruction of the early days of the Convention, such

[8] *Id.* at 2–3.

[9] *Id.* at 2 [again citing Lester].

[10] *Id.* at 5.

[11] Y.S. Klerk & L. van Poelgeest, *Ratificatie à contre coeur: de reserves van de Nederlandse regering jegens het Europese Verdrag voor de Rechten van de Mens en het individueel klachtrecht*, RECHTSGELEERD MAGAZIJN 220–43 (1991).

negative results were so predictable that not only human rights activists, but even the PACE membership that had prepared the initial drafting of the Convention in 1949, viewed the Convention signed in 1950—complete with its two essential "optional" provisions—as a major disappointment.[12]

Given the intentionally tightly confined nature of the Convention system as originally constructed, it is easy to understand why legal scholars studying the ECtHR's judicial appointment processes begin their analyses in 1998, when Protocol 11 profoundly changed the structure of the Court. Protocol 11 effectively did away with a great many of the compromises that had been built into the original Convention system some fifty years earlier. The Commission, which had in truth long served as the primary decisional institution of the Convention system, was abolished, thereby granting the Court original jurisdiction in all cases brought to Strasbourg under the Convention. Individuals were accordingly granted the right to petition the Court directly, while the Court was granted compulsory jurisdiction.

Furthermore, because the Court was clearly going to carry a much greater workload in the absence of the Commission, it was finally turned into a full-time institution. As originally constructed, the Court and its judges were only to function on a part-time basis. Indeed, ECtHR judges were expected to have full-time jobs at home and to come only intermittently to Strasbourg to handle the odd case: the original Convention actually included a provision stating that judges of the Court would be paid a daily compensation for their work.[13]

For all that Protocol 11 profoundly changed the structure and nature of the ECtHR, it is nonetheless a mistake to consider the Court only in its post-1998 iteration. To do so obscures important continuities between the "new" and "old" Court, between the interests, reservations, and conflicts of such key actors as the Contracting Parties or the domestic judiciaries, and between the fundamental historical developments that have helped to transform the European political, legal, and institutional landscapes over the last fifty years.

Protocol 11 did not come as a lightning bolt from the sky. It was part of an ongoing cycle of transformations of Europe and of the Convention system. Early rumblings about moving toward a "single" Court (i.e., one that merged the Court and the Commission) date back as early as the 1980s, when a number of Council of Europe institutions began mooting the issue in a long series of discussions, reports, and proposals, ranging from a 1982 meeting of the Committee of Experts for the Improvement of the Procedure under the European Convention on Human Rights (known technically as "DH-PR"), to a 1985 European Ministerial Conference on Human Rights, to assorted international conferences.[14] The DH-PR was eventually

[12] *See* Bates (2011) at 22, 29–31.

[13] Article 42 stated: "The members of the Court shall receive for each day a duty of compensation to be determined by the Committee of Ministers."

[14] For a more detailed account of these early debates, *see* Council of Europe, "Explanatory Report to Protocol No. 11 to the Convention for the Protection of Human Rights and Fundamental Freedoms, restructuring the control machinery established thereby," ["Explanatory Report

called upon by the Council of Europe's Steering Committee for Human Rights to examine the issue, leading to a report that was finally declassified by the Committee of Ministers and published in 1989.[15] But fundamental disagreements over the merits of "merging" into a "single" Court led to impasse, notwithstanding a steady flow of initiatives pointing in that general direction.

The impasse was not broken until 1993, when the Committee of Ministers finally decided to back the merger idea and the European Heads of State endorsed this decision in the Vienna Declaration.[16] And yet, after ten plus years of ongoing discussions, both the PACE and Committee of Ministers suddenly stressed the urgency of reform. Why? What had happened that suddenly made it so important that the Commission's traditional management of complaints via "friendly settlements" (i.e., diplomatic compromise) needed to be replaced by formal judicial decisions handed down by a European Court with compulsory and original jurisdiction that could be directly petitioned as of right by individuals? What could be so important to have actually gotten the Contracting Parties to finally accept what they had so vehemently refused since 1950, namely, to subject themselves directly to review and liability before a supranational European human rights court?[17] What had changed?

The technical answer is caseload. As the Explanatory Report to Protocol 11 describes, "The number of applications registered with the Commission has increased from 404 in 1981 to 2,037 in 1993."[18] As a result:

> The backlog of cases before the Commission is considerable. At the end of the Commission's session in January 1994, the number of pending cases stood at 2,672, more than 1,487 of which had not yet been looked at by the Commission. It takes on average over 5 years for a case to be finally determined by the Court or the Committee of Ministers.[19]

A growing number of applications had led to an increasing number of cases referred to the Court, which resulted in backlogs and increasingly unacceptable delays. This is only logical. But why the sudden urgency?

to Protocol 11"] 3–4, available at https://rm.coe.int/CoERMPublicCommonSearchServices/DisplayDCTMContent?documentId=09000016800cb5e9.

[15] Doc. H (89)2, republished in 14 HUMAN RIGHTS LAW JOURNAL 31–48 (1993).

[16] *See* Explanatory Report to Protocol 11 at 5.

[17] As Brian Simpson bluntly states: "The truth was that a majority [of the governments] in the Council of Europe were, whatever their pretensions in public, unenthusiastic at the prospect of international European human rights protection." A.W.B. SIMPSON, HUMAN RIGHTS AND THE END OF EMPIRE 667 (2001).

[18] *See* Explanatory Report to Protocol 11 at 5.

[19] *Id.*

The real answer, of course, just as for the ECJ, was *accession*. As the Explanatory Report to Protocol 11 states:

> The number of applications registered with the Commission has increased from 404 in 1981 to 2,037 in 1993. This figure can be expected to increase significantly in view of the fact that the system has become better known to individuals in member States, and in view of the fact that new States have and will become Parties to the Convention. By the year 2000, there may well be 35–40 States party to the Convention. The number of judges and members of the Commission will increase in a corresponding manner.[20]

Accession of former Eastern Bloc countries was the game changer. Hungary opened the floodgates by becoming the first to accede to the Convention in 1990, followed swiftly by some thirteen others by the time Russia itself acceded in 1996. As a result, the number of Contracting Parties, which had risen modestly from fourteen in 1950 to twenty-one in 1987, would explode to forty-one by 2000.

And while the importance of the purely numerical dimension of the problem should not be minimized, accession obviously involved far more. In a 1992 Recommendation, the PACE thus declared:

> 2. [The PACE] notes that the number of Council of Europe member states has risen to twenty-seven and will continue to rise in the next few years and that a considerable increase in the number of applications submitted to the Commission and to the Court is thus to be expected.
>
> 3. It expects that *the number of individual applications will increase disproportionately to the population of the new member states as, contrary to older member states, the Council of Europe's system for the protection of human rights constitutes for them an important element for the building-up of fundamental rights, democracy and the rule of law*.[21]

With these paragraphs, the PACE had expressed the crux of the matter. Yes, accession would profoundly affect caseload. But the Convention system would represent something fundamentally different to the "new member states" than it did for the "older" ones. For the new states, the Convention would be an important means of constructing or establishing "fundamental rights, democracy and the rule of law."

The inferences were dual. First, the new states did not in fact possess such constitutional, legal, political, and social goods; hence the need to use the Convention system as a tool for gaining them. Second, and in contradistinction, the older states did not need to make use of the Convention system in this manner. Exactly why

[20] *Id.*

[21] PACE Recommendation 1194 (1992) (emphasis added).

is not exactly spelled out. One possibility is that they had already availed themselves of the Convention system in such a manner, to good effect. The other, and far more likely option, is that the Convention represented something fundamentally different to these older members. For them, it was but a *subsidiary* means of protection: (a) a backstop meant to guard against particular and localized fundamental rights violations and (b) a bulwark in the last instance against potential slides toward totalitarianism.

The distinction between the old and new Member States, while obviously realistic in many respects, was also loaded. For one thing, it reflected and even reinscribed many of the assumptions of the immediate post-War period, i.e., those that governed precisely the foundational period of the Convention system. As Ed Bates explains so well, in the foundational period, the Convention system was broadly seen as an "alarm bell" that would allow a siren to sound should any (Western) Member State begin to teeter toward totalitarianism.[22] By inference—and this was also rather self-evidently part of the publicity component of the Council of Europe—the Eastern bloc countries under Soviet influence were not teetering toward totalitarianism: they were already there.

One need hardly stress that, given this historical background, the PACE was surely being realistic about the state of socio-political life in most Eastern European countries in the early 1990s. To saddle emerging democracies with such a legacy of 1950, however, was not only to reinforce unflattering and estranging distinctions, but also to grant them important prescriptive power moving forward.

This prescriptive component becomes evident when one recognizes the longstanding European distinction between two fundamentally different visions of the Convention system: a thinner "alarm bell" anti-totalitarian vision and a more robustly justiciable and human-rights-oriented one. This latter vision had fought hard for enshrinement in the Convention system from the very beginning. But it had for the most part been defeated in the early days. On the one hand, such a vision was said to be "unnecessary for the European nations where human rights were already well protected" (i.e., the very ones to accede to the Convention); and on the other, it was too often associated with advocates striving for a more sweeping European-wide federation (an arguably utopian European Union).[23] This defeat became manifest with the rejection—thanks to the Convention's two "optional" opt-in provisions—of a Court with compulsory jurisdiction over individual complaints.

By the early 1990s, however, it was precisely these foundational assumptions that were being retrieved and recast in the service of a new project: managing the accession of the new Member States from the East. The Convention was no longer to be conceived as a merely subsidiary or backstop system of protection. It was

[22] *See* Bates (2011) at 21–27.
[23] *See id.* at 25–26.

instead to be deployed, to be used as a tool "for the building-up of fundamental rights, democracy and the rule of law."[24] By recasting the Convention system in these familiar—yet inverted—terms, both the Convention system and the Court could now be affirmatively tasked to supervise the new Member States in a manner that could actively generate results. As Leo Zwaak revealingly stated in the aftermath of the passage of Protocol 11:

> Still, it can be said that the enlargement of the Council of Europe with "new democracies", the recent ratification of the Convention by the Russian Federation and the existing human rights situation in Turkey are only some indicators that a more active role of a supervisory body would be desirable.[25]

It was the 1990s mass accession that enabled a fundamental reconceptualization of the Court, one that called for the Court to adopt "a more active" and constructive supervisory role, rather than a more modest, intermittent, and subsidiary "alarm bell" function.

This shift in the Council of Europe's perspective also emerges quite clearly in the sudden explosion of interest in another set of debates alongside those regarding the role of the Court and of the Convention: debates over "judicial independence." These debates are sufficiently important that I dedicate Part III to analyzing them in detail.[26] For our current purposes, it is sufficient to underline that these debates arose in exactly the same period as did the Protocol 11 debates about the structure of the Convention system and the remit of the Court.

Thus, for example, in 1994, the very same year that the Committee of Ministers of the Council of Europe signed onto Protocol 11, the Committee suddenly passed a Recommendation "On the Independence, Efficiency and Role of Judges."[27] The Ministers open this Recommendation by making a series of conceptual links that effectively encapsulate the issues on the table:

> Noting the essential role of judges and other persons exercising judicial functions in ensuring the protection of human rights and fundamental freedoms;
> Desiring to promote the independence of judges in order to strengthen the rule of law in democratic states;
> Aware of the need to reinforce the position and powers of judges in order to achieve an efficient and fair legal system;

[24] PACE Recommendation 1194 (1992) (emphasis added).

[25] Leo Zwaak, *The Reform of the Supervisory Mechanism under the European Convention on Human Rights: Does it Really Matter?*, *in* To Baehr in Our Minds: Essays on Human Rights From the Heart of the Netherlands 195 (Mielle Bulterman, Aart Hendriks, & Jacqueline Smith eds., 1998).

[26] *See infra* Part III.

[27] Committee of Ministers, 1994 Recommendation on the Independence of Judges.

> Conscious of the desirability of ensuring the proper exercise of judicial responsibilities which are a collection of judicial duties and powers aimed at protecting the interests of all persons,
>
> Recommends that governments of member states adopt or reinforce all measures necessary to promote the role of individual judges and the judiciary as a whole and strengthen their independence and efficiency, by implementing, in particular, the following principles: ... [28]

The Ministers' Explanatory Report is even more explicit about the links between judicial independence, democracy, the separation of powers, and the rule of law:

> 1. Within the framework of the activities undertaken to promote and guarantee the efficiency and fairness of civil and criminal justice, it was decided to prepare a recommendation on the independence, efficiency and role of judges.
> 2. Indeed, the Council of Europe includes among its aims the institution and protection of a democratic and political system characterised by the rule of law and the establishment of a constitutionally governed state, as well as the promotion and protection of human rights and fundamental freedoms.
> 3. The recommendation on the independence, efficiency and role of judges recognizes and emphasises the pre-eminent and significant role played by judges in the implementation of these aims. The independence of judges is one of the central pillars of the rule of law. The need to promote the independence of judges is not confined to individual judges only but may have consequences for the judicial system as a whole.[29]

Indeed, the Ministers' explanation even offers the following striking paragraph:

> 38. The independent allotted task of judges is that of safeguarding the rights and freedoms of all persons within the scope of their duty to administer justice (see paragraph 1). The judge is responsible for protecting the rights and freedoms granted to individuals. This obligation should not only be seen as a duty to protect the minimum rights as expressed in the European Convention of Human Rights. The obligation goes further but it is difficult to define in precise terms its scope. Ultimately, the obligation has to do with the defence of democracy and the rule of law, safeguarding against oppression and the totalitarian state as expressed in the Statute of the Council of Europe.[30]

The change in tone and emphasis could hardly be more apparent. The Council of Europe was now in the business of promoting constitutionalism and the rule

[28] *Id.* at 1
[29] *Id.* at 6.
[30] *Id.* at 14.

of law in emerging democracies, "safeguarding against oppression and the totalitarian state." The foundational era's "alarm bell" vision was being fused with the more robust and justiciable human rights vision to yield a particularly active and powerful Court, whose judges were suddenly portrayed as the linchpins of democracy.

This new state of affairs, however, was going to put the Court in a very difficult position. On the one hand, it was going to have to assert a "more active" supervisory role in order to deal with new accession states. But on the other, it was itself going to be increasingly composed of judges put forward by those very states. The judicial appointments reforms manifest all of the tensions and inconsistencies implicit in this delicate state of affairs.

This brief historical reconstruction allows us therefore to place the current judicial appointments debates in their proper frame. These debates are but the latest step in an ongoing set of discussions about the nature, goals, and remit of the Convention system; about the respective roles of the Court, the Commission, and the Committee of Ministers in that system; about the role of the Court as a court; and about the nature of its membership and of the States it needs to supervise.

In these long-term debates, the transformations effectuated by Protocol 11 were not a brand new beginning. The "new" Court did not suddenly emerge fully formed in 1998 like Athena from Zeus's head. Rather, Protocol 11 was but another stage—if undoubtedly a particularly important one—in the ongoing development of the Convention system. And as we shall see, those changes interacted with historical developments, institutional realities, and intellectual debates in a manner that are intimately connected to the judicial appointments disputes.

II. The Judicial Appointments Developments

Having briefly laid out the backstory, we can now turn to the developments in the ECtHR's judicial appointments process itself. These developments began over twenty years ago and, perhaps surprisingly, show little sign of stopping. They are also a little byzantine, insofar as they involve multiple institutional actors, ranging from the PACE, to important PACE committees and subcommittees, to the Committee of Ministers, to members and ex-members of the Court, to assorted national actors. Finally, these developments include both substantive and procedural reforms, including numerous procedural appointments reforms that generate—and are often intended to generate—particular substantive effects.

Given the history outlined above, it should not be terribly surprising that the first major moves directed at reforming the ECtHR's judicial appointment process took place at almost exactly the same period as the judicial independence debates and the Protocol 11 developments. In 1995, a key PACE institution, the Committee on

Legal Affairs and Human Rights,[31] proposed a Draft Resolution and Report "on the procedure for examining candidatures for the election of judges to the European Court of Human Rights."[32] The Committee explicitly framed its proposals in terms of the expected ratification and entry into force of Protocol 11:

> With the entry into force of Protocol No. 11 to the European Convention on Human Rights, expected in the course of 1997, a single and full-time Court of professional judges will be set up. However, the election procedure of judges by the Parliamentary Assembly will not be substantially modified.
>
> Nevertheless, the Assembly wishes to take advantage of the short time left to improve its own procedure for examining the candidatures and for the selection of candidates, for more efficiency and professionalism.[33]

The PACE would continue to elect ECtHR judges from a slate of three judicial candidates put forward by each Member State. But the Committee proposed two modifications to these traditional procedures once Protocol 11 took effect. First, "[f]uture candidates will be invited to fill in a model curriculum vitae, so that the Assembly will have comparable information at its disposal." The Committee Rapporteur, Lord Kirkhill explained that such a "model CV"—i.e., a pre-formatted CV form—"would make it easier to compare the candidates among themselves."[34] Although this explanation is true insofar as it goes, Kirkhill and the Committee were being discreet. The real problem had long been that Member States had found an effective means of signaling their preference for one of the three candidates they put forward for PACE election to the Court: they would vary the form of the CVs in accordance with their preferences. Their favored candidates would be put forward with impressively long and rich résumés, while disfavored candidates would be put forward with meager ones![35]

The Committee's second proposal was that the candidates "be interviewed by a sub-committee of the Assembly, for their qualities to be assessed."[36] Kirkhill explained:

[31] In addition to playing an important role in the PACE election of ECtHR judges, the Committee effectively operates as the Parliamentary Assembly's legal advisor. *See* Committee on Legal Affairs and Human Rights, Work of the Committee on Legal Affairs and Human Rights (AS/Jur): an overview, Information document prepared by the Secretariat, AS/Jur/Inf (2014) 01.

[32] PACE Committee on Legal Affairs and Human Rights (Rapporteur: Lord Kirkhill), Report on the procedure for examining candidatures for the election of judges to the European Court of Human Rights 1, Doc 7439, 1403-15/12/95-1-E (1995) ["PACE Report for Examining ECtHR Judicial Candidatures"].

[33] Ratification of Protocol 11 clearly proved more difficult than the Committee expected and thus did not come into effect until 1998.

[34] PACE Report for Examining ECtHR Judicial Candidatures at 6.

[35] *See* John Hedigan, *The Election of Judges to the European Court of Human Rights*, *in* PROMOTING JUSTICE, HUMAN RIGHTS AND CONFLICT RESOLUTION THROUGH INTERNATIONAL LAW: LIBER AMICORUM LUCIUS CAFLISCH 238 (MARCELO KOHEN ed., 2007).

[36] PACE Report for Examining ECtHR Judicial Candidatures at 1. When the Committee's Draft was eventually passed as a PACE Resolution, it was the Committee itself (or a sub-committee thereof) that would run the candidate interviews and make its recommendations to the PACE. Importantly, the key

> It is clear that if one really wants to assess the qualities of the candidates this cannot be done on their CV alone. This would already be very difficult at national level but becomes impossible when one has to judge candidates from completely different cultural and other backgrounds. Even if one uses exactly the same terminology, the meaning of the words may be completely different and errors of translation and appreciation are likely to arise. The committee has therefore come to the conclusion that it would not be sufficient merely to examine the CVs of all the candidates but that, in addition, they should be invited to a hearing. This hearing could be held by the Sub-Committee on Human Rights or by a special *ad hoc* sub-committee of the Committee on Legal Affairs and Human Rights.[37]

In short, the Committee had come to "the opinion that—with the establishment of the new single, full-time European Court of Human Rights—there should be *a more professional approach* to the election procedure."[38]

It is worth pausing for a moment to make a few passing remarks on these initial procedural proposals. First, they clearly tie the need for appointments reform to Protocol 11's creation of a single and full-time ECtHR, i.e., with the obvious increase in the importance within the Convention system of the Court *qua* court. Second, they respond to this rise in judicial importance with procedural reforms. By establishing the model CV and the candidate interviews, the Committee suggests that formal and thorough bureaucratic procedures can lend appropriate rationality to the appointments process. Third, this technocratic rationality is explicitly couched in the language of "professionalism" and "quality." This draws an important—if tactfully implicit—dichotomy between the Committee's disinterested attention to electoral procedural regularity and to the candidate's substantive merits on the one hand, and the proposing governments' self-interested tactical hijinks on the other.[39]

Finally, three more issues are worth quickly flagging, although a fuller discussion will have to be postponed for now. First, it is an open question whether the proposed changes—and especially the model CV—could reasonably have been imagined to do very much to solve the problem of Member States trying to control the Strasbourg election process. Those Member States have always had a long

institutional figure for this Committee was long the affable *eminence grise* and institutional powerhouse, Andrew Drzemczewski, who officially served as the Committee's Head of Secretariat. *See* http://assembly.coe.int/nw/Committees/as-jur/as-jur-main-EN.asp. Tellingly, he then served in the same capacity for the newly freestanding Committee on the Election of Judges to the European Court of Human Rights. *See* http://assembly.coe.int/nw/Committees/as-cdh/as-cdh-main-EN.asp. Until his recent retirement, he was the Head of the Legal Affairs and Human Rights Department of the Parliamentary Assembly of the Council of Europe.

[37] PACE Report for Examining ECtHR Judicial Candidatures at 6.

[38] *Id.* at 6–7 (emphasis added).

[39] Amusingly, the status of the PACE in this dichotomy, unlike that of the Committee and of the national governments, is not entirely clear.

list of methods at their disposal to let their preferences be known, starting with the most obvious solution of using national representatives on the PACE to spread the word. After all, the PACE is composed of representatives of national parliaments. How hard would it really be, therefore, for national governments, especially from countries with parliamentary systems of government, to have national PACE representatives make governmental preferences be known?

Indeed, the model CV did nothing to curtail the elegantly simple tactic of Member States submitting the three CVs in the order of national preference. As the PACE Committee on Legal Affairs and Human Rights recognized in 1999: "In the past, given that it did not know the candidates, the Assembly very often merely ratified the choice of the High Contracting Party (in reality, the choice of the government) by electing the candidate whose name appeared first on the list."[40] This eventually led to a new PACE Recommendation and Resolution asking that the CVs be submitted in alphabetical order![41]

Second, if the PACE and its pivotal Committee on Legal Affairs and Human Rights were truly serious about the critical importance of interviews as a means "to assess the qualities of the candidates,"[42] then one can only be quite suspicious of the Committee's later refusal to allow the proposed Advisory Panel of Experts to conduct candidate interviews of its own[43] (or for that matter, their refusal to countenance a joint interview session held by both the Committee and the APE).[44]

Finally, it is surely worth noting what is *missing* from the discussion of the PACE Committee's proposed reforms in anticipation of the ratification of Protocol 11: neither the Committee's Draft Resolution nor Lord Kirkhill's explanation voiced a single word about *accession*. Given that the Report dates from 1995, i.e., the absolute highpoint of mass accession of new Member States from the former Eastern Bloc, this was clearly the elephant in the room: after all, some seventeen new Member States acceded to the Convention between 1990 and 1996, of which only Andorra did not hail from someplace east of Berlin. This public silence may have been politic, but it is nonetheless astounding: Protocol 11 was coming into force, the Court's jurisdictional and supervisory powers were being massively

[40] PACE Committee on Legal Affairs and Human Rights, Report on National procedures for nominating candidates for election to the European Court of Human Rights 3, Doc. 8505 (Rapporteur Wohlwend) (September 8, 1999) ["1999 Report on National Procedures for Nominating Candidates"].

[41] *See* PACE Recommendation 1429 (1999); 2004 PACE Recommendation 1649; and 2005 PACE Resolution 1432.

[42] *See supra* text accompanying notes 36–37.

[43] PACE Committee on Legal Affairs and Human Rights, Report on National procedures for the selection of candidates for the European Court of Human Rights, Doc. 12391 at para. 11 (October 7, 2010) ["2010 Report on National Procedures for Selecting Candidates"]. Of course, senior jurists qualified to sit in Strasbourg would bristle all the more at yet another round of vaguely demeaning interviews.

[44] Such a refusal is perfectly understandable as a matter of institutional jurisdiction and prerogative (i.e., the PACE wishing to retain its exclusive authority to elect ECtHR judges); but this political reality is hardly a substantive justification for denying the APE to conduct its own interviews.

increased, judicial independence was on the agenda, and reforms to the judicial appointments process were being proposed, yet accession was never once overtly mentioned. But the results followed as a matter of course: after minor tinkering, the PACE quickly passed the Committee Report's recommendations regarding the model CVs and the candidate interviews.[45]

Meanwhile, the PACE quite logically turned its attention to the national part of the appointment process. After all, the Convention establishes that the PACE elects from among a list of three candidates put forward by the Member State. But the Convention says nothing about how those three candidates are to be selected in the first place. The PACE first focused on this national selection process for the simple reason that far too many of the candidate lists were all male. In 1996, it therefore "instructed its Committee on Legal Affairs and Human Rights to examine the question of the qualifications and manner of appointment of judges to the European Court of Human Rights, with a view to achieving a balanced representation of the sexes."[46]

This focus on domestic selection practices had two primary effects. First, it opened a long-term struggle to try to remedy the gender imbalance on the Court. In a series of resolutions and recommendations that were then taken up by the Committee of Ministers and interpreted by the Court itself, the PACE tried to ensure that all national lists include at least one woman.[47] In the end, the PACE had a good deal of success on this front. In the judicial elections following the passage of PACE Order No. 519 (1996), which called on Member States to include at least one woman in their list of three candidates, only fourteen of the forty Member States then party to the Convention complied (i.e., two thirds of the countries nonetheless presented all male lists). But as things now stand, except in rather narrowly defined circumstances, the PACE will only consider national lists containing candidates of both sexes.[48]

The second effect was to establish a beachhead for examining domestic selection practices beyond the gender context. In 1997, the Committee on Legal Affairs and Human Rights sent to each of the Member States a questionnaire regarding the procedures they used for selecting the three judicial candidates they put forward

[45] *See* PACE Resolution 1082 (1996).

[46] PACE Order No. 519 (1996). *See* Committee on Legal Affairs and Human Rights, 1999 Report on National Procedures for Nominating Candidates.

[47] *See, e.g.*, PACE, Resolution 1366 (2004); PACE, Resolution 1426 (2005); and PACE, Resolution 1627 (2008); ECtHR, *Advisory opinion on certain legal questions concerning the lists of candidates submitted with a view to the election of judges to the European Court of Human Rights*, February 12, 2008, available at http://hudoc.echr.coe.int/app/conversion/pdf/?library=ECHR&id=003-2268009-2419060&filename=003-2268009-2419060.pdf.

[48] *See* PACE, Resolution 1627 (2008). David Kosař has claimed that the PACE compromised its position somewhat in the case of Belgium's 2012 submission of an all-male list. *See, e.g.*, David Kosař, *Selecting Strasbourg' Judges: A Critique*, *in* SELECTING EUROPE'S JUDGES: A CRITICAL REVIEW OF THE APPOINTMENT PROCEDURES TO THE EUROPEAN COURTS (MICHAL BOBEK ed., 2015) at Part 4.1. But Kosař's assessment is vehemently contested within the Council of Europe.

for election by the PACE to the Court. This resulted in a 1999 Report and Draft Recommendation on "National procedures for nominating candidates for election to the European Court of Human Rights." The Report stated:

> 5. In the light of the replies provided by national delegations to a questionnaire, and of the experience gained on the occasion of the procedure for electing judges to the Court, the following observations may be made:
>   i. the method of selecting candidates varies considerably from one country to another;
>   ii. in the majority of cases there are no rules governing the selection of candidates;
>   iii. a substantial number of governments did not include a woman on their list of three candidates;
>   iv. the candidates put forward did not always meet the criteria established by the Convention: either they lacked experience in human rights, or had never held judicial office, or were not sufficiently fluent in at least one of the Council of Europe's two official languages.[49]

Clearly, the Report was going to recommend changes.

The Report placed much of the blame for the shortcomings of the ECtHR judicial appointments process on national governments. Answers to the Committee's questionnaire demonstrated that the "process of selecting candidates was almost exclusively the preserve of national governments."[50] In this domestic part of the appointments process, effectively governed therefore by national governments, crude politics played a distressingly important role:

> Lists [of judicial candidates] were often the result of an arbitrary political decision. Partisan considerations lay behind the elimination of numerous candidates in the national selection procedures. Thus, several outgoing judges or commissioners were subject to political sanctions.[51]

The reality of governmental political control could therefore be correlated to a series of failures in judicial appointment outcomes. Too many candidates were simply unqualified to serve as judges in a major human rights court:

[49] PACE Committee on Legal Affairs and Human Rights (Rapporteur: Wohlwend), Report on National procedures for nominating candidates for election to the European Court of Human Rights 3, Doc. 8505 (September 8, 1999). ["1999 Report on National Procedures for Nominating Candidates"].

[50] *Id.* at para. 14.

[51] *Id.* at para. 35, citing Jean-François Flauss, "Radioscopie de l'élection de la nouvelle Cour européenne des droits de l'homme," Rev. trim. dr. h. H. 437, 440 (1998).

> The proportion of candidates with recognised experience in the field of human rights is not in keeping with the requirements of the Convention. Some candidates did not even conceal their lack of experience in their curriculum vitae, and others concealed it very clumsily. States should take greater pains to select candidates who, being called to hold such prestigious office, can demonstrate human rights activities worthy of the name.[52]

Similarly, "Bearing in mind the technical expertise required, it was essential that the future judges were legal practitioners. In addition, the lists submitted by states should better reflect the range of judicial professions, by including more practising legal experts (lawyers)."[53] Even more, "it is regrettable that a significant proportion of the candidates had an insufficient grasp of English or French."[54]

Compounding these problems, explained the Report, was the reality that national governmental preferences were usually ratified automatically at the European level. The PACE usually followed express governmental preferences when electing from among its list of three judicial candidates:

> More often than not, the ranking of candidates as established by states was approved, because the first candidate was quite simply the best. When the sub-committee changed the order of the candidates, its recommendation was not always followed by the Assembly ... The official state candidate was rarely defeated.[55]

Clearly, the Committee recognized that it had only a limited capacity to intervene effectively in the face of revealed national governmental preferences.

The best the Committee could do was to propose a series of guidelines for Member State governments to follow when drawing up their lists of judicial candidates. Composing its proposal in delicate terms, the Committee framed its draft PACE recommendation as follows:

> In order to remedy these shortcomings and assist the governments of the member states in their procedures for selecting candidates for the next elections, the Assembly recommends that the Committee of Ministers invite the governments of the member states to apply the following criteria when drawing up lists of candidates for the office of judge in the European Court of Human Rights:

52 1999 Report on National Procedures for Nominating Candidates at para. 36.
53 *Id.* at para. 37.
54 *Id.* at para. 27.
55 *Id.* at paras 29, 34.

i. issue a call for candidatures through the specialised press, so as to obtain candidates who are indeed eminent jurists satisfying the criteria laid down in Article 21 (1) of the Convention;
ii. ensure that the candidates have experience in the field of human rights, either as practitioners or as activists in non governmental organisations working in this area;
iii. select candidates of both sexes in every case;
iv. ensure that the candidates are in fact fluent in either French or English and are capable of working in one of these two languages;
v. put the names of the candidates in alphabetical order.[56]

Finally, perhaps as a means of further counterbalancing the relatively unchecked power of national governments in the appointments process, the Committee proposed that these governments "consult their national parliaments when drawing up the lists so as to ensure the transparency of the national selection procedure."[57] The PACE passed these recommendations verbatim some two weeks later.[58]

Despite these advances, the judicial appointments issues simply refused to go away at either the domestic or the European level. To the contrary, the issues were repeated sufficiently often for the panoply of connected debates to become ever more firmly entrenched. Thus, in 2003, a group of eminent European judges (mostly national constitutional court judges) with strong academic connections met under the aegis of an international human rights center named "Interights" to consider the ECtHR's judicial appointments process. They soon published a highly influential Report, tellingly entitled "Judicial Independence: Law and Practice of Appointments to the European Court of Human Rights,"[59] which reiterated the increasingly familiar and intertwined critiques. Its "executive summary" states:

> In the last forty years, the European Court of Human Rights has been at the forefront of the development of regional and international human rights jurisprudence. While paying tribute to the Court, this report notes that its credibility and authority risk being undermined by the ad hoc and often politicised processes currently adopted in the appointment of its judges.
>
> As a leading human rights court internationally, it would be anomalous and unacceptable if appointments to the Court failed to meet the international human

[56] *Id.* at para. 5.
[57] *Id.* at para. 6.
[58] PACE Recommendation 1429 (1999).
[59] Jutta Limbach et al., "Judicial Independence: Law and Practice of Appointments to the European Court of Human Rights" (2003), available at http://www.interights.org/jud-ind-en/index.html ["Interights Report"].

> rights standards that it is charged with implementing, including those requirements relating to the independence and impartiality of judges. In addition, flawed appointment procedures leave open the prospect that judges selected will lack the requisite skills and abilities to discharge their duties. This risks having an adverse effect on the Court's standing and on the development of authoritative human rights jurisprudence in Europe.
>
> The current system of appointments to the Court involves the nomination of three candidates at a national level, followed by an election by the Council of Europe's Parliamentary Assembly. At both stages, the processes lack transparency and accountability.
>
> At a national level, States are given absolute discretion with respect to the nomination system they adopt. The Council of Europe does not provide guidelines on appropriate procedures; nor does it require States to report on or account for their national procedures. Even in the most established democracies, nomination often rewards political loyalty more than merit.
>
> At the international level, the Convention provides that the power to appoint judges lies solely with the Parliamentary Assembly. The Committee of Ministers has adopted a limited review role, which on paper allows it to question States' lists of nominees and nomination procedures. However, in practice the Committee of Ministers gives the impression of being more interested in safeguarding State sovereignty, than in ensuring the quality of candidates nominated.[60]

This summary reproduces once again the now classic alignment of issues. Judicial appointments trigger concern for judicial independence. Politicization of the process at the domestic level, reinforced at the European level, risks the appointment of unqualified candidates, which threatens the Court's standing and jurisprudential authority.

The Report's recommendations were fairly specific:

- The Council of Europe should devise and distribute minimum standards for national nomination procedures. These would include requiring States to establish an independent body to arrive at the list of nominees and to submit an account of their nomination procedures to the Council of Europe. The report also recommends that the Council of Europe should provide a template to States for interviewing candidates.
- The list of nominees submitted by States and the description of nomination procedures adopted should be scrutinised by the Council of Europe. Those lists that have been devised pursuant to procedures that do not meet the prescribed minimum standards should be returned to States.

[60] *Id.* at 4.

- The body making recommendations to the Parliamentary Assembly on the eligibility or suitability of candidates should itself be independent, possess the requisite expertise to fulfil its role, and follow a fair and open procedure. This could be done either by engaging a group of independent experts to provide advice on candidates to the Parliamentary Assembly, or by making an expert group of judicial assessors available to the existing Sub-Committee. In both cases, candidates would be interviewed by an independent group expert in international human rights law and would provide reasons for its ranking of candidates.[61]

This set of recommendations focuses on both the domestic and the European dimensions of the appointments process. At both levels, the Report calls for the establishment of independent bodies to play the key procedural and decision-making roles. And should domestic procedures fail to meet "prescribed minimum standards," then the Council of Europe should simply decline altogether to consider the national list of candidates.

The Interights Report's analysis and recommendations built upon existing PACE recommendations, helped to put new potential reforms on the agenda, and continued to develop the core set of conceptual connections. The Report linked the lack of consistent domestic procedural structures to the exercise of arbitrary political whim at the domestic level, then tied this to a lack of judicial independence, to a corresponding lack of confidence in the Strasbourg Court, and to a resulting loss of jurisprudential authority.

The alignment of this basic constellation of issues has continued to define the ECtHR appointments discussions in almost all the ensuing debates. In a 2004 Recommendation on Candidates for the European Court of Human Rights, for example, the PACE—acting on the advice of its clearly frustrated Committee on Legal Affairs and Human Rights—reiterated all of the requirements that the PACE had expressed in its 1999 Recommendation on national procedures for nominating ECtHR candidates. It stated:

> 19. In addition to the moral qualities and experience rightly expected of candidates, laid down in Article 21, paragraph 1, of the Convention, the Assembly recommends that the Committee of Ministers invite the governments of the member states to meet six other criteria before submitting lists of candidates for the office of judge in the European Court of Human Rights, namely to ensure:
>
> 19.1. that a call for candidatures has been issued through the specialised press;
>
> 19.2. that candidates have experience in the field of human rights;

[61] *Id.* at 5.

19.3. that every list contains candidates of both sexes;
19.4. that the candidates have a sufficient knowledge of at least one of the two official languages;
19.5. that the names of the candidates are placed in alphabetical order;
19.6. that as far as possible no candidate should be submitted whose election might result in the necessity to appoint an ad hoc judge.[62]

In this respect, the PACE was merely repeating itself, which of course underlines just how little progress had actually been achieved in the intervening five years. But this time, the PACE took a page from the Interights Report by framing its Recommendation in terms of judicial independence. In fact, it did so in decidedly more loaded terms:

1. An independent judiciary is indispensable for the protection of human rights and fundamental freedoms.
2. In order for the European Court of Human Rights to continue to inspire confidence, it is vital that the process by which judges are selected and appointed also inspire confidence.
3. The Parliamentary Assembly insists that the process of appointment must reflect the principles of democratic procedure, the rule of law, non-discrimination, accountability and transparency.[63]

As should be obvious, the PACE was combining its 1999 proposals regarding national processes for constructing lists of candidates for the Court with the "rule of law" discourse that burst onto the scene during the period of mass accession Eastern States in the early to mid-1990s.[64] The result was a compelling mix of arguments. As Kevin McNamara, Rapporteur for the Committee on Legal Affairs and Human Rights, stated in the opening of the 2003 Report that proposed the 2004 PACE Recommendation:

> If the European Court of Human Rights is to command confidence, the process by which the judges are elected must echo the principles of the democratic method, the rule of law, accountability and transparency.
>
> National procedure for nominating candidates must therefore meet a number of requirements, otherwise the Assembly should not consider the list of candidatures.[65]

[62] PACE Recommendation 1649 (2004) at 2. *Cf.* PACE Recommendation 1429 (1999).
[63] PACE Recommendation 1649 (2004) at 1.
[64] *See supra* text accompanying notes 21–30.
[65] PACE Committee on Legal Affairs and Human Rights, Report on Candidates for the European Court of Human Rights 1, Doc. 9963 (Rapporteur McNamara) (October 7, 2003).

The topic of judicial appointments was gradually becoming a watershed issue for an increasingly familiar package of concerns.

Even as the debates were thus congealing into a patterned and arguably repetitious set of arguments, they developed and triggered ongoing reforms. Thus, when the PACE and its Committee on Legal Affairs and Human Rights repeated in 2003–04 the recommendations that it had made in 1999, they also proposed a new reform: the term of office for ECtHR judges should be changed from six-year renewable terms to nine-year nonrenewable ones. Committee Rapporteur McNamara explained:

> **Security of tenure**
>
> . . .
>
> 68. Renewable terms of office carry risk of threats to judicial independence. The Sub-Committee is aware both of anecdotal reports and one specific case concerning judges who have expressed views or ruled contrary to the wishes of their nominating government coming under pressure from that government. The threat of non re-nomination may carry with it substantial adverse consequences for the individual concerned.
>
> *Terms of Office*
>
> 69. The Rapporteur considers that a 9-year period of appointment would contribute to the greater efficiency and continuity of the Court and would consolidate its independence. Accordingly, he supports amendment being made to the Convention to this effect.[66]

The Committee followed its Rapporteur's position, as did the PACE as a whole: the 2004 PACE Recommendation proposed that the Convention be revised in order to establish nine-year nonrenewable terms of judicial office.[67] Almost immediately incorporated into Protocol 14's amendment to the Convention, the change would, however, have to wait another six years to take effect: the Protocol only came into force in 2010.[68]

Similarly, the discussions continued about what should be done when, as was clearly all too often the case, a Member State simply refused to heed the Council of Europe's recommendations about how national lists of judicial candidates should be composed and transmitted. Just as PACE Recommendation 1649 (2004) reiterated the demands placed on Member states five years earlier by PACE

[66] *Id.* at 15. The suggestion was put forward some two years earlier in the Report of the Evaluation Group to the Committee of Ministers on the European Court of Human Rights, EG Court(2001)1 September 27, 2001, at para. 89, available at https://wcd.coe.int/ViewDoc.jsp?id=226195&Lang=-fr#P1176_114799.

[67] *See* PACE Recommendation 1649 (2004).

[68] By refusing to ratify Protocol 14 as a means of objecting to unfavorable ECtHR judgments, Russia held up the Protocol's entry into force for almost six years. *See, e.g.*, Bill Bowring, *The Russian Federation, Protocol No. 14 (and 14bis), and the Battle for the Soul of the ECHR*, 2 GoJIL 589 (2010).

Recommendation 1429 (1999),[69] so did the PACE have to deal with the ongoing insistence by certain Member States to express a preference among the judicial candidates they put forward on their lists for election by the PACE. In response, the PACE adopted the following measure in amusingly prickly terms:

> The Assembly confirms its practice of listing candidates for the post of judge in alphabetical order on the ballot paper. This shall also remain the practice in those cases where the government, disregarding the Assembly's position as set out in Recommendations 1429 (1999) and 1649 (2004), has expressed a preference for one of the candidates. Any such expressions of governmental preference shall play no role in the deliberations of the Ad hoc Sub-Committee on the Election of Judges to the European Court of Human Rights, where only the criteria provided for in the European Convention on Human Rights and those established by the Assembly itself shall be relevant.[70]

Indeed, the PACE was clearly getting sufficiently annoyed with Member States refusing to take their recommendations seriously that it began taking more high-handed measures. In 2009, the PACE, now sounding like a broken record, repeated the gist of its requirements regarding national selection procedures, which

[69] *See supra* text accompanying note 62.

[70] Appendix 1 to PACE Resolution 1432 (2005). As Rapporteur Rudolf Vis made clear, the Committee of Ministers refused to support the PACE position in the face of what could only have been the strong insistence of certain Member States to continue to express their preference among the three candidates they were putting forward for election. As the Report stated:

> 9. The Parliamentary Assembly has long requested that states submitting lists of candidates for the post of judge to the European Court of Human Rights should present them in alphabetical order (Recommendations 1429 (1999) and 1649 (2004)) and avoid expressing any official preference for a particular candidate (Recommendation 1429 (1999)). In its reply to that recommendation (Doc. 8835), the Committee of Ministers considered that it was a matter for individual states to decide in the light of their domestic procedures for nominating candidates, whether they wish to express a preference or not. The Committee of Ministers also noted that neither itself (in its examination of states' lists), nor the Parliamentary Assembly in its selection procedure, were obliged to accept the expressed preference of a state for a particular candidate.
>
> 10. It should be noted that the Committee of Ministers has, according to the legal text governing the election procedure for the three senior posts of the Council of Europe's Secretariat, the possibility of listing the names in order of preference. However, at least since the seventies it has no longer done so.
>
> 11. The Committee on Rules of Procedure and Immunities proposes that the Assembly confirms its practice to list candidates for the post of judge in alphabetical order on the ballot paper. This should remain the practice also when a government - disregarding the Assembly's position as set out in Recommendation 1429 (1999) - has expressed a preference for one of the candidates. Any such expressions of governmental preference will play no role in the deliberations of the ad hoc sub-committee on the election of judges to the European Court of Human Rights, where only the criteria provided for in the European Convention on Human Rights and those established by the Assembly itself will be relevant.

PACE Committee on Rules and Procedure (Rapporteur: Rudolf Vis), Report on Procedure for Elections Held by the Parliamentary Assembly other than those of its President and Vice-President, Doc. 10385, December 21, 2004.

it had formally established in 1999 and already reiterated in 2004: Member States, when selecting and nominating candidates to the Court, should "issue public and open calls for candidatures," "describe the manner in which [the candidates] were selected," "transmit the names ... in alphabetical order," ensure that the candidates "possess an active knowledge of one official language of the Council of Europe and a passive knowledge of the other," etc.[71] Picking up on the 2003 Interights Report on Judicial Independence, the PACE Resolution also "urge[d] the governments of member states which have still not done so, to set up—without delay—appropriate national selection procedures to ensure that the authority and credibility of the Court are not put at risk by ad hoc and politicised processes in the nomination of candidates."[72]

But now the PACE followed up these repeated requirements with a pair of clear threats:

> Despite a marked improvement in national selection procedures in several countries, there is still significant variance as concerns fairness, transparency and consistency. Referring to its Recommendation 1649 (2004) on candidates for the European Court of Human Rights, the Assembly yet again reiterates that the process of nominating candidates to the Court must reflect the principles of democratic procedure, transparency and non-discrimination. *In the absence of a real choice among the candidates submitted by a state party to the Convention, the Assembly shall reject lists submitted to it. In addition, in the absence of a fair, transparent and consistent national selection procedure, the Assembly may reject such lists.*[73]

Both the substantive quality of the national lists of three judicial candidates and the procedure by which such lists were constructed were grounds for the PACE to reject the lists altogether. Furthermore, this statement of principle, passed as a PACE Resolution, merely formalized a "long-standing practice" that the PACE had already instituted and deployed. As Rapporteur Christopher Chope of the Committee on Legal Affairs and Human Rights explained in the Report that led to this Resolution:

> Indeed, where the sub-committee is not satisfied that the candidates on the list meet the requirements under the ECHR and in various Assembly resolutions and recommendations—usually after having interviewed the three candidates—it proposes to the Bureau that the list be sent back to the national authorities.

[71] PACE Resolution 1646 (2009) on the Nomination of Candidates and Election of Judges to the European Court of Human Rights at para. 4.
[72] PACE Resolution 1646 (2009) at para. 5.
[73] *Id.* at para. 2 (emphasis added).

> This has recently occurred with respect to lists submitted by Azerbaijan (twice), Bulgaria, Cyprus, Luxembourg, Moldova, San Marino and Turkey.[74]

The explicit formalization of this practice as a policy officially enshrined as a PACE Resolution, when combined with the overt shaming of such a list of Member States, could hardly have escaped notice.[75]

But the really major development was about to break. In 2010, the sitting President of the ECtHR, Jean-Paul Costa, took the initiative of sending a letter to the "permanent representatives" of the Member States of the Council of Europe (i.e., the national ambassadors in Strasbourg) in order to put forward an important proposal: a panel of senior experts should be established to "advise" Member States regarding the list of three judicial candidates they intended to put forward to the PACE for election to the ECtHR.

President Costa began by explaining in rather dramatic terms why the selection of judges of sufficient quality was so important to the ECtHR:

> In terms of the future of the Court and therefore the Convention system, one of the decisive factors will be the quality of its Judges. Whatever reforms are undertaken, the system will fail if judges do not have the necessary experience and authority.
>
> The quality of the Judges is important not only to guarantee the high standard of the decisions delivered and the jurisprudence developed. It is also essential because, in a subsidiary system where human rights protection falls primarily to the national courts, the European Court as the ultimate arbiter of human rights issues must be composed of persons of sufficient standing and authority to command the respect of national judges, including senior national judges. If this is not the case, the Court itself will suffer from a deficit of authority and the system will lose credibility and effectiveness.
>
> This aspect is also particularly important in view of the prospect of the European Union's accession to the Convention. One of the critical issues in this context will be the future relationship between the Court of Justice of the European Union and the Strasbourg Court. For that relationship to function it must be based on mutual respect.[76]

In these key paragraphs, President Costa framed the issues in stark and even rather alarming terms. The entire Convention system, including its Court, was apparently

[74] PACE Committee on Legal Affairs and Human Rights (Rapporteur: Christopher Chope), Report on the Nomination of Candidates and Election of Judges to the European Court of Human Rights, Doc. 11767, Explanatory Memorandum at para. 8 (December 1, 2008).

[75] As we shall see, these threats have only become more formalized over time. *See infra* Chapter 5(IV).

[76] Jean-Paul Costa, Letter from the President of the European Court of Human Rights, addressed to member states' Permanent Representatives (Ambassadors) on June 9, 2010 ["Costa Letter"].

at risk of "failing." And the key variable, it seems, was the "quality" of the Court's judges.

Although Costa recognized that the quality of these judges is "important ... to guarantee the high standard of the decisions delivered and the jurisprudence developed," it does not take much insight to sense that this was not his only, and maybe not even his primary, concern. His true focus lay instead in the relationship between the ECtHR and *other courts*; and this relationship, it seems, hinges on reputation and status. As Costa explained, the Convention is a subsidiary system of protection, in which national courts carry the primary load, but in which the ECtHR must then function as "the ultimate arbiter of human rights issues." For such a system to function properly, Costa declared, the ECtHR "must be composed of persons of sufficient standing and authority to command the respect of national judges, including senior national judges. If this is not the case, the Court itself will suffer from a deficit of authority and the system will lose credibility and effectiveness." Without judges of sufficient status, supreme court judges at the domestic level will apparently not respect the Court sufficiently for the Convention system to function. In other words, they will not willingly follow the Court's jurisprudence. And as those domestic high courts represent the primary line of defense for human rights, the entire Convention system is at risk of "failure."

Costa made the same basic point regarding the operation of the Convention system at the European level. This time, the issue was the evolving relationship between the ECtHR and the ECJ. In particular, the EU's Treaty of Lisbon called for the EU to accede to the Convention. This accession would profoundly affect the relationship between the ECJ and the ECtHR, as the latter would suddenly become—to use Costa's words—"the ultimate arbiter of human rights issues" with regards to the EU, just as it had already become with regards to national authorities. Accession would effectively grant the ECtHR judicial supremacy with regards to any human rights challenge brought against any EU institution, *including the ECJ*. This, needless to say, would prove a *very* difficult pill for the ECJ to swallow;[77] and it would require, Costa explained, that "the relationship [between the two courts] be based on mutual respect."

President Costa could not voice what all knowledgeable observers undoubtedly recognize, namely, that the ECJ has always commanded greater respect than the ECtHR; hence the importance that the ECtHR command sufficient ECJ respect for EU accession to operate properly. The "mutual respect" language was a face-saving device: the real concern was that the ECJ respect the ECtHR, not the other way around. But Costa could at least leverage that anxiety for the purposes

[77] Indeed, the ECJ has since spit out the pill altogether: in its notorious Opinion 2/13 of December 18, 2014, the ECJ effectively blocked EU accession to the European Convention (and with such accession, its own potential subservience to the ECtHR). *See* http://curia.europa.eu/juris/document/document.jsf?docid=160882&doclang=EN.

of supporting his proposed reform: the ECJ, he makes sure to note, had itself recently adopted an "independent panel" (the 255 Panel) to review appointments to the ECJ. Without a parallel arrangement in Strasbourg, Costa implies, the ECtHR would be unable to command the authority necessary to function as the "ultimate arbiter" of human rights controversies emanating from the EU and initially supervised by the ECJ.

Starting from this baseline concern, President Costa turned immediately to the work of two high-level groups that had been convened to consider how to deal with the ECtHR's enormous caseload and related institutional difficulties. The first was the "Group of Wise Persons" convened in 2005 by the Heads of State of the Council of Europe Member States "to consider the long-term effectiveness of the ECHR control mechanism, including the initial effects of Protocol 14."[78] The second was the Interlaken Conference on the Future of the European Court of Human Rights, held in February 2010 under the Swiss Chairmanship of the Committee of Ministers. Both had produced long reports that covered a very wide set of topics, ranging from caseload and case-management issues, to national remedies and implementation of ECtHR judgments, to instituting new advisory and other procedures.[79]

Within the long list of suggestions put forward by these two high-level groups, each had considered a proposal to establish some kind of panel to screen candidates put forward by the Member States to fill judicial vacancies on the ECtHR. The 2006 Report of the Group of Wise Persons stated:

> [T]he Group considers that the professional qualifications and knowledge of languages of candidates for the post of judge should be carefully examined during the election procedure.
>
> For this purpose, before the Parliamentary Assembly considers the candidatures, an opinion on the suitability of the candidates could be given by a committee of prominent personalities possibly chosen from among former members of the Court, current and former members of national supreme or constitutional courts and lawyers with acknowledged competence.[80]

Similarly, at the Interlaken Ministerial Conference, Secretary General Thorbjørn Jagland, using language and arguments that would soon be taken up by President Costa, proposed:

[78] Report of the Group of Wise Persons to the Committee of Ministers, CM(2006)203 at para. 1 ["Report of the Wise Persons"]. As we have seen, it later turned out that the Protocol would not be ratified and put into effect until 2010. *See supra* note 68 and accompanying text.

[79] *See id.*; High Level Conference on the Future of the European Court of Human Rights, Interlaken Declaration of February 19, 2010, available at http://www.coe.int/t/dgi/hr-natimplement/Source/interlaken_declaration_en.pdf.

[80] Report of the Wise Persons at paras. 117–18.

18. The authority of the Court's case law depends in part on the **standing and credibility of the Court** itself, including in the eyes of the judges of the highest national courts whose own decisions may be subject to its scrutiny. Along with independence and impartiality, therefore, it is important also to ensure the highest levels of expertise and relevant experience on the part of the Court's judiciary. Bearing in mind the various Parliamentary Assembly proposals, as well as the 2003 Interights report, States should ensure that they have transparent national selection procedures for candidates for election as judge. The criteria for office and election procedures could also be reviewed. In this context, we should examine the idea of a mixed screening panel composed of prominent former high level national or international judges before transmitting the list of candidates to the Parliamentary Assembly for election.[81]

Both proposals envisaged some kind of committee or panel composed primarily of prominent judges to vet judicial candidates prior to the PACE election of judges.

President Costa first underlined the importance of selecting judges that truly meet the Convention's stated criteria for office, namely, that they "be of high moral character and must either possess the qualifications required for appointment to high judicial office or be jurisconsults of recognized competence."[82] Returning implicitly to the issue of "baby judges,"[83] he stressed that "jurisconsults of recognized competence" must necessarily possess "extensive experience," which would involve "publication of important works" and be indicated by sufficient "length of occupation of a professorial chair." Then he stressed that the Member States have the "fundamental role" of ensuring that they submit lists of three candidates who are "of equivalent standing" and who have been selected by "a fair and transparent procedure," so that the PACE can exercise "a real choice" in its judicial elections.

Having reiterated these now well-worn points, President Costa then made this key proposal:

However, this is not enough. That is why I would urge the Committee of Ministers to set up rapidly a panel along the lines proposed by the Wise Persons and the Secretary General. Such a panel, which should be composed of senior figures from a relevant background, would intervene before a list was submitted to the PACE by the contracting party so as not to interfere with the PACE's Convention responsibilities in this area. Moreover, its role would be advisory; in other words it would make recommendations to the nominating state including, as necessary,

[81] Secretary General of the Council of Europe, Contribution to the Preparation of the Interlaken Ministerial Conference, SG/Inf(2009)20 December 18, 2009 (emphasis in original).

[82] Costa letter at 7, quoting Article 21(1) of the Convention.

[83] *See supra* text accompanying notes 44–47.

> proposals to modify the list. Such a Panel could be set up without amending the Convention by a decision of the Committee of Ministers.
>
> I intend to raise this matter as soon as possible with the President of the PACE. I very much hope that you and your colleagues, Ministers' Deputies, will be able to discuss this important issue in the near future.
>
> For my part, I am prepared to make more detailed proposals on the operation of the Panel and the appointment of its members.[84]

Costa had intervened directly.

President Costa's letter was to prove the critical moment in the establishment of what would soon become the APE: the Advisory Panel of Experts, eventually chaired by former ECtHR President Luzius Wildhaber (Costa's predecessor as ECtHR President). But as can be surmised from Costa's language, his APE proposal represented a difficult institutional high wire act. In particular, the establishment and operation of the APE would have to tread very carefully between two potential dangers. On the one hand, the APE must not "interfere with the PACE's Convention responsibilities." That is, the APE's assessment of the judicial candidates must not take away from what may, as a practical matter, be the PACE's single most important function in the Convention system: the election of ECtHR judges. As a result, Costa made sure to specify that the APE would "intervene *before* a list was submitted to the PACE by the contracting party," so that the PACE could perform its electoral role as defined by the Convention. On the other hand, the APE must not appropriate the power of the Member States under the Convention to nominate the list of three candidates to be put forward for election by the PACE. As a consequence, Costa made sure to underline that the APE's role would be merely "advisory." Finally, given that amendment of the Convention could prove quite difficult (as ratification of Protocol 14 had demonstrated quite clearly), Costa proposed that the APE "could be set up without amending the Convention by a decision of the Committee of Ministers."

President Costa's proposal was both bold and delicate. It argued forcefully for a screening panel that could not help but tread on the toes of Member States, the PACE, or – most likely – both. But it worked hard to finesse those threats by inserting the APE somewhere between the Member States and the PACE in a manner that would not eviscerate the role of either. How exactly this would work was not, however, entirely clear. But Costa was far too experienced to float too many specifics in writing: hence his intentionally uninformative closing remark that he was "prepared to make more detailed proposals on the operation of the Panel and the appointment of its members."

[84] Costa letter at 7–8.

The difficulty of President Costa's institutional high wire act—which one can detect in his letter—would soon become much more apparent. The PACE's Committee on Legal Affairs and Human Rights responded to the Costa proposal in a decidedly cool and, at best, guardedly positive fashion. In a draft resolution adopted in October, 2010 (undoubtedly penned by Andrew Drzemczewski),[85] the Committee stated:

1. It is the Parliamentary Assembly's task, by virtue of Article 22 of the European Convention on Human Rights (ETS No. 5) ("the Convention"), to elect judges of the highest calibre to the European Court of Human Rights (the Court) from a list of three candidates nominated by states parties. This provides "democratic legitimacy" to judges elected by the Assembly.
2. This presupposes that states parties to the Convention transmit to the Assembly a list of three jurists with the necessary qualifications, experience and stature, as required by Article 21, paragraph 1, of the Convention ("The judges shall be of high moral character and must either possess the qualifications required for appointment to high judicial office or be jurisconsults of recognised competence"), so that member states, and in particular their highest judicial authorities, fully acknowledge the Court's authority.
3. Hence, in order to be in a position to choose between candidates with the necessary standing and authority, the Assembly reiterates the need for rigorous, consistent, fair and transparent national selection procedures, as specified in its Resolution 1646 (2009) on the nomination of candidates and election of judges to the Court.
4. It follows that, as "[t]he authority of the Court is contingent on the stature of judges and the quality and coherence of the Court's case law" (paragraph 7 of Assembly Resolution 1726 (2010) on the effective implementation of the European Convention on Human Rights: the Interlaken process), the Assembly fully supports all attempts by states parties to enhance the quality of candidates transmitted to it, in particular by improving, where necessary, national selection procedures. Seen from this perspective, the recent initiative of the President of the Court to set up a panel to advise governments before lists of candidates are transmitted to the Assembly is welcome.[86]

The Committee could hardly have accepted President Costa's proposal in more unenthusiastic terms.

The PACE Committee's framing of the APE proposal echoes the institutional balancing act implicit in Costa's letter, further revealing the tensions that would eventually prove so debilitating for the APE. The Committee draws a categorical distinction between the role of the PACE and that of the Member States in the

[85] *See supra* note 36.
[86] 2010 Report on National Procedures for Selecting Candidates.

judicial appointments process. The former elects "judges of the highest caliber" to the ECtHR from a list of three candidates nominated by the Member States, thereby providing "democratic legitimacy" (left both undefined and in quotation marks) to the judges. This leaves the latter to provide the PACE with an appropriate list. End of story: the division of labor is cut and dried.

Once the Committee had parceled out the responsibilities in this fashion, all the reform work would necessarily fall into the sole purview of the States. The PACE thus "fully supports all attempts by states parties to enhance the quality of candidates transmitted to it, in particular by improving, where necessary, national selection procedures." But the Committee intimates that such reforms are not really its business at all; indeed, "seen from this perspective" (to use the Committee's prickly language), the APE merely emerges as the next in a long line of domestic selection procedures that need to be "rigorous, consistent, fair and transparent" in order to put the PACE in a position to do its job properly. In some important sense, therefore, the Committee effectively turns its back on the APE, making sure to reserve to itself and the PACE complete and unfettered authority to elect ECtHR judges from among the candidates put forward by sovereign nations.

The Explanatory Memorandum of the Committee's Rapporteur, Renate Wohlwend, frames its discussion of the Costa proposal in just this manner. The first two thirds of her Memorandum work methodically through the many PACE Resolutions and Recommendations designed to improve the process by which the Member States put together their list of candidates. Only then, after having thereby suggested the full extent to which the proposed APE must be viewed as a domestic procedural matter (note that the Report is tellingly entitled "National procedures for the selection of candidates for the European Court of Human Rights"), does Wohlwend broach the Costa proposal.

She begins by relaying some more information about how President Costa imagined the panel might function:

> 9. Briefly put, the idea mooted by President Costa is the creation of an advisory panel of seven persons, from among former judges of the Strasbourg Court, other international courts, members of the highest national courts and lawyers of recognised competence. The panel would need to be geographically and gender balanced. Members of the panel, appointed by the Committee of Ministers for a term of three years, renewable once (upon proposal of the Court's President), would (and here I quote from President Costa's appended letter), "intervene before a list was submitted to the Assembly by the contracting party so as not to interfere with Assembly's Convention responsibilities in this area. Moreover, its role would be advisory; in other words it would make recommendations to the nominating state including, as necessary, proposals to modify the list. Such a panel could be set up without amending the Convention by a decision of the Committee of Ministers."

10. My understanding of the manner in which the proposed panel of experts would function is this: the panel would provide advice to governments by examining the curriculum vitae of the candidates selected before transmission of the list of the three candidates to the Assembly. This procedure would be obligatory. If the panel were to find, after an examination of the curriculum vitae, that the list to be forwarded to the Assembly is composed of suitable candidates, it would so inform the state concerned without further comment. If, however, the panel were of the view that one or more of the persons on the list (to be) put forward to the Assembly was not suitable, it would provide its views, in a confidential procedure, to the state concerned, indicating to it why the said person or persons should not be on the list. Then, if ever the state concerned were not to heed the "advice" of the panel and transmit, to the Assembly, a list containing one or more persons deemed by the panel not to meet the criteria for office—as provided in Article 21, paragraph 1, of the Convention,—the panel would inform the Assembly of its reasons.[87]

The proposed APE would therefore be exactly the same size as the EU's 255 Panel, established the year before, although its members would serve slightly shorter terms (three vs. four years, renewable once).[88] Like the 255 Panel, the APE was to be geographically balanced:[89] in accordance with the PACE's long-time concern, it was also to be gender balanced.

The APE would apparently function as a quasi-advisor to the State. I say "quasi-advisor," but one could also describe its function as "advisor-or-else." The idea was that "the panel would provide advice to the [nominating] governments ... *before* transmission of the list of three candidates to the [PACE]." This indeed looks advisory, especially if the Panel were to find the list to be composed of suitable candidates. In fact, things still look advisory if one or more of the candidates were found not suitable, as the Panel would inform the government confidentially, so that the government could take appropriate measures to remedy the problem before the list were ever transmitted to the PACE for election.

But then came the all-important "or else" component of the proposal, which would transform the APE into something more than a merely "advisory" body: "if ever the state concerned were *not* to heed the 'advice' of the panel and transmit, to

[87] *Id.* at paras. 9–10 (footnote omitted).

[88] *See* Council Decision 2010/124/EU of February 25, 2010, relating to the operating rules of the panel provided for in Article 255 of the Treaty on the Functioning of the European Union [2010] OJ L50/18.

[89] As we have seen, however, the 255 Panel never made good on this commitment. *See supra* Chapter 3(I).

[8] As the Assembly's Sub-Committee on the Election of Judges to the European Court of Human Rights undertakes interviews with all candidates prior to election ..., it would be important to ensure that this new advisory panel, if created, operates only by means of a written procedure ... [Footnote in original].

the Assembly, a list containing one or more persons deemed by the panel not to meet the criteria for office . . ., the panel would inform the Assembly of its reasons." This proviso was obviously a threat: if the government stubbornly refused to withdraw an unsuitable candidate, the APE would publicly shame both the government and the candidate. Needless to say, it was hard to imagine either that a government would ever be willing to expose itself or its problematic candidate(s) to such shaming or, even if it were, that the PACE would ever be willing to ratify the decision of such a government by electing such a candidate. The proposal therefore seemed to be a *de facto* mechanism for allowing unsuitable candidates to be quietly if effectively vetoed by the Panel of Experts prior to their being proposed the PACE for election.

Having thus put some more detailed meat on the bare bones of President Costa's proposal, Wohlwend gave her assessment. It was hardly glowing. She explained:

> 11. This initiative by President Costa is welcome, in that the clear intention behind it is to ensure that lists transmitted to the Assembly consist of three candidates of the highest quality . . . That said, even if I am of the view that this, and any other attempt to help us—the states concerned and the Assembly—ensure that lists of candidates transmitted to the Assembly are composed of three jurists of outstanding calibre, certain critical comments can nevertheless be made with respect to this proposal. This idea, modelled on the independent panel (Article 255 of the Treaty on the Functioning of the European Union) set up with the entry into force of the Lisbon Treaty, relates to another type of "animal". Under the European Convention on Human Rights it is the Assembly which elects judges from a list of three persons (in other words, it has a choice: Article 22), whereas the European Union panel looks at the suitability of (single) candidates put forward for appointment by governments to the Court of Justice of the European Union. Election of judges by the Assembly, in the Strasbourg system, provides "democratic legitimacy", something which no other international court possesses. Similarly, states parties to our Convention might consider such a "hybrid creation" as an inappropriate interference in their own national, hopefully rigorous, transparent and fair, selection procedures (as might also the Assembly, were it ever suggested that such a panel provide the Assembly, rather than states parties, with advice).[8] That said, as the initiative of President Costa is made in the spirit of enhancing the quality of candidates to be transmitted to the Assembly, I believe that this proposal is worthy of serious consideration.[90]

This important and revealing paragraph foreshadows all of the difficulties that the APE would eventually encounter.

[90] 2010 Report on National Procedures for Nominating Candidates at para. 11.

What were Wohlwend's objections? The first is somewhat inchoate. She objects to modeling the APE on the EU's 255 Panel, because the latter is "another type of 'animal.'" The 255 Panel intervenes in the EU's judicial appointment process, in which Member States put forward only one judicial candidate for appointment to the ECJ. In the Convention system, however, the PACE elects each ECtHR judge from a list of three candidates. This is of course true. But so what? Wohlwend states: "Election of judges by the Assembly, in the Strasbourg system, provides 'democratic legitimacy', something which no other international court possesses." The logic behind Wohlwend's objection is a little difficult to divine: after all, does the mere fact that the selection processes are different for ECJ and ECtHR judges mean that vetting panels may not be useful for both? Does judicial election by parliamentarians hailing from forty-seven countries lead to greater "democratic legitimacy" than judicial appointment by the representative government of each of those forty-seven? Should human rights and the machinery designed to defend them be subject to "democratic legitimacy" concerns? And if so, how? Although one might venture reasonable and potentially compelling answers to such questions, Wohlwend does not even attempt to do so. Her logic remains completely opaque.

Her motivation, however, is easier to understand: it is important for her to claim such "democratic legitimacy" (though she too leaves the term both undefined and in quotation marks) and to do so in the name of the PACE. Doing so elevates the status of the PACE and of its primary task (judicial elections); and it thereby defends them against potential encroachment by the proposed APE.

She soon made this turf-protecting impulse more explicit. The States proposing the judicial candidates might consider the APE (unflatteringly described as a "hybrid creation") to be "an inappropriate interference in their own national, hopefully rigorous, transparent and fair, selection procedures." And so too would the PACE, "were it ever suggested that such a panel provide the Assembly, rather than states parties, with advice." Having taken such an obvious shot across the bow of the Costa proposal, Wohlwend does not bother to condemn it altogether: "That said, as the initiative of President Costa is made in the spirit of enhancing the quality of candidates to be transmitted to the Assembly, I believe that this proposal is worthy of serious consideration." Hardly a ringing endorsement!

The Committee's Draft Resolution and Wohlwend's Explanatory Memorandum are essential documents for trying to figure out why the APE was fated to meet with such resistance. They demonstrate just how jealously the PACE would likely protect its own turf, i.e., its power to elect ECtHR judges. Similarly, it anticipates just how jealously the Member States might do the same with regards to their capacity to select judicial candidates. But it also reiterates the fundamental argumentative and conceptual parameters of the ECtHR appointments debates: the Convention system is claimed to possess a special "democratic legitimacy" (as always, left completely undefined) due to the fact that the PACE elects ECtHR judges from a list of three candidates nominated by each Member State; and each Member State has a legitimate right to run its "own national, hopefully rigorous, transparent and fair, selection procedures," which should not be subject to "inappropriate interference." Only within those settled parameters could attempts to improve the "quality" of judicial candidates (again, left virtually undefined) be addressed.

One final observation should be made before we leave this foundational Committee Report behind. It concerns a relatively subtle, but ultimately quite important, pair of remarks in Wohlwend's Explanatory Memorandum. The first is the following statement: "If the panel were to find, after an examination of the curriculum vitae, that the list to be forwarded to the Assembly is composed of suitable candidates, it would ... "[91] The key piece of information in this remark concerns the parameters of the APE's examination of judicial candidates: was the APE's review to be limited to "examination of the curriculum vitae"? Apparently so. Confirmation arrives in a footnote to the sentence warning against "inappropriate interference" by the APE in national selection and PACE election procedures: "As the Assembly's Sub-Committee on the Election of Judges to the European Court of Human Rights undertakes interviews with all candidates prior to election ..., it would be important to ensure that this new advisory panel, if created, operates only by means of a written procedure ..."[92] In other words, the APE's procedural capacities were being intentionally compromised from the very beginning, lest the Panel compete (i.e., engage in "inappropriate interference") with either the national selection or with the PACE election processes, including, in particular, the interview and assessment process performed by the Sub-Committee on Election of Judges to the ECtHR within the PACE's Committee on Legal Affairs and Human Rights. This was hardly an auspicious start.

The Committee of Ministers nonetheless voted to establish the Advisory Panel of Experts the very next month. In a Resolution recalling "the importance of ensuring the impartiality and quality of the Court," the Ministers established a Panel "of seven members, chosen from among members of the highest national courts, former judges of international courts, including the [ECtHR] and other lawyers of recognized competence."[93] This Panel, which would be "geographically and gender balanced," would therefore be composed primarily of domestic and international high court judges, who would be appointed to once renewable three-year terms by the Committee of Ministers, "following consultations" with the President of the ECtHR.[94]

91 *See supra* text accompanying footnote 87.

92 *See* 2010 Report on National Procedures for Nominating Candidates at note 8.

93 Committee of Ministers, Resolution CM/Res(2010)26 on the Establishment of an Advisory Panel of on Candidates for Election as Judge to the European Court of Human Rights (November 10, 2010) ["2010 Resolution on the Establishment of an Advisory Panel of Experts"]. According to this Resolution, the Contracting States may submit proposal for appointment to the Panel. *Id.* at para. 3.

94 *Id.* at paras. 2–3. Furthermore, "Proposals for appointment [to the Panel] may be submitted by the High Contracting Parties." *Id.* at para. 3.

The Committee of Ministers also delineated the manner in which the APE was to function:

> Before submitting a list to the Parliamentary Assembly as provided for in Article 22 of the Convention, each High Contracting Party will forward to the Panel, via its secretariat, the names and curricula vitae of the intended candidates. On the basis of these written submissions, the Panel shall perform its function in accordance with the operating rules appended to this resolution.
>
> Where the Panel finds that all of the persons put forward by a High Contracting Party are suitable candidates, it shall so inform the High Contracting Party without further comment.
>
> Where it is likely that the Panel may find one or more candidates not suitable for office, the chair of the Panel shall contact the High Contracting Party concerned to inform it and/or to obtain any relevant comments. If, in the light of the written submissions and any comments obtained, the Panel considers that one or more of the persons put forward by a High Contracting Party are not suitable, it shall so inform the High Contracting Party, giving reasons for its view, which shall be confidential. The Panel shall in a similar manner consider one or more new candidates who would subsequently be presented by the High Contracting Party.
>
> When a list of three candidates nominated by a High Contracting Party is being considered in accordance with Article 22 of the European Convention on Human Rights, the Panel shall make available to the Parliamentary Assembly in writing its views as to whether the candidates meet the criteria stipulated in Article 21§1 of the Convention. Such information shall be confidential.[95]

The APE was born.

As should be apparent, the APE was hamstrung in the manner suggested by Rapporteur Wohlwend's Explanatory Memorandum.[96] It was to review the suitability of candidates on the basis of extremely limited information. As the Resolution stated, the Panel must "perform its function" "on the basis of these written submissions," i.e., on the basis of nothing more than "names and curricula vitae of the intended candidates." Indeed, the appended Operating Rules specified: "The Panel's procedure is a written one. Members shall transmit their views to the Chair in writing."[97] Although the Rules allowed that the Panel "may hold a meeting where it deems this necessary to the performance of its function,"[98] the exceptional nature

[95] *Id.* at para. 5. As we shall see, this paragraph was later amended to require Member States to submit its list to the Panel at least three months before required submission to the PACE, in order to leave sufficient time for the APE process to unfold properly. *See* CM/Res(2014)44, with effect from November 26, 2014).

[96] *See supra* text accompanying notes 87.

[97] 2010 Resolution on the Establishment of an Advisory Panel of Experts at Operating Rules (iii).

[98] *Id.* at Operating Rules (iv).

of this permission ("*may* hold *a* meeting") made it clear that the Panel was effectively to work by mail, using nothing more than a CV. Although this would obviously reduce financial expenses, it also would limit the capacity of the Panel to develop into an active institution with its own identity, ethos, and agenda.

The Committee of Ministers' Resolution also regulated the interactions between the APE and the nominating States in interesting ways. The Resolution appears to envisage three basic scenarios. First, should the APE find the national list suitable, it so informs the State and that is the end of the story without further ado. Second, if "it is likely that the Panel may find one or more candidates not suitable for office," then the APE tells the State why. This appears to be a process of informal warning, opening up a conversation that will hopefully lead to a simple resolution of the problem (most likely the replacement of any such candidate on the national list). Third, should "the Panel consider[] that one or more of the persons put forward by a High Contracting Party are not suitable," then the APE "shall so inform the High Contracting Party, giving reasons for its view, which shall be confidential." This final scenario appears to imply that scenario #2 had failed to lead to a happy conclusion, i.e., the State had refused to remove the problematic candidate(s) and the APE did not alter its views as a result of its correspondence with the State.

Finally, regardless of which of the three scenarios between the APE and the nominating State have actually materialized, "the Panel shall make available to the Parliamentary Assembly in writing its views as to whether the candidates meet the criteria stipulated in Article 21§1 of the Convention." In other words, the Committee of Ministers appeared to maintain the "or else" component of the Costa proposal. As described by Wohlwend, this component held that "if ever the state concerned were *not* to heed the 'advice' of the panel and transmit, to the Assembly, a list containing one or more persons deemed by the panel not to meet the criteria for office . . ., the panel would inform the Assembly of its reasons."[99] The APE's assessment and "advice" were thus backed up by the threat of shaming.

But then the Resolution made an all-important adjustment. It specified that the APE's "views," transmitted "in writing" to the PACE, "shall be confidential." While such confidentiality is obviously essential for preserving the reputation of any judicial candidate that the APE may eventually find unsuitable, it also greatly compromised the APE's potential effectiveness. After all, the key to the APE is its capacity to function as a screening device. But in a calculating world, this capacity hinges on the credibility of the threat that the APE represents, namely, that national governments withdraw unsuitable candidates lest the APE call them out publicly. But if that "public" shaming is minimized and contained by a confidentiality requirement, the APE's deterrent effect is reduced accordingly, especially when the appointing body would ultimately be composed of several hundred

[99] *See supra* text accompanying notes 87–90.

fractious parliamentarians voting by majority (i.e., the PACE) rather than two dozen Ministers of Justice meeting face to face as a small college and voting by unanimity (i.e., the Council of the EU). Put differently, the confidentiality requirement lowers the price for a State's intransigence in proposing and refusing to withdraw an unsuitable judicial candidate. As we shall see, this was not merely a game theoretic exercise: the seemingly minor and thoroughly understandable addition of the confidentiality language in the Committee of Ministers' Resolution would soon have quite tangible consequences.

5
The APE in Operation

I. The Early Days

In December 2010, the Deputies of the Committee of Ministers agreed on the composition of the inaugural Advisory Panel of Experts (APE). Its members would be Katarzyna Gonera (Justice of the Polish Supreme Court); Renate Jaeger (former Justice of the German Supreme Court and retiring Justice of the European Court of Human Rights (ECtHR)); John L. Murray (Chief Justice of the Irish Supreme Court and former Justice of the European Court of Justice (ECJ)); Matti Pellonpää (Justice of the Finnish Supreme Administrative Court and former Justice of the ECtHR); Professor Sami Selçuk (former First President of the Turkish Court of Cassation); Professor Luzius Wildhaber (the Swiss former President of the ECtHR and former Justice of the Supreme Court of Liechtenstein); and Valery Zorkin (Chairman of the Russian Constitutional Court).[1] All seven had important judicial careers. Each, without exception, had served as a Justice or Chief Justice of a national supreme or constitutional court; and four of the seven had also served as a Justice of the ECtHR (Jaeger, Pellonpää, Wildhaber) or of the ECJ (Murray). The geographic diversity of the Panel was considerable, as two of the seven hailed from the East (Gonera of Poland and Zorkin of Russia) and another came from Turkey (Selçuk). But despite the Parliamentary Assembly's (PACE) efforts regarding the ECtHR, gender parity was still clearly lacking (only two of the seven were women).

How, then, did the Panel's first three-year term of operation work out? At first, things appeared to be functioning in an acceptable manner. In April 2012, after a little more than a year of the APE's operation, its Chair, Luzius Wildhaber, held an "Exchange of Views" with the Steering Committee for Human Rights of the Committee of Ministers. After recalling that the Panel was established in order to ensure that the Convention's criteria for judges on the Court be fully respected, he opined:

> This is clearly an eminently delicate but necessary task: the credibility of the European system of protection of human rights and fundamental freedoms obviously depends on the quality of the judgments and decisions pronounced by

[1] CM/Del/Dec(2010)1101/1.7E / December 10, 2010.

> the Court, which depend in turn on the quality, aptitudes and experience of the Court's members.[2]

Thankfully, this "delicate task" appeared to be going fairly well. "It gives me pleasure to highlight," Wildhaber wrote, "that during its first months of existence the Panel has benefitted from a most satisfactory level of co-operation both from the Contracting Parties and from the Parliamentary Assembly."[3]

In its first few meetings, Wildhaber explained, "the Panel discussed its internal working methods and criteria for the assessment of the qualification of candidates." On this front, the APE made an interesting choice. Noting that "in the European Union there is a similar committee which has the task of advising on the aptitude" of ECJ judicial candidates, Wildhaber explicitly quoted "the six elements" for assessing judicial candidates that the EU's Article 255 Panel had elaborated in its Annual Reports.[4] In contrast, however, he offered a much more vague and impressionistic image of the Panel's own mode of assessment:

> The Panel shares this endeavour to get a comprehensive picture of candidates. It believes that there should be a global assessment of all the qualities of a candidate, whatever his or her professional career path, with a view to determining whether a candidate has an aptitude for the judicial interpretation and application of the law at such a level in a constitutional and international context (of which knowledge of human rights would be only one component).[5]

Reading between the lines, one can infer what had actually occurred: despite the objection of some of its own members, the Panel had refused to adopt the 255 Panel's explicit and detailed criteria. For that matter, the Panel had refused to generate detailed criteria of its own, lest they eventually prove cumbersome. It opted instead to engage in a more "global assessment" of a judicial candidate's "aptitude for the judicial interpretation and application of the law at such a level in a constitutional and international context."

Contrary to President Sauvé and his 255 Panel, Wildhaber therefore did not attempt to spell out a detailed (and arguably binding) list of criteria by which candidates would be assessed. Speaking for the APE, he only touched briefly upon a few points regarding qualifications. While the Convention's requirement that ECtHR judges "must either possess the qualifications required for appointment

[2] Steering Committee for Human Rights, Ministers' Deputies Exchange of Views with Mr. Luzius Wildhaber, Chairman of the Advisory Panel of Experts on Candidates for Election to the European Court of Human Rights (April 4, 2012), in DH-GDR (2013)005, February 5, 2013 at para. 2 (translation by the author) ["2012 Exchange of Views"].

[3] *Id.* at para. 18 (in English).

[4] *Id.* at para. 9. For a detailed description and analysis of this list of six criteria, *see supra* Chapter 3(II)(B).

[5] 2012 Exchange of Views at para. 9

to high judicial office or be jurisconsults of recognised competence" "would seem to exclude judges from lower national first-instance courts," the Panel held the opinion that judges holding positions in higher national courts "should not, for that reason alone, be considered qualified" to serve on the Court. Instead, "additional factors," such as "significant length of service at a high level, service on international tribunals, together with the publication of important books or articles" "may constitute key elements in qualification for such an appointment." Similarly, to qualify as "jurisconsults of recognized competence," candidates must have "extensive experience." Taking up President Costa's cause against unacceptably young candidates, he explained that "the level of 'recognised competence' is normally reached when a person has been professor at a well-known university for a significant number of years and has published important works, including works relating directly or indirectly to human rights protection."[6] In addition to such seniority and status issues, however, Wildhaber had little more to add to the qualifications analysis. The Panel had accepted and applied the PACE's rules on gender balanced lists; and it fully supported the PACE's language requirements. But that was all.

Wildhaber did, however, have a little more to say on the procedural front; and his comments are revealing. First, he went to the bother of noting that the Panel could not really do much to assess the "high moral character" of the candidates:

> Since—contrary to the situation in the European Union—the Panel is not empowered (at least not expressly) to convoke the candidates for interviews, it will probably find it difficult, or delicate, to make judgments concerning the character of candidates unless it is manifestly apparent.[7]

The Panel's inability to interview the candidates was clearly vexing.

Second, the Panel wanted to ensure that it could engage in fruitful dialogue with the Member States about the lists they were submitting. This demonstrated "the importance of submitting the list of candidates to the Panel well in time before it is submitted to the [PACE.]" What was the problem? Wildhaber explained:

> On a few occasions Contracting Parties have submitted their list simultaneously to both [the PACE and the APE], something which deprives the work of the Panel of an important part of its possible impact and reduces or even suppresses the possibility of a dialogue conducive to the submission to the Assembly of a list of suitable candidates.[8]

[6] *Id.* at paras. 11–12.
[7] *Id.* at para. 10.
[8] *Id.* at para. 17.

With this comment, Wildhaber gave a fleeting glimpse into what was soon going to become all too obvious: the Panel was starting to experience significant difficulties. But what could they be? Why would national governments submit their lists of candidates simultaneously to the APE and the PACE? How could it do them any good?

II. The Storm Hits

The problems burst into the open less than a year later, when, in January 2013, Wildhaber made a stunningly public scene in his next "Exchange of Views" with the Steering Committee. His opening comments are sufficiently ominous to warrant quotation in full:

> I am overjoyed that you have granted me this opportunity to exchange views with you for the second time since the constitution of the Panel in January 2011. The first exchange took place in April 2012 in order to keep you informed on the Panel's activities during the first year of its existence.
>
> This second exchange of views pursues a goal that risks to be less pleasant, namely, to give me the opportunity to inform you of problems that the Panel has confronted since our encounter of April 2012. I have been charged by the other members of the Panel to inform you of the growing concerns that are raising doubts about the usefulness of performing the work for which you elected us in December 2010.[9]

Something had clearly gone terribly wrong.

Here, then, was Wildhaber's striking description of what had happened:

> I remind you that there were nine elections of new judges in 2012 during the June and October sessions of the [PACE]. The governments concerned having submitted their lists of candidates, the Panel considered that the candidates of six of the lists possessed all of the competences required by Article 21(1) of the European Convention of Human Rights. In two cases, doubts were expressed regarding the qualifications of certain candidates, but these doubts were then allayed thanks to supplementary information furnished by the governments concerned. Nonetheless, one of these lists, which had been plainly approved by the Panel, was then rejected by the PACE's Sub-Committee on the Election of Judges.

[9] Steering Committee for Human Rights, Ministers' Deputies Exchange of Views with Mr. Luzius Wildhaber, Chairman of the Advisory Panel of Experts on Candidates for Election to the European Court of Human Rights (January 30, 2013), in DH-GDR (2013)005, February 5, 2013 at 1 (translation by the author) ["2013 Exchange of Views"].

> In the case of two other lists, the members of the Panel considered one candidate of each list not to possess the qualities required by Article 21(1) of the Convention. One of these later withdrew his candidacy prior to [PACE] election, which permitted the Government concerned to present a new list. In the second case, the candidate deemed unfit by the Panel was [nonetheless] maintained on the list. Nor did he withdraw his candidacy. He was elected by the PACE after a very active lobbying campaign.
>
> In addition, I must also inform you of several cases in which the governments did not await the opinion of the Panel before submitting their respective lists of candidates to the PACE, and this despite the fact that the Panel had duly informed them that it needed more time to evaluate the candidates concerned. In these cases, the PACE simply proceeded to elect judges without having received the opinion of the Panel.
>
> The Panel can only regret that it was neither consulted nor informed of these events or of reasons justifying these decisions.[10]

These are, of course, stunning statements for the substance of what they disclose. Oddly, however, the underlying facts cannot confidently be pieced together from this account. Wildhaber explains that for the nine elections that were to take place in 2012, six government lists presented fully qualified candidates. Furthermore, the Panel expressed doubts concerning two lists; but further government information resolved those doubts. Does Wildhaber mean (which seems more likely) that two of the six "good" lists nonetheless presented candidates about whom the Panel had entertained doubts? If so, then only four of the nine lists were truly unproblematic—less than half! But even if the two doubtful lists were *not* part of the six "good" ones, then fully a third of the government lists were nonetheless deemed deficient, which is still not altogether ideal. The explanation was hardly clear; but either way, the message was less than encouraging.

As if this were not enough, Wildhaber's account gets more alarming. The next problem was institutional: although the Panel had expressly resolved its doubts concerning those two other lists (i.e., it had ultimately given them a clean bill of health), the PACE's Sub-Committee on the Election of Judges nonetheless chose to reject one of them. In other words, the inter-institutional tensions that we identified in Renate Wohlwend's Committee Report were apparently leading to bad blood. The PACE's Sub-Committee was clearly unwilling to cede its own assessment powers to the APE: it could (and did) decide on its own to reject a list that the APE had just approved. But to do so was obviously to slight the APE: why should such a panel of unusually high-powered judicial experts go to the bother of examining the judicial candidates' qualifications if a committee of relatively

[10] *Id.*

unqualified politicians could simply override its professional assessments?[11] This power to override only aggravated the already irksome procedural anomaly to which Wildhaber had alluded when discussing the Panel's inability to make effective assessments regarding the character of candidates: the Panel, unlike the PACE Sub-Committee on the Election of Judges, had been refused the power to interview the candidates.[12]

These festering inter-institutional rivalries between the APE and the PACE Committees were hardly the worst of it. Wildhaber goes on to explain that two other national lists contained an unqualified candidate. In one case, the new Panel system appears to have functioned as intended: the problematic candidate withdrew and the national government was thus able to present a new list.[13]

But the other case was an unmitigated disaster: not only did the candidate refuse to withdraw, but his government even went so far as to engage in "a very active lobbying campaign" that apparently bore fruit: the PACE actually proceeded to elect the candidate the APE had explicitly deemed unfit![14] The disrespect shown to the APE by the PACE's Sub-Committee on the Election of Judges was therefore surpassed by that shown by the PACE as a whole!

Finally, that disrespect was compounded by the utter dismissiveness demonstrated by "several" other governments, who, after having been "duly informed" that the Panel "needed more time to evaluate [their list of] candidates," had apparently not even bothered to await the opinion of the Panel before submitting their respective lists of candidates to the PACE. But this raises the same question as in the case of the "few" governments who, as Wildhaber had explained the year before, had submitted their list of candidates simultaneously to the APE and the PACE:[15] leaving aside the lack of consideration that such behavior demonstrates toward the APE, what good could such behavior possibly accomplish for the governments involved? It would create a procedural irregularity that would be immediately obvious to all: as we have seen, the Committee of Ministers' Resolution establishing the APE directed that the APE opinion be made (confidentially) available in writing to the PACE.[16] Without the confidential APE assessment, the

[11] The Interights Report had been scathing on the amateurishness of the Committee members. It stated, for example: "The Sub-Committee is comprised of approximately 27 members of the Parliamentary Assembly's Committee on Legal Affairs and Human Rights.... There is no requirement of legal expertise, although some members of the Sub-Committee are lawyers. Others are qualified in other disciplines. Very few have any knowledge or experience of international human rights law. The Sub-Committee's composition significantly inhibits its ability to provide a competent, independent assessment of candidates' legal professional capability ... " Jutta Limbach et al., "Judicial Independence: Law and Practice of Appointments to the European Court of Human Rights" (2003), available at http://www.interights.org/jud-ind-en/index.html ["Interights Report"]. at 21.

[12] *See supra* text accompanying note 7.

[13] As we shall see, this must have been the French case. *See infra* Chapter 10(V).

[14] As we shall see, this must have been the Czech case. *See infra* Chapter 10(VI).

[15] *See supra* text accompanying note 10.

[16] *See supra* Chapter 4, text accompanying notes 95–99.

candidate files before the PACE would obviously be incomplete. So what was the good? The answer is as revealing as it was distressing to the APE: despite the obvious procedural irregularity, the PACE simply went ahead and held the judicial election without further ado!

The reaction of President Wildhaber and of the Panel members was thoroughly understandable:

> This experience has left the Panel members with feelings of frustration. These feelings have been exacerbated by a perceived lack of co-operation, or even interest, on the side of the other stakeholders in the election procedure. This explains probably why, at a Panel meeting in October 2012 the members decided to raise these issues with other stakeholders in the election procedure.[17]

Wildhaber was overtly stating the obvious: as such disheartening procedural developments and appointments episodes demonstrate all too clearly, the APE was apparently at risk of being frozen out by both major sets of institutional players in the ECtHR judicial appointments system. On the one hand, a significant number of governments were willing to bypass or ignore the APE in one way or another; and on the other, the PACE and its Sub-Committee were willing to turn a blind eye to these governmental tactics or, at the very least, were unwilling to do anything meaningful to correct them. After all, had the PACE or its Sub-Committee simply refused to move forward on the election of candidates until their national lists had been properly reviewed by the APE, the resistant national governments would have had no real choice but to follow the mandated procedures. Worse, not only had the PACE failed to put an end to governmental resistance, it had done the opposite: it had actually elected a candidate expressly deemed unfit by the APE, thereby *rewarding* a national government that had intentionally ignored the APE's negative assessment. Needless to say, this was hardly an inducement for national governments to take the APE process more seriously.

In response, Wildhaber was taking multiple forms of action. First, he was meeting with everyone possible: the President and Secretary General of the PACE, the Chair of the Sub-Committee, the Chair of the Committee of Ministers, the President of the ECtHR, etc. Second, he was supporting procedural modifications proposed by himself and others. Wojciech Sawicki, Secretary General of the PACE, had, for example, started to give national governments more time to submit their lists to the PACE, which would in turn leave more time for the APE to be usefully consulted.

But Wildhaber, as Chair of the APE, was pressing for a much more straightforward solution: "The Panel would consider important the introduction of new

[17] 2013 Exchange of Views at 1.

criteria for the rejection of lists, for example, when a list contains candidates declared unsatisfactory by the Panel or when a list was not submitted in time to the Panel." The APE, in short, was asking for the effective power to veto national lists containing unqualified candidates.

Wildhaber was fully aware of the delicacy of such a proposal:

> The Panel's contribution to the overall aim of ensuring the quality of the elected judges can only be meaningful if its opinion is sought in time, respected and taken into account by the High Contracting Parties. And here I am touching a soft point. While the Panel is aware that its opinions are not legally binding, there is a political undertaking to respect the Panel's opinions on suitability of the candidates proposed. This would seem to include an agreement not to submit to PACE candidates which have been rejected as unfit by the Panel. This is, precisely, the rationale of the creation of the Panel; its very *raison d'être*.[18]

Of course, the existence of this supposed "political undertaking" was precisely what was being contested by the recalcitrant national governments, on the one hand, and by the PACE and its Sub-Committee on Election of Judges on the other. Their actions demonstrated quite clearly that, contrary to Wildhaber's claim, they did not in fact consider themselves bound to follow the APE's assessments of the suitability of judicial candidates.[19]

Wildhaber was sensitive to the dual powers he was seeking to tame. First, "The Panel members, of course, understand that the Governments might sometimes disagree with the Panel's first assessment of one or more candidates or might not comprehend the Panel's reasons." But "constructive dialogue" (and eventual acquiescence by the national government) undoubtedly represented "the way things should be." Second, "The Panel understands that the election of judges is attributed to a political body [i.e., the PACE]. A touch of political atmosphere is unavoidable. However, any political choice should be exercised exclusively among sound candidates possessing the knowledge and skills required by Article 21(1) of the [Convention]."

Wildhaber thus overtly recognized that the APE's professional assessment of candidates was operating alongside the work of two political entities: the national governments and the PACE. But, he was asserting, the assessment of professional qualifications and the exercise of political choice were both distinguishable and reconcilable. Professional assessment fell under the remit of the APE. Political

18 *Id.* at 2.

19 Indeed, one can readily argue that the Resolution establishing the APE impliedly countenanced such a governmental refusal to follow a negative assessment authored by the APE. *See* Committee of Ministers, Resolution CM/Res(2010)26 on the Establishment of an Advisory Panel of on Candidates for Election as Judge to the European Court of Human Rights (November 10, 2010) ["2010 Resolution on the Establishment of an Advisory Panel of Experts"] at para. 5.

decision-making belonged of course to the governments and the PACE; but these entities could only legitimately exercise such political choice within the professional parameters duly ratified by the APE. Wildhaber's synthesis was elegant: "The Panel's role is precisely to ensure that three candidates of comparable qualities are presented to the Parliamentary Assembly in order to give the Parliamentarians a real choice."[20] It was not at all evident, however, whether Wildhaber's political interlocutors would accept such a framing of the division of their respective provinces.

The APE and its Chair formalized their proposals in a list that it submitted six months later to the Steering Committee for Human Rights of the Committee of Ministers, with whom Wildhaber had had the two "exchanges of view" we have just analyzed.[21] The first two proposals bluntly stated:

i. The PACE Sub-Committee should not accept any list of candidates containing names of candidates who were not considered qualified by the Panel.
ii. The Sub-Committee should not proceed with an election as long as it has not received the Panel's opinion on the candidates' qualifications.[22]

These two proposals demonstrate the pivotal role that the APE wished to play in the ECtHR appointments process. If adopted, these proposals would to put an end to the precariousness of the APE's influence. If judicial elections could not go forward before the APE's opinion on the candidates' qualifications had been duly produced and transmitted, the national governments would be unable to continue to ignore the APE process altogether.[23] And if judicial elections ought not to go forward should the national list include candidates that the APE had found unsuitable, then the PACE would no longer vote on such tarnished lists, never mind elect such a candidate to the Court.[24] The APE was effectively proposing that its assessment process and its conclusions bind the duo of political institutions: the national governments and the PACE.

These proposals also do something both pointed and subtle: they specify not that the PACE, but that the PACE's *Sub-Committee on Elections* should not move forward on judicial elections until and unless a positive opinion on a candidate list has been received from the APE. As a result, these proposals locate the specific source of the inter-institutional rivalry: the Sub-Committee (now a full-fledged Committee[25])—unlike the accordingly disempowered APE—is the PACE entity most directly responsible for managing the judicial elections process. It is

[20] *Id.*
[21] Advisory Panel of Experts on Candidates for Election as Judge to the European Court of Human Rights, Proposals made by the Panel in its submission to the CDDH in May 2013, in Final Activity Report for the Committee of Ministers ["APE Proposals of May 2013"] at Appendix 2.
[22] *Id.*
[23] *See supra* text accompanying note 18.
[24] *See supra* text accompanying note 22.
[25] *See* PACE Resolution 2002 (2014).

the procedural initiator and institutional heavyweight within the PACE process: not only does it conduct the candidate interviews, but it also has the responsibility and power to assess their qualifications and rank them accordingly.[26] It also has the power to refuse candidate lists altogether.[27] In other words, the Sub-Committee could undoubtedly preempt any attempt by a national government to bypass the APE procedure or to flout a negative APE assessment of the qualifications of particular judicial candidates. The APE therefore logically called upon the Sub-Committee to support its procedural role: efficiency would undoubtedly be improved if the Sub-Committee nipped all problems in the bud by refusing to move forward on a given judicial election until the APE's opinion on that candidate list had been duly produced and transmitted.

That said, the APE proposal was not merely arguing for procedural efficiency. It was effectively blaming the Sub-Committee for much of the problems. After all, the Sub-Committee must have been allowing the elections to move to a vote in the PACE, even in those cases where the APE had delivered a negative opinion or even no opinion at all. In so doing, the Sub-Committee was effectively dismissing the importance of the APE and its work. But why would it do so?

The reality, as Renate Wohlwend's Report had tacitly suggested in response to the original APE proposal, is that the APE represented a relatively direct challenge not only to the national governments who were putting forward the judicial candidates, but also to the PACE and to its Sub-Committee. After all, the election of ECtHR judges is one of the most—and arguably the most—important of the PACE's tasks. And needless to say, it obviously is (and always had been) *the* defining task of the Sub-Committee on the Election of Judges (which, far from falling in importance, has since become the full-fledged Committee on the Election of Judges to the ECtHR).[28] From the perspective of the PACE and its (now) Committee, the APE was therefore something of an interloper.

The travails of the APE have thus been in great measure the product of a turf war over overlapping jurisdiction. The APE was effectively replicating the assessment work of the (then) Sub-Committee, which was understandably unwilling to hand over its own, never mind the PACE's, powers to this new and independent entity.

The procedural effects followed straightforwardly from this jurisdictional battle. Instead of operating as a gatekeeper that would limit access *of national candidate lists* to the plenary PACE (by only granting access to those lists approved by the APE), the Sub-Committee was functioning as a gatekeeper that was limiting access *of the APE*: the confidential APE opinions were forwarded not to the PACE as a whole, but only to its Sub-Committee, which thereby exercised a great deal of control over the eventual impact of those opinions. Due to this procedural set-up,

[26] The Committee now publishes its ranking of the candidates prior to PACE elections.
[27] *See supra* Chapter 4, text accompanying note 74.
[28] *See* PACE Resolution 2002 (2014).

the PACE members received not the APE's opinion, but only the Sub-Committee's assessment and ranking of the candidates.

Indeed, the Sub-Committee's gatekeeping function bothered the APE sufficiently that the APE's third reform proposal actually read: "The flow of information between the Sub-Committee and the Plenary of the PACE should be improved by making the Panel's opinion available to all PACE members before the election."[29] This proposal was effectively (and self-evidently) the APE's attempt to bypass the Sub-Committee in order to have a direct effect on the PACE's judicial elections. This desire to have a real impact also shines, however tentatively, through the APE's fourth proposal: "The Committee of Ministers may consider suggesting to the members of the PACE not to vote for candidates not considered qualified by the Panel."[30] The APE was proposing a series of alternatives designed to increase the direct and indirect impact of its opinions on PACE judicial elections.

The APE's "Final Activity Report" for its first three-year term of operation, published later that year, reinforced this basic project, first by giving a rough numerical breakdown of its candidate assessments and then by reiterating how its work should figure in the judicial appointments process.

The Report relayed its assessment figures as follows:

> 38. To date the Advisory Panel has examined the *curricula vitae* of candidates submitted by seventeen Governments.
>
> 39. In respect of eight country lists the Panel considered all candidates to be qualified within the meaning of Article 21(1) of the Convention.
>
> 40. In the case of eight other lists of candidates the Panel requested additional information on one or more of the nominated candidates (seventeen in total). In respect of eight candidates, the Panel came to the final conclusion that the candidates met the requirements of Article 21(1) of the Convention. In six cases, the Panel concluded that the candidates were not qualified. Two candidates were replaced by their governments with candidates who were then considered qualified within the meaning of Article 21(1) of the Convention. In another case, a candidate withdrew during the process and the replacement candidate was considered qualified by the Panel. In case of three candidates the Governments concerned maintained the candidatures and submitted the lists as such to the PACE.
>
> 41. In the case of another list the Government submitted the *curricula vitae* to the PACE before the Panel could assess the additional information provided in respect of three candidates.
>
> 42. Finally in the case of one list, the Panel considered one candidate not to be qualified, but decided not to request any additional information as the list had already been submitted to the PACE and could, therefore, no longer be changed.[31]

[29] APE Proposals of May 2013 at Appendix 2.
[30] *Id.*
[31] APE Final Activity Report 2013.

As these numbers attest, the APE had been all too active. It had given a clean bill of health to *less than half* (eight of seventeen) of the national lists it had examined. Of the remaining nine lists, eight provided additional information that the APE had requested regarding seventeen of the candidates. In other words, the APE had reservations about seventeen of the twenty-four candidates on those eight problematic lists, i.e., an average of more than two out of the three candidates per list! This is an astonishingly high number, even if, in the end, the APE ultimately concluded that only six of these candidates were unqualified.

What happened to these six candidates deemed unqualified is revealing as well. Two were replaced by suitable candidates. One more withdrew in favor of a suitable replacement. But three—fully half of those rejected by the APE—were nonetheless maintained on the lists that their national governments proposed to the PACE for election.

As if this were not bad enough, three more candidates, all apparently on a uniformly dubious list, were sent before the PACE for election before the APE could assess the additional information that it had requested of their national government. And yet another list, which contained one candidate deemed unfit, was submitted to the PACE before the APE could even request further information (apparently regarding one or both of the other candidates on the list).

The final tally suggests that the APE approved of eight lists outright (twenty-four candidates). Nine lists were questionable. Of the twenty-seven candidates on these problematic nine lists, only seven were approved outright by the APE. Eight more were approved upon receipt of further information. A further seven were formally rejected. And five remained questionable, as their candidacies were sent before the PACE without the APE receiving further information in time to make an assessment.

These figures suggest three important conclusions. First, the APE considered a very large percentage of all the candidates (some 40%) to be questionable to one degree or another: the APE "requested additional information" regarding twenty of the fifty-one candidates. Second, the APE formally concluded that a significant percentage of the candidates (seven of forty-six) were ultimately unqualified, and another five remained suspect (as the APE was never in a position to give its final assessment). This means that the APE would ultimately have declared somewhere between 14% and 24% (between seven and twelve of fifty-one) of the candidates to be unfit to serve as ECtHR judges. Finally, a distressing number of candidates and lists had been forwarded to the PACE despite the APE having declared the candidates outright unqualified (four candidates) or suspect (five candidates). That nine of fifty-one candidates (almost 20%) would be put before the PACE under such conditions demonstrates the precariousness of the APE's position: several Member States were perfectly willing to thumb their noses as the APE and its assessment process; and the Sub-Committee was unwilling and/or unable to stop them.

In one pithy paragraph addressed to the PACE, the APE's Report therefore reiterated the key proposals that had already been put before the Steering Committee for Human Rights some six months before:[32]

> 49. The prerogative for the election of judges to the Court lies with the PACE. It is its Sub-Committee on the Election of Judges that interviews the candidates and gives a recommendation to the members of the PACE. The Panel would, therefore, also invite the PACE and in particular its Sub-Committee to benefit from the Panel's expertise to the fullest extent possible by taking into account the Panel's opinion. The Sub-Committee should, therefore, not proceed with an election until it has received the Panel's final opinion on the candidates' qualification. The Sub-Committee may also consider not accepting any lists of candidates containing names of candidates who were rejected as not qualified by the Panel. Lastly, the PACE may also consider disseminating the Panel's opinion among all members of the PACE and not only among the members of the Sub-Committee.[33]

In the eyes of the APE, it was clearly the PACE's Sub-Committee that represented the key stumbling block at the European level.

III. The Response

How, then, did the Committee of Ministers' Steering Committee for Human Rights (CDDH) respond to the APE's complaints and proposals? On the one hand, the Committee recognized the APE's fundamental complaints about how the governments and the PACE (and in particular, the PACE's Sub-Committee on Elections) were sometimes failing to respect the APE's contributions. Governments had indeed dismissed the APE and its assessments in assorted ways; and in such cases, the PACE had accepted to proceed with the election process nonetheless. On the other hand, the Committee accepted only a few of the APE's proposed reforms and even imposed certain restrictions on the APE for good measure.

The Steering Committee was maintaining a delicate balancing act. Although the Steering Committee went to great pains to insist that "in the overwhelming majority of cases, the Advisory Panel has interacted with the other actors as foreseen in Resolution CM/Res(2010)26"[34] and that "fruitful working relations have been the general rule and misunderstanding or disagreement the rare exception,"[35] it

[32] *See* 2013 Exchange of Views.

[33] APE Final Activity Report 2013.

[34] Steering Committee for Human Rights, CDDH Report on the Review of the Functioning of the Advisory Panel of Experts on Candidates for Election as Judge to the European Court of Human Rights, ["CDDH 2013 Report"] CDDH(2013)R79 Addendum II (November 29, 2013) at para. 28.

[35] *Id.* at para. 55.

recognized the need to make "adjustments."[36] Those adjustments, while undoubtedly important, nonetheless quashed any attempt by the APE to play an authoritative role in the ECtHR appointments process.

In probably its most important passage, the CCDH Report directly addressed the APE's annoyance at the periodic refusal of the PACE and of certain governments to follow the APE's opinions. President Wildhaber, it will be recalled, had publicly wondered about the future usefulness of the APE should its opinions be dismissed in this manner.[37] Although he had recognized that the APE's opinions "are not legally binding" and that the election of ECtHR judges "is attributed to a political body" (i.e., the PACE), Wildhaber had nonetheless maintained:

> there is a political undertaking to respect the Panel's opinions on suitability of the candidates proposed. This would seem to include an agreement not to submit to PACE candidates which have been rejected as unfit by the Panel. This is, precisely, the rationale of the creation of the Panel; its very *raison d'être*.[38]

The Steering Committee flat out refused to accept this account. Addressing the notorious case of the PACE electing a candidate that the APE had officially found unqualified, the CCDH categorically stated that "neither is the government concerned required to follow the Advisory Panel's advice, nor is the Parliamentary Assembly required to act consistently with it."[39] The Committee was intransigent:

> CM Resolution (2010)26 reflects the fact that competence for the election of judges to the Court is attributed under the Convention to the Parliamentary Assembly. This implies that the (Sub-Committee of the) Parliamentary Assembly is free to conduct the election procedure according to its internal working procedures and enjoys a certain discretion when it wishes to create additional criteria for the assessment of the candidates' qualifications, and that its assessment of a candidate's qualifications is autonomous and independent. The Parliamentary Assembly may weigh the qualifications of a particular candidate differently from the Advisory Panel. This is so as the Sub-Committee conducts interviews with the candidates, which the Advisory Panel is not empowered to do.[40]

The APE thus gained no ground whatsoever in its attempt to claim more authoritative status or a more determinative role. The national governments and the PACE (including especially its Sub-Committee on Elections) were the duly authorized institutions in the ECtHR appointments process. The APE merely helped

36 *Id.* at para. 29.
37 *See supra* text accompanying notes 13–22.
38 *See supra* text accompanying note 18.
39 CDDH 2013 Report at para. 30.
40 *Id.* at para. 31.

those institutions; it did not bind them. The most the CDDH was willing to offer the APE was patently patronizing language: "While the opinion of the Advisory Panel is non-binding, it may be assumed that the Sub-Committee of the Parliamentary Assembly gives due consideration to an opinion of the Advisory Panel on a particular list of candidates."[41]

Having made clear its position of principle regarding the secondary status of the APE relative to the PACE and the governments, the CDDH was willing, however, to support the APE when those primary institutions failed to allow the APE to perform its proper (i.e., merely supportive) role in the assessment process. In particular, the Steering Committee condemned those instances in which a Member State had submitted its list of candidates simultaneously to the PACE and the APE or had forwarded its list to the PACE without awaiting the Advisory Panel's opinion:

> The CDDH considers such practices by States Parties to be incompatible with the *raison d'être* of CM Resolution (2010) 26. States Parties are reminded of the need to submit lists of candidates well before the deadline by which they must submit their list to the Parliamentary Assembly. Likewise, the Parliamentary Assembly is invited not to proceed with the election process without allowing the Advisory Panel a reasonable time within which to inform the State Party concerned of its views on the intended candidates.[42]

At least the APE had won support for the relatively self-evident—though recurrently ignored—proposition that it should not be openly dismissed by its intended interlocutors.

In addition to condemning such clear abuses of the ECtHR's appointments process, the CDDH endorsed a straightforward procedural adjustment that could significantly help the APE in doing its work. The existing practice had been to ask Member States to submit their proposed list of candidates to the APE six weeks prior to when those lists were due to be submitted to the PACE for elections purposes. The problem was that this could leave insufficient time for the APE and national governments to hash out problems that the initial list may have posed; i.e., back-up plans and new sets of candidates could be quite difficult to negotiate and propose in so little time. The CDDH therefore recommended that national lists be forwarded to the APE a full three months prior to their PACE due dates, thereby granting the APE twice as much time to exert influence over the national governments.[43]

[41] *Id.*

[42] *Id.* at para. 34.

[43] The Committee of Ministers formally adopted this new three-month standard in its Resolution CM/Res(2014)44 amending Resolution CM/Res(2010)26 on the Establishment of an Advisory Panel of Experts on Candidates for Election as Judge to the European Court of Human Rights (November 26, 2014).

By the same token, however, the Steering Committee pushed back against the APE's awkward delineation of the sources of information and the standards it used to assess judicial candidates. On these issues, the APE had made a series of clumsy decisions. Its starting point on standards clearly had to be Article 21(1) of the Convention, which simply states that ECtHR judges "shall be of high moral character and must either possess the qualifications required for appointment to high judicial office or be jurisconsults of recognised competence." This vague provision is, however, of little practical use. As a result, the Committee of Ministers had gone to the bother of drawing up Guidelines that synthesized the numerous PACE Recommendations and Resolutions on ECtHR judicial appointments that we have been discussing,[44] complete with an extensive explanatory memorandum that provided examples of "good practices" for each of the required standards.[45] But the APE's Final Activity Report published at the end of its first term all but brushed those Guidelines aside with the dismissively summary notation that the Panel "has had due regard to the Guidelines of the Committee of Ministers on the selection of candidates for the post of judge at the European Court of Human Rights."[46] Instead of adopting, or simply elaborating upon, the guidelines delineated by the very institution that had created the APE in the first place, the APE Report turned immediately to the qualifications standards that the EU's Article 255 Panel had elaborated in its Annual Reports, even going so far as to quote its sister institution for the "six elements" that it had established for candidates for positions on the ECJ.[47]

Worse, the APE then muddled matters by disclosing that it did not shy away from using what can only be termed "informal" sources of information regarding the candidates it was assessing. In an oddly self-aggrandizing passage, its Final Report stated:

> In addition to the *curricula vitae* and any further information provided by the Governments upon the Panel's request, the Panel has received on several occasions unsolicited information from various sources (e. g. non-governmental organisations). The Panel does not actively seek information from such sources. It should be emphasised that the Panel has never rejected any candidate as not qualified based on information received from a different source than the Government. However, it should not be forgotten that the Committee of Ministers appointed the seven Panel members *ad personam* because of their considerable personal and professional experience and their high standing. The Panel members are

[44] *See* Committee of Ministers' Deputies, Guidelines of the Committee of Ministers on the selection of candidates for the post of judge at the European Court of Human Rights, CM(2012)40 final (March 29, 2012).

[45] *See* Committee of Ministers' Deputies, Guidelines of the Committee of Ministers on the selection of candidates for the post of judge at the European Court of Human Rights—Explanatory Memorandum, CM(2012)40 addendum final (March 29, 2012).

[46] APE Final Activity Report 2013 at para. 25.

[47] *Id.* at para. 26.

> well-known in the legal profession and they have naturally personal contacts with judges at the highest national courts, other legal professionals or non-governmental human rights organisations, who may use such personal contacts to transmit information to the Panel.[48]

Even though the APE explained that it had recently decided that "only information from reliable and objectively verifiable sources should be used" and, "[f]urthermore, if such information put into question the qualification of a candidate, the Panel would ask the Government concerned for clarifications before possibly using such information to the detriment of a candidate," the APE was not only playing a little fast and loose with its assessment guidelines and with the information on which it would base those assessments, but was also saying so publicly in a clumsy bid to underline the status and connections of its members.

The Steering Committee pushed back rather forcefully. First, it expressed grave misgivings about the APE's use of informal information:

> There is however an inherent risk in taking into account materials from undisclosed sources concerning individual candidates without those candidates having the possibility of responding to, or even being aware of that information. In particular, the pro-active use of a "judicial network" may lead to unjustified considerations influencing the Advisory Panel's opinion. In general, where the Advisory Panel envisages making greater use of other (undisclosed) sources of information, it should give the government concerned an opportunity to reply.[49]

In its conclusions, the CDDH bluntly stated: "The CDDH would propose giving further careful consideration to the (non-)use of non-official sources of information by the Advisory Panel."[50] It was reining in the APE, which had made the amateurish decision to be indiscreet.

Second, the Steering Committee criticized not only the sources of the APE's information, but also the standards by which it was assessing the information that it received. Clearly annoyed that the APE had failed to adopt the Committee of Ministers' own Guidelines as the formal basis for its assessment of ECtHR candidates, the Committee insisted:

> The CDDH proposes to amend the Committee of Ministers' Resolution to indicate that the Committee of Ministers' Guidelines on the selection of candidates for the post of judge at the European Court of Human Rights, alongside the Convention itself, form the basis of the Panel's assessment. It takes note that the

48 *Id.* at para. 18.
49 CDDH 2013 Report at para. 43.
50 *Id.* at para. 57.

> Advisory Panel draws useful inspiration for a substantive and reliable interpretation also from other sources, including the practice of the panel instituted by Article 255 TFEU. It is important for the functioning of the Advisory Panel and in particular its interaction with the government concerned that the assessment of the qualification of the candidates be based upon foreseeable and commonly shared criteria.[51]
>
> The APE, in short, should not be allowed to substitute its own (vague) assessment criteria for those formally adopted by the Committee of Ministers.

Finally, and probably most importantly, the Steering Committee refused to go along with any suggestion that the APE be empowered to intervene more directly in the appointments process by distributing its opinions more broadly, for example, by sending them to all members of the PACE.[52] If the APE wanted "to enhance the authority of the Advisory Panel's opinion that a particular candidate does not meet the required criteria," then it should simply provide the candidate's government "with a reasoned written opinion stating the exact reasons why a particular candidate is not deemed to fulfil the necessary criteria for election."[53] The APE would not be freed from the control exercised by the PACE's Sub-Committee on Elections: "[W]hat is essential is that the Advisory Panel continues its practice of informing the (Sub-Committee of the) Parliamentary Assembly when the government submits a list featuring a candidate who was not deemed qualified by the Advisory Panel, including the name(s) of the candidate(s) concerned."[54] The flow of information and the fundamental distribution of competences were not to change.

The Steering Committee further maintained the status quo in the face of two other suggestions. The first potential reform was fascinating: the APE's opinion might be distributed not only to the government proposing a given list, but to all the other governments as well. The Committee explained:

> This would enable governments to exert (albeit non-public) political peer pressure on a government disregarding a negative assessment of the Advisory Panel. As the Panel was set up in light of the shared responsibility of the States Parties for the effective operation of the Convention system, the nomination of a candidate who is not qualified in accordance with the Convention is a matter of concern to all States Parties. One option would be ... to permit an assessment by the Panel that a candidate is unqualified to be transmitted, on a strictly confidential basis, to all States Parties, if after a specified and reasonable time the nominating State

[51] *Id.* at para. 48.
[52] *See supra* text accompanying notes 28–29.
[53] CDDH 2013 Report at para. 45.
[54] *Id.*

has not withdrawn the candidate in question. However, views in the CDDH were divided.[55]

Such a reform would have transformed the ECtHR assessment mechanism into something closer to the one that had developed for the ECJ. Why? Because once the APE's negative opinion regarding a candidate had been distributed to all the Member States, it would have been extremely difficult for the proposing government not to withdraw a problematic candidate on its list. For one thing, the reputational cost for the government would have been high: it would have had to deal with its governmental counterparts face to face. And for another, the odds of getting such a candidate elected would have been severely damaged: once the negative opinion was clearly known by all the governments, many of the other governments—most of which are parliamentary in nature—would naturally flag this to their national delegations sitting in the PACE, who would then be far less likely to throw their electoral support behind a candidate clearly branded as unqualified. This reform would therefore have transformed the APE's institutional position into one significantly more reminiscent of the EU's Article 255 Panel. The APE, like the 255 Panel, might have begun to exert something more akin to a veto power with regard to candidates it deemed unqualified. But "views in the CDDH were divided"; so the reform proposal died.

The Steering Committee also explicitly torpedoed the APE's second attempt to address its opinion on a given list to a broader audience than merely the proposing government (and, secondarily, the Sub-Committee). Framing this as a confidentiality issue, the Steering Committee argued that changing the APE's confidentiality provisions "may have significant repercussions for the Advisory Panel, the nature of its work and its relations with States Parties and/ or the Parliamentary Assembly." The APE might become less effective in dealing with national governments, which, the CDDH implied, might become less flexible should their concessions to the APE become known. Worse, "any change in the confidentiality requirements surrounding the Advisory Panel's contacts with the Parliamentary Assembly" could result in publicizing the information that the APE might give to the PACE, which "could change the relationship between the two bodies." What might ensue? "There may be some outside expectation that the Parliamentary Assembly would follow the Advisory Panel's views"; and this, in turn, might "impact on the autonomous freedom enjoyed by the Parliamentary Assembly to elect judges."[56]

The Steering Committee, though speaking in somewhat veiled and convoluted terms, had clearly grasped the stakes of the APE's proposed reforms. Changing the flow of information between the APE and its potential interlocutors would likely change—and, the APE hoped, *would* change—their respective power relations

55 *Id.* at para. 47.
56 *Id.* at para. 54.

concerning judicial appointments. A negative assessment by the APE might trigger peer pressure on proposing governments; and/or it might effectively force the PACE to vote against particular judicial candidates. While the APE would clearly be in favor of such changes, the governments, the PACE (and especially its influential Sub-Committee on Elections) and—perhaps not terribly surprisingly—the Committee of (national) Ministers' Steering Committee clearly were not. In sum, the APE had won a few concessions, especially regarding patently dismissive governmental and Sub-Committee behavior; but it had lost its core struggle to influence the ECtHR judicial appointments process in a more significant fashion. Indeed, its proposals were rejected precisely because they might prove successful.

IV. Conclusion

The path to the current state of the ECtHR's judicial appointment process has passed through a series of stages. Over the last sixty plus years, the Court has transitioned from its passive Cold War beginnings, through its post-'89rebirth as an active agent of rights-based constitutional democracy and the rule of law, to its current APE-assisted and powerful if controversial self.

In its first phase, the Court was only a minor part of a byzantine institutional architecture that was devised in the Cold War era to provide an anti-totalitarian alarm bell while making sure not to pose too much of a threat to the wary States that had signed onto the European Convention on Human Rights. The result was a complex set of (largely diplomatic) institutional and procedural arrangements that effectively rejected a more aggressive and justiciable approach.

The second phase marked the gradual judicialization of the Convention system as the Member States of the Council of Europe progressively accepted that their institutional and procedural creation was indeed worthy of trust. The dominance of the Commission, and the concomitantly part-time and secondary nature of the Court, gradually induced the Member States to opt into the Convention's two notorious optional provisions, eventually leading to a Court with compulsory jurisdiction over individual complaints.

In phase three, the Council of Europe considered the possibility of restructuring its institutions and procedures. The underlying idea was to fuse the Commission and the Court. This would transform the ECtHR into a new, single, full-time, and permanent Court, simultaneously abolishing its traditional diplomatic screening mechanism (i.e., the Commission) and thereby granting individuals direct access to what would now be the dominant institution of the Council of Europe: the newly reorganized Court. But these debates made little headway until the mid-1990s, when the Member States, now facing imminent and large-scale accession of new Member States from the former Soviet Bloc, suddenly broke through their impasse and signed onto Protocol 11 of the Convention.

The fourth phase marked the rapid transformation of the ECtHR into its modified judicial form, complete with its new procedural, institutional, and conceptual features. In this period of mass Eastern accession, the new Court was no longer to be a passive and symbolic alarm bell to be rung in rare moments of Western European backsliding. It was instead to act in an active manner to help fashion the newly acceded States into properly democratic constitutional orders characterized by the rule of law and the judicial protection of fundamental rights. The newly central place of the judiciary at both the domestic and European levels called for the elaboration of judicial independence and judicial appointments measures that would cement this leading role. The Council of Europe accordingly passed (and passed again) a panoply of measures designed to put this new regime into effect.

Finally, this focus on judicial independence and judicial appointments ultimately led to a crowning institutional and procedural achievement: the establishment of the Advisory Panel to vet candidates proposed by the Member States for election to the Strasbourg Court. The APE, formally proposed by ECtHR president Jean-Paul Costa and eventually chaired by his predecessor Luzius Wildhaber, was modeled loosely on the EU's Article 255 Panel, but suffered a very different fate. Trapped in an institutional and procedural vice between the Member State governments, on the one hand, and the PACE and its Committees, on the other, the APE has fought hard to play the kind of leading role in judicial appointments that the 255 Panel has been able to cut out for itself. Openly snubbed by recalcitrant Member States unwilling to heed its advice, undermined by the PACE (and its Committees) leery of losing any institutional prerogatives, and only intermittently and cautiously supported by a Committee of Ministers torn between its more political and its more technocratic component parts, the APE was quickly frustrated by its increasing inability to exercise its vetting mission with the zeal it thought appropriate.

In short, the tensions apparent from the very inception of the European Convention on Human Rights continue to endure, albeit in different institutional forms and contexts. Wary from the start of a powerful human rights court before which they might repeatedly be hauled as defendants, the Member States of the Council of Europe made sure to design an institutional and procedural structure that defanged the ECtHR while providing the ideological and signaling benefits they sought to promote in the post-War and Cold War eras. The resulting institutional and procedural architecture was an imaginative, if byzantine, edifice that fused political, diplomatic, and legal sensibilities. Even once the Court was established and its jurisdiction settled, the ECtHR remained a part-time and relatively secondary institution.

Only the prospect of large-scale accession of the former Soviet Bloc countries from the East finally induced a fundamental change in the Court's basic operational set-up. Suddenly, the reforms came in rapid succession. The ECtHR was to be a single, full-time, and permanent Court, directly available to plaintiffs who would no longer need to run the gauntlet of the Commission's conciliatory screening mechanism. The Court's appointment procedures needed to be standardized and professionalized, complete with beefed-up guarantees of judicial independence. Its initially imaginative institutional structure would become increasingly classical over time, with its judges gradually looking more important and more purely judge-like over time. The Court's authority *qua* court needed to be properly settled.

The old tensions and reticence have nonetheless persisted. Few of the old or new Member State governments have proven unreservedly in favor of subjecting their chosen judicial candidates to the increasingly formalized, professionalized, and intrusive judicial appointments process. They have therefore resisted in a host of ways, some more direct and blatant than others, as APE Chair Luzius Wildhaber bitterly complained in his 2013 "Exchange of Views." Indeed, the Council of Europe's Committee of Experts on the System of the ECHR (DH-SYSC) has confirmed that such problems have continued unabated:

> **The opinions [of the APE] are not always followed**: during the period between January 2014 and June 2017, among the 29 lists examined by the Panel, in 9 cases the candidates were maintained on the list despite the Panel's negative opinion.[57]

This astonishing passage reveals that in the four years following Wildhaber's public row, in almost a third of all cases, Member State governments have not only proposed lists that contained at least one candidate deemed unsuitable by the APE, but have also refused to replace such candidate(s) from the list eventually presented to the PACE for election.

That said, one can now also find signs that the inter-institutional dynamics have begun to shift. These signs, rather well buried in the administrative thicket of Council of Europe procedure, suggest that some of the tensions between the PACE Committee on the Election of Judges and the APE have begun to thaw. The thrillingly entitled Memo "Procedure for the election of judges to the European Court of Human Rights," prepared by none other than the longstanding Secretary General of the PACE, Wojciech Sawicki, lays out several key developments that have modified the interactions between the institutions we have been discussing.[58] First, "the list [of judicial candidates] should be submitted to the Assembly only after the

[57] Steering Committee for Human Rights, Committee of Experts on the System of the ECHR (DH-SYSC), [Draft] Report on the process of selection and elections of judges of the [ECtHR], DH-SYSC(2017)R4 Addendum at para. 81 (November 10, 2017) (emphasis in original) ["2017 Report on the process of selection and election of ECtHR judges"]. For more on this 2017 Report, *see infra* Chapter 6(V) and Chapter 8(I).

[58] Secretary General of the Assembly, "Procedure for the election of judges to the European Court of Human Rights," SG-AS (2019) 05 ["Sawicki Memo"]. Sawicki's authorship represents the concrete, if opaque, sign of the document's importance. As a formal matter, most of the modifications laid out in the Sawicki Memo were passed by the PACE in its Resolution 2278 (2019) on Modification of various provisions of the Assembly's Rules of Procedure.

Panel's opinion on the suitability has been obtained."[59] This wording makes it fairly clear that the Member State governments should no longer play games with—never mind ignore—the APE: if the APE opinion must have been "obtained" for a list of judicial candidates to be submitted to the PACE for election, then surely the government should no longer be able to submit their list to the APE and the PACE at the same time, never mind categorically refuse to submit their list the APE in the first place. And indeed, the nearly contemporaneous 2019 PACE Resolution 2278 specifies that "The [PACE] decides not to consider lists of candidates where . . . the Advisory Panel was not duly consulted."[60]

Second, Sawicki's Memo demonstrates an increasing commitment to taking ever more seriously the PACE's vetting process of the candidates and of the national selection procedures. It states not only that "The Assembly for its part also assesses the fairness, transparency and consistency of the national selection procedure including public and open calls for candidatures," but also that its Committee on Elections has "begun to place greater emphasis on this issue."[61] Beyond offering such bromides, however, the Memo also overtly states that in 2016 alone, the PACE Committee "rejected two [national] lists [of judicial candidates] on purely procedural grounds."[62] Sawicki even follows this reality check with details: "In one case . . . the list was transmitted simultaneously to the panel [i.e., the APE] and the Assembly. In another case, no meaningful national selection procedure was carried out at all." Finally, "[f]ollowing discussions in yet another case, in January 2019, the committee decided that it would no longer consider lists of candidates when no interviews had been carried out during the national selection procedure."[63] The PACE Committee on Elections was increasingly playing hardball with uncooperative governments.

Next, the Sawicki Memo reveals a shift in the dynamics within and surrounding the Committee. First, the Committee would now be able to reject a list by a simple majority vote (rather than the two-thirds supermajority vote previously in place).[64] Second, Committee members from the country submitting a list would no longer be allowed to vote on that list in Committee.[65] And repeatedly absentee members would now be removed from the Committee "[t]o ensure an appropriate level of participation."[66] The Committee, it appears, increasingly means business.

[59] Sawicki Memo at para. 7(8).

[60] PACE Resolution 2278 (2019) at para. 2.4.2.

[61] Sawicki Memo at para. 8.

[62] *Id.*

[63] *Id.*

[64] *Id.* at para. 17. *See also* PACE Resolution 2278 (2019) at para. 2.4.1.

[65] *Id.* at para. 24. *See also* PACE Resolution 2278 (2019) at para. 2.4.1. Note, however, that they are nonetheless "permitted to participate in [the Committee's] discussions" on the matter, which does significantly limit the effects of the change. *See* Sawicki Memo at para. 24.

[66] *Id.* at para. 14.

Perhaps most interesting, however, is a shift in the working relationship between the Committee and the APE. Sawicki's Memo explains: "The Chairperson of the panel [the APE] is invited to join the briefing sessions in order to explain the panel's views on the list and reply to possible questions by members."[67] This seemingly bland sentence marks a meaningful change. Now that the APE Chair will attend the briefing sessions in which the APE Committee on Elections reviews the applicant dossiers and prepares its interviews, it will be far more difficult for the Committee to override the APE's assessment regarding the suitability of judicial candidates. While such divergences and overrides might theoretically be possible, socio-political pressures would undoubtedly make them highly unusual.[68] There can be no doubt but that the tensions between the PACE Committee (then sub-Committee) on the Election of Judges and the APE have been significantly reduced since the early days, when their respective Chairs (Klaas de Vries and Luzius Wildhaber) found it so difficult to find common ground.

There are at least two divergent ways to interpret these ongoing developments, both of which are compelling. The first emphasizes the general direction of the substantive and procedural reforms and of the shifting dynamics between the Committee on the Election of Judges, the APE, and the Member States. Under this reading, the general trend has clearly been toward ever-stronger substantive norms, ever more stringent procedural requirements, and—especially recently—a somewhat more constructive working relationship between the Committee and the APE. Under the second reading, conversely, these general trends merely underscore the ongoing resistance of Member State governments, the hardwired tensions between the institutions and actors in play, and the endless succession of debates and measures that predictably result in ever more debates and reforms. How, then, should we understand not only the direction of these reforms, but also the never-ending need for ever more of them?

In our examination of these seemingly interminable reform efforts, one can begin to make out the broad outlines of interesting cleavages and alignments, ranging from national and regional divisions (e.g., East vs. West or recent vs. established Member States) to institutional ones (e.g., the APE vs. the PACE and its committees). To these should be added the less evident tensions between political institutions (such as the national governments and the PACE), on the one hand,

[67] *Id.* at para. 16.

[68] One can safely presume that it would be much harder for the Committee to find a candidate suitable that the APE had found unsuitable than for the Committee to find unsuitable one that the APE had found suitable. To take a real-world example: a seemingly qualified judicial candidate represents on his/her CV that (s)he has sufficient linguistic capacities in English and French. The APE, limited to examining the candidates' CVs, has no reason to question this representation. In its personal interview, however, the Committee immediately recognizes the unhappy reality that the candidate's linguistic capacities are not as represented. Based on this extra information, the Committee would be obliged to declare unsuitable a candidate that the APE had (properly) found suitable.

and judicial and academics players (such as the APE, ECtHR presidents Costa and Wildhaber, and the Interights authors), on the other, with the Committee of Ministers teetering somewhere in between. With these political, institutional, procedural, and ideological divisions in mind, it is time to start examining how we might decipher and make sense of what has been going on.

PART III
JUDICIAL INDEPENDENCE? AGAIN?

Now that we have patiently worked our way through much of the primary material regarding the European judicial appointments debates and reforms, the time has come to start explaining and theorizing in a more thoroughgoing manner what these developments have been all about. I have made no attempt to hide what I believe to be the single most important triggering factor in these developments, namely, the rapid and large-scale accession of new Member States from the former Eastern Bloc in the wake of the fall of the Berlin Wall. But calling attention to this momentous historical change hardly suffices, in and of itself, to explain the judicial appointments debates and reforms. Accession was certainly the great triggering event; but that event was embedded in a series of institutional, political, and conceptual structures that profoundly affected the course of the debates and their ensuing reforms.

As we shall see over the next few Parts, there are many ways that one might try to make sense of the judicial appointments reforms. The most straightforward approach, which is also the one most in keeping with the European debates of the last twenty plus years, is to understand these reforms as the product of a concerted struggle over judicial independence. This Part addresses this account head-on.

Focusing on judicial independence raises three important complications. I am flagging them immediately, so that we may keep them in mind right from the start. The first is that the academic literature on judicial independence now comes in two principal and almost incompatible variants. One variant, which one might call "classical," is very straightforward. Unfortunately, it is also of no theoretical interest. It offers little more than vague and rather trite statements about the importance of judicial independence to the separation of powers, the threats that judicial hierarchy can pose to the independence of individual judicial decision-makers, the dangers that excessive judicial independence might pose to the rule of law, and so on. In reading these bland if well-meaning statements of the obvious, one cannot help but be reminded of the statue of the founder of Faber College in the movie *Animal House*, on whose pedestal is engraved the amusingly insipid college motto: "Knowledge is good." Yes, indeed, judicial independence is good. Although, as this literature dutifully if laboriously points out, one can always have too much of a good thing . . .

The other variant is very much the opposite. It offers a highly skeptical, even corrosive, take on the judicial independence literature of the first type. This variant, which I confess to find quite genial both in substance and in style, makes a series of insightful points. Most importantly, it stresses that as soon as one gets beyond the obvious (i.e., the outright corruption of anyone's reasonable definition of appropriate judicial behavior), the classical judicial independence literature hinges on a series of misleadingly vague terms and fuzzy ideas about judicial interpretation and decision-making, about the relationship between the judicial and the political, about the separation of powers, and so on. Its basic point, which it often states quite overtly, is that the classical debates over judicial independence are terribly vague and overblown.

Although I am inclined to agree wholeheartedly with such critiques, I think it is important to take two points seriously nonetheless. To begin with, the mere fact that the classical judicial independence debates tend to be stunningly vacuous does not explain why they remain so remarkably persistent. Indeed, the very fact that these debates appear so sterile makes their persistence all the more notable and worthy of analysis. This drives us, however, toward a second-order analysis: the judicial independence debates are important not because they are compelling, but, to the contrary, because they are so inane. Such a perspective suggests that those debates must be productive on some other register, for example, as an acceptable language for advancing particular policy proposals.

The next point is less amusing. As the current Hungarian and Polish examples demonstrate all too clearly, people, institutions, and governments really do periodically behave in ways that violate just about anyone's reasonable idea of judicial independence. One can of course view such instances as pathological, either as one-off anomalies in an otherwise legitimately democratic regime or as systemic failures indicative of large-scale authoritarian dangers. But even if one treats such occasions as anomalies, they do offer useful vantage points for examining fundamental assumptions about appropriate judicial decision-making practice, about the nature of "the political," about the relation of the judicial to the political, and so on. With some notable exceptions, most of the skeptical literature is directed primarily to a pre-Trump American audience and does not really mean to be addressing post-Soviet scenarios. In the case of more frontal attacks on judicial independence, the classical literature can therefore be more on point, even if it is rather basic: sometimes subtlety is just not in order.

The second complication in our judicial independence analysis is that judicial independence does not simply function as an external—one might almost say "independent"—analytic framework that we can bring to bear on the European judicial appointments debates "from the outside." Instead, judicial independence is itself a major theme within those European judicial appointments debates. As a result, the judicial independence debates are themselves a significant part of the object of our analysis.

This somewhat confusing state of affairs means that this Part must address judicial independence in at least two different ways. It must bring the judicial independence literature to bear *on* the judicial appointments debates that we have presented in Parts I and II. But this Part must also examine the emergence and development of the judicial independence debates *within* these European judicial appointments debates. This creates a certain "hall of mirrors" effect, as the judicial independence literature functions as both a subject and object of the analysis.

The take-away point is that this dual quality of the judicial independence debates, in which judicial independence emerges both as a framework for understanding the judicial appointments reforms and as an important component of the appointments debates, reveals something important. Judicial independence is not merely a straightforward or objective framework for making sense of the judicial appointments debates. It is also a particular rubric that specific and interested players define and deploy as a means to inflect and influence European legal developments. In other words, "judicial independence" functions as a legal, political, institutional, and conceptual *intervention.*

The third complication is that although judicial independence has undoubtedly surfaced again and again as a major theme and concern in the European judicial appointments debates, it has gradually been accompanied, and at times been overshadowed, by another: judicial quality. This Part will therefore prepare the next, which will take a first crack at explaining not only how the topic of judicial quality interacts with the topics of judicial independence and judicial appointments, but also how and why it has effectively become *the* dominant theme in both the primary and secondary literatures about European judicial appointments reform.

This Part is organized as follows. Chapter 6 presents and examines the primary literature on European judicial independence. This literature consists of a surprisingly long list of measures adopted on a regular and ongoing basis by institutions attached to the Council of Europe over the course of the last twenty plus years. Some of these measures are more formally authoritative than others. Most carry titles that explicitly address judicial independence, although a few are framed slightly differently, such as the pompously entitled "Magna Carta of Judges" adopted in 2010 by the Consultative Council of European Judges. Over the course of time, these European institutions have of course sharpened their analyses, modulated the focus, and expanded the scope of their measures, and done so in a manner that indicates a certain evolution in perceived areas of concern. That said, these measures demonstrate a degree of overlap and even repetition that is striking in its own right. For the most part, the institutions have passed and re-passed measures that re-till the same ground as before, with only modest substantive changes.

The first measure to be passed was a Recommendation "On the Independence, Efficiency and Role of Judges" adopted by the Committee of Ministers in 1994.[1] This Recommendation, which we examined briefly in Chapter 4,[2] is couched heavily in terms of "the defence of democracy and the rule of law"; it accordingly bears the imprint of its time, as it dates from the high point of mass accession of the new Member States from Eastern and Central Europe.

The second was the "European Charter on the Statute for Judges," passed in 1998 and 1999 by a more informal group of European participants, judges, and judicial associations organized by the Council of Europe.[3] This document covered much the same ground, but began to focus attention more concertedly on the establishment and functioning of independent judicial councils as a means to promote "the competence, independence and impartiality" of the judiciary.[4]

The third was the Opinion No. 1 on "Standards Concerning the Independence of the Judiciary and the Irremovability of Judges" adopted in 2001 by the newly created Consultative Council of European Judges, which had been established the year before by the Committee of Ministers of the Council of Europe.[5] This comparatively hard-hitting document took a relatively hardline approach that reveals a growing frustration with Eastern European judicial developments and an increasing conviction in the importance and stature of the judiciary at both the domestic and the supranational levels.

The list of such measures goes on and on; and it shows no sign of abating. Not only have other institutions, such as the Venice Commission (formally entitled "The European Commission for Democracy through Law") jumped on the judicial independence bandwagon, but the Committee of Ministers and the Consultative Council of European Judges (CCJE) have even returned to the issue several times, generating updated or expanded versions of their earlier measures. For all of the apparent blandness of the topic of judicial independence, its persistence borders on the extraordinary.

Chapter 7 turns to the secondary literature on judicial independence. For the sake of brevity, and in the interest of maintaining the interest of my readers, I will spend a minimum of space on the classical literature. I will instead turn very quickly to the main variants of the skeptical literature. I will pause first on Lewis Kornhauser's devastating critique of the classical concept of judicial independence, which he dismisses as categorically "not useful," for the simple reason that it cannot be isolated from other closely associated analytic terms, such as the separation

[1] Committee of Ministers, Recommendation Rec R (94)12 on Independence, Efficiency and Role of Judges (October 13, 1994) ["1994 Recommendation on the Independence of Judges"].

[2] *See supra* Chapter 4(I).

[3] *See* European Charter on the Statute for Judges, DAJ/DOC (98) 23 (1998) at para. 1.1.

[4] *See id.*

[5] Consultative Council of European Judges, "Opinion No. 1 on Standards Concerning the Independence of the Judiciary and the Irremovability of Judges," CCJE (2001) OP No. 1 ["CCJE Opinion No. 1 on the Independence of the Judiciary"], available at https://rm.coe.int/1680747830at para. 4.

of powers or the rule of law, and inevitably hinges on fundamentally contested notions of adjudication.[6]

Having cleared the ground a bit in this manner, the chapter will turn to more tactical accounts of judicial independence. I will begin by paying appropriate respects to Martin Shapiro's seminal analysis of the role played by constitutional courts, which stresses the importance of constitutional courts as acceptable "third party adjudicators" to resolve assorted types of constitutional conflicts and, relatedly, their function as "junkyard dogs" knowingly set loose to police constitutional bargains and boundaries, albeit at some risk to all involved.[7]

This perspective modifies significantly the way in which one might approach judicial independence. Such independence now emerges not as a virtue in its own right, nor just as a mechanism to help promote other rule of law virtues, but as a tool to advance the interests of particular institutional players in their struggles against others. This rather realist (some might say rather cynical) approach to the judicial independence debates thus calls attention to the particular players and interests involved and stresses how judicial independence can be tactically deployed as weapon or shield, as the case may be.

This tactical turn is central to the work to which this Part will devote the greatest attention: a chapter by Lee Epstein, Jack Knight, and Olga Shvetsova on selecting judicial selection mechanisms in the Burbank/Friedman volume on *Judicial Independence* and two sister articles co-written by Nuno Garoupa and Tom Ginsberg on judicial independence and judicial councils.[8] This trio of important pieces offers a fascinating set of perspectives on judicial independence and its relation to judicial selection mechanisms.

For Epstein et al., judicial independence represents a mechanism for self-interested political actors to account for future political conditions. When such actors are relatively certain that they will remain in power, they prefer to decrease judicial independence in order to ensure judicial subservience to the entrenched political order. But the more they face a likely fall from power, the more they seek to increase judicial independence in order to prevent judicial capture by a succeeding regime. On this view, political actors modulate the quantum of judicial

6 *See* Lewis Kornhauser, *Is Judicial Independence a Useful Concept*, *in* JUDICIAL INDEPENDENCE AT THE CROSSROADS: AN INTERDISCIPLINARY APPROACH 45 (STEPHEN B. BURBANK and BARRY FRIEDMAN eds., 2002).

7 *See* Martin Shapiro, *The European Court of Justice*, *in* JUDICIAL INDEPENDENCE IN THE AGE OF DEMOCRACY: CRITICAL PERSPECTIVES FROM AROUND THE WORLD 273 (Peter H. Russell & David M. O'Brien eds., 2001).

8 *See* Lee Epstein, Jack Knight, & Olga Shvetsova, *Selecting Selection Systems*, *in* JUDICIAL INDEPENDENCE AT THE CROSSROADS: AN INTERDISCIPLINARY APPROACH 191 (STEPHEN B. BURBANK and BARRY FRIEDMAN eds., 2002); Nuno Garoupa & Tom Ginsberg, *The Comparative Law and Economics of Judicial Councils*, 27 BERKELEY J. INT'L L. 53 (2009); Nuno Garoupa & Tom Ginsberg, *Guarding the Guardians: Judicial Councils and Judicial Independence*, 57 AM. J. COMP. L. 103, 109 (2009). For simplicity's sake, and with due apologies to her coauthors, I will simply refer to author of the "Selecting Selection Systems" chapter as "Epstein."

independence as a means to account for their own political futures, effectively discounting or hedging their bets in the face of increased political uncertainty.

For Garoupa and Ginsberg, however, judicial independence is part of a larger tension between judges, politicians, and public policy. When judges are weak and politically dependent, reformers may push for a stronger and more independent judiciary in order to gain the advantages of judicial decision-making. But as that increasingly independent judiciary gains more power over public policy, and as politics thus becomes increasingly judicialized, pressure will mount to subject that judiciary to greater political accountability. As a result, a strong judiciary may shrink back into an increasingly weak and dependent one. On this view, judicial independence can be seen as a rather cyclical process, in which the judiciary becomes subject to greater independence or accountability in response to governing politico-judicial conditions; and judicial councils are valuable institutional mechanisms because they can be designed and operated in such a manner as to promote either greater judicial independence or greater judicial accountability, as conditions require.

As this and ensuing chapters will demonstrate, I am very much in favor of deploying such tactical accounts as a means to make sense of the judicial independence debates and their relation to European judicial appointments reforms. There can be little doubt that very savvy players have been driving the European debates and reforms. As Parts I and II already made clear, the cast of characters involved in the assorted reform measures have almost always tended to be highly experienced judicial, academic, and political players, well versed in the practice of international relations and international and supreme court judicial decision-making. And as those Parts emphasized, those players have undoubtedly been operating against a backdrop of unusually large-scale and particularly evident political, institutional, and ideological flux. It is hard, therefore, not to see the judicial independence debates, complete with their associated impact on judicial appointments reforms, as a process of relatively sophisticated and self-interested bargaining during a period of particularly large-scale uncertainty. In such a context, the tactical approaches offer an extremely useful prism for addressing the judicial debates and reforms.

As will become apparent, however, I do not necessarily agree with the specific conclusions suggested by the proposed tactical accounts, at least as they may operate in the European context under study in this book. But I do not see this as a problem. The theories prove extremely useful for teasing out the particular complexities and tensions that actually define the multi-level European judicial/political arena; and they offer a clear and straightforward framework for discussing these complexities and tensions. These theories are thus a very helpful bridge toward arriving at my destination, allowing me to refine my arguments while differentiating them from other ways of approaching the issues.

Chapter 7 then offers my initial take on the judicial independence debates and their relation to the European judicial appointments reforms. I quickly state the key points now in order to help frame the intervening exposition and analysis. First, these European judicial independence and appointments debates/reforms are a multi-level game. This remark, though painfully simple, has tremendous repercussions on our analysis. The European judicial debates cannot be approached as if they were operating at a single level, with the "European" judiciary and its independence and/or accountability being placed into a straightforward relation to "European" political institutions. I put the term "European" in quotation marks to underline the essential point that many of the thorny issues stem from the relationship between "European" judges and/or judicial candidates (i.e., at/to the European Court of Justice (ECJ) and European Court of Human Rights (ECtHR)) and "domestic" political players operating at the national level.

Indeed, one of the defining features of the European judicial environment is precisely that it involves a constant overlap between the domestic and European realms. In this multi-level environment, European judges or judicial candidates can simultaneously be very weak relative to domestic political players (e.g., relative to executive branch actors at the judicial appointment or reappointment phase) and yet colossally powerful at the European level (e.g., as ECJ or ECtHR judges at the judicial decision-making phase). This leads to enormous tensions.

Once we recognize the domestic dimension of this "European" judicial environment, we can take proper account of the fact that different judges, hailing from different Member States, are situated quite differently than others with respect to judicial independence and appointments. Czech judges and judicial candidates are simply not in the same position as Belgian ones. Furthermore, different Member States are also situated quite differently than others with respect to these judicial issues. The relationship of the Bulgarian government to judicial independence and selection issues, as well as to European supranational judicial decision-making in general, cannot help but be quite different than that of the German government.

Indeed, we should go further. The point is not simply that different judges, judicial candidates, Member States, or governments are differently situated with respect to these judicial issues; they obviously are. Rather, the difference between their respective positions has been actively motivating these judicial debates and reforms. Thus, the judicial independence and appointments reforms represent in large measure an attempt by interested parties in some parts of Europe to manage judges and governments from others.

Given these complex and multi-level realities, the key insight of this judicial independence Part and the next on "judicial quality" is that "judicial independence" relative to some judges and Member States can actually function as "judicial accountability" relative to others. To boil this insight down to its most basic—and most important—manifestation: to promote the judicial independence of Czech judicial candidates relative to their own Member States may well function as the imposition of a certain judicial accountability on both the Czech government and on its judges relative to Germany, the UK, and France. Thus, even if we could put our finger on just what "judicial independence" really means or requires, we would still have to recognize that it operates completely differently in different contexts, relative to different players, and so on. And in the multi-level European context, this highly context-dependent reality means that procedures that appear to promote judicial independence can in the very same case induce not only certain kinds of judicial accountability, but also assorted kinds of subservience.

Fostering such a contextual approach to our subject matter allows us to increase our sensitivity to the particular interests of different players in the debates, which only calls further attention to the number of such players and the number of different registers in which they may be confronting each other. These players are not limited to self-evidently "political" actors, such as Member State governments or European supranational institutions; and their fields of action are not limited to overtly "political" matters, such as struggles over left/right divisions, vertical divisions of power between national and supranational governmental entities, divisions between old and new Member States, and so on.

Such recognizably "political" players and their classic structural and substantive struggles are persistent and important. But we should not lose sight of the fact that the judicial independence debates and the judicial appointments reforms also bring to bear vital institutional and professional interests. Judges and academics are in fact major players in all these struggles; and it would be naïve to deny that they too have interests of their own, that these interests vary depending on differentiations within their respective professional groupings, and that the judicial independence and appointments debates represent a pivotal field of engagement for these institutional and professional interests. As we shall see, there exist many struggles of this sort, ranging from those between judges and Member State executive branch actors, between Member State supreme (including constitutional) court judges and European ones, between elite academics and Member State governments, and so on. All such interests intersect with each other, creating a rich overlay that further complicates the self-evidently "political" interactions between national governments, European institutions, and so on.

Finally, the attention that we give to the tactical dimension of the judicial independence and appointments debates should not blind us to the fact that these debates also represent an earnest fight over ideas; and ideas really do matter. These debates construct an identifiable set of conceptual associations and their supposed implications. These debates and reforms therefore constitute a deeply ideological endeavor and not just the playing out of brute self-interest in the judicial independence and appointments field. In other words, it would be a mistake to reduce the judicial independence and appointments debates to no more than an institutional manifestation of strategic political and/or professional calculations. Such calculations undoubtedly play a very major role in the development of the debates. But as will become obvious, the ideological endeavor is deeply important in its own right. It includes the very construction of the judicial independence and appointments fields as appropriate sites for concerted action. It creates ideological commitments and forges their supposed entailments; and the players intervening in the debates really are invested in and molded by the conceptual prisms thereby constructed.

As we shall then see in Part IV, the keystone of this intellectual organization is the all-important concept of judicial "quality." It reconciles—or at least satisfies—the seemingly conflicting judicial independence and accountability demands suggested by the Garoupa/Ginsberg and Epstein analyses while constructing a conceptual framework that permits particularly interested groups (especially elite judges and academics) to claim authoritative status and to wield increasingly significant institutional power.

6

The Primary Literature

Taking Measures (and More Measures)

Over the last twenty odd years, the institutions attached to the Council of Europe have passed a seemingly endless series of measures more or less directly focused on judicial independence. This Part presents the most important of them in quick succession in order to develop a sense of the basic contours of the primary materials, of their principal concerns and associations, of their relation to legal and political developments, and of their ongoing trajectory. Once we have a sufficient grasp of these judicial independence measures, we will be in a position to bring the secondary literature to bear on our analysis.

I. The Committee of Ministers' 1994 Recommendation "On the Independence, Efficiency and Role of Judges"

In April 1994, the high point of the accession of new Member States from the former Eastern Bloc, the Committee of Ministers of the Council of Europe adopted Protocol 11 to the Convention, which would do away with the previously all-important and conciliatory Commission and create the "new" ECtHR of full-time professional judges before which individuals would directly lodge complaints once the Protocol took effect in November 1998. Barely six months later, in October 1994, the Committee of Ministers passed its Recommendation "On the Independence, Efficiency and Role of Judges."

The temporal connection between the mass accession of previously socialist States from the former Soviet sphere of influence, the new entrenchment of the Strasbourg Court as an authoritative judicial institution to which individuals could directly bring justiciable claims of right, and the sudden preoccupation with judicial independence is therefore immediate. For this reason, it is hardly surprising that when the Committee of Ministers passed its new measure on judicial independence that same year, it deployed language that made clear conceptual and rhetorical links between judicial independence, judicial power, the protection of human rights and fundamental freedoms, constitutional democracy, the separation of powers and the rule of law. Their work was therefore utterly representative of the 1990s' "transitional democracy" period.[9]

The hortatory preamble language of the Ministers' 1994 Recommendation on Judicial Independence does an excellent job of suggesting these links. It states:

> Noting the essential role of judges and other persons exercising judicial functions in ensuring the protection of human rights and fundamental freedoms;
>
> Desiring to promote the independence of judges in order to strengthen the rule of law in democratic states;
>
> Aware of the need to reinforce the position and powers of judges in order to achieve an efficient and fair legal system;
>
> Conscious of the desirability of ensuring the proper exercise of judicial responsibilities which are a collection of judicial duties and powers aimed at protecting the interests of all persons,
>
> Recommends that governments of member states adopt or reinforce all measures necessary to promote the role of individual judges and the judiciary as a whole and strengthen their independence and efficiency, by implementing, in particular, the following principles: ...[10]

It is hard to miss the centrality of judges in this depiction of democratic States governed by the rule of law. But the Ministers' Explanatory Report offers even more grandiose and explicit language about the importance of the judiciary to constitutional democracy and the rule of law:

> 1. Within the framework of the activities undertaken to promote and guarantee the efficiency and fairness of civil and criminal justice, it was decided to prepare a recommendation on the independence, efficiency and role of judges.
> 2. Indeed, the Council of Europe includes among its aims the institution and protection of a democratic and political system characterised by the rule of law and the establishment of a constitutionally governed state, as well as the promotion and protection of human rights and fundamental freedoms.
> 3. The recommendation on the independence, efficiency and role of judges recognizes and emphasises the pre-eminent and significant role played by judges in the implementation of these aims. The independence of judges is one of the central pillars of the rule of law. The need to promote the independence of

[9] *See, e.g.*, Robert Cooter, *The Rule of State Law and the Rule-of-Law State: Economic Analysis of the Legal Foundations of Development*, *in* ANNUAL WORLD BANK CONFERENCE ON DEVELOPMENT ECONOMICS 1996 191 (1997); Martin Golding, *Transitional Regimes and the Rule of Law*, 9 RATIO JURIS 387–95 (1996); NEIL KRITZ ed., TRANSITIONAL JUSTICE: HOW EMERGING DEMOCRACIES RECKON WITH FORMER REGIMES, VOLS. I–III (1995); Andrzej Rapaczynski, *The Rule of Law in Theoretical and Comparative Perspective*, *in* THE BALANCE OF FREEDOM: POLITICAL ECONOMY, LAW, AND LEARNING 81 (ROGER MICHENER ed., 1995).

[10] 1994 Recommendation on the Independence of Judges at 1.

> judges is not confined to individual judges only but may have consequences for the judicial system as a whole.[11]

Clearly, the Ministers' sudden preoccupation with judicial independence in the 1990s could not be separated from the large-scale political and economic transformations that quickly followed in the wake of what was still, at that time, the very recent fall of the Berlin Wall.

The Ministers made no attempt whatever to downplay the dimension of the political transformations underway or to minimize the critical role that they imagined the judiciary and fundamental rights would have to play in the emerging political order. They intoned:

> The independent allotted task of judges is that of safeguarding the rights and freedoms of all persons within the scope of their duty to administer justice (see paragraph 1). The judge is responsible for protecting the rights and freedoms granted to individuals. This obligation should not only be seen as a duty to protect the minimum rights as expressed in the European Convention of Human Rights. The obligation goes further but it is difficult to define in precise terms its scope. Ultimately, the obligation has to do with the defence of democracy and the rule of law, safeguarding against oppression and the totalitarian state as expressed in the Statute of the Council of Europe.[12]

In this highly pedantic passage, the Ministers effectively present an independent judiciary as not merely an agency to "protect the minimum rights" of the Convention, but as the linchpin of democracy and the rule of law and as the active and central bulwark against totalitarian oppression.

This understanding of the role of the judiciary in safeguarding fundamental rights and in opposing the threats posed by totalitarian political authority provides the central prism for the Ministers' 1994 Recommendation. It leads first to the attempt to entrench judicial independence in the domestic legal orders: the Recommendation proposes that judicial independence be formally constitutionalized "by inserting specific provisions" providing, for example, that "decisions of judges should not be the subject of any revision outside any appeals procedures as provided for by law," that "the terms of office of judges and their remuneration should be guaranteed by law," that "no organ other than the courts themselves should decide on its own competence, as defined by law," and that "the government or the administration should not be able to take any decision which invalidates judicial decisions retroactively."[13] Such guarantees are clearly directed at the classic

[11] *Id.* at Explanatory Memorandum, 6.
[12] *Id.* at 14.
[13] *Id.* at 2.

powers of the political leadership in socialist countries to revise or overturn judicial decisions or even to divest the judiciary of cases.[14]

This understanding of the essential role of the judiciary also leads to the Recommendation's second major contribution, which would prove to have important and long-lasting effects. The Recommendation categorically states:

> All decisions concerning the professional career of judges should be based on objective criteria, and the selection and career of judges should be based on merit, having regard to qualifications, integrity, ability and efficiency. The authority taking the decision on the selection and career of judges should be independent of the government and the administration. In order to safeguard its independence, rules should ensure that, for instance, its members are selected by the judiciary and that the authority decides itself on its procedural rules.[15]

This recommendation was directed above all at new Member States regarding judicial appointments, promotion, and discipline at the domestic level. But it would prove to have a great deal of purchase in two other domains: domestic judicial appointments, promotion, and discipline (in established as well as in new Member States) and judicial appointments at the European level (i.e., appointments to the ECJ and the ECtHR).

The Ministers were obviously quite conscious that several of the established Member States did not in fact possess the type of independent authority on the selection and career of judges that the Recommendation was demanding. The Recommendation therefore made allowances:

> However, where the constitutional or legal provisions and traditions allow judges to be appointed by the government, there should be guarantees to ensure that the procedures to appoint judges are transparent and independent in practice and that the decisions will not be influenced by any reasons other than those related to the objective criteria mentioned above.[16]

The Explanatory Memorandum explains the Ministers' reasoning a little further:

> Although the recommendation proposes an ideal system for judicial appointments, it was recognised (see sub-paragraph 2) that a number of the member states of the Council of Europe have adopted other systems, often involving the government, parliament or the head of state. The recommendation does not

[14] For a particularly thought-provoking conceptualization of these powers, *see* Mirjan Damaška, The Faces of Justice and State Authority: A Comparative Approach to the Legal Process 178–80 194–201 (New Haven and London: Yale University Press, 1986).

[15] 1994 Recommendation on the Independence of Judges at 2.

[16] *Id.* at 3.

> propose to change these systems which have been in operation for decades or centuries and which in practice work well. But also in states where the judges are formally appointed by the government, there should be some kind of system whereby the appointment procedures of judges are transparent and independent in practice. In some states, this is ensured by special independent and competent bodies which give advice to the government, the parliament or the head of state which in practice is followed or by providing a possibility of appeal by the person concerned. Other states have opted for systems involving wide consultations with the judiciary, although the formal decision is taken by a member of government.[17]

As the above passages suggest, the Ministers were in a bit of a bind. On the one hand, they sought to impose a hard and fast rule, directed primarily at new accession States with a history of judicial subservience to authoritarian political power, regarding the establishment of independent authorities to govern judicial selection and careers. On the other hand, they had to contend with the reality that the established Member States by no means uniformly satisfied such a straightforward rule. The compromise solution was obviously imperfect—indeed, one might say that it was blatantly imbalanced—and it would, as we shall see, lead to further difficulties.

Finally, the 1994 Recommendation offered a few general statements about the need for judges to be able to decide cases in a manner that was independent and free from improper influence:

> In the decision-making process, judges should be independent and be able to act without any restriction, improper influence, inducements, pressures, threats or interferences, direct or indirect, from any quarter or for any reason. The law should provide for sanctions against persons seeking to influence judges in any such manner. Judges should have unfettered freedom to decide cases impartially, in accordance with their conscience and their interpretation of the facts, and in pursuance of the prevailing rules of the law. Judges should not be obliged to report on the merits of their cases to anyone outside the judiciary.[18]

The Explanatory Memorandum specified: "The purpose of this provision is to ensure that no pressure of any kind and from any quarter obliges the judge to deliver judgment along the lines desired by a party, the administration, the government or any other person."[19] Emphasizing that "The independence of judges is first and foremost linked to the maintenance of the separation of powers," the Memorandum stressed that "the organs of the executive and the legislature have a

[17] *Id.* at Explanatory Memorandum, para. 16.
[18] *Id* at 2.
[19] *Id.* at Explanatory Memorandum, para. 17.

duty to ensure that judges are independent" and "must refrain from adopting any measure that could undermine the independence of judges."[20]

In conclusion, the Ministers' 1994 Recommendation took the first step in what was to become a long list of European measures directed toward promoting judicial independence. As might have been expected from the analysis offered in Parts I and II of this book, this concern over judicial independence burst onto the scene during the period of mass accession of new Member States from the former Eastern Bloc. The 1994 Recommendation bears the clear imprint of this historical context. It proposes measures that ideally would constitutionally entrench judicial independence; establish an independent authority to govern judicial selection, promotion, and discipline; and guarantee independent judicial decision-making free of party, executive, legislative, or other improper influence. But no less important than such relatively specific proposals is the general tone and framework of the Recommendation, which stresses the need to empower an independent judiciary as a means to safeguard individual rights and freedoms, defend democracy and the rule of law, guarantee the separation of powers, and protect against oppression and the totalitarian state. In its first manifestation, this judicial independence measure was a 1990s civics lesson in the basics of constitutional democracy.

II. The 1998 European Charter on the Statute for Judges

The European Charter on the Statute for Judges is not an official European legal measure.[21] It was passed in 1998 by a more informal group of European participants, judges, and judicial associations organized by the Council of Europe under the auspices of the "Themis Plan," which, along with the "Demo-droit" program, was designed to help ease the transition of Central and Eastern European countries to democracy and to Council of Europe norms.[22] Working under the telling rubric of "Activities for the development and of consolidation of democratic stability," the authors took the next important step in the development of the European judicial independence debates.

After making the classic textual references, the Charter's preamble states its concerns and objectives:

> Being concerned to see the promotion of judicial independence, necessary for the strengthening of the pre-eminence of law and for the protection of individual liberties within democratic states, made more effective;

[20] *Id.* at Explanatory Memorandum, para. 15.

[21] *See* CCJE Opinion No. 1 on the Independence of the Judiciary at para. 4.

[22] *See* XLVI European Yearbook 1998 (1998) 64. Allow me the liberty to suggest that there must be a fine dissertation to be written on the nomenclature of European measures and programs.

Conscious of the necessity that provisions calculated to ensure the best guarantees of the competence, independence and impartiality of judges should be specified in a formal document intended for all European States;
Desiring to see the judges' statutes of the different European States take into account these provisions in order to ensure in concrete terms the best level of guarantees;
Have adopted the present European Charter on the statute for judges.[23]

Although typically vague, this language does offer a few insights. At a basic level, these opening paragraphs underline once again the all-important link between judicial independence, the protection of rights ("individual liberties"), and democracy that was so characteristic of the time. But they also add a new and important twist, the full significance of which will become apparent later in this chapter: they stress the need to guarantee not only the independence/impartiality of judges, but also their competence.

The addition of "competence" to the judicial debates is hardly subtle. The Charter's substantive language opens with a statement of "General Principles." The very first paragraph states:

> 1.1. The statute for judges aims at ensuring the competence, independence and impartiality which every individual legitimately expects from the courts of law and from every judge to whom is entrusted the protection of his or her rights. It excludes every provision and every procedure liable to impair confidence in such competence, such independence and such impartiality.[24]

The term "competence" is used five times in the four-page Charter; and it reappears another ten times in the nine plus pages of the Charter's Explanatory Memorandum.

The unmistakable rise of judicial competence in the judicial independence debates works in tandem with the fleshing out of another crucial institutional theme: the establishment of an appropriately independent authority to govern judicial selection, promotion, and discipline. As we have seen, the Committee of Ministers' 1994 Recommendation on Judicial Independence had already expressed the gist of this idea. But the Charter devotes its primary space and attention to this institutional feature of the independence debates. After stating its General Principles in about a page, the Charter then spends the remaining two and a half pages discussing institutional and professional issues, in which the independent authority must play a key role: judicial selection, recruitment and initial training, appointment and irremovability, career, liability, remuneration, and termination.

[23] European Charter on the Statute for Judges, DAJ/DOC (98) 23 (1998) at 5.
[24] *Id.* at para. 1.1.

Indeed, the Charter's fundamental contribution is that this independent authority should govern all aspects of the judicial profession. The Charter's General Principles categorically state:

> In respect of every decision affecting the selection, recruitment, appointment, career progress or termination of office of a judge, the statute envisages the intervention of an authority independent of the executive and legislative powers within which at least one half of those who sit are judges elected by their peers following methods guaranteeing the widest representation of the judiciary.[25]

The Charter's Explanatory Memorandum offers significant insight into the underlying reasoning. Two points are particularly worthy of note. First, it addresses, albeit somewhat uncomfortably, how older and more recent Member States of the Council of Europe might regulate judicial independence:

> The question arose whether the provisions of the Charter should be mandatory, i.e., whether it should be made compulsory to include them in national statutes regulating the judiciary, or whether they should have the force of recommendations, so that different provisions deemed capable of ensuring equivalent guarantees could be implemented instead.
>
> The latter approach could be justified by a reluctance to criticise national systems in which a long-standing, well-established practice has ensured effective guarantees on statutory protection of the judiciary, even if the system barely mentions such protection.
>
> However, it has also been argued that in a fair number of countries, including new Council of Europe member States, which do not regulate the exercise by political authorities of powers in the area of appointing, assigning, promoting or terminating the office of judges, the safeguards on competence, independence and impartiality are ineffective.
>
> This is why, even though the Charter's provisions are not actually mandatory, they are presented as being the optimum means of ensuring that the aforementioned objectives are attained.[26]

This awkward, almost embarrassed, passage effectively recognizes that older Member States may well possess "long-standing, well-established practice has ensured effective guarantees on" judicial independence that others—"including new Council of Europe member States," as the passage demurely states—do not. Hence the need to limit the Charter to the status of mere recommendations.[27]

[25] *Id.* at para. 1.3.
[26] *Id.* at Explanatory Memorandum, para. 1.1.
[27] *See id.*

The second important feature of the Memorandum is the attention that it continues to pay to judicial "competence." It states early on:

> The Charter endeavours to define the content of the statute for judges on the basis of the objectives to be attained: ensuring the competence, independence and impartiality which all members of the public are entitled to expect of the courts and judges entrusted with protecting their rights . . .
>
> These safeguards on individuals' rights are ensured by judicial competence, in the sense of ability, independence and impartiality.[28]

Although the Memo is at some pains to explain what such competence actually entails, it does not shrink from attempting to do so. The clearest language appears in the Memo's discussion of judicial "selection, recruitment and initial training." It explains:

> Judicial candidates must be selected and recruited by an independent body or panel . . .
>
> The choice made by the selection body must be based on criteria relevant to the nature of the duties to be discharged.
>
> The main aim must be to evaluate the candidate's ability to assess independently cases heard by judges, which implies independent thinking . . . The ability to apply the law refers both to knowledge of the law and the capacity to put it into practice, which are two different things . . .
>
> In order to ensure the ability to carry out the duties involved in judicial office, the rules on selection and recruitment must set out requirements as to qualifications and previous experience . . .
>
> Candidates selected to discharge judicial duties must therefore be prepared for the task by means of appropriate training, which must be financed by the State.
>
> Certain precautions must be taken in preparing judges for the giving of independent and impartial decisions, whereby competence, impartiality and the requisite open-mindedness are guaranteed in both the content of the training programmes and the functioning of the bodies implementing them. This is why the Charter provides that the [independent authority] must ensure the appropriateness of training programmes and of the organization which implements them, in the light of the requirements of open-mindedness, competence and impartiality which are bound up with the exercise of judicial duties.[29]

This Charter and its Memo thus make a notable attempt to define "competence" and to institutionalize the means to promote it. Not only must criteria be

[28] *Id.*

[29] *Id.* at Explanatory Memorandum, paras. 2.1–2.3.

established and requisite qualifications and experience be defined, but appropriate training must be instituted and financed to prepare judges for their weighty task. Finally, this preparation must aim to generate not only competence and impartiality, but also "open-mindedness" (which, though left undefined, appears to be derived from the "independent thinking" mentioned earlier in the passage).

Although the 1998 Charter on the Statute for Judges carries no formal legal authority, it nonetheless represents an important intervention in the developing European primary literature on judicial independence. It reinforced and expanded upon the Committee of Ministers' 1994 Recommendation on Judicial Independence, especially by spelling out in greater detail the need to establish an independent authority (effectively a "judicial council") that would govern all aspects of the judicial profession, ranging from selection, to training, to promotion, to discipline. It further insisted that this authority must be at least 50% judicial in composition, elected by the judiciary itself. And it promoted the developing notion of the professionalization of the judiciary by stressing not only judicial training, but also judicial competence.

III. The CCJE's 2001 Opinion No. 1

The year after its creation by the Committee of Ministers, the CCJE adopted its first policy paper: its Opinion No. 1 on "Standards Concerning the Independence of the Judiciary and the Irremovability of Judges." A notably sharp, forthright, and explicitly pragmatic document, this Opinion took the next important step in the development of European legal measures concerning judicial independence.

The Opinion trumpets its deeply pragmatic orientation right from the start. Immediately after making the standard textual references, it offers the following bold, almost pugnacious statement: "**Throughout the CCJE discussions, members of the CCJE emphasised that what is critical is not the perfection of principles and, still less, the harmonisation of institutions; it is the putting into full effect of principles already developed.**"[30] The CCJE was planning to put explicit implementing measures on the table.

The CCJE undoubtedly protested too much. Despite its claims to the contrary, the CCJE was in fact keen to make explicit one essential point on the level of first principles: the judiciary is, to use US constitutional parlance, one of the three "coequal" branches of government.[31] The Opinion declares:

[30] CCJE Opinion No. 1 on the Independence of the Judiciary (emphasis in original).

[31] *See, e.g.*, Mistretta v. United States, 488 U.S. 361, 380–84 (1989) (discussing separation of powers and "Madison's view of the appropriate relationship among the three coequal Branches."). *See also* Edward Hirsch Levi, *Some Aspects of Separation of Powers*, 76 Colum. L. Rev. 371 (1976) (discussing generally separation of powers doctrine in a US context)

The rationales of judicial independence

10. Judicial independence is a prerequisite to the rule of law and a fundamental guarantee of a fair trial . . .

11. This independence must exist in relation to society generally and in relation to the particular parties to any dispute on which judges have to adjudicate. The judiciary is one of three basic and equal pillars in the modern democratic state. It has an important role and functions in relation to the other two pillars. It ensures that governments and the administration can be held to account for their actions, and, with regard to the legislature, it is involved in ensuring that duly enacted laws are enforced, and, to a greater or lesser extent, in ensuring that they comply with any relevant constitution or higher law (such as that of the European Union). To fulfil its role in these respects, the judiciary must be independent of these bodies, which involves freedom from inappropriate connections with and influence by these bodies. Independence thus serves as the guarantee of impartiality. This has implications, necessarily, for almost every aspect of a judge's career: from training to appointment and promotion and to disciplining.[32]

This confident statement of the coequal and independent nature of the judiciary relative to the political branches should not, however, be taken for granted. In fact, one need only look at the French constitutional example to recognize that the claim to judicial coequal status is just that: a claim. Far from referring to a "judicial power" that might be on an equal footing with the political branches, Title VIII of the 1958 French Constitution explicitly reduces the judiciary to a mere "*autorité judiciaire*."[33] Furthermore, the entire public law branch of the French judiciary—the administrative tribunals headed by the Conseil d'Etat—is literally part of the executive branch. And as one of the two leading Civilian models (the other being the German), the skeptical French approach to judicial authority is hardly anomalous. Indeed, until 2011 (i.e., ten years after the CCJE's Opinion No. 1), the Swedish constitution did not even list the judiciary as a separate governmental power at all![34]

The CCJE's confident—if empirically and legally dubious—claim of coequal judicial status must therefore be understood not as a statement of *fact*, but as a key feature of its judicial independence *project*; and it guides the pragmatic institutional conclusions that the Opinion would then explicitly draw.[35] Its key development is to insist not only on the existence of such an independent (and likely

[32] CCJE Opinion No. 1 on the Independence of the Judiciary at paras. 10–11.

[33] Constitution du 4 octobre 1958, available at http://www.conseil-constitutionnel.fr/conseil-constitutionnel/francais/la-constitution/la-constitution-du-4-octobre-1958/texte-integral-de-la-constitution-du-4-octobre-1958-en-vigueur.5074.html.

[34] *See* The Constitution of Sweden: The Fundamental Laws and the Riksdag Act (with an Introduction by Magnus Isberg) 21, Chapter 11 (2016), available at https://www.riksdagen.se/en/SysSiteAssets/07.-dokument--lagar/the-constitution-of-sweden-160628.pdf/.

[35] CCJE Opinion No. 1 on the Independence of the Judiciary at para. 13.

predominantly judicial) council/authority (as suggested by the European Charter), but also on the establishment of formal and public procedures to govern its operation. Although the CCJE claimed "general acceptance" for the proposition "both that appointments should be made 'on the merits' based on 'objective criteria' and that political considerations *should* be inadmissible,"[36] it recognized that these objectives were proving difficult to attain. Two problems were complicating matters. The first was the sheer diversity of national legal regimes and institutional approaches. The second was that any legal definition of these "aspirations" was bound to be frustratingly vague: "[A]ny 'objective criteria', seeking to ensure that the selection and career of judges are 'based on merit, having regard to qualifications, integrity, ability and efficiency', are bound to be in general terms."[37]

In order to solve these dual problems of diversity and vagueness, the CCJE put forward a deeply pragmatic solution that could be applied across the board in any and all national systems regulating judicial selection and promotion:

> **The CCJE recommended that the authorities responsible in member States for making and advising on appointments and promotions should now introduce, publish and give effect to objective criteria, with the aim of ensuring that the selection and career of judges are "based on merit, having regard to qualifications, integrity, ability and efficiency".** Once this is done, those bodies or authorities responsible for any appointment or promotion will be obliged to act accordingly, and it will then at least be possible to scrutinize the content of the criteria adopted and their practical effect.[38]

With this recommendation, the CCJE made an important contribution to the European judicial independence debates. It demanded that "objective criteria" for "merit-based" judicial appointments be *formally published* as governing norms in order that they be open to public scrutiny, both as to their content and as to their application.

The CCJE's second step was to marry this call for formal norms with a call for the establishment of "formal procedures" to be applied ideally by a formally established "independent authority" or "non-political body." Dissatisfied with the permissive approach previously taken with respect to established Member States, it bluntly stated:

> 34. There is room for concern that the present diversity of approach may tacitly facilitate the continuation of undue political influence over appointments. The CCJE noted ... that informal appointment procedures and overtly political

[36] *Id.* at para. 17 (emphasis in original).
[37] *Id.* at para. 25.
[38] *Id.* (emphasis in original).

influence on judicial appointments in certain States were not helpful models in other, newer democracies, where it was vital to secure judicial independence by the introduction of strictly nonpolitical appointing bodies....

In contradistinction to the Committee of Ministers' 1994 Recommendation,

the CCJE is concerned now about [the Recommendation's] somewhat vague and open nature in the context of the wider Europe, where constitutional or legal "traditions" are less relevant and formal procedures are a necessity with which it is dangerous to dispense. **Therefore, the CCJE considered that every decision relating to a judge's appointment or career should be based on objective criteria and be either taken by an independent authority or subject to guarantees to ensure that it is not taken other than on the basis of such criteria.**[39]

As if this were not clear enough, the CCJE reiterated its point in the conclusion of this section of its Opinion:

45. Even in legal systems where good standards have been observed by force of tradition and informal selfdiscipline, customarily under the scrutiny of a free media, there has been increasing recognition in recent years of a need for more objective and formal safeguards. In other states, particularly those of former communist countries, the need is pressing. **The CCJE considered that the European Charter—in so far as it advocated the intervention (in a sense wide enough to include an opinion, recommendation or proposal as well as an actual decision) of an independent authority with substantial judicial representation chosen democratically by other judges—pointed in a general direction which the CCJE wished to commend. This is particularly important for countries which do not have other longentrenched and democratically proved systems.**[40]

In short, the CCJE called for the blanket establishment of formal norms, to be applied via "formal procedures" by a formally established "independent authority with substantial judicial representation."

But the paragraphs contain several secondary messages as well. The most explicit is that well-established democracies with "long-entrenched and democratically proved systems" and a certain "force of tradition and informal self-discipline" may in some cases be able to curtail "undue political influence" over judicial appointments by informal means, but "newer democracies," "former communist countries," and "countries which do not have other longentrenched and democratically proved systems" are in no position to do so. To the contrary, the examples set by

[39] *Id.* at paras. 32–36 (emphasis in original).
[40] *Id.* at para. 45 (emphasis in original).

some of the older democracies are downright unhelpful. They set bad/inapplicable models for the former communist countries, which do not have powerful constitutional or informal traditions and for whom the need for "formal safeguards" is therefore "pressing."

Furthermore, the creation of regulatory exceptions to assuage a few European Convention on Human Rights (ECHR) Member States with traditionally informal approaches has effectively preempted the blanket adoption of formal norms, procedures, and institutions that would be better suited to a Europe increasingly defined by large-scale Eastern enlargement. The paragraphs therefore transmit not only the message of East/West and old/new differentiation, but also a sober plea for regulatory unification: overall European judicial independence would be greatly improved by the adoption of a consistent regulatory framework that would entrench formal norms, procedures, and institutions for the purposes of judicial appointments, promotions, discipline, and so on.

Finally, the CCJE's inaugural Opinion makes one more significant contribution: it overtly extends its analysis to reach appointments to the European supranational courts. As the CCJE explicitly recognized, such an extension lay beyond the four corners of its official mandate.[41] But the obligations imposed by the ECHR required that due attention be paid to the supranational European dimension of independent judicial appointments:

> The CCJE considered that the ever increasing significance for national legal systems of supranational courts and their decisions made it essential to encourage member States to respect the principles concerning independence, irremovability, appointment and term of office in relation to judges of such supranational courts.[42]

Indeed, the CCJE went even further. It extended its analysis not only to the Convention system of which it was, after all, a part (it had been established by the Committee of Ministers), but also to the EU:

> 56. **The CCJE agreed that the importance for national legal systems and judges of the obligations resulting from international treaties such as the European Convention and also the European Union treaties makes it vital that the appointment and reappointment of judges to the courts interpreting such treaties should command the same confidence and respect the same principles as national legal systems. The CCJE further considered that involvement by the independent authority referred [to above] should be encouraged in relation to appointment and reappointment to international courts.** The Council of Europe

[41] *Id.* at para. 54.
[42] *Id.* at para. 55.

> and its institutions are in short founded on belief in common values superior to those of any single member State, and that belief has already achieved significant practical effect. It would undermine those values and the progress that has been made to develop and apply them, if their application was not insisted upon at the international level.[43]

The CCJE had effectively applied its analysis not only to domestic judicial courts, but also to the ECtHR and even to the ECJ.

The contribution of the CCJE's Opinion to the European judicial independence debates was to cement a series of earlier recommendations and to fuse them together into an increasingly coherent, pragmatic, and programmatic whole. Working off the baseline assumption that the judiciary represents one of the three truly equal branches of government, the CCJE argued forcefully that judicial independence on both the domestic and the supranational levels required that formally established judicial councils apply formally established norms, using formally established procedures. While older democracies with long-standing traditions might be able to do without such formal mechanisms, the newer democracies of the formerly communist States of the Eastern Bloc simply could not.

Finally, it is worth noting that these positions, put forward so clearly by the CCJE in 2001, correspond particularly well to those adopted by the EU's Article 255 Panel some ten years later. This may not be entirely coincidental: the inaugural chairman of the CCJE was none other than Lord Mance,[44] who has since gone on to play such a prominent role as a two-time member of the Article 255 Panel.[45]

IV. The Venice Commission Reports

The European Commission for Democracy through Law (known as "the Venice Commission"), created in the immediate aftermath of the fall of the Berlin Wall, works in two primary modes. It provides legal advice at the behest of specific Member States "wishing to bring their legal and institutional structures into line with European standards and international experience in the fields of democracy, human rights and the rule of law."[46] And it drafts more general reference documents about a wide range of topics related to such issues, ranging from the design and functioning of democratic institutions, to the protection of fundamental rights, to electoral processes, and so on.[47] In drafting such reference documents,

[43] *Id.* at para. 56 (emphasis in original).

[44] *See* http://www.coe.int/t/dghl/cooperation/ccje/presentation/Bio-Mance_en.asp.

[45] *See supra* Chapter 3.

[46] *See* http://www.venice.coe.int/WebForms/pages/?p=01_Presentation.

[47] For a list of the Venice Commission's most important reference documents, *see* http://www.venice.coe.int/WebForms/pages/default.aspx?p=01_main_reference_documents&lang=en.

the Venice Commission usually synthesizes the work of Council of Europe institutions and adds some new analysis of its own, often incorporating experience it has gathered from providing legal advice to Member States.

The Venice Commission has drafted two such reference documents that intersect directly with the judicial independence debates. The most obvious is its 2010 "Report on the Independence of the Judiciary—Part I: The Independence of Judges."[48] The other, which predates it, is its 2007 "Report on Judicial Appointments."[49] Neither, frankly, adds a great deal to the other measures we have been discussing. I nonetheless pause briefly over them in order to stress a few points. First, they offer yet another example of European institutions jumping onto the judicial independence bandwagon, even if only to rehash what had already been developed on several occasions by sister institutions. Second, they demonstrate the ongoing salience of these debates and the purchase they continue to have on the European legal imagination; after all, the Venice Commission's 2010 Report on judicial independence was written over fifteen years after the Committee of Ministers' original 1994 Recommendation. Third, even if they do not add much to the debates, they certainly do continue to entrench the issues and shore up the links forged between them. Finally, each iteration of these measures does of course offer some variation from the others, however minor it may be.

The Venice Commission Reports effectively synthesize the basic positions delineated by the measures we have analyzed above. The Reports hit all the usual points that had gradually been developed over the previous fifteen years. They (1) assert the need to entrench the independence in the judiciary "in the Constitution or equivalent texts," (2) insist that "all decisions concerning appointment and the professional career of judges should be based on merit applying objective criteria within the framework of law," (3) urge "the establishment of an independent judicial council" composed in "substantial part if not the majority" of judges elected by their peers, (4) recommend that such judicial councils "have decisive influence on the appointment and career of judges," (5) instruct that judges "be appointed permanently until retirement," and so on.[50] In this respect, they demonstrate the ongoing salience of these judicial issues and consolidate the intellectual connections and pragmatic institutional solutions that the European institutions have forged to respond to them.

What may be somewhat surprising, however, is the tenacity of the East/West and old/new distinctions that were of such obvious importance in the early to mid-1990s. The 2007 Venice Commission Report on Judicial Appointments thus opens as follows:

[48] CDL-AD(2010)004, available at http://www.venice.coe.int/webforms/documents/default.aspx-?pdffile=CDL-AD(2010)004-e ["Report on the Independence of Judges"].

[49] CDL-AD(2007)028, available at http://www.venice.coe.int/webforms/documents/default.aspx-?pdffile=CDL-AD(2007)028 ["Report on Judicial Appointments]".

[50] *See* Venice Commission, "Report on the Independence of Judges" at para. 82.

> Introduction
>
> 2. Choosing the appropriate system for judicial appointments is one of the primary challenges faced by the newly established democracies, where often concerns related to the independence and political impartiality of the judiciary persist. Political involvement in the appointment procedure is endangering the neutrality of the judiciary in these states, while in others, in particular those with democratically proved judicial systems, such methods of appointment are regarded as traditional and effective.[51]

As if introducing the entire Report in such a manner were not sufficient, the Venice Commission underlines the basic point once again in its conclusions:

> Conclusions
>
> 44. In Europe, a variety of different systems for judicial appointments exist and that there is not a single model that would apply to all countries.
>
> 45. In older democracies, the executive power has sometimes a decisive influence on judicial appointments. Such systems may work well in practice and allow for an independent judiciary because these powers are restrained by legal culture and traditions, which have grown over a long time.
>
> 46. New democracies, however, did not yet have a chance to develop these traditions, which can prevent abuse, and therefore, at least in these countries, explicit constitutional and legal provisions are needed as a safeguard to prevent political abuse in the appointment of judges.[52]

One would be hard-pressed to foreground more explicitly the divisions between the older Member States and the newer accession States from the former Eastern Bloc.

In its 2010 Report on Judicial Independence, the Venice Commission continues in the same vein. Not only does it quote in full the passage directly above,[53] but it also adds two more specific objections to characteristic features of Eastern European judicial procedure. The first involves the powers of the Soviet and post-Soviet Prokuratura:

> 9. Final character of judicial decisions
>
> 65. Recommendation (94) 12, Principle I(2)(a)(i) provides that "decisions of judges should not be the subject of any revision outside the appeals procedures as provided for by law". . . .

[51] Venice Commission, "Report on Judicial Appointments" at para. 2.
[52] *Id.* at paras. 44–46.
[53] *See* Venice Commission, "Report on the Independence of Judges" at para. 31, quoting Venice Commission, "Report on Judicial Appointments," at paras. 44–50.

> 66. … [T]he experience of the Venice Commission and the case law of the ECHR indicate that the supervisory powers of the Prokuratura in post-Soviet states often extend to being able to protest judicial decisions no longer subject to an appeal.
>
> 67. The Venice Commission underlines the principle that judicial decisions should not be subject to any revision outside the appeals process, in particular not through a protest of the prosecutor or any other state body outside the time limit for an appeal.[54]

The second, also used in "certain post-Soviet countries," is "the practice of guidelines adopted by the Supreme Court or another highest court and binding on lower courts . . . ."[55] This practice violated "the principle of the independence of each individual judge," that is, "independence within the judiciary."[56] As can be seen from the Venice Commission's critiques, the distinctions between East/West and old/new democracies have continued to be drawn despite the passage of time. Indeed, the Venice Commission has sharpened the language by refusing to use the classic euphemisms of older/newer democracies or "transition democracies," or even vague references to "former communist countries"; instead, it points directly to "post-Soviet" countries and to their characteristic legal institutions.

Finally, it is worth mentioning two final features of the Venice Commission Reports, if only in passing. First, in addition to continuing the trend of pushing more and more explicitly for the establishment of judicial councils (a term that it uses forthrightly, instead of deploying a more bland designation, such as an "independent authority"), the Venice Commission also continues the gradual development of the discourse of judicial "quality." This important theme, which first surfaced under the rubric of "competence" in the European Charter on the statute of Judges,[57] emerges in a very prominent manner the Report on the Independence of Judges. Having explained its procedural background, the Report opens with a section entitled "Preliminary Remarks," which serves to underline the importance of promoting judicial independence. The Report explains: "Without independent judges there can be no correct and lawful implementation of rights and freedoms."[58] It continues:

> 7. The independence of the judges and—as a consequence—the reputation of the judiciary in a given society depends on many factors. In addition to the institutional rules guaranteeing independence, the personal character and the

[54] Venice Commission, "Report on the Independence of Judges" at paras. 65–67.
[55] *Id.* at para. 70.
[56] *See id.* at paras. 68–71.
[57] *See supra* Chapter 6(II).
[58] *See* Venice Commission, "Report on the Independence of Judges" at para. 6.

professional quality of the individual judge deciding a case are of major importance. The legal culture as a whole is also important.

8. Institutional rules have to be designed in such a way as to guarantee the selection of highly qualified and personally reliable judges and to define settings in which judges can work without being unduly subjected to external influence.[59]

The Report thus forges a direct link between judicial independence, judicial selection institutions, and "the professional quality of the individual judge," a link whose importance will become fully apparent in Part IV below.[60]

Second, it is worth noting that the Venice Commission goes out of its way to remove two categories of judges from the ambit of its Report on in the Independence of the Judiciary. It states: "It should be noted that some principles are applicable only to the ordinary judiciary at the national level but not to constitutional courts or international judges, which are outside the scope of the present report."[61] Although the Report then does a very poor job of explaining which principles are subject to such exceptions, we should file away for future reference that the Report, like the CCJE's Opinion 1, is quite conscious of the vexing question of which types of courts should be subject to its judicial appointments and judicial independence principles. As we shall see in Chapter 12, the distinction between "ordinary" domestic judges on the one hand, and constitutional or international judges on the other, is practically and theoretically important.

In conclusion, then, the Venice Commission Reports add yet another gloss to the European judicial independence debates. Although they do not add a great deal substantively to the other measures we have discussed, they do demonstrate the ongoing salience of these debates and the willingness (one might almost say "compulsion") of European institutions to rehash the issue over and over again. In addition to entrenching ever more the same set of issues, the links between them, and the potential institutional policy responses they might inspire, the Venice Commission does make two notable contributions. It gives an increasingly prominent place to the issue of "the professional quality" of judges. And it underlines particularly starkly the now classic distinctions between East and West and between older and newer democracies, going so far as to point the finger quite directly at "post-Soviet" judicial institutions and practices. Let me therefore note that the 2010 Report on the Independence of the Judiciary, which made these unusually specific and pointed objections, was adopted "on the basis of comments" of four members of the Venice Commission, one of whom was none other than the Russian Member: Valery Zorkin, the Chairman of the Russian Constitutional Court. It is probably no accident that in December 2010, Zorkin was himself appointed to

[59] *Id.* at paras 7–8.
[60] *See infra* Chapters 8 and 9.
[61] Venice Commission, "Report on the Independence of Judges" at para. 11.

the inaugural Advisory Panel of Experts on Candidates to the European Court of Human Rights.[62]

V. Concluding Trends

The stream of measures more or less directly related to judicial independence and appointments has not stopped flowing. The CCJE—demonstrating a marked penchant for grandiose titles—produced its Opinion No. 10 "on the Council of the Judiciary at the service of society" in 2007. It also published its "Magna Carta of Judges" in late 2010, on the very same day that the Committee of Ministers released a revised version of its original 1994 Recommendation "On the Independence, Efficiency and Role of Judges."[63] The stream therefore continues unabated. Such recent additions to the European judicial independence measures may not make contributions sufficiently important to warrant detailed presentation and analysis. But we should nonetheless scan them quickly to highlight the trajectory of their modifications.

The first interesting trend is the rise of a decidedly defensive tone in some of the newer measures.[64] This is particularly noticeable in the Committee of Ministers' 2010 reworking of its original 1994 Recommendation on judicial independence. This new Recommendation contains several remarks that stress the selfless motives for judicial independence. Its hortatory introductory paragraphs, for example, include the following language:

> Underlining that the independence of the judiciary secures for every person the right to a fair trial and therefore is not a privilege for judges, but a guarantee of respect for human rights and fundamental freedoms, allowing every person to have confidence in the justice system ...[65]

As if this remark were not enough, the Recommendation reiterates the same basic idea less than a page later: "The external independence of judges is not a prerogative or privilege granted in judges' own interest but in the interest of the rule of law and of persons seeking and expecting impartial justice."[66] In addition to

[62] *See* Committee of Ministers, Establishment of an Advisory Panel of Experts on Candidates for Election as Judge to the European Court of Human Rights—Implementation, CM/Del/Dec(2010)1101/1.7E (2010).

[63] *See* CCJE, "Magna Carta of Judges (Fundamental Principles)," CCJE (2010) 3 final (November 17, 2010); CM/Rec(2010)12 (November 17, 2010).

[64] This tone presages the virulent anti-European diatribes that were only to increase in the run-up to the 2016 Brexit vote and its aftermath. *See infra* Chapter 13.

[65] CM/Rec(2010)12.

[66] *Id.* at para. 11.

advancing such selfless motives for judicial independence, the Recommendation also urges governmental restraint in criticizing or questioning the judiciary:

> 18. If commenting on judges' decisions, the executive and legislative powers should avoid criticism that would undermine the independence of or public confidence in the judiciary. They should also avoid actions which may call into question their willingness to abide by judges' decisions, other than stating their intention to appeal.[67]

Indeed, the CCJE's Opinion No. 10 goes so far as to include an entire section suggesting that Judicial Councils may well be "the appropriate agency to play a broad role in the field of the promotion and protection of the image of justice" and "to provide the correct perception of the judge's role in society."[68] The judicial independence measures thus appear to have acquired a judicial public relations dimension.

The second notable feature of the recent measures is their growing call for the adoption, publication, and application of formal norms and procedures in all matters related to judicial selection and careers and for these norms to be oriented toward the merits and qualities of the candidates. The updated 2010 Committee of Ministers' Recommendation again makes the point particularly clearly. It states:

> Decisions concerning the selection and career of judges should be based on objective criteria preestablished by law or by the competent authorities. Such decisions should be based on merit, having regard to the qualifications, skills and capacity required to adjudicate cases by applying the law while respecting human dignity...
>
> Where judicial authorities establish systems for the assessment of judges, such systems should be based on objective criteria. These should be published by the competent judicial authority.[69]

The CCJE's Opinion on Judicial Councils is no less explicit:

> It is essential for the maintenance of the independence of the judiciary that the appointment and promotion of judges are independent and are not made by the legislature or the executive but are preferably made by the Council for the Judiciary...

[67] *Id.* at para. 18.

[68] *See* Consultative Council of European Judges, "Opinion No. 10 on the Council of the Judiciary at the Service of Society," CCJE (2007) OP No. 10 ["CCJE Opinion No. 10 on the Independence of the Judiciary"] 10 and paras. 80–86.

[69] CM/Rec(2010)12 at paras. 44, 58.

> Although this appointment and promotion system is essential, it is not sufficient. There must be total transparency in the conditions for the selection of candidates, so that judges and society itself are able to ascertain that an appointment is made exclusively on a candidate's merit and based on his/her qualifications, abilities, integrity, sense of independence, impartiality and efficiency. Therefore, it is essential that, in conformity with the practice in certain States, the appointment and selection criteria be made accessible to the general public by every Council for the Judiciary.[70]

The formalization of norms and procedures and their ever-increasing orientation toward judicial quality therefore continues.

Finally, these new measures encourage an increasingly systematic entrenchment of judicial councils as the key institutional mechanism for promoting judicial independence as well as for managing judicial selection and almost all other important aspects of the judicial profession, ranging from training, to promotion, to discipline, to budgets and administration, and so on. The title and subject matter of the 2007 CCJE "Opinion No. 10 on the Council of the Judiciary at the service of society" is telling in this regard.[71] But the 2010 Committee of Ministers' Recommendation on judicial independence also includes an entire chapter on judicial councils, which are to be composed predominantly of judges elected by their peers and whose primary task is "to safeguard the independence of the judiciary and of individual judges."[72] Furthermore, the CCJE's 2010 "Magna Carta of Judges" categorically states:

> 13. To ensure independence of judges, each State shall create a Council for the Judiciary or another specific body, itself independent from legislative and executive powers, endowed with broad competences for all questions concerning their status as well as the organisation, the functioning and the image of judicial institutions.[73]

The trajectory of the judicial independence debates thus leads increasingly clearly toward the required establishment of judicial councils. Indeed, because the Magna Carta explicitly states, "These principles shall apply *mutatis mutandis* to judges of all European and international courts,"[74] there is good reason to believe that such provisions enshrining not only the principle of judicial independence but

[70] *Id.* at paras. 48, 50.

[71] The Opinion also states: "It is essential for the maintenance of the independence of the judiciary that the appointment and promotion of judges are independent and are not made by the legislature or the executive but are preferably made by the Council for the Judiciary." *See* CCJE Opinion No. 10 on the Independence of the Judiciary at para. 48.

[72] *See* CM/Rec(2010)12 at Chapter IV.

[73] CCJE, "Magna Carta of Judges (Fundamental Principles)."

[74] *Id.* at para. 23.

also the institutional mechanism of judicial councils are to be applied at the supranational as well as the domestic level.

Given this policy trajectory and its increasingly evident institutional endpoint, one should no longer be terribly surprised that the EU's Article 255 Committee and the ECtHR's Advisory Panel of Experts were established in the first place, and established at almost the same time. Indeed, a telling hortatory remark in the preamble of the Committee of Ministers' 2010 reworking of its Recommendation on judicial independence appears to invite such intellectual and institutional convergence: "Wishing to promote relations among judicial authorities and individual judges of different member states in order to foster the development of a common judicial culture ... "[75] At least in the area of judicial independence and judicial councils, such commonality appears to have been increasingly called for and attained.

[75] *See* CM/Rec(2010)12 at 1.

7

The Secondary Literature

What to Make of Judicial Independence?

The secondary literature on judicial independence is voluminous and varied. I confess that I find most of it to be rather plodding, characterized above all by oft-repeated, if well-meaning, platitudes that add little to our understanding of judicial practice. The good news, however, is that a number of new analyses have shaken up the classic secondary literature, adding an increasingly skeptical and potentially fruitful set of perspectives. This chapter begins with a very quick presentation of more traditional analyses. I will not linger on them very long: I present them merely by way of background in order to set up the tactical approaches that will be the true focus of our attention. The first is the arch-classical analysis of political scientist Peter H. Russell; and the second is the more skeptical position adopted by constitutional scholar Stephen Burbank.

We will then move quickly to the tactical analyses. After setting the table with Martin Shapiro's seminal analysis of the role played by constitutional courts, this section will concentrate on three specific tactical works: a chapter by political scientists Lee Epstein, Jack Knight, and Olga Shvetsova on selecting judicial selection mechanisms and two sister articles co-written by economist Nuno Garoupa and comparative constitutional scholar Tom Ginsberg on judicial independence and judicial councils.[1] This set of important works transforms the way we might approach judicial independence: no longer conceived simply as a virtue in its own right, nor just as a mechanism to help promote other rule of law virtues, judicial independence emerges as a tool to advance the interests of particular institutional players in their struggles against others. Finally, the section pays respect to the tactical analysis adopted by Landes and Posner in their classic article propounding an interest group theory of judicial independence.[2] Having worked through this

[1] *See* Lee Epstein, Jack Knight, & Olga Shvetsova, *Selecting Selection Systems*, *in* Judicial Independence at the Crossroads: An Interdisciplinary Approach 191 (Stephen B. Burbank and Barry Friedman eds., 2002) ["Epstein (2002)"]; Nuno Garoupa & Tom Ginsberg, *Guarding the Guardians: Judicial Councils and Judicial Independence*, 57 Am. J. Comp. L. 103 (2009) ["Garoupa & Ginsberg, *Guarding the Guardians*"]; Nuno Garoupa & Tom Ginsberg, *The Comparative Law and Economics of Judicial Councils*, 27 Berkeley J. Int'l L. 53 (2009) ["Garoupa & Ginsberg, *The Comparative Law and Economics of Judicial Councils*"].

[2] *See* Martin Shapiro, *The European Court of Justice*, *in* Judicial Independence in the Age of Democracy: Critical Perspectives from Around the World 273 (Peter H. Russell & David M. O'Brien eds., 2001) ["Shapiro (2001)"]; William Landes & Richard Posner, *The Independent Judiciary in an Interest-Group Perspective*, 18 J. Law & Econ. 875 (1975) [Landes & Posner (1975)].

literature, I will then be in a better position to begin laying out my analysis of the European judicial independence debates.

I. By Way of Introduction: Classics Old and New

The venerable Canadian political scientist Peter Russell devoted significant effort toward elaborating a general theory of judicial independence.[3] His work faithfully summarizes and organizes the classic understandings of the key features of judicial independence. These key features are organized by a set of basic distinctions. Judicial independence can refer to the judiciary as a whole or to the individual judge. When referring to the judiciary as a whole, the issues focus on the separation of powers: can the judiciary act in a manner that is sufficiently free from undue external interference from the legislative and the executive, i.e., the political branches of government? When referring to the individual judge, the issues also include an internal element: can the judge decide cases in a manner that is sufficiently free from undue pressure from within the judicial hierarchy? These classic distinctions thus themselves rest on the fundamental distinction between law and politics: judicial independence distinguishes between judicial decision-making on the basis of unfettered judicial application of law and judicial decision-making on the basis of political factors, be they of an external/political or internal/professional nature.

Russell further summarizes and organizes the classic vectors of analysis by delineating four basic types of infringement on judicial independence. "Structural" problems involve "the power of governmental bodies outside the judiciary to create and modify judicial institutions," such as court packing or imposing jurisdictional limitations.[4] "Personnel" issues involve all aspects of "appointing, remunerating, and removing judges ... as well as promotions and transfers, modes of discipline short of removal, professional evaluation" and so on.[5] "Court administration" involves issues such as "the assignment of judges to cases and courtrooms, the sittings of the courts, and court lists."[6] Finally, "direct approaches" to interfering with judicial independence include "[a]ttempts at bribery or threats," as well as non-criminal options that "can most certainly occur in well-established liberal democracies" and that "range all the way from telephone calls and private visits through huddled conversations at social events to high-pressure media campaigns."[7] As

[3] *See*, e.g., Peter H. Russell, *Toward a General Theory of Judicial Independence*, *in* JUDICIAL INDEPENDENCE IN THE AGE OF DEMOCRACY: CRITICAL PERSPECTIVES FROM AROUND THE WORLD 1, 3 (PETER H. RUSSELL & DAVID M. O'BRIEN eds., 2001) ["Russell (2001)"]; Peter H. Russell, *Conclusion: A General Theory of Judicial Independence Revisited*, *in* JUDICIAL INDEPENDENCE IN CONTEXT 599 (ADAM DODEK & LORNE SOSSIN eds.,2010).

[4] Russell (2001) at 13.

[5] *Id.* at 14.

[6] *Id.* at 20.

[7] *Id.* at 21.

this last sentence demonstrates, Russell's classic analysis includes a final and firmly embedded distinction between "liberal democracies" and "illiberal, authoritarian regime[s]."[8] As Russell straightforwardly asks in the opening sentence of his section on "the rationale of judicial independence": "What do we expect of the judiciary in a liberal democracy?"[9] Russell's work thus does an excellent job of synthesizing the classic concerns of the judicial independence literature. Indeed, it reflects quite well the central preoccupations of the European primary literature that we studied in Chapter 6.

Stephen Burbank adds a more skeptical, contextualized, and even relativist sensibility to his analysis, which has become as canonical as Russell's. Burbank offers several important contributions to the scholarly debates. First, he presents judicial independence as the flip side of judicial accountability. In his words, "judicial independence and judicial accountability are different sides of the same coin."[10] Second, he maintains that judicial independence does not exist for its own sake: it is a means to an end. This instrumental perspective urges scholars to focus on the goal(s) to be served by judicial independence and accountability and "suggests that the quantum and quality of independence (and accountability) enjoyed by different courts in different systems, and indeed by different courts within the same system, may not be the same."[11] This leads to a third conclusion: judicial independence is by no means monolithic. It (like judicial accountability) can therefore be suitably modulated in order to account for contextual factors and goals.

Burbank's analysis proves useful in many respects for the European debates. In particular, it underlines just how monochromatic and acontextual the European judicial independence measures have tended to be, offering one-size-fits-all solutions that advance insufficiently defined goals and make little if any connection between judicial independence and judicial accountability.

It is true that Burbank does not do much himself to define just what the goals of judicial independence might actually be. He and his co-author Barry Friedman, for example, merely ask such open-ended questions as, "Is there a goal that any enlightened architect of any judicial system would want courts in that system to be able to achieve and for which a measure of decisional independence would be necessary?"[12] To such broad questions, they only offer rather vague, skeptical and somewhat relativist responses, such as: "It remains for polities to define what it is that they want from their courts and the measure (or quality) of judicial independence they believe is necessary or appropriate in order to secure it."[13] Furthermore,

[8] *See id.* at 9.
[9] *Id.*
[10] Stephen Burbank & Barry Friedman, *Reconsidering Judicial Independence*, *in* Judicial Independence at the Crossroads: An Interdisciplinary Approach 9, 11 (Stephen B. Burbank & Barry Friedman eds., 2002) ["Burbank & Friedman (2002)"]
[11] *Id.*
[12] *Id.* at 21.
[13] *Id.* at 35.

although they insist that in making such decisions, polities "should not treat judicial independence and judicial accountability as dichotomous but rather different sides of the same coin,"[14] they never say anything about what the nature of that "coin" might be. Such vagueness is undoubtedly frustrating, as it offers no clear normative, programmatic, or even analytic conclusion. But Burbank's work does nonetheless help to promote a more fine-grained and contextual understanding of judicial independence that links this independence not only to particular courts in particular legal cultures at particular moments in time, but also to judicial accountability and to the particular goals that a polity wishes its courts to promote. By fostering such a varied, contextualized, and instrumental view, Burbank has moved the ball a good ways down the road.

II. The Tactical Turn

Burbank's attention to the goals that a polity wishes to promote via both judicial independence and judicial accountability lays the groundwork for a more tactical approach to the subject matter at hand. I use the term "tactical" to cover a broad range of theoretical work that might be categorized under one or more specific variants of such positive political theory as public choice theory, game theory, or new institutionalism. The basic idea is that one should approach the judiciary as a political institution among others (albeit perhaps a distinctive one), governed by the same type of self-interested and coldly calculating behavior that characterizes all the other political institutions that surround it (and probably any individual working with or within them).

Martin Shapiro is doubtless the central proponent of such an approach, especially in the realm of constitutional law in general and European judicial politics in particular. In Shapiro's framework, the judicial independence of constitutional courts (including the European Court of Justice (ECJ)) is but a shorthand description of two core features of courts generally (including constitutional courts). The first is in effect *the* central requirement of effective "triadic conflict resolution": parties to a conflict must be able to turn to mutually acceptable "third party adjudicators" to resolve their disputes in a manner that losers will tolerate.[15] The second is that in the constitutional context, political institutions understand that the judiciary, acting as such a third party adjudicator in vertical (federal) and horizontal (inter-branch) constitutional disputes, will function as a "junkyard dog": political institutions establish the judiciary and set it loose specifically to police constitutional bargains and boundaries, despite the risks that the judiciary obviously poses for all constitutional actors whenever it exercises this authority.[16] Political

[14] *Id.*
[15] *See* Shapiro (2001) at 273–74.
[16] *Id.* at 275–75.

institutions thus create and accept judicial independence because they believe that it is in their self-interest to do so, even though they understand perfectly well that they will periodically rue its existence due to unexpected and unwelcome judicial interventions. Indeed, as the design of the Maastricht "pillar" system demonstrated quite clearly in the EU context, political institutions have become sufficiently clear-eyed about the dangerous (if necessary) independence of the judicial junkyard dog (i.e., the ECJ) that they have taken to adopting jurisdictional and other strategies to help manage the associated risks and limit the resulting damage.[17]

It is hard to overestimate the importance of the contribution that Shapiro's work has made in this domain. It fundamentally reorients the way that one might conceive of judicial independence, which now emerges as a deeply pragmatic and even hard-bitten mechanism for political institutions to advance their self-interest within a constitutional framework. Political institutions create an independent judiciary and modulate its field of operation not because they value judicial independence as such, or because they see it as a means to promote other rule of law values, but simply because it helps to secure a state of constitutional affairs that those institutions deem to be in their own self-interest.

Shapiro's perspective sets the table for two other scholarly interventions on the judicial independence front. The first is an important 2001 chapter by Lee Epstein, Jack Knight, and Olga Shvetsova on selecting judicial selection mechanisms.[18] Epstein's chapter offers a thorough debunking of the myth that successive waves of American reformers have imposed their respective noble conceptions of proper judicial selection mechanisms. According to this hackneyed tale, the Founders favored an independent judiciary; Jeffersonians and Jacksonians, a more accountable one; Progressives, a less politicized one; Pound-style progressives, a more meritorious one, and so on.[19]

To Epstein, this standard narrative is borscht. It offers "a rather naïve picture": "No one in this story, or so it seems, is out for their own individual political gain."[20] Generalizing her analysis, Epstein proposes the following explanation of what motivates the institutional design choices regarding the judicial selection systems for constitutional courts in general:

> To apply this general framework to explain the choice of selection and retention systems for judges, we begin with the basic assumption that designers of constitutional courts prefer institutional rules that will best serve their long-term political goals. But, because attaining this goal requires them to determine the relationship between their present political preferences and the long-term effects of the rules

[17] *Id.* at 297–98. We shall return to this example. *See infra* Chapter 7(III)(A)(2).
[18] *See* Epstein (2002) at 191.
[19] *See id.* at 202–03.
[20] *Id.*

> governing constitutional courts, their preferences over judicial selection and retention mechanisms will vary depending on their beliefs about present and future political conditions. So, for example, the more uncertain those conditions—in the fundamental sense that the actors do not know the political circumstances they will face in the future—the less the designers of the court will be able to constrain (with confidence) the court and, thus, the greater the independence the institutional rules will provide the justices.[21]

Epstein's approach to judicial independence differs in several important respects from Shapiro's. Most importantly, Shapiro focuses on the major political institutions of government (the legislative and executive branches, the federal and state governments, etc.); but Epstein focuses on individuals (and perhaps on clearly identifiable political interests), who then act as "the designers of the [constitutional] court." The types of conflicts and concerns that dominate Shapiro's analysis of constitutional courts therefore revolve around such large-scale structural problems as "two against one" struggles between the three branches of government, in which the constitutional court backs one or the other side to some structural constitutional law dispute.[22] But Epstein is far more interested in the calculations made by specific "political actors." As she states: "The effect of [political] uncertainty . . . necessarily directs our attention to the types of information available to political actors at the time they are establishing beliefs about the long-term effects of institutional rules."[23]

Epstein's focus on these specific political actors turns the issue of judicial independence into a coldly self-interested calculation of present and future political conditions and their likely effects on their (largely personal) political fortunes.[24] The attitude of these actors toward judicial independence therefore hinges entirely on the level of personal and systemic political uncertainty that those actors believe they face. The more those actors are certain that they will remain in power, the more they will seek to do away with judicial independence: they have no interest in an independent judiciary that might unsettle their political dominance or frustrate their political preferences. They will instead promote institutional arrangements that will ensure judicial subservience to the (one might say "their") entrenched political order.[25]

[21] *Id.* at 214.

[22] *See*, e.g., Shapiro (2001) at 273–77.

[23] Epstein (2002) at 214.

[24] Epstein is not terribly clear about who exactly constitutes this class of "political actors." We can certainly surmise that it includes leading political figures. I think that the analysis can probably be extended to cover, for example, identifiable groups of such individuals whose interests are bonded together by political affiliation; but Epstein does not offer a clear statement on such matters.

[25] Ramseyer and Eric Rasmusen propounded this basic position in the 1990s. *See* J. Mark Ramseyer & Eric Rasmusen, *Why Are Japanese Judges So Conservative in Politically Charged Cases?*, 95 Am. Pol. Sci, Rev. 331, 333 (2001). *See generally* J. Mark Ramseyer, *The Puzzling (In)Dependence of Courts: A Comparative Approach*, 23 J. Legal Stud. 721 (1994) (discussing political uncertainty and politicians' corresponding desire for independent courts).

The more those actors believe, however, that future political conditions (both personal and systemic) are uncertain, the more they will seek to enhance judicial independence. For them, judicial independence represents not a threat but an insurance policy. An independent judiciary can function as a bulwark against a complete reversal of political fortunes, as it would resist its outright capture by a politically unfriendly successor regime.[26]

Epstein's theory therefore suggests that political actors who are in a sufficiently powerful position at the time of constitutional design will modulate the amount of judicial independence they will build into the constitutional order as a means to account for their own political futures. The less secure they believe their political futures to be, the more they will hedge their bets by entrenching a more independent judiciary. In Epstein's econometric parlance, which she then cashes out in more colloquial terms:

> As uncertainty increases, the probability of adopting (or changing to) institutions that lower opportunity costs of justices (again, the political and other costs justices may incur when they act sincerely) also increases. In other words, political uncertainty produces selection mechanisms that many scholars associate with judicial independence (e.g., life tenure or long terms of office). Under certain conditions, the converse also holds ... This follows from the fact that the designers believe they will remain in power and, thus, hope to inculcate a beholden judiciary.[27]

For Epstein, therefore, judicial independence is but a tool wielded by constitutional designers to protect their political fortunes over time.

In two important articles published a few years later, Nuno Garoupa and Tom Ginsburg offer a less personalized and less self-contained account. For them, judicial independence does not exist in isolation, rising or falling in response to the predictions of personal political fortunes. Judicial independence exists instead in a constant dialectical relationship with judicial accountability. Like the two pans of an old-fashioned balance scale, each rises and falls in opposition to the other. And like a pendulum, the dominance of each tends to swing back and forth alternatingly between the two extremes. In the key theoretical passage that is repeated almost verbatim in their two co-authored articles on the subject, Garoupa and Ginsburg state:

> It is our view that the periodic reforms of judicial appointments and management that we observe within and across countries reflect a dialectic tension between the need to de-politicize the judiciary and the trend toward judicializing politics.

[26] Needless to say, it would not hurt to stack the judiciary with judicial allies before making the transition to a system of judicial independence ...

[27] Epstein (2002) at 195.

> Independence is needed to provide the benefits of judicial decision-making; once given independence, judges are useful for resolving a wider range of more important disputes. As the judiciary begins to take over functions from democratic processes, however, the pressure for greater accountability mounts.
>
> When judges have little influence over public policy and politics, concerns over independence tend to dominate, and reformers may push for a move from a politically dependent, weak judiciary to a strong, self-regulated judiciary. This shift gives rise to a judiciary that has some control over its own affairs. Frequently, though not inevitably, judges use this independence to increase their influence over public policy, perhaps because of exogenous events. However, once politics is judicialized in a significant way, pressures arise for greater political accountability. The judiciary remains strong but is subject to more oversight and control. Sometimes these pressures for more accountability can lead to assaults on judicial independence, particularly if a small group of principals is able to control the process of supervision. In such circumstances, a politically accountable, strong judiciary may revert back to a politically dependent, weak judiciary, as in a rising authoritarian regime. This dynamic framework provides a tool for understanding the various institutional adjustments observed in different countries.[28]

In this relatively disembodied account, judicial independence does not rise or fall (as per Epstein) in accordance with the personal political predictions and tactical calculations of the particular political actors who are in a position to effectuate such changes. It rises and falls instead in accordance with an almost mechanical swinging between an overly politicized judiciary and an overly judicialized politics.

Agency, in this account, appears almost nonexistent, despite the fact that Garoupa and Ginsburg explicitly adopt a principle-agent model. As they state: "[W]e develop a principle-agent model of judicial councils. We treat judges as the agents and society as the principle, on whose behalf the judges exercise power."[29] This tremendously broad framing of the relevant actors ("judges" and "society") does of course make it rather difficult to locate exactly who might be driving the push for greater or lesser judicial independence or accountability, as the case may be. But perhaps that is the point: excessive judicial independence or accountability, or, stated otherwise, an excessively judicialized politics or an excessively politicized judiciary, will necessarily generate countervailing pressures that will start the pendulum swinging in the opposite direction.

According to Garoupa and Ginsburg, judicial councils should be understood within this general framework of the "eternal struggle for a balance between [judicial] independence and accountability."[30] They function as "monitoring devices

[28] Garoupa & Ginsberg, *The Comparative Law and Economics of Judicial Councils* at 61; Garoupa & Ginsberg, *Guarding the Guardians* at 117–18.

[29] Garoupa & Ginsberg, *The Comparative Law and Economics of Judicial Councils* at 62.

[30] *Id.* at 55.

designed to maintain the relationship between the principal, society, and its agents, the judges."[31] Although there exist many different variations on such judicial councils, they are all basically mechanisms for managing the tensions between these values and players:

> Judicial councils are bodies designed to take appointment and promotion of judges away from the partisan political process, while ensuring some level of accountability. Judicial councils fall somewhere in between the polar extremes of letting judges appoint their own successors and maintain internal responsibility for judicial discipline, and the alternative of complete political control of appointments, discipline, and promotion. The first model of judicial self-selection arguably errs too far on the side of independence, while pure political control may make judges too accountable, in the sense that they will consider the preferences of their political principals in the course of deciding specific cases. As an intermediate body between politicians and judges, the judicial council pro- vides a potential device to enhance both accountability and independence.[32]

Judicial councils thus emerge as an institutional manifestation and reconciliation of the opposing poles of judicial independence and accountability.

Garoupa and Ginsburg examine different models of judicial councils in *Guarding the Guardians: Judicial Councils and Judicial Independence*, studying variations in their competences, composition, and legal basis. Their competences tend to include varying admixtures of three basic components: "(i) Housekeeping functions (managing budget, material re- sources, operations); (ii) Appointment of judges; and (iii) Performance evaluation (promotion, discipline, removal and retention of judges, and judicial salaries)."[33] Their varying composition consists of "three possible types of members, (i) judges, (ii) members of other government bodies or their appointees, and (iii) lawyers. Judges on the Council are typically appointed by the Supreme Court or by other courts, while lawyers are appointed by the law society/bar association. Members of government bodies are typically appointed by their organizations."[34] Finally, judicial councils can be established by ordinary legal means (i.e., legislation); or they can be established and entrenched by constitutional means.

Working on the same basic theoretical assumptions as in their *The Comparative Law and Economics of Judicial Councils*, Garoupa and Ginsberg organize the variations in the competences, composition, and legal basis of judicial councils in terms

[31] *Id.* at 61–62.
[32] *Id.* at 57.
[33] Garoupa & Ginsberg, *Guarding the Guardians* at 119.
[34] *Id.* at 120.

of their core distinction between judicial independence and accountability. As for composition,

> We can frame this as the question of whether judicial councils are set up to ensure independence of judges from the principals or accountability to the principals. If judges are a majority on the council, the assumption is that judges utilize the council to exercise self-government and maintain independence. If judges are a minority on the council, the assumption is that the council is a device to constrain the judges and render them more accountable. These two types of councils reflect quite different goals.[35]

As for competences, "We view extensive competence of a judicial council as enhancing judicial accountability."[36] And as for legal basis,

> Note that the issue of whether or not a council is constitutionalized is itself interesting. If the composition and powers of the council are left to ordinary law, they are subject to enhanced manipulation by the government and other actors and hence less of a guarantee of independence. Presumably those councils lean more toward the accountability pole than the independence pole. Conversely, when the council structure is entrenched in the constitution, it is beyond the reach of ordinary politics and hence likely to reflect a desire for greater levels of judicial independence and insulation. In the results that follow, we predict and find systematically lower independence scores for countries with non-constitutionalized councils.[37]

Each of the key design variables thus maps cleanly onto the independence/accountability distinction.

For Garoupa and Ginsberg, judicial councils are therefore a mechanism for negotiating the "eternal struggle for a balance between [judicial] independence and accountability."[38] Their design can be intentionally modulated in order to set the pendulum swinging toward one of these two goals; and if the pendulum has a traditional tendency to overshoot the mark, one might hope that the council would moderate the excesses before the pendulum swings back with excessive force.

According to such an analysis, judicial councils can function as a potentially important moderating device. But it is important to recognize that for Garoupa and Ginsberg, the key forces that animate the fundamental dynamics of the judicial/political order lie elsewhere. Those animating forces are the dialectically

[35] *Id.* at 121 (references omitted).
[36] *Id.*
[37] *Id.* at 123.
[38] *The Comparative Law and Economics of Judicial Councils* at 55.

opposed drives toward judicial independence on the one hand and judicial accountability on the other. When the judiciary is weak, it will be dominated by, and be subservient to, the political branches: the judiciary will be politicized. Under such circumstances, pressure will mount to empower and depoliticize the judiciary, granting it the independence necessary for it "to provide the benefits of judicial decision-making." Once empowered in this manner, however, the judiciary may well overshoot the mark, gradually arrogating to itself the power to engage in increasingly expansive and intrusive policy-making: politics will be judicialized. Under such circumstances, pressure will mount to hold the judiciary to account, tethering it more closely to the policy preferences of the political branches. Once disempowered in this manner, however, the judiciary may well find itself once again in the subservient role that prompted the initial calls for judicial independence. To Garoupa and Ginsberg, these are the key animating forces and dynamics. Judicial councils are but a mechanism for trying to manage them.

In conclusion, then: the tactical perspectives adopted by Shapiro, Epstein et al., and Garoupa/Ginsberg fundamentally reorient the way one might approach judicial independence. They allow us to develop a far more dynamic understanding of European developments regarding not only judicial independence, but also judicial appointments in general. Their approaches prompt us to conceive of judicial independence as a tool and not merely as a freestanding principle operating in its own right or in the furtherance of other rule of law values. By thinking of judicial independence in this manner, we can better visualize and examine the ways in which judicial independence interacts with political forces and political actors to advance specific interests and projects over time.

III. An Independent Take on European Judicial Independence and Accountability

The judicial independence literature has long been structured by the distinction between judicial independence and judicial accountability. Some fifteen years ago, Stephen Burbank was already challenging the notion that the two are "analytically discrete concepts."[39] Burbank sought instead to recast judicial independence and accountability as "different sides of the same coin" in order to argue in favor of trying to achieve "the proper balance between them."[40] Although Burbank was trying to put a new spin on the distinction, he therefore did not intend to efface the distinction altogether. To the contrary, the idea was simply to put the two notions

[39] *See* Burbank & Friedman (2002) at 14; Stephen Burbank, *What Do We Mean by 'Judicial Independence'?*, 64 OH. ST. L. REV. 323, 325 (2003); Stephen Burbank, *The Architecture of Judicial Independence*, 72 S.CAL. REV. 315 (1999).

[40] Burbank & Friedman (2002) at 15.

explicitly in relation to each other (although how this relation was meaningfully different from what had previously been described by such classical judicial independence scholars as Peter Russell remains less than clear).[41]

Within the tactical literature, Garoupa and Ginsberg take the analysis of the relationship between judicial independence and judicial accountability particularly seriously. As we have just seen, their entire analysis hinges on the theoretical claim that judicial orders oscillate between these two concerns as their judiciaries swing between the Scylla and Charybdis of an excessively politicized judiciary and an excessively judicialized politics. This elegant conceptual framework leaves us, however, with an important question that, for all its apparent simplicity, turns out to be fiendishly difficult: at their core, are the European judicial appointments reforms primarily judicial independence measures or, to the contrary, judicial accountability measures?

A. Judicial Independence or Judicial Accountability?

1. Judicial independence

According to Garoupa and Ginsberg, reformers push for judicial independence in order to counteract an excessive politicization of the judiciary: "When judges have little influence over public policy and politics, concerns over independence tend to dominate, and reformers may push for a move from a politically dependent, weak judiciary to a strong, self-regulated judiciary."[42]

In the European context, however, this first Garoupa/Ginsburg thesis immediately runs into a great deal of trouble. To be sure, the EU and Convention systems have been passing an endless series of judicial independence measures. Yet, one would be very hard-pressed to suggest that the ECJ or the European Court of Human Rights (ECtHR) "have little influence over public policy and politics" or that they have been excessively subservient to the political branches. Frankly, such a suggestion borders on the absurd. Almost every reputable history of the EU puts the ECJ at the very center of the Union's development at every stage of its history, with the ECJ functioning as a vital player on all levels. In fact, the centrality and importance of the ECJ has become so taken for granted that the ECJ has become a veritable lightening rod in the Brexit debates.[43] Indeed, the canonical story has the ECJ making, at the very least, massive contributions to the fundamental constitutional architecture of the EU: it was the ECJ, after all, that established the

[41] *See*, e.g., Russell (2001).

[42] Garoupa & Ginsberg, *Guarding the Guardians* at 61; Garoupa & Ginsberg, *The Comparative Law and Economics of Judicial Councils* at 117–18.

[43] *See*, e.g., David Allen Green, "Brexit: Why did the ECJ become a UK 'Red Line'?" available at https://www.ft.com/content/32cd1e87-c7d1-3026-86fc-bce5229711d1. For more on this issue, *see infra* Chapter 13.

supremacy and direct effect of European law in the seminal *Costa* and *Van Gend* judgments and that elaborated such key doctrines as the principle of state liability for breaches of European law in the *Francovich* judgment.[44]

As if such "constitutional" contributions were not enough, the Court has developed and wielded tremendous regulatory power to help construct the European common market. The story of how a court could perform such a leading role is well documented and need not be repeated at length here.[45] Suffice it to say that when Member State governments proved unable to overcome their divergent interests in order to generate concerted regulatory action, the Court stepped into the regulatory vacuum: it aggressively elaborated its "negative integration" jurisprudence, thereby fashioning the basis of a European common market.[46]

Given such seminal constitutional and regulatory interventions, no one could reasonably argue that the ECJ has been anything other than a pivotal and colossally powerful player in the development of European policy. Faced with this self-evident reality, the only remaining questions have been (1) whether to applaud or critique the ECJ's exercise of power and (2) how to account for it in the first place. On the first question, most scholars of the EU have traditionally offered distinctly positive assessments of the role played by the ECJ, although notable dissenters, such as Hjalte Rasmussen, have periodically been heard.[47] And on the second, most Europeanists have tended to line up with neo-functionalist and new institutionalist accounts (such as those offered by Ernst Haas, Martin Shapiro, and Alec Stone Sweet) of the ECJ's unintended interventions, although a smattering of liberal intergovernmentalists, such as Andy Moravcsik, have tried to make the (very) difficult argument that even the ECJ's most imaginative and far-reaching interventions actually reflected the latent wishes of the EU's Member States.

One need hardly perform lengthy analysis to arrive at a similar conclusion regarding the self-evident policy-making power of the ECtHR. True, the Strasbourg Court was undoubtedly quite timid in the early days of its operation. But over the last few decades, it has clearly become an active and often threatening judicial institution, routinely generating rather daring judgments regarding a host of volatile issues, from State liability,[48] to fundamental rights (Irish policing[49]) (gay rights[50]) (Iraqi detentions[51]) (suppression of international terrorism[52]), and on and on.

[44] *See* Van Gend en Loos v. Nederlandse Administratie der Belastingen, (26/62) [1963] E.C.R. 1; Costa v. ENEL, Case 6.64 [1964] C.M.L.R. 425; Francovich v. Italy, Cases C-6/90 & C-9/90, [1991] E.C.R. I-5357.

[45] For the classic accounts, *see, e.g.*, Joseph Weiler, *The Transformation of Europe*, 100 YALE L.J. 2403 (1991).

[46] *See* PAUL CRAIG & GRAINNE DE BURCA eds., THE EVOLUTION OF EU LAW 613–14 (1999).

[47] *See* HJALTE RASMUSSEN, ON LAW AND POLICY IN THE EUROPEAN COURT OF JUSTICE. A COMPARATIVE STUDY IN JUDICIAL POLICYMAKING (1986) [Rasmussen (1986)].

[48] Francovich v. Italy, Cases C-6/90 & C-9/90, [1991] E.C.R. I-5357.

[49] Ireland v. UK, App. No. 5310/71 (1978) Eur. Ct. R.H. 1.

[50] Dudgeon v. UK, App. No. 7525/76, (1989) Eur. Ct. R.H. 5.

[51] Al-Jedda v. UK, App. No. 27021/08, (2011) Eur. Ct. R.H. 1092.

[52] Kadi v. Commission, Cases C-402 & C-415/05, [2008] E.C.R. I-6351.

These judgments have regularly challenged the constitutional traditions and policy judgments of the Conventions' signatory States.

The tremendous and imaginative power exercised by both the ECJ and ECtHR and the far-reaching policy interventions they have consistently authored would therefore seem to falsify quite thoroughly the first Garoupa and Ginsberg thesis. As this Part has demonstrated, the European judicial independence reforms began in the mid-1990s, which is to say long after the ECtHR and especially the ECJ had demonstrated themselves to be major players in the European constitutional, legal, and political fields; and the flow of judicial independence measures have continued unabated ever since, even as the powers of those courts reached ever greater heights and touched ever greater geographical and substantive domains.

This historical and jurisdictional experience would appear to leave us with two basic options with regards to Garoupa and Ginsberg. The first is quite simply to conclude that these two scholars seem to have gotten their analysis exactly wrong: calls for judicial independence have come precisely when the European courts have been universally recognized as unusually powerful judicial institutions that have been making massive and often controversial policy interventions on a host of hot button issues.

The second option, however, is altogether different. It consists of adopting a more suspicious stance about European reforms passed in the name of "judicial independence." This approach would attempt to salvage the analysis of Garoupa and Ginsberg by treating such reforms not as judicial independence measures, but instead as judicial accountability measures. This initially counterintuitive stance would throw us into the realm of the second Garoupa and Ginsberg thesis.

2. Judicial accountability

One might therefore approach the European reforms from the other direction, focusing not on their nomenclature but on their context. Given the apparent collapse of the first Garoupa and Ginsberg thesis in the face of the ECJ's and the ECtHR's large-scale policy interventions, one might instead treat those interventions as a sign that the European reforms should, to the contrary, be analyzed in accordance with the second Garoupa and Ginsberg thesis. According to this second theory, a judiciary bolstered by judicial independence measures may well trigger blowback:

> Frequently, though not inevitably, judges use this independence to increase their influence over public policy, perhaps because of exogenous events. However, once politics is judicialized in a significant way, pressures arise for greater political accountability. The judiciary remains strong but is subject to more oversight and control. Sometimes these pressures for more accountability can lead to assaults on judicial independence, particularly if a small group of principals is able to control the process of supervision. In such circumstances, a politically accountable,

> strong judiciary may revert back to a politically dependent, weak judiciary, as in a rising authoritarian regime.[53]

This prism certainly offers food for thought, especially in a supranational European environment characterized by such prominently policy-making high courts as the ECJ and ECtHR. Two insurmountable problems do however present themselves to adopting this second thesis in the European context. The first manifests on the discursive level: more or less *none* of the endless judicial independence measures passed over the last twenty years say anything at all about judicial accountability. Can one really believe that all of these judicial independence reforms have actually been elaborate masquerades that have been consistently sustained for decades in order to produce the exact opposite of their stated purpose? Skepticism is one thing; conspiracy theory is another.[54]

The second problem manifests on the programmatic level; and it is probably even more important than the first. The problem, frankly, is that it is hard to see how any of the judicial reforms undertaken by the EU or the Council of Europe has subjected the ECJ, the ECtHR, or their respective judges to any greater level of judicial accountability at all. The ECtHR, for example, did away with reappointment altogether in 2010, having moved to a single nonrenewable nine-year term after discussions and internal recommendations dating back at least since 1999.[55] For its part, the ECJ has maintained the possibility of reappointment; but the discussions undertaken at the time of the Constitutional Convention made it quite clear that renewable terms were very much under threat.[56] The trend on the reappointment front has therefore been quite clearly—and quite expressly—in favor of greater judicial independence, not judicial accountability.

One could reasonably counter that the Article 255 Panel can in fact review candidates nominated for reappointment, which adds greater teeth to the reappointment process that remains in the EU system. But this is not terribly convincing. For one thing, Member State governments nominating such candidates always could (and periodically did) exercise such accountability by themselves. And for another, the 255 Panel itself has shown no interest in exercising meaningful authority of this kind in the first place. As we have seen, the Panel has declined to interview anew those candidates nominated for reappointment, as it deemed sufficient the interview conducted at the time of the candidates' nomination for a first term. Even more telling is that, in stark contrast to its frequently negative assessment of

[53] Garoupa & Ginsberg, *Guarding the Guardians* at 61; Garoupa & Ginsberg, *The Comparative Law and Economics of Judicial Councils* at 117–18.

[54] In describing judicial independence as the opposite of judicial accountability, I am merely relating the theoretical prism that links the two theses of Garoupa and Ginsberg. Personally, I am not interested in arguing over the veracity of this ontological question.

[55] *See supra* Chapter 4 (II).

[56] *See supra* Chapter 2(IV).

first-term judicial candidates,[57] the Panel has given its stamp of approval to every single candidate who has ever been nominated for reappointment.[58] This hardly bespeaks increased judicial accountability. Nor is there anything with respect to judicial promotion, discipline, funding, tenure, or anything else that suggests rising judicial accountability at either the ECJ or the ECtHR.

One might try to argue that certain developments on the jurisdictional front could be seen as a means to hold the ECJ in particular accountable for having been too activist in assorted domains. This reading was rather compelling at the time of the 1992 Maastricht Treaty's establishment of the "three pillar system," which did indeed keep the ECJ from exercising jurisdiction in entire swaths of new EU regulatory domains, such as in foreign policy and military matters (the second pillar's Common Foreign and Security Policy (CFSP)) and in criminal justice and cooperation in civil matters (the third pillar's Justice and Home Affairs).[59] As Martin Shapiro rightly argued, it was "quite natural" to exclude ECJ jurisdiction in the EU's foreign relations pillar; but it was "quite another matter" to "exclude the ECJ from a pillar actually named justice and home affairs."[60]

But this jurisdictional argument holds less and less water. Even at the time, the argument would not have been perfectly convincing. To be sure, the EU was refusing the ECJ jurisdiction in some new domains of EU competence. This certainly implied leeriness about subjecting political decision-making in such sensitive domains to ECJ review, which also entailed an implied rebuke. But this was hardly the same as limiting (never mind removing) ECJ jurisdiction in domains that already existed. Nor is it entirely clear that such jurisdictional haggling could ever really be cleanly assimilated to "judicial accountability." More importantly, however, the three pillar system has since been collapsed by the Treaty of Lisbon, which significantly expanded ECJ jurisdiction in many such matters (especially in "Freedom, security and justice" issues), even if it did maintain some exclusions in others (especially in sensitive CFSP issues).[61] What is more, the ECJ's 2008 *Kadi* judgment subjected even such CFSP measures to fundamental rights review by the ECJ itself, thereby undermining quite significantly whatever jurisdictional firewall remained.[62]

[57] *See supra* Chapter 3(II)(A)(2).

[58] *See* Jean-Marc Sauvé, *Selecting the European Union's Judges: The Practice of the Article 255 Panel, in* Selecting Europe's Judges: A Critical Review of the Appointment Procedures to the European Courts 83 (Michal Bobek ed., 2015) ["Bobek (2015)"]; Article 255 Panel, Activity Report of the Panel provided for by Article 255 of the Treaty on the Functioning of the European Union, Third Report of December 13, 2013 (No. SN 1118/2014) at 9; Fourth Report of February 10, 2017 at 11; Fifth Report of February 22, 2018 at 12 .

[59] *See* Treaty on European Union, available at https://europa.eu/european-union/sites/europaeu/files/docs/body/treaty_on_european_union_en.pdf.

[60] Shapiro (2001) at 297.

[61] *See* Article 24 TEU and Article 275 TFEU.

[62] *See Kadi*.

In short, there is very little indeed to suggest that anything meaningful has been done to increase the judicial accountability of the ECJ or the ECtHR, never mind of their respective judges. Almost nothing in the primary or secondary literature overtly suggests—either discursively or programmatically—that the judicial reforms of the last twenty-five years were undertaken in order to effectuate such judicial accountability, despite the unmistakable and sometimes decried judicialization of European politics during that period.[63] To conclude, the second Garoupa/Ginsberg thesis appears to fail as badly as the first.

B. *Judicial* Accountability?

I say that the second Garoupa and Ginsberg thesis "appears to fail" for a reason. One can always produce more or less generous readings of a given text; and I often find it most helpful to produce both, as this allows one to draw the most out of a text while also being sensitive to its limitations. With this in mind, we can return to Garoupa and Ginsberg, reading their work generously for its maximum value.

The second Garoupa/Ginsberg thesis suggests that mounting judicialization of politics is eventually likely to generate mounting pressures for judicial accountability. Given the undeniably forceful exercise of judicial power by the ECJ and ECtHR, the Garoupa/Ginsberg thesis would therefore lead us, as we have just seen, to expect a drive in that direction. But our examination of the discursive and programmatic thrust of the European judicial reforms shows no indication of such a drive. Can we nonetheless detect something that recovers as much as possible of the Garoupa/Ginsberg theory?

The answer is a qualified "yes." Even though the European judicial reforms of the last twenty-five years have been framed overwhelmingly in terms of judicial independence, it is hard to deny that the EU's Article 255 Panel and the Council of Europe's Advisory Panel of Experts (APE) both look a great deal like accountability devices, as they subject candidates for high European judicial office to the scrutiny of blue ribbon European panels. But here is the key: in order to make sense of the European judicial reforms, we need to distinguish clearly between *judicial* accountability and accountability *tout court*.

The distinction we must draw is between (1) judicial accountability, that is, accountability *of* judges, and (2) accountability *for* judges, and for our purposes especially, accountability for judicial nominations and appointments. The two are really not the same (although there can obviously be a certain amount of crossover). As soon as we have made the distinction, it is suddenly easy to recognize that

[63] *See*, e.g., Rasmussen (1986); Alec Stone Sweet, Governing with Judges: Constitutional Politics in Europe (2000); Joseph Weiler, The Constitution of Europe: Do the New Clothes Have an Emperor? (1999).

the two European judicial panels (i.e., the 255 Panel and the APE) do indeed create accountability *for judicial appointments decisions*, but that this is by no means straightforwardly assimilable to accountability *of the European courts or of their judges*.

We can of course collapse the distinction, for instance, by adopting the rather common if relatively contrived notion that the pre-screening of judicial candidates represents some type of front-loaded judicial accountability mechanism. But this muddles matters far more than clarifies them. The reality is that the accountability at issue in the European reforms runs not to the judges themselves, but to the Member States (and especially to Member State governments) who propose the judicial candidates in the first place, and perhaps to the European institutions who may appoint them and in whose name they would eventually render judgments.

Once we have drawn this key distinction, however, it is difficult to see how accountability of Member States and European institutions for judicial appointments decisions has much to do with what Garoupa and Ginsberg are talking about: using judicial accountability in order to reign in an excessive judicialization of politics. Why would checking judicial candidates prior to their appointment to the European bench lead those candidates, once appointed as ECJ or ECtHR judges, to cut back on their own policy-making decisions in order to hew more closely to the policy preferences of the political branches? Unless one believes that one could somehow identify in advance "modest"—i.e., non-policy-activist—judges (whatever that means),[64] it is hardly evident why it would. Indeed, one could argue that such pre-vetting might give those judges greater standing to promote their own judicial policy preferences.

The only other option is to argue that accountability of the Member States (and arguably of the European institutions) for judicial appointment decisions would reduce the judicialization of politics because there exists a fairly firm link between selection by the Member States (and/or the European institutions) and policy-making by European judges in the course of their later judicial decision-making. But note the difficulty of the argument, as it requires at least two leaps: (1) from the appointers to the judges themselves; and (2) from judicial appointments to judicial decisions. Both links look quite tenuous, unless one is prepared to treat European judges as mere vessels or conduits for the policy preferences of the appointers.

Indeed, the problem with this line of argument is even more fundamental. The reason is simple, if not immediately obvious: the more one is prepared to make this double leap (from judicial appointments by the appointers to judicial decisions by the judges), the more the supposed problem of the judicialization

[64] Note that Mikael Madsen has actually tried to make such a claim by correlating the professional background of European judges to their judicial philosophies. *See* Mikael Rask Madsen, *The Legitimization Strategies of International Judges: The Case of the European Court of Human Rights*, *in* Bobek (2015) 259, at 276–78.

of politics vanishes. After all, judges operating as such conduits would merely be heeding the policy preferences of the appointers, rather than overriding them with their own judicial preferences. For Garoupa and Ginsberg, such a scenario would actually do away with the need for more judicial accountability. To the contrary, it might well raise the opposite question of whether there existed a need to bolster judicial independence in the face of such a politicization of the judiciary!

But note: the problem with the Garoupa/Ginsberg analysis is neither with its theorization of the interplay between judicial independence and accountability, nor with its dynamic depiction of the oscillation between politicizing judging and judicializing politics. These contributions are actually quite thought provoking; and they offer insights that, as we shall soon see, prove quite useful. The problem lies instead with the tremendous oversimplification of the model, especially in the multilevel European context. A clue to this can be found in their distressingly simplified depiction of agency dynamics in the context of judicial councils:

> **III. Theory**
>
> This section presents a theory of judicial councils drawn from the economic concept of principles and agents. Judicial councils are monitoring devices designed to maintain the relationship between the principal, society, and its agents, the judges.[65]

Although such a description may be useful as a simple heuristic for basic economic or political theory purposes, it is far too blunt an instrument to help us make sense of the judicial appointments reforms at the intersection of the European and domestic arenas. Can "society" really function as a useful category for the purposes of generating incisive analysis? At the very least, we would need a far more sensitive and realistic account of who the assorted players are and what their interests might be in assorted legal and political contexts. This is just another way to underline once again that we are studying a set of multilevel exchanges between multiple possible players and interests that all interact at once.

Lee Epstein really helps in this regard, as she offers a far more agent-sensitive approach. She explains:

> On our account, the creation of and changes in the institutions used to select justices serving on (constitutional) courts of last resort must be analyzed as a bargaining process between relevant political actors, with their decisions reflecting their relative influence, preferences, and beliefs at the moment when the new

[65] Garoupa & Ginsberg, *The Comparative Law and Economics of Judicial Councils* at 61–62 (footnote omitted).

institution is introduced—along with (and critically so) their level of uncertainty about future political circumstances.[66]

This agent-sensitive approach adds a key element to the interplay of independence and accountability and of the politicization of the judiciary and judicialization of politics described by Garoupa and Ginsberg. It invites us to shift our attention at least partially from the relevant judges to the "relevant political actors." This suggests that we ought to consider whether what may appear at first blush to be *judicial* accountability devices—especially, the 255 Panel and the APE—may actually function primarily as *political* accountability devices. Viewed in such a light, the central figures in the drama may of course include the judges who serve on the high European courts; but the primary protagonists and targets would actually be the governments that nominate them.

C. *European* Judges?

Once we have taken Lee Epstein's suggestion to heart, and thus broadened our perspective in order to include Member State governments as central political actors in the judicial developments we have been examining, we can finally make good and proper use of the insights offered by Garoupa and Ginsberg. The first Garoupa/Ginsberg thesis posited that a push for greater judicial independence would likely result from a period of excessive politicization of the judiciary, in which a weakened judiciary had become overly subservient to the will of powerful political leaders. As we explained, this portrait of a weak and dependent judiciary hardly fits the ECJ or the ECtHR, which have been universally recognized as enormously powerful institutions whose "constitutional" and policy-making judgments have routinely transformed the legal and political landscapes of Europe. This led us to reject out of hand the idea that the first Garoupa/Ginsberg thesis could be fruitfully deployed to describe European judicial developments.

What we need to recognize, however, is that this description of the tremendous power of the European high courts applies to those *courts* when operating as *institutions* in their *European* legal domain. But this tremendous institutional power ought to be distinguished from the very limited power of those courts' *judges* and judicial *candidates* when they operate as *individuals* at the *domestic* level. For this is quite a different matter. After all, and as we have seen, neither the EU nor the Council of Europe have traditionally done much at all to liberate ECJ or ECtHR judges from the appointment and reappointment powers of their national governments.

[66] Epstein (2002) at 195.

To the contrary, the EU has from its very inception done almost everything in its power to ensure that Member States would retain all but complete and unfettered power to appoint whomever they wished to the ECJ: as we saw in Chapter 2, the 1950 ECSC negotiations led to the adoption of the French proposal that European judges be appointed by common accord of the governments for renewable six-year terms. This process effectively guaranteed maximum national governmental control. On the front end, appointment by "common accord" granted each Member State government the power to play tit for tat with judicial appointments, which effectively shielded their judicial nominations from challenge by other Member States. And on the back end, the short and renewable judicial terms empowered the governments to police their judges with the threat of nonrenewal.[67]

The ECtHR has traditionally done little better. True, appointment at the Council of Europe level involved election by the PACE from a slate of three candidates put forward by each Member State government, which would appear to reduce the control that a national government could exercise over which national candidate would serve in Strasbourg. But as we have seen, it took little effort for the Member State governments to make known their preferred candidate. National parliamentary representatives simply conveyed governmental preference to their colleagues on the Parliamentary Assembly (PACE); or the Member State governments overtly ranked the candidates and submitted the three candidate names and CVs in order of national preference; or the governments made no express statement of preference, but cunningly submitted long and rich résumés for their favored candidates that contrasted neatly with the meager ones submitted for disfavored ones.[68] And until very recently—2010, to be precise—ECtHR judges served the same renewable six-year terms as their ECJ counterparts.[69]

Thanks to these more realistic appraisals of the European judicial appointments processes, we can now see more plainly that there exists a radical—and to my mind, quite characteristic and perhaps even defining—disconnect between (1) the extraordinary power of ECJ and ECtHR judges when they function in their judicial capacities at the European institutional level and (2) these judges' traditional dependence on, and vulnerability to, national governmental authorities when they function in their individual capacities at the domestic level, first at the initial candidacy phase and eventually at the reappointment phase. Indeed, this fundamental disconnect motivates a great deal of the judicial reforms that we have been examining.

On the one hand, the traditional capacity of Member States to call the shots on judicial appointments to the two European high courts undoubtedly generates—as the first Garoupa/Ginsberg thesis would suggest—calls for greater judicial

[67] *See* Chapter 2(I).
[68] *See* Chapter 4(II).
[69] The nine-year nonrenewable term only came into effect with Protocol 14.

independence. But it is essential that we recognize that such calls for judicial independence are not directed toward European institutions, but toward the Member State governments, precisely because they have traditionally held almost all the cards in the judicial appointments process.

On the other hand, the tremendous power wielded by the ECJ and the ECtHR also generates—as the second Garoupa/Ginsberg thesis would suggest—calls for greater accountability. But it is even more essential that we recognize that such calls for accountability are not directed toward the *European judges* at all, but toward the *Member State governments*, once again because they have traditionally held almost all the cards in the judicial appointments process. Such calls are therefore not properly understood as demands for *judicial* accountability. In short, we need to appreciate that these calls for *governmental* accountability (for their judicial appointments) have little to do with curtailing the judicialization of politics, even if they tacitly recognize that such a judicialization has indeed occurred.

D. European *Judges*? On European Uncertainty

It should now be apparent that although the European judicial appointments reforms obviously revolve around judges (how could they not?), the central figures in this drama are not so much those judges as the national governments that propose them. Those national governments are the entities from which the European judges must enjoy the requisite independence; and at the same time, those governments are the entities that must be held accountable for the judicial candidates nominated to serve as ECJ and ECtHR judges. This increasingly puts those national governments in the awkward position of being held accountable for, yet urged to be independent of, their judicial candidates. Indeed, this demand for governments to be more responsible for their judicial appointments while simultaneously being called upon to leave their judges more independent has played out in the context of what almost everyone recognizes as the ever increasing power of the European courts. This represents a patently difficult charge, albeit one that—as we shall see—affects different governments differently.

Once we have properly placed the national governments at the center of the European judicial appointments developments, we can ask forthrightly: what has changed? Why did the national governments that had long zealously guarded their prerogative to control the nomination and reappointment of their judicial candidates suddenly do an about face, promoting and accepting reforms that progressively increased both their accountability for judicial nominees and the independence that those nominees would enjoy relative to their governments?

The primary answer, as I hope the reader will by now anticipate, is the large-scale Eastern enlargement that took place in the wake of the fall of the Berlin Wall. Lee Epstein's analysis can help us to tease out the dynamics involved. As we have explained, Epstein theorizes that support for judicial independence is a function of how the relevant political actors assess their political futures. To boil her theory down to its core: the more comfortably entrenched these politicians believe themselves to be, the less interested they are in an independent (as opposed to a beholden and subservient) judiciary; but the more they feel threatened by future political uncertainty, the more they seek to establish judicial independence as a means to protect themselves and their programs from political reversals.[70]

Epstein's theory does a good job of explaining much of the European judicial reforms. For as long as the European Member States were a relatively closed group of Western European countries, their governments had little or no interest in fostering an independent European judiciary in Luxembourg or Strasbourg. To the contrary, they had every reason to try to keep as short a leash as possible on judges who, as anyone of any perspicacity clearly realized, were fully capable of wielding European norms to great effect. Indeed, as we have seen, national representatives clearly foresaw the dangers that a powerful European-level judiciary might pose and did so since the 1950s, i.e., since long before the ECJ or ECtHR were actually in a position to exercise such powers: hence the appointments solutions adopted for the ECJ and the jurisdictional, procedural, and institutional limitations placed on the still nonfunctioning ECtHR.[71]

Of course, both the EU and the Council of Europe had seen their membership gradually increase over time. The EU, which had begun as a Community of six in 1952 and 1958, had added three new Member States in 1973, one in 1981, two in 1986, and three in 1995, leaving the EU with a total of fifteen. In over forty years, the EU had therefore added a grand total of nine Member States. These changes, while not trivial, were moderate and fairly easily managed.

But by 1995, something very different was on the immediate horizon: accession of countries of the former Eastern Bloc would almost double the size of the fifteen-member EU, bringing its membership to twenty-seven by 2004, including ten new entrants in 2004 alone. And the Council of Europe, whose fourteen Contracting Parties in 1950 had risen very modestly to twenty-one in 1987, would explode to forty-one by 2000. The sheer numbers were formidable. But the political implications were even more daunting: to admit Spain, Finland, and Portugal was one thing, but to admit Bulgaria, Poland, and Russia was quite another.[72] And the speed at which these changes were occurring was nothing less than breathtaking. The Council of Europe, which included twenty-three Member States at the dawn of the 1990s, would add seventeen new Member States by 1996; and the EU would all but double from fifteen Member States to twenty-seven in all of four years.

70 *See* Epstein (2002) at 214.

71 *See supra* Chapter 2(I) and Chapter 4(I).

72 For an interesting description of the misgivings that some had regarding the rapid admission of former Eastern Bloc countries into the Council of Europe, *see* Andrew Drzemczewski, *Human Rights in Europe: An Insider's Views* EHRLR 134 [2017].

This sea change in European membership obviously generated enormous political uncertainty; and this uncertainty was perhaps especially acute in the judicial domain. After all, political bargaining on the institutional and substantive fronts could be managed in any number of ways. Voting weights in Council could be (and were) haggled over rather freely; and the application of free movement norms could be (and was) delayed in a manner that was shamelessly directed at the labor force of prospective Member States.[73] But the straightforward one State, one judge principle was itself almost impossible to finesse. However one looked at the problem, the math was simple: the ECJ and ECtHR were going more or less to double in size in short order. And at least as a brute numerical matter, the one Romanian judge would carry as much weight as his/her one German colleague.[74]

For the established Member States, this impending state of judicial affairs offered two disturbing possibilities. The first was that the new accession States from the former Eastern Bloc would reproduce the sort of subservient judiciary that was thought typical of the Soviet era.[75] This would of course be quite destabilizing—and even rather threatening—for the EU and the Council of Europe as well as for their existing Member States. There was no way to predict with confidence how the new "transition democracies" of the East would develop over time, how they might respond to—and wield—powers newly acquired via accession, and so on. But it was entirely reasonable for the older Member States to fret at the prospect of the ECJ and ECtHR being stacked with political hacks of highly unpredictable States from the former Soviet sphere. The second prospect was that the new Member States would start afresh and nominate truly independent judges. Although this prospect would undoubtedly have looked better, it could still not be terribly reassuring: no one could really know what the profile or proclivities of such candidates might actually be.

Both of these scenarios represented wild cards—and perhaps outright threats—for the established European order. The first raised the prospect of judicial hacks operating not only as shills for their national governments, but also as prospective tools for the exercise of concerted action by potentially aligned new Member States. It also raised the possibility, which would become more plausible over time, that the Euroskeptic government of a new Member State might plant friends within the high European courts. The second was less overtly threatening, but no

[73] For an excellent report on the effects of the transitional arrangements regarding labor rules for the EU's 2004 and 2007 enlargements, *see* Agnieszka Fihel, Anna Janicka, Paweł Kaczmarczyk, and Joanna Nestorowicz, "Free Movement of Workers and Transitional Arrangements: Lessons from the 2004 and 2007 Enlargements," available at ///Users/mitchellasser/Downloads/CMR_report_final_08052015.pdf.

[74] The risks involved were apparent to all. *See* Drzemczewski (2017).

[75] There was of course a good deal of variation within Socialist/Communist States and even within given States over time. But in none was the judiciary held to be a truly independent, never mind "coequal," branch of State authority. *See* e.g., Adras Sajo, *The Judiciary in Contemporary Society: Hungary*, 25 CASE W. RES. J. INT'L. L. 293(1993); Alan Uzelac, *Survival of the Third Legal Tradition?*, 49 SCLR (2) 377, 382–88 (2010).

less unpredictable: independent judges might not be under governmental orders, but could still develop novel and disruptive judicial doctrines. Both of these scenarios clearly put established expectations and long-term political, legal, and constitutional bargains at risk.

Now that we can fully recognize the immense instability that accession therefore threatened to bring to the European legal orders and their existing Member States, we can properly appreciate its importance to European judicial developments. Indeed, this connection between political uncertainty and judicial developments should not come as a surprise: the American theoretical literature has repeatedly placed the notion of uncertainty at the very center of its tactical accounts of judicial independence.

We have seen the centrality of uncertainty in Lee Epstein's analysis, in which judicial independence emerges as a calculated response by relevant actors to manage their own perceived political uncertainty moving forward. But the connection between uncertainty and judicial independence goes back much further. Thus, Martin Shapiro theorizes constitutional courts (including the ECJ) as acceptable "third party adjudicators" specifically empowered to police constitutional bargains and boundaries, despite the risks that the judiciary obviously poses for all interested constitutional actors whenever it exercises this authority.[76] Better to set loose such an independent "junkyard dog" than to live with the uncertainty of unenforceable constitutional bargains.

But the truly path-breaking text in this line of analysis is certainly "The Independent Judiciary in an Interest-Group Perspective," published in 1975 by Bill Landes and Dick Posner.[77] Yet this truly seminal article, which generated an enormous and ongoing degree of interest in the political science literature,[78] has been all but ignored in the contemporary judicial independence debates, including those in Europe. In the primary edited volumes on judicial independence, for example, none of the ten chapters of the 300-page Burbank/Friedman volume ever refers to it in any way;[79] and in the fifteen chapters of the Russell/O'Brien 300-page volume, it is cited only once and in passing.[80] Similarly, it never appears at all in the fourteen chapters of the 300-page Bobek volume on European judicial appointments reform.[81] Yet its analysis resonates a great deal not only with the work of

[76] Shapiro (2001) at 273–75.

[77] 18 J. L. & Econ. 875 (1975).

[78] For useful discussions of the literature surrounding the Landes and Posner article, *see*, e.g., Donald Boudreaux & A.C. Pritchard, *Reassessing the Role of the Independent Judiciary in Enforcing Interest-Group Bargains*, 5 Constit. Pol. Economy 1 (1994); Stefan Voigt, *Positive Constitutional Economics: A Survey*, *in* Constitutional Political Economy in a Public Choice Perspective 11 (Charles Rowley ed., 1997) at 39–41; Georg Vanberg, *Establishing and Maintaining Judicial Independence*, *in* The Oxford Handbook of Law and Politics 99 (Keith E. Whittington, R. Daniel Kelemen, & Gregory A. Caldeira eds., 2008).

[79] *See* Burbank & Friedman (2002).

[80] *See* David M. O'Brien & Yasuo Ohkoshi, *Stifling Judicial Independence from Within: The Japanese Judiciary*, in Russell & O'Brien, Judicial Independence in the Age of Democracy 37, at 37.

[81] *See* Bobek (2015).

Martin Shapiro and Lee Epstein, but also with European judicial developments in the judicial independence domain.

The basic thrust of the Landes/Posner article is elegantly simple. Legislative bargains won by interest groups are of limited value if they do not endure beyond the term of the enacting legislature. Indeed, the value of such bargains necessarily depends on how long interested parties can expect the deals to be enforced. The key to instituting such endurance is to limit the capacity of the legislature to overturn its prior bargains. This can be done by two primary means. The first is obvious: making it difficult (procedurally or otherwise) for the legislature to overturn its prior decisions; the second is less so: making it difficult for the legislature to induce the judiciary to overturn those prior decisions by interpretive means. The second approach—judicial independence—frees the judiciary from kowtowing to the political whims of the currently sitting legislature and thus allows it to seek in good faith to enforce the original legislative deal.

To Landes and Posner, therefore, judicial independence is effectively an entrenchment mechanism: it is a means for interest groups to guard against political uncertainty over time. In this regard, Landes and Posner state the core of Lee Epstein's position some thirty-five years earlier. Indeed, one could reasonably argue that Landes and Posner foreshadow a great deal of Martin Shapiro's analysis of constitutional courts. For them, as for Shapiro, such a court functions effectively as a mutually acceptable mechanism for enforcing political bargains, constitutional bargains being little more than expensive variants on ordinary legislative ones. In fact, Landes and Posner recognize explicitly the phenomenon that Shapiro later describes quite brilliantly as the junkyard dog: independent judges empowered to enforce prior bargains will occasionally frustrate interested parties by refusing to apply the original bargains or by generating unexpected interpretations. In other words, interested parties will sometimes get bitten by those empowered to police their boundaries: "But that is just a necessary price to pay for a system in which interest groups will have incentives to invest in legislation that yields them benefits over an extended period of time."[82] In amusingly deadpan economic terms, they go so far as to state that this is but "the expected 'tax' resulting from the independence of the judiciary"![83]

In sum, Landes and Posner, then Martin Shapiro, and eventually Lee Epstein all stress that judicial independence is a mechanism for generating stability over time in the context of uncertain and changing political realities. Their respective takes on judicial independence do of course vary in numerous respects. Most notably, they place different actors at the center of their respective stories. For both Shapiro and Epstein, the main protagonists are overtly political actors: in Shapiro's case, the branches of government; in Epstein's, specific political players or parties.

[82] Landes & Posner (1975)at 879.
[83] *Id.* at 884.

For Landes and Posner, however, the true protagonists are the interest groups that motivate the workings of government. But even this difference may not represent a major theoretical disagreement, as the distinction between institutional actors and interests groups can obviously be collapsed relatively easily, as Landes and Posner's interest group theory of government itself suggests.[84]

IV. Conclusion

These theoretical insights of the American tactical literature are deeply suggestive as we return our gaze to Europe. They support the basic historical claim I have been propounding, namely, that the European judicial reforms undertaken over the last twenty-five years are deeply related to the large-scale accession of former Eastern Bloc States after the fall of the Berlin Wall. The enormous uncertainty raised by this accession quickly led to strident, recurrent, and strikingly persistent calls for judicial independence.

This Part has presented the most important of these European judicial independence measures. These measures have stressed certain recurring themes. At the most fundamental level, they elaborated a set of governing principles regarding the importance of the judiciary for a properly functioning constitutional democracy. This pedantic theoretical construct was clearly directed toward the "transition democracies" of Central and Eastern Europe; but it also crystallized and propounded political theory claims that were by no means self-evident, never mind universally recognized, in all Western European Civilian jurisdictions at the fall of the Berlin Wall. This theoretical construct placed courts at the very center of the national and supranational constitutional orders, ideally as a coequal branch of government. Judges and courts were the central institution for safeguarding individual rights and freedoms, defending democracy and the rule of law, guaranteeing the separation of powers, and protecting against oppression and the totalitarian state.

This 1990s civics lesson (whose economic consequences were being heavily theorized by neoliberal writers of the time[85]) also coalesced into a recognizable set of institutional demands, almost all framed in terms of "judicial independence." This led to a long series of increasingly specific measures that were designed to guarantee independent judicial decision-making free of party, executive, legislative, or other improper influence. At the most general level, judicial independence should be constitutionally entrenched. At the more nitty-gritty level, judicially chosen and judicially staffed judicial councils should be formally established to govern all aspects of judicial appointment, training, promotion, and discipline; and these

[84] *Id.* at 877.
[85] For more on this, *see infra* Chapter 12(V)).

councils should exercise these powers by applying formally established norms on the basis of formally established procedures.

In order to make sense of these developments, I have turned to a series of theoretical accounts of judicial independence. By far the most suggestive have been those drawn from such positive political theory as public choice theory, game theory, or new institutionalism. These accounts propound a tactical understanding of judicial independence that, when transposed to the European context, stress the centrality of governmental and other political actors and the tremendous political, juridical, economic, institutional, and ideological uncertainty produced by the massive Eastern enlargement of the EU and of the Council of Europe in the post-1989 period.

These tactical accounts can only take us so far, however. If taken at their word, they can often lead, as we have seen most clearly in the case of Garoupa and Ginsberg, to explanations that simply do not square with realities on the ground. No one could plausibly argue, for example, that the rise of judicial independence measures at the European supranational level has been driven by the weakness of the ECJ and ECtHR. Nor has the tremendous power of those institutions generated judicial accountability measures worthy of the name, nor, frankly, to judicial accountability measures that even use the name.

But these tactical accounts are nonetheless extremely useful. They raise a series of themes, such as political uncertainty, that are patently crucial to European judicial developments. They raise others, such as the politicization of the judiciary and the judicialization of politics, that are deeply suggestive. They call attention to political actors who are every bit as central to the European judicial developments in question as the judges themselves. And when we try in good faith to read these tactical accounts in a generous fashion in order to derive as much explanatory benefit from them as possible, they provoke us to refine our analyses and to tease out a set of relationships that might not otherwise become apparent.

PART IV
A QUALITY DISCUSSION

Part III traced the sudden explosion of European judicial independence measures to the period following the fall of the Berlin Wall, when a dauntingly long list of former Eastern Bloc countries prepared to accede to the Council of Europe and to the EU. Leaving behind the more classical accounts of judicial independence, it then leveraged the more tactical conception of judicial independence prevalent in several strands of American theoretical literature as a means to link this accession to the sudden blossoming of European judicial independence measures: given the unmistakable policy-making power of the European Court of Justice (ECJ) and the European Court of Human Rights (ECtHR), large-scale accession from Central and Eastern Europe created sufficiently troubling political uncertainty to induce existing European Member States to shift away from their long-standing policy of zealously protecting national control over the selection and retention of "their" judges on the European courts to a new and seemingly contrary policy of demanding judicial independence. These Member States and their representatives in assorted European institutions suddenly began insisting on the independence of all judges at all levels and at every stage, from selection, to training, promotion, retention, and discipline. And as we explained, they increasingly converged on the institutional form of the judicial council as a key mechanism for promoting such independence. These developments finally culminated in paradigm-shifting reforms at the European level with the adoption in 2009–10 of the EU's Article 255 Panel and the Council of Europe's Advisory Panel of Experts (APE).

In Chapter 7, I read the American "tactical" theoretical literature not only to call attention to the link between the rise of political uncertainty and calls for judicial independence, but also to shift our attention at least in part from the judges themselves to the governments that now adopted such a pro-independence stance. This focus on Member State governments leaves us with unfinished business. First, the historical record strongly suggests that the primary objective of the judicial independence and appointments reforms has been to manage the instability threatened by the new accession States. This obviously implies that established and new Member States hold different interests with respect to judicial independence, interests that we need to examine in our ongoing analysis of the European judicial appointments reforms.

Second, this asymmetry between Member States also suggests that in the European context we are studying, judicial independence should be understood as more than just judicial independence: judicial independence is also a means to minimize the potential impact that the new Member State governments might effectuate through their judicial nominees to the ECJ and the ECtHR. In other words, we need to conceive of the judicial independence developments, at least in part, as a means for some Member State governments to control others. We need, in short, to start conceptualizing judicial independence at the European level, at least in part, as a system for such governments to *impose* (political and other) control, not merely as a system to *remove* such control.

Third, we can now see clearly that, in the shadow of impending mass accession, the established Member States were suddenly willing to make a trade: they were willing to sacrifice control over their own judicial appointments to the European courts in order to take away that of their new counterparts. But given the undeniable power of the ECJ and ECtHR, this sacrifice would hardly have been attractive. Far better, of course, would have been to remove the latter without completely forfeiting the former. This posed an interesting tactical conundrum: might there be some way for the old Member States to have their cake and eat it too?

To address this question, this Part examines two deeply related themes that have gradually emerged in the European judicial appointments debates. As sequencing is important, I will discuss the two in chronological order. The first theme is the long-standing and ongoing tendency to formalize judicial relations on the European level. This formalization is immediately visible in the judicial appointments domain on which we have been focusing. It appears in the formalization of appointment procedures demanded by assorted European measures and institutions. In order to satisfy Council of Europe requirements, for example, Member States must make formal and public calls for candidacies to fill judicial positions on the European courts; they should formally adopt and apply formal procedures for examining candidates, and so on. The same holds true at the European level, where the assorted institutions involved in judicial appointments must now abide by such formal procedures as well: one need only think, for example, of the elaborate committee and sub-committee procedures spelled out by the Council of Europe, the Parliamentary Assembly (PACE), the EU's Council, and Article 255 Panel, etc. But this formalization goes well beyond the procedural realm, as is demonstrated, for example, by the PACE's adoption of painstakingly elaborated norms about the required gender breakdown of candidate lists, the linguistic proficiency of candidates, and so on. Indeed, this tendency has even manifested itself on the institutional front, as the establishment of such formal and dedicated institutional mechanisms as the Article 255 Panel, the APE, and domestic judicial councils clearly attests.

The second theme, deeply intertwined with the first, is the more recent, often quite strident, and at times frankly alarmist, discourse of judicial "quality."

Tellingly, this theme, upon which we briefly touched in the course of our discussions in the last few chapters, burst onto the scene at two specific moments. For the EU/ECJ, it suddenly appeared in 2003, that is, on the very eve of the great 2004 accession of twelve new Member States, which almost doubled the size of the EU and ECJ from fifteen to twenty-seven. Not coincidentally, this was also precisely the moment when the first serious discussions were held regarding the establishment of what would eventually become the Article 255 Panel. For the Council of Europe and its ECtHR, these discussions also reappeared quite suddenly in 2009–10, which is to say, on the eve of the establishment of the APE. We will therefore examine the emergence of this theme in several key documents: the 2003 Interights Report, the EU's Constitutional Convention's 2003 Discussion Circle on the Court of Justice, the 2010 Interlaken Conference on the Future of the European Court of Human Rights, and the 2010 letter that ECtHR President Jean-Paul Costa sent to the ambassadors of the Member States of the Council of Europe. As this chapter demonstrates, the emergence of the theme of judicial quality merged with the ongoing formalization process to forge a common solution: the establishment of the 255 Panel and the APE.

As we shall see, however, the "quality" debates hardly came to an end with the creation of the two Panels. Instead, the establishment of the Panels provided, as we saw in Parts I and II, the impetus for the elaboration of criteria for the assessment of candidates to the ECtHR and especially the ECJ. That is, it gave rise to the impulse to define the attributes of a proper European judge. At least as important, the theme of judicial quality became (and has remained) utterly central to the assessment of the European judicial appointments reforms in the ongoing academic and institutional debates. As Chapter 8 explains, academics have enthusiastically joined their European institutional colleagues in this respect: they too have ardently espoused the cause of judicial quality, rallying for its promotion and decrying its absence or loss. Indeed, the concern for judicial quality has become so dominant that it is now—perhaps even more than judicial independence—*the* central intellectual prism of the European judicial appointments debates, at least in the academic/doctrinal literature.

Chapter 9 argues that the overlapping European development of (1) the formalization of judicial institutions, procedures, and norms and (2) the theme of judicial quality represents a two-pronged solution to the dilemmas triggered by mass accession of former Eastern Bloc countries. These two developments offer a tactical resolution to the judicial appointments and judicial independence debates that permit the established Member States to go as far as possible toward having their cake and eating it too.

8
Formalization and Judicial Quality

I. Formalization

The first important feature of the "formalized judicial quality" solution elaborated since the fall of the Berlin Wall has been the unmistakable formalization of almost all aspects of the European judicial appointments process. I have already presented most of the key developments over the course of the last three chapters. I organize and briefly reintroduce them again here in order to underline just how thoroughly this procedural, normative, and institutional formalization has come to permeate the European judicial appointments domain.

A. Procedural Formalization

The Parliamentary Assembly of the Council of Europe (the PACE) has been the most aggressive player in the development of formalized European judicial appointment procedures. It has passed a long list of measures that explicitly address judicial appointment processes at both the domestic and the European levels.

As we have seen, the first major moves directed at reforming the ECtHR's judicial appointment process occurred at the height of large-scale accession, precisely when the judicial independence debates rose to prominence and when Protocol 11 was being fashioned to create the single full-time ECtHR.[1] In 1995, the PACE's powerful Committee on Legal Affairs and Human Rights proposed its Draft Resolution and Report "on the procedure for examining candidatures for the election of judges to the European Court of Human Rights," which, in anticipation of the entry into force of Protocol 11, was designed "to improve [the PACE's] own procedure for examining the candidatures and for the selection of candidates, for more efficiency and professionalism."[2] This led to two significant procedural developments. First, candidates to fill vacancies on the ECtHR were now "invited to fill in a model curriculum vitae, so that the Assembly will have comparable information at its disposal" when selecting among the slate of three candidates put forward

[1] *See supra* Chapter 4.

[2] PACE Committee on Legal Affairs and Human Rights (Rapporteur: Lord Kirkhill), Report on the procedure for examining candidatures for the election of judges to the European Court of Human Rights 1, Doc 7439, 1403-15/12/95-1-E (1995). ["PACE Report for Examining ECtHR Judicial Candidatures"].

by the Member States. Furthermore, these three CVs were then to be transmitted in alphabetical order, lest the PACE be influenced by a Member State's expression of its preference for particular candidates.[3] Second, the three candidates would "be interviewed by a sub-committee of the Assembly, for their qualities to be assessed," leading to a recommendation to the Assembly.[4]

An entire second layer of procedure was then added to these formal procedures: the APE would vet the candidates proposed by the national governments to fill ECtHR vacancies. As we have seen, the addition of this new layer of procedure posed all sorts of delicate problems vis-à-vis both the Member State governments and the PACE's Committee on Legal Affairs and Human Rights (and in particular its Sub-Committee on Elections of Judges to the ECtHR).[5] This led to the carefully formalized—if rather byzantine—procedure under which the APE would operate at the intersection between the national selection and the PACE election processes.[6] These processes, furthermore, were later formally amended in a revealing attempt to pre-empt recalcitrant national governments from doing an end-run around the APE.[7]

It is important to recognize, however, that this litany of procedural rules represents only a fraction of the measures adopted to govern judicial appointments to the ECtHR. It includes the rules addressed to the European level of the appointments process; but that still leaves all of the rules directed at the domestic level of the process. And here again, the list of measures is long and detailed. These often redundant measures include the 1999, 2004, and 2009 PACE measures on "National procedures for nominating candidates for election to the [ECtHR]," "Candidates for the [ECtHR]," and "Nomination of candidates and election of judges to the [ECtHR]."[8] These measures call attention to the national part of the appointment process, insisting that the domestic authorities institute and abide by formal and transparent procedures for the selection and nomination of candidates to fill vacancies on the ECtHR, that they issue a formal call for candidates in the

[3] *See* PACE Recommendation 1429 (1999); 2004 PACE Recommendation 1649; and 2005 PACE Resolution 1432.

[4] PACE Report for Examining ECtHR Judicial Candidatures at 1.

[5] *See supra* Chapter 4(II). I have chosen to list the APE procedures under the rubric of European-level measures, although one could just as easily classify them as domestic/national level procedures: in theory, at least, the APE intervenes at the domestic level, where it provides advice to Member State governments regarding their candidates. *See, e.g.*, PACE Committee on Legal Affairs and Human Rights, Report on National procedures for the selection of candidates for the European Court of Human Rights, Doc. 12391 (October 7, 2010) at para. 11.

[6] Committee of Ministers, Establishment of an Advisory Panel of Experts on Candidates for Election as Judge to the European Court of Human Rights—Implementation, CM/Del/Dec(2010)1101/1.7E (2010) at para. 5.

[7] *See* CM/Res(2014)44, with effect from November 26, 2014.

[8] PACE Recommendation 1429 (1999); PACE Recommendation 1649 (2004); PACE Resolution 1646 (2009) on the Nomination of Candidates and Election of Judges to the European Court of Human Rights.

appropriate specialized press, that they include at least one woman in their slate of three nominated candidates, and so on.[9]

As if this were not enough, the measures listed above are only those formally addressed to appointments to the ECtHR. As soon as one would also include the long list of measures passed, for example, under the rubric of "judicial independence," including the formal adoption of formal institutions applying formal rules in all domestic judicial matters, the list would explode in length.[10]

Furthermore, I have not even begun to list any of the measures adopted by the institutions of the EU. While the list of such measures pales in comparison to the blizzard of rules instituted under the auspices of the Council of Europe and especially the PACE, the EU has nonetheless significantly formalized its judicial appointment procedures.

Prior to the mass accession of former Eastern Bloc countries, there were essentially *no* formal EU rules regarding judicial appointment other than the basic Treaty provisions concerning the ECJ, which, as we have seen, effectively granted each Member State government a free hand to appoint whomever it wished. This changed with the Treaty of Lisbon, which established the Article 255 Panel. The Council accordingly passed a pair of decisions establishing the Panel's operating rules and appointing its members.[11] In addition to specifying that Panel members serve four-year terms and can be reappointed once, these rules formally establish the Panel's working methods, which specify, inter alia, that new judicial candidates shall be given a private hearing before the Panel, that the "deliberations of the panel shall take place *in camera*," that the Panel is to generate a "statement of reasons" that sets out "the principal grounds on which the panel's opinion is based," which "shall be forwarded to the Representatives of the Governments of the Member States," and so on.[12]

But the most important source of formal procedural rules has been the 255 Panel itself. As we have seen, the Panel decided unilaterally to publish an Activity Report (at first published annually), which it then leveraged to impose an impressive set of procedural requirements at the Member State level:

> [T]he panel, pursuant to point 6 of its operating rules, asks the government proposing the application to pass on the essential reasons why it chose the proposed

[9] *See id.*

[10] *See supra* Chapter 6.

[11] Council Decision 2010/124/EU of February 25, 2010 relating to the operating rules of the panel provided for in Article 255 of the Treaty on the Functioning of the European Union [2010] OJ L50/18; Council Decision 2010/125/EU of February 25, 2010 appointing the members of the panel provided for in Article 255 of the Treaty on the Functioning of the European Union [2010] OJ L50/20. *See* Vassilio Skouris, Recommendation relating to the operating rules of the panel provided for in Article 255 TFEU, Brussels, January 11, 2010, 5195/10, JUR 5 INST 2 COUR 1; Vassilio Skouris, Recommendation concerning the composition of the panel provided for in Article 255 TFEU, Brussels, February 2, 2010, 5932/10 JUR 57 INST 26 COUR 13.

[12] *See* Council Decision 2010/124/EU of February 25.

> candidate and a letter explaining the reasons for the application and a bibliographic list of the candidate's publications. The panel also asks for information on the national procedure that led to the candidate being selected, inviting the government to say inter alia whether there was a public call for applications, whether a national selection committee was set up and if so how the national selection committee was made up and what it recommended.[13]

The Panel then laid out detailed procedural rules governing its own European-level appointments assessments. Of these, the most important govern the hearing that the Panel conducts with each judicial candidate. They are formal and specific: the hearing lasts an hour, begins with a short candidate self-presentation, continues with a question and answer session in which questions are posed "in English or French, for 50 minutes, on the various aspects of the candidature (skills/expertise, experience, motivation, etc.)" to which the candidate "is asked to respond in the language in which the question was asked," [14] and which now proceeds "in two stages: a presentation by the candidate of the reasons for his or her candidature and a description of a legal case, followed by a discussion with the members of the panel."[15] In short, the Panel accomplished a degree of procedural formalization in its first Activity Report that rivals what the Council of Europe institutions achieved in its mountain of measures.

B. Substantive/Normative Formalization

As we noted in passing in Chapter 4, the European preference in the judicial appointments domain has been to institute procedural, rather than substantive, reforms. But this procedural preference (which can easily be read in substantive or normative terms) has by no means precluded the adoption of more explicitly substantive norms. The PACE has once again been a particularly active player in this regard. Its efforts in support of gender balance straddle the border between procedural and substantive reforms. Starting once again in the mid-1990s, the PACE passed a series of measures designed to ensure that all national judicial lists include at least one woman.[16] And in a clearly substantive vein, the PACE also repeatedly insisted that national authorities ensure that candidates have appropriate professional experience and linguistic capacities. In 1999, the PACE thus called upon

[13] Article 255 Panel, Activity Report of the Panel provided for by Article 255 of the Treaty on the Functioning of the European Union, First Report of February 17, 2011 (No. 6509/11) at 6.

[14] *Id.*

[15] Fourth Activity Report of February 10, 2017at 17.

[16] *See, e.g.*, PACE Order No. 519 (1996); 1999 Report on National Procedures for Nominating Candidates; PACE Resolution 1366 (2004); PACE Resolution 1426 (2005); and PACE Resolution 1627 (2008);

Member States to "ensure that the candidates have experience in the field of human rights, either as practitioners or as activists in non-governmental organisations working in this area" and "ensure that the candidates are in fact fluent in either French or English and are capable of working in one of these two languages."[17] It then reiterated these substantive requirements with growing impatience in 2004 and 2009.[18] As we have seen, the PACE eventually got to the point of threatening to reject entire national lists of candidates should its procedural and substantive requirements not be satisfied by the national authorities submitting lists to fill vacancies on the ECtHR,[19] a threat eventually concretized and explained in the Sawicki Memo we examined in Chapter 5.[20]

Although the APE itself did relatively little to delineate specific substantive norms that ECtHR candidates must satisfy, APE President Luzius Wildhaber, writing in his "Exchange of Views" with the Council of Europe's Ministers' Deputies, nonetheless elaborated on the Convention's requirement that ECtHR judges "must either possess the qualifications required for appointment to high judicial office or be jurisconsults of recognised competence": "the level of 'recognised competence' [for jurisconsults] is normally reached when a person has been professor at a well-known university for a significant number of years and has published important works, including works relating directly or indirectly to human rights protection."[21] Furthermore, this Treaty norm "would seem to exclude judges from lower national first-instance courts," although judges holding positions in higher national courts "should not, for that reason alone, be considered qualified" to serve on the Court.[22]

For its part, the Article 255 Panel had a great deal more to say regarding the substantive criteria required of ECJ candidates. Using the megaphone it had itself created by the invention and publication of its Activity Report, the Panel explained:

> Although the criteria established by the Treaty on the Functioning of the European Union are exhaustive, the panel nevertheless considers that they could be more clearly and precisely explained. The panel's assessment ... is therefore

[17] PACE Recommendation 1429 (1999).

[18] *See* PACE Recommendation 1649 (2004); PACE Resolution 1646 (2009) on the Nomination of Candidates and Election of Judges to the European Court of Human Rights.

[19] *See* PACE Resolution 1646 (2009) at para. 2 ("In the absence of a real choice among the candidates submitted by a state party to the Convention, the Assembly shall reject lists submitted to it. In addition, in the absence of a fair, transparent and consistent national selection procedure, the Assembly may reject such lists.")

[20] *See* Secretary General of the Assembly, "Procedure for the election of judges to the European Court of Human Rights," SG-AS (2019) 05 ["Sawicki Memo"]at para. 8; PACE Resolution 2278 (2019) at para. 2.4.2.

[21] 2012 Exchange of Views at paras. 11-12. 11–12.

[22] Steering Committee for Human Rights, Ministers' Deputies Exchange of Views with Mr. Luzius Wildhaber, Chairman of the Advisory Panel of Experts on Candidates for Election to the European Court of Human Rights (April 4, 2012), in DH-GDR (2013)005, February 5, 2013 at para. 2 (translation by the author).

> made on the basis of six considerations: the candidate's legal expertise, professional experience, ability to perform the duties of a Judge, assurance of independence and impartiality, language skills and aptitude for working as part of a team in an international environment in which several legal systems are represented.[23]

Although it stressed "that its assessment of the candidature is an overall assessment," the Panel nonetheless warned that "if a candidature is clearly lacking in one of these areas, this could be grounds for an unfavourable opinion."[24] As the Panel proved quite willing to reject candidates (it rejected about one out of every four first-time candidacies during its first four-year term of operation),[25] it soon became perfectly clear that it would be rash to flout the substantive norms that the Panel was elaborating. Indeed, the Panel's First Activity Report expounded on these norms in significant depth and detail, as we explained in Chapter 3.[26] It even took it upon itself to institute rather bright-line rules, such as those governing the second of the criteria listed above, i.e., the professional experience of candidates: absent "exceptional" circumstances, ECJ candidates must have at least "twenty years' experience of high level duties" (and General Court candidates, "twelve or even fifteen years") for their experience "to be deemed sufficient."[27]

In the end, the 255 Panel thus proved at least as willing as the PACE to elaborate and institute substantive norms to govern the assessment of judicial candidates to the high European courts. The formalization of the appointments process thus moved forward on the substantive front in addition to the procedural one.

C. Institutional Formalization

Finally, and as can be inferred from the analysis above, formalization also took new and important institutional shapes at both the ECtHR and the ECJ, and at both the domestic and the European levels. The most obvious manifestation of formal institutional reform is of course the establishment of the APE and the Article 255 Panel; but this represented only the culmination of a longer-term process of institutional formalization. At the PACE, for example, the Assembly has repeatedly reformulated its committee structure in order to address ECtHR judicial appointments ever more specifically. In 1995, for example, in preparation for Protocol 11's coming into effect, the PACE's Committee on Legal Affairs and Human Rights proposed that the review of newly formalized "model CVs" and of newly instituted candidate interviews be undertaken by "the Sub-Committee on Human Rights or

23 First Activity Report at 8–9.
24 *Id.* at 9.
25 *See* Third Activity Report of December 13, 2013 (No. SN 1118/2014)at 9.
26 *See supra* Chapter 3(II)(B).
27 *See* First Activity Report at 9.

by a special ad hoc sub-committee of the Committee on Legal Affairs and Human Rights."[28] In fact, the increasing formalization of such institutions continues to this day: in 2015, the PACE increased the profile and status of the Sub-Committee by formally re-establishing it as a newly freestanding "Committee on the Election of Judges to the European Court of Human Rights."[29] This new and full fledged Committee "interviews each of the three candidates in person, scrutinises their CVs and makes recommendations to the plenary Assembly concerning the qualifications of these candidates."[30]

Such institutional formalization has also been forcefully promoted at the domestic level. As we saw in detail in Chapter 6, a plethora of judicial independence measures have pushed Member States to establish formal institutions to govern all aspects of the judicial profession, including selection, training, promotion, retention, and discipline, and to formally report on them to the European authorities whenever candidates are proposed to the European courts.[31] This led to an increasing convergence on the institutional form of the judicial council, which functioned in turn as a prototype—or at the very least as an inspiration—for the European version of such institutions: the APE and the Article 255 Panel.

These two European panels obviously represent the crown jewel of the institutional formalization process for European judicial appointments. Both have been formally constituted by positive European legal measures: the Article 255 Panel by its namesake Article in the EU's Treaty of Lisbon and the APE by the (tellingly) less august avenue of a Resolution of the Council of Europe's Committee of Ministers.[32] As we have seen, they function on the basis of formal procedural rules and have become key institutional mechanisms that link the national nomination of judicial candidates and their eventual appointment to the high European Courts.[33]

Finally, we should not lose sight of what might well be the single most important example of institutional formalization in the European judicial domain as a whole: Protocol 11 to the European Convention on Human Rights (ECHR). This Protocol, negotiated during the heyday of accession of former Easter Bloc countries in the 1990s, transformed quite fundamentally the nature and structure of the ECtHR and its surrounding institutional apparatus: the Commission was abolished, the role of the Committee of Ministers was sharply

[28] PACE Committee on Legal Affairs and Human Rights (Rapporteur: Lord Kirkhill), Report on the procedure for examining candidatures for the election of judges to the European Court of Human Rights 1, Doc. 7439, 1403-15/12/95-1-E (1995) at 6.

[29] *See* http://assembly.coe.int/nw/Committees/as-cdh/as-cdh-main-EN.asp.

[30] *Id.* For a particularly knowledgeable description of the Committee and its work, *see* Andrew Drzemczewski, *The Parliamentary Assembly's Committee on the Election of Judges to the European Court of Human Rights*, 35 HRLJ 269 (2015).

[31] *See supra* Chapter 6.

[32] Committee of Ministers, Resolution CM/Res(2010)26 on the Establishment of an Advisory Panel of Experts on Candidates for Election as Judge to the European Court of Human Rights (November 10, 2010).

[33] *See supra* Parts I and II.

reduced, and individuals gained direct access to the Strasbourg Court, which, in gaining compulsory jurisdiction, thereby became the fulcrum of the Council of Europe.

Protocol 11 changed the nature of the European Convention system, which had originally been structured in such a manner as to minimize the effective role of the Strasbourg Court. By radically modifying the institutional "control machinery" in Strasbourg, Protocol 11 transformed the pre-existing ECHR regime, which had been primarily *diplomatic* in nature: in the great majority of instances, cases had been rejected or negotiated settlements had been worked out between Member State governments and the Commission rather than litigated before the ECtHR.[34] Protocol 11 changed this diplomatic state of affairs quite dramatically: suddenly, each and every dispute would go directly to the Court, where it would be litigated to its formal legal conclusion. A predominantly diplomatic and negotiated regime of informal settlements was thereby replaced by an overwhelmingly judicialized and legalized regime of formal norms and litigated disputes leading to formal judgments. Given this fundamental shift in the nature of the Convention system, it is hardly surprising that judicial appointments would become a focal point of attention.

The instantiation of all of these procedural, substantive, and institutional reforms has undoubtedly led to a depth and breadth of formalization in the judicial appointments domain that could hardly have been imagined prior to the mass accession of new Member States from the former Eastern Bloc, when national executive branch actors zealously guarded their traditional power to govern their judicial appointments according to their own political calculations. This formalization process began shortly after the fall of the Berlin Wall and has continued unabated to this day, eventually coming to dominate (if at times somewhat uneasily) the appointments process to the European high courts on both the national and the European levels. But this formalization represents but one of the two key developments in the European judicial appointments field. We now turn to the other: the promotion of judicial quality.

II. The Rise of Judicial Quality

A. The EU and Council of Europe Debates

The emergence of judicial quality as an important theme in debates over appointments to the European high courts can be traced directly to February 2003, when

[34] Y.S. Klerk & L. van Poelgeest, *Ratificatie* à contre coeur: *de reserves van de Nederlandse regering jegens het Europese Verdrag voor de Rechten van de Mens en het individueel klachtrecht*, RECHTSGELEERD MAGAZIJN ATHEMIS 220, 243 (1991).

the issue suddenly began to be actively discussed in two different official venues: (1) the Interights group of seven eminent and academically connected judges (mostly constitutional court judges), who met in London on February 14 to discuss the ECtHR's judicial appointments process and (2) the Discussion Circle on the Court of Justice, which met in Brussels on February 17, 2003 under the framework of the European Constitutional Convention.

The Interights discussions led to the publication the ensuing spring of a Report that was unusually blunt in its critique of the ECtHR's appointment system. It argued that the Court's "credibility and authority risk being undermined by the ad hoc and often politicised processes currently adopted in the appointment of its judges."[35] In addition to questioning "the independence and impartiality" of the Court's judges, it argued that "flawed appointment procedures leave open the prospect that judges selected will lack the requisite skills and abilities to discharge their duties ... ,which risks having an adverse effect on the Court's standing and on the development of authoritative human rights jurisprudence in Europe." The problems lay at both the national and the European levels:

> At a national level, States are given absolute discretion with respect to the nomination system they adopt. The Council of Europe does not provide guidelines on appropriate procedures; nor does it require States to report on or account for their national procedures. Even in the most established democracies, nomination often rewards political loyalty more than merit.
>
> At the international level, the Convention provides that the power to appoint judges lies solely with the Parliamentary Assembly. The Committee of Ministers has adopted a limited review role, which on paper allows it to question States' lists of nominees and nomination procedures. However, in practice the Committee of Ministers gives the impression of being more interested in safeguarding State sovereignty, than in ensuring the quality of candidates nominated.[36]

This framing of the issues, stated bluntly in the "executive summary" of the Interights Report, crystallized the alignment of issues: the politicization of the appointments process at the domestic level, reinforced at the European level, both threatens judicial independence and risks the appointment of unqualified candidates, which then threatens the Court's standing and jurisprudential authority. The key division, immediately recognizable in the passage above, is between politics/sovereignty on the one hand, and quality/merit on the other.

[35] Jutta Limbach et al., "Judicial Independence: Law and Practice of Appointments to the European Court of Human Rights" 4 (2003), available at http://www.interights.org/jud-ind-en/index.html ["Interights Report"].

[36] *Id.*

The Interights Report went further. It offered specific proposals designed to remedy the problems it had identified. Some addressed national selection procedures, for example, by proposing that States establish independent panels to arrive at the list of nominees to the Court. But others addressed the "international" (i.e., European) level of the appointments process. In particular, the Interights group proposed not only that the national candidates' lists and the procedures by which they were selected "be scrutinized by the Council Europe" and "be returned to the States" should they "not meet the prescribed minimum standards," but also that an independent body be established at the European level in order to advise the PACE on "the eligibility or suitability of candidates":

> The body making recommendations on the eligibility or suitability of candidates to the Parliamentary Assembly should itself be independent, follow a fair and open procedure and possess the requisite expertise to fulfil its role. This could be done by engaging a *body of independent persons* with relevant expertise, including persons with judicial experience, to provide advice to the Assembly on the candidates submitted to it. It would review the submitted curricula vitae and interview candidates thoroughly, with a view to identifying the most suitable professional judge. The independent body would provide reasons for its views. In the alternative, the existing Sub-Committee should be strengthened by having available to it a group of independent judicial assessors. The judicial assessors would be involved in the interviewing of candidates and would provide reasoned advice to the Sub-Committee with a view to identifying the most qualified candidate.[37]

The Interights Report had taken a major step. It had raised the issue of judicial quality; and it had linked it to the establishment of "a body of independent persons" to assess whether judicial candidates put forward by the Member States passed professional muster.

The Discussion Circle met in Brussels three days later. The record of its meeting, published by the end of the week, reinforced the same key step, this time in the EU context. Despite encountering opposition during its debates, the Discussion Circle elected to put forward the controversial proposal of establishing "a panel to assess the candidates," which would work hand in hand with the establishment of formal "criteria which would guarantee the professional quality, independence and impartiality of the candidates":

[37] *Id.* at 5 (emphasis in original). In 2017, the Open Society Justice Initiative offered similar recommendations in a broader international context. *See* Open Society Justice Initiative, Strengthening from Within: Law and Practice in the Selection of Human Rights Judges and Commissioners (2017). Its assessment of the Strasbourg appointments process was ultimately more positive, if only because of its juxtaposition to the Inter-American Court of Human Rights and the African Court on Human and Peoples' Rights.

> The idea of setting up a panel to assess the candidates was well received, although some members preferred to keep the present system; some members proposed that governments should put forward more than one candidate while others preferred a single candidate; the importance of establishing criteria which would guarantee the professional quality, independence and impartiality of the candidates was stressed . . . [38]

With the benefit of hindsight, we can of course see clearly that this proposed institutional innovation was in effect the embryo of the Article 255 Panel.

The Discussion Circle's generative moment not only launched the creation of the 255 Panel, but also framed it in a manner that has held sway ever since: it proposed the establishment of a formal institutional mechanism precisely in order to assess whether judicial candidates satisfied formal criteria of "professional quality, independence and impartiality." In other words, the Discussion Circle explicitly linked its institutional innovation not only to the judicial independence theme that had exploded during the period of mass accession of former Eastern Bloc States, but also to the emergent issue of judicial quality. On the eve of the mass accession of 2004, the Discussion Circle had reinforced the same key institutional and conceptual links as the Interights group: judicial quality and independence were to be secured via a combination of formalization and institutionalization.

Article 255 of the Lisbon Treaty is the "constitutional" manifestation of this alignment of issues. It establishes the Panel, which is "set up in order to give an opinion on candidates' suitability to perform the duties of Judge and Advocate-General . . . " As these candidates must "possess the qualifications required for appointment to the highest judicial offices in their respective countries or who are jurisconsults of recognised competence" (for the ECJ) or "possess the ability required for appointment to high judicial office" (for the General Court), the Panel would—at least as a practical matter—have to elaborate its conception of these "qualifications" and of this "ability."

As we saw at some length in Chapter 2, that is exactly what the Panel did: in its very first Activity Report, it formally published and elaborated upon the six substantive criteria by which it would make its assessment of candidates. In the words of the Panel,

> Although the criteria established by the Treaty on the Functioning of the European Union are exhaustive, the panel nevertheless considers that they could be more clearly and precisely explained. The panel's assessment . . . is therefore made on the basis of six considerations: the candidate's legal expertise, professional

[38] Record of the meeting on February 17, 2003 of the Discussion Circle on the Court of Justice, CONV 573/03, available at http://european-convention.europa.eu/pdf/reg/en/03/cv00/cv00573.en03.pdf.

> experience, ability to perform the duties of a Judge, assurance of independence and impartiality, language skills and aptitude for working as part of a team in an international environment in which several legal systems are represented.[39]

The Panel then spent the next two and a half pages working methodically through these six criteria.[40] Indeed, by the time of its Third Activity Report, the Panel's section of the "Assessment of candidates' suitability," though largely duplicative of its First Activity Report, would nonetheless run over four pages long, including subsections on "Assessment criteria" and "Clarification of the specific assessment of these criteria by the panel."[41] Happily, however, the Panel was able to report, as it already had the year before, that most of the candidates passed muster:

> In most cases, candidates have been able to demonstrate, by means of the information provided in the dossier and at their hearing, that they **fulfil the requirements** for appointment to the offices for which they were proposed. The quality of some candidatures—particularly in terms of legal abilities and professional experience—has even been extremely impressive, if not outstanding.[42]

The language of quality, which had appeared on the scene at the critical historical juncture when the great collection of former Eastern Bloc countries was about to accede to the EU, when the constitutional Convention was taking place, and when the Article 255 Panel was formally proposed, had now emerged in the Panel's own Report.

This set of associations has proven to be solid and enduring. The Council of Europe's APE, for example, clearly represents the product of combining a concern for judicial quality with calls for the establishment of a formal institutional mechanism for assessing judicial candidates. As we saw in Chapter 4, the proposal to establish the APE was advanced by the work of three important groups: the 2003 Interights group, the "Group of Wise Persons" convened in 2005 by the Heads of State of the Council of Europe Member States "to consider the long-term effectiveness of the ECHR control mechanism,"[43] and the 2010 Interlaken Conference on the Future of the ECtHR. Each stressed the quality, qualifications, expertise, experience, etc. of ECtHR judicial candidates; and each proposed the establishment of some sort of panel of eminent jurists to vet the candidates put forward by the Member States for election by the PACE.

39 First Activity Report at 8–9.

40 *See id.* at 9–11.

41 *See* Third Activity Report at 17–21. The same holds true for the Fourth. *See* Fourth Activity Report at 22–26.

42 *Id.* at 20 (emphasis in original). *See also* Second Activity Report of January 22, 2013 (No. 5091/13) at 13.

43 Report of the Group of Wise Persons to the Committee of Ministers, CM(2006)203 at para. 1.

The 2006 Report of the Group of Wise Persons followed up on the 2003 Interights Report (discussed above) by proposing the formation of a "committee of prominent personalities" to vet the professional and linguistic qualifications of judicial candidates:

> Secondly, the Group considers that the professional qualifications and knowledge of languages of candidates for the post of judge should be carefully examined during the election procedure.
>
> For this purpose, before the Parliamentary Assembly considers the candidatures, an opinion on the suitability of the candidates could be given by a committee of prominent personalities possibly chosen from among former members of the Court, current and former members of national supreme or constitutional courts and lawyers with acknowledged competence.[44]

The Group of Wise Persons had added some detail to the Interights proposal; but the underlying logic remained the same.

The 2010 Interlaken Ministerial Conference on the Future of the European Court of Human Rights offered the next iteration. In preparation for the Conference, Secretary General Thorbjørn Jagland linked "the idea of a mixed screening panel composed of prominent former high level national or international judges" not only to "ensur[ing] the highest levels of expertise and relevant experience on the part of the Court's judiciary," but also to "the standing and credibility of the Court itself" and to the "authority of the Court's case law":

> 18. The authority of the Court's case law depends in part on the **standing and credibility of the Court** itself, including in the eyes of the judges of the highest national courts whose own decisions may be subject to its scrutiny. Along with independence and impartiality, therefore, it is important also to ensure the highest levels of expertise and relevant experience on the part of the Court's judiciary. Bearing in mind the various Parliamentary Assembly proposals, as well as the 2003 Interights report, States should ensure that they have transparent national selection procedures for candidates for election as judge. The criteria for office and election procedures could also be reviewed. In this context, we should examine the idea of a mixed screening panel composed of prominent former high level national or international judges before transmitting the list of candidates to the Parliamentary Assembly for election.[45]

[44] *Id.* at paras. 117–18.

[45] Contribution of the Secretary General of the Council of Europe to the Preparation of the Interlaken Ministerial Conference, SG/Inf(2009)20, December 18, 2009 (emphasis in original).

Although the Conference as a whole did not specifically endorse the panel suggestion put forward by its Secretary General, it did adopt an "Action Plan" that wholeheartedly adopted the language of quality while calling upon the Member States and the Council of Europe to take necessary action:

> 8. Stressing the importance of maintaining the independence of the judges and of preserving the impartiality and quality of the Court, the Conference calls upon States Parties and the Council of Europe to:
>
> a) ensure, if necessary by improving the transparency and quality of the selection procedure at both national and European levels, full satisfaction of the Convention's criteria for office as a judge of the Court, including knowledge of public international law and of the national legal systems as well as proficiency in at least one official language. In addition, the Court's composition should comprise the necessary practical legal experience.[46]

The table was now set for a specific proposal to be formally put forward.

That proposal was advanced in June of 2010, when the sitting President of the ECtHR, Jean-Paul Costa, sent a letter to the "permanent representatives" of the Member States of the Council of Europe (i.e., the national ambassadors in Strasbourg) advocating the establishment of a panel of senior experts to "advise" Member States about the list of candidates they intended to put forward to the PACE for election to the ECHR. His letter opens as follows:

> Dear Ambassador,
>
> As you know, point 8 of the Interlaken Action Plan calls upon the states parties and the Council of Europe to "ensure, if necessary by improving the transparency and quality of the selection procedure at both national and European levels, full satisfaction of the Convention's criteria for office as a judge of the Court, including knowledge of public international law and of the national legal systems as well as proficiency in at least one official language."
>
> In terms of the future of the Court and therefore the Convention system, one of the decisive factors will be the quality of its Judges. Whatever reforms are undertaken, the system will fail if judges do not have the necessary experience and authority.
>
> The quality of the Judges is important not only to guarantee the high standard of the decisions delivered and the jurisprudence developed. It is also essential because, in a subsidiary system where human rights protection falls primarily to the

46 High Level Conference on the Future of the European Court of Human Rights, Interlaken Declaration of February 19, 2010, Action Plan at para. 8, available at http://www.echr.coe.int/Documents/2010_Interlaken_FinalDeclaration_ENG.pdf.

> national courts, the European Court as the ultimate arbiter of human rights issues must be composed of persons of sufficient standing and authority to command the respect of national judges, including senior national judges. If this is not the case, the Court itself will suffer from a deficit of authority and the system will lose credibility and effectiveness.[47]

With this dramatic *cri de cœur*, President Costa made judicial "quality" the linchpin of the very survival of the ECHR: he solemnly declared not only that that the "quality of [the Court's] Judges" was a "decisive factor" for "the future of the Court," but that the entire ECHR "system will fail if judges do not have the necessary experience and authority."[48]

Faced with the publication of such an alarming—and arguably alarmist—claim penned by such an important figure, the Member States and the Council of Europe could not help but seriously consider President Costa's proposal to establish the APE to help vet judicial candidates that might be put forward for election to the Strasbourg Court. And as we know, the APE quickly came into existence: it was established by a Resolution of the Committee of Ministers on November 10, 2010, barely six months after Costa had signed his letter.[49]

But it is also worth noting the full extent to which the establishment of the APE went hand in hand with the full-throated adoption of the language of "quality." In almost every relevant Council of Europe measure or report beginning from the 2010 period, the issue of the quality of the Court, its judges, and/or its case-law was raised in one way or another. In a string of instances, these measures stated, for example:

> The authority of the Court is contingent on the stature of judges and the *quality* and coherence of the Court's case law. In this context it is the Assembly's responsibility to elect judges of the *highest calibre* to the Court from a list of three candidates nominated by states parties. Recalling its Resolution 1646 (2009) on the nomination of candidates and election of judges to the European Court of Human Rights, the Assembly reaffirms its call that national selection procedures must be rigorous, fair and transparent in order to enhance the *quality*, efficacy and authority of the Court.[50]
>
> Recalling the Interlaken Declaration whereby the High Contracting Parties to the Convention and the Council of Europe were invited to ensure the full

[47] Jean-Paul Costa, Letter from the President of the European Court of Human Rights, addressed to member states' Permanent Representatives (Ambassadors) on June 9, 2010.

[48] *See id.*

[49] *See* Committee of Ministers, Resolution CM/Res(2010)26 on the Establishment of an Advisory Panel of Experts on Candidates for Election as Judge to the European Court of Human Rights (November 10, 2010).

[50] PACE Resolution 1726 on "Effective implementation of the European Convention on Human Rights: the Interlaken process" (April 19, 2010) at para. 7 (emphasis added).

> satisfaction of the Convention's criteria for office as a judge of the Court and the importance of ensuring the impartiality and *quality* of the Court.[51]
>
> It follows that, as "[t]he authority of the Court is contingent on the stature of judges and the *quality* and coherence of the Court's case law" (paragraph 7 of Assembly Resolution 1726 (2010) on the effective implementation of the European Convention on Human Rights: the Interlaken process), the Assembly fully supports all attempts by states parties to enhance the *quality* of candidates transmitted to it, in particular by improving, where necessary, national selection procedures. Seen from this perspective, the recent initiative of the President of the Court to set up a panel to advise governments before lists of candidates are transmitted to the Assembly is welcome.[52]
>
> The Parliamentary Assembly, whose task, by virtue of Article 22 of the European Convention on Human Rights (ETS No. 5—the Convention), is to elect judges of the *highest calibre* to the European Court of Human Rights (the Court) from a list of three candidates nominated by states parties, underlines the importance of appropriate national selection procedures in order to ensure and reinforce the *quality*, efficacy and authority of the Court.[53]
>
> This initiative by President Costa is welcome, in that the clear intention behind it is to ensure that lists transmitted to the Assembly consist of three candidates of the highest *quality* ... That said, even if I am of the view that this, and any other attempt to help us—the states concerned and the Assembly—ensure that lists of candidates transmitted to the Assembly are composed of three jurists of *outstanding calibre*, certain critical comments can nevertheless be made with respect to this proposal ... That said, as the initiative of President Costa is made in the spirit of enhancing the *quality* of candidates to be transmitted to the Assembly, I believe that this proposal is worthy of serious consideration. [54]

The language of judicial quality has become an utterly central feature of the European judicial appointments debates.

Indeed, the rapid establishment of the APE did nothing to stop the ongoing flow of such language. To the contrary, it was fully incorporated within the formal language of the governing Council of Europe measures and has visibly resurfaced, especially in moments of tension. Thus, for example, when the Committee of Ministers of the Council of Europe published its "Guidelines of the Committee of Ministers on the selection of candidates for the post of judge at the European Court of Human Rights" in 2012, it opened the document as follows:

[51] Resolution CM/Res(2010)26 on the Establishment of an Advisory Panel of Experts on Candidates for Election as Judge to the European Court of Human Rights (November 10, 2010) (emphasis added).

[52] PACE Doc. 12391, National procedures for the selection of candidates for the European Court of Human Rights (October 7, 2010) at para. 4 (emphasis added).

[53] *Id.* at Wohlwend Report, para. 1 (emphasis added).

[54] *Id.* at para. 11 (emphasis added).

> The Committee of Ministers,
>
> Underlining the fundamental importance of the High Contacting Parties' role in proposing candidates of the highest possible *quality* for election as judges of the European Court of Human Rights (hereinafter "the Court"), so as to preserve the impartiality and *quality* of the Court, thereby reinforcing its authority and credibility;
>
> Recalling Articles 21 and 22 of the European Convention on Human Rights (hereinafter "the Convention", ETS No. 5), which, respectively, set out the criteria for office and entrust the Parliamentary Assembly with the task of electing judges from a list of three candidates nominated by each High Contracting Party;
>
> Recalling the Declaration adopted at the High Level Conference on the Future of the European Court of Human Rights (Interlaken, Switzerland, 18 and 19 February 2010), which stressed the importance of maintaining the independence of the judges and of preserving the impartiality and *quality* of the Court;
>
> Recalling also the Declaration adopted at the High Level Conference on the Future of the European Court of Human Rights (Izmir, Turkey, 26 and 27 April 2011), which cited the need to encourage applications by good potential candidates for the post of judge at the Court, and to ensure a sustainable recruitment of competent judges, with relevant experience, and the impartiality and *quality* of the Court... [55]

The Ministers could hardly have done more to foreground the centrality of quality in the judicial selection process. But just to underline the point, the first paragraph of their "Explanatory Memorandum" attached to those Guidelines boldly states:

> 1. The human rights protection system based upon the European Convention on Human Rights ("the Convention") is in large part distinguished and made effective by the judicial nature of its control mechanism, the European Court of Human Rights ("the Court"). The authority and credibility of that Court, and thus of the Convention system as a whole, depends upon the *quality* of its judges. Each judge of the Court is elected by the Parliamentary Assembly from a list of three candidates nominated by a High Contracting Party. It is therefore vital that these candidates are of the highest possible *quality*.[56]

President Costa's highly dramatic depiction of how the entire ECHR "system will fail" should its judges not be of sufficient "quality" and possess "the necessary

[55] CM(2012)40 (March 28, 2012) (emphasis added).

[56] CM(2012)40 addendum final, Guidelines of the Committee of Ministers on the selection of candidates for the post of judge at the European Court of Human Rights (March 29, 2012) (emphasis added).

experience and authority" had effectively been internalized by the Ministers and incorporated into their core descriptions of the Convention system.[57]

Similarly, when the APE's Chair, Luzius Wildhaber, was eventually driven to complain to the Ministers about the assorted ways in which Member States and the PACE were failing to allow the APE to play the key role that he had envisaged, he framed his objection in the same terms:

> The Panel's contribution to the overall aim of ensuring the *quality* of the elected judges can only be meaningful if its opinion is sought in time, respected and taken into account by the High Contracting Parties. And here I am touching a soft point. While the Panel is aware that its opinions are not legally binding, there is a political undertaking to respect the Panel's opinions on suitability of the candidates proposed. This would seem to include an agreement not to submit to PACE candidates which have been rejected as unfit by the Panel. This is, precisely, the rationale of the creation of the Panel; its very *raison d'être*.[58]

To President Wildhaber, the APE was all about policing the quality of judicial candidates.

Finally, when the Committee of Ministers' Steering Committee for Human Rights responded to President Wildhaber's complaints in its own report on the functioning of the APE, it too adopted the same language of judicial quality, even though it hardly granted the APE the significant procedural power it was seeking. Linking the legitimacy of the ECtHR to "the integrity and *quality* of its judgments," it immediately made the now obligatory incantation of judicial quality: "The Parliamentary Assembly has exclusive competence for electing Court judges, but the *quality* of those judges depends in the first place on the *quality* of the candidates that are nominated by the States Parties. If a list is not composed of *qualified* candidates, the most that the Assembly can do is reject it."[59] This is precisely why President Costa had "called on the States Parties to set up a panel of independent experts to ensure the quality of the candidates for election"; and this is why the APE had been established.[60] As was the case in the EU context, the establishment of the expert panel to vet judicial candidates went hand in hand with the rise of this language of judicial quality.

[57] *See id.*

[58] Advisory Panel of Experts on Candidates for Election as Judge to the European Court of Human Rights, Proposals made by the Panel in its submission to the CDDH in May 2013, in Final Activity Report for the Committee of Ministers at 2 (emphasis added).

[59] CCDH(2013)R79 Addendum II, CDDH Report on the review of the functioning of the Advisory Panel of experts on candidates for election as judge to the European Court of Human Rights (November 29, 2013) at paras. 1–2 (emphasis added).

[60] *See id.* at paras. 4–5.

B. The Academic Debates

When discussing judicial appointments reform, scholars have been no less keen than the European institutions to harp on the goal of increasing the quality of judicial candidates to the ECJ and the ECtHR. Although a more dedicated analysis of the European academic literature will have to await the next Part, it is important for us to recognize here that the discourse of judicial quality has thoroughly permeated scholarly discussions on the subject.

Probably the most outspoken critic of European judicial appointment practices is the heretofore impassive German publisher Norbert Paul Engel. In a short but altogether remarkable 2012 article tellingly entitled "More Transparency and Governmental Loyalty for Maintaining Professional Quality in the Election of Judges to the European Court of Human Rights"[61] (which we will discuss at length in Part V), Engel harped repeatedly on the "quality" and "qualifications" of judges on the European bench. In the opening section of his article, entitled "The unresolved quality problem in brief," Engel laid out the core of the issue. ECtHR President Costa had sent out his "signal of alarm" to the Committee of Ministers ("The [Convention] system will fail if judges do not have the necessary experience and authority") in response to the recent appointment of unacceptable candidates to fill positions on the Court. In "a reluctant minimalist reaction" to this "urgent warning," the Ministers had established the APE, but "vested [it] with less than real power." And they had done so "despite the existence of a convincing blueprint of a panel solution established by the European Union to make maintenance of judicial quality a matter of public record for the nomination of judges for the [ECJ]."[62]

In response to this state of affairs, Engel put forward "Four proposals for improving the professional quality on the Strasbourg bench." The proposals were quite straightforward: (1) the APE should formally submit its review of judicial candidates not only to the government that proposed them, but also to all forty-seven of the Member States and (2) to the PACE Sub-Committee in charge of judicial elections; (3) the Sub-Committee's ensuing recommendation ranking the candidates should be made public rather than confidentially sent to the MEPs; and (4) the Sub-Committee should not move forward on a national list that had not been "certified" by the APE.[63] The reader should easily recognize that these four proposals would significantly alter the dynamics of the judicial appointments process at the ECtHR, in effect bringing the APE far more into line with the EU's Article 255 model. Indeed, Engel does not hide that he would consider this a great improvement: "Contrary to the EU system for ensuring quality on the bench, the solution of the Committee of Ministers of the Council of Europe has proven its inefficacy."[64]

61 32 Hum. Rts L.J. 448 (2012).
62 *Id.* at 448–49.
63 *Id.* at 449.
64 *Id.*

As can readily be surmised, Engel's seminal article revolves around the issue of judicial "quality." Not only does the term figure prominently in the title and subtitles of the article, but it also emerges no fewer than thirteen times over the course of the article's seven printed pages. To this one can add nine further references to "qualification(s)" and to "qualified" or "unqualified" judicial candidates; and this is to say nothing of the numerous references to "(un-)suitable" candidates and so on.

And yet, the article does characteristically little to define what judicial quality might actually mean. It does, however, give two examples of problematic candidacies that shed some light. The first involved a candidate (eventually elected) who was professionally inexperienced and unusually young ("just 33 years of age at the time of her nomination").[65] The second involved another (who eventually withdrew) who was linguistically deficient: he "had so little knowledge of the second official language (English) that both [the APE and the Sub-Committee] considered him unsuitable."[66] For all that the Engel article endlessly refers to judicial quality, it therefore does little if anything to define or elaborate on it; it merely reiterates the by now classic minimum demands of age/experience and linguistic capacity.

Writing insightfully on the "social legitimacy" of the ECtHR, Başak Çali, Anne Koch, and Nicola Bruch touch repeatedly on the perceived quality of ECtHR judges in the eyes of domestic political, legal, and judicial elites, but also offer no insight into what such quality might entail. Thus, "UK interviewees were strikingly negative in their assessments of the quality of the judges of the Strasbourg Court,"[67] "Irish respondents ... shared the concern about the quality of Strasbourg judges with their British counterparts,"[68] and "[t]he quality of Strasbourg judges is one concern that figured in German interviews";[69] but the authors do not plumb what the nature of such quality might be. Instead, they simply note the inverse correlation between the respondents' trust in domestic institutions and their esteem for the quality of ECtHR judges. Hence, "the quality of the Strasbourg judges is not a significant concern where the trust in the domestic decision-making is low";[70] and, conversely, "if domestic institutions are valued highly and/or the human rights situation is assessed as positive ... stronger forms of judicial review by the Court ... and concerns about the quality of international judges ... are not only routine criticisms but signal legitimacy erosion and inform deeper trends that undermine respect for the institution."[71] Once again, therefore, judicial quality emerges

[65] *Id.* at 451.

[66] *Id.*

[67] Başak Çali, Anne Koch, & Nicola Bruch, *The Social Legitimacy of Human Rights Courts: A Grounded Interpretivist Theory of the Legitimacy of the European Court of Human Rights*, 35 Hum. Rts. Q. 955, 970 (2013).

[68] *Id.* at 971

[69] *Id.*

[70] *Id.* at 979.

[71] *Id.* at 981.

as an important area of concern in the academic literature; yet such quality remains oddly undefined and unexamined.

Even the recent publication of the volume edited by Michal Bobek, SELECTING EUROPE'S JUDGES: A CRITICAL REVIEW OF THE APPOINTMENT PROCEDURES TO THE EUROPEAN COURTS—which, taken together, undoubtedly represents by far the best and most complete scholarly work to date on the subject—does little to clarify matters, despite the obvious importance that its contributors attach to the issue. As Koen Lemmens states in a manner that reproduces quite faithfully the "signal of alarm" sent by President Costa to the Committee of Ministers, "The reform of the selection process has two clear goals: it aimed at preserving the impartiality of the Court and at assuring the quality of the judges. Nothing less than the credibility of the Court is indeed at stake."[72] Lemmens embeds this quality concern in a "conflict of values ... between technocratic legitimacy and democratic legitimacy": the APE and the PACE's Sub-Committee represent a means to navigate the conflict between what he describes as the meritocratic and quality-oriented selection panels that have increasingly been established at the national level and the politically-oriented electoral process of the PACE.[73] On this procedural reading, the APE and the PACE's Sub-Committee function to "double-check" quality in order to ensure that a mistake was not made at the national level, which then removes the sting from the political machinations at the European level:

> Undeniably, at the level of the Parliamentary Assembly, politics play a dominant role; however, since the improved quality-check has already filtered out unfit candidates, political games should not have an impact on the quality of the judges to be elected.[74]

Although this analysis effectively captures some of the key conceptual dynamics in play and does advance eminently reasonable pragmatic conclusions, it too makes little attempt to explain what such "quality" might actually entail.

Even more pronounced is the chapter authored by David Kosař, which gives no quarter in its critique of the operation of the ECtHR's judicial selection process. Building explicitly off of the articles by Engel and Çali et al. we have just discussed, Kosař paints a dramatic picture of the lack of professional standing of the ECtHR's judges:

> The key message of this cross-country comparison is that the qualifications and experience of Strasbourg judges have been questioned not just in the United

[72] Koen Lemmens, "(S)electing Judges for Strasbourg: A (Dis)appointing Process?," in MICHAL BOBEK ed., SELECTING EUROPE'S JUDGES: A CRITICAL REVIEW OF THE APPOINTMENT PROCEDURES TO THE EUROPEAN COURTS 95, 100 (2015) ["Bobek (2015)"].

[73] *See id.* at 117.

[74] *Id.*

Kingdom. Interviewees from all countries covered by Çali's study, apart from Bulgaria, were very critical and dissatisfaction with the quality of Strasbourg judges is thus more widespread than expected.

In sum, there is a growing consensus that how judges are selected has an impact on the ECtHR's legitimacy. Çali's findings show how widespread and deep the negative perception of the quality of Strasbourg judges is. The criticism raised by other authors confirms the depth and breadth of the problems concerning the selection of Strasbourg judges. The current situation might have become worse than Çali's findings suggest. It is important to take into account the fact that interviews were conducted between 2008 and 2010, which is before several recent controversies broke concerning the selection of Strasbourg judges, and before the problems concerning the selection of judges became a salient issue in academic literature.[75]

Focusing on deeply practical and problematic features of the ECtHR's selection procedure—ranging from (a) the unwillingness of risk-averse candidates to submit themselves to an uncertain fate at the hands of the Strasbourg electoral process to (b) adopting a retirement age sufficiently low to pre-empt "very top candidates from certain old Council of Europe States ... to [be 'hired'] after their compulsory retirement in their home countries"[76]—Kosař poses the straightforward question: "how can one attract top candidates?"[77] And here, as in all the other academic analyses, the analysis stops: what exactly constitutes such a top quality candidate is just never really developed.

For Kosař, as for Engel, the solution is nonetheless clear: the ECtHR must reform its selection process in such a manner as to bring it into line with the single candidate veto system of the ECJ. As Kosař argues: "[T]hat is the way it works in Luxembourg and it works much better than the Strasbourg rule. To my knowledge, no one has questioned the qualifications, experience or stature of Luxembourg judges."[78] Indeed, Kosař believes so strongly in the primacy of judicial quality over other selection considerations that he flatly states: "It is thus critical to move beyond second-tier principles such as non-politicization, diversity and the transparency of national procedures, and pay more attention to the higher-level principles of professional competence and integrity."[79]

As a final example of the attention paid by the scholarly literature to the issue of judicial quality, let me turn to the contribution of Michal Bobek, who edited the important new volume on judicial appointments to the European courts.[80] To

[75] David Kosař, *Selecting Strasbourg' Judges: A Critique*, *in* Bobek (2015) at 120, 126–27 (citations omitted).
[76] *Id.* at 139.
[77] *Id.* at 156.
[78] *Id.* at 160.
[79] *Id.* at 161 (citations omitted).
[80] *See* Michal Bobek, *Epilogue: Searching for the European Hercules*, *in* Bobek (2015) at 279.

Bobek—now an Advocate General at the ECJ—there is just no question but that the advisory panels were created in order to promote the quality of candidates to the European courts. Although the EU and the Council of Europe are obviously different, "both are international organisations, both have supranational courts, and in both organisations questions of the quality of judicial appointments arose recently together with the desire of carrying out some reforms in this regard."[81] As a result, "both introduced institutional changes at roughly the same time with a similar goal: to strengthen the quality and professionalism of their judges, and thus to enhance the authority and legitimacy of their respective courts."[82]

Viewed as such quality-oriented institutions, Bobek concludes that the Panels—and especially the Article 255 Panel—have been fairly successful. "On the whole," he writes, "there is no doubt that having and enforcing at least some minimalist criteria for the appointment to European courts is a progress in terms of ensuring basic quality of the appointees." But this does not mean that problems no longer remain:

> The positive overall assessment of the operation of the expert panels in European judicial selections, in particular as far as the 255 Panel is concerned, should nonetheless not be stretched too far. There has certainly been an improvement contrasted with several years ago. It might be criticized as a rather pragmatic progress by stealth, focused on the technocratic outcome and not on the democratic process, but it is clearly an improvement in terms of ensuring the quality of judicial appointees. This should, however, not lull the observer into believing that all is now fine . . . [83]

As this passage demonstrates, quality has become one of the most central focal points of scholarly analysis of the European judicial appointments reforms; but it functions in a conceptual field populated by other related terms. In particular, Bobek (like Lemmens) places quality within a straightforward binary opposition between the technocratic and the political, locating it firmly on the technocratic side.[84] Meanwhile, this opposition is itself accompanied by yet another: the distinction between transparent and veiled appointment processes.

This set of distinctions yields a seemingly straightforward alignment of issues, values, and institutions. On one side is the technocratic and transparent; on the other, the political and veiled. Bobek states, for example, in response to the PACE "upgrading its Sub-Committee on the Election of Judges to the European Court of

[81] *Id* at 281.
[82] *Id.*
[83] *Id.* at 306
[84] *Cf.* Lemmens, *(S)electing Judges for Strasbourg in* Bobek (2015) at 117.

Human Rights into a permanent and full committee," which might empower this political institution relative to the APE:

> In sum, the search for a new balance between the democratic and the technocratic within the Council of Europe's judicial selections following the insertion of the new Advisory Panel might eventually be resolved by a re-affirmation of the political element. On the whole, however, this victory might be quite short-lived, unless serious attention starts being given also to the professional quality of the candidates by the political bodies in charge.[85]

The binary oppositions thus yield normative payoffs: If the political element is to be empowered at the expense of the technocratic element, then it must adopt some of the latter's quality-orientation. But if the technocratic is to be empowered, then it must deliver at least some of the transparency that distinguishes it from unprincipled political deal-making:

> Last, apart from the functional or legal arguments, there are powerful symbolic considerations. Three of them may be highlighted. First, there is a certain justificatory narrative that accompanied the birth of the expert panels. It pictured knowledgeable experts who will bring the light of rational quality decision-making into the dark corridors of shabby political deals, disguised behind the veil of state sovereignty. Such a narrative, if it is to be believed and to provide on-going legitimacy for these expert bodies, brings with it an implied promise of a different operation, a different style, and also a different level of transparency and control than those uncontrolled and unprincipled diplomats could ever provide.[86]

In Bobek's analysis, quality must not therefore operate "by stealth." If it does, then technocratic governance loses its claim to offer greater democratic legitimacy than its crude political rival.

As should now be apparent, the emergence of the language of judicial quality has been a major development in both the institutional realm of the EU and the Council of Europe and the scholarly realm of academic debate. This focus on judicial quality has provided a focal point for discussions on the need for, and success of, judicial appointments reform. At the same time, however, it should be reasonably apparent that this turn to judicial quality has not been accompanied by a concomitant discussion about just what such judicial quality might actually mean or entail. Judicial quality has instead been deployed as a very vaguely defined, if very frequently invoked, term that stands at the confluence of several basic if recurring

[85] Bobek (2015) at 288.
[86] *Id.* at 297.

distinctions: the technocratic vs. the democratic, the judicial vs. the political, the European vs. the domestic, the transparent vs. the opaque, and so on. It is time, therefore, to start deciphering the role that judicial quality and the formalization of judicial appointment criteria, processes, and institutions have played in the development of European judicial institutions over the last ten to twenty years.

9
Formalized Quality in Operation

I. Removing and Imposing Control

The first and probably most obvious consequence of both the formalization and the quality-orientation of the European judicial appointments process is to free judges and judicial candidates from some degree of national governmental control. Take formalization, for example. As we discussed in Chapter 8, the formalization process has been conspicuously aggressive, extensive, and persistent, even if it remains forever incomplete. The Parliamentary Assembly of the Council of Europe (PACE) has passed and passed again umpteen measures that formalize the process by which judges are to be selected, nominated, and appointed at both the domestic and the European levels. These measures formalize not only such substantive norms as those governing the qualifications for judicial office and the gender makeup of candidate lists, but also the procedural and institutional structures under which judicial nominations and appointments are to proceed at both the domestic and the European levels.

It is undoubtedly true that this formalization process, for all of its conspicuousness, remains in important respects incomplete, especially at the Council of Europe. These imperfections notwithstanding, the hoops that Member State governments must now regularly jump through to select and nominate their candidates for European judicial office are relatively clear, thorough, and significant. Indeed, the annoyance transparently shown by institutions such as the Consultative Council of European Judges at the persistence of some "informal appointment procedures and overtly political influence on judicial appointments in certain"[1] established Western European Member States only serves to underline the relatively exceptional character of such holdovers. Furthermore, even such governmental outliers must now run the gauntlet of the formalized European norms, processes, and institutions, notwithstanding their refusal to accept similarly formalized mechanisms at the domestic level.

These assorted modes of formalization represent a clear change from the prior regime, under which European judicial appointments were governed by highly informal, decentralized, and deferential mechanisms that effectively accorded

[1] Consultative Council of European Judges, "Opinion No. 1 on Standards Concerning the Independence of the Judiciary and the Irremovability of Judges," CCJE (2001) OP No. 1 ["CCJE Opinion No. 1 on the Independence of the Judiciary"], available at https://rm.coe.int/1680747830at para. 34.

national governments the unilateral power to place their chosen candidates in European judicial office. As the European judicial independence measures make quite explicit, the purpose of the appointment and other judicial reforms has been precisely to free the judiciary from such political (especially, executive branch) control.

The judicial quality measures have done a similar job of limiting the capacity of domestic governmental actors to exert unilateral and unfettered political control over their national candidates for European judicial office (including those already sitting on the European bench). Of course, judicial quality is—even more than bare formalization—a value in its own right. But to state the obvious, this value clearly did not rank sufficiently highly in the recent Western European context for it to be promoted at the European level, despite the fact that no knowledgeable observer would have been so naïve as to believe that the quality of European judges (or domestic ones, for that matter) was uniformly sublime. To the contrary, the established Member States had guarded their influence over European judicial appointments rather zealously, as we have seen in some detail.[2] But mass accession reordered priorities.

As a result, judicial quality has functioned as a thinly veiled critique. Given that its emergence as a subject of controversy can be dated quite clearly to the post-accession period, no well-informed analyst could fail to grasp what had triggered the newfound concern. As with the judicial independence literature, the judicial quality concerns were obviously not directed by German, French, English, or Dutch observers toward their own judicial candidates; they were aimed at the new Member States and at their potentially troublesome nominees.

Viewed in this light, it becomes increasingly clear that the judicial quality debates—in parallel to and in tandem with the formalization process—function as a rather clever means of *imposing* control over judicial appointments and not merely as a means of *freeing* judges *from* control. This proposition calls for more sustained analysis. So let's walk through the reasoning step by step.

To begin the analysis, we can easily recognize that formalization and quality both operate to free judges and judicial candidates from some measure of Member State government control. Hemmed in by formal norms, processes, and institutions as well as by the demands imposed by quality requirements, judicial appointments (and reappointments) can move forward in a manner less beholden to political power. In this respect, both formalization and quality function in large part as judicial independence mechanisms. But that is only part of the story.

Recall that for Garoupa and Ginsburg and to some extent Epstein and Burbank, judicial independence exists in counterpoint to judicial accountability. In the Garoupa/Ginsburg version, calls for judicial independence are a response to

[2] *See supra* Chapters 2 and 4.

judicial weakness relative to the governing political power; this occurs when a servile and non-policy-making judiciary is overly beholden to the political powers-that-be, as in the paradigmatic authoritarian regime.[3]

As we suggested in Chapter 7, the key to making use of this insight is to recognize that European judicial appointments are a multi-level game. True, almost no one would suggest that the two European Courts have done anything but grow their power exponentially and to exercise that power in deeply policy-making (and even constitutionally formative) ways. But this judicial policy-making power *on the institutional level* should not mask the reality that European judges can be quite weak and vulnerable *as individuals* relative to their own domestic governments, especially when they are candidates for appointment or reappointment to European judicial office. Indeed, the same holds true for those judges when they look forward toward their *departure* from European judicial posts, when they will likely be seeking judicial, academic, or governmental positions back home.[4]

Under these conditions, the domestic and European establishment of formal institutions to manage judicial appointments, of formal norms to govern them, and of formal appointment processes to run them, all undoubtedly functions to promote judicial independence: such measures limit the capacity of Member State governments to monkey around with judicial appointments to the European courts or, at least, make it significantly more difficult for them to do so. The less effectively governments can pull the strings on European judicial appointments, the more European judges and judicial candidates can behave independently of those governments.

Let me therefore state the interaction of the issues clearly and succinctly. First, the calls for judicial independence have undoubtedly been a response to judicial weakness, but on the *domestic*, as opposed to the *European*, level. Second, this weakness is of an *individual*, as opposed to an *institutional* nature. Third, this individual judicial *weakness* on the home front is aggravated by what is, on the contrary, the tremendous institutional *strength* of the Luxembourg and Strasbourg Courts operating on the European level. In other words, judges who are individually vulnerable to their own national governments can wield enormous power over all national governments when functioning as members of the European high courts. Finally, this potentially toxic combination of individual weakness and institutional power only became truly threatening in the face of mass accession of former Eastern Bloc countries, i.e., when it raised the prospect that a large number of judicial hacks and cronies drawn from the *nomenklatura* might be appointed to

[3] *See, e.g.*, Nuno Garoupa & Tom Ginsberg, *The Comparative Law and Economics of Judicial Councils*, 27 Berk. J. Int'l L. 53, 61 (2009).

[4] *See, e.g.*, Jean-François Flauss, *Radioscopie de l'élection de la nouvelle Cour européenne des droits de l'homme*, 35 Rev. tr. d. h. 437, 440 (1998) (relating the Dutch government's apparent refusal to promise its sitting ECtHR Judge Van Dijk that he would be reintegrated into the Dutch Conseil d'Etat upon his retirement from the ECtHR).

the European Courts. The only way out of this bind was to weaken the bonds between national governments and European judges/judicial candidates.

But note the tension that this solution created. Prior to mass accession, the established Member States had shown little inclination to subject their own judicial nominations to formal norms, processes, or institutions. To the contrary, the representatives of those Member States had made sure to foster judicial appointment processes that maximized their traditional power over their own judicial appointees. This approach simply gave institutional form to their classical view of the appropriately dominant role that national governments should play in the appointment of judges to international courts. As the French legal advisor Paul Reuter had argued when negotiating the original judicial appointments provisions for the European Court of Justice (ECJ), such a predominant position reserved to the governments "their rightful role" ("*le rôle qui leur revenait*").[5]

In other words, the increased judicial independence that appeared desirable in the post-accession context conflicted with the judicial accountability that the Member States had traditionally wished to entrench via short and renewable terms of judicial office. As Anne Boerger-De Smedt explains, "The appointment process for the judges and the temporary nature of their employment offered reassuring guarantees for the governments." To those governments, their "rightful role" included of their ability to "keep the upper hand over the Court by controlling [its membership] and by assuring themselves that any judge who became undesirable could be tossed aside after his first term."[6] The judicial independence promoted by the formalization of European judicial appointments thus naturally interfered with the judicial accountability that established (i.e., Western) Member State governments traditionally wished to exercise over "their" judges on the European high courts.

This is where the richly variable notion of "judicial accountability" comes into play. As I elaborated in Chapter 7, the mode of accountability that takes precedence in the post-accession context is not in fact *judicial* accountability, and certainly not judicial accountability in the Garoupa/Ginsburg sense, i.e., accountability of European judges for their potentially intrusive policy-making.[7] As we saw, almost nothing has been done on that front at all. Indeed, *no one* in the debates over European judicial appointments explicitly argues that the power or policy-making authority of the European Courts should be curtailed.[8] Instead, the accountability at issue is the accountability of *national governments* for

[5] *See* Anne Boerger-De Smedt, *La Cour de justice dans les négociations du traité de Paris instituant la CECA*, 14(2) J. of Eur. Integration Hist. 7, 21 (2008).

[6] *See id.*

[7] *See supra* Chapter 7(III) and (IV).

[8] This is not to say that there does not exist in fact an unstated undercurrent of sentiment in this direction. For more on this important issue, *see infra* Chapter 12(V).

their *judicial appointments*—or more precisely, for their nominations (i.e., their attempted appointments)—to the European Courts.

II. Judicial Quality as a Loaded Mediating Device

It is in this environment that judicial "quality" emerges to make its fundamental contribution to the European judicial debates. The newfound stress on judicial quality links together at least four competing impulses: (1) promoting the judicial independence of Eastern European judges from their national governments and (2) imposing accountability on those new Member State governments for their judicial appointments (especially given the tremendous power of the two European Courts), while (3) minimizing the accountability that the governments of long-standing (Western) Member States had always refused to shoulder for their own judicial appointments and (4) maintaining some measure of judicial accountability of Western European judges to their own governments. Let us work through all four dimensions of the problem.

At a first level, the notion of judicial quality imposes a minimum standard that limits the capacity of potentially problematic new Member States to appoint beholden hacks to the European Courts (or, for that matter, to scuttle the European Courts from the inside by intentionally appointing incompetents). This limitation can be visualized in different ways. The most straightforward would be that the more incompetent the nominated judges, the more beholden they are likely to be. After all, why else would a national government nominate an incompetent? Another variation would be to recognize that the higher the quality of the candidates or judges, the more likely they would be to have attractive career options; and these options would increase their independence from the nominating government. Yet another variant would suggest that the more high-grade the judicial nominees, the more likely they would be to understand just how far they could go to advance governmental preferences without visibly violating professional norms. Such jurists would recognize (and remain safely within) the limits of (beholden) behavior in which they could reasonably engage when acting as European judges. Though not ruling out politically motivated judicial behavior, this would at least put professional and deontological constraints on the judicial actor. In addition, judicial quality should also be understood as a matter of professional and perhaps political socialization: quality might well stand as a proxy for adherence to the values of the European legal orders as understood from within those orders: external indicia of quality can denote mastery of, and eventually allegiance to, those values. As I explained in Chapter 3, for example, it is relatively difficult to imagine how someone fulfilling the professional criteria established by the Article 255 Committee would not be fundamentally congenial to the European project, as traditionally understood.[9]

A final and deeply practical point should also be made about the relationship between the imposition of judicial quality standards and taming the threat of new Member States appointing beholden judicial hacks. The reality on the ground is that in the new Member States of the former Eastern Bloc, and all the more so for the many small countries within that new group, there actually exists a finite—and often distressingly small—pool of viable judicial candidates qualified (by almost any reasonable standard) to sit on the high European courts. This should not be terribly surprising. After all, the EU's great eastward enlargement occurred in 2004, when eight new Member States acceded to the Union. And of these eight, most are really quite small. Indeed, the entire population of all eight countries—the Czech Republic (10 m.), Estonia (1.3 m.), Hungary (9.8 m.), Latvia (2 m.), Lithuania (3 m.), Poland (38.5 m.), Slovakia (5.5 m.), Slovenia (2 m.)—currently represents a grand total of some 72 million, a figure that barely surpasses the national population of France (66 m.), the UK (64 m.), or Italy (60 m.), never mind reaches the 80 plus million that Germany represents all by itself. Indeed, if one removes Poland (which accounts for well over half of the Eastern total), the population of Spain (46 m.) singlehandedly dwarfs the combined population of the other seven new Member States (33.5 m.).

The effect of these demographic realities on the pool of viable judicial candidates should be obvious. High quality European jurists—*however* defined—do not grow like annual flowers. Given the current complexity of the EU legal regime, it takes many years for most of them to be educated and trained; in fact, it takes many years for most of their teachers to be educated and trained. This multi-generational process necessarily means that for a significant period of time, there will necessarily be a very real shortage of highly trained candidates for high European judicial office.

Another way to look at this is simply to recognize the long-standing paucity of law school programs in Eastern Europe that were preparing students to specialize in European law. Take Croatia, for example, whose population of 4.3 million puts it roughly in the middle of the new EU Member States from Eastern and Central Europe. To this day, it possesses all of four law schools (Zagreb, Osijek, Rijeka, and Split); and of these, only Zagreb (and perhaps Rijeka) was in a position to offer a meaningful education in EU law prior to accession. And even this was of *very* recent vintage: a chair in European Public Law was only spun off from the chair in Constitutional Law in the early 2000s; and it has only produced some two doctorates a year. Under such circumstances, how many "quality" candidates could one reasonably expect to apply for posts at the high European Courts in Strasbourg and Luxembourg in the wake of accession, as opposed to engaging in high-level

[9] *See supra* Chapter 3(II)(B).

private sector legal practice, serving in national ministries, or on the national high courts, joining the Commission in Brussels, etc.? As one can imagine, the number is vanishingly small.

In such a context, the demand for "quality" judicial candidates represents a potentially major constraint on Member State governmental actors. Given the paucity of well-trained Eastern or Central European jurists ready and willing to put themselves forward for nomination to the European Courts, the governments of the newly acceded States are significantly hampered in their ability to pick and choose among viable candidates. With so few "quality" potential candidates available in the first place, those governments are simply not in a very good position to play favorites and thus to demand subservience from the few candidates potentially in play. Indeed, those governments are at some pains to generate gender-mixed lists of qualified candidates on a recurring basis. In the context of the new accession States, therefore, a call for judicial quality operates in effect as a fairly strong judicial independence device: if they want their judicial candidates to make it through the vetting process, the governments need to select candidates who can afford *not* to be subservient to them.

The judicial independence thus afforded in the new accession States by the demand for judicial quality does not simply operate, however, to readjust the relationship between the judicial candidates and their national governments. The second part of the equation is that the mechanism chosen to promote such judicial independence was to impose a meaningful dose of accountability on the new Member State governments for their judicial appointments. As a result, the relationship between the new Member States and their judicial candidates became actively linked to the relationship between the older Member States and the newly acceded ones.

Of course, there had always been some version of intergovernmental interaction on judicial appointments. As we have seen, however, that link was extremely weak. For ECJ openings, appointment "by common accord" effectively gave each Member State the capacity to call the shots on the appointment of its own chosen candidates;[10] and for European Court of Human Rights (ECtHR) openings, PACE election from a slate of three candidates gave ample room for Member State governments to make their intentions clear (and thus for the PACE to ratify those national governmental preferences in the overwhelming majority of cases).[11] And in the grand old diplomatic days of a much smaller and more homogenous EU, Member State governments would even do each other the courtesy of quietly notifying one another in advance of the judicial nominations they intended to make.[12]

But the establishment of the 255 Panel and of the Advisory Panel of Experts (APE), complete with these Panels' review of candidate quality, represented

[10] *See supra* Chapter 2.
[11] *See supra* Chapter 4.
[12] Interview with former Advocate General Carl Otto Lenz, Schönberg, Germany (August 7, 2015).

something else altogether. Suddenly, the Member States were in a position to vet each other's judicial candidates (even if only indirectly) via the Panels, to rebuff governmental attempts to appoint judicial hacks, and, depending on the particularities of the Panels, to shame those governments more or less publicly for failed judicial candidacies. This intergovernmental accountability mechanism held out the very real possibility of a self-reinforcing fall in status of the following (rather predictable) type: "Look at those miserable Bulgarians, who can't even propose a proper European judge!"[13] The establishment of such scandal-inducing mechanisms, which we will study at greater length in Part V, clearly changes the nature of the judicial appointments process.

Of course, such new accountability mechanisms apply not only to new Member States, but to established ones as well. But the key is to recognize that accountability for one is not the same as accountability for the other. Several reasons explain this disparity; but the fundamental reason is simple: numbers. The established Member States are just that: established. They have had decades of active involvement in the European project and thus possess legal and academic cultures that are thoroughly acquainted with, invested in, and intertwined with European law and politics. For them, European law has gradually become part and parcel of their legal heritage, even if it exhibits at times a difficult and tension-laden relationship with their domestic legal orders.

Furthermore, the decades-long interconnection between the Western European domestic and supranational legal regimes has been further strengthened by sheer continuity. Western European law faculties, unlike their sisters behind the Iron Curtain, were not made to languish for several decades under authoritarian regimes uninterested in European legal developments, and arguably in legality *tout court*. As a result of such regulatory and educational realities, the established Western Member States tend to possess a relatively deep pool of highly knowledgeable European legal specialists, not to mention the even deeper pool of domestic jurists whose specific areas of expertise—be it constitutional law, administrative law, antitrust law, and so on—have long been significantly intertwined with European legal and regulatory developments.

Finally, simple demographics play a very meaningful role. The five biggest EU countries by population (Germany, France, the UK, Italy, and Spain) have all been long-standing Member States: three are founding members and the UK and Spain joined their ranks in 1973 and 1986.[14] At the other end of the scale, however, seven of the EU's eight smallest countries (Malta, Cyprus, Estonia, Latvia, Slovenia,

[13] *See, e.g.*, N.P. Engel, *More Transparency and Governmental Loyalty for Maintaining Professional Quality in the Election of Judges to the European Court of Human Rights*, 32 Human Rights L.J. 448, 450 (2008).

[14] Needless to say, the EU status of the UK has been very much in question over the course of writing this book.

Lithuania, and Croatia) only joined the Union upon mass accession of the former Eastern Bloc countries in the post-2004 period.[15]

Given such major historical, professional, educational, and demographic disparities, it should not be difficult to understand why the establishment of "quality" standards for European judicial candidates does far less to constrain established Member States in their choice of nominees. These countries tend to have the luxury of relatively large pools of professionally viable candidates. This is not to say that such candidates are all sublime (indeed, there has always been a certain amount of *sotto voce* griping about the middling standing of particular judges and even of the judges typically appointed by certain long-standing Member States); but these candidates do nonetheless tend to meet whatever minimum professional qualifications might be imposed Europe-wide (although, as we shall see, there are always exceptions[16]). The practical consequence is fiendishly loaded: a focus on judicial "quality" operates in effect to *maintain* a good deal of nominating discretion for the governments of established Member States while tending to *foreclose* much of this discretion for the newly acceded Member States of the former Eastern Bloc.

III. Recognizing Historical Exceptions

But the focus on judicial quality has done more than just maintain uneven levels of governmental discretion in the face of seemingly neutral standards. A further development has been the refusal of several long-standing Member States to formalize their judicial selection processes in the manner suggested more or less explicitly by the PACE, the APE, the Article 255 Panel, and so on. Unwilling or unable to confront such recalcitrance, the European institutions have chosen instead to grant the more established Member States an extra degree of leeway not granted to the newer Member States.

The institutions of the Council of Europe have been particularly brazen in this regard. As I explained in Chapter 6, during the period of mass ECHR accession of the mid-1990s, the Committee of Ministers had formally recommended that:

> All decisions concerning the professional career of judges should be based on objective criteria, and the selection and career of judges should be based on merit, having regard to qualifications, integrity, ability and efficiency. The authority taking the decision on the selection and career of judges should be independent of the government and the administration. In order to safeguard its independence, rules should ensure that, for instance, its members are selected by the judiciary and that the authority decides itself on its procedural rules.[17]

[15] The eighth small country is Luxembourg, which is a Founder Member State.
[16] *See infra* Chapter 10(V) for the notorious French example.
[17] Committee of Ministers Rec R (94) 12 (October 13, 1994) at 2.

In addition, the PACE has since explicitly stated: "In addition, in the absence of a fair, transparent and consistent national selection procedure, the Assembly may reject such lists."[18]

But the Ministers nonetheless overtly created a tradition-based exception to their own rules. Its Explanatory Memorandum clarifies:

> Although the recommendation proposes an ideal system for judicial appointments, it was recognised (see sub-paragraph 2) that a number of the member states of the Council of Europe have adopted other systems, often involving the government, parliament or the head of state. The recommendation does not propose to change these systems which have been in operation for decades or centuries and which in practice work well.[19]

The Committee of Ministers had therefore created a tradition-based distinction that simultaneously *imposed* independence-based procedures on the newly acceded Member States of the East and *excused* established Member States of the West from having to abide by those procedures!

Although the Consultative Council of European Judges (CCJE) criticized this approach on practical grounds several years later, the criticism was not that the distinction left too much discretion in the hands of the governments of established Member States. Instead, the problem was that the exception set a bad example for the former Socialist countries—a criticism that, though perhaps well valid, nonetheless reinforced the underlying logic of the Ministers' original distinction.[20] So the exception has stood ever since. As the Venice Commission concluded in 2007:

> In Europe, a variety of different systems for judicial appointments exist and that there is not a single model that would apply to all countries.
>
> In older democracies, the executive power has sometimes a decisive influence on judicial appointments. Such systems may work well in practice and allow for an independent judiciary because these powers are restrained by legal culture and traditions, which have grown over a long time.
>
> New democracies, however, did not yet have a chance to develop these traditions, which can prevent abuse, and therefore, at least in these countries, explicit constitutional and legal provisions are needed as a safeguard to prevent political abuse in the appointment of judges.[21]

[18] PACE Resolution 1646 (2009) at para. 2.

[19] Committee of Ministers Rec R (94) 12 (October 13, 1994) at Explanatory Memorandum, para. 16. The Ministers' exception included only one rather vague proviso: "However, where the constitutional or legal provisions and traditions allow judges to be appointed by the government, there should be guarantees to ensure that the procedures to appoint judges are transparent and independent in practice and that the decisions will not be influenced by any reasons other than those related to the objective criteria mentioned above." Committee of Ministers Rec R (94) 12 (October 13, 1994) at 3.

[20] *See* CCJE Opinion No. 1 at para. 45.

[21] Venice Commission, "Report on Judicial Appointments," CDL-AD(2007)028 at paras. 44–46.

By instituting such a blatantly loaded distinction, the Council of Europe has thus maintained as much flexibility as possible for old Member State governments to wield their traditional discretion over judicial nominations, even as it formally claimed to be removing such discretion across the board.

For its part, the Article 255 Panel has been far more discreet. It simply instituted a procedural demand that it be apprised of the national selection procedure by which each Member State had chosen its candidate for judicial appointment in Luxembourg. The Panel explained in its Third Activity Activity Report:

> Since the start of its work, the panel has requested information on the *national selection procedure* whenever this information was not provided directly by the Member State proposing the candidature. The purpose of the request is to know whether there was a call for applications, whether an independent body had decided on the merits, i.e. the professional merits of the candidature proposed with regard to the post to be filled, or whether any other selection procedure offering at least equivalent guarantees, such as choice of the candidate by a Member State's highest court, had been used. Lastly, it wishes to know what conclusions the government drew from such a procedure, if it exists.[22]

This would seem to be a thinly veiled "suggestion" that Member States institute and abide by formal selection procedures run by "an independent body" that would "decide . . . on the merits."

On the other hand, the Panel then explained that the failure to institute such a national selection mechanism could not be held against a candidate:

> The panel specifies that the method for selecting the candidate chosen at national level *may not be prejudicial to him or her*. In particular, the lack of a procedure enabling candidates' merits to be assessed in an independent and objective manner may not in itself constitute a handicap. It would, after all, be illogical to disadvantage candidates whose merits are to be assessed on the grounds of a selection process over which they have no control. Furthermore, the panel is aware that the selection procedure is the sole responsibility of Member States and is not framed by the TFEU. As a result, the panel naturally gave favourable opinions on suitable candidatures within the meaning of the Treaty, even in the absence of public call for applications or an independent national procedure for assessing merits.[23]

[22] Article 255 Panel, Activity Report of the Panel provided for by Article 255 of the Treaty on the Functioning of the European Union, Third Report of December 13, 2013 (No. SN 1118/2014) at 14 (emphasis in original).
[23] *Id.*

Member States and their candidates would not be punished for a governmental refusal to adopt formal and independent judicial selection mechanisms, although adopting one might help borderline candidates squeak past the Panel:

> In other words, the existence of a national procedure enabling the merits of candidates to be assessed in an independent and objective manner *may*, when in the eyes of the panel a candidature has certain weak points, *work in the candidate's favour* as the panel's doubts and questions can be put aside by the trust it places in the national procedure.[24]

The Article 255 Panel thus adopts an approach to national selection mechanisms that looks quite different from the one deployed in Strasbourg, but that, as a practical matter, arrives at a fairly similar place. It strongly suggests that independent and merit-based procedures be adopted at the national level for the selection of judicial nominees. But it refuses to hold fast to its own recommendation, thereby opening the door for the maintenance of domestic selection on the basis of unilateral executive branch command. When push comes to shove, what matters in the end is that the quality of the candidate (ECJ) and/or of the "constitutional tradition" (ECtHR) be deemed sufficient.

Finally, the escape hatches thus built into the national judicial selection procedures, both of which undoubtedly favor long-standing Western European Member States (either because of their pre-existing constitutional traditions or because of their relatively deep pool of highly trained judicial candidates), necessarily affect the relationship between Member State governments and their potential judicial nominees. The reason for this is very simple: the very discretion afforded to these Western Member State governments puts "their" judges at a certain disadvantage. Far more than their Eastern European counterparts, the Western governments have decisional leeway and appointment options. Stated simply, their potential judicial nominees (including sitting judges in Luxembourg, who are eligible for reappointment) are replaceable, and replaceable largely at the pleasure of their governments. Such increased governmental options create increased judicial accountability—i.e., increased judicial vulnerability—to those governments.

The key to understanding the importance of the turn to judicial "quality" in the European appointments debates is therefore to recognize that it represents a wonderfully supple mechanism for bridging the twin impulses toward judicial independence, on the one hand, and judicial accountability, on the other. Judicial independence is gained above all by those judicial candidates who must deal with the governments of their newly acceded States. At the same time, this gain in judicial independence is purchased by means of increased accountability of those

[24] *Id.*

new Member State governments to their more established counterparts in the West, via the establishment of formal, quality-based norms, procedures, and institutions. But the creation of loopholes at both the Council of Europe ("constitutional traditions" can substitute for formal national selection procedures) and at the EU (quality candidates cannot be penalized for their governments' failure to use formal procedures) effectively works to shelter a good measure of Western governmental discretion, which in turn maintains a concomitant measure of judicial vulnerability (or "accountability") to those governments inclined to exercise it.

That said, one should not summarily conclude that the establishment of the increasingly formalized and quality-oriented appointments processes do not in fact impose constraints upon the established Western Member States as well as upon their newly acceded counterparts. They do. But these constraints can be both accepted and managed. First of all, the constraints imposed on established Member States may simply be worth it to those Western governments. Yes, the two new European Panels (the APE and the 255 Panel) will subject their judicial nominations to some measure of scrutiny. But with this scrutiny comes the assurance that the appointments hailing from the former Eastern Bloc meet some threshold level of independence and quality (however defined)—an assurance made all the more precious by the self-evident policy-making and even quasi-constitutional power of the ECJ and the ECtHR.

Second, the constraints placed on the Member State governments, while uniform in theory, function asymmetrically in practice, as we have just seen. Western States, far more than their Eastern partners, tend to possess a relatively deep roster of viable judicial candidates. Their luxury to pick and choose from among this deep roster of candidates, especially when coupled with their capacity to maintain executive-driven appointments processes due to long-standing "constitutional traditions," significantly loosens the constraints placed on their appointments decisions. This is not to say that there are no constraints at all. As we shall see in Chapter 10, Western Member States can and do periodically run afoul of the APE and the 255 Panel. But frankly, such episodes require some combination of both pigheadedness and incompetence.

Third, the nature and degree of the constraints placed on Member State governments hinges a great deal on the two Panels themselves. This in turn depends not only on the Panels' processes and practices (which we have already examined at length), but also on their membership. Needless to say, a serious analysis of that membership is a rather daunting task, as it would have to consider a rather wide range of potentially meaningful factors, such as professional background and commitments, intellectual and political biases, and so on. Mikael Madsen has taken a good first stab at tackling such issues, to which we will return in in the forthcoming chapters.[25] But in the context of our current discussion about the

[25] *See* Mikael Rask Madsen, *The Legitimization Strategies of International Judges: The Case of*

asymmetric effects of the "quality" orientation of the European judicial appointments regimes, one factor is particularly striking: the geographic distribution of the Panels' membership.

As we explained in Parts I and II, the two European Panels are composed overwhelmingly of national supreme or constitutional court judges with strong European ties.[26] Despite such similarities, the initial geographic distribution of the two Panels varied significantly.[27] For its part, the membership of the Article 255 Panel was and has remained skewed overwhelmingly toward established and wealthy Member States from Western Europe. Of the eleven figures who have served on the Panel in either its first or second term, only *one*—let me repeat only *one*—Justice Peter Paczolay of Hungary, has hailed from Eastern Europe.[28] And even now, in its third incarnation, it *still* only possesses a single such member: Mirosław Wyrzykowski of Poland.[29]

The APE, by contrast, originally possessed somewhat greater geographic diversity, as two of its original seven members hailed from the East (Justices Gonera of Poland and Zorkin of Russia) and another came from Turkey (Professor Selçuk). But the geographic distribution of the APE has only deteriorated since, as only *one* of its current members—once again, this is not a misprint, only *one*—hails from Central or Eastern Europe (Maria Gintowt-Jankowicz of Poland), despite the fact that fully half the forty-seven Member States of the Council of Europe were located somewhere east of Germany, including not only a plethora of Central European nations, but also numerous former republics of the USSR, such as Armenia, Azerbaijan, Estonia, Georgia, Latvia, Lithuania, Moldova, the Ukraine, and Russia itself.[30]

This striking geographic imbalance clearly results in a near total domination of the two Panels by the long-standing Western Member States of the EU and of the Council of Europe. True, Western governments may feel some degree of constraint as a result of the mere existence of the Panels, which can indeed impose some limit on their capacity to appoint their chosen judicial candidates to the European Courts. But given the geographic provenance of the Panels' members, who could really be blamed for regarding the two Panels primarily as agents who police

the European Court of Human Rights, *in* Selecting Europe's Judges A Critical Review of the Appointment Procedures to the European Courts 259 (Michal Bobek ed., 2015).

[26] This is no accident. Interview with Chief Justice Koen Lenaerts, Luxembourg, November 9, 2016.

[27] *See supra* Chapter 3(I); Chapter 5, text accompanying note 1.

[28] *See supra* Chapter 3(I).

[29] Council Decision 2017/2262 of 4 December 2017, appointing the members of the panel provided for in Article 255 of the Treaty on the Functioning of the European Union, available at https://eur-lex.europa.eu/legal-content/EN/TXT/?uri=CELEX%3A32017D2262. The gender imbalance also remains outrageous: only one of the seven members of the 255 Panel, the Portuguese judge Maria Eugénia Martins de Nazaré Ribeir, is a woman.

[30] *See* https://www.coe.int/en/web/dlapil/advisory-panel. Its gender representation is not much better, as only two of its seven members are women. *See id.*

the newly acceded Member States from the East on behalf of the long-standing Member States of the West?

IV. Conclusion: A Supple Formalization

Mass accession of former Eastern Bloc countries to the EU and the Council of Europe prompted a newfound eagerness among long-standing European Member States to subject proposed candidates for European judicial office to external scrutiny. This clearly presented a dilemma for such Western States, which had heretofore guarded their appointment prerogatives rather zealously. But the tremendous power of the two European high courts, when combined with the one State, one judge principle, put these long-standing Member States in a bind. They wanted to be assured that the governments of newly acceded States from the East would not appoint judicial hacks who might profoundly transform the existing legal/constitutional state of affairs.

This chapter has argued that this appointments dilemma prompted the development of a two-pronged solution: (1) the formalization of judicial institutions, procedures, and norms and (2) the thematization of judicial quality. This clever and supple solution to the judicial dilemmas triggered by mass Eastern accession has permitted the established Member States to go as far as possible toward having their cake and eating it too. It promotes a good deal of judicial independence of Eastern judicial figures from their governments, while subjecting those governments to a good deal of accountability to the West for their judicial nominations. Furthermore, the historical and demographic asymmetry between Eastern and Western Europe means that this accountability could be purchased with a minimum of disruption to the traditional appointment prerogatives of Western European governments: an orientation toward formalization and quality—at least as actually instituted in the European judicial appointments context—does not in the end present major challenges to the long-standing Western Member States. The same cannot be said for most of the new accession States from the former Eastern Bloc.

Before turning the page on this chapter, I would like to make two final points. The first I will only mention quickly in passing, as I will discuss it at much greater length in Part V. It would be a mistake to adopt only a State-centered prism on these European judicial appointments developments. Other institutional interests are clearly at stake, not the least of which would be judicial and academic in nature, as well as domestic and European in provenance. We will need, therefore, to consider how these interests interact with the developments we have been discussing.

For now, however, I would like to pause momentarily on a second point. The two-pronged approach developed to manage judicial appointments in the post-accession period—an approach that we might dub "formalized quality"—represents in some respects a willful ossification of political and theoretical understandings on both the domestic and the European levels. It offers what appears to be, at least on the surface, a removal of nuance, a foreclosing of more potentially creative understandings of the relationship between political and judicial institutions, between domestic and international/supranational law, between the legal and the diplomatic, and so on. It represents a conspicuous turn toward a more formalist/positivist and technocratic vision of judicial appointments and judicial practice, one that maps quite easily onto one of the classic sides of the long-standing American debates on judicial appointments: the more bar-oriented professionalism vision, as opposed to the political and representational one.[31]

Whether this value-laden choice is to be praised or regretted is of course very much open to debate. Nothing says, furthermore, that the answer need be the same everywhere for all courts in all eras. Indeed, it may be that this currently prized approach has much to offer, especially in the ECtHR context in the post-Soviet era. After all, the ECtHR addresses human rights violations, which, though notoriously difficult to define and manage in specific cases, could perhaps—at least in certain core instances—be amenable to more bright-line and positivist analyses than the more obviously policy-oriented regulatory, trade, and harmonization issues routinely faced in the EU context.

Even if the formalized quality approach—complete with its increasingly codified process of judicial selection on the basis of formalized criteria of professional quality—may not offer a great deal in the way of imaginative rethinking of the relationship between political and judicial institutions, or between domestic and international or supranational law, or between the legal and the diplomatic, etc., it may very well promote the appointment of professionally competent positivists from the newly acceded Member States from the East.

If the approach accomplishes no more than this, it would nonetheless have to be considered a success for the long-standing Member States from the West. After all, the Eastern Member States and their judges represented a significant wildcard for

[31] Koen Lemmens and Michal Bobek both tend to frame this division in terms of the meritocratic/technocratic vs. the political. *See* Koen Lemmens, *(S)electing Judges for Strasbourg: A (Dis)appointing Process?*, *in* Bobek (2015)95, 117; Bobek, *Epilogue: Searching for the European Hercules in id.* at 306. There exists an enormous US literature on judicial selection mechanisms. *See, e.g.*, CHRIS BONNEAU & MELINDA GANN HALL, IN DEFENSE OF JUDICIAL ELECTIONS (2009); Paul Carrington, *Judicial Independence and Democratic Accountability in Highest State Courts*, 61 L. & CONTEMP. PROBS 79 (1998); Stephen Croley, *The Majoritarian Difficulty: Elective Judiciaries and the Rule of Law*, 62 U. CHIC. L. REV. 618 (1995); Jay Daugherty, *The Missouri Non-Partisan Court Plan: A Dinosaur on the Edge of Extinction or a Survivor in a Changing Socio-Legal Environment?*, 62 MISSOURI L. REV. 315 (1997); Brian Fitzpatrick, *The Politics of Merit Selection*, 74 MISSOURI L. REV. 675 (2009); Henry Glick, *The Promise and Performance of the Missouri Plan: Judicial Selection in the Fifty States*, 32 U. MIAMI L. REV. 509 (1978); Melinda Gann Hall, *State Supreme Courts in American Democracy: Probing the Myths of Judicial Reform*, 95 AM. POL. SCI. REV. 315 (2001); Roy Schotland, *New Challenges to States' Judicial Selection*, 95 GEORGETOWN L.J. 1077 (2007); CHARLES SHELDON & LINDA MAULE, CHOOSING JUSTICE: THE RECRUITMENT OF STATE AND FEDERAL JUDGES (1997); MATTHEW STREB ed., RUNNING FOR JUDGE: THE RISING POLITICAL, FINANCIAL, AND LEGAL STAKES OF JUDICIAL ELECTIONS (2007).

the European project. Their sheer numbers, when combined with their decades-long separation from their Western European counterparts, could undoubtedly disrupt the relatively settled understandings and arrangements that had been painstakingly elaborated since the 1950s under the umbrella of the EU and the Council of Europe.

In this historical context, a turn to conventional judicial formalism or positivism would go a long way toward calming the instability threatened by mass Eastern accession. In a manner deeply reminiscent of Landes and Posner's understanding of judicial independence,[32] such an approach would tend toward long-term stability by reinforcing the deals long worked out at the European level between the established Member States. Of course, one could and should question—far more than did Landes and Posner—just what "enforcing the original deal" might really mean in actual cases (which, frankly, is less than clear). But the threshold question—at least in the brave new world of the post-accession era—is first and foremost whether the judges of newly acceded European Member States would understand themselves to be committed to maintaining settled arrangements and understandings, whatever this might really mean in practice.

Indeed, such settled arrangements and understandings—by which I can only mean *relatively* settled, as such matters are always heavily contested in their own right—has been sufficiently essential in the history of the EU and of the accession of new Member States that they have long been referred to by a specific term: the *acquis communautaire*, that is, the accretion of Community law that has been painstakingly developed ("acquired") over the course of the EU's history.[33] In fact, the idea of such a settled *acquis* and the importance attached to its maintenance was so great that the EU formally listed and organized the *acquis* into no fewer than thirty-one chapters for the purposes of arranging accession with the ten prospective Member States of the great 2004 enlargement.[34]

In such a context, the prospect of appointing competent if unimaginatively formalist or positivist Eastern judges would have looked quite comforting indeed. In fact, it would provide an important twist on Kim Scheppele's brilliantly insightful piece, "Declarations of Independence: Judicial Responses to Political Pressure."[35]

[32] William Landes & Richard Posner, *The Independent Judiciary in an Interest-Group Perspective*, 18 J. Law & Econ. 875 (1975).

[33] For an interesting account of the genealogy of the notion of the *acquis*, *see* Stephen J. Silvia & Aaron Beers Sampson, *Acquis Communautaire and European Exceptionalism: A Genealogy*, ACES Working Paper, July 1, 2003, available at https://www.researchgate.net/profile/Stephen_Silvia/publication/29998554_Acquis_Communautaire_and_European_Exceptionalism_A_Geneaology_ACES_Working_Paper_20031_July_2003/links/0a85e52fa5a459100c000000/Acquis-Communautaire-and-European-Exceptionalism-A-Geneaology-ACES-Working-Paper-20031-July-2003.pdf.

[34] The *acquis* has now been broken down into no fewer than thirty-five chapters. *See* http://ec.europa.eu/enlargement/policy/conditions-membership/chapters-of-the-acquis/index_en.htm.

[35] Kim Lane Scheppele, *Declarations of Independence: Judicial Responses to Political Pressure*, *in* Judicial Independence at the Crossroads: An Interdisciplinary Approach 227 (Stephen B. Burbank & Barry Friedman eds., 2002).

Writing especially in the Central and Eastern European context, Scheppele undermines the distinction between a judge acting under political orders and a judge dutifully applying legislation. She argues that judicial formalism or positivism may not, as conventionally thought, be a mark of judicial independence. It may instead function as an effective mode of judicial subservience to political masters constituted, as it happens, as authoritative lawgivers. Under such conditions, judges actually *lack* judicial independence: they faithfully apply formal political enactments without making appropriate and independent reference to higher law principles.

Scheppele's troubling insight leads to fascinating results in the European post-accession context, where the whole point was to bind those new Eastern Member States and their judges to the pre-existing *acquis*. To the extent that such judicial positivism might represent subservience to political power, the argument would run, so much the better: it would represent subservience to pre-existing (i.e., pre-accession) power. In other words, it would provide just the type of continuity and stability that the established Member States would be seeking. Landes and Posner would be proud.

On the other hand, the Article 255 Panel has provided its own twist on the formal quality approach. For all of the institutional, procedural, and substantive formalization that the Panel both represents and institutes, it also promotes a distinctly more reflective understanding of a quality European judge. Embedded within a dauntingly long set of highly formalized criteria regarding specific language skills, years of professional experience, and so on, the Panel offers a more nuanced take on the "legal expertise" it seeks a candidate to demonstrate. The Panel explains:

> Using the content of the dossiers and the hearing, the panel seeks to determine the breadth and solidity of the candidates' knowledge of the major judicial issues, the challenges involved in the rule of law, and the key aspects of the Union's legal system and EU law, as well as the candidates' ability to reflect on the application of this law by Member States' legal systems, and on the relationships between these systems and European law. The panel emphasises that knowledge of EU law is a factor that it takes into consideration in its assessment of candidatures, but that this is less important than being able to demonstrate a real ability to analyse and reflect on the conditions and mechanisms for applying this law, particularly within the Member States' national legal systems, and the major ongoing challenges involved.[36]

Although this description includes a telling reference to the candidate's knowledge of "the challenges involved in the rule of law," which could only have been directed eastward, it de-emphasizes the candidate's formal legal knowledge in favor of his/

[36] First Activity Report of February 17, 2011 (No. 6509/11) at 9.

her capacity to adopt a more reflective posture relative to the complex relationship between the domestic and European legal orders. The judicial consideration of such high-grade and perspective-laden considerations hardly squares with a simplistically positivist and/or formalist approach to judging.

Indeed, the 255 Panel has further emphasized this reflective tendency by instituting a new component to its interview of judicial candidates: the discussion of difficult cases. The Panel explained this new feature of its procedure in its Fourth Activity Report, published in 2017. In addition to asking for "the text of one to three recent publications, of which the candidate is the author, written in or translated into English or French," the Panel would now require "the presentation of one to three sensitive legal cases which the candidate has handled in his or her professional practice, which must not exceed five pages per case."[37] This written exercise in thoughtful legal tact and self-reflection would then have to be performed orally during the candidate's interview with the Panel.[38] Clearly, the Panel must not be interested in rote descriptions of mechanical exercises in positivist legal application.

As a result, the relationship between the development of (a) "formalized quality" criteria for judicial appointments and (b) a formalist/positivist approach to European judging is not perfectly clear. On the one hand, there is no doubt that the formalized quality criteria promote a distinctly professionalized and technocratic judicial profile. And there is good reason to believe that adopting such criteria would promote the appointment of appropriately professionalized judges who would seek dutifully to apply the *acquis*, now formally organized into a non-negotiable laundry list of positive law groupings, such as free movement of goods, public procurement, competition policy, fisheries, taxation, and so on.[39] Indeed, in the wake of mass Eastern accession, the resulting gain in stability was apparently sufficient to outweigh the seemingly dramatic limitation that the formalized quality approach might place on the traditional government prerogative to appoint European judges more or less at will.

On the other hand, the formal criteria actually established by the Article 255 Panel do more than promote a boringly positivist vision of European judging. True, for most judicial candidates, the threshold issue will be how to satisfy the Panel's specific criteria, including language requirements and formal indicia of professional experience and standing. But for the high-grade candidates that the Panel describes, the issue will also involve their capacity to reflect upon the EU's fundamental constitutional relationships. And as we suggested in Chapter 3, this combination of formal indicia and reflective capacities will tend to lead the judicial appointments process in certain institutional and programmatic directions: i.e., toward candidates committed to the European project even as they have the

[37] Fourth Activity Report of February 10, 2017 at 17–18.
[38] *Id.* at 18.
[39] *See* http://ec.europa.eu/enlargement/policy/conditions-membership/index_en.htm.

seniority and experience to be serious players on the domestic judicial or academic scenes. Such reflective candidates, in the mold of Justices Sauvé and Mance themselves, would not be simplistic positivists merely squeaking through the gauntlet of the Panel's formal criteria. They would to the contrary be thoughtful judges self-consciously managing the ongoing development of the European legal and political orders. In the end, adding judges with this "sophisticated" Europhilic profile to those bearing a more dutifully, if crudely, positivist one may well offer a compelling compound of enlightened stability congenial both to established Member States and to important professional, governmental, economic, and other elites.

PART V
SCANDAL!

The aim of science is to seek the simplest explanations of complex facts. We are apt to fall into the error of thinking that the facts are simple because simplicity is the goal of our quest. The guiding motto in the life of every natural philosopher should be, "Seek simplicity and distrust it."

Alfred North Whitehead[1]

The last two Parts deployed a loosely intergovernmentalist perspective: they examined the development of European judicial independence measures, the formalization of judicial appointment processes, and the thematization of judicial quality primarily in terms of Member States (and especially Member State governments) and their state interests. This vantage point put us in a position to recognize the divergence of interests between the established Western European Member States and the new accession States from the East. This in turn enabled us to appreciate how European judicial appointment developments have served to manage the instability threatened by large-scale accession of former Eastern Bloc nations.

I hope the last two Parts have demonstrated the tremendous explanatory power of this realist perspective. The impressive explosion of judicial appointments and independence measures, the rising formalization of the appointments processes, and the sudden preoccupation with judicial quality can only be properly understood as a reaction to mass Eastern accession in the context of the persistently rising power of the two European high courts.

That said, it would be a mistake to stop the analysis there. As a historical matter, and as we shall see in Part VI, these European measures, though initially developed in the context of Eastern enlargement, were later reinforced in the context of the financial and immigrant crises that would manifest in the following decade. But on a more fundamental analytic level, Member State governments represent only part of the story, albeit a very important part. Other actors and other interests are also clearly at play. Judicial institutions and players—ranging from the two high European courts themselves, to domestic supreme courts, to judges on all those courts, to European institutions such as the two European appointments panels

[1] Alfred North Whitehead, The Concept of Nature: Tarner Lectures Delivered in Trinity College, November 1919 at 163 (1920).

and the Parliamentary Assembly of the Council of Europe (PACE) Committee on the Election of Judges, to assorted academic and administrative players, and so on—have all played pivotal roles in these ongoing developments.

This Part adopts a methodology designed to turn our attention toward these different institutional players and interests. This methodology can be seen as a loose hybrid of two others. The first, a realist cousin (if traditional antagonist) of the broadly intergovernmental perspective that I deployed in the last two Parts, is more neo-functionalist and neo-institutionalist in orientation.[2] It gives these other institutional actors and interests their due: it recognizes the full extent to which such institutions have gone their own way, despite their initial creation and empowerment predominantly by national governmental actors. It therefore examines how these institutions have developed and advanced their own agendas and interests, sometimes in ways that are evidently at variance with what the national governments might have predicted and might reasonably have wished *ex ante* (and perhaps *ex post*).

The second perspective is more constructivist in orientation:[3] it resists treating European judicial independence, judicial authority, or judicial quality—or even the judicial maintenance of European legal stability (such as the *acquis communautaire*)—as self-evident and exogenous values and interests that predate their elaboration by the assorted players involved. Indeed, even the players, their groupings, and their alignments ought not to be treated as fixed, never mind foreordained. This approach invites us to pay attention to the gradual elaboration of a series of conceptual linkages that help to generate ideas and interests over time. Such an approach suggests that we ought to treat the issues of judicial independence, authority, or quality—indeed, even the issue of judicial appointments as a whole—not as pre-existing values whose contours and content are predetermined, but as sites for debate and contention, even more, as interventions that shape not only the contours and content of those values, but that reformulate the interests, identities, and alignments of all the players involved.

This Part moves these institutional and ideological factors to center stage. The point is not to displace the more state-centered prisms that characterized the last few chapters, but to supplement them in very important ways. The idea is to generate a layering effect, one that allows us to grasp something of the intricate interweaving of ideas, interests, issues, institutions, reforms, and so on that has, over the

[2] For classic statements of neo-functionalist and neo-institutionalist theory, *see, e.g.*, ERNST HAAS, THE UNITING OF EUROPE: POLITICAL, SOCIAL, AND ECONOMIC FORCES, 1950–1957 (3rd ed., 2004); WAYNE SANDHOLTZ & ALEC STONE SWEET, ALEC (eds.), EUROPEAN INTEGRATION AND SUPRANATIONAL GOVERNANCE (1998); WAYNE SANDHOLTZ, ALEC STONE SWEET, & NEIL FLIGSTEIN (eds.), THE INSTITUTIONALIZATION OF EUROPE (2001).

[3] For classic statements of constructivist theory in the political science and international relations literature, *see, e.g.*, Emanuel Adler, *Seizing the Middle Ground: Constructivism in World Politics*, 3 EUR. J. INT. RELAT. 319 (1997); PETER J. KATZENSTEIN (ed.), THE CULTURE OF NATIONAL SECURITY: NORMS AND IDENTITY IN WORLD POLITICS (1996); John G. Ruggie, *What Makes the World Hang Together? Neo-utilitarianism and the Social Constructivist Challenge*, 52 INT. ORG. 855 (1998); Alexander Wendt, *Anarchy is What States Make of It*, 46 INT. ORG. 391 (1992).

last fifteen to twenty years, permitted the heretofore sleepy issue of European judicial appointments to rise to the level of an increasingly pressing matter of concern.[4]

In order to move beyond the primarily state-centered approach that I have been deploying so far in this book, I now turn our attention to a persistent feature of the European judicial appointment debates over the last fifteen to twenty years: *scandal*. These European debates have included a steady diet of unsavory revelations concerning judicial appointments, especially regarding appointments to the European Court of Human Rights (ECtHR). Member States have retaliated not only against their own judges who had failed to tow the national line, but also against foreign judges who had made embarrassing statements in sensitive cases. Member State governments have made ham-fisted attempts to appoint obviously unqualified judicial candidates for patently self-serving and inappropriate reasons. The PACE's Sub-Committee on Elections has kowtowed to vengeful governments by favoring less over more qualified candidates. And the PACE itself has not only turned a blind eye to Member States thumbing their noses at the Advisory Panel of Experts (APE), but has also knowingly elected seemingly unqualified or otherwise dubious judges.

In short, European judicial appointments have been marred by a series of scandalous—if likely exceptional and not entirely surprising—incidents. Clearly, something is amiss. Indeed, these notorious episodes have strongly motivated European judicial appointments reforms, including the establishment of the APE in 2010. But as we shall soon see, the reforms, including the establishment of the APE, have by no means put an end to such episodes or to their underlying causes. The problems persist, reforms notwithstanding. Indeed, some suggest that matters may be getting worse.[5]

Before we advance any further, however, it is worth pausing momentarily to call attention to a fundamental research problem. Given that so much of the ECtHR's judicial appointments processes are confidential, it is difficult—even for a dedicated researcher—to know what exactly is going on. After all, the APE's interactions with the Member States are almost completely confidential (and intentionally so). The APE's remit is "to advise governments before lists of candidates are transmitted to the [PACE.]"[6] But that advice is quite confidential. As the Resolution establishing the APE declares:

> Where it is likely that the Panel may find one or more candidates not suitable for office, the chair of the Panel shall contact the High Contracting Party concerned

[4] For the now classic statement regarding "matters of concern," see Bruno Latour, *Why Has Critique Run Out of Steam? From Matters of Fact to Matters of Concern*, 30 Critical Inquiry 225 (2004).

[5] The 2013 plaint penned and published by the APE Chair Luzius Wildhaber is a particularly prominent example. *See* Steering Committee for Human Rights, Ministers' Deputies Exchange of Views with Mr. Luzius Wildhaber, Chairman of the Advisory Panel of Experts on Candidates for Election to the European Court of Human Rights (January 30, 2013), in DH-GDR (2013)005, February 5, 2013 ["2013 Exchange of Views"].

[6] PACE Committee on Legal Affairs and Human Rights, Report on National procedures for the selection of candidates for the European Court of Human Rights, Doc. 12391 (October 7, 2010).

to inform it and/or to obtain any relevant comments. If, in the light of the written submissions and any comments obtained, the Panel considers that one or more of the persons put forward by a High Contracting Party are not suitable, it shall so inform the High Contracting Party, giving reasons for its view, which shall be confidential.[7]

Furthermore, the opinion eventually produced by the APE concerning the suitability of a Member State's slate of candidates is itself a confidential document. More yet, it is not even made available to the 324 members of the PACE: it is only shown to the members of the PACE's subgroup on elections (long the thirteen-member Sub-Committee on Elections, and now the twenty members of the full-fledged Committee on Elections[8]). These committee members handle the APE document with such care that copies are not allowed to leave the room in which the committee meetings are held.[9] As we have seen, the APE would dearly love to loosen such confidentiality strictures, as doing so would increase its leverage over other institutional actors in the ECtHR judicial appointments process; but its attempts to change these confidentiality requirements have been expressly rejected.[10]

Indeed, even the Sub-Committee's (now Committee's) own ensuing recommendation to the PACE was traditionally confidential. This became painfully clear in a notorious incident in which the President of the PACE silenced a member of the Assembly when he tried to question the qualifications of a judicial candidate by referring to such a Sub-Committee recommendation in open Assembly. The remarkable—if rather opaque—exchange was as follows:

> THE PRESIDENT (Translation)—I call Lord Tomlinson on a point of order.
>
> Lord TOMLINSON *(United Kingdom)*—My point of order concerns the election of judges to European Court of Human Rights. I have the document that was produced by the Sub-Committee on the Election of Judges to the European Court of Human Rights, and I see that there is a difference in how different candidates have been treated. As I look at it, I find that of the five elections that came to a successful conclusion—
>
> Mr CHOPE *(United Kingdom)*—Point of order.
>
> Lord TOMLINSON *(United Kingdom)*—You cannot have a point of order in the middle of my point of order.

[7] Committee of Ministers, Resolution CM/Res(2010)26 on the Establishment of an Advisory Panel of Experts on Candidates for Election as Judge to the European Court of Human Rights (November 10, 2010).

[8] *See* Advisory Panel of Experts on Candidates for Election as Judge to the European Court of Human Rights, Second activity report for the attention of the Committee of Ministers 2, Advisory Panel(2016)1 (February 25, 2016).

[9] Interview with Andrew Drzemczewski, Strasbourg, November 10, 2016.

[10] *See supra* Chapter 5.

Mr CHOPE *(United Kingdom)*—You are going to disclose a document that is confidential.

Lord TOMLINSON *(United Kingdom)*—It is not confidential at all. That is what a plenary is entitled to do. I am amazed to see a British Conservative in this Assembly trying to stifle free speech.

When it comes to the Czech Republic, they selected—

THE PRESIDENT said that the document to which Lord Tomlinson was referring was confidential and therefore he was in violation of the Rules of Procedure.

He declared the ballots open.

Lord TOMLINSON *(United Kingdom)*—When it comes to the United Kingdom—

THE PRESIDENT (Translation)—I am sorry, I am just going to have to speak more loudly than you, Lord Tomlinson. [11]

As should be quite evident, the inner working of the ECtHR's judicial election process is therefore treated as highly sensitive and confidential. This necessarily means that it is very difficult indeed for an interested observer to learn about what is really going on behind the scenes in Strasbourg. But the full analytic significance of this informational problem can only be grasped if one asks a simple but puzzling question: if such a thick veil of secrecy covers the judicial appointment process in Strasbourg, then how does one know about embarrassing appointments episodes in the first place?

The answer is that confidential (or at least non-public) information has been leaked. This seemingly straightforward response does more, however, than answer the question. It also demonstrates that these embarrassing episodes do not simply exist or come into being all by themselves. Of course, a number of underlying facts exist and a series of actual events have taken place. But the scandals, as scandals, have been *produced*. Specific people leaked specific information to others; specific players framed and published that information and thereby leveraged it for specific purposes. That information was then used to advance particular reform proposals/agendas, to promote certain institutional interests over others, to support or critique the ensuing reforms, and so on.

This Part is designed to make the most out of these simple but essential insights. It describes the privileged information that has been made more or less publicly available. It examines who has disclosed such information and what they have

[11] PACE, 2012 Ordinary Session (Third part), Report, Twenty-first Sitting, Tuesday June 26, 2012 at 10 a.m., Document AS (2012) CR 21, available at http://assembly.coe.int/Documents/Records/2012/E/1206261000E.htm. For more on this notorious judicial candidacy, *see infra* Part (II)(F).

The Committee has since adopted the practice of publishing rather cryptic summary statements of its analysis of the qualifications of the judicial candidates for election by the PACE. *See, e.g.*, http://website-pace.net/documents/1653355/1653736/TableForthcomingJudgesElections-EN.pdf/775de55c-67b8-4f46-befd-1063dca1b5e0.

done with it. It uses this set of disclosures as a means to study the perspectives and interests of classes of players who cannot be easily assimilated to State governments, such as particular groupings of academics, civil servants, judges, and institutions (such as the PACE Sub-Committee on Elections). And it elaborates explanations by adopting a dynamic understanding of the relationship between these players and the normative, institutional, and ultimately conceptual structures within which—and on which—they operate.

Finally, the key to elaborating this set of understandings will be to make good use of a particular set of sociological, anthropological, and political science readings. There exists a fairly small, but very rich and sophisticated theoretical literature on scandal; and this literature proves immensely useful for teasing out and making sense of the European judicial appointments debates we have been studying over the course of this book.

This Part is organized as follows. Chapter 10 summarizes a handful of the most notorious episodes in the ECtHR appointments process of the last fifteen to twenty years. These episodes represent a spectrum of bad behavior by a broad range of pivotal actors in the appointments process, ranging from Member State governments, to the PACE Sub-Committee on Elections, to the plenary PACE itself. These episodes, now fairly well known within Council of Europe circles, shape the contours of the ongoing debates concerning European judicial appointments reform.

Chapter 11 presents the core of scandal theory, as it has been elaborated in a body of notable contemporary work by such political sociologists as John B. Thompson, Cyril Lemieux, and Damien de Blic and by political scientists Andrei Markovits, Mark Silverstein, and Alain Garrigou, all of which builds on the earlier work of social anthropologists Max Gluckman and Eric de Dampierre. These works, for all of their methodological, theoretical, and substantive differences, hold a great deal in common. Above all, they treat scandal as an unpredictable struggle over norms and values that unfolds dynamically over time. It is a process of making public revelations in an attempt to mobilize forces to challenge and eventually change an existing state of normative, institutional, and/or political affairs. A scandal is thus not a pre-existing event, but a complex and precarious intervention.

Chapter 11 then re-examines the European judicial appointments scandals through the prism provided by the scandal theory. As we shall see, this is a rather tricky enterprise. On the one hand, the scandals that have been publicized regarding European judicial appointments *reveal* a good deal about the pre-existing state of legal, judicial, and political affairs. They expose tensions and fissures not only between long-standing and newly acceded Member States, between European and other institutions, between professional and other interest groups, and so on, but also between competing visions of the judicial role and its relation to politics, governmental interests, etc. On the other hand, the scandals *do* something. They forge—or at the very least seek to forge—a novel set of alignments. They seek to create a sense of outrage and to mobilize the ensuing reaction, pointing it in particular directions in order to arrive at new ends. The scandals are therefore a form of political engagement that aims to reorganize existing institutions, interests, and ideologies into new constellations. And as we shall see, it is often the case that the more artfully a scandal performs its novel reconstruction, the more it portrays itself as merely validating a pre-existing set of values and understandings. As a result, the European judicial appointments scandals offer both (1) a static snapshot of *pre-existing* fault lines within the European legal/political landscape and (2) a privileged perspective on the dynamic transformation that this European landscape is *currently* undergoing. The core of the analytic and conceptual problem—and perhaps the core of scandal as a technique—is that it is never quite clear whether a given scandal presents a static or dynamic depiction of its subject matter.

10
The Juicy Bits

This chapter briefly describes the events underlying half a dozen ECtHR judicial appointments scandals that have broken into the open over the last fifteen to twenty years. Some of these episodes are quite straightforward; others a little more complex. Some appear distinctly more serious than others. Viewed as a whole, however, they often yield a decidedly unflattering portrait of the ECtHR appointments process.

Let me therefore pause for a moment to make something clear right from the outset. It is absolutely not my intention to heap scorn on the European Courts or to call them into disrepute. Nor will I add meaningfully to the pool of known examples by making further public disclosures.[12] The point here is not to reveal scandals, nor to harp unduly on them, but to analyze them—not only for the substance of what they claim to reveal, but also for the process by which these claims are made by particular actors in particular contexts.

The first three examples involve infamous examples of Member State governments refusing to nominate sitting ECtHR judges for reappointment (via reelection) to another judicial term in Strasbourg. They are in effect instances of governmental retribution against their own sitting ECtHR judges.

I. The 1998 Bulgarian Appointment

The first example is probably the most straightforward. In 1998, Bulgaria refused to re-nominate its sitting judge, Dimitar Gotchev, for another term in Strasbourg. Judge Gotchev had been the first and only Bulgarian judge to serve at the ECtHR: Bulgaria had only ratified the European Convention in 1992.

Why did this refusal to re-nominate draw attention? Because the refusal appeared to be in retribution for Judge Gotchev's role (or perhaps more accurately, non-role) in the *Lukanov* judgment that the ECtHR had handed down just the year before.[13] Andrei Lukanov had been the last Prime Minister ("Chairman of the Council of Ministers") of the old Bulgarian Communist/Socialist regime.

[12] Knowledgeable insiders will undoubtedly notice that I flesh out or correct certain details concerning scandals already in the public domain.

[13] Lukanov v. Bulgaria, Application no. 21915/93 (March 20, 1997), 1997-II, 529, available at http://cambodia.ohchr.org/WebDOCs/DocAnnotatedCode/ECHR_Decisions/Lukanov%20v.%20Bulgaria%20[20%20Mar%201997]%20[EN].pdf.

When that regime fell, Lukanov was charged (along with several other major old regime figures) with misappropriating funds allocated to such friendly countries as Nicaragua, Cuba, Laos, Kampuchea (Cambodia), Afghanistan, Angola, and Yemen, the allocated funds totaling tens of millions of dollars. He was arrested and placed in detention for some four months on the grounds that he might abscond and commit further offenses.[14]

Lukanov had challenged his arrest and detention from the very beginning and, having exhausted his domestic remedies, had eventually brought his case to Strasbourg. The case offered little in the way of legal interest. The ECtHR already had a well-settled jurisprudence on pre-trial detention; and it was easy to recognize that the Lukanov detention would fail to satisfy that ECtHR jurisprudence.[15] But the case would nonetheless be quite politically sensitive. This stood to be the first time that the ECtHR would formally sanction one of the newly acceded States of the former Eastern Bloc. And the case did involve, after all, the post-communist government's detention of the final premier of the Bulgarian Communist/Socialist regime.

Predictably, the ECtHR sanctioned Bulgaria for the detention, which was held to violate Article 5-1 of the Convention, which guarantees "the right to security and liberty of the person": there could have been no "lawful detention" without "reasonable suspicion of [his] having committed an offence."[16] Yes, the Lukanov government had made decisions to grant funds to "developing countries." But no, there was no indication whatsoever that Lukanov or others could reasonably be suspected of having gained any personal advantage from such an allocation of funds.[17] Indeed, the violation was apparently so obvious that the government had even stated to the Court "that they were prepared to accept the Commission's opinion that there had been a violation of the Convention"![18]

When the ECtHR's judgment came down, the Bulgarian government—then led by the leading anti-communist party, the Union of Democratic Forces—was nonetheless furious. Why? Because the Court's decision had been unanimous. In other words, the Bulgarian judge, Dimitar Gotchev, had not dissented. The government presented him with the bill: upon the expiration of his first term, it refused to renominate him for re-election to the Court. As Professor Jean-François Flauss, long the foremost observer of the ECtHR's inner workings, explained at the time, Judge Gotchev "had plainly and simply been the victim of a 'settling of accounts,' as the national authorities had not forgiven him the vote that he had cast in favor of condemnation in the *Lukanov* affaire."[19] Flauss explained:

14 *See id.* at paras. 9, 11, 39, 52.

15 Jean-François Flauss, *Radioscopie de l'élection de la nouvelle Cour européenne des droits de l'homme*, 35 Rev. trim. dr. h. 437 (1998) ["Flauss (1998)"].

16 *See* Lukanov at 15.

17 *Id.* at 14.

18 *Id.* at 12.

19 Flauss (1998) at 440.

> In that case, the vote in favor of the finding of a violation was taken to be treason. The plaintiff, Lukanov, was in fact a leader of the old communist regime. Whatever may otherwise have been the legitimate reasons for not including Gotchev on the list [of three] candidates [proposed by the Bulgarian Government for election to the ECtHR]—and they undoubtedly existed—it goes without saying that his eviction demonstrates quite clearly that [political] "detachment" is not a virtue widely shared within Bulgarian governing circles ... Given the circumstances of the *Lukanov* affaire, the application of settled case law demanded a finding of a violation [of the Convention]. Judge Gotchev therefore had no room whatsoever to maneuver, lest he appear to be the spokesman of the challenged government.[20]

Gotchev was not re-nominated in Strasbourg. The end of the story was even worse for ex-Premier Lukanov: long rumored to be in physical danger, he was shot dead in broad daylight outside his apartment building in Sophia.[21] The lone gunman has never been identified.

II. The 2001 Moldovan Appointment

The 2001 Moldovan incident is roughly similar to the Bulgarian one. This time, the offending ECtHR judge was Tudor Pantîru, the first Moldovan to sit in Strasbourg (Moldova acceded to the Convention in 1995). Once again, the problem was the refusal of the judge to dissent from a unanimous ECtHR judgment in a sensitive case.

The case involved the Moldovan government's refusal to recognize the Metropolitan Church of Bessarabia, an Orthodox Christian Church that had broken away from the Metropolitan Church of Moldova. Under the Religious Denomination Act, religious denominations active in Moldova are required to obtain official recognition by government decision. The Church of Bessarabia had sought such recognition since 1992 (shortly after the passage of the Act), but had never succeeded, despite protracted administrative debates within the Moldovan State. The government ultimately claimed that recognizing the schismatic Church of Bessarabia would have required it to intervene in the internal matters of a recognized church (the Church of Moldova), thereby violating the religious neutrality required of the State. The Church of Bessarabia, unable to gain redress in the Moldovan courts (if for no other reason than the fact that it had not gained legal recognition to sue in the first place), eventually filed its claim in Strasbourg.

The claim put the ECtHR in the unenviable position of having to walk into the minefield of Moldovan politics. In telegraphic summary, the problem was as

[20] *Id.* at note 20.

[21] *See* Jane Perlez, *A Bulgarian is Shot and Motives are Many*, NY Times, November 3, 1996, available at http://www.nytimes.com/1996/11/03/world/a-bulgarian-is-slain-and-motives-are-many.html.

follows. Moldova declared independence in 1991 in the midst of the breakup of the Soviet Union. Very quickly, the question became whether Moldova should unify with Romania, its immediate neighbor to the West, with whom it shared not only its primary language but also a long and complicated history. This was a deeply fraught question. The Soviets had long promoted a separate (i.e., non-Romanian) Moldovan identity as a means of buttressing its own position in the region: Moldova was one of the fifteen republics of the USSR. This left the newly independent Moldovan State torn in three directions: toward Moscow to the East, toward Bucharest to the West, and toward its own small, independent, but fractured Moldovan country. These inherently difficult political, cultural, and other identity questions were also sharpened by particularly brutal economic realities: Moldova remains to this day by far the poorest country in Europe as a whole and even in its own region. Its per capita GDP is less than two thirds of neighboring Ukraine's and less than *one quarter* of Romania's.[22]

The church struggle arose in this highly charged atmosphere of competing loyalties and patrons. As the Moldovan courts had explained, "the Metropolitan Church of Moldova was part of the Russian Orthodox Church and therefore dependent on the patriarchate of Moscow, whereas the Metropolitan Church of Bessarabia was attached to the Romanian Orthodox Church and therefore dependent on the patriarchate of Bucharest."[23] As the case made quite apparent, these fractured devotional loyalties mapped all too easily onto contemporary political fault lines: the Church of Bessarabia—which claimed almost a third of the entire population of Moldova—wished to renew ties with Bucharest precisely when the issue of (re-) unification with Romania was the most pressing and divisive political issue in Moldova.

The Moldovan government opposed such unification and thus treated the Church of Bessarabia as a schismatic church that, by reviving Russo-Romanian rivalries, threatened the social stability and territorial integrity of the young republic.[24] Indeed, the Church of Bessarabia was recognized by every Orthodox patriarchate with one telling exception: the patriarchate of Moscow. The Moldovan government followed Moscow's lead by refusing to recognize the Church and—at the very least—stood idly by as its churches, clergy, and adherents were subjected to a long list of abuses.[25]

Faced with likely ECtHR condemnation for its refusal to recognize the Church of Bessarabia, the Moldovan government apparently had one last card to play: it pressured its judge on the Court to defend its position, if necessary by dissenting in

[22] According to the World Bank, the 2017 per capita GDP for Moldova is $5,697, for Ukraine is $8,666, and Romania is $25,840. *See* World Bank, "GDP per capita, PPP (current international $)," available at https://data.worldbank.org/indicator/NY.GDP.PCAP.PP.CD.

[23] Metropolitan Church of Bessarabia v. Moldova, Application no. 45701/99 (December 13, 2001).

[24] *Id.* at 25–26.

[25] *See id.* at 12–17.

the impending judgment. But Judge Pantîru would not dissent: the ECtHR judgment would be unanimous. The Moldovan government, which had, just to aggravate matters, recently returned to the control of the Moscow-aligned Communist Party, played hardball. Norbert Engel explains:

> The Moldovan Judge Tudor Pantîru had refused to cede to his Government, which had called on him with an ultimatum in [the Church of Bessarabia case] to vote ... in accordance with its instructions and to justify its position in a dissenting opinion. Thereafter, the Government obstructed the re-election of the judge who had insisted on his independence. The body that, under domestic law, selects the three candidates for Strasbourg from the total number of applications nevertheless placed Judge Pantîru at the top of the list.
>
> The Moldovan Government, using the criminal justice system for its own ends, brought criminal proceedings against the judge for allegedly misusing public property, asserting that he had not vacated a State-owned flat allocated to him as a diplomat. He therefore allegedly lacked the integrity necessary for the Strasbourg office. The judge stated that he had acquired and paid for the flat. The Moldovan selection committee stood by its decision in favour of Mr Pantîru, whereupon the Government replaced the committee members and was finally rewarded with a compliant decision at the third attempt. The Parliamentary Assembly raised no objection to the Government's action and elected a successor instead of rejecting the list under protest.[26]

In short, the Communist government scrapped the slate of three candidates on which Judge Pantîru had previously figured (if only conditionally, i.e., subject to his return of the contested apartment!). It instead sent Strasbourg a new slate altogether, from which Judge Pantîru was simply missing.

The next question was what the European institutions would do about these governmental hijinks. The answer proved to be: nothing. Jean-François Flauss concludes:

> The Committee of Ministers could have objected to the retraction [of the earlier slate of nominated judges] and held that the transmission of the list of candidates was final and irrevocable, except in the case of death. Lacking political courage, it failed to do so. Similarly, it should have ruled out the possibility of a conditional candidacy. Clearly, from a pedagogical point of view, such a health and safety

[26] N.P. Engel, *More Transparency and Governmental Loyalty for Maintaining Professional Quality in the Election of Judges to the European Court of Human Rights*, 32 Human Rights L.J. 448, 450 (2008) (footnotes omitted) ["Engel (2008)"].

> measure should have been imposed on certain European "new democracies," for whom the Rule of Law is sometimes but an empty slogan.[27]

The European institutions did no such thing. Instead, the PACE simply elected one of the three candidates on the new Moldovan slate; and Judge Pantîru would have to do his best to get along. Norbert Engel concludes:

> [T]he Secretary General of the Council of Europe, Waller Schwimmer, offered him in 2001 a subordinate position at secretary level (below the category for lawyers) as a financial stop-gap. As it emerged that Pantîru could not return to his country without risking his own safety, he was subsequently dependent on part-time posts in Bosnia and Herzegovina and Kosovo that had to be filled by international lawyers.[28]

III. The 2004 Slovak Appointment

The Bulgarian and Moldovan incidents each offer examples of national governments exacting retribution against their respective judges for failing to do their bidding in highly politically sensitive cases brought before the ECtHR. The 2004 Slovak appointment was arguably less pernicious, but decidedly more comedic: the Slovak government was apparently dead set on appointing a political ally, Ján Drgonec, who was then an MP of a party that was part of the ruling governmental coalition.[29] The difficulty was not with the qualifications of this former judge, who had recently served as a Justice of the Slovak Constitutional Court. The first problem was instead that Drgonec was a sitting member of the Slovak Judicial Council,[30] i.e., a member of the very institution called upon to propose the three candidates to be nominated to Strasbourg! Indeed, he had been appointed to the Council by the ruling government.[31] The second problem was that Drgonec's obvious rival for the

[27] Jean-François Flauss, *Le Renouvellement triennial de la Cour européenne des droit de l'homme*, 47 Rev. tr. d. h. 693, 698 (2001).

[28] Engel (2008) at 450–51. The political situation having since changed, Pantîru served as a judge on the Constitutional Court of Moldova starting in 2013 (and President in 2017–18). *See* https://constcourt.md/pageview.php?l=en&id=1142&idc=31&t=/Composition-and-organization/Resigned-judges/Tudor-PANTIRU/.

[29] Drgonec had been a member of the Presidium of the ANO Party. *See* Doc. 10263, Election of a judge to the European Court of Human Rights with respect to Slovakia, Letter from the Secretary General of the Council of Europe to the President of the Parliamentary Assembly (September 16, 2004), available at http://assembly.coe.int/nw/xml/XRef/X2H-Xref-ViewHTML.asp?FileID=10634&lang=EN. The ANO Party was part of the governing coalition in the (second) Mikuláš Dzurinda government from 2002 to 2005. *See* http://www.europarl.europa.eu/enlargement_new/applicants/pdf/slovakia_profile_en.pdf.

[30] http://www.sudnarada.gov.sk/1st-term-members/.

[31] *Id.*

ECtHR position was none other than the Slovak judge then sitting in Strasbourg, Viera Strážnická (one of the minority of female ECtHR judges).

Events played out in a manner bordering on the burlesque. In Act I, which took place in December 2003, the Judicial Council produced its first decision concerning which candidates to nominate to Strasbourg. Drgonec ran for the ECtHR post against the other candidates, including the sitting Judge Strážnická. As Drgonec was a member of the Council, he left the room so as not to take part in the Council's deliberations. The Council found that three candidates, including Drgonec and Strážnická, met the statutory conditions for nomination; but one—and only one—received sufficient Council votes to be proposed: Council-member Drgonec![32] And this despite the fact that each Member State must nominate three candidates for election to the Court in Strasbourg.

Act II took place after Judge Strážnická had raised a constitutional complaint regarding the selection process used in the December 2003 proceedings. Six candidates presented themselves in February 2004 (including the three found in December to meet the statutory conditions for nomination); and the Judicial Council tried again.[33] This time, the Council succeeded at least in putting forward a list of three candidates. But the list had a rather insurmountable problem: it failed to satisfy the PACE requirement that it contain candidates of both sexes.[34] This meant two things. First, Judge Strážnická had once again been left off the list. And second, that list would immediately be rejected in its entirety in Strasbourg.

Act III took place after the inevitable rejection of that list in April. The Judicial Council tried yet again in June 2004.[35] This time, the Judicial Council considered eight candidates, including Drgonec, Judge Strážnická, and six others. In an impressively lopsided vote, the Council selected its three nominees: Drgonec and two appellate court judges, Ján Šikuta (who had been one of the other candidates nominated in February) and Soňa Smolová. Judge Strážnická, who was after all the sitting Slovak judge in Strasbourg, was nowhere close to being re-nominated. In contrast to Drgonec, for example, who received a perfect fifteen votes in favor, none opposed and no abstentions, Strážnická received but two in favor, three opposed (the most of any of the eight candidates), and double-digit abstentions.[36] If the election were to go forward in Strasbourg, Drgonec would not have to face competition from the obvious candidate: the sitting Judge Viera Strážnická.

But would that election go forward? In Act IV of the farce, it did. This was by no means inevitable. After all, the Slovaks had rather mysteriously left off the sitting ECtHR judge from its list of three candidates, despite the fact that she had

[32] www.sudnarada.gov.sk/data/att/623_subor.doc.

[33] *See* http://domov.sme.sk/c/1261387/sudna-rada-bude-volit-troch-kandidatov-na-post-sudcu-do-strasburgu.html.

[34] *See* http://www.slovensko.com/news/1192.

[35] *See* http://www.sudnarada.gov.sk/data/att/649_subor.pdf.

[36] *Id.*

steadfastly persisted in trying to get re-nominated. In addition, the lead candidate in every iteration of the Slovak nomination process was none other than Ján Drgonec. Though seemingly qualified for the job (arguably even more so than the sitting Judge Strážnická), Drgonec was nonetheless a member of the very selection committee that was selecting the candidates . . . hardly an ideal procedural arrangement. Then came the debatable quality of the other two nominees. Both were unexceptional appellate court judges; and one of them (Smolová) effectively had no experience whatever in the human rights area and could not speak, read, or write in English at all.[37] The end result was a tremendously imbalanced list of candidates that, while formally gender mixed, had merely added a makeweight female candidate: Smolová could not reasonably be considered a viable electoral alternative to Drgonec. Indeed, even Šikuta could hardly be considered a distinguished candidate; and he too could only claim to be "learning" French.[38]

But the Strasbourg institutions did nothing meaningful to stand in the way of the Slovak vote. The Committee of Ministers forwarded the list of candidates to the PACE. Worse, the Sub-Committee on Judicial Elections, despite the assorted anomalies and deficiencies described above, took the perplexing position that all three candidates were actually of "high quality."[39] Indeed, the Sub-Committee—which, furthermore, had met with barely half its membership—did not even squawk at the fact that the Slovak government had improperly ranked the candidates in order of preference.[40] The vote simply proceeded to the floor of the PACE.

In the final Act, the PACE took center stage. With only some 120 members present (out of more than 300), the PACE proceeded to elect Šikuta overwhelmingly over the objectively more qualified Drgonec, who, furthermore, could do no better than muster the same number of votes as the borderline candidate Smolová.[41] As Professor Flauss concluded:

> The PACE vote should obviously be understood as a snub inflicted on the Slovak government, which in this case had provided the canes for its own beating. The fact remains that the election of Mr. Šikuta (whose probity is in no way in doubt)

[37] *See* Doc. 10263, Election of a judge to the European Court of Human Rights with respect to Slovakia, Letter from the Secretary General of the Council of Europe to the President of the Parliamentary Assembly (September 16, 2004), available at http://assembly.coe.int/nw/xml/XRef/X2H-Xref-ViewHTML.asp?FileID=10634&lang=EN.

[38] *See id.*

[39] Jean-François Flauss, *Brèves observations sur le second renouvellement triennal de la Cour européenne des droits de l'homme*, 61 Rev. tr. d. h. 5, 31 (2005) ["Flauss (2005)"].

[40] *See id.*

[41] *See* PACE, Official Report of Debates, 2004 Ordinary Session, Twenty-ninth Sitting, Wednesday October 6, 2004 at 3 p.m., at 1076, available at https://books.google.com/books?id=f-eGY2asFKbUC&pg=PA1047&lpg=PA1047&dq=%C5%A0ikuta+drgonec+smolova&source=bl&ots=gOCnxUxs4L&sig=_I0t6bxFLBAwxTr-l9TDOZmQU9o&hl=en&sa=X&ved=0ahUKEwjT76qi4PrMAhWB2SYKHWs0DYcQ6AEIMjAD#v=onepage&q=%C5%A0ikuta%20drgonec%20smolova&f=false.

> is nonetheless deeply regrettable. First, the new Slovak judge has no knowledge of French, which remains until further notice one of the Court's two official languages. Second, Mr. Šikuta will exercise authority over the Registry staff, of which many members will possess a level of experience and qualifications far superior to his own. This disparity will be even greater in his working relationships with his [new judicial colleagues on the Court] …
>
> In the end, the new appointment of the Slovak judge turned into a farce. The Sub-Committee on Elections, the PACE, and the Committee of Ministers has each been seriously discredited in turn. True, the crude and clumsy ploy of the Slovak government has been turned aside. But, ultimately, at what cost?[42]

IV. The 2004 Estonian Appointment

The three incidents we have related so far all involve a Member State's unwillingness to re-nominate its sitting ECtHR judge. But they also increasingly reveal a second feature of such struggles, namely, the ensuing response (or lack thereof) by the European institutions in Strasbourg. The national authorities can play hardball politics of one kind or another with their judges, or their judicial candidates, or their judicial councils; but how the European authorities respond to such behavior obviously impacts not only upon the effectiveness of these national tactics, but also upon communal understandings of what may or may not constitute the boundaries of acceptable governmental behavior at the intersection of the political and judicial realms. Such responses to domestic political action simultaneously reflect upon, and ultimately implicate, the European institutions themselves: their decisions about whether and how to react to domestic governmental pressures help to define the nature of the European political and judicial spheres as much as they influence and define their domestic counterparts.

Domestic political hijinks therefore offer much of what is compelling in the three incidents described immediately above. But the European institutional responses, non-responses, and mixed responses all represent key features of those incidents. The refusal of the Committee of Ministers, the PACE Sub-Committee on Judicial Elections, and the PACE to react visibly and forcefully to the Bulgarian or Moldovan governments helps to set the ground rules of the relationship between the domestic and the European on the one hand, and between the political and the legal on the other. Meanwhile, the mixed set of European responses to the Slovak debacle (silence by the Committee of Ministers, surprising permissiveness by the Sub-Committee, and arguably self-defeating contrariness by the PACE) does a

[42] Flauss (2005) at 31–32.

great deal to demonstrate the complexity and delicacy of these multi-level inter-institutional interactions.

In the fourth and final re-nomination incident that we will consider, the national political maneuvers share center stage with the European institutional responses. As in the Bulgarian and Moldovan scenarios, the Estonian nomination battle of 2004 involved retribution against a sitting ECtHR judge for his action in a politically sensitive case. What makes the incident so interesting, however, is that it was not the Estonian government that was exacting retribution against the Estonian judge.

The judge in question was Rait Maruste, who had been the Estonian judge at the ECtHR since 1998. He decided to run for reappointment (i.e., re-election) upon the expiration of his six-year term in 2004. The Estonian government duly put his name forward on the list of three candidates that it forwarded to the authorities in Strasbourg. That list included two other candidates: Mai Hion, then the agent of the Estonian government before the ECtHR,[43] and Heike Pisuke, a law professor at the University of Tartu.[44] None of this was at all exceptional or even terribly noteworthy.

The surprise came when the PACE's Sub-Committee on Elections made its recommendation to the PACE: it favored Mrs. Hion over the sitting Judge Maruste. This choice against a sitting judge at the Court was all the more unexpected because Maruste had been chosen over Mrs. Hion in 1998.[45] What could explain this odd turn of events?

All indications pointed toward Moscow. The previous year, the ECtHR had handed down its decision in the highly divisive *Slivenko v. Latvia* litigation.[46] The case involved a family of ex-Soviet military personnel who had been transferred to, and ultimately settled in Latvia as early as 1959. When Latvia finally gained its independence from the USSR at the time of its dissolution in 1991, this left a host of difficulties about how to disentangle the two countries, including the vexing question of how to deal with Russian/ex-Soviet military personnel living in Latvia. This eventually led to a 1994 Latvian-Russian Treaty on the withdrawal of Russian troops, which provided for the complete withdrawal of Russian military troops and their families. After some five years of bitterly contested legal proceedings in the Latvian courts, the Slivenko family was finally deported to Russia in 1999.

[43] The "agent" functions in essence as the solicitor general of the government before the Court.

[44] *See* Comité des Ministres, *Communication Addendum*, Doc. 10099, in 2004 Session Ordinaire (deuxième partie) [of the PACE], Documents de séance, 26–30 avril 2004 at 225, available at https://books.google.com/books?id=AoiSVp9n5HQC&pg=PA225&lpg=PA225&dq=maruste+hion+-pisuke+2004&source=bl&ots=lO6YTCKwIt&sig=LaSmdVO0sisSZtNZ3UZwqPPdF30&hl=en&sa=X-&ved=0ahUKEwjptuaSkf3MAhWENz4KHZIqAI8Q6AEIKDAC#v=onepage&q=maruste%20hion%20pisuke%202004&f=false.

[45] *See* Flauss (2005) at 12.

[46] Slivenko v. Latvia, Application no. 48321/99 (October 9, 2003).

The Slivenkos argued that their removal from Latvia violated their right to respect for their private life, family life, and their home as guaranteed by Article 8 of the European Convention. The mother had lived there since 1959, when she was one month old. The father had been there since the 1970s, where he had met and married his wife. Their daughter was born there in 1981; and there she had been raised and spent her entire life. The Russian government supported the Slivenkos in their ECtHR litigation as third party interveners. It claimed, alongside the Slivenkos, that the family had been fully integrated into Latvian society: after all, they had been nationals of the Latvian Soviet Socialist Republic and had lived there for almost their entire lives.[47]

The Latvian government responded that their deportation pursued legitimate national aims and was compatible with both Latvian law and the Latvia-Russian Treaty. Furthermore, the removal should also be examined "in the context of the eradication of the consequences of the illegal occupation of Latvia by the Soviet Union, which had been completed by the withdrawal of the Russian troops from the territory of Latvia."[48] Clearly, the case turned in significant measure on how to construe the historical record that formed the factual background of the case. How, in particular, should one conceive of the fifty years of Soviet Russian dominance over Latvia? Indeed, how should one conceive of the USSR? And thus, how should one conceive of Soviet military officers and their families who had been sent to—and eventually settled in—Latvia?

The majority of the ECtHR held in favor of the Slivenko family. The Latvian extradition was an unjustified interference with the family's right to respect for their private life and their home. Notwithstanding the Treaty and the Latvian government's legitimate national security objectives, the application of the Latvian scheme for removal of foreign troops and their families needed to make it possible for exceptions to be made on the basis of individual circumstances. In this case, the deportation of the Slivenkos was not "necessary in a democratic society."[49] The Latvian authorities had "failed to strike a fair balance between the legitimate aim of the protection of national security and the interest of the protection of the applicants' rights under Article 8."[50] The Slivenko family, supported by the Russian government, had won their case. And the Russians, by extension, had won as well: the Court had refused to treat the ex-USSR and its Russian personnel in the harsh terms put forward by the Latvian government.

But the Russian government was infuriated nonetheless. The problem stemmed from the fact that several members of the ECtHR dissented from the majority decision. Most joined a Dissenting Opinion that simply disagreed with the majority

47 *Id.* at para. 91.
48 *Id.* at paras. 76–78.
49 *Id.* at para. 128.
50 *Id.* at para. 128.

about whether Latvia was justified in removing the Slivenko family. Such an Opinion, however couched, necessarily offered a less conciliatory assessment of the legacy of Soviet rule in Latvia. But far worse for the Russians was the Separate Dissenting Opinion by Judge Rait Maruste of Estonia.

Maruste's Dissent added little of substance to the joint Dissent's reasoning. Indeed, Maruste cosigned that Dissent. But he nonetheless felt compelled to write separately; and he did so in blunt terms that could only have been calculated to be as explicit and jarring as possible. In what can only be seen as a *cri-de-cœur* on behalf of the liberated Baltic States, Maruste wrote:

> While sharing the views expressed in the joint dissenting opinion, I would like to express here some more reasons why I am unable to agree with the majority.
>
> Firstly, I think the case is particular in its historical background. From that background flow consequences under constitutional and international law which cannot be disregarded. It is well known and recognised in international law that the Baltic States, including Latvia, lost their independence on the basis of the "Hitler-Stalin Pact" between Nazi Germany and the USSR, which actually refers to the Molotov-Ribbentrop Pact, or the secret protocols that were appended to the non-aggression treaty between the Soviet Union and Germany, which was signed on 23 August 1939. The result of this secret agreement was that Eastern Europe was divided into two spheres of influence, leaving the Baltic States, including Latvia, in the Soviet Union's sphere of interests. This was followed by Soviet threats of force in the form of an ultimatum addressed in 1940 to the Baltic States, including Latvia, in which the USSR demanded a change of government and the entry of Soviet armed forces (in addition to those already stationed in Soviet military bases). The actual entry of military forces and the change of government took place in June 1940.
>
> According to Article 42 of the Hague Regulations on the Laws and Customs of War on Land, a territory is considered occupied "when it is actually placed under the authority of the hostile army". By way of comparison, the Nuremberg Military Tribunal included the ultimatum delivered by Germany to Austria in 1938 among the acts to be judged as "crimes against peace" within the meaning of the 1945 London Charter.
>
> The above actions by the Soviet Union were not recognised by a majority of the international democratic community, including the European Parliament and the Council of Europe. The latter, for example, expressed its attitude in Resolution 189 (1960) on the situation in the Baltic States, noting, "on the twentieth anniversary of the occupation and forcible incorporation into the Soviet Union of the three European States of Estonia, Latvia and Lithuania" that "this illegal annexation took place without any genuine reference to the wishes of the people".
>
> It has been an established principle in international law which is now also enshrined in the Statute of the International Criminal Court (Article 8) that the

> transfer, directly or indirectly, by the occupying power of parts of its own civilian population into the territory it occupies is not allowed. Indeed, according to the same Article 8, it is a war crime.[51]

One can certainly understand why the Estonian Judge Maruste would pen such an extraordinary passage, which not only referred explicitly to the "Hitler-Stalin Pact"—as if the "Molotov-Ribbentrop Pact" were not bad enough!—but also went so far as to label the continued presence of Russians in Latvia as a potential war crime. After all, the Soviet takeover of Latvia was effectively indistinguishable from its takeover of Estonia.

But the Russians were in no mood to be understanding; and they apparently did their best to make the Estonian judge pay. This, then, was the explanation for the otherwise confounding decision by the PACE's Sub-Committee on Elections to place the sitting Judge Maruste behind Mrs. Hion in its ranking of the three candidates for the Estonian seat on the Court (despite the fact that the same Committee had preferred Judge Maruste over Mrs. Hion six years before). Professor Flauss writes:

> The Sub-Committee had not recommended his name and had instead chosen Mrs. Hion, the agent of the Estonian government before the Court. Now, everyone will understand that this choice was not fundamentally motivated by a desire to promote better female representation on the Court, nor was it dictated by Judge Maruste's inferior competence (he was found superior to Mrs. Hion in 1998). It was instead the result of a lobbying effort conducted by the Russian delegation to the PACE, and also, in all likelihood, by the very hot-tempered agent of the Russian government before the Court. In this matter, the point was to make the Estonian judge pay dearly for the perhaps blunt, but nonetheless perfectly justified, statements that he had expressed in his dissenting opinion in the *Slivenko* case.[52]

The Russians had apparently thrown their weight around in Strasbourg; and although they did not manage in the end to unseat Judge Maruste, they had certainly succeeded in making him sweat: in the (once again poorly attended) PACE vote, he barely squeaked by Mrs. Hion, with eighty-eight votes to her seventy-five.[53] If nothing else, a clear warming shot had been fired across the bow of the ECtHR: a sitting judge would be wise to think twice before publicly humiliating the Russians.

[51] Separate Dissenting Opinion of Judge Maruste, in *id.* at 50.
[52] Flauss (2005) at 12.
[53] *See* Council of Europe: Parliamentary Assembly, Official Report of Debates: 2004 Ordinary Session (Second Part), Thirteenth Sitting, Wednesday April 28, 2004 at 3 p.m., at 479.

In one sense, this case was only yet another instance of a sitting ECtHR judge being subjected to retribution at reappointment for actions taken (or not taken) during the course of his/her duties. But there was an important twist: this time, the pressure was being applied not by the judge's own government, but that of another Member State (Russia). This novel feature of the incident was deeply meaningful. For starters, it was one thing for a Member State to police its own judge for failing properly to represent the legal interests of his/her country: indeed, the structural requirement that the judge from the defendant State sit on every case in which his/her country is in question all but guarantees that the judge would often play some version of such a defensive role, even if only in an attenuated explanatory fashion. As a practical matter, this means that every ECtHR judge in every case in which her country is legitimately in question will be placed in the uncomfortable position of having to decide between defending the Convention system and defending her country.[54]

Everyone at all familiar with the Strasbourg system therefore fully understands that the national judge on the deciding panel necessarily faces this bind, which, furthermore, must be resolved in a public manner: the ECtHR (unlike the ECJ) permits dissenting and concurring opinions, which allows everyone (including the national government) to observe whether that judge has decided to defend her country (by dissenting), or to break with her country by joining in the Court's condemnation, or to try to finesse the tension through some form of artful compromise. Because ECtHR judges are therefore always subject to the umbrage of their own national governments, everyone understands why the sitting national judge must be particularly tactful in the cases involving her home country. But it was another thing altogether for the *other* judges on the panel to be cowed into pulling punches. One could reasonably expect, and account for, the national judge. But all the other judges? This threatened the integrity of the ECHR system as a whole.

This Estonian/Russian episode also revealed another threat arguably as fundamental. After all, if a given Member State wished to punish its own judge, it had merely to refuse re-nominate him/her for reelection. As long as it dotted its i's and crossed its t's by proposing a viable list of three other suitable candidates, the

[54] It goes perhaps without saying that a judge can theoretically (and even practically) do both at the same time and even that this is precisely what s/he should always do. But that is not an easy point to make to a national government that is being publicly shamed before an international tribunal for having engaged in fundamental rights violations. As Flauss explains:

> There are [ECtHR] judges who have never voiced, by means of a separate opinion, the slightest critique of the positions propounded by "their" State, nor ever even voted against the latter. The restraint thus demonstrated by some judges manifests, at least for them, their intention not to enter into conflict with their principals and/or to appear to be a bad patriot or a traitor plain and simple.

Flauss (2005) at 28–29, n. 81.

For more on this representational conception of European judges, *see infra* Chapter 12(II)(A) and Chapter 13.

government could effectively fire its judge at the end of the judge's term. But how could a different Member State fire this same judge? Without the power to nominate three potential replacements, it theoretically could not.

This practical tactical reality reveals the distinctive challenge raised by the 2004 Estonian appointment. The Bulgarian, Moldovan, and Slovak episodes were fundamentally domestic affairs: the national governments could simply refuse to re-nominate their judges; and the most the European institutions could do was to try to resist, for example, by making it difficult for those governments by refusing to accept their new lists for one (potentially pretextual) reason or another. But the Estonian appointment was by necessity a European affair: the Russians, unable to refuse independently to re-nominate (the judge was, after all, Estonian), had to enlist the support of other actors at the European level to punish Judge Maruste; and it apparently did so quite effectively. It was the Sub-Committee of the PACE that took the surprising action of preferring Mrs. Hion, thereby putting Judge Maruste in a very precarious position. And as the razor thin margin of Maruste's re-election by the PACE makes quite clear, the Russian intervention, backed by the Sub-Committee, came ever so close to succeeding. In some sense, therefore, the key feature of the Estonian episode is just how clearly it implicated not only a national government, but also the institutions of the Council of Europe in these bare-fisted judicial appointment struggles.

V. The 2011 French Appointment

The newer Member States have undoubtedly provided the overwhelming majority of the judicial appointment scandals; but they have by no means cornered the market. Though not a terribly exciting example, probably the best-known episode starring a long-standing Member State was the 2011 French appointment to replace Jean-Paul Costa, the retiring President of the Court, who had been the French judge in Strasbourg ever since it had become a single and permanent court in 1998. Faced with the task of replacing such an emblematic figure, the Sarkozy government made a stunningly amateurish and ultimately ineffectual attempt to get a political ally appointed to the Court for reasons unrelated to the Court itself.

The episode began during the summer of 2010, when the French Minister of Justice made a public call for applications for the Strasbourg post. Some twenty applications were filed, which were then forwarded to a group of exceptionally senior group of jurists to make a first cut. These four eminent (if particularly elderly) figures—Gilbert Guillaume (ex-president of the International Court of Justice), Prosper Weil (the *doyen* of French public law), Jean-Pierre Puissochet (former ECJ judge), and Marc Perrin de Brichambaut (Secretary General of the Organization for Security and Co-operation in Europe)—constituted the French delegation to the Permanent Court of Arbitration in the Hague; and they were charged with producing a list of six candidates, from which the government would select the three to nominate to Strasbourg.[55]

These senior jurists ended up producing a list of five, instead of six. And they did more. They underlined that two candidates appeared "particularly worthy of nomination": Edwige Belliard (the Director of Legal Affairs at the Foreign Ministry and the Agent of the French government before the ECtHR) and André Potocki (Justice of the French Court of Cassation and former Vice-President of the Court of First Instance of the European Communities).[56] Importantly, they also refused to include in their list the name of a centrist political ally of President Sarkozy: Michel Hunault, a Member of the French National Assembly since 1993.

The Sarkozy government responded by trying to push through its preferred candidate nonetheless. It simply added Hunault's "complementary" name to the two "particularly worthy" candidates and presented this list of three to the Strasbourg authorities.[57] Why had it done this? Word on the street was that the Sarkozy government was playing a crass, if intricate, political game. The French President was facing a likely loss in the impending 2012 presidential elections; and his young friend and communications advisor, Franck Louvrier, was hoping for a seat in parliament in order to keep his budding political career afloat after Sarkozy left office. Hence the seemingly clever ruse: Hunault would be put forward for the prestigious judicial post in Strasbourg, opening up his seat in the French national assembly, into which Louvrier could be "parachuted."

Things went badly from there. First, the newly created APE advised the French that Mr. Hunault was not a suitable candidate.[58] Although Hunault had a master's degree in law, he had spent the overwhelming majority of his career as a parliamentarian, not as a practicing lawyer. Worse, he did not speak English. As his CV suggested all too tellingly, he had been undergoing "intensive training" in English ... for the previous month![59]

But the Sarkozy government forged ahead nevertheless: it presented the list of three for review by the PACE's Sub-Committee on Elections. The Sub-Committee was no more charitable toward the list. Indeed, when the Sub-Committee convened to interview the nine French, Norwegian, and Swiss candidates to the Court, it simply refused to meet with the French candidates at all. The French delegation proceeded to make an unseemly row in full earshot of mortified staff. But the Sub-Committee's Vice-Chairman, Klaas de Vries, simply informed them that

[55] PACE, Election of judges to the European Court of Human Rights, List and curricula vitae of candidates submitted by the Governments of France, Norway and Switzerland, Doc. 12527 (February 25, 2011) at 4.

[56] *Id.*

[57] *Id.*

[58] *See* Engel (2008) at 451.

[59] PACE, Doc. 12527, at 11.

the French list had already been rejected.[60] There would be no interviews with the French candidates.

Eventually, matters were resolved in an uncontroversial manner. Hunault came to understand that he had no real shot at the Strasbourg position; so he finally withdrew his name from consideration. The French government submitted the name of an appellate court judge to complete the list of three candidates. And the PACE elected the distinguished Judge Potocki of the Cour de cassation to the ECtHR by a wide margin. One might be tempted, therefore, to think that all's well that ends well: the Strasbourg institutions had indeed managed to stop the French government from ramming through its desired appointment; and a particularly graceful and worthy candidate was ultimately appointed.

But real damage had been done. The French government had publicly embarrassed itself in a manner that was extremely unusual for such an established and leading Member State. Indeed, the episode was rather widely publicized in the French press and even managed to cross national boundaries.[61] Perhaps more important, by running roughshod over the newly instituted APE in one of its very first engagements, the French government had shown a degree of disdain for the new institution that would prove infectious and from which, one could reasonably argue, the APE has never really recovered.

VI. The 2012 Czech Appointment

The most notorious of the ECtHR appointment scandals undoubtedly involves the election of Aleš Pejchal as the Czech judge in 2012. The reason for this is simple. The French and Estonian cases, for all of their backstage intrigue, eventually resulted in the appointment or reappointment of respected judicial candidates. And while the Bulgarian, Moldovan, and Slovak cases ended up *denying* reappointment of more

[60] Franck Johannès, *Petite manœuvre pour placer un ami*, LE MONDE, March 14, 2011, available at http://libertes.blog.lemonde.fr/2011/03/14/petite-manoeuvre-de-lelysee-pour-placer-un-ami/.

[61] *See, e.g.*, *id.*; Corinne Lepage, "Copinage en Sarkozie: la double honte de la France à Strasbourg," available at http://rue89.nouvelobs.com/blog/corinne-lepage/2011/03/24/copinage-en-sarkozie-la-double-honte-de-la-france-a-strasbourg-196747; Antoine Spohr, , "Cour européenne des droits de l'homme: les trois candidats français ajournés," (April 12, 2011), available at https://blogs.mediapart.fr/aspohr/blog/120411/cour-europeenne-des-droits-de-lhomme-les-trois-candidats-francais-ajournes; Europe1, "Election à la CEDH: La France retire sa liste," (April 11, 2011), available at http://www.europe1.fr/international/election-a-la-cedh-la-france-retire-sa-liste-494725; Le Parisien, "Juge à la CEDH: la France devra présenter une nouvelle liste de candidats," (April 11, 2011), available at http://www.leparisien.fr/strasbourg-67000/juge-a-la-cedh-la-france-devra-presenter-une-nouvelle-liste-de-candidats-11-04-2011-1403429.php#xtref=https%3A%2F%2Fwww.google.com%2F; Giornalettismo, "Si libera un posto al Parlamento francese? Sarkozy ci mette un amico suo," (March 16, 2011), available at http://www.giornalettismo.com/archives/117940/si-libera-un-posto-al-parlamento-francese-sarkozy-ci-mette-un-amico-suo/; Koen Lemmens, *(S)electing Judges for Strasbourg: A (Dis)appointing Process?*, *in* SELECTING EUROPE'S JUDGES A CRITICAL REVIEW OF THE APPOINTMENT PROCEDURES TO THE EUROPEAN COURTS 95, 113–15 (MICHAL BOBEK ed., 2015).

or less worthy ECtHR judges, the scandals did not involve the appointment of candidates officially branded as unqualified. For this, 2012 Czech appointment broke new ground.

At its core, the Czech case is fairly straightforward, despite the intricacies described by the Czech scholar David Kosař.[62] The Czech ECtHR seat was to be vacated in the fall of 2012. Due to a number of relatively unrelated circumstances, such as the opening of other desirable positions at about the same time, the Czech government's call for applications for the Strasbourg post led to an unusually small number of candidates.[63] The Czech authorities could easily fill two of the three slots on the list to be submitted to Strasbourg with Mahulena Hofmannová (law professor at the University of Luxembourg) and Zdeněk Kühn (law professor at the Charles University in Prague and a judge of the Czech Supreme Administrative Court), even if both were relatively young. But they had sufficient trouble finding a legitimate candidate for the third slot that they had to take the unusual step of putting out a separate call in order to fill it: none of the other candidates who had already presented themselves were suitable to put forward to Strasbourg. This new call yielded two more candidates: an undistinguished lower level professor and Aleš Pejchal, an attorney in private practice in Prague who, it later turned out, happened to be a personal advisor to the far-right and Eurosceptic Czech President Václav Klaus (although, tellingly, this relationship was not disclosed on his application's CV).[64] The government therefore added Pejchal to Hofmannová and Kühn and sent the list to Strasbourg.

Neither the APE nor the PACE Sub-Committee on Elections was impressed with Pejchal's addition. The APE declared him unqualified to sit on the Court. Despite its best efforts, however, the APE was ultimately unable to work out a face-saving solution in its confidential dealings with the Czechs. It is not entirely clear whether this was because the Czech government was prepared to push through the appointment of its favorite candidate at all costs[65] or whether it was simply desperate due to its lack of plausible reserve candidates.[66] For either reason or both, the Czech government refused to back down by taking Pejchal off its list. Nor was Pejchal

[62] *See* David Kosař, *Selecting Strasbourg Judges: A Critique*, *in* Bobek (2015) at 120, 150–56 ["Kosař (2015)"].

[63] As Kosař explains, the extension of the mandate of the Czech seat from 2010 to 2012 due to the delayed ratification of Protocol 14 resulted in the loss of a number of qualified candidates: a number of other prestigious domestic and international judicial positions had opened up and been filled in the interim. *See id.* at 151–52.

[64] *See* PACE, Election of Judges to the ECHR: List and curricula vitae of candidates submitted by the Governments of Bosnia and Herzegovina, Croatia, the Czech Republic, the Netherlands, Poland, the Russian Federation, Sweden and the United Kingdom, Doc. 12936 (May 22, 2012), available at http://assembly.coe.int/Documents/WorkingDocs/2012/COE.PACE.WD.COM.12936.2012.EN.pdf, at 57–60.

[65] This is the thesis of Norbert Engel. *See* Engel (2008) at 450.

[66] This is the thesis of David Kosař. *See* Kosař (2015) at 153–54.

himself willing to withdraw, as Hunault had eventually done in the French struggle the year before.

The position of the Czech government was soon to look even worse: the Sub-Committee also found Pejchal unacceptable. It did not, however, find him unqualified: he was, after all, the serving Vice-President of the Czech Bar Association, although he had twice been rejected for a position on the Czech Constitutional Court.[67] For the Sub-Committee, the key problem lay instead in his close advisory relationship with the deeply problematic Czech President Václav Klaus.

Rather than formally refuse the entire list, however, which would have forced the Czech government to try to dig up another suitable candidate (which was by no means assured, especially given the added risk that one of the two qualified candidates might simply withdraw out of frustration), the Sub-Committee chose to forward only two of the three names to the PACE for consideration: Hofmannová and Kühn. This rather clever solution would allow the vote to move forward in the PACE while effectively taking Pejchal out of play. The APE would be satisfied; the Czech government would be spared public humiliation; and the judicial election could proceed in a timely fashion.

Unfortunately, this solution proved too clever by half. The Czech government not only stuck by its list but now actively lobbied to maintain it: the Minister of Justice went so far as to bypass the APE altogether by sending a letter directly to PACE members (although, once again, it is not entirely clear whether this was to support Pejchal in particular or the list as a whole).[68] Worse, Pejchal himself went on a lobbying campaign that raised eyebrows.[69] As Kosař writes: "According to Czech sources, the Czech Bar Association and the Archbishop of Prague, among other actors, wrote letters of support for Mr. Pejchal to [the] PACE."[70] This was all the more unseemly because Pejchal was serving at the time as Vice-President of the Czech Bar Association.

But matters became even more distasteful. Pejchal's wife, who was working at the Chamber of Deputies of the Czech Parliament, was—in a heretofore unprecedented act—suddenly "assigned" to the Council of Europe in Strasbourg. From this tactical perch, she successfully joined in the lobbying campaign for her husband. It worked, despite Lord Tomlinson's attempt—ultimately overridden on confidentiality grounds—to quote from the Sub-Committee recommendation on the floor of the PACE in order to question Pejchal's suitability for the judicial post.[71] Ultimately, not only was the Czech list not rejected, but Pejchal—who had, after

[67] *See* PACE Doc. 12936 at 57; Kosař (2015) at 155.

[68] *Cf.* Engel (2008) at 450 and Kosař (2015) at 153–54.

[69] *See* Engel (2008) at 450.

[70] Kosař (2015) at 154. *See* PACE Doc. 12936 at 57.

[71] *See supra* text accompanying note 11; PACE, 2012 Ordinary Session (Third part), Report, Twenty-first Sitting, Tuesday June 26, 2012, at 10 a.m., Document AS (2012) CR 21, available at http://assembly.coe.int/Documents/Records/2012/E/1206261000E.htm.

all, been deemed unsuitable by both the APE and the PACE's own Sub-Committee on Elections—was duly elected by the General Assembly of the PACE as the Czech judge on the ECtHR.

This result was sufficiently scandalous that a number of the members of the APE considered resigning. They eventually tasked their Chair, Luzius Wildhaber, to meet with figures in key leadership positions of the PACE, the Committee of Ministers, and the Court in order to express their outrage and try to work out some solutions moving forward. This led to the "Exchange of Views" between Wildhaber and the Committee of Ministers' Steering Committee for Human Rights, in which Wildhaber strongly voiced their frustrations.[72] This led in turn to modest reforms, that, as we explained in Chapter 5, nonetheless fell far short of the effective veto power that the APE wished to exercise over candidates it deemed unqualified to sit on the Court.[73] And of course, the notorious Judge Pejchal continues to serve as the Czech judge in Strasbourg, much to everyone's dissatisfaction.

VII. Temporary Conclusion

The six unhappy episodes described in this chapter offer an unflattering portrait of appointments conflicts at the Strasbourg Court. As the ensuing chapter should make clear, I have no interest whatever in undermining the Court or the Council of Europe, or in calling their good work into question. Nor is my purpose straightforwardly reformist: unlike Professor Jean-François Flauss, I am not leveraging these sordid episodes in order to promote a particular procedural or professional program. For the purposes of this book, the interest of these scandalous episodes lies in the window they offer onto the politics of the European judicial appointments, judicial independence, and judicial quality debates. In order to make the most of this perspective, let us now turn to scandal theory.

72 *See* 2013 Exchange of Views.
73 *See supra* Chapter 5(III).

11
Scandal Theory in Context

I. The Core of Scandal Theory

I propose that we now pause in our analysis of such European appointment incidents in order to turn to contemporary scandal theory. I use the term scandal theory to refer to a relatively small, but conceptually rich, body of literature that focuses on scandal, and especially political scandal. Building off of the groundbreaking work of social anthropologists Max Gluckman and Eric de Dampierre, this fascinating literature has been elaborated most successfully by such political sociologists and political scientists as John B. Thompson, Andrei Markovits, Mark Silverstein, Cyril Lemieux, Damien de Blic, and Alain Garrigou.

This literature comes in different shapes and sizes, addresses different political and social contexts, and offers a good deal in the way of methodological, theoretical, and substantive variation. I will intentionally downplay such differences in order to emphasize instead the many fundamental points that these texts hold very much in common. To the extent that this framing of the field and that transposing it to the European appointments debates represents a modest intervention in the field of scandal theory, so much the better. But that is not the primary point of the exercise, which is simply to generate a coherent set of analytic insights that we might fruitfully bring to bear on our materials. As we shall see, scandal theory does in fact offer a rich set of analytic perspectives that can help us to work through the players, processes, and stakes in the European judicial appointment debates.

A. The Scandalous Event

Scandal theory stresses that scandal tends to present itself as a pre-existing event: some person or institution has engaged in scandalous behavior that is now appropriately subject to opprobrium. In some respects, this common sense notion of scandal is accurate; but in others, it is not. It is of course true that a scandal usually depends on the prior occurrence of some kind of problematic event. But to qualify the event as scandalous is tautological: such a circular definition does little to describe what makes the scandal a scandal in the first place.

The common sense notion therefore obscures the building blocks of scandal. The key to a scandal is not the event itself, so much as the public revelation of the violation of particular sorts of norms. In the words of Alain Garrigou:

> When speaking of a scandal . . ., everything proceeds as if people were speaking not of what they are doing [when speaking in such terms], but speaking about the object of their speech. These moments are oriented towards the past, and secondarily towards the future (via the potential consequences of the denouement). The present seems totally absent, except as elucidation of the past. And yet, it is the publication of evidence, of revelations, of police and legal action, and the taking of positions that actually constitutes the raw material of scandal.[1]

Scandal, in other words, is not so much a prior event as the process of revealing that event, of invoking the allegedly violated and purportedly vital norms, and of summoning the community's opprobrium for that violation. Let us therefore briefly work through these assorted component parts.

B. Claim of Violation of Norms

A scandal almost inevitably stems from a claim that a given norm has been violated. As we shall see, there is a good deal to say about each of the terms that compose such a statement. But let us begin with the norm itself. The literature exhibits some disagreement regarding what kinds of norms are liable to give rise to scandalous violation. On the one hand, a number of scholars—often arguing from a comparative perspective—argue that the nature of the transgressed norms or values depends on the political culture in question. Thus, Theodore Lowi notes that "[s]ince politically relevant moral values vary from culture to culture and country to country, conduct that offends values deeply and widely enough to become a serious scandal will vary accordingly."[2] As a result, to use the wry terms of John Logue, not only "is what is a scandal a question of political culture," but also "each country gets the scandals it deserves."[3]

Other scholars, however, try to delimit what kinds of norms are likely to be in play. Cambridge sociology professor John Thompson, for example, explains that the violated norms can be neither too minor (such as a trivial act of jaywalking) nor too major (such as genocide): they must occupy a contested middle ground

[1] Alain Garrigou, *Le boss, la machine et le scandale. La chute de la maison Médecin*, 5 Politix (no. 17) 7, 16 (1992) ["Garrigou (1992)"].

[2] Theodore Lowi, *Forward*, *in* Andrei Markovits & Mark Silverstein eds., The Politics of Scandal: Power and Process in Liberal Democracies vii, ix (1988)>>>["Markovits & Silverstein (1988)"].

[3] John Logue, *Conclusion*, *in* Markovits & Silverstein (1988) at 254, 259, 265.

with such ill-defined boundaries as those concerning sex, finances, or the abuse of political power.[4] In the context of political scandals, however, it is the duo of Markovits and Silverstein that offers by far the most precise and restrictive demarcation: they claim that a true political scandal always involves the violation of the due process norms that manage the classic tension in liberal democracies between (a) the public exercise of democratically sanctioned political power and (b) the liberal protection of private interests against such democratic rule. To Markovits and Silverstein, therefore, a true political scandal violates the core divisions that both define and threaten liberal democracy itself.[5]

C. Revelation to a Public

Although a scandal thus depends on the violation of some kind of norm, it is not the breech alone that "makes" the scandal. That breech must provoke a scandal. This means that the breech must somehow be revealed and communicated to a public that is called upon to respond with opprobrium, it must generate the requisite response, and so on. Scandal, in other words, is an *unfolding process*, not a mere one-shot (never mind pre-existing) event.

If the literature is consistent on one point, it is that the *sine qua non* of a scandal is therefore the public revelation of the problematic and previously concealed deed. In Lowi's terms, "the primary political element of scandal is concealment and its exposure."[6] This process of exposure involves widening the circle of those who are aware of the transgression from the immediate participants (such as the alleged transgressor and victim) to a public of some kind,[7] however small: "By definition, there is no scandal as long as the transgression remains secret."[8]

This broadening of the public requires publicizing the act. As Thompson writes, not only is scandal is "*a drama of concealment and disclosure*,"[9] but it "can arise only if the tacit agreement which keeps gossip and rumor at the level of private communication among friends or acquaintances is broken and the revelations ... are articulated in public."[10] This implies a great deal. In particular, it implies both agency

[4] John Thompson, Political Scandal: Power and Visibility in the Media Age 14–15 (2000) ["Thompson (2000)"].

[5] Andrei Markovits & Mark Silverstein, *Introduction: Power and Process in Liberal Democracies*, *in* Markovits & Silverstein (1988) at 1, 5–9.

[6] Lowi, *Forward*, *in* Markovits & Silverstein (1988) at x.

[7] *See* Markovits & Silverstein (1988) at 3.

[8] Damien de Blic & Cyril Lemieux, *The Scandal as Test: Elements of a Pragmatic Sociology*, 71 Politix 9, 21 (2005) ["Blic & Lemieux (2005)"]. English language edited version available at http://www.cairn-int.info/article-E_POX_071_0009--the-scandal-as-test.htm#anchor_citation, at para. 20, citing Thompson (2000) at 18.

[9] Thompson (2000) at 18 (emphasis in original).

[10] *Id.* at 21.

(i.e., someone who chooses to publicize) and means (i.e., some form of media). As Eric de Dampierre explained magisterially in *Annales* as early as 1954:

> The third working hypothesis is that to constitute a scandal, the scandalous event does not suffice; it must find a public. There is no scandal without a public, without the dissemination of the scandalous event within the public that it thereby helps to form, and without mass communication.[11]

Finally, this implies the existence, selection, and/or formation of some kind of community or communities that will serve as the scandal's public(s).

Each of these components is deeply suggestive. The agency required to publicize the scandal raises the issue of interests, motivations, and tactical decision-making. The means of publication suggests the existence and mobilization of mechanisms for disseminating information to a chosen public. And the existence of such a public raises the issue of its membership and nature, which raises in turn the questions of identity formation and the construction of political or other community.

The theoretical literature thus posits a core relationship between scandal and community. Max Gluckman, the noted leader of the "Manchester School" of social anthropology, was especially interested in this relationship: in a seminal 1963 article, he put forward an account according to which gossip and scandal are mechanisms for reinforcing the membership, identity, and values of a given community.[12] His central insight was that gossip and scandal are community-based: they are not recounted to just anyone. To the contrary, to be granted access to them is to granted access to the community:

> The important things about gossip and scandal are that generally these are enjoyed by people about others with whom they are in a close social relationship. Hence when we try to understand why it is that people in all places and at all times have been so interested in gossip and scandal about each other, we have also to look at those whom they exclude from joining in the gossiping or scandalizing. That is, the right to gossip about certain people is a privilege which is only extended to a person when he or she is accepted as a member of a group or set. It is a hallmark of membership. Hence rights to gossip serve to mark off a particular group from other groups.[13]

[11] Eric de Dampierre, *Thèmes pour l'étude du scandale*, in ANNALES. ÉCONOMIES, SOCIÉTÉS, CIVILISATIONS, 9e année, N. 3, 328, 332 (1954) ["Dampierre (1954)"].

[12] *See* Max Gluckman, *Gossip and Scandal*, 4(3) CURRENT ANTHROPOLOGY 30 (1963) ["Gluckman (1963)"]. Gluckman made little or no attempt to distinguish between gossip and scandal; but for our purposes, it is not worth critiquing this analytic imprecision.

[13] *Id.* at 313.

Gossip and scandal thus possess what Gluckman terms "positive virtues": they offer a community the means to differentiate between insiders and outsiders, and thus the means to reinforce group unity, identity, and values.

To Gluckman, this community-oriented feature of gossip and scandal was essential not only for distinguishing between a community and its outsiders (who would not be granted entry into the circle of those to whom gossip and scandal would be revealed), but also for regulating the relationship between different factions and cliques *within* the community itself. As he saw it, gossip and scandal also offered a means for these different internal interests and players to compete for normative and socio-political authority:

> I propose to illustrate the social affiliations of this process and to suggest that gossip, and even scandal, have important positive virtues. Clearly they maintain the unity, morals and values of social groups. Beyond this, they enable these groups to control the competing cliques and aspiring individuals of which all groups are composed. And finally, they make possible the selection of leaders without embarrassment.[14]

Thus, "Scandalizing is one of the principal means by which the group's separateness is expressed, even though it is also the principal manner in which internal struggles are fought."[15] On this reading, gossip and scandal are important mechanisms for "competitively aligned" cliques within a community to "struggle for status and prestige" by acceptable means, while simultaneously policing the boundary between that community and all others.

Gluckman accordingly suggests that scandal is a highly competitive process by which a community regulates both its internal and its external relationships. If a prospective leader mishandles his use of scandal, for example, by "scandalizing too far," then "he himself oversteps the values of the group and his scandal will turn against him, will prove that he or his small clique is unworthy of the larger group."[16] The struggle for leadership within the community via the proper use of scandal accordingly generates community unity, even as it empowers the internal leaders to then deploy scandal against both outsiders and internal rivals.

Perhaps the most concise and effective manner to recast Gluckman's analysis of the community-based aspect of gossip and scandal is therefore to say that scandal has *representative* value. Scandal is a central means by which an internal faction struggles to gain primacy within a given community; and having achieved such primacy, the faction not only takes on leadership of the whole community relative to all outside communities, but can also deploy scandal as a means both to refuse

[14] *Id.* at 308.
[15] *Id.* at 312.
[16] *Id.* at 313.

access to the domestic community and to express that community's superiority over others. Gluckman thus states: "Scandal when directed by members of a group against another group is unifying in another, and an obvious, way—it asserts the superiority of the scandalizing group."[17]

D. Contested Norms or Values

If we accept that rival factions do indeed choose to reveal the scandalous violation of community norms as a means to gain some measure of internal and external ascendency, this nonetheless leaves unclear the relationship between the transgressions and the norms they violate. One possibility is that the question of violation hinges on merely empirical facts: i.e., did the alleged transgression actually take place? The other possibility, however, is that the question of violation hinges instead on normative schisms: i.e., the real question is not so much whether the allegedly transgressive act was committed as whether the act should be considered scandalously transgressive in the first place—a question that hinges in turn on the existence, status, and proper construction of the asserted norm.

Although this distinction between what might be termed "factual" and "normative" struggles is reasonably clear in theory, the reality is that most scandalous charges work hard to efface the distinction: a scandal always claims (almost by definition) that the norm in question self-evidently exists and that its application to the alleged facts self-evidently demonstrates the existence of a scandalous transgression. Such pretensions have left their mark on the literature: some strands of scandal theory take scandal more or less at its word, taking for granted that the existence of a scandal implies the pre-existence of a norm or value that is sufficiently anchored in the community for its violation to trigger the requisite opprobrium. Other strands, however, stress that one should treat a scandal's assertions as no more than heated claims regarding the existence and applicability of the asserted community norms.

The former set of analyses—which effectively take scandal at its word—tend to take a self-consciously Durkheimian cast. For them, scandal performs the fundamentally conservative function of reinforcing established communal norms and values. Markovits and Silverstein explain:

> Within sociology, research building on Emile Durkheim's work in social integration has dominated studies dealing with scandals. Durkheim argued that even the most asocial, amoral, pathological actions (e.g., murder, theft, suicide) are ultimately functional to the integration of society. By violating a shared belief, sacred

[17] *Id.* at 314.

> or profane, such a transgression helped to reaffirm not only the belief itself but the social collectivity that upholds and sustains that belief. Hence for Durkheim, transgressions are not only normal in everyday life but necessary for the maintenance of any social order.
>
> Scandals fit this model perfectly. Invariably, scandals serve to strengthen the *conscience collective*. In addition to reaffirming and ultimately strengthening the bonds of a common morality, scandals help to create the scapegoats, enemies and pariahs needed by all communities. This, in turn, aids the social processes of legitimation and mass mobilization. While a scandalous act invariably challenges the norms and values of the community, the public ritual of investigation, discussion, and punishment ultimately serves to reinforce the primacy of those shared norms and values. According to Durkheim, criminal behavior and subsequent punishment serve much the same function ... [T]he ritual of scandal and punishment provides social systems with a means for self-legitimation and purification. Scandals, in short, constitute an important opportunity for reaffirming the social order.[18]

Gluckman adopts a fundamentally similar approach, overtly recognizing that his "argument about gossip and scandal is similar" to the classic Durkheimian analysis of the combination of crime and punishment, which "serves useful ends in maintaining the law, and therefore society."[19]

But a second set of analyses adopts a much less mechanical view of the relationship between community norms and scandal. That is, they are far less likely to infer the existence of a self-evidently pre-existing and powerful community norm from the mere fact that a scandal has broken out. To them, the existence of a scandal more likely indicates that a struggle has broken out over a contested norm. As Thompson explains in a particularly important paragraph:

> I have suggested that the transgression of a value or norm can give rise to a scandal only if the value or norm has some degree of moral force or "bindingness" for some of the individuals who become aware of its transgression. But this is not to say that these values or norms are likely to elicit general or widespread consensus in a particular socio-historical context, nor is it to say that these values or norms are matters about which most people feel very strongly or with reference to which they organize their own lives. On the contrary, values or norms are often contested features of social life, adhered to by some individuals and groups and rejected (or simply ignored) by others. Hence scandals are often rather messy affairs, involving the alleged transgression of values or norms which are themselves subject to contestation. Moreover, values and norms are always embedded

[18] Markovits & Silverstein (1988) at 2–3.
[19] Gluckman (1963) at 315.

> in relations of power; they structure social life in ways that permit certain kinds of activity and exclude or forbid others (or force them underground). In many cases, scandals are not just about actions which transgress certain values or norms: they are also about the cultivation or assertion of the values or norms themselves. Thus the making of a scandal is often associated with a broader process of "moralization" through which certain values or norms are espoused and reaffirmed—with varying degrees of effectiveness and good faith—by those who denounce the actions as scandalous.[20]

For Dampierre, and later Blic and Lemieux, a scandal clearly depends on the existence of some pre-existing norm or value; but the progress and eventual outcome of a scandal hinges on the community's current relationship to this norm or value. Blic and Lemieux thus argue that a scandal is effectively a "test" of a community's commitment to a "transgressed value" and thus "whether or not the denounced scandal is really a scandal":

> It is thus up to the actors themselves, and to them alone, to show us through their indignant reactions or their relativistic attitudes whether the offense really is an offense. Indeed, as De Dampierre would say, they are the ones who will test their adherence to the transgressed values and who will put their common sense of injustice to the test.[21]

And indeed, Dampierre put forward this crucial idea that a scandal was in effect a test of social values:

> Amongst the effects that a scandalous event produces on received values, some are at the very least unexpected. If a scandal [i.e., a scandalous event] is corrosive insofar as it demonstrates that socially recognized values are neither absolute nor equally respected by all, and thus subject to discussion, it also reinforces these same values by the very fact that it undermines them; in truth, it is the touchstone of these values, a test that demonstrates that these values are not irrelevant, that they still survive as values. The scandal that lapses into indifference is no longer a scandal (was it ever?).[22]

For this set of authors, therefore, a scandal does not so much *reveal* the prior existence of a social norm as it *tests* that norm's continued relevance and resonance in a given community. One might add, furthermore, that according to this logic, a scandal might also test the emergence of a new social norm or, at least, the

[20] Thompson (2000) at 16.
[21] Blic & Lemieux (2005) at 16, English version at para. 13.
[22] Dampierre (1954) at 335–36.

development of an existing norm in new directions that may—or may not—garner community adherence.

The literature never does resolve this difficult tension between the conservative and the contestatory nature of scandal, i.e., whether a scandal manifests (a) the existence of an anchored social norm or (b) a contest over the existence, vitality, relevance, and meaning of an old, new, or emerging social norm. Far from considering this a flaw, I see it as completely appropriate. By its very nature, scandal walks a very fine line between reinforcing existing community values and putting those values, their elaboration, and their following to the test. Although it is fair to say that a scandal that leads to opprobrium demonstrates that a value actually garnered sufficient community support to produce such a result, this can only be affirmed with the benefit of hindsight: had the scandal played out otherwise, the value would instead have been abandoned or relativized. This demonstrates both the uncertain and the diachronic nature of scandals: they play out over time, leading to potentially unpredictable conclusions.

E. Unfolding over Time

John Thompson describes scandal as exhibiting a "sequential structure," with a succession of phases that unfold with the uncertainty and speculation of a good novel.[23] Markovits and Silverstein spell out those phases or "stages" as follows:

> Typically, a period of normalcy is disturbed by an unusual event. Initially confined to a small circle of active participants, the transgressor and the immediate victim, the event "takes off" through the efforts of a third party, often the purifier. In the third stage, the event becomes public and demands are made for punishment and restitution. Stage four comprises the process of reaffirmation in which transgressors are punished and reforms are instituted. The cycle is completed when normalcy is again restored, incorporating the reforms designed to safeguard the system from similar transgressions in the future. The reforms are only successful in preventing very similar events from recurring shortly after the initial transgression. Different transgressions, however, are bound to occur later; ... scandals are inherent in the very structure of politics and confirm Durkheim's point that each social system needs pathologies for its successful reproduction. In short, political scandals constitute important ingredients in the maintenance and development of political life.[24]

[23] *See* Thompson (2000) at 72–73.
[24] Markovits & Silverstein (1988) at 3.

This sequential account underlines once again the precarious nature of scandal. On the one hand, it demonstrates its conservative function, which leads to the "re-affirmation," "maintenance," and "successful reproduction" of political life and values, leading to a restoration of "normalcy" in the wake of some disturbance created "by an unusual event." But on the other, it suggests a far more fluid and contested politics, in which specific actors, such as "the transgressor and the immediate victim" and "a third party, often the purifier," take the event "public" and press for particular outcomes, including not only "punishment and restitution," but also "reforms."

This dualism, which leads to "the maintenance and development of political life," can be seen as "confirm[ing] Durkheim's point that each social system needs pathologies for its successful reproduction." But it can also be understood to challenge Durkheim's fundamentally static framework. Markovits and Silverstein thus argue that there is "an important element missing a Durkheimian analysis: the exercise of, and struggle for, political power. Durkheim's framework misses the single most important ingredient in any political scandal: the central role of power in the construction of social reality, public morality, and the *conscience collective*." [25] Indeed, scandal functions precisely at this delicate intersection between the static reproduction of communal political structures and the struggle to take control of them and of their development.

F. Public Disapproval ... or not

Regardless of its potentially conservative or contestatory/reformist orientation, a scandal requires, to use the terms of Thompson, "visible disapproval," publicly expressed.[26] As he pithily states: "No response, no scandal."[27] For Blic and Lemieux, Thompson's insight yields a methodological desideratum and a theoretical conclusion:

> This pragmatic methodology, which consists of following the actors in how they publicly remark upon contradictions (or conversely, stifle them) or respond positively to public disapproval (or, conversely, show themselves to be indifferent) leads us to seek the meaning of scandal not in an essentialist definition of the offense but in terms of the reactions aroused by an act of public denunciation.[28]

[25] *Id.* at 4.
[26] *See* Thompson (2000) at 20. *See also* Blic & Lemieux (2005) at 71, English version at para. 8.
[27] *See* Thompson (2000) at 20.
[28] Blic & Lemieux (2005) at 15–16, English version at para. 11.

Two conclusions follow. First, as Thompson recognizes, scandal is effectively a "speech act." It requires that someone make a public show of opprobrium: *sotto voce* gossip, rumor, or disapproval is not sufficient.[29] Furthermore, this act of disclosure and denunciation must find a public that is responsive to the scandalous charge and that acts on it with the requisite opprobrium.

Second, scandal is in essence an invitation. The public denunciation is a "proposition of engagement" "made by a denunciator who now awaits a response."[30] Blic and Lemieux explain:

> It is what follows this proposition for engagement that will give meaning to the offense thus denounced. In other words, it is what follows that will determine whether or not the denounced scandal is really a scandal. It is thus up to the actors themselves, and to them alone, to show us through either their indignant reactions or their relativistic attitude whether an offense is really an offense.[31]

If the charge fails to illicit the necessary response, no scandal.

This underlines the tenuous, perhaps even risky, nature of scandal. As Thompson states, a scandal's "eventual outcome is intrinsically unclear."[32] The denunciator seeks to elicit a scandalized response, but may find little more than indifference. Sometimes, a scandal simply "does not take."[33] Scandal therefore lays down a challenge, one that can fail as well as succeed, whether through opposition or indifference.

Dampierre specified that there exist eras when a scandal would have great difficulty finding purchase in a given community:

> It appears quite clear that a scandal immediately creates a "malaise"; whatever its type, it buts up against the clear conscience of its public. And when there is attached to this clear conscience all of the amalgamated beliefs, representations and emotions that characterize the mentality of a social group, one can expect that the scandal will have trouble breaking out … "Let it go: it's ancient history," "Let bygones be bygones."[34]

[29] *See* Thompson (2000) at 20–25.

[30] Blic & Lemieux (2005) at 16, English version at para. 13, *citing* Luc Boltanski, Distant Suffering. Morality, Media and Politics (G. Burchell, trans.,1999).

[31] Blic & Lemieux (2005).

[32] Thompson (2000) at 73.

[33] Blic & Lemieux (2005) at 26, English version at para. 24.

[34] Dampierre (1954) at 334 (citation omitted).

[1] The exploitation of scandal becomes in turn a scandal for the camp of good conscience. And when a mounting revolution denounces the scandals of the established regime, it becomes in turn the ultimate scandal. Attaching the label of scandal to a revolution simultaneously minimizes its importance and gathers energies against it.

From this, Dampierre deduced that a scandal's capacity to break out hinges on its public, whose attachment to the values of the day will either fuel or smother the scandal's progress:

> We explained above that a scandal requires a public. But we must now add that it is precisely one of the effects of scandal that it creates its public, or more precisely, its publics; because a scandal tends to split its public into two camps: those who seek to reestablish the lost clear conscience and bliss, and those who seek to tear down this clear conscience in order to create a new one. The first group "buries" the scandal, while the second "exploits" it. Scandal is often the appetizer of revolution.[1][35]

Scandal, in other words, depends on a certain anxiety and instability. If the existing social regime is too well settled in its ways, then a scandal challenging those ways is buried. But if the regime has already adopted new values, then a scandal challenging the old ones is met with indifference. The French philosopher René le Senne thus wrote:

> Scandal emerges less from organic periods, which are governed by rigid and respected structures, or from troubled periods, which are torn apart by warlike or revolutionary periods, than from transitional ones, in which the old law has lost its vigor, in which the young one has not yet acquired its own. As long as the attachment to certain historical values are too strong, they discourage potential assailants; if they become too weak, they provoke no interest: it is in the interval that scandal is a prelude to more materially violent offensives. The *Marriage of Figaro* was a pre-revolutionary symptom.[36]

It is therefore in periods of potential transition that scandal is most likely to prove explosive.

In such potentially transitional periods, transgressions that might once have been buried or that might soon elicit mere shrugs are now the occasion for public demonstrations of opprobrium. "Once the transgression is made public, that is, 'scandalous,' … it becomes socially necessary to punish it, even though such a transgression was tolerated as long as it was still possible to turn a blind eye to it."[37] In such an environment, in which a particular set of values is simultaneously shared and disputed, strategic actors seek to leverage claimed transgressions as a means either to shore up the existing regime or to undermine, reform, or even

35 *Id.* at 334–35 (citation omitted).
36 René le Senne, *Le Scandal*, *in* L'Existence 127, 142 (1945).
37 Blic & Lemieux (2005) at 22, English version at para. 20.

overthrow it. This leads to the deployment of "strategies of scandalization," as strategic actors compete to enlist a divided public to support their particular agendas.

Scandals thus emerge as intrinsically political interventions. And like all such interventions, they carry risk. They can succeed or fail. As Thompson states in the corruption context:

> A disclosure of corrupt activities that elicits no response, no publicly articulated condemnation or rebuke, will not give rise to a scandal. In circumstances where corruption is pervasive, is widely known to exist and is accepted as a quasi-legitimate way of conducting public affairs, the disclosure of a case of corruption may give rise to little more than a sigh of resigned indifference. The disclosure is a gauntlet thrown down but not yet taken up.[38]

Worse, the "gauntlet" may be picked up and returned in kind: the person making the scandalous accusation can often become subject to counter-accusations, most often that making the initial accusation was scandalous in its own right.

The risk of counter-accusation is sufficiently common that the literature often classifies the phenomenon as the transition from a scandal to an "affair." Elisabeth Claverie offers the best-known framework for analyzing this transition. She explains that a scandalous charge can take three possible paths. It can lead to a scandal. It can lead to indifference. Finally, it can lead to an "affair"; i.e., the charge can be flipped back on the accuser, who now faces a counter-charge. As Blic and Lemieux recognize, "an affair constitutes a particularly troubled moment of social transformation and reversibility of positions."[39]

The potential transformation of a scandal into an affair further underlines several key elements of scandal in general. First, it demonstrates that a scandal is a political intervention that accomplishes a great deal. In a particularly important passage, Blic and Lemieux argue:

> [S]candal . . . never leaves things as they were. As a "status degradation ceremony," it leads to repositionings, a redistribution of institutional cards, that is, a brutal challenge to established relations. It often gives rise to organizational reworkings, the production of new legal provisions, and the collective validation of new practices. Put another way, it is one of the "effervescent moments" discussed by Durkheim. This is one reason why the researcher should make the effort to grasp it in its performative or rather in its *institutionalizing* dimension. We thus go from the question "How does scandal reveal a pre-existing order?" to questions such

[38] Thompson (2000) at 30.

[39] Blic & Lemieux (2005) at 17, English version at para. 15. *See* Elisabeth Claverie, *L'affaire du Chevalier de la Barre: La naissance d'une forme politique*, *in* CRITIQUE ET AFFAIRES DE BLASPHÈME À L'ÉPOQUE DES LUMIÈRES (Philippe Roussin ed.,1998) ["Claverie (1998)"].

> as "What does scandal change in social relations?," "What does it transform in terms of ways of reacting, institutional functioning, categories, and judgment practices?," in other words, "What does it do?" It is true that recognizing an institutionalizing power in scandal condemns us to a particularly dynamic form of sociology, a sociology that, no longer satisfied with deducing the event from the structure after the fact and interpreting what happened *ex post* as what was bound to happen, forces itself to take the measure of the fact that every scandal produces a state of social organization that did not fully pre-exist it and was not fully predictable.[40]

Indeed, even when a scandal "merely" reinforces existing understandings, it changes the existing state of affairs:

> The institutionalizing perspective remains perfectly valid when scandal leads to a reinforcement of initial positions and dominant beliefs. However, reinforcing these positions and beliefs does not leave them as they were. Only an excessively static perspective would cause us to liken their reaffirmation to a simple mechanism of reproduction.[41]

Second, the potential for scandal to turn into an affair illustrates scandal's precarious nature. To use the terms of Alain Garrigou, scandal is above all an ideological intervention whose outcome is not mechanically produced from the initial state of political affairs or from the initial transgression. Scandal does not follow a "natural course." It is a "political mobilization,"[42] one that addresses a (likely) divided public, attempting to shape, unify, and direct both its consciousness and its collectivity in a particular manner. As Dampierre explains:

> It would be inaccurate to say that scandal attacks institutions and laws of the state: in truth, it aims primarily to undermine the emotions and beliefs that lie fundamentally at the source of these institutions and that provide them with their coherence.
>
> And if, nevertheless, in activating these beliefs, scandal reinforces them, it is because it creates collective emotions and behaviors. Scandal creates its public, creates or activates a "we," and makes this "we" manifest by a communion, by a partial fusion of consciousness.[43]

[40] Blic & Lemieux (2005) at 11–12, English language version at para. 4 (citations omitted).
[41] *Id.* at footnote 6.
[42] Garrigou (1992) at 11–13, 16–17.
[43] Dampierre (1954) at 336.

Scandal thus emerges as an intentional challenge to—or rallying cry in support of—existing ideological presuppositions and commitments, one that the relevant strategic actors hope will generate important normative, communal, and institutional consequences. As a result, scandal straddles a very delicate line between enforcing and challenging existing social norms, ideological connections, community structures, and political/institutional/power relations. It is therefore a political act that carries risk: it can only be resolved over time, and this in a decidedly uncertain environment.

II. Scandal Theory in Action

Scandal theory provides an immensely valuable framework for our analysis of the ongoing European judicial appointments reforms. Its common threads invite us to approach the appointments debates with a measure of caution. They suggest that these debates, framed so often in scandalized terms, not only offer revealing windows onto the existing tensions and fissures between assorted governmental, institutional, and other actors, but also represent important interventions by savvy players determined to elicit opprobrious responses that might generate desired normative, conceptual, institutional, and ultimately political developments. Let us therefore reread the European judicial appointments debates in terms of the scandal theory we have just presented.

A. The Scandalous Event

The first important insight provoked by scandal theory is that one ought to question what the scandalous appointments event really was or what we should consider it to have been. On the one hand, one could follow the lead of publisher Norbert Engel and Professor Jean-François Flauss (who first reported the events most prominently in the specialized international press) by treating any one of the six selected juicy stories I related in Chapter 10 as a scandalous event in its own right. Each—whether the 1998 Bulgarian, the 2001 Moldovan, the 2004 Slovak or Estonian, the 2011 French, or 2012 Czech debacle—represents in its own way a sordid tale of governmental overreach, institutional and professional incompetence, and the like. Each gets reported, publicized, and criticized by one of the informants (Engel and/or Flauss), who treats it as a meaningful transgression worthy of attention and response.

On the other hand, one might consider the underlying scandal to be a more general and pre-existing failure that triggered the European judicial reforms in the first place. To adopt this tack would also be to follow the lead of the informants

Engel and Flauss, who, as we shall soon see, each embed their specific examples in a broader critique of European appointments practice.

And of course, the scandal could be both particular and general in nature. In other words, our understanding of the scandalous event depends on what we want to think of as the underlying scandal: is it particular instances of abuse (such as each of the six tawdry appointments sagas reported in Chapter 10) or are such instances merely examples of the *real* scandal (such as European judicial appointments practice in general)? Needless to say—and quite tellingly, as we shall see—there is no clear answer to such a question.

The important point is that scandal theory urges us to pay attention to the framing of the scandalous event(s). On the one hand, each of the unseemly episodes is presented as a scandal in its own right; and on the other, each is presented as but an instantiation of a more general failure in European judicial appointments. But what exactly *is* this large-scale—if never quite overtly stated or defined—scandal? Clearly, it is the violation of some kind of norm (or set of norms). The substance of such a norm(s), however, requires some analysis, which brings us to the next section.

Before we launch into this analysis, however, let us pause quickly to recognize one more feature of how the appointments scandal is framed. As Alain Garrigou insightfully explained, a scandal tends to be presented as a pre-existing event: this past scandalous event must soon lead to appropriate consequences. This framing tends to elide the all-important work that is being performed in the present. As Garrigou states: "The present seems totally absent, except as elucidation of the past. And yet, it is the publication of evidence, of revelations, of police and legal action, and the taking of positions that actually constitutes the raw material of scandal."[44] As we move forward in our analysis, therefore, we should bear clearly in mind that the appointments scandal, like any other scandal, entails not so much a prior event as the process of making revelations, of invoking allegedly violated and purportedly vital norms, and of summoning the community's opprobrium for that violation in order to effectuate some kind of response. Scandal, in other words, far from being a *fait accompli*, is an act very much in progress.

B. Claim of Violation of Norms

As will soon become apparent, the norms in play in the European judicial appointment scandals and reforms are unclear, developing, and profoundly contested.[45] For the moment, however, it is important that we identify the claims themselves about which norms have been violated. Some of these claims are extremely easy to

[44] Garrigou (1992) at 16.
[45] *See infra* Chapter 11 I(D).

ascertain: one need only scan the relevant source material, ranging from the official institutional documents discussing proposed reforms, to academic revelations and/or critiques concerning current appointments practices, and so on, in order to gather a list of the norms that are said to have been violated, or to be at risk, or to need support, etc. Other claims are less immediately apparent: one must read further into these sources in order to ascertain claims that, often of a more general nature, are proposed in a more implicit or oblique manner.

If we scan the six notorious scandalous events related in Chapter 10 above, it takes little to compile a list of the norms that those events are claimed to have violated. The key sources for the accounts of the six scandals are above all Professor Jean-François Flauss and publisher Norbert Engel. In the first scandal, Flauss wryly explained that the Bulgarian government's refusal to re-nominate Judge Gotchev was "plainly and simply ... a 'settling of accounts,' as the national authorities had not forgiven him the vote that he had cast in favor of condemnation in the *Lukanov* affaire."[46] Gotchev's failure to dissent from the European Court of Human Rights' (ECtHR) condemnation of the Bulgarian government "was taken to be treason"; and thus, "it goes without saying that his eviction demonstrates quite clearly that [political] 'detachment' is not a virtue widely shared within Bulgarian governing circles ... "[47]

In the second scandal, Norbert Engel explained that the "Moldovan judge Tudor Pantîru had refused to cede to his Government, which had called on him with an ultimatum in [the Church of Bessarabia case] to vote ... in accordance with its instructions and to justify its position in a dissenting opinion." When he refused to do so, "the Government obstructed the re-election of the judge who had insisted on his independence," eventually going so far as not only to put forward the apparently bogus charge that Judge Pantîru had failed to vacate a State-owned diplomatic flat, but also to replace the entire national judicial selection committee in order to be "rewarded with a compliant decision" (i.e., one that left Pantîru off of the slate of national candidates forwarded for election in Strasbourg).[48]

In the third, the Slovak government adamantly refused to re-nominate the sitting ECtHR judge Viera Strážnická in order to promote the appointment of Ján Drgonec, who was not only an MP of an allied party that was part of the ruling governmental coalition, but who the government had itself appointed to the national judicial selection committee. "According to a broadly shared opinion," Professor

[46] Jean-François Flauss, *Radioscopie de l'élection de la nouvelle Cour européenne des droits de l'homme*, 35 Rev. trim. dr. h. 437, 440 (1998) ["Flauss (1998)"].

[47] *Id.* at note 20.

[48] N.P. Engel, *More Transparency and Governmental Loyalty for Maintaining Professional Quality in the Election of Judges to the European Court of Human Rights*, 32 Human Rights L.J. 448, 450 (2008) ["Engel (2008)"]. Of course, the national governments were under no formal obligation to put forward any given candidate for election to the Court, including the sitting judge from that country. But the refusal to put forward the name of the sitting judge, especially under such circumstances, certainly raised eyebrows. The end of renewable judicial terms at the ECtHR has done away with the issue.

Flauss explained, "a refusal to renominate the sitting judge [as one of the three candidates for appointment] is equivalent to the exercise of a 'veto right' contrary to judicial independence . . . "[49]

In the fourth, the Russians had thrown their weight around in Strasbourg in an attempt to punish the sitting Estonian Judge Maruste for his dissent in the *Slivenko* case, in which he had made a point of stressing the illegality—indeed, he used the term "war crime"[50]—of the Soviet occupation of Latvia as a result of the "Hitler-Stalin Pact." As Flauss explained, "the point was to make the Estonian judge pay dearly for the perhaps blunt, but nonetheless perfectly justified, statements that he had expressed in his dissenting opinion."[51]

In the fifth scandal, the French government tried to play a crass political game in order to promote the career of a political ally. Contrary to the recommendation of the French delegation to the Permanent Court of Arbitration in the Hague (which served as the committee charged with producing a list of six candidates from which the government would select the three to nominate to Strasbourg), the Sarkozy government chose to add the name of Michel Hunault in the hope that this would open up a seat in Parliament for President Sarkozy's young friend and communications advisor, Franck Louvrier. As Engel explained, this "political manœuvre by the Elysée Palace to place an unsuitable candidate on the list of three," though ultimately a "manifest failure," demonstrated a "misled feeling of unlimited State power."[52]

Finally, in the sixth, the Czech government refused to back down in the face of the Advisory Panel of Experts' (APE) negative assessment of the suitability of one of the three candidates the government had proposed for election in Strasbourg. As Engel wrote:

> Instead of replacing the candidate by another one, which it would have been expected to do, the Czech Government intensified its lobbying in favor of its preferred candidate. The Minister of Justice sent a letter—bypassing the [APE]—to [PACE] members in which, with the forceful insistence typical of a power-conscious Government, he underlined his support for the election of the candidate considered unsuitable.[53]

[49] Jean-François Flauss, *Brèves observations sur le second renouvellement triennal de la Cour européenne des droits de l'homme*, 61 Rev. tr. d. h. 5, 10 (2005) ["Flauss (2005)"] (citations omitted).

[50] Slivenko v. Latvia, App. No. 48321/99 (October 9, 2003) at 50 (Separate Dissenting Opinion of Judge Maruste).

[51] Flauss (2005) at 12.

[52] Engel (2008) at 451.

[53] *Id.* at 450. It should be noted that the PACE has followed the recommendations of its Committee on the Election of Judges in almost all recent cases. *See* Andrew Drzemczewski, "Election of Judges to the ECtHR," in Hélène Ruiz-Fabri (ed.), Max Planck Encyclopedia of International Procedural Law at para. 34 (2019), https://opil.ouplaw.com/view/10.1093/law-mpeipro/e3367.013.3367/law-mpeipro-e3367 (explaining that it had done so for nineteen of the previous twenty elections). The figure is now thirty out of thirty-one. *See* https://assembly.coe.int/LifeRay/CDH/Pdf/TableForthcomingJudgesElections-EN.pdf.

This willingness to "crash[] all gates" to get "their preferred candidate" elected was, Engel stated, "an astonishing lack of loyalty to the other Contracting Parties to the Convention."[54]

These six accounts offer significantly overlapping portrayals of the types of norms that had been violated. In each depiction, it was the national government that had committed the violation, heavy-handedly throwing its weight around in a manner that overstepped its proper boundaries. Most often, this governmental hubris had infringed upon judicial independence in decision-making. Thus, the first three episodes were instances of alleged governmental retribution against a sitting ECtHR judge who had violated governmental wishes in a particular case. The Bulgarian government had "settled accounts" with its judge, who had failed to dissent in the *Lukanov* case, demonstrating that " 'detachment' is not a virtue widely shared within Bulgarian governing circles . . . "[55] The Moldovan government had "obstructed the re-election of the judge who had insisted on his independence" by refusing to follow its command to dissent in the *Church of Bessarabia* case.[56] And as for the Russian government's attempt to block the reappointment of Judge Maruste, "the point was to make the Estonian judge pay dearly for the perhaps blunt, but nonetheless perfectly justified, statements that he had expressed in his dissenting opinion" in the *Slivenko* case.[57] In each of these three cases, the national government was thus shown to have breached the firewall separating it from judicial decision-making, thereby threatening judicial independence.

The remaining three reported episodes are somewhat different. They depict heavy-handed governmental behavior that allegedly impinged not so much on independent judicial decision-making as on the integrity of the judicial appointments process itself. The Slovak government had obstinately refused to re-nominate sitting judge Viera Strážnická in order to support its own preferred candidate, thereby validating "the broadly shared opinion" that "a refusal to renominate the sitting judge is equivalent to the exercise of a 'veto right' contrary to judicial independence . . . "[58] The French government had demonstrated a "misled feeling of unlimited State power" by refusing to back away from the "political manœuvre by the Elysée Palace to place an unsuitable candidate on the list of three" in order to place an ally in an open seat in the French National Assembly.[59] And the Czech government, "with the forceful insistence typical of a power-conscious Government," had lobbied intensively for a judicial candidate officially deemed unqualified by the APE.[60]

54 Engel (2008) at 449.
55 *Id* at note 20.
56 *Id.* at 450.
57 Flauss (2005) at 12.
58 *Id.* at 10 (citations omitted).
59 Engel (2008) at 451.
60 *Id.* at 450.

Although the notion of judicial independence is undoubtedly in play in these last three accounts, it is not the type of decisional independence that was at stake in the first three. Rather, the fundamental claim revolves around governmental overreach on a more institutional level: each national government had not only backed a particular judicial candidate for its own political purposes, but had also run roughshod over the judicial appointments process in order to force through its desired outcome. Indeed, in the last two cases, such misguided behavior—indicative of "a power-conscious Government" and a "misled feeling of unlimited State power"—had resulted in an attempt to appoint a seemingly unqualified candidate to sit on the ECtHR.

We can therefore readily identify a family of interrelated yet distinct claims put forward by these six accounts. All involve "judicial independence"; but they do so in significantly different ways, depending on whether they foreground (a) the independence of individual judges in their decisional capacities or (b) the independence of the judicial appointments process from executive branch control. Under these two important variations, all six accounts advance a common underlying theme: inappropriate exercises of political power by domineering national governments. At the most basic level, this theme calls urgently into question the fundamental tenets of the separation of powers: what kind of democratic State permits its executive branch to issue marching orders to sitting judges about how to rule in the cases before them? And/or to punish judges who refuse to abide by those diktats? And/or to abuse their power by appointing cronies or favorites to the judiciary in the first place (and unqualified ones at that)?

With this set of interrelated questions, we arrive at a key thrust of the appointments scandals: these scandals make a point of stressing the democratic *bona fides*—or, more accurately, the *lack* of democratic *bona fides*—of the Member State governments involved. Indeed, this is the most common and recurrent theme of these episodes: the Member State governments in question are flouting the basic tenets that characterize (or, at least, should characterize) the separation of powers and the exercise of judicial independence in a democratic State worthy of the name. The scandals are object lessons about what *not* to do in a democratic State.

And this is the point; for the object lessons have been made precisely in the era when mass accession of new Member States from the former Eastern Bloc has resulted in large-scale European enlargement. In other words, the scandals have emerged in the period when the "transition democracies" from the East have sought to assimilate into the supranational European entities of the West. The scandals have effectively called into question the appropriateness of allowing these transition democracies to gain full entrance into the inner sanctum of what was once an elite "rich country club."[61] They call out and make a public issue out of the

[61] As Heather Grabbe wrote in 2006: "In enlarging to 25 member-states and beyond, the EU will change its nature. It will move from being a predominantly rich country club to a truly continental

problematic appointments behavior committed primarily by the governments of newly acceded states from the former Eastern Bloc.

It is important to recognize, however, that the sudden publication of such episodes, which call into question the decisional and structural independence of the new Eastern European judicial appointments, strongly suggests double standards, if not outright hypocrisy. As we explained in Chapter 2, for example, the judicial appointments process instituted from the very beginning at the European Court of Justice (ECJ) was designed precisely to *maximize* national governmental control over judicial appointments and appointees: appointment by common accord of the governments for renewable six-year terms quite obviously gave every national government the unilateral power not only to dismiss any of "its" judges who earned its displeasure, but also to replace any judge at reappointment time with another judge more in tune with the government of the day. Thus, it has long been common knowledge, for instance, that the Germans—hardly European bad apples—have felt no obligation to reappoint their sitting European judges; to the contrary, new German governments have routinely and unapologetically changed them out for others of their own choosing. Why, then, the suddenly scandalous connotation attached to robust governmental interventions in the judicial appointments process?

As Blic and Lemieux explain, the arrival of new actors on the institutional scene can trigger a re-examination of "hitherto concealed" institutional behavior "according to current norms and described retroactively as scandalous."[62] These actors can disturb the balance within a given institution as well as the balance between that institution and adjacent ones. As a result, the existing division of social sectors can be jostled, leading to a challenge to "the prerogatives claimed, little by little, by one institution vis-à-vis another."[63]

This description meshes extremely well with the arrival of new actors on the European scene. The new accession States clearly represented a disruption *within* the European judicial and political spheres. But they also represented a disturbance of sufficient scope to disrupt not only those two spheres, but also the relationships *between* them: the arrival of the newly acceded Member States from the East prompted a reconsideration of the borders demarcating the judicial from the political sectors.

The problem, of course, was that the new impulse to call into question the relationship between the judicial and the political would logically call into question how the long-standing Member States had themselves managed their judicial appointments. In other words, redrawing the lines between the judicial and the

union." Heather Grabbe, *What Hope for Solidarity in the Enlarged European Union?*, *in* WHAT HOLDS EUROPE TOGETHER? CONDITIONS OF EUROPEAN SOLIDARITY 42 (Krzysztof Michalski ed., 2006).

[62] Blic & Lemieux (2005) at 34, English version at para. 34.
[63] *See id.*

political in a manner that would capture the current behavior of new Member States would likely ensnare the past and even ongoing behavior of longstanding Member States.

The *ex-post* redrawing of the lines between the judicial and the political, and the associated tarring of long routine behavior as scandalous, thus yielded historical and geo-political difficulties: they effectively established new norms of behavior, rather than enforcing pre-existing ones. These new normative borders accordingly ran the risk of recasting traditional government behavior as scandalous; but none of the institutional, academic, judicial, or other players was prepared to make such a charge overtly. The closest anyone ever came was in 2001, when the Consultative Council of European Judges tellingly called upon established Member States to adopt formal institutions and norms to govern their judicial appointments, if only to model good behavior for the "newer democracies," "former communist countries," and "countries which do not have other longentrenched and democratically proved systems."[64] And perhaps needless to say, this call to model good behavior hardly puts the established Member States in the same boat as their new colleagues.

The ultimate solution, however, as seen most clearly in the ECtHR context, was quite the opposite. It was to generate a blatantly discriminatory set of rules that simultaneously put forward a requirement that Member States establish an independent (and largely) judicial authority (likely a judicial council) to take all decisions "on the selection and career of judges," only to carve out an explicit exception for those established Member States whose long-standing constitutional or legal traditions were deemed sufficient to protect the judicial appointments process.[65]

In other words, the solution to the historical problem (i.e., the fact that the governments of established Member States had long protected their capacity to exercise unilateral authority over their judges via the (re-)appointment process) was to draw, formalize, and thus entrench a geopolitical distinction between (Western) Member States with long-standing constitutional traditions and those (Eastern) ones lacking "longentrenched and democratically proved systems."[66] The scandal of politically dominated judicial appointments would thus be thrown *geographically eastward* rather than *temporally backward.*

This construction of the judicial appointments scandal has externalized longstanding national practices and then projected them primarily onto the new Member States, suddenly treating such practices as a foreign and disqualifying sign of insufficient democratic pedigree. This subjects the new Member States to a civics

[64] *See* Consultative Council of European Judges, "Opinion No. 1 on Standards Concerning the Independence of the Judiciary and the Irremovability of Judges," CCJE (2001) OP No. 1 ["CCJE Opinion No. 1 on the Independence of the Judiciary"], available at https://rm.coe.int/1680747830 at paras. 32–36, 45.

[65] *See* Committee of Ministers Rec R (94) 12 (October 13, 1994) at 3 and at Explanatory Memorandum, para. 16.

[66] *See* CCJE Opinion No. 1 at para. 45.

lesson that the long-standing Member States had expressly rejected to apply to themselves, most explicitly in the ECJ context. The framing of the scandal, in other words, paints an implicit portrait of the new Member States that simultaneously accentuates their seemingly recurrent democratic shortcomings, whitewashes the long-standing Member States' history of zealously protecting their own capacity to engage in just such governmental control over the judiciary, and accordingly prompts an exception-based regulatory solution that effectively enables the established Member States to continue to do precisely what is described as scandalous when attributed to the new accession States.

Of course, these normative struggles over the appropriate (non-)relationship between the political and the legal spheres also hinge on a more basic factual/empirical claim, namely, that the supposed governmental offenses—assuming that they can or should appropriately be defined as offenses—actually occurred. And here, once again, scandal theory is informative. As Dampierre insightfully explains:

> It matters little whether the scandalous event be true or false; what matters is that it be taken as true. The Templars were likely innocent of the crimes charged by Philip the Fair's lawyers, as were probably the Franciscans that the Nazis dragged before the courts under analogous claims. The study of scandal is related to that of blackmail and denunciation as means of social control.[67]

Indeed, it is unclear how non-insiders might assess the truth-value of each of the reported scandals. How, for example, did Professor Jean-François Flauss or publisher Norbert Engel know what they claimed to know? After all, the commentators' sources are—understandably—almost never revealed; and without any citation to sources, how can one determine whether their accounts are true? Yes, one can confirm that the Bulgarian and Moldovan governments had failed to re-nominate their respective ECtHR judges in 1998 and 2001. But how can we really know whether the commentators had accurately conveyed the reasons for which those governments had actually refused to re-nominate those judges? How, in other words, can we really know whether each declined to re-nominate as retribution for the judge's refusal to support his government's position in a very specific case?

To be clear, it is not my purpose to call such accounts directly into question. By any measure, Flauss and Engel (to cite the two most prominent commentators) have been exceptionally well-informed and insightful observers of the European judicial scene. But every appointments story is subject to complicating factors, countervailing explanations, and so on. And it is worth pausing momentarily over such complications in order to draw some useful lessons.

[67] Dampierre (1954) at 330.

Let us therefore return quickly to the notorious 2012 appointment of the Czech ECtHR judge, Aleš Pejchal. According to Norbert Engel, the Czech government was specifically championing its preferred ECtHR candidate and was prepared to do so at all costs.[68] According to David Kosař, however, the Czech government was driven by less sinister motives: the real problem was the dearth of plausible reserve candidates should Pejchal be dropped from the list of Czech candidates for the ECtHR post.[69] How is one really to assess the truth of the matter? Frankly, good luck!

Furthermore, how is one to assess the actions undertaken by the APE and the PACE Sub-Committee on Elections in response to the Czech machinations? As I explained in Chapter 10,[70] from the point of view of the PACE Sub-Committee on Elections, the truly problematic feature of the Pejchal candidacy was not so much that he was egregiously unqualified; he was, after all, serving as Vice-President of the Czech Bar Association. True, he had twice been rejected for a position on the Czech Constitutional Court. Appointing him to the ECtHR would therefore not reflect particularly glowingly on the Strasbourg Court.[71] But the bigger problem was that he was the personal advisor of the rightwing and Eurosceptic Czech President Václav Klaus.

In addition to missing this important factual element, the existing accounts of this episode have failed to grasp that the APE chose not to confront directly the problem of Pejchal's relationship with President Klaus; it opted instead to take the less overtly confrontational (if more factually disputable) tack of simply declaring Pejchal unqualified.[72] This left the PACE Sub-Committee in a delicate position. It could confront both the Czech government and the APE by doing what the APE had not: declare a spade a spade and object to Pejchal on the grounds of his close relationship with the problematic President Klaus. Or it could avail itself of the cover conveniently provided by the APE by simply declaring Pejchal unqualified, despite the fact that his qualifications were arguably—if only arguably—sufficient to pass muster. As we have seen, however, the Sub-Committee chose to try to finesse the problem: it adopted the brilliantly subtle (if ultimately disastrously

[68] *See* Engel (2008) at 450.

[69] *See* David Kosař, *Selecting Strasbourg' Judges: A Critique, in* Selecting Europe's Judges: A Critical Review of the Appointment Procedures to the European Courts 120 at 153–54 (Michal Bobek ed., 2015) ["Kosař (2015)"].

[70] *See supra* Chapter 10(VI).

[71] *See* PACE Doc. 12936 at 57; Kosař (2015) at 155.

[72] It is worth stressing that one could very reasonably argue that a judicial candidate who has been rejected for a position on a national Constitutional Court should *ipso facto* be deemed unqualified to sit on one of the two great European Courts. But that would be an argument, not a self-evident conclusion. After all, Article 21 of the ECHR states that ECtHR judges "must either possess the qualifications required for appointment to high judicial office or be jurisconsults of recognised competence." The fact that an ECtHR candidate was once rejected for appointment to a national constitutional court (typically by political means) does not necessarily indicate that s/he does not "possess the qualifications required for appointment to high judicial office."

unsuccessful) administrative solution of refusing to forward Pejchal's name to the PACE as a viable judicial option, only to find—to its horror—that a majority of those (relatively few) PACE members voting in Strasbourg that day was prepared to elect him anyway.

The point here is not to call the commentators into question: after all, they each captured significant (if somewhat different) facets of the story, which is no mean feat in such an opaque environment. The point is instead to underline that what matters in such scandal situations is not so much that the scandalous accounts actually *be* true, so much as that they be *taken* to be true . . . and for what propositions.

In the judicial appointments context, the Pejchal appointments scandal did indeed cast a shadow over the ECtHR appointments process. But far more, it painted a picture of woefully inadequate judicial candidates from the new accession States from the East, supported by their scheming governments. It yielded an ongoing story of contagion and perversion, in which the blatant democratic insufficiencies of the transition democracies from Eastern and Central Europe are introduced to, and eventually subvert, the very institutions, structures, and procedures that were designed by the long-standing Western European democracies to promote the rule of law on the European level.

Indeed, it is worth noting that for every story that makes it into the published press (even if only the specialized international press), there are a great many more circulating in the professional and institutional circles loosely connected to the European legal and judicial scene. Since most Civilian countries have very close connections between the academic and judicial fields,[73] this means that almost every high-level academic with European or international interests is acquainted with some juicy story or other about some candidate or appointment cycle, the more titillating the better. Such tales, which typically remain at the level of insider gossip rather than publicized scandal, now utterly permeate the European judicial and academic milieus.

Perhaps the most archetypical insider gossip was about the Chief Justice of a Balkan country who wished to resign from his/her position in favor of a position on the bench in Strasbourg: s/he wished to avoid directing a series of politically delicate corruption cases in the domestic courts. The candidate list(s) on which s/he appeared were said to have been rejected *in toto* for no other reason than to keep that judge in charge of the problematic prosecutions, as no one else was trusted to perform this difficult job properly. Indeed, the job was all the more important given the Balkan country's accession to the EU.[74]

[73] *See* Mitchel Lasser, Judicial Deliberations: A Comparative Analysis of Judicial Transparency and Legitimacy 195–99 (2004).

[74] I hope the reader will excuse my deliberate imprecision: I would like insofar as possible to convey the tenor of the gossip, not to partake in it.

Such a Byzantine tale does a magisterial job of weaving together so many of the themes that characterize the current judicial appointments debates. It rests above all on an underlying portrait of large-scale and endemic political corruption. It expresses the fear of admitting this corruption into the European body politic upon accession.[75] It assumes a dearth of qualified and trustworthy judicial candidates in the Balkan country in question, which leads to the need to keep the Chief Justice in the domestic corruption-fighting job. And finally, it suggests that knowing elites from the West are resorting to fiendishly clever—if underhanded and domineering—institutional and administrative machinations to minimize the damage.

The point here is not so much that the stories underlying the gossip or scandals are (or are not) true, but that they are pervasive, that they are generally taken to be true, and that the stories and their lessons apply in the first instance to the newly acceded States from the old Eastern Bloc. But even more, the stories are deeply thematically related; and this thematic coherence is quite telling: the stories all stress a fundamental breakdown in the method by which the brute exercise of political power is tamed and legitimated by the proper exercise of democratic and institutional process.

The political scientists Andrei Markovits and Mark Silverstein have been especially interested in theorizing this link between scandal and proper political process. As they see it, "political scandals can only occur in liberal democracies":

> The modern liberal democracy merges these two [liberal and democratic] traditions, and, in so doing, evidences both a fear and an acceptance of state power. Liberal democracies are ambiguous constructs: While they need power like any other kind of state, they also curtail this very same power in order to maximize the individual's autonomy from the state. There thus exists a constant tension that is inherent in liberal democracies. Political scandals in the modern world can be understood only by developing an appreciation for this ambiguity concerning the use of political power–an ambiguity present to varying degrees in all liberal democracies.[76]

To Markovits and Silverstein, this tension-laden ambiguity means that all liberal democracies necessarily "exhibit a deep-seated schizophrenia over the uses of political power"[77] and must therefore find a way to manage this fundamental tension:

[75] For the European preoccupation with immigration and the body politic, *see* ELIZABETH S. ANKER, FICTIONS OF DIGNITY: EMBODYING HUMAN RIGHTS IN WORLD LITERATURE, Chapter 1 (2012).

[76] Markovits & Silverstein (1988) at 5.

[77] *Id.*

> Liberal democracies seek both to ensure the separation of the private and public realms and to overcome (hide) their ambiguity over the use of political power. They perform these miracles through a faith in process. It is only via the firm institutionalization—almost sanctification—of due process that liberal democracies can legitimately curtail the randomness, secretiveness, and exclusive character inherent in the exercise of political power. Any violation of the formal arrangements of due process is tantamount to a frontal attack on the very nature of the liberal democratic system proper.[78]

Process thus become more than simply the marker of the legitimacy of a given liberal democracy: "To the liberal, the process *is* the public interest and hence any attempt to escape from the strict rules of the political process—regardless of the ultimate goals—is contrary to the common good."[79]

The analysis of Markovits and Silverstein could hardly inform the European judicial appointments scandals (and, for that matter, the judicial appointments reforms) more directly. Over and over again, the scandals (and the reforms) focus on the establishment and violation of the proper process for selecting, appointing, and/or electing judicial candidates for European judicial office, almost always as a result of the abusive exercise of brute political power. Given this framing, it should not be surprising that the judicial appointments scandals tend overwhelmingly to address precisely those "transition democracies" that appear to teeter uncertainly between their authoritarian past and a properly democratic future, as well as, on occasion, those established democracies that happen to be led at a given moment by domineering political actors and regimes (such as the Sarkozy regime in France) who appear ready to flout traditional procedural expectations. In either variant, the punch line of the scandals is fundamentally the same: the governments in question do not understand, or care about, or live up to, the procedural requirements that lie at the very heart of a proper liberal democratic order.[80] This, quite clearly, is the fundamental conceptual lesson of the judicial appointments scandals and reforms.

For all of the descriptive and explanatory appeal of this scandal-based theoretical account, one should nonetheless resist the temptation to accept it uncritically. True, all indications suggest that numerous governments have indeed intervened

[78] *Id.* at 6.

[79] *Id.* Thompson puts forward a very similar account of "power scandals":

> It is partly because power scandals are the purest form of political scandal that they have come to assume such significance within the political field. What we see in power scandals is not the illicit intrusion of extraneous factors – sex, money – into the field of political power, but rather the illicit use of political power itself. This phenomenon is particularly troubling in liberal democratic societies, precisely because these are societies in which the exercise of political power is based on the rule of law; hence the flouting of these rules can be seen or portrayed as an activity which undermines the very foundations of legitimate power.

Thompson (2000) at 196.

[80] It is difficult indeed not to read the myriad scandals of the Trump administration in such a light.

heavy-handedly in the European judicial appointments process, trying in one way or another to promote or obstruct the appointment of particularly favored or disfavored candidates. No independent observer could reasonably contest such an assessment of the factual evidence. But this factual element represents only a portion of the claims made not only by those publishing on the appointments scandals, but also by those theorizing such scandals: for those authors supplement their factual assertions with both implicit and explicit claims about the nature and requirements of liberal democracy and about the relationship of specific judicial appointments procedures to those liberal democratic demands.

In other words, the judicial appointments scandals (buttressed by certain strains of scandal theory) suggest that we actually know *ex ante* what liberal democracy requires (both in general and in the specific context of judicial appointments): a resolutely apolitical judicial appointments process. On this view, the parameters of the appointments struggles are completely set; and all that remains is to flush out the facts that establish instances of scandalous appointments behavior, which is to say, appointments behavior that violates such a settled due process understanding of the rigid separation of the judicial and the political.

But this is patently misleading: *there has never been* a settled European understanding of the need to maintain such a rigid separation of the judicial and the political. The European courts had apparently been functioning perfectly well enough for decades without the appointments reforms that, in anticipation of the mass accession of former Eastern Bloc countries, began to appear in the mid-1990s. As the Interights 2003 Report forthrightly stated: "Even in the most established democracies, nomination [to the ECtHR] often rewards political loyalty more than merit."[81] And as we saw in the ECJ context, the Member State governments had knowingly adopted an appointments process that was designed precisely to maximize their capacity to select, supervise, and control their judicial appointees.[82]

At the domestic level, furthermore, appointment to national judicial office in many Western European democracies has long been deeply connected to executive and even legislative power. Indeed, this has been the case especially for high judicial positions and particularly for constitutional courts. One need only think, for example, of the appointments process to the French or German constitutional courts. Every three years, the French President and the presidents of the upper and lower houses of the French Parliament each appoint a judge to serve nine years on the Constitutional Council.[83] The candidates must satisfy no professional qualifications; and the appointments are subject to no meaningful review. As for the German Constitutional Court, the Bundesrat and the Bundestag elect half of

[81] Interights (Dr. Jutta Limbach, Chair), "Judicial Independence: Law and Practice of Appointments to the European Court of Human Rights" 9 (May 2003) ["Interights Report"] at 4.

[82] *See supra* Chapter 2(I).

[83] French Constitution, Article 56, available at https://www.conseil-constitutionnel.fr/le-bloc-de-constitutionnalite/texte-integral-de-la-constitution-du-4-octobre-1958-en-vigueur.

the judges by supermajority vote and obviously do so with a keen awareness of party loyalties.[84] Similarly, until 2009, the British Law Lords were appointed by the Queen on recommendation of the Prime Minister.[85] And this is to say nothing of more complex and hardwired linkages between the judicial and political authorities, such as the traditional executive branch status of the Conseil d'Etat judges in Belgium, France, Italy, Luxembourg, the Netherlands, etc.[86]

Indeed, the most telling indication that the parameters of the appropriate relationship between the judicial and the political had hardly been resolved in either the domestic or the international appointments arenas is probably the simple fact—as we explained in detail in Parts III and IV—that European institutions such as the CCJE (the Consultative Council of European Judges), the Venice Commission, and so on have been actively working to promote judicial appointment reforms. That they have had to do so—never mind the ongoing resistance with which their efforts have been met—is immensely revealing. First, these institutions have had to work hard to promote the adoption of such reforms, even within the most long-standing liberal democracies of Europe; and second, those democracies generated resistance that was sufficiently staunch to lead to the creation of (loaded) exceptions to those very reforms.[87] This indicates quite clearly that, far from operating in a settled conceptual environment, the debated reforms have been taking place on actively contested turf.

In other words, the judicial appointment scandals have not been simple factual disputes over alleged governmental abuses. They have been ideological and

[84] This is certainly not news. Ginsburg and Garoupa summarize the classic literature as follows:

> As a consequence of the appointment mechanism, which requires a supermajority (two-thirds) in the federal parliament, there is a need for a consensus between major political parties.[80] Over time, a norm has developed so that constitutional judges are effectively appointed on party tickets without public hearings.[81] The supermajority requirement has created a de facto quota system;[82] the two major parties divide the seats, with the occasional appointment of a judge from one of the minor parties to reflect parliamentary composition and ongoing governmental coalitions.[83]
>
> 80. *See* Georg Vanberg, The Politics of Constitutional Review in Germany 83 (2005).
> 81. *See* Rainier Nickel, "The German Federal Constitutional Court: Present State, Future Challenges," *in* Building the UK's New Supreme Court: National and Comparative Perspectives 175, 183–84 (Andrew Le Sueur ed., 2004) (arguing those package deals lack transparency); Grimm, *supra* note 42 (arguing that such package deals eliminate the possibility of electing extremists to the court and therefore reduce polarization).
> 82. *See* Donald P. Kommers, Judicial Politics in West Germany: A Study of the Federal Constitutional Court 89 (1976); Vanberg, *supra* note 80, at 83–85.
> 83. Kommers, *supra* note 10, at 22; Vanberg, *supra* note 80, at 83, 85.

Nuno Garoupa and Tom Ginsburg, *Building Reputation in Constitutional Courts*, 28 Ariz. J. Int'l & Comp. L. 539, 556 (2011).

[85] https://www.parliament.uk/business/lords/whos-in-the-house-of-lords/members-and-their-roles/how-members-are-appointed/; David Fedman ed., English Public Law 301–302 (2009).

[86] The ECtHR's 1995 *Procola* judgment triggered some reforms on this front, most notably in Luxembourg. *See* Procola v. Luxembourg, App. No. 14570/89, September 28, 1995; Luxembourg constitutional reform of July 12, 1996.

[87] *See supra* Chapter 6(III); Chapter 9(III).

institutional interventions concerning both (a) the contested relationship between the judicial and the political and (b) the contested nature of the European courts (i.e., are they to be assimilated to domestic courts, and if so, to "ordinary," "administrative," or "constitutional" ones?). As a result, the scandals tend to present themselves as factually demonstrating the violation of proper democratic norms and their procedural requirements; but they represent in truth much more: they are struggles over the definition of those norms and the elaboration of their supposed institutional consequences.

C. Leadership Struggles: The Construction of Inter-Institutional Allegiances

Approaching the appointment scandals and debates as interventions in ongoing conceptual and institutional struggles suggests that we should work to identify, and distinguish between, the institutional players primarily interested in these developments. The appointment debates are undoubtedly lively conceptual disputes. But they are also institutional struggles that pit certain classes of players against others at the intersection of the judicial, political, and academic arenas.

Clearly, the most directly implicated group consists of the European judges themselves. Much of the appointments discussion represents in effect a concerted attempt by those judges to free themselves from the heavy-handed control that the national governments have traditionally exerted over them. This control has obviously long manifested at the initial appointments phase, when the governments had a rather free hand in choosing their candidates to the ECJ and the ECtHR: in the case of the ECJ, by exercising their more or less unfettered capacity to appoint "their" judge on the Court (thanks to the tit for tat dynamic established by the appointment "by common accord" of the Member States), and in the case of the ECtHR, by signaling—and stacking the deck in favor of—their preferred judicial candidate.[88] But as we have seen, this control was further strengthened by the traditional possibility of reappointment, which effectively placed the European judges under the ongoing supervision of their home governments. This supervision has been particularly delicate for ECtHR judges, who must sit on all of their home country's cases and who can publish dissenting opinions. And finally, all these judges are often at the mercy of their governments for the purposes of professional reinsertion into the domestic sphere upon the eventual termination of their judicial mandates.

Indeed, the pressures exerted by the domestic governments may well have been significantly more direct than commentators have overtly recognized. In the

[88] *See supra* Chapters 2(I) and 4(I).

course of my research, I have periodically been plied with lengthy, detailed, and surprisingly blunt accounts of how, for example, certain governments have given explicit directions to "their" ECJ judges on how to rule in particular cases.[89]

I confess that I have found such accounts/revelations rather startling. I suppose that they should not have been: after all, the apparent fury of the Moldovan government, for example, when Judge Pantîru allegedly refused to go along with its directions to dissent in the *Church of Bessarabia* case,[90] should have served as an indication that such governmental demands might not be altogether unusual. But I found them startling nonetheless. Above all, they were offered in a straightforward and non-dramatic fashion in formal interview settings by former judges and other officers of the Luxembourg and Strasbourg Courts, naming not only the countries involved (which commonly were large Western European democracies, *not* new accession States from the East), but also the specific former judicial colleagues concerned, and often enough the precise cases in play. In other instances, the former judges explained how some of their colleagues routinely reported back to their national governments in order to debrief them on the meaning and likely further consequences of recently decided cases, and so on.

It is essential that we recognize, however, the true import of such revelations. The point here is not that such judicial and governmental behavior was routinely presented as scandalous; but rather that it frequently was *not*. I do not mean to suggest the amusingly circular—if substantively important—idea that the scandal is that such behavior would not necessarily be deemed scandalous. The point is instead to take the data more seriously: we need to recognize that, at least for many of the players involved, such behavior was not in fact deemed scandalous.

This realization is important in and of itself. It is a reminder that we ought not take the judicial appointments debates and reforms entirely at face value. These reforms were not merely self-evident responses to novel historical challenges arriving from the East. That is, they were not straightforwardly dictated by some preexisting Western European consensus regarding the nature of the judicial function (and of the relationship between the judicial and the political) that needed only to be exported Eastward. They were instead active interventions and meaningful reforms that affected the West as well as the East. But this realization has further implications.

The fact that it could be considered relatively routine for judges to meet with governmental players both to advise them on the consequences of their judgments and to listen to their own views on how cases might be approached speaks volumes regarding long-standing understandings of the judicial role and its relation to governmental authority. The whole point is that such judges did not truly understand themselves as radically distinct from their national administrations. To

89 With apologies, I cannot divulge any further details regarding sources, cases, countries or judges.

90 *See supra* Chapter 10(II).

the contrary. They functioned in a complex and nuanced relationship with those administrations, to which they were connected in various ways. Sometimes they were high-ranking members of the high administrative court structure (such as the Conseil d'Etat), which meant that they were themselves part of the administration (if undoubtedly a distinctive part). Sometimes they were part of the high ordinary judiciary, in which case they were used to being part of a large college of seasoned jurists well accustomed to dealing in an organized fashion with important matters of state policy. Sometimes they were highly influential academic jurists whose status may well have led them to advise the administration in assorted ways, perhaps eventually leading to appointment to their national constitutional court.

Under any of these permutations, it would be terribly simplistic and naïve (as well as patently tone-deaf) to conclude that the judges were either hermetically sealed off from the exercise of governmental authority or utterly subservient to it. They were instead more or less directly or indirectly implicated in it. They were part and parcel of it, albeit in ways that were functionally or deontologically distinguished from other players located in adjacent state institutions. To quote the utterly self-conscious French public law maxim descended from the 1641 Edit de Saint-Germain-en-Laye, "To judge the administration is also to administer."

As a consequence, the development of a class of high-level European judges who would work to free themselves from their traditional attachments to their national governments represents a rather novel and significant development. There existed no such pre-existing class of European judges who would have imagined themselves as pre-emptively cut off from public authority or who would have possessed pre-existing "interests" in such a state of affairs. That class of European judicial actors, complete with its interest in such a rigid division of authority, was progressively constructed precisely by the ongoing judicial appointments debates and by the gradual elaboration of their procedural, institutional, and conceptual entailments. Neither that class of judges, nor their role definition, nor their interests ever really existed as such prior to those debates.

The impending mass accession of former Eastern Bloc states to both the EU and the Council of Europe thus provided the historical impetus for what would eventually become such a self-identified class of European judges who would come increasingly to understand themselves as distinct from—or, at least, suitably independent of—public authority, as appropriately in charge of the European judicial appointments process, as representatives of a class of truly high-quality jurists of a particular type, and so on. And as we have seen, once that high-grade, pan-European judicial identity was formed, it has certainly promoted the aggressive development of its prerogatives vis-à-vis other actors in the European judicial fields.

These developments can be seen most clearly in the institutional developments we have described concerning judicial appointments to both the Luxembourg and the Strasbourg Courts. Thus, the EU's Article 255 Panel was effectively the brainchild of the 2000 "Ole Due Working Report," which stated:

> The Working Party would also suggest that the appointment of all Members of the Court of Justice and the CFI should be scrutinised on the basis of a comprehensive file submitted by each Member State. To assist the Member States in their deliberations, an advisory committee consisting of highly-qualified independent lawyers should be set up to verify the legal competence of candidates.[91]

And as we have seen, the Ole Due Working Party was composed of an extremely high-powered group of seven jurists, five of whom were themselves former ECJ Justices or Advocates General and one more who was about to be.[92] Having been conceived by such an eminent group of judges, it should probably come as no surprise that the first 255 Panel was itself composed overwhelmingly of other eminent judges, proposed by none other than the sitting ECJ President, Vassilios Skouris. Other than the one member put forward by the European Parliament (Ana de Palacio), it consisted entirely of high-level judges: Jean-Marc Sauvé (the leader of the French Conseil d'Etat), Peter Jann (former Justice of the Austrian Constitutional Court and of the ECJ), Lord Mance (Justice of the UK Supreme Court), Torben Melchior (President of the Danish Supreme Court), Peter Paczolay (President of the Hungarian Constitutional Court) and Virpi Tiili (former Finnish Judge of the Court of First Instance).[93] Indeed, the overwhelmingly judicial composition of the first 255 Panel was strictly maintained in the second: all three outgoing judicial members were replaced by other judges, leading once again to a 255 Panel composed of six judges and only one non-judicial member (appointed by the European Parliament).[94] Indeed, the same composition holds true once again with the current Panel, which consists of President Christiaan Timmermans (Dutch former ECJ Judge), Simon Busuttil (Maltese MEP), Frank Clarke (Chief Justice of the Supreme Court of Ireland), Carlos Lesmes Serrano (Chief Justice of the Supreme Court of Spain), Maria Eugénia Martins de Nazaré Ribeiro (Portuguese ex-Judge of the General Court), Andreas Vosskuhle (President of the German Federal Constitutional Court), and Mirosław Wyrzykowski (ex-Justice of the Polish Constitutional Tribunal).[95]

The judicial domination of the EU's 255 Panel has been faithfully reproduced by the ECtHR's APE. This too should come as no surprise. The idea of such a vetting

[91] Report by the Working Party on the Future of the European Communities' Court System (January 2000) ["Ole Due Report"], available at ec.europa.eu/dgs/legal_service/pdfdue_en.pdf at 51.

[92] The group consisted of former ECJ President Ole Due (Chair), former ECJ Justices Yves Galmot, Ulrich Everling, former ECJ Justice and Advocate General Lord Slynn of Hadley, former ECJ Advocate General José Luis da Cruz Vilaça, soon-to-be ECJ Justice Rosario Silva de Lapuerta, and the antitrust specialist professor/lawyer/former General Director of Competition at the Commission Aurelio Pappalardo. Ole Due Report at 52.

[93] *See supra* Chapter 3(I).

[94] *See id.*

[95] *See* Council Decision 2017/2262 of December 4, 2017, appointing the members of the panel provided for in Article 255 of the Treaty on the Functioning of the European Union, available at https://eur-lex.europa.eu/legal-content/EN/TXT/?uri=CELEX%3A32017D2262.

panel for ECtHR judicial candidates was first proposed by the influential "Group of Wise Persons" convened in 2005 by the Heads of State of the Council of Europe Member States "to consider the long-term effectiveness of the ECHR control mechanism."[96] This high-powered Group—itself composed of eleven members, seven of whom were former high-level judges of national supreme or constitutional courts or of the ECJ or ECtHR[97]—put forward the idea in the following terms:

> [T]he Group considers that the professional qualifications and knowledge of languages of candidates for the post of judge should be carefully examined during the election procedure.
>
> For this purpose, before the Parliamentary Assembly considers the candidatures, an opinion on the suitability of the candidates could be given by a committee of prominent personalities possibly chosen from among former members of the Court, current and former members of national supreme or constitutional courts and lawyers with acknowledged competence.[98]

And indeed, the composition of the first APE followed an exclusively judicial model; its members were Katarzyna Gonera (Justice of the Polish Supreme Court), Renate Jaeger (former Justice of the German Supreme Court and retiring Justice of the ECtHR), John L. Murray (Chief Justice of the Irish Supreme Court and former Justice of the ECJ), Matti Pellonpää (Justice of the Finnish Supreme Administrative Court and former Justice of the ECHR), Sami Selçuk (former First President of the Turkish Court of Cassation), Luzius Wildhaber (the Swiss former President of the ECtHR and former Justice of the Supreme Court of Liechtenstein), and Valery Zorkin (Chairman of the Russian Constitutional Court).[99] All seven had served as a Justice or Chief Justice of a national supreme or constitutional court; and four of the seven had also served as a Justice of the ECtHR or of the ECJ.

This exclusively judicial model has remained unsullied. Since its first meeting in January 2011, five of the seven members of the APE have been replaced (only Justices Murray and Pellonpää remain, the former having taken over from Luzius Wildhaber as Chair). All five new members are or have been justices of their national supreme or constitutional courts and/or judges of the ECJ or ECtHR: Nina Vajic (former Croatian Justice of the ECtHR), Jean-Paul Costa (former Justice of the French Conseil d'Etat and President of the ECtHR), Christoph Grabenwarter (Justice of the Austrian Constitutional Court), Lene Pagter Kristensen (Justice of the Danish Supreme Court), and Maria Gintowt-Jankowicz (former Justice of the Polish Constitutional Court).

[96] Report of the Group of Wise Persons to the Committee of Ministers, CM(2006)203 at para. 1.

[97] For the list of the members of the Group, *see id.* at para. 3.

[98] Report of the Group of Wise Persons to the Committee of Ministers, CM(2006)203 at paras. 117–18.

[99] CM/Del/Dec(2010)1101/1.7E / December 10, 2010.

The first and most obvious institutional result of the judicial appointments debates has thus been the establishment and swift entrenchment of unmistakably judicial colleges at the European level. These colleges—the 255 Panel and the APE—have already succeeded not only at reproducing themselves over time by renewing their almost exclusively judicial membership at each iteration (literally the only exception among the fourteen positions on these two Panels has been the selection made by the European Parliament to the 255 Panel), but also at significantly modifying the relationship between themselves and their European judicial colleagues, on the one hand, and the national administrations, on the other.

Of these two judicial colleges, the 255 Panel has clearly had the greater success at profoundly modifying the pre-existing nature of the judicial–executive relationship. Working with impressive speed and professional acumen, the 255 Panel has effectively established and entrenched itself as the final arbiter of the EU's judicial appointments. It has established and exercised this powerful institutional position both by effectively vetoing the judicial choices of national governments and by elaborating in some detail the profile of acceptable candidates to the EU's judiciary.[100]

As we have seen, the APE has had a significantly more difficult time establishing its authority in the judicial appointments domain. It has not succeeded in occupying the dominant gatekeeping position of the 255 Panel; nor has it imposed a well-elaborated set of criteria for vetting—and thus selecting—judicial candidates to the Strasbourg Court. But that does not mean that the APE has not been extremely successful in its own right. As we have seen, however, the reality is that it has been working on far more difficult ground: it has had to deal with more diverse and less tractable Signatory States, a far less congenial institutional framework and political ecosystem, and so on.[101]

Despite these constraints, the APE has helped to foster an environment in which ECtHR judges can—and indeed should—to use the term proposed to me by former ECtHR President Jean-Paul Costa, function as "ingrates" relative to the governments that put their names forward for election to the ECtHR.[102] The APE has successfully pushed those governments on several occasions to drop candidates whose profiles or qualifications were suspiciously thin or politically compromised, forcing them to replace them with others less vulnerable to professional critique or political pressure. While these largely behind-the-scenes efforts have periodically run into real difficulties, such as those described in the "scandal" section above, this should not blind us to the constraints that the APE has nonetheless imposed on the national governments.

[100] *See supra* Chapter 3(II) and (III).
[101] *See supra* Chapter 5.
[102] Interview with Jean-Paul Costa, Strasbourg, France, March 2013.

If nothing else, the operation of the APE has significantly increased the price of concerted governmental action in the ECtHR appointments arena. A government must now, for example, work much harder to generate three viable candidates than it did when any three names would do: the APE is positioned to look over the governmental work and impose reputational and institutional costs should that work be substandard. If the government nonetheless choses to plow ahead with its original slate of candidates, the APE will impose further costs, even if the government may—as in the extraordinary Czech scenario—periodically succeed in ramming through its preferred candidate notwithstanding the high price of scandal for everyone involved.

D. The Formation of Identities and Interests

The net result of these interactions has been the forging of a new set of professional groups, identities, and expectations. The most glaring example of this process is actually to be found in a seemingly negative context: the self-evident fury of the APE members resulting from the Czech appointment scandal. As the reader may recall,[103] the APE declared Aleš Pejchal unqualified to sit on the Court. But the Czech government obstinately refused to pull his name from its list, perhaps because he was its preferred candidate, perhaps because it had no viable back-up candidate, or perhaps both. The PACE's Sub-Committee on the Election of Judges to the ECtHR also found Pejchal unacceptable, though apparently not for the same reasons as those publicly espoused by the APE: Pejchal was not entirely unqualified, but he was unacceptably closely tied to the right-wing Czech President Václav Klaus. Trying to finesse the problem, the Sub-Committee simply forwarded the names of the other two Czech candidates to the APE as viable candidates, only to have the PACE—in the wake of unseemly (and perhaps inappropriate) electioneering—elect the candidate deemed unqualified/unacceptable: Judge Pejchal.

The APE was absolutely incensed. Its fury was all the greater given that its professional pride had been slighted in other respects. On one occasion, the Sub-Committee on Elections had rejected a governmental list of candidates that the APE had just "fully approved."[104] And on several others, national governments had not bothered to await the APE's opinion on their lists of candidates before submitting them to the PACE, which—amazingly enough—proceeded to vote on those lists nonetheless.[105]

[103] *See supra* Chapter 10(6).

[104] *See* Steering Committee for Human Rights, Ministers' Deputies Exchange of Views with Mr. Luzius Wildhaber, Chairman of the Advisory Panel of Experts on Candidates for Election to the European Court of Human Rights (January 30, 2013), in DH-GDR (2013)005, February 5, 2013 ["2013 Exchange of Views"] ("Malgré cela, l'une de ces listes, pleinement approuvée par le Panel, a été ensuite rejetée par la Sous-Commission sur l'élection des juges de l'Assemblée Parlementaire.")

[105] *Id.*

The language used by the APE Chair, Luzius Wildhaber (former President of the ECtHR), to express the APE's anger speaks volumes not only about the APE's self-perception, but also its perception of the assorted interests that surround it:

> This experience has left the Panel members with feelings of frustration. These feelings have been exacerbated by a perceived lack of co-operation, or even interest, on the side of the other stakeholders in the election procedure. This explains probably why, at a Panel meeting in October 2012 the members decided to raise these issues with other stakeholders in the election procedure.[106]

As this paragraph expresses so well, Wildhaber and his APE colleagues clearly see themselves as a cohesive unit. The APE can be slighted; and if so, it can react. But what is perhaps most interesting is how Wildhaber describes that response: the APE members "decided to raise these issues with other stakeholders in the election procedure." With this passage, we can undeniably see the gelling of an identity formation; the APE understands *itself* as an identifiable "stakeholder" in the ECtHR judicial election process.[107]

To identify who might be the other such "stakeholders," one need only look at the list of institutional players that Wildhaber arranged to meet to voice the APE's frustrations. The first set of meetings were with leaders of the PACE and of its Sub-Committee on Elections:

> On 5 November 2012 I met with the Chair of the Sub-Committee on the Election of Judges, Mr Klaas de Vries, in The Hague in order to share with him the Panel members' concerns. In order to pursue this discussion I then met with the President of the Parliamentary Assembly, Mr Jean-Claude Mignon, and the Secretary General of the Parliamentary Assembly, Mr Wojciech Sawicki on 3 December 2012. We discussed concrete measures.

The second set of meetings were held with the institutional representatives of the Member States as well as with the President of the Court:

> I have also held meetings with the Chair of the Committee of Ministers, the President of the European Court of Human Rights and the Secretary General of the Council of Europe on 3 and 4 December 2012 in order to address the above difficulties encountered by the Panel.

[106] *Id.*

[107] Note that Wildhaber stresses this notion of "stakeholders," repeating the term in successive sentences. *See id.*

The Committee of Ministers is composed of the Foreign Ministers of the Member States of the Council of Europe.[108] It is therefore the chief intergovernmental institution operating at the European level in Strasbourg. As for the Secretary General of the Council of Europe, he is in essence the administrative point man for the Council of Europe, acting as administrative and managerial liaison between the Committee of Ministers (which selects him) and the PACE (which formally appoints him) in order to effectuate the overall purposes of the Council of Europe.[109] And of course, the Court is the Court.

At first blush, Wildhaber's account of the meetings therefore suggests several discrete classes of stakeholders: the APE itself, the PACE (including its Sub-Committee—now the Committee—on the Election of Judges), the Member State governments, and the Court. This raises several interesting issues. In particular, it suggests that the APE, though composed exclusively of high-level European and domestic judges (and Chaired by the former President of the ECtHR), should not be automatically lumped together with the ECtHR. In a similar vein, this suggests that we ought to question whether the PACE and its Sub-Committee should be treated uncritically as a single, undifferentiated entity.

But perhaps most important is the issue of the Member State governments. While it is true that Committee of Ministers is composed of the Foreign Ministers of the Member States of the Council of Europe, it is by no means obvious that it ought to be automatically assimilated to the governments of the Member States. The key is to recognize that although the Committee of Ministers is formally composed of the Foreign Ministers of the Member States, it very rarely functions in that manner. Indeed, it does so only once a year (in May or November). Instead, each Member State appoints a "Permanent Representative" (who almost always functions as that country's "Deputy"), who resides in Strasbourg and takes part in the Committee of Ministers' weekly meetings, known as the "Meetings of the Ministers' Deputies" and in the meetings of subsidiary groups (usually organized thematically). This is how the Committee of Ministers actually functions.

Why does this institutional detail matter? Because it helps us to grasp the institutional, professional, and sociological profiles of the actors in play. In short, it is somewhat misleading to describe the Committee of Ministers as the governments of the Member States. True, it is formally composed at the top of the national Foreign Ministers. But it is really run by ambassadorial Permanent Representatives in Strasbourg. Even more, the Committee of Ministers is operated on a daily level by "representatives" designated by the Member State governments; these representatives function in "intergovernmental committees and subordinate bodies" of the Committee of Ministers, such as the important Steering Committee for Human Rights (CDDH), which has its own "subordinate structures," such as the

[108] *See* http://www.coe.int/en/web/cm/about-cm.
[109] *See* http://www.coe.int/en/web/secretary-general.

Committee of Experts on the System of the European Convention on Human Rights (DH-SYSC), and so on.[110]

In other words, the Committee of Ministers is actually a sizable institution of senior civil servants, most of whom are long-term executive branch diplomats and/or legal specialists committed to the common project that is the European Convention on Human Rights, the Council of Europe, and the Court. Although these career technocratic civil servants obviously come from their respective Member States, and although they have been designated by them to Strasbourg, these civil servants should not be readily assimilated to the governments that sent them. They are simply not the same kind of executive branch actors as those who would naturally come to mind when one speaks of "national governments," such as national politicians who reside in their national capitals and bargain primarily in their country's self-interest. They are, for the most part, very high-grade professionals with significant legal expertise and a commitment to the European human rights project and its institutions.

Indeed, one need only look at the list of participants at the meetings of the sub-groups of the DH-SYSC (under the CDDH, which is under the Committee of Ministers), to recognize the overall level and expertise of the professionals involved: the dominant profile is of seasoned members of the national legal services of the Member States, often specialized in the human rights field, and commonly the "Agent" of the Member State before the ECtHR (who serves in effect as the country's primary legal representative—i.e., its "solicitor general"—before the Court and whose office also often serves as a primary vector for the transmission of ECtHR developments into the domestic legal order).[111]

It is no accident, therefore, that Wildhaber's meetings with "stakeholders" led to the indirect introduction of a final—and implicitly distinct—class of interested parties: the Member State governments themselves. Wildhaber states:

> As a first step the Secretariat of the Parliamentary Assembly, under the impulsion of its Secretary General, Mr Sawicki, has already started to provide the Contracting Parties with more time for the submission of their lists of candidates. This will have the immediate positive consequence to allow the governments more time to consult the Panel before submitting the list to the PACE.[112]

[110] *See* Steering Committee for Human Rights (CDDH), Terms of reference of the CDDH and its subordinate bodies for the biennium 2016–2017, as adopted by the Committee of Ministers at their 1241st meeting, November 24–26, 2015), available at www.coe.int/t/dghl/standardsetting/cddh/Mandats CDDH 2016-2017_EN.asp.

[111] *See, e.g.*, Meeting Report of Drafting Group I on the Follow-Up to the CDDH Report on the Longer-Term Future of the Convention (DH-SYSC-I), 2nd meeting, October 19–21, 2016, DH-SYSC-I (2016)R2. For an excellent presentation of the role of the Agent as intermediary between Strasbourg and the domestic legal systems, *see* Magda Krzyzanowska-Mierzewska, *The Reception Process in Poland and Slovakia*, *in* A EUROPE OF RIGHTS: THE IMPACT OF THE ECHR ON NATIONAL LEGAL SYSTEMS 531, 594–99 (HELEN KELLER & ALEC STONE SWEET eds., 2008).

[112] *See* 2013 Exchange of Views.

This subtle paragraph reveals and confirms a great deal. Most importantly, it introduces a new class of actors, the Contracting Parties and their governments, who are therefore (accurately) understood as separate from the seemingly intergovernmental Committee of Ministers. In other words, the PACE leadership does not contact the national governments through the Committee of Ministers, despite the fact that the Committee is formally composed of the Foreign Ministers of each of those Contracting Parties' governments: it goes directly to the source.

Indeed, the socio-professional distinctiveness of the Committee of Ministers and the Committee's resulting (partial) separation from the national governments "back home" provides insight into the otherwise vexing question that underlies much of this book: why would the Member State governments have agreed to the creation of the APE in the first place? After all, the APE represents a significant potential threat to a Member State's capacity to promote the election of judicial candidates of its own choosing. This is of course an enormously complex question that I have already discussed a great deal throughout the book. The primary answer I have suggested so far has been the mass accession of former Eastern Bloc States in the wake of the fall of the Berlin Wall.

But it is now worth considering a second, perhaps subsidiary, answer: the APE is *not really* the creature of the Council of Europe as a whole, nor of the PACE, nor of the Court, nor of the Member State governments as such. It was instituted by the Committee of Ministers, i.e., by high-grade civil service professionals heavily informed by the legal and human rights expertise of its key cadres. For such players, allegiance has come to run more strongly toward the legal institutions they serve and the transnational legal/professional projects they embody than toward the relatively blunt and fleeting political calculations of domestic politicians back home. In other words, the establishing of the APE was only formally the work of the Member State governments. Once we move beyond such formalities, however, we can recognize that the APE was actually created by a relatively distinctive and pan-European class of committed civil service professionals, many of whom commonly practice and/or argue before the Strasbourg Court. Indeed, one of the classic paths to the Strasbourg bench has been to serve as a national Agent before the Court.[113]

The Committee of Ministers' socio-professional formation does much to explain why its institutional and intellectual commitments came to line up so well with those of the ECtHR's judges. Indeed, the Committee's responsibilities as enforcement arm of the Court further reinforce this natural alliance: after all, it is

[113] Even now, when the PACE has repeatedly recommended that Member States should propose judicial candidates who would not often have to recuse themselves from the cases before the Court, four of the sitting ECtHR judges were once national Agents. Those judges are Guido Raimondi (Italy), Erik Mose (Norway), Alena Polackova (Slovak Republic), and Jolien Schukking (Netherlands). *See* https://www.echr.coe.int/Pages/home.aspx?p=court/judges&c. This is not to mention the significantly larger number of national Agents and former Agents who have been put forward as candidates to fill those judicial positions.

the Committee that supervises the execution of the Court's rulings by the Member States.[114] It is no accident, therefore, that the Committee of Ministers, functioning through its Deputies and, in particular, in its "DH" (Human Rights) meetings, has overseen both the Member States' execution of the Court's judgments and the APE reforms to the ECtHR's judicial appointments/election process.

That being the case, it makes a good bit of sense that it was the Secretary General of the PACE—and not the Committee of Ministers—who acted as the indirect channel for hammering out a partial solution to the governments' willful dismissal of the APE: to "provide the Contracting Parties with more time for the submission of their lists of candidates," which "will allow the governments more time to consult the Panel before submitting the list to the PACE."[115] Indeed, this settlement between the PACE leadership and the national governments raises an intriguing issue, which I mention only briefly now, namely, whether—at least for the purposes of judicial appointments—the national governments may often be more closely aligned with the PACE than with the (nominally intergovernmental) Committee of Ministers: at least those exchanges are between politicians and politicians. Furthermore, the PACE is composed of representatives drawn in a politically representative fashion from the national parliaments; and given that most Council of Europe countries are parliamentary democracies, those PACE representatives necessarily reflect the basic political orientation of their governments back home. This further reinforces the links between the plenary assembly of the PACE and the national governments.

Finally, the relative affinity between the Committee of Ministers and the ECtHR judges, on the one hand, and between the national governments and the PACE members, on the other, informs the dominant response of academics to the judicial appointments reforms. In that socio-professional context, prominent academics almost always default toward the professionals who possess technical expertise akin to their own.[116] Indeed, this comfortable association of prominent scholars with high judicial authority is particularly strong in the modern Civilian tradition of Continental Europe. After all, the dominant praxis in post-War Civilian countries has been that such scholars should serve as the primary class of appointees to sit on national constitutional courts.[117] Over time, this tradition has largely carried over into the supranational realm of Europe.[118] An examination of the biographies of

[114] Article 46 of the European Convention on Human Rights.

[115] *See* 2013 Exchange of Views.

[116] Mikael Madsen, who has done substantial work on European judicial appointments, has been a notable exception. *See* Mikael Rask Madsen, *The Legitimization Strategies of International Judges: The Case of the European Court of Human Rights*, *in* Bobek (2015) at 259 ["Madsen (2015)"].

[117] *See, e.g.*, John Ferejohn, *Constitutional Review in the Global Context*, 6 N.Y.U. J. Legis. & Pub. Pol'y 49, 55 (2002–2003); Michaela Hailbronner, *Rethinking the rise of the German Constitutional Court: From anti-Nazism to value formalism*, I•Con 623, 646 (2014).

[118] Madsen, however, notes (and bemoans) a gradual trend away from appointing elite law professors with strong political and diplomatic connections to more judicially oriented legal technicians. *See* Madsen (2015).

the members of the two high European Courts bears this out extremely clearly: in the spring of 2017, for example, fully half of the forty-seven ECtHR judges and thirty-nine ECJ judges and Advocates General had been tenured academics prior to their election or appointment to the Strasbourg or Luxembourg Courts—easily making university professors *the* leading profile of ECJ and ECtHR judges.[119]

By way of example, one need only look at Professor Michal Bobek, the Czech scholar who edited SELECTING EUROPE'S JUDGES, the leading volume on judicial appointments to the ECJ and the ECtHR. In the book's twenty-three-page Prologue, written when he held teaching and research positions at Oxford and the College of Europe (Bruges), Bobek could hardly have been more focused on the criteria of quality and merit that so permeate academic debates on the European judicial selection process: in those twenty-three pages, Bobek uses the term "quality" no fewer than twenty-one times and the term "merit" yet another fourteen, never mind the times he also uses closely associated terms. It could hardly be more appropriate or more telling, therefore, that Bobek has since been appointed Advocate General at the ECJ, where he is currently serving. True, Bobek is for our purposes an emblematic figure, given his prominent publishing on the topic of this book. But the professional, intellectual, and sociological links between the European professorial community and the national constitutional and European judicial institutions are undeniably strong and ongoing.

III. Conclusions

This chapter constructed a unified account of scandal theory and deployed it to help make sense of the scandalous development of the European judicial appointments debates and reforms of the last twenty years, especially in the ECtHR context. The theory proves immensely valuable for teasing out features of these debates and reforms that may not have been immediately obvious and that we will have occasion to examine in further detail over the final Part of this book. Most importantly, scandal is not some straightforward prior event. It is the uncertain, contested, and unfolding process of making public disclosures about alleged prior events in an effort to construct and mobilize a targeted public whose outrage is enlisted to support controversial normative assertions and to promote the leadership claims of those endorsing them.

To conclude this chapter by means of an organized summary, let us therefore walk quickly through our findings by following the six main points suggested by scandal

[119] See http://www.echr.coe.int/Pages/home.aspx?p=court/judges; http://curia.europa.eu/jcms/jcms/Jo2_7026/en/. In fact, the professorial component of the professional profiles is so strong that a large number of the non-academics (judges, Ministry of Justice attorneys, etc.) have held university lecturing positions of one kind or another.

theory. First, the scandalous event is not simply a straightforward, completed event. The earliest disclosures date precisely from 1998;[120] that is, they coincide perfectly with the coming into effect of Protocol 11, which established the "new" ECtHR, whose task would now be to adjudicate all claims directly and openly, transforming the Court abruptly into an active agent of human rights norms in the transitional East.[121] But this was only the beginning of a long dribble of disclosures, first by Professor Flauss, then by publisher Norbert Engel, and eventually by the former ECtHR President Luzius Wildhaber himself. The appointments scandal therefore developed over time, unfolding not only before, but also well after, the establishment of the judicial vetting Panels. Even after all of this Part's analysis, it remains unclear whether the scandalous event actually consists of any one—or even a group—of the unsavory episodes such as those recounted in Chapter 10 or, more likely, whether it is also something more fundamental (if never quite clearly or openly stated), be it the deplorable lack of status and respect afforded to the Strasbourg Court and its judges, the shameful overreaching of domineering national governments, or the distasteful incorporation of unsuitable Eastern partners into the European fold.

Second, the scandal revolves around the claim that norms have been violated. As we shall reiterate below, the specific normative claims are deeply and perpetually contested. What matters for now, however, is that the norms in question are precisely the type of "mid-range" and "due process" claims that scholars have identified as characteristic of political scandals in liberal democracies.[122] They occupy a contested middle ground with such ill-defined boundaries as those concerning the abuse of political power.[123] The scandalous events have all involved governments running roughshod over judges exercising their duties in good faith and over the proper procedures for the selection and appointment/election of judges to the European Courts. In other words, they strike precisely at the cherished procedural protections that constitute and define liberal democratic orders.[124]

Third, the scandal required, and to some extent consisted of, the making of revelations to a public. This process began with Professor Flauss, who published his first series of revelations in his 1998 article, *Radioscopie de l'élection de la nouvelle Cour européenne des droits de l'homme* and who then updated his scandalous revelations every few years until his early death in 2010.[125] Norbert Engel took up the task in 2012,[126] followed eventually by the startling revelations made by the

[120] *See* Flauss (1998).
[121] *See supra* Chapter 4(I).
[122] *See* Markovits & Silverstein (1988) at 5–9.
[123] *See* Thompson (2000) at 14–15.
[124] *See* Markovits & Silverstein (1988) at 5–9.
[125] *See* Flauss (1998); Jean-François Flauss, *Le Renouvellement triennial de la Cour européenne des droit de l'homme*, 47 Rev. tr. d. h. 693 (2001) ["Flauss (2001)"]; Flauss (2005); Jean-François Flauss, *Les élections de juges à la Cour européenne des droits de l'homme (2005–2008)*, 75 Rev. tr. d. h. 5 (2008) ["Flauss (2008)"].
[126] Engel (2008).

sitting President of the APE: former ECtHR President Luzius Wildhaber.[127] All of these revelations were truly shocking, not only for the information they contained, but also for their mere publication. To this day, it is impossible to mention these publications in Strasbourg without eliciting disapproving head shakes—and often outright shudders—from players aligned with such Council of Europe political institutions as the PACE, its (Sub-) Committee on the Election of Judges, and so on: these players do not hesitate to express their belief that the public airing of such dirty laundry is unseemly and deeply unproductive.

The Strasbourg judges and their closest academic observers and allies, however, not only nod knowingly, but also happily and conspiratorially divulge every sordid episode they can. In fact, I have been perpetually amazed during interviews that they make no effort whatever to demand confidentiality or even to ask for discretion. With few exceptions, my problem has been how to remember it all without using a recording device (which I do not, for fear of creating barriers) or developing advanced stenographic skills! True, most of my interlocutors have at least a vague sense of who I am or know that I come recommended by a friend or colleague; and true, I go to some effort to convey from the beginning that I am already very much in the know. But I get little sense that any of this matters a great deal. These interlocutors *want* me to be in the know; they assume that I am a friendly; and they routinely go to some bother to demonstrate that they know even more titillating stories than my other sources.

As Max Gluckman stressed, gossip and scandal construct and police community and membership:

> The important things about gossip and scandal are that generally these are enjoyed by people about others with whom they are in a close social relationship. Hence when we try to understand why it is that people in all places and at all times have been so interested in gossip and scandal about each other, we have also to look at those whom they exclude from joining in the gossiping or scandalizing. That is, the right to gossip about certain people is a privilege which is only extended to a person when he or she is accepted as a member of a group or set. It is a hallmark of membership. Hence rights to gossip serve to mark off a particular group from other groups.[128]

Indeed, I cannot deny the flush of pleasure (and the attendant gratitude) at being entrusted with such sensitive information and at the rewarding social and professional inclusion that this implies. True, this trust may reflect little more than the comfortable alliance that already exists between European judges and academics. And true, these revealing discussions clearly serve as a welcome outlet for highly

[127] 2013 Exchange of Views.
[128] Gluckman (1963) at 313.

placed judges to express their strong views on their professional tasks and milieus. And yet, it is hard not to experience the flattering sensation of being invited into a clan.

But I would have to be very naïve indeed not to recognize that in addition to serving as a sympathetic sounding board, I am also being leveraged: I am being put to use to advance my interlocutors' institutional and programmatic interests in their battles with internal and external rivals. Indeed, there can be no doubt but that these quiet discussions demonstrate the existence and the development of significant internal schisms. To listen to well-placed figures in the PACE, its (Sub-) Committee on the Election of Judges, the Committee of Ministers, the ECtHR, or the APE is to listen to very different accounts and analyses of facts and events, and to witness very different understandings of which players and institutions should legitimately be playing the dominant role in the Council of Europe and in its interactions with the wider political and legal universe, and thus of who should represent the Council of Europe (and, perhaps to a lesser degree, its human rights mission) (a) within the Council of Europe and (b) between the Council of Europe and its external interlocutors, including domestic governments and judges.

To my political interlocutors, the unseemly public disclosures by judicial and academic figures (and the audacity they imply) are scandalous in their own right, rising almost to the level of an *affaire*.[129] Not only are these disclosures indiscrete, they challenge the legitimate role of the political sphere: they treat political figures as bumbling idiots incapable of comprehending—never mind advancing—the rule of law. They demonstrate the rise of an unjustifiably sanctimonious judicial posture, in which only a duly authorized caste of judicial priests can legitimately care about human rights and take appropriate action to protect them. The disclosures are, in short, the self-interested and weaponized manifestation of the sectarian professional interests of an increasingly powerful and self-righteous judicial guild. On this view, the judicial appointments reforms are in effect an elaborate purification ritual that serves to empower and justify judicial rule.

Needless to say, my judicial interlocutors—and, almost all of my academic ones—do not share this assessment! To them, the unsavory revelations are but representative examples of a shameful lack of respect for fundamental rights, of improper political interference with the judicial role, of disregard for the dictates of the separation of powers, of non-comprehension of the importance of independent judicial decision-making, and so on. For them, the scandals are above all self-evident lessons in the perils of political overreach, exemplified by transition "democracies" from the recently acceded countries from Central and Eastern Europe. On this view, public revelation of such scandalous political behavior serves to rally well-meaning actors to find ways to combat their reoccurrence.

[129] For the classic explanation of how a scandal can be flipped back on he who reveals it, thereby creating an *affaire*, *see* Claverie (1998).

Fourth, the scandalous nature of the revelations hinges on the normative assessment of the acts in question. For this, the key question—contrary to what one might initially have assumed—is probably less whether the alleged acts have occurred than whether those acts qualify as scandalous in the first place. Those making the disclosures (especially Flauss, Engel, and Wildhaber) obviously claimed so; hence, the irascible disclosures. But as we have seen, the scandalous nature of those acts is not as consistently self-evident as the disclosures have presented them to be. The norms governing the relationship between the political branches (especially the executive) and the judiciary were far less settled than the scandalous publications treated them as being; and whatever those norms had been, they certainly did not lead automatically to the conclusions that Flauss, Engel, and Wildhaber loudly propounded regarding judicial appointments. This is not to say that there do not exist very good reasons to adopt the normative positions pressed by such authors. It is simply to recognize that for all their self-confident and indignant rhetoric, these judicial and academic figures have been advocating reformist agendas while working hard to present them as the self-evident entailments of long-standing and universally recognized constitutional values and normative rules.

Fifth, because the scandalous publications were reformist interventions rather than the expression of self-evident and uncontroversial truths, the elaboration of their outcomes would take some time. And indeed, over twenty years have passed since Professor Flauss published his initial set of revelations.[130] During that time, all of the developments dutifully recounted by this book have taken place: the meetings, the debates, the proposals, the pushback, the reforms, the resistance, the new reforms, the set-backs, the repeated reforms, and on and on. When viewed in the fullness of time, it becomes rather clear that the scandals represent much more than a static, Durkheim-ian mechanism for the successful reproduction of a given social system: the scandals argued for, prompted, and defended a whole series of reforms on issues ranging from judicial appointments to judicial independence to judicial councils, etc.

Sixth, and finally, it is not entirely clear whether the unseemly appointments disclosures have generated the degree and type of outrage that would qualify them as veritable "scandals." It is true that the sordid disclosures and the charged debates contributed significantly to advancing the judicial reform agenda. In that sense, there really has been a judicial appointments/independence scandal; far from eliciting indifferent shrugs, these public denunciations have generated a meaningful institutional, professional, procedural, and normative response.[131] That said, the scandals have generally remained contained within the professional circles

[130] *See* Flauss (1998).

[131] *See* Blic & Lemieux (2005) at 16, English version at para. 13.

surrounding the European Courts. The disclosures by Flauss and Engel, for example, were published in the specialized press.[132] Only the French fiasco seems to have broken fleetingly into the general press.[133]

Furthermore, it is hard to gauge the degree of actual outrage. On the one hand, it certainly appears to be significant, given not only the initial impetus for reform in the 1990s, but also the staying power of the reform movement ever since. But on the other, it takes but a little perspective to recognize the flip side to these endless reforms. The mere fact that the reforms have been deemed necessary on such an ongoing basis, that there exists a felt need to pass ever more precise and exhaustive measures, and especially that such measures have had to be reissued over and over again should clue us into the fact that their reformist zeal must not be universally shared.

Indeed, the depth and persistence of the resistance to the reforms shines brightly through the very literature that has made the unseemly disclosures. The Wildhaber "Exchange of Views" with the Committee of Ministers' Steering Committee for Human Rights demonstrates the point all too well.[134] In this strikingly plaintive missive, which we examined in some depth in Chapter 5, Wildhaber indignantly recounts a long series of willful slights that the Member State governments and Strasbourg institutions had directed toward the APE and toward the procedural and institutional reforms that the Council of Europe had enacted over the previous fifteen years. Within a few months of its creation, the APE was being strong-armed—or perhaps worse, ignored—by even the French government. Not only was an increasingly long line of governments refusing to abide by the APE's judgments concerning the suitability of proposed judicial candidates to the ECtHR, but others were also refusing to submit those candidacies to the APE in a manner that would allow it to perform its vetting duties in the first place. Far from standing firm in the way of such hijinks, the PACE and its (Sub-) Committee on the Election of Judges to the ECtHR all but ratified them by moving forward on judicial elections despite such obvious procedural irregularities.[135]

Tellingly, these problems have hardly vanished over time. In its 2017 "[Draft] Report on the process of selection and Elections of judges of the [ECtHR]," the Council of Europe's Committee of Experts on the System of the ECHR ("DH-SYSC") made clear that the problems that APE Chair Luzius Wildhaber had complained of so bitterly in his 2013 "Exchange of Views" had persisted. In particular,

[132] *See* Flauss (1998); Flauss , (2001); Flauss (2005); Flauss (2008); Engel (2008).
[133] *See supra* Chapter 10(V).
[134] *See* 2013 Exchange of Views.
[135] *See supra* Chapter 5(II) and (III).

> **The opinions [of the APE] are not always followed**: during the period between January 2014 and June 2017, among the 29 lists examined by the Panel, in 9 cases the candidates were maintained on the list despite the Panel's negative opinion.[136]

This startling revelation demonstrates that in almost one out of every three cases, the Member State governments have not only proposed lists that contained at least one candidate deemed unsuitable by the APE, but have also refused to replace the problematic candidate(s) from the list they eventually presented to the PACE for election! And this is in the four-year period *after* President Wildhaber's public revelation of the APE's frustrations with the lack of cooperation that it had been receiving from "other stakeholders in the election procedure."[137]

And that is not all. The Report continues:

> Another crucial question was that of governments not submitting the list to the Panel before its presentation to the Assembly [i.e., the PACE]. This issue was examined in light of three incidents in 2016 whereby the lists were submitted to both instances almost simultaneously or by completely circumventing the Advisory Panel. In two cases, the lists contained replacement candidates on which the Panel did not have the opportunity to express a view either because the government did not wait for its view or because it did not even submit the replacement candidate's curriculum vitae to the Panel. In the third case, the government submitted simultaneously the list of candidates to both the Panel and the Assembly, in which case the Panel immediately suspended its examination of that list.[138]

And yet, in the face of such blatant governmental subversion of the carefully elaborated ECtHR judicial election process, even the Committee of Ministers' Committee of Experts on the System of the ECHR refused to adopt the seemingly sensible proposal that "without the consultation of the [APE], the list would automatically be rejected."[139] Things would go on as before.

The point here is not to determine conclusively whether these unseemly disclosures succeeded in eliciting sufficient outrage for them to qualify officially and authoritatively as a "scandal." Rather, the varying responses demonstrate the precariousness of the reform enterprise, complete with its attendant disclosures. The disclosures were examples calibrated to generate a response of outrage and to lead toward the adoption of programmatic reforms. That this approach offered

[136] Steering Committee for Human Rights, Committee of Experts on the System of the ECHR (DH-SYSC), "2017 Report on the process of selection and election of ECtHR judges" at para. 83 (emphasis in the original).

[137] *Id.*; 2013 Exchange of Views.

[138] 2017 Report on the process of selection and election of ECtHR judges, at para. 89.

[139] *Id.* at para. 88.

no guarantees is all too apparent from ensuing developments. On the one hand, a coalition of high-grade judges, academics, and other institutional players (such as sub-parts of the Committee of Ministers) coalesced sufficiently to push through the long set of reforms we have studied throughout this book. But on the other, numerous Member State governments and institutional players (such as the PACE and its sub-parts) have been far more reticent, demonstrating significant and even strident resistance to the reforms that have been put in place.

The scandals/disclosures/reforms thus offer a mixed bag of responses. Indeed, these responses have been sufficiently disparate and inconsistent that one need not be a jaded European institutional veteran to recognize that many of the reforms have been formally and passively approved as a public relations matter, but substantively and actively opposed as an international relations matter. Whether this demonstrates the "success" of the strategy of scandal (or even whether this result qualifies as a scandal in its own right) depends a great deal on one's interlocutors.

At the same time, the judicial appointment scandals and the varied responses to them effectively demonstrate the complex nature of scandal in general. On the one hand, they can be understood to "confirm Durkheim's point that each social system needs pathologies for its successful reproduction."[140] On the other hand, they represent a concerted effort to drive debates and reforms in specific directions. As this Part has shown, scandal functions precisely at this delicate intersection between the static reproduction of communal political structures and the struggle to take control of these structures and of their development.

[140] Markovits & Silverstein (1988) at 3.

PART VI
MAKING SENSE OF THE REFORMS

This book has given a sustained look at the judicial appointments debates and reforms that have taken place at the European level since the creation of the two great European courts in the 1950s, and especially since the explosion of interest in such topics in the 1990s. I have sought to demonstrate how the seemingly sudden and nearly simultaneous addition of screening panels to vet judicial candidates to the Luxembourg and Strasbourg Courts actually marked the culmination of an extended set of debates and reforms that need to be dated not to 2009–10, when the Panels were eventually instituted, but all the way back to the fall of the Berlin Wall. What matters in this story, in other words, is far more visible in the *longue durée* of historical, political, institutional, and intellectual developments than in snapshots of recent developments. At the same time, I have also tried to convey the full extent to which contingency really does matter: who, for example, happened to be appointed to which institution and what happen to be the structural particularities of that institution can yield impressively large and long-term effects.

The most important methodological feature of the analysis has been to refuse to treat the judicial appointments reforms as freestanding developments. The judicial appointment reforms, in other words, are not just about judicial appointments. The reforms are instead embedded in a long series of interwoven debates and concerns, such as those involving judicial independence, judicial quality, judicial councils, and so on.[1] All of these debates are connected to and responsive to each other; so their full meaning and import are not really accessible without a proper reconstruction of the web of interconnected associations in which they are embedded and of which they are important component parts.

Having methodically presented the key interconnected issues, debates, and reforms, the time has come to be more explicit about exactly how they are aligned and thus about what they really mean and what they really do. But there is a catch: these connections are complex. By this, I do not simply mean that they are thorny and thus difficult to decipher (although this is undoubtedly often the case).

[1] Indeed, since each of those debates is itself interwoven with many others, one could theoretically continue the analysis ad infinitum.

I also mean something more: the connections are multifaceted and variable. They sustain multiple, competing, and at times frankly contradictory readings.

I believe that this hermeneutic complexity is utterly central to the prolonged success of the judicial appointments, independence, and quality debates as a multifaceted site for ongoing judicial, political, institutional, and academic engagement. It permits a host of different players to contribute actively to these debates and to the ensuing reform efforts, to laud and critique their effects, and so on, despite the fact that these players may not agree with each other about very much at all, including, most importantly, what the debates and reforms are "really" all about. In other words, it is precisely the capacity of these interrelated issues to mean different things to different people in different contexts that gives them their flexibility, strength, and appeal. It would therefore be a grave analytic oversimplification (not to say "mistake") to try to impose a single, coherent meaning onto this interconnected web. What matters in the end is how these multiple and divergent meanings work together to yield a productive site for engagement.

For all of this complexity, however, I believe that there is in fact a relatively small number of dominant takes on these issues and on how they connect with each other, and that we can identify which types of players tend to adhere to which takes and why. I will therefore do my best to present straightforwardly the key conceptual, institutional, and professional connections that explain the connotation and the import of the assorted issues in play. As I hope the previous chapters already suggest, such an analysis should yield significant insights on the state of European legal, political, and judicial affairs, on the forces pushing for institutional and other reforms, and on the direction that ongoing developments appear most likely to take.

In order to make some sense out of these debates and reforms, this chapter therefore presents a series of contending interpretations of the materials we have been studying over the course of this book. To be plain: I believe that each of these numerous readings is correct, in the sense that each accurately conveys an important strand in the rise, development, and salience of the judicial appointments debates. To the extent that these interpretations appear supportive of, or inconsistent, or even contradictory with, each other, that is just a fact of life. After all, it should come as no great surprise that highly contested debates and reforms give rise to contested understandings, conflicted motivations, inconsistent and at times counterproductive claims, and so on. Indeed, were it not for such competing understandings, it is hard to imagine how such potentially tedious appointment issues could have turned into important and revealing sites of engagement.

12
Different Ways to Connect the Dots

I have not hidden from the reader what I believe to be the single most important explanatory matrix for making sense of the appointments debates and reforms: managing the accession of a large number of new Members States from Central and Eastern Europe. As this book has already discussed this explanation at some length, I will reserve further dedicated discussion on this front until the later sections of Chapter 13. I will instead turn to a series of alternative prisms that play important roles in framing the debates and driving the reforms.

I. Strand #1: The Supranational Transplantation of Institutional Forms: The Rise and Spread of Judicial Councils

The first major theme, which we first had occasion to discuss in Chapter 6, surfaces explicitly and repeatedly in the political, judicial, and academic debates: the establishment of national judicial councils tasked with overseeing a wide panoply of judicial matters, ranging from appointments, to training, to discipline, to organization. As Garoupa and Ginsburg explain, there has been an undeniable worldwide boom in such judicial councils: France established the modern version of its *Conseil supérieur de la magistrature* as a constitutional organ in the immediate post-war period, followed by Italy in 1958, Spain and Portugal in the 1970s. From there, judicial councils spread to the countries of Eastern Europe and Latin America, and so on.[2] Indeed, the establishment of national judicial councils became so routine that "the World Bank and other multilateral donor agencies have made judicial councils part of the standard package of institutions associated with judicial reform and rule of law programming."[3]

Given the rapid spread of judicial councils as an institutional form on the national level, it is only logical that they would eventually have emerged on the

[2] Nuno Garoupa & Tom Ginsberg, *Guarding the Guardians: Judicial Councils and Judicial Independence*, 57 AM. J. COMP. L. 103, 106–07 (2009) [Garoupa & Ginsberg, *Guarding the Guardians*]. France had possessed a *Conseil supérieur de la magistrature* since 1883, but it was the 1946 Constitution of the Fourth Republic that officially enshrined the *Conseil* in the Constitution itself. *See* http://www.conseil-superieur-magistrature.fr/le-csm/histoire-et-patrimoine; Title IX of the 1946 Constitution.

[3] Garoupa and Ginsberg, *Guarding the Guardians* at 109. Needless to say, cause and effect blurs: the World Bank not only reflects but promotes such a rise in judicial councils.

supranational level as well. In Europe, the first step remained national in orientation: international and supranational institutions supported the establishment of national judicial councils. As we saw in Chapter 6, the institutions of the Council of Europe eagerly jumped on this bandwagon.[4] National judicial councils were becoming increasingly ubiquitous.

But the supranational European contribution to the development of judicial councils was not limited to giving encouragement to the deployment of the councils at the national level, where they might play pivotal roles in staffing, organizing, and overseeing the national judiciaries. The second development was the proposal that judicial councils also be used as the mechanism to select candidates to serve as judges at the European and international levels. The idea was simple: the national selection, appointment, and reappointment of such European judicial candidates should follow the same procedures and benefit from the same protections as those governing the selection of judges serving in the national judiciaries.[5] In a few short years, the institutional form of the judicial council had migrated from the domestic to the supranational judiciaries.[6]

Then came the third step: the establishment of the Article 255 Panel and of the Advisory Panel of Experts (APE) in 2009–10. This time, such institutions were actually to operate at the European, rather than the national, level. True, few openly stressed that the Panels were effectively inspired by and modeled on national judicial councils.[7] But it would be hard not to recognize the close family resemblance: a small and elite group of predominantly judicial figures would now vet candidates proposed to fill European judicial vacancies on the basis of their professional qualifications and character fitness.

Sure enough, it was only a matter of time before the genetic link between the new European Panels and domestic judicial councils would be overtly made. Indeed, it was none other than the impressive figure of Jean-Marc Sauvé, the inaugural President of the 255 Panel, who boldly presented the Panel in such terms.

[4] *See, e.g.*, Committee of Ministers Rec R (94) 12 (October 13, 1994) at 2. The 1998 European Charter on the Statute for Judges echoed these recommendations. *See* European Charter on the Statute for Judges, DAJ/DOC (98) 23 (1998) at Parts II–VII. So did the CCJE's 2001 Opinion No. 1 on "Standards Concerning the Independence of the Judiciary and the Irremovability of Judges": Consultative Council of European Judges, "Opinion No. 1 on Standards Concerning the Independence of the Judiciary and the Irremovability of Judges," available at https://rm.coe.int/1680747830. *See id.* at paras 32–37, 45.

[5] *See, e.g.*, *id.* at para. 56.

[6] It takes little imagination, furthermore, to suggest that this transplantation of the judicial council from country to country and from the national to the supranational levels is subject to all of the sorts of difficulties that Katarina Pistor and others have analyzed under the rubric of the "transplant effect." *See, e.g.*, Daniel Berkowitz, Katharina Pistor, & Jean-Francois Richard, *Economic Development, Legality and the Transplant Effect*, 47 Eur. Econ. Rev. 165 (2003). In other words, it might not be so surprising that the adoption of the 255 Panel by the twenty-seven Member States of the EU has gone more smoothly than the adoption of the APE by the Member States of the Council of Europe, which consists of a much larger and more diverse group of countries that is less dominated by Western European traditions.

[7] Even in the recent Bobek volume, there are only rare and fleeting suggestions of the genetic link between the national judicial councils and the 255 Panel and APE. The one notable exception is offered by the President of the 255 Panel, Jean-Marc Sauvé, discussed immediately below.

In 2013, on the ceremonial occasion of the 130th anniversary of the creation of the original French judicial council (the *Conseil supérieur de la magistrature*), Sauvé proudly described the 255 Panel as "a sort of minimalist judicial council or judicial council *light*,"[8] thereby explicitly linking it to its venerable French progenitor.

In fact, President Sauvé and Lord Mance have had such ambitions for their 255 Panel that they have steadfastly argued in favor of expanding its role in the European judicial appointments process beyond the one it was tasked to perform by Article 255 of the Lisbon Treaty. In addition to vetting the judicial candidates proposed by the Member State governments for appointment (and/or reappointment) to the European Court of Justice (ECJ) (and to the lower General Court), Sauvé and Mance have proposed that the 255 Panel play a key role in their selection.

They have proposed such a selection role in two different appointments contexts. Both have been overtaken by events, but are nonetheless worth relating. First, the lower Court of the EU, now known as the General Court (which previously went by the more accurate if apparently insufficiently august name, "Court of First Instance"), has long been swamped by an ever-increasing caseload. This should hardly be surprising: since its creation in 1989, the General Court was composed of only one judge per country, which was hardly sufficient to manage a caseload consisting, inter alia, of all direct actions brought by all European citizens challenging the legality of the acts of the EU's institutions.[9] The obvious solution was to enlarge the size of the Court.

In 2011, the ECJ thus proposed expanding the General Court by twelve new judges.[10] The problem was that any proposal to increase the size of the General Court by something other than a straightforward multiplying factor (such as, e.g., doubling it), would necessarily mean that some countries would have more judges than others. There was simply no obvious way to select or rotate the extra twelve positions between twenty-seven Member States.

Faced with this conundrum, President Sauvé had a solution: the 255 Panel might evaluate and rank—on the basis of "their competences and capacities"—the judicial candidates who might respond to a public call for applications.[11] In the end, this proposal never got off the ground. The Member State governments were so

[8] Jean-Marc Sauvé, "Le rôle du comité 255 dans la séparation des pouvoirs au sein de l'Union européenne," 10, intervention lors du colloque pour le 130ème anniversaire du Conseil supérieur de la magistrature le 24 octobre 2013, available at http://www.conseil-etat.fr/fr/discours-et-interventions/la-separation-des-pouvoirs-l-union-europeenne-et-le-comite-255-.html ["Sauvé (2013)"].

[9] The easiest way to visualize the math is as follows. Any international court that is composed of one judge per country effectively requires each judge to handle at least the number of cases originating from her entire country. And since such international courts usually sit in panels of at least three judges, each judge must also be sit on all the cases originating from at least two other countries. Absent draconian filtering mechanisms (such as a system of *certiorari*), any such court that permits individuals to press their own actions will necessarily be swamped.

[10] *See* Document 8787/11, available at http://register.consilium.europa.eu/doc/srv?l=EN&f=ST%20 8787%202011%20INIT.

[11] *See* Sauvé (2013) at 9.

incapable of coming up with a solution for distributing or rotating the extra judicial seats, and yet were so unwilling to imperil their capacity to appoint their fair share of the Court's judges, that another solution had to be found. In the end, the answer was to take the relatively drastic action of literally doubling the size of the Court.[12]

This episode is important for two reasons. On the one hand, it demonstrates how attached the Member States continue to be to their capacity to select "their" judges on the European bench. But on the other, it shows how keen President Sauvé was to continue transplanting the logic and operation of judicial councils from the domestic to the supranational spheres. Not only did he propose that the 255 Panel become involved in selecting the extra judges for an expanded General Court, but he proposed ranking candidates who would present themselves through an open call for applications. Sauvé, in other words, was proposing to transplant the judicial council form quite thoroughly from the national to the supranational spheres.[13]

The second proposal put forward by Sauvé was arguably even more audacious. This time, the issue was the expected accession of the EU to the European Convention on Human Rights. Were this accession to take place, the EU would, like any of the forty-seven existing Member States, be called upon to put forward a list of three candidates to fill the judicial position that would thereby be created at the Strasbourg Court. But how would the twenty-seven EU Member States select the three candidates to fill the EU's one judicial position on the European Court of Human Rights (ECtHR)? Once again, Sauvé openly volunteered—one might almost say "lobbied"—for the 255 Panel to play the pivotal role. The 255 Panel could once again evaluate and rank—on a basis "founded essentially on merit"—those candidates who might respond to a public call for applications. This would allow the EU to compose the traditional list of three candidates to put forward to the Council of Europe for selection and appointment by the Parliamentary Assembly (PACE). Sauvé concludes: "These two developments would ultimately serve to reinforce the role played by the 255 Panel in strengthening the independence and legitimacy of the judicial power within the European Union."[14]

[12] The price tag was made more acceptable by folding the EU's Civil Service Tribunal (and its jurisdiction) into the General Court. *See* Document 14448/14, available at http://data.consilium.europa.eu/doc/document/ST-16576-2014-INIT/en/pdf; Regulation of the European Parliament and of the Council amending Protocol No. 3 on the Statute of the Court of Justice of the European Union, Doc PE-CONS 62/15 (November 18, 2015), available at http://data.consilium.europa.eu/doc/document/PE-62-2015-INIT/en/pdf.

[13] Georges Vandersanden appropriately stresses the theoretical importance of the selection mechanism that was briefly used for the EU's Civil Service Tribunal. *See* Georges Vandersanden, *The Real Test—How to Contribute to a Better Justice: The Experience of the Civil Service Tribunal*, *in* SELECTING EUROPE'S JUDGES: A CRITICAL REVIEW OF THE APPOINTMENT PROCEDURES TO THE EUROPEAN COURTS 86 (Michal Bobek ed., 2015) ["Bobek (2015)"].

[14] Sauvé (2013) at 9. *See also* Sauvé in Bobek (2015) at 84–85 ("Further improvements of the system put in place within the EU could certainly be envisaged or desired. They could follow in particular from further evolution of the role of the Panel, be it in relation to the potential increase of the number of judges at the General Court or, once it becomes relevant, the appointment of the EU Judge to the European Court of Human Rights. In both of these cases, a public call for applications could be envisaged and

This ECtHR selection dilemma, like the one posed by the proposed expansion of the EU's General Court, has since been overtaken by events: in the famous 2014 Opinion 2/13, the ECJ held that the EU could not currently accede to the Council of Europe.[15] But this Opinion, which put everything on hold, does not efface Sauvé's impulse, which was once again to transplant the roles played by judicial councils at the national level to those that the 255 Panel might play at the supranational level. The Panel need not be limited to vetting judicial candidates put forward by the EU's Member States to sit in Luxembourg; it could begin to take on the role of ranking (and thus effectively selecting) the EU's potential judges, be it for the General Court or the ECtHR. It was therefore no accident that President Sauvé described the 255 Panel as "a sort of minimalist judicial council or judicial council *light*."[16] Indeed, he repeated the idea in Michal Bobek's book on SELECTING EUROPE'S JUDGES: the 255 Panel "could perhaps be seen . . . as a germ of a council of the judiciary within the European Union."[17] Far from downplaying the Panel's role, Sauvé has consistently described it in terms that mirror those of judicial councils in general: the Panel "exercises its full responsibilities and contributes, within the limits of its charge, to strengthening the independence and legitimacy of the European courts within the European Union's horizontal and vertical separation of powers. The Panel's field of action therefore carries much further than the apparent modesty of its powers might suggest."[18]

In conclusion, it is ultimately quite compelling to understand the establishment of the APE and of the 255 Panel as the gradual transplantation of the institutional form of the judicial council from the domestic to the supranational realms. This transplantation took place in stages, starting with the supranational support for the further adoption of national judicial councils, leading to the use of such national judicial councils to help select European and international judges, leading to the establishment of quasi-judicial councils at the European level in the form

the Panel might in particular be asked to evaluate and rank the candidates according to their merit, a task which would be certainly attainable."); Lord Mance, "The Composition of the European Court of Justice" (The text of a talk given to the United Kingdom Association for European Law, 19th October 2011) 27, available at https://www.supremecourt.uk/docs/speech_111019.pdf ["Mance (2011)"]; Jean-Marc Sauvé, "The Future of the European Union Courts; Increased Workload: Organisation, Appointment and Training of Judges," Conference organized by the Council of Bars and Law Societies of Europe, Monday April 28, 2014, available at http://www.conseil-etat.fr/content/download/4032/12124/version/1/file/28_04_2014_discours_president_sauve_en.pdf ["Sauvé (2014)"].

[15] Opinion 2/13 (2014), available at http://curia.europa.eu/juris/document/document.jsf?docid=160882&doclang=EN.

[16] Sauvé (2013) at 10.

[17] Jean-Marc Sauvé, *Selecting the European Union's Judges: The Practice of the Article 255 Panel, in* Bobek (2015) at 84. Though he does not specifically address such potential expansion of the Panel's remit, Lord Mance does pay a great deal of attention to judicial appointment commissions (especially at the domestic level), whose "scope and diversity" he openly favors expanding. The framing of his analysis suggest that his views are quite consonant with those of his colleague Sauvé. *See* Mance (2011) at 6–7 .

[18] Sauvé (2013) at 10.

of the 255 Panel and the APE to vet candidates to the Luxembourg and Strasbourg Courts, leading to the proposed use of the 255 Panel to rank (and thus effectively to select) the judicial candidates applying to serve as judges of the General Court or the ECtHR.

II. Strand #2: The Legal and Professional Normalization of the European Courts

The transplantation of the domestic institutional form of the judicial council to the supra—or inter-national level demonstrates an impulse to normalize the European Courts, that is, to treat them increasingly as recognizable and routine legal and judicial fora that happen to function at the international level. This represents a significant conceptual shift both for the European Courts and for the judges who serve on them. This process of legal and professional normalization can be understood in two ways: as the de-internationalization or as the de-constitutionalization of those courts and of their judges.

A. The Legalization and De-Internationalization of the International/Supranational

In order to appreciate the institutional and conceptual import of the European judicial developments we have been studying, it is essential to recognize that judicial quality control, testing, and so on have traditionally been a strong feature of the ordinary domestic courts in European civilian jurisdictions. These features have been further associated with national judicial schools or centers, such as the French *Ecole Nationale de la Magistrature*, the *Escuela Judicial Española*, the Italian *Scuola Superiore della Magistratura*, the Portuguese *Centro de Estudios Judiciários*, etc.[19] These institutions are associated in turn with demanding entrance examinations ("*concours*"), testing, and ranking of assorted kinds. And then come the strong professional structures for review and advancement currently characterized by—and controlled by—the national judicial councils. In other words, the "ordinary" national judiciaries function on the basis of a rather well elaborated conception of a professionalized, career, civil service judiciary.

This idea of a professional judicial corps has traditionally been quite distinct from the one governing international judges. This is perfectly apparent in the European context. As we have seen at length, judicial appointments to the ECJ and the ECtHR have traditionally run in a very different direction: political

[19] *See* https://e-justice.europa.eu/content_national_training_structures_for_the_judiciary-406-en.do.

discretion—not professional and institutional qualification—has been the governing principle behind such appointments. As a practical matter, national governments have from the very beginning appointed "their" candidates to sit in Luxembourg, effectively free of significant review; and until recently, they have been more or less free to put forward their three candidates to Strasbourg, where relatively deferential political elections in the PACE traditionally yielded their preferred results in the great majority of cases. And as a final safety valve, short and renewable judicial terms meant that national governments could effectively recall judges who had somehow earned their displeasure in order to replace them with others essentially of their own choosing.

But the distinctiveness (or even peculiarity) of the international judicial sphere was hardly limited to such appointments processes. It also manifested in the very composition of the sitting judicial chambers of the courts in question. Take the ECtHR: it *requires* that in every case, the national judge of the country at bar sit on the judicial bench. Rule 26 of its Rules of Court thus specifies: "the Chamber shall in each case include the President of the Section and the judge elected in respect of any Contracting Party concerned."[20] Even the modern State-oriented French tradition, which was developed in the revolutionary and Napoleonic periods, never called for such representation on the sitting judicial panel. To this day, a governmental or quasi-judicial agent can argue before the French ordinary courts on behalf of the law and of the general interest;[21] but this is quite different than empowering such figures to sit as voting judges in the case.

This ECtHR institutional/procedural feature strongly suggests that the national judge would play at least some kind of ambassadorial role on behalf of her country's legal and political orders. That ambassadorial role can of course be understood as more or less assertive. At one (benign) extreme, the national judge would merely offer her judicial colleagues knowledge of, and insight into, the actual operation of her home system. Her role would thus be ambassadorial/informational. At the other (vigorous) extreme, the national judge would actively represent the perspective and interests of the domestic system. Her role would be ambassadorial/representative.

Although judicial professional norms push strongly in the direction of the more benign pole, one can readily understand why the Member States would wish their ECtHR judges to function as judicial ambassadors. By definition, almost any time a given Member State is party to an action before the Strasbourg Court, it plays the unenviable role of defendant: the plaintiff claims that the State has violated human rights and has refused proper redress. It is no accident, therefore, that the ECtHR

[20] http://www.echr.coe.int/Documents/Rules_Court_ENG.pdf. As we have seen, this rule, when combined with the possibility of writing concurrences and dissents, leaves the national judge publicly exposed in every case in which his or her country is concerned.

[21] *See* Mitchel Lasser, Judicial Deliberations: A Comparative Analysis of Judicial Transparency and Legitimacy (2004) Chaps. 2 and 6 ["Lasser (2004)"].

has traditionally had a strong international court ethos that the Member States made sure to build into its very decision-making structure and that distinguishes it from ordinary domestic judicial venues.

The ECJ, on the other hand, hears a much broader range of cases than its Strasbourg cousin. A given Member State might, for example, appear in the capacity of a plaintiff instead of a defendant; and very often, no Member State is party to the litigation at all (e.g., if the case stems from a private dispute or if it involves an individual challenge to EU institutional acts). So it should not be surprising that the ECJ's decision-making procedures do not similarly guarantee the presence of the national judge.[22]

That said, one should not be fooled. From the ECJ's inception, its Rules of Procedure called for the use of a plenary formation in any case in which a Member State was a defendant; and this obviously guaranteed that the national judge would sit on the case. Although this rule was eventually relaxed, the Member State could nonetheless demand decision by a plenary formation, which effectively maintained the guarantee of the national judge.[23] By now, the use of smaller chamber formations has been consistently expanded and routinized. Even so, Member State parties still possess the right to demand that a case be heard by the Grand Chamber.[24] This at least makes it a coin flip as to whether "their" judge will sit on those cases that matter most to them: the Grand Chamber is composed of fifteen of the Court's twenty-eight judges.

[22] Of course, the ECJ is nonetheless composed of one judge per country. The influential ECJ Judge Pierre Pescatore stated bluntly that it would have been "impossible in the long term to maintain community ties as tightly as stipulated by the Treaties ... if the Member States are unable to have the conviction that the Court of Justice includes for each case, at the very least, one member with direct knowledge of the national law and of the particulars of the national interests involved." Pierre Pescatore, in Institut für das Recht der Europäischen Gemeinschaften, Zehn Jahre Rechtsprechung des Gerichtshofs der Europäischen Gemeinschaften 614 (1965), quoted in Antoine Vauchez, Brokering Europe: Euro-Lawyers and the Making of a Transnational Polity 48 (2015) ["Vauchez (2015)"].

[23] Matthew Gabel, Michael Malecki, Clifford Carrubba, & Joshua Fjestul, *The Politics of Decision-Making in the European Court of Justice: The System of Chambers and Distribution of Cases for Decision*, Meetings of the European Consortium for Political Research, Marburg, Germany (September, 2003), available at http://www.uky.edu/~mjgabe1/GabelMarburg.pdf.

[24] The Statute of the Court of Justice of the European Union states, in pertinent part:

> Article 16
> The Court of Justice shall form chambers consisting of three and five Judges ...
> The Grand Chamber shall consist of 15 Judges ...
> The Court shall sit in a Grand Chamber when a Member State or an institution of the Union that is party to the proceedings so requests.

Statute of the Court of Justice of the European Union (consolidated version), available at https://curia.europa.eu/jcms/upload/docs/application/pdf/2016-08/tra-doc-en-div-c-0000-2016-201606984-05_00.pdf. *See also* Article 60 of the Consolidated version of the Rules of Procedure of the Court of Justice of September 25, 2012, available at https://curia.europa.eu/jcms/upload/docs/application/pdf/2012-10/rp_en.pdf ("The Court shall assign to the Chambers of five and of three Judges any case brought before it ... unless a Member State or an institution of the European Union participating in the proceedings has requested that the case be assigned to the Grand Chamber...").

Even at the ECJ, the international dimension of the European Courts has therefore been maintained fairly strongly, although it has been weakened somewhat over time. That said, and as we have seen in the context of the potential expansion of the size of the General Court, the possessive representational impulse nonetheless remains strong: the Member States simply could not come up with an acceptable solution for expanding the Court other than doubling it outright, thereby guaranteeing that they could each appoint their fair share of their own nationals.[25]

Given this ongoing Member State concern to protect insofar as possible the prerogative to have "their" judges sit on their cases, it is no small development for the European Courts to have moved noticeably in the direction of treating European judges as if they were normal judges akin to those appointed by bureaucratic and examination-based means to the ordinary national judiciaries. This development represents an impulse—if not quite a formal policy—to legalize and de-politicize the European Courts, to turn them increasingly into professional law appliers as opposed to discretionary legal ambassadors, and thus to turn the European systems into classic positivist legal orders rather than policy-based systems of intergovernmental negotiation and accommodation. At the very least, it represents an impulse to make the European Courts look as if they were becoming ordinary judicial institutions.[26] This attempt to reconstruct the European judicial field aims not only to legalize the international, but also to normalize the European judiciary. Given that national political actors have not traditionally favored such a formally legal approach when operating in the international space, such normalization and legalization of the European judicial sphere represents a potentially major development.

B. The Legalization and De-Constitutionalization of the International/Supranational

The last section approached the normalization and legalization of the European judicial sphere in vertical terms: the European appointment reforms and their adjacent institutional and procedural developments suggested a de-internationalization of the European Courts and judges that render them more akin to ordinary domestic courts and judges. But these developments can and should also be approached in horizontal terms.

There are two reasons for doing so. First, the discussion above suggests that a shift along the "vertical" axis between the supranational and the domestic simultaneously entails a shift along the horizontal axis between the governmental/executive and the judicial. At the extreme, this would raise a crass separation of powers issue: the national executives would violate the judicial independence of "their"

[25] *See supra* Chapter 12(I).
[26] For more on how this shift raises important legitimacy issues, *see infra* Chapter 13(II)(C)(2).

European judges whenever they might put them under orders. But even at the less extreme ambassadorial level, those judges might function in effect as knowledgeable, information-bearing representatives of the national/governmental at the European judicial level, thereby blurring not only the distinction between the supranational and the national, but also the horizontal distinction between the governmental and the judicial.

Second, once we start paying attention to vertical and horizontal divisions of state power, it becomes evident that there has long existed a second set of "courts" that, like their international/supranational brethren, cannot traditionally be readily assimilated to the "ordinary" domestic courts, whether in their jurisdiction, their ethos, their professional and deontological makeup, or their modes of appointment: namely, the national constitutional courts.

The "ordinary" courts—to use a telling term-of-art within contemporary European Civilian jurisdictions—handle private, commercial, and criminal law matters. They are the ones that are typically governed by the types of professional entrance, training, review, and promotion mechanisms of the kind now typically handled in significant measure by judicial councils. They demonstrate the bureaucratic and technocratic qualities of civil service judiciaries functioning in the classic Civilian world of the civil law.[27]

These courts are to be radically distinguished from the national constitutional courts. The latter institutions, derived from the neo-Kelsenian model and increasingly important in the post-war period, are in some sense the polar opposite of their ordinary counterparts. They are the ones that handle constitutional determinations; indeed, their existence is precisely what permits the ordinary courts to remain in their purely legal realms without having to stray into the charged political world of constitutional decision-making. Far from being subject to the kind of bureaucratic entrance, training, appointment, and promotion mechanisms that characterize the technocratic legal world of the ordinary courts and judges, the constitutional courts are typically constituted by predominantly political means.[28]

The French Constitutional Council, for example, is composed of nine judges who serve nine-year terms. One third of these judges are turned over every three years, when the President of the Republic, the President of the Senate, and the President of the Chamber of Deputies each unilaterally selects a new judge entirely of his or her own choosing. These judges are subject to no meaningful political or professional vetting process, require no formal educational or professional qualifications, or anything else of the sort.[29] The German example is less extreme, but still highly political: sixteen judges of the Federal Constitutional Court are elected

[27] *See* Lasser (2004) at Chapters 2, 6, 10, and 11.

[28] *See* Alec Stone Sweet, *Constitutional Courts*, *in* The Oxford Handbook of Comparative Constitutional Law 816, 824 (Michel Rosenfeld & András Sajó eds., 2012).

[29] *See* Article 56 of the French Constitution of 1958.

by two-thirds majorities of the Bundestag and the Bundesrat, although, six of those sixteen must have served as federal judges and all must be qualified jurists.[30] Although the German constitutional bench is therefore significantly more legally professionalized than its French counterpart, it is nonetheless appointed by explicitly political means.

The political profile of these "neo Kelsenian" constitutional courts and the overtly political appointments processes that characterize them are no accident. The basic idea was to recognize and segregate large-scale political/constitutional questions from the "ordinary" courts; for these courts are not, and should not be, equipped or empowered to handle such major political issues. The creation of specialized constitutional courts would simultaneously allow important (vertical and horizontal) separation of powers issues and fundamental rights matters to be properly addressed by appropriately political institutions, while creating a firewall to protect the legal/judicial from the incursion of the political/constitutional. As Alec Stone Sweet explains, this approach is especially evident when the constitutional court performs abstract a priori review, at which point the constitutional court can almost be thought of as a third legislative chamber.[31]

The appointment processes to the ECJ and the ECtHR are quite in line with such national appointments processes for constitutional judges. Each establishes mechanisms for the political selection of judges—whether by political appointment or election or some combination thereof; i.e., they all deploy politically oriented mechanisms that differ fundamentally from the civil service approaches (education, examination, training, review, promotion) that dominate the selection and advancement of "ordinary" judges at the national level.

Indeed, it makes a good bit of sense for ECJ and ECtHR appointments to mirror such constitutional appointment mechanisms. While I do not intend to enter into the endless definitional and ontological arguments about whether the European Courts actually *are* constitutional courts,[32] one would be hard-pressed to deny that the ECJ and the ECtHR do in fact make judgments that have broadly "constitutional" consequences at both the European and the national levels. They define the vertical distribution of powers between the European and domestic institutions; they define the horizontal distribution of powers between the European institutions themselves and between, for example, the domestic courts and the domestic

[30] *See* Article 94 of the German Basic Law. *See also* https://www.bundesverfassungsgericht.de/EN/Das-Gericht/Organisation/organisation_node.html.

[31] *See* Alec Stone Sweet, *The Third Chamber Model: A Review and Defense*, *in* The Birth of Judicial Politics in France: The Constitutional Council in Comparative Perspective 209 (1992).

[32] *See, e.g.*, Alicia Hinarejos, *Introduction: The ECJ as a Federal Constitutional Court*, *in* Judicial Control in the European Union: Reforming Jurisdiction in the Intergovernmental Pillars 1 (2009); Bo Vesterdorf, *A Constitutional Court for the EU*, 4 I•Con 607 (2006), available at https://academic.oup.com/icon/article/4/4/607/640268; Alec Stone Sweet, Governing with Judges: Constitutional Politics in Europe 153–93 (2000).

political branches; they establish and elaborate the constitutive doctrines of supremacy and direct effect; they institute, define, and impose fundamental rights doctrine, and so on. It is therefore entirely reasonable to have adopted politically oriented appointment processes for the ECJ and ECtHR that are broadly similar to those deployed for staffing the national constitutional tribunals.

But the European judicial appointments reforms run distinctly counter to this constitutional court paradigm. As in the de-internationalization context discussed above, the reforms push distinctly toward a more professionalized, technocratic, and qualification-based direction, with the application of formalized qualification norms by expert panels operating at the European level in a manner highly reminiscent of judicial councils at the domestic level.

This normalization of the profile of the European courts and of their judges not only represents a shift from a more constitutional to a more ordinary judicial appointment method, but also mirrors a concomitant shift in successful European judicial profiles. The Danish academic Mikael Madsen has studied and theorized these judicial profile changes in some detail. In the Strasbourg context, for example, he concludes that today's ECtHR judges are far more technically trained and specialized in the field of human rights law, but possess far less political capital and diplomatic savvy, than their predecessors. He writes:

> The current profile of the Strasbourg bench is fundamentally different from the original cast of judges, which largely consisted of high-profile jurists with contacts in multiple legal and political milieux ...; that is, the current bench does simply not have the social and political capital than enabled the original incarnation of the Court to move fairly easily in between law and politics and, by doing so doing, legitimize the institution ...
>
> With regard to the contemporary selection of judges, the schism basically relates to the fact that recruitment patterns in recent years have favoured judges with mainly legal capital at the expense of other relevant capital, notably exposure to the politics of international law. If we look at the sociological configuration of the current ECtHR, the first main difference between it and the former Court consisting of a well-connected legal-academic elite is that is lacks access to constituencies outside law.[33]

The judicial profiles, like the judicial appointments procedures, are being "legalized"; or, to use Madsen's terms, they are stressing "legal capital" over "political" or other capital.

This legalization impulse reinforces the formalization process that we observed in the ECtHR context. Not only have formal appointments norms proliferated,

[33] Mikael Rask Madsen, *The Legitimization Strategies of International Judges: The Case of the European Court of Human Rights*, *in* Bobek (2015) at 276–77.

but these norms are also to be formally applied by formal institutions formally established to do so at both the domestic and the European levels (ranging from domestic judicial councils, to the PACE Committee on Election of Judges, to the APE, etc.). And this is not to mention the most fundamental legalization development: Protocol 11 to the European Convention on Human Rights, which all but put an end to the diplomatic work done by the Commission in favor of systematic and formal litigation before the Strasbourg Court.[34]

For its part, the ECJ also appears to have moved in the direction of formalizing and legalizing its appointment procedures in a manner that evokes ordinary, rather than constitutional, courts. The establishment of the 255 Panel, its elaboration of formal professional qualifications, and its intense examination of candidates all push toward a more classic legal model that characterizes ordinary, as opposed to constitutional, courts.

But that movement has hardly been total. First, the vetting by the 255 Panel does not completely make up for the fact that the Member States do still unilaterally pick their judicial candidates to sit in Luxembourg. Second, the 255 Panel has demonstrated a desire to promote the candidacy of jurists who demonstrate a reflective, big-picture, one might almost say "constitutional," understanding of the systemic role played by the EU Courts. As the Panel states in its Annual Report:

> Using the content of the dossiers and the hearing, the panel seeks to determine the breadth and solidity of the candidates' knowledge of the major judicial issues, the challenges involved in the rule of law, and the key aspects of the Union's legal system and EU law, as well as the candidate's ability to reflect on the application of this law by Member States' legal systems, and on the relationships between these systems and European law.[35]

The Panel therefore plays down the importance of the candidate's knowledge of EU law: while it is a "factor" in its assessment of a candidate, it is "less important" than capable reflection on the application of EU law with the Member States and on the primary stakes currently involved.[36] As a result, even though the creation of the 255 Panel and the establishment of its norms represent an institutional and conceptual move toward the kind of professional qualification model that typically characterizes ordinary courts in the Civilian tradition, the Panel has been sufficiently savvy to incorporate a certain supranational constitutional perspective into its qualification criteria.

[34] *See supra* Chapter 8(II). Madsen decries this formalization/legalization of the Strasbourg system as simplistic, formalist, and thus as limiting the ECtHR's "strategic room for manoeuvre." *See id.* at 277–78.

[35] Article 255 Panel, Activity Report of the Panel provided for by Article 255 of the Treaty on the Functioning of the European Union, First Report of February 17, 2011 (No. 6509/11) at 9.

[36] *See id.*

In conclusion, the European judicial appointments developments represent a powerful—if not quite complete—shift toward treating the ECJ and the ECtHR as routine legal and judicial fora that happen to function at the international level. This normalization of the European Courts suggests a de-internationalization and de-constitutionalization of those Courts and of their judges: it denotes a movement toward turning those institutions into ordinary courts, staffed in accordance with the civil service procedures, standards, and mentalities that characterize the classic national judicial branches.

III. Strand #3: Judicial/Judicial Dynamics

In addition to identifying and calling attention to the vertical and horizontal relationships of the type we have been examining in the first two strands above, we should also recognize dynamics of a different kind: judicial/judicial ones. I confess that I find such dynamics inherently fascinating; so much so that I dedicated my last book to studying them as cause, effect, and field of engagement in the context of the European fundamental rights revolution.[37] What I would like to convey now is something of the complex reciprocity that I sought to describe in detail in that context. The key is to recognize that such intra-judicial dynamics function in multiple directions at the same time.

A. Practical Inter-Institutional Politics: The European Courts' Efforts to Promote Buy-In from Member State Courts

The status/standing of the European Courts represents the most straightforward—and probably the most important—facet of the intra-judicial dynamics of the judicial appointment reforms. The European judicial appointments debates betray a deep-seated anxiety held by the European Courts (and echoed by major European jurists) that their rulings will not be sufficiently respected, especially by what may well be their primary professional audience: the domestic courts.

This brooding anxiety over the status of the European Courts surfaces as endlessly recurring declarations about the tenuous "authority" of those courts and of their rulings. The Executive Summary of the influential 2003 Interights Report entitled "Judicial Independence: Law and Practice of Appointments to the European Court of Human Rights"[38] thus opened as follows:

[37] *See* Mitchel Lasser, Judicial Transformations: The Rights Revolution in the Courts of Europe (2009) ["Lasser (2009)"].

[38] Interights (Dr. Jutta Limbach, Chair), "Judicial Independence: Law and Practice of Appointments to the European Court of Human Rights" 9 (May 2003) ["Interights Report"].

> In February 2003, a group of eminent European jurists met in London to consider the issue of judicial independence with respect to the current procedure for judicial appointments to the European Court of Human Rights. This report details their deliberations and contains their recommendations.
>
> In the last forty years, the European Court of Human Rights has been at the forefront of the development of regional and international human rights jurisprudence. While paying tribute to the Court, this report notes that its credibility and authority risk being undermined by the ad hoc and often politicised processes currently adopted in the appointment of its judges.[39]

The prominent Interights jurists could not have been more emphatic or clear: what was at stake in the judicial appointments process was the "credibility and authority" of the Court.

Similarly, when President Jean-Paul Costa of the ECtHR sent his 2010 letter about the urgent need to establish the APE, he wrote:

> In terms of the future of the Court and therefore the Convention system, one of the decisive factors will be the quality of its Judges. Whatever reforms are undertaken, the system will fail if judges do not have the necessary experience and <u>authority</u>.
>
> The quality of the Judges is important not only to guarantee the high standard of the decisions delivered and the jurisprudence developed. It is also essential because, in a subsidiary system where human rights protection falls primarily to the national courts, the European Court as the ultimate arbiter of human rights issues must be composed of persons of sufficient standing and <u>authority</u> to command the respect of national judges, including senior national judges. If this is not the case, the Court itself will suffer from a deficit of <u>authority</u> and the system will lose credibility and effectiveness.[40]

The entire APE proposal, including the need to ensure the quality of the ECtHR's judges, hinged on the capacity of the Court to maintain the authority necessary for national judges—and especially the "senior national judges"—to follow its lead "as the ultimate arbiter of human rights issues."

This near obsessive concern for the authority of the Court and of its jurisprudence has hardly abated.[41] To the contrary, it has progressed from alarmist passages

[39] *Id.* at 4.

[40] Jean-Paul Costa, Letter from the President of the European Court of Human Rights, addressed to member states' Permanent Representatives (Ambassadors) on June 9, 2010 ["Costa Letter"] (emphasis added).

[41] Nor is the obsession at all recent for the European courts. Antoine Vauchez describes in detail the struggles that the ECJ encountered in its early relations with the domestic high courts. *See, e.g.*, Vauchez (2015) at 31–32. He even recounts the following amusing—but highly telling—anecdote: "Oral history accounts report that the judges broke out the champagne each time a new appeal [from the domestic

of the type just cited to remarkably extensive and systematic analyses. The best example is the "Report on the Longer-Term Future of the System of the European Convention on Human Rights," published in late 2015 by the Committee of Ministers' Steering Committee for Human Rights.[42] This exhaustive seventy-five-page Report, generated after two full years of study, opens with a dozen pages of introductory materials before moving on to its five substantive chapters. Chapter I offers a straightforward seven-page summary of the Convention system. Then the next four chapters get to the heart of the matter. Chapter II, entitled "The Authority of the Convention: National Implementation," spends ten pages examining how domestic institutions, including the political branches and especially the domestic courts and legal actors, respond to the Strasbourg Court's interpretations of the Convention.[43] Chapter III, entitled "The Authority of the Court," spends seven pages addressing the "Challenge of the Caseload" before dedicating some ten pages to "The Challenge Regarding the Authority of the Case Law."[44] These pages work methodically through a panoply of judicial "quality" issues ("The quality of judges," "The quality of the Registry," and "The quality and consistency of the case law") that should, after our analysis in Part IV of this book, strike the reader as quite familiar. As if these "authority" discussions regarding the Convention, the Court, and the Court's case law were not sufficient, the Report then adds a twelve-page Chapter IV, entitled "The Authority of the Court's Judgments: Execution of Judgments and its Supervision." In short, the three central "Authority" chapters represent three out of the Report's four substantive chapters and forty-one of the Report's seventy-three pages.[45] The authority of the European Courts could hardly be more emphatically emphasized.

Of course, the issue of the judicial authority of the European Courts and of their rulings has always been delicate and important. A great deal of excellent scholarly work has addressed these intra-judicial power dynamics. Such analyses have typically started with the question of why the domestic courts would be willing to play ball with European Courts at all: after all, the ECJ and ECtHR would appear to be disruptive forces, barging into relatively settled domestic legal fields, threatening their stability, sovereignty, and priority.

courts] was notified." *Id.*, *citing* Catherine Barnard & Elenor Sharpston, *The Changing Face of Article 177 References*, 34 COMMON MKT. L. REV. 1113, 1117 (1997).

[42] Steering Committee for Human Rights, CDDH Report on the Longer-Term Future of the System of the European Convention on Human Rights, CDDH(2015)R84 Addendum I, available at http://www.coe.int/t/dghl/standardsetting/cddh/reformechr/CDDH(2015)R84_Addendum%20I_EN-Final.pdf [Report on the Longer-Term Future of the ECHR System].

[43] *See id.* at 20–30.

[44] *See id.* at 31–47.

[45] Excluding the Table of Contents and the Appendix, but including the Executive Summary and all other introductory materials.

The judicial empowerment thesis, put forward most famously by Joseph Weiler, offered a compelling explanation for why they would. Especially for traditionally marginalized Civilian courts, European law was both exciting and empowering. These ordinary courts were traditionally deeply subservient to the political branches, dutifully applying their commands without further ado. Such self-effacing judicial actors could be immensely empowered by working with European law and the European Courts. After all, the ECJ had declared European law to be both directly applicable before the domestic courts and hierarchically superior to any and all national norms. This meant that the domestic courts could now not only handle interesting and powerful new legal materials, but they could also effectively exercise judicial review over their national legislative and executive branches (traditionally unthinkable in Western European Civilian jurisdictions): if domestic law contravened European law, the national courts could—indeed, they were required to—put aside that domestic law in favor of European law. With this magical turn of legal events, the most modest domestic court was suddenly a powerful European court.

But it is important to recognize that the judicial empowerment of the domestic courts had variegated effects, working better for some than for others. For starters, power is not just an objective thing. It is also a relative one. Although all domestic courts were now empowered to exercise judicial review over the political branches in the name of European law, some domestic courts—namely, most constitutional ones—already had that power under domestic constitutional law. The ordinary courts thus stood more to gain from the advent of supreme European law than did the constitutional ones. Indeed, these constitutional courts had lost the supremacy of their constitutional norms and could therefore easily be understood to have come out behind in the bargain. Worse, they had lost their monopoly to challenge legislative acts.

Furthermore, other non-constitutional domestic courts could already challenge their national political branches, if only to a limited extent. In particular, the administrative courts could already challenge the acts of the executive branch, albeit under domestic public law. True, European law added to this existing capacity the power to challenge the legislative branch under European law. But the ordinary courts had now joined the administrative courts in their capacity to exercise judicial review. The ordinary courts were thus greater winners than the administrative ones, who could easily feel that the prestige of their august domestic mission was diminished in the process.

But even this oversimplifies. True, the high ordinary courts—such as the Courts of cassation—could now challenge the legislative or executive acts of their national political branches on the basis of European law. But the lower ordinary courts could now effectively challenge the higher courts' judicial judgments on the same grounds. Indeed, the easiest tack for lower domestic courts was simply to make preliminary references to the ECJ in Luxembourg whenever they disagreed with any domestic legal position, regardless of whether that position was taken by the legislative or executive branches or, for that matter, by the superior courts (or some combination thereof). It is precisely for this reason that the domestic judiciaries have repeatedly tried to insist on the lower courts passing legal questions through their national judicial hierarchy rather than independently and immediately sending references to Luxembourg; and it precisely for the same reason that the ECJ has repeatedly refused to let the domestic high courts succeed in this endeavor.[46]

The ECJ's open door policy toward the lower domestic courts not only invited a steady stream of cases from the domestic judiciaries and thereby fostered a European legal consciousness in, and allegiance from, those national courts; it also foreclosed the capacity of the higher domestic courts to challenge the authority of the ECJ and of its rulings. The ECJ could enlist the help of the lower courts if ever the higher courts were tempted to refuse to send cases to Luxembourg, never mind if they ever decided to flout the ECJ's jurisprudence. The lower courts, now operating as important European courts, could bypass their superior courts by going directly to Luxembourg, shaking free of rigidly hierarchical domestic judicial supervision. This was an unmitigated gain in judicial power for the lower ordinary domestic courts. But it was far more of a mixed bag for the higher courts, even in the ordinary judiciary. True, they had gained great power to review the acts of the political branches. But this review was performed in the name of European—not domestic—law. Probably worse, this power was purchased at significant institutional cost: the lower courts could now flout their own jurisprudence on the same grounds.

These complex dynamics have played out quite methodically in the ECJ's jurisprudence. The most prominent domestic judicial resistance had come at the hands of the constitutional courts, whose own authority and prestige has been most obviously compromised by the ECJ.[47] But the domestic lower courts have systematically undermined any such constitutional—or, for that matter, any supreme

[46] *See, e.g.*, Case 166/73, Rheinmühlen-Düsseldorf v.Einfuhr—und Vorratsstelle für Getreide und Futtermittel, [1974] ECR 33 (January 16, 1974); Case 146/73, Rheinmühlen-Düsseldorf v.Einfuhr—und Vorratsstelle für Getreide und Futtermittel, [1974] E.C.R. 139 (February 12, 1974).

[47] The 1974 German *Solange I* judgment serves as the prototype of such national constitutional court resistance. *See* 2 BvL 52/71 *Solange I*, May 29, 1974—BVerfGE 37, 27. But as Bruno de Witte and Wojciech Sadurski have explained so well, this sort of resistance has been repeated throughout many Western, Central, and Eastern European jurisdictions. *See* Bruno de Witte, *Direct Effect, Supremacy, and the Nature of Legal Order*, *in* The Evolution of EU Law (Paul Craig & Grainne de Burca eds., 1999); Wojciech Sadurski, *"Solange, chapter 3": Constitutional Courts in Central Europe—Democracy—European Union*, EUI Working Paper Law No. 2006/40, available at http://cadmus.eui.eu/bitstream/handle/1814/6420/LAW-2006-40.pdf?sequence=1&isAllowed=y. And this is not to mention the well-known refusal of certain constitutional courts to refer questions to the ECJ at all. *See* Fruzsina Gárdos-Orosz, *Preliminary Reference and the Hungarian Constitutional Court: A Context of Non-Reference*, 16 German L.J. 1569 (2015).

court—resistance by taking the independent decision to raise the issues directly with the Luxembourg Court.[48] This gradually led to all the supreme courts falling more or less into line, accepting the supremacy and direct effect of European law, as propounded, needless to say, by the ECJ's own jurisprudence.[49]

The ECtHR has had a somewhat different—and more straightforward—relationship with the domestic supreme courts. Under the Convention's system of admissibility, "The Court may only deal with [a complaint] after all domestic remedies have been exhausted."[50] According to the ECtHR's own Department of the Jurisconsult:

> The rationale for the exhaustion rule is to afford the national authorities, primarily the courts, the opportunity to prevent or put right the alleged violations of the Convention. It is based on the assumption, reflected in Article 13, that the domestic legal order will provide an effective remedy for violations of Convention rights. This is an important aspect of the subsidiary nature of the Convention machinery.[51]

The exhaustion rule has thus concentrated power in the hands of the domestic supreme courts, which operate in effect as the final authorities regarding the operation of human rights norms in their respective domestic systems. These supreme courts therefore function as the centralized point of contact between the domestic orders and the European Convention system: unlike in the EU system, there exists no effective mechanism for the lower courts to work around (not to say "subvert") their supreme courts by bypassing them and going straight to the European Court. Precisely because all domestic human rights claims must effectively go through those domestic supreme courts as a last resort, it is critically important for the ECtHR to enlist those courts' adherence, if not their active support.

Now that we have these practical inter-institutional dynamics clearly in mind, we can appreciate the barely concealed panic in the tone and substance of President Costa's 2010 letter proposing the APE to the Member States' Permanent Representatives to the Council of Europe. A great deal of the effectiveness of the Convention system does in fact hinge on the willingness of the domestic high courts to follow the lead of the Strasbourg Court. As Costa explains, the Court

[48] *See, e.g.*, the Rheinmühlen I and II cases, *supra* note 46.

[49] *See* Karen Alter, Establishing the Supremacy of European Law: The Making of an International Rule of Law in Europe (2003).

[50] Article 35(1) of the European Convention of Human Rights.

[51] European Court of Human Rights Directorate of the Jurisconsult, Practical Guide on Admissibility Criteria 22 (3rd ed. 2014) (citations omitted), available at http://www.echr.coe.int/Documents/Admissibility_guide_ENG.pdf.

"must be composed of persons of sufficient standing and authority to command the respect of national judges, including senior national judges. If this is not the case, the Court itself will suffer from a deficit of authority and the system will lose credibility and effectiveness."[52] From the point of view of the ECtHR and of its President Costa, to lose the support of the domestic high courts is effectively to lose the Convention system as a whole.

Viewed from this perspective, the rise of the APE and of the 255 Panel—complete with the proliferation of formal norms and processes for regularized, professionalized, and quality-based judicial appointments to the two European high Courts—is best understood as a concerted attempt by those European institutions and players to promote buy-in from the domestic courts (and especially the domestic supreme courts). It addresses as directly as possible the relatively low esteem in which European (specifically ECtHR) judges are held by some political, legal, and judicial elites within certain national systems.[53] It offers assurances not only to the domestic legal elites, but also, and more importantly, to the domestic high courts, that the processes used to fill European judicial vacancies will be at least minimally transparent, standardized, independent, professionalized, and quality-based.

But this straightforward picture of the European institutions addressing the substantive concerns of Member State juridical actors should not be viewed in isolation. True, the new Panels and procedures have in fact taken steps to provide professional comfort to, and thus to enlist ongoing support from, high-ranking national judges. And true, these steps represent a signaling device to the effect that the European Courts (1) can be trusted—as a matter of professional competence, independence and quality—to make truly difficult decisions in an immensely delicate legal, constitutional, and political environment and (2) should accordingly be followed.

But the new Panels and procedures have done significantly more. They have actively enlisted the support of leading figures from within the domestic supreme and constitutional courts. Indeed, the Panels effectively represent a mode of institutional assimilation of these leading domestic judicial figures by the European institutions. This assimilation comes in two flavors. The first is personal. By enlisting the personal engagement of leading domestic judicial figures within the institutional framework of the European Courts, the new Panels disarm the most important potential sites of judicial resistance: those very same judicial figures working in their national supreme or constitutional courts.

[52] Costa Letter.

[53] *See* Başak Çali, Anne Koch, & Nicola Bruch, *The Social Legitimacy of Human Rights Courts: A Social Interpretivist Theory of the Legitimacy of the European Court of Human Rights*, 35 Hum. R.Q. 955 (2013).

Let us return briefly to the composition of the two Panels in order to demonstrate the point. As we saw in Parts I and II, these Panels—and especially the 255 Panel—have traditionally been composed of leading figures from leading courts. It is surely no accident that the 255 Panel has been headed from its inception by the impressive leader of the French Conseil d'Etat, Jean-Marc Sauvé. Nor is it unimportant that his most visible colleagues over the course of his two terms have been the highly respected Lord Mance, Justice of the UK's Supreme Court, and Peter Paczolay, President of the groundbreaking Hungarian Constitutional Court. For the second term of the 255 Panel, this trio has been further reinforced with other highly prominent and esteemed judges, of which the most important is undoubtedly Andreas Vosskuhle, President of what is likely the most influential and powerful national court in Europe: the German Federal Constitutional Court. In short, the 255 Panel boasts the leading judges from some of the most powerful, iconic and respected Member State courts.[54]

The European Panels (and especially the 255 Panel) have thus done an excellent job of enlisting the support of highly prominent judicial figures hailing from especially influential and tactically important national courts. In doing so, they make it significantly more difficult for those leading judges and their leading courts to call into question the authority of the high European Courts and to disrespect their judges and jurisprudence: after all, these prominent figures have themselves vetted the judges now sitting in Luxembourg and Strasbourg. As a result, these leading national figures have in effect been incorporated—one might be tempted to say "coopted"—into the very institutional and professional structure of the European judiciary.

Finally, the ongoing participation of these national judicial figures in the European institutional structure lends an important aura of professionalism and quality to all the judges who sit in Luxembourg and Strasbourg. In effect, the establishment and operation of the Panels trades on the status and respect of the leading judicial figures who compose them. The Panels operate as a signal to all domestic judges that the European Courts and their jurisprudence should be properly respected.

[54] Not terribly surprisingly, one might argue that the APE has been somewhat less successful in securing the membership of equally prominent domestic judges. Though studded with fine judges from important courts, the APE's leading figures have been European judges (ex-ECtHR presidents Wildhaber and Costa) and respected domestic judicial figures from respected—but not truly leading—domestic supreme courts, such as current APE Chair John L. Murray (former Chief Justice of the Irish Supreme Court and former Justice of the ECJ), Renate Jaeger (former Justice of the German Supreme Court and former Justice of the ECHR), Valery Zorkin (Chairman of the Russian Constitutional Court), and perhaps most impressively Bernard Stirn (French Conseil d'Etat). This is an excellent roster of judges; but no one could reasonably argue that it rivals the personal or institutional authority of the judges of the 255 Panel and of the national courts from which they hail.

B. Inter-Institutional Domestication: The Member State Judiciaries' Influence over the European Courts

The inter-institutional politics are not, however, as unidirectional as the analysis directly above might suggest. It is undoubtedly true that the European Courts and institutions have integrated national supreme/constitutional court judges into their institutional structures via the 255 Panel and the APE, which simultaneously (1) Europeanizes and thus to some extent disarms them and (2) leverages their support for reputational and prudential purposes. But this assimilation of prominent national supreme/constitutional court judges can—and should—also be read in a very different manner: the establishment and operation of the European Panels also represent a successful intervention by the national high courts in the European judicial arena.

At a first level, the national judicial intervention can be inferred from the European institutional response. The mere creation of the Panels and establishment of the assorted appointments norms strongly suggest that judicial resistance by the national supreme courts prompted this European response in the first place. Indeed, the alarmist language used by ECtHR President Costa in his 2010 letter proposing the APE conveys all too clearly his fear of serious and high-level national judicial opposition to the Strasbourg Court. Indeed, he openly stated that the Court "must be composed of persons of sufficient standing and authority to command the respect of national judges, including senior national judges. If this is not the case, the Court itself will suffer from a deficit of authority and the system will lose credibility and effectiveness."[55] In other words, the fear of high-level national judicial resistance—whether real or imagined, and whether extant or anticipated—helped to prompt the European judicial institutional responses that culminated in the APE.

Viewed through this prism, it was actually the national supreme/constitutional courts that had successfully triggered European-level judicial developments. Furthermore, the national high courts and their leading judges have gone significantly further than merely playing this triggering role. All one has to do to see this is to return to the very composition of the European Panels, which, after all, consists overwhelmingly of prominent national judicial figures. Although one should certainly read the participation of these national judges on the Panels as a form of *European cooptation*, one should not hesitate—to the contrary—to read it as a form of *domestic infiltration*: a collection of particularly prominent national supreme/constitutional court judges have successfully taken over the task of reviewing all candidacies for judicial positions on the European courts.

[55] Costa Letter.

Indeed, these leading national judges have gone further. As can be seen most clearly in the EU context, they not only vet the candidates for European judicial office, they have also effectively granted themselves the power to define the standards by which such candidacies shall be measured. In so doing, they have effectively become the arbiters of what sorts of judges should fill European judicial positions and thus what the European judiciary in general should look like. Viewed in the long term, therefore, one can readily argue that the high domestic judiciary has come to exercise professional control over the European judicial institutions, even if the latter appears to control a good deal of the European jurisprudence and judicial relations (including its constitutional dimensions).[56]

Jean-Marc Sauvé, the head of the French Conseil d'Etat who served as the President of the 255 Panel from its very inception, all but stated as much when framing the 255 Panel as "a sort of minimalist judicial council or judicial council *light*"[57] and as "a germ of a council of the judiciary within the European Union."[58] By moving to vet rather aggressively all candidates for European judicial office, to establish and define quite explicitly the standards by which such candidacies shall be measured, to elaborate the procedures by which the candidacies shall tested, and to propose rather audaciously to expand the role of the 255 Panel from the examination into the selection of judicial candidates, Sauvé has only underlined the full extent to which domestic judicial leaders have been influencing—if not fully *domesticating*—European judicial institutions.

In sum, the European Panels offer a complex picture of reciprocal interactions between the European Courts and the national supreme/constitutional courts. By folding domestic judicial luminaries into their European institutional constructs, they simultaneously respond to—and defuse—assumed resistance by domestic high courts, enlist the support of those courts, and partake of their status and reputation, including by drafting (coopting?) domestic judicial leaders. At the same time, these judicial leaders can also be seen as having successfully taken the reins of the institutional structures that increasingly regulate the European judicial institutions themselves. They were apparently at the root of the initial creation of those Panels; constitute the overwhelming majority of their membership; have leveraged those positions to elaborate, impose, and apply their own definitions of appropriate European judicial qualifications; and have made bold proposals to extend even further the power they have come to yield from within the European institutions they helped to create and have come to control and leverage.

[56] I say "a good deal" of that jurisprudence in order to stress that it hardly controls it all. As I have stressed elsewhere, the domestic courts also exercise significant power to shape such constitutional arrangements. *See* Lasser (2009) at Chap. 7.

[57] Sauvé (2013) at 10.

[58] Sauvé in Bobek (2015) at 84.

IV. Strand #4: Separation of Powers Developments

At the same time, the European judicial appointments reforms have undoubtedly had a significant impact on the separation of powers, insulating and empowering the judiciary relative to executive branch authority. The list of developments of this front is long and fairly evident; but let us briefly recap the primary changes in order to get a more panoramic sense of their importance.

First come all of the judicial independence measures passed by the Council of Europe. Of these, one need only refer to the Recommendation of the Committee of Ministers 2010 Recommendation "on judges: independence, efficiency and responsibilities," which calls for all Member States to establish their own independent "councils for the judiciary," composed primarily of "judges chosen by their peers."[59] This judicial entity, governed by formal rules and procedures, would be responsible for all judicial selection, training, appointment, promotion, and discipline. In essence, the judiciary was to become an increasingly independent and largely self-sufficient and self-governing institution, virtually free of executive branch influence.

Second, this framework for judicial self-governance was effectively extended from the domestic to the European arena. The Council of Europe demanded that Member State nominations for election to the ECtHR be put forward via a similarly independent and procedurally formalized process, run by a similarly independent and judicialized institution. Absent a showing to this effect, the PACE would simply refuse to consider the candidates put forward for election to the Strasbourg Court.[60]

As we have seen, the 255 Panel was less categorical in this regard. It refused to announce a categorical rule rejecting any judicial candidate chosen by dubious national governmental processes. That said, it did insist that each Member State explain in detail the process by which any proposed candidate was selected. Given the 255 Panel's effective veto power over proposed judicial candidates for the EU Courts, few could fail to understand that this requirement was a thinly veiled "invitation" for Member States to adopt an appropriately independent and professional selection procedure (or face the consequences).

Third, the new appointment processes and institutions established at the European level were overtly designed to limit the capacity of Member State governments to dominate not only the appointments process, but also their own judicial candidates. On the appointments front, the Council of Europe passed (and re-passed) a whole range of measures expressly designed to limit the capacity of

[59] Committee of Ministers, Recommendation Rec R (94)12 on Independence, efficiency and role of judges (October 13, 1994) at paras. 26–27.

[60] *See, e.g.*, PACE Committee on Legal Affairs and Human Rights, Report on Candidates for the European Court of Human Rights 1, Doc. 9963 (Rapporteur McNamara) (October 7, 2003).

Member States to rig the PACE voting process in favor of their preferred judicial candidates: candidates had to use a standardized CV form, their names had to be listed in alphabetical order, the PACE Sub-Committee on Judicial Elections would conduct its own interview of the candidates, and so on.

The appointments developments have also limited the capacity of Member State governments to influence the judges they put forward to sit on the European Courts. The establishment of domestic judicial councils reduces the ability of the governments to call the shots on European judicial appointments in the first place. The APE and 255 Panel then vet the candidates in order to help ferret out any who may nonetheless be improperly beholden to political authority. ECtHR judicial terms have been lengthened and made un-renewable, which significantly reduces the incentives for sitting ECtHR judges to tow the domestic governmental line when deciding sensitive cases; and recent debates suggest that the EU Courts may well be headed toward a similar change in the near future. The professional qualifications demanded by the 255 Panel (even more forcefully than by the APE) not only makes it more likely that judicial candidates will be more professionally than politically oriented to begin with, but also makes it less likely that they would need governmental patronage to land high-grade professional work at the end of their European judicial terms. In short, the long series of European judicial appointments developments has created a web of norms, practices, and institutions that significantly reinforce the horizontal separation of powers between national political authority (viz., national executives) and the judicial branch functioning on the European level.

That said, these changes, which can and should be read as "separation of powers" developments, should themselves be interpreted in several ways. For example, they clearly should, as we have stressed, be read as East-West political interventions in the post-'89 context. The European developments generate effects that are distributed differently across different domestic jurisdictions. Given political, legal, professional, and demographic realities, the developments undoubtedly generate more significant impacts on the small new Member States from the East than on the large established ones from the West. And in this respect, the developments should be understood as significant political interventions that have allowed established governments from the West to exercise some control over the governments of new Member States from the East, albeit at some cost to their own ability to master their own European judicial appointments.[61]

But there is yet another way to read these "separation of powers" developments: as political developments not so much on the East-West front, but on the democratic theory front. The point this time is not so much to control unpredictable new Eastern European governments in order to maintain the *acquis*

[61] *See supra* Chapter 9(II)–(IV).

communautaire, i.e., to maintain the legal, political, regulatory, and economic arrangements painstakingly elaborated over decades at the European level. Nor is it to protect the domestic and European judiciaries in the name of "judicial independence" as such.

The idea is instead that the judiciary ought to be empowered plain and simple. As the Consultative Council of European Judges (CCJE)—led after all by Lord Mance—went to some pains to stress:

> The judiciary is one of three basic and equal pillars in the modern democratic state. It has an important role and functions in relation to the other two pillars. It ensures that governments and the administration can be held to account for their actions, and, with regard to the legislature, it is involved in ensuring that duly enacted laws are enforced, and, to a greater or lesser extent, in ensuring that they comply with any relevant constitution or higher law (such as that of the European Union).[62]

The CCJE's claim was far from self-evident, however, especially in Civilian jurisdictions (in the West as well as the East). Instead, this claim to judicial "coequal" status was an aggressive effort to produce and entrench a reordering of constitutional arrangements in favor of judicial power in a time of great political uncertainty.

V. Strand #5: The "Neoliberal" Turn: The Empowered and Disempowered Judiciary

One way to understand this reordering is therefore in constitutional terms. But the impulse to move courts into the heartland of the national and supranational constitutional orders, ideally as a coequal branch of government, also included more: judges and courts must be *the* central institution for defending individual rights and freedoms, safeguarding democracy, and the rule of law, guaranteeing the separation of powers, and protecting against oppression and the totalitarian state.[63] This package of ideas represents of course a 1990s civics lesson utterly typical of the "rule of law" and "law and development" literatures of the post-1989 period.[64] But now that the lesson would apply as much in France as in Poland, the

[62] CCJE Opinion No. 1 at para. 11.

[63] *See, e.g.*, CCJE Opinion No. 1.

[64] *See, e.g.*, Robert Cooter, *The Rule of State Law and the Rule-of-Law State: Economic Analysis of the Legal Foundations of Development*, *in* ANNUAL WORLD BANK CONFERENCE ON DEVELOPMENT ECONOMICS 1996 (1997) 191–17; Martin Golding, *Transitional Regimes and the Rule of Law*, RATIO JURIS 9(4):387–95 (1996); Andrzej Rapaczynski, *The Rule of Law in Theoretical and Comparative Perspective*, *in* THE BALANCE OF FREEDOM: POLITICAL ECONOMY, LAW, AND LEARNING 81 (Roger Michener ed., 1995).

theory had deeper commitments than merely providing guidance to the "transition democracies" of Central and Eastern Europe.

The underlying conviction was tied instead to more "neoliberal" tenets.[65] As numerous European judicial and ministerial figures have repeatedly informed me in interviews, this conviction—sometimes held by the speaker and sometimes relayed as a conviction held by others—is that the solid judicial application of settled law is far preferable to indiscriminate legal and regulatory changes instituted by volatile and self-serving political leadership. It is a conviction that combines a deep distrust of governmental political power with a strong neoliberal faith in judicially enforced vested rights: far better to govern the new Europe via judicially enforced fundamental rights and fundamental market freedoms than to leave matters in the hands of unpredictable, unreliable, and often unsophisticated governments.

As voiced by these important judicial and ministerial figures, one cannot help but recognize the influence of the work of Andrei Shleifer, Forencio Lopez-de-Silanes, Rafael La Porta, Hernando de Soto, and so on.[66] In this more neoliberal mode, the "separation of powers" agenda not only moves decisively from (a) the classic (French) Civilian tenet of shielding appropriately political decision-making from a potentially power-hungry and retrograde judiciary to (b) an inclination to divide public authority more symmetrically between three "coequal" branches, but also to (c) a valorization of judicial rights enforcement over the governmental exercise of political power as the ideal mode of governance.

This new governance approach—stressed by Ran Hirschl as underpinning the worldwide rise of constitutionalism since at least the 1970s[67]—did, however, put a lot of eggs in the judicial basket, as it suggested that the judiciary should function as a central and arguably dominant governance institution. The European judiciary and its membership accordingly became a critically important focus of attention: thus empowered, European judges needed to be carefully chosen in

[65] I place "neoliberal" in quotation marks one last time in order to stress that I am not interested in entering into the endless definitional and ideological controversies over the term. For more on such debates, *see, e.g.*, GÉRARD DUMÉNIL & DOMINIQUE LÉVY, CAPITAL RESURGENT: ROOTS OF THE NEOLIBERAL REVOLUTION, trans. Derek Jeffords (2004); Taylor C. Boas & Jordan Gans-Morse, *Neoliberalism: From New Liberal Philosophy to Anti-Liberal Slogan*, 44 STUDS. IN COMP. INT'L DEV. 137 (2009); WENDY BROWN, UNDOING THE DEMOS: NEOLIBERALISM'S STEALTH REVOLUTION (2015); SIMON SPRINGER, KEAN BIRCH, & JULIE MACLEAVY eds., THE HANDBOOK OF NEOLIBERALISM (2016); PETER BLOOM, THE ETHICS OF NEOLIBERALISM: THE BUSINESS OF MAKING CAPITALISM MORAL (2017).

[66] *See, e.g.*, WORLD BANK, DOING BUSINESS IN 2004: UNDERSTANDING REGULATION (2004); Simeon Djankov, Rafael La Porta, Florencio Lopez-di-Silanes, & Andrei Shleifer, *The Regulation of Entry*, 117 QUARTERLY JOURNAL OF ECONOMICS 1 (2002); Simeon Djankov, Rafael La Porta, Florencio Lopez-di-Silanes, & Andrei Shleifer, *Courts*, 118 QUARTERLY JOURNAL OF ECONOMICS 453 (2003) [Djankov et al. (2003)]; HERNANDO DE SOTO, THE OTHER PATH (1989).

[67] *See* RAN HIRSCHL, TOWARDS JURISTOCRACY: THE ORIGINS AND CONSEQUENCES OF THE NEW CONSTITUTIONALISM (2004); Ran Hirschl, *The Political Origins of the New Constitutionalism*, 11 IND. J. GLOB. STUDS. 71 (2004).

order to make sure that the European Courts would not go off the rails. The judicial appointments developments followed as a matter of course.

On this neoliberal view, the latent problem was the recurrent tendency for judges to engage in naïve and misguided activism. The resulting desire to control judicial activism can (and should) of course be read as demonstrating a fear of the horde of new European judges descending from the East. But to attribute the fear entirely to this Eastern peril would be to oversimplify. At its core, this anxiety was arguably as neoliberal as it was intergovernmental in nature: the danger of judicial activism (i.e., judges disrupting settled expectations via aggressive judicial decision-making) was every bit as pressing as the danger of judicial hack-tivism (i.e., judges acting under governmental orders).

From this conservative perspective, the dilemma was that an appropriately powerful judiciary could exercise its power inappropriately, leading to destabilizing jurisprudential interventions on a wide range of important fronts. The aggressive judicial elaboration of imaginative doctrines, including the jurisprudence of fundamental rights and freedoms, could lead to everything from abusive levels of social benefits, to out of control immigration, to economic and jurisprudential uncertainty, to governmental liability, to emasculated policing, and so on.[68]

The key, then, was to find a way to promote an appropriately conservative judicial approach. From this neoliberal vantage point, the solution was none other than the establishment of the judicial screening panels (i.e., the 255 Panel and the APE) and their forceful imposition of judicial quality standards.[69] This institutional device would best manage the delicate task of putting the plenary exercise of judicial power on a firm footing precisely by limiting its tendency to go rogue.

This conviction that the institutional device of the judicial screening panels could limit unwarranted judicial activism was potentially naïve. In its simplistic form, it suggested a surprisingly straightforward and old-fashioned belief in positivism: properly professionally qualified judges would just "apply the law" as they should. Full stop. In this respect, it reproduced some of the more crude assumptions about judicial interpretive practice that shine through neoliberal theory of the period, ranging from the World Bank's Doing Business reports to Djankov, La Porta, Lopez-di-Silanes, and Shleifer's *Courts*.[70]

But in my experience, this conservative perspective has generally functioned in a somewhat more sophisticated European vein, one that reflects a sincere deontological conviction that professionalism and quality lead to a shrewd and deliberate

[68] *See, e.g.*, CJEU judgment of 03.07.1986, C-66/77 Lawrie-Blum; CJEU judgment of 20.09.2001, C-184/99 Grzelczyk; Francovich & Ors v. Italy (C-6/90 & C-9/9) [1991] ECR 5357; McCann and Others v. UK (Case No. 17/1994/464/545) 21 ECHR 97 GC (September 27,1995); Big Brother Watch and Others v. UK, App. Nos. 58170/13, 62322/14, & 24960/15 (September 13, 2018), available at https://hudoc.echr.coe.int/eng#{%22itemid%22:[%22001-186048%22]}.

[69] Djankov, La Porta, Lopez-di-Silanes, and Shleifer did attempt (however crudely) to define what judicial "quality" might mean. *See* Djankov et al. (2003).

[70] *See id.*

judicial modesty, rather than to the mechanically deductive production of required judicial outcomes in specific cases: qualified judges just "apply the law" because that is the mark of a good judicial professional. Even as early as in the 1960s, André Donner—the Dutch former President of the ECJ—demonstrated this turn of mind when explaining the benefits of steering clear of such politically explosive issues as de Gaulle's "empty chair crisis":

> People have regretted that in last year's differences between France and its partners, the legal implications of the French absence in the Council was never submitted to the Court. That is much too legal an approach; it would have been the definite end of the Communities as Communities if the opposing parties had gone to law and asked a ruling of the Court on details that were no more than the juridical top of a political iceberg. Under the existing conditions, the capacity of the legal framework to support the weight of such controversies is yet only a limited one—just as political science teaches us that no constitution has the unlimited ability to withstand any social or political disintegration.[71]

On this view, activism (or even excessive legalism) reflects some combination of ignorance, inexperience, naïveté, and unprofessionalism. Truly high quality and professionalized judges can be counted on to shoulder important and delicate governance work precisely because they know the limitations incumbent on a properly functioning judiciary. Such judges exercise what Alexander Bickel might have considered the "passive virtues" of wise judging.[72] They know enough to support settled expectations rather than rock the boat.

In either the more simplistic or more sophisticated version, however, the parameters of the neoliberal judicial dilemma remain fundamentally the same: an appropriately powerful, stable, and apolitical law must be enforced by an accordingly powerful—and thus potentially disruptive—judiciary. For this neoliberal model to function properly required two things. First, the judiciary had to be freed from the capricious domination of executive branch actors (and their attendant evils). Second, the necessarily powerful European judiciary had to be freed from the capricious temptations of judicial activism. The solution was to establish professional requirements and institutional mechanisms (i.e., the judicial screening panels) that would promote and enforce judicial quality standards; these standards could then be relied upon to function as proxies for the type of stable and rights-based governance that neoliberals prized so highly in the post-transition period.

[71] André Donner, The Role of the Lawyer in the European Communities 63 (1968).

[72] *See* Alexander Bickel, *The Supreme Court, 1960 Term—Forward: The Passive Virtues*, 75 Harv. L. Rev. 1940 (1961).

VI. Strand #6: Neo-Institutionalism: Unintended Consequences?

The establishment and ensuing operation of the European judicial vetting Panels do not demonstrate, however, the type of judicial modesty that neoliberals would appear to value. To the contrary, they have functioned in a manner that calls for neo-institutionalist analysis: those Panels appear to have taken matters into their own hands, leading to a great deal of unintended consequences.

In order to run such an analysis of unintended consequences, however, one must first address a threshold issue: whose intent should we be considering? This seemingly straightforward question tends toward an implicitly straightforward answer: the entities that created those institutions, i.e., the Member State governments. Both this question and its answer, however, mask devilish assumptions.

The first point is that whichever entity one picks as the one whose intent matters, such as the most likely candidate—Member State governments—that entity is bound to be composed of a long series of distinguishable sub-entities whose "intents" (however constructed) cannot help but be in tension with each other. In other words, even such a seemingly self-evident entity as a "Member State government" is inevitably constructed by the person examining the unintended consequences; and this construction requires making a whole series of prior analytic assumptions and simplifications about who or what, exactly, should count as this Member State government. Should it be the Parliament? The Prime Minister or Foreign Minister's office? The powerful interests that tend to drive the national economy? Some combination of these or other possibilities? This analytic rabbit hole offers no clear or unitary way out, as attests the energy that intergovernmentalists such as Moravcsik have expended in the attempt to model some semblance of an answer to such questions.[73]

The second point is that one need not—and likely should not—resolve the issue of whether it was "really" this or that player whose intent should be treated as controlling. To return to the perspective suggested by the neoliberal analysis above, one need not decide whether it was the established Member State governments who were driving judicial appointments developments in order to control new Member State governments or whether it was neoliberal elements within old and new Member State governments (as well as within the European institutions, and so on). It could be, and indeed it likely was, both (and many more).[74] Needless

[73] *See, e.g.*, Andrew Moravcsik, *Liberalism and International Relations Theory*, Harvard University CFIA Working Paper No. 92-6 (1992); Andrew Moravcsik, *Preferences and Power in the European Community: A Liberal Intergovernmentalist Approach*, 31 J. Com. Mkt. Studies 473 (1993). One of the most frustrating aspects of the existing literature regarding the European judicial appointments reforms has been how rarely it examines such issues. The intent of the reforms, as well as their authors, appear utterly unitary.

[74] At times, Ran Hirschl appears to suggest a stronger version of such overlapping intentions than I feel comfortable adopting. He argues, for example:

to say, however, diversifying our understanding of the range of actors driving the appointments developments makes it increasingly difficult to elaborate an understanding of the "intent(s)" that motivated their actions. In this respect, talking about "unintended consequences" has all of the weaknesses that bedevil talking about "legislative intent."[75]

The third point is that once one gets beyond a rather simplistic understanding of the key actors in play ("Member State governments"), it becomes immediately clear that assorted institutional forces have been at work. As I explained in Chapter 11, for example, the APE was established not so much by Council of Europe as a whole, nor by the PACE, nor by the Strasbourg Court, nor by the "Member State governments" as such. It was established in the first instance by the Committee of Ministers, i.e., by a group of seasoned executive branch diplomats and legal specialists, including especially specialists in the human rights field, such as each Member State's Agent (effectively, its solicitor general) before the Strasbourg Court. In other words, the APE was created in large measure by long-term European specialists committed above all to the common project that is the European Convention on Human Rights, the Council of Europe, and the Court, and who were therefore all too happy to respond swiftly to the urgent call put out by then ECtHR President Jean-Paul Costa for the creation of a panel of experts to vet the judicial candidates who might sit on his Court.[76]

Of course, these European specialists theoretically represent their Member State governments. But it would be quite misleading to understand them in such simplistic terms. They rarely represent the policy/political vision of their "governments back home" in some straightforward manner. Both as individuals and as a functioning group, their commitments usually lie far more in their professional tasks and institutional goals: European fundamental rights promotion. Their motives for advancing judicial appointments reform are therefore quite distinct from (though sometimes reconcilable with) those of the politicians back home. This group of

> My account of judicial empowerment suggests that the constitutionalization of rights and the fortification of judicial review result from a strategic pact led by hegemonic yet increasingly threatened political elites seeking to insulate their policy preferences against the changing fortunes of democratic politics, in association with economic and judicial elites who have compatible interests. The changes that emerge reflect a combination of the policy preferences and professional interests of these groups.

Hirschl, *The Political Origins of the New Constitutionalism* at 98.

This account strikes me as too strategically deliberate and conceptually static to be quite right, given the fluid and constructed character of the interests and alliances in play.

[75] For more on the classic debates regarding interpretation based on legislative intent, *see, e.g.*, Kent Greenawalt, Statutory and Common Law Interpretation (2013); Ronald Dworkin, Law's Empire 320–21, 336 (1986); Antonin Scalia & Bryan Garner, Reading Law: The Interpretation of Legal Texts 388–93 (2012); Richard Ekins, The Nature of Legislative Intent (2012).

[76] *See supra* Chapter 11(II)(D).

specialists believes in the European high Courts—or at least wants to believe in them—and is committed to improving and promoting them.

Like the neoliberals, they too look somewhat askance at crassly political governmental decision-making. But that is not really because they believe in the generative force of private interests supported by judicially enforced vested rights (although some may believe this in part). They trust instead in the civilizing force of the European Courts and are inclined to do what they can to support it, not because they believe that European judicial decision-making consists of apolitical rule application, but because they believe in the European project as a whole, in the independent value of fundamental rights institutions and jurisprudence, as well as in productive and intelligent market regulation/creation via the enlightened elaboration of a jurisprudence of fundamental rights and market freedoms. Their commitment is to the European project, not to the defense of vested property and contract rights as such. And for them, the European Courts are an essential component of that project: they need to be of the utmost quality, not because they need to be conservative in their interpretations, but, to the contrary, because they need to know when to pick their battles. Of course it is important to lay low and not rock the boat much of the time; but this is precisely to be in the best possible position to press forward with the development of impactful European jurisprudence when the occasion calls for it and the time is ripe.

To summarize, the new institution of the APE was itself created by yet another institution, the Committee of Ministers. If, then, one wishes to consider the "unintended consequences" that have flowed from unexpectedly headstrong Strasbourg institutions that have grown independent of the governments who created them, then the first institution to look at might not be the APE, but the Committee of Ministers, despite the fact that this institution itself consists, in principle, of executive branch actors! Indeed, it was the Committee of Ministers that took up the call of ECtHR President Costa to establish the APE, much to the annoyance both of the PACE's Committee on Legal Affairs and Human Rights and Sub-Committee on the Election of Judges to the ECtHR and of the assorted governments that soon came to resist and increasingly flout the APE.[77] It pressed forward doggedly with its own agenda, passing its own judicial appointments measures even as the PACE Committees that dealt most directly with the Court and with human rights enforcement, such as the Committee on Legal Affairs and Human Rights, continued to pass and re-pass their own long list of measures.[78] Having taken matters into its own hands, the Committee of Ministers thus crowned the emerging European judicial appointments regime by establishing the APE, which was in effect its own version of the EU's 255 Panel.

[77] *See supra* Chapter 5(II).
[78] *See supra* Parts II–IV.

Once the Committee of Ministers (and maybe even the PACE committees) had gone off on their own paths, the Panels followed suit by going off on theirs. Indeed, depending on who one considers to be the primary players in the establishment of those Panels (i.e., the "Member State Governments" and/or the Committee of Ministers, etc.), and depending thus on what one imagines to be those players' intents/motives/desires, one might say that the Panels went not only "on their own paths," but also "off the rails." The 255 Panel did so right off the bat: not only did it reject a stunningly high percentage of candidates put forward by the Member States to fill judicial positions in Luxembourg, but no less importantly, it also began on its own initiative to compose and publish its Activity Reports on an almost annual basis. This greatly leveraged the 255 Panel's position and power, effectively putting the Panel in the position not only to veto and approve candidacies unilaterally, but also to dictate the profile of acceptable EU judicial candidates and to twist arms regarding the Member States' establishment of appropriate selection mechanisms at the national level.

Similarly, the APE went off on its own path in ways that rattled the cage of assorted national and European players. The Panel not only snubbed the Committee of Ministers' Guidelines and Explanatory Memorandum regarding candidate assessment in favor of its own relatively informal standards modeled on the criteria formally elaborated by the EU's 255 Panel, it even took it upon itself to use information supplied by the APE's "personal contacts with judges at the highest national courts, other legal professionals or non-governmental human rights organisations, who may use such personal contacts to transmit information to the Panel."[79] When, furthermore, several Member State governments refused to bow to the APE's assessment of specific judicial candidates by replacing those candidates with others, and/or when the PACE and its Sub-Committee on the Election of Judges to the ECtHR disagreed with those assessments, the APE and its Chair Luzius Wildhaber made a public row. They chose to publish their "Exchange of Views" with the Steering Committee for Human Rights of the Committee of Ministers, in which (1) they claimed that the APE's expert assessments should effectively function to veto any candidate that had earned its negative assessment and (2) they all but threatened to resign when the Member State governments and the PACE failed to show the APE and its members the deference they believed they deserved.[80]

Indeed, the full extent of the Panels' institutional power grab can be seen in the proposals put forward by the 255 Panel's leadership (especially President Sauvé

[79] *See* Committee of Ministers' Deputies, Guidelines of the Committee of Ministers on the selection of candidates for the post of judge at the European Court of Human Rights—Explanatory Memorandum, CM(2012)40 addendum final (March 29, 2012); APE Final Activity Report 2013 at paras. 18–26.

[80] *See* Steering Committee for Human Rights, Ministers' Deputies Exchange of Views with Mr. Luzius Wildhaber, Chairman of the Advisory Panel of Experts on Candidates for Election to the European Court of Human Rights (January 30, 2013), in DH-GDR (2013)005, February 5, 2013 ["2013 Exchange of Views"] at 1.

and Lord Mance) to use the Panel to select judicial candidates for appointment (a) to an enlarged General Court and (b) to the ECtHR. The mere fact that institutional developments eventually overtook those proposals should not blind us to the important dynamics at play: once established, the Panels evinced a marked tendency to seek to enlarge their effectiveness, influence, and, most creatively, their very mandate. Far from limiting itself to vetting national candidates for European judicial office, the 255 Panel had taken upon itself (1) to fashion and impose on the Member States detailed criteria for office that reflected its own idea of a proper European judge, (2) to "invite" each national government to explain and justify the procedure by which it had selected its judicial candidate for Luxembourg, thereby inducing—if not quite ordering—Member States to adopt a selection procedure that included "a public call for applications," an appropriately established and composed "national selection committee" whose recommendations would be followed by the Member State governments themselves, etc.,[81] (3) to reject a surprisingly high percentage of judicial candidates put forward by the Member States, and (4) to propose running on its own the selection processes for judicial candidates to an enlarged General Court and to the ECtHR. One would be hard-pressed to argue that the "Member State governments" (however construed) had foreseen, never mind intended, such a broad panoply of consequences.

The analysis of such unintended consequences can also lead in somewhat different directions. One can, of course, run the analysis in the manner we just have; i.e., one can read this institutional mission creep as a product of the Panels, once constituted. But one can also read it as mission creep generated by the specialist elements of European institutions as a whole (i.e., the EU and Council of Europe) or of institutions composed of actors drawn from the Member States' own executives and/or parliaments (i.e., the Committee of Ministers, the PACE's Committee on Legal Affairs and Human Rights), and so on. In each analytic iteration, institutions formed by or of other institutions have gone their own way, taking on tasks, formulating agendas, and provoking outcomes that would have been unforeseen and unintended by the creators of those new institutions.

VII. Strand #7: The Construction of Elite Judicial Power

These unintended consequences clearly also include the formation and emergence of a judicial and academic professional elite that straddles the Member State/Europe divide. To examine the profiles of the current judges of the ECJ and ECtHR is to recognize the existence of a tremendously coherent professional caste. These judges are, as a general rule, rather far removed from the politically experienced

[81] *See* First Annual Report at 6.

jurists championed by Mikael Madsen.[82] Instead, this European judicial corps is primarily academic in orientation. In April, 2019, for example, some twenty-seven of the forty-seven judges at the ECtHR and some twenty of thirty-nine judges and Advocates General at the ECJ were once full-time university professors.[83] In other words, the majority of all high European judges are academic jurists.

As Antoine Vauchez magisterially demonstrates in BROKERING EUROPE: EURO-LAWYERS AND THE MAKING OF A TRANSNATIONAL POLITY, the rise of the European institutions in the 1950s and 1960s was strongly linked to a process of legalization that had a distinctly academic character. This academic legalism was exemplified by the first President of the EEC Commission, Walter Hallstein, a theoretically inclined private law specialist and law school dean who had served as Rector of the University of Frankfurt and who, according to Vauchez's wry description, "purportedly made a point of keeping the title of professor in all circumstances"; by the European parliamentary figure Fernand Dehousse (Professor of International Law at the University of Liège); and such judicial figures as Andreas Donner, Roberto Monaco, and Alberto Trabucchi of the ECJ, all of whom had pursued academic careers.[84] Indeed, the first five ECtHR Presidents (McNair, Cassin, Rolin, Walcock, Pallieri) were all accomplished scholars.[85] The link between the European high Courts—and for that matter, between the European institutions in general—and the legal professoriate is thus deep and long-standing.

That said, not only may Madsen be correct that ECtHR judges in the post-1989 period possess a narrower professional focus and less political capital than their predecessors, but one cannot miss the increasingly professorial turn at the head of the ECJ since the mid-1990s. Among the first eight Presidents of the Luxembourg Court, only one—Andreas Donner, professor of constitutional and administrative law at the University of Amsterdam[86]—was primarily an academic. For thirty-six of its first forty-two years of existence, the ECJ was therefore led by a judicial, political, or executive branch figure: Massimo Pilotti was President of the Italian Court of Cassation; Charles-Léon Hammes was a judge and member of the Conseil d'Etat of Luxembourg; Robert Lecourt was a French Minister of Justice; Hans Kutscher was a Ministry official and legislative legal advisor before serving as judge on the German Constitutional Court; Josse Martens de Wilmars was a Dutch parliamentarian; John Mackenzie-Stuart was a British QC and, briefly, a judge; and Ole Due was a Danish Ministry Director. Since 1994, however, the Court has been led

82 *See* Madsen in Bobek (2015) at 276–77.

83 *See* https://www.echr.coe.int/Pages/home.aspx?p=court/judges&c; https://curia.europa.eu/jcms/jcms/Jo2_7026/en/.

84 Vauchez (2015) at 24–25.

85 *See* https://curia.europa.eu/jcms/jcms/Jo2_7014/en/.

86 For a valuable examination of the profiles of the early ECJ judges, *see* Antonin Cohen, *The European Court of Justice in the Emergent European Field of Power: Transnational Judicial Institutions and National Career Paths*, *in* LAWYERS AND THE CONSTRUCTION OF TRANSNATIONAL JUSTICE 239 (YVES DEZALAY & BRYANT G. GARTH eds., 2012).

uninterruptedly for twenty-five years by a university professor: the last three ECJ presidents have been the Spanish International Law professor Gil Carlos Rodríguez Iglesias, the Greek Public Law Professor Vassilios Skouris, and the Dutch EU Law Professor Koen Lenaerts. There is no mistaking the shift.

Further cementing this Euro-national judicial-academic alliance is the fact that the second leading background for these ECJ and ECtHR judges consists of having been a national supreme court or constitutional court judge.[87] In April, 2019, for example, some seventeen of the forty-seven judges at the ECtHR and some twelve of thirty-nine judges and Advocates General at the ECJ had previously served in such a capacity.[88] As a result, the overwhelming percentage of judges at the ECJ and the ECtHR consists of former academics and supreme court judges. In fact, even among the remaining European judges who do not fit this description, most of whom have served primarily in national Ministries of Justice, it is common for them to have also been supreme court judges or law professors at other points in their careers.[89] This is not to mention the very high percentage of non-professors who have nonetheless taught consistently in law faculties over the course of their judicial (and sometime ministerial or prosecutorial) careers. The European judicial-academic link is hard to overstate.

But the European judicial-judicial link is rather interesting in its own right. Contrary to what one might have imagined, the cohort of former high national judges skews heavily toward supreme court, cassation, and high administrative (e.g., Conseil d'Etat) judges, rather than constitutional ones. Of the twelve former high national judges sitting in Luxembourg in April 2019, nine are former national supreme court judges and only four former constitutional court judges.[90] Similarly, of the seventeen in Strasbourg, twelve are former national supreme court judges and only six former constitutional court judges. This 2:1 ratio may be a little surprising, as one might have expected a strong preference for judges with experience in the kinds of *organstreit*/separation of powers, federalism, and fundamental rights issues that characterize constitutional court jurisprudence. The consistent and large numerical inclination in the other direction strengthens instead the all-important link between the European high Courts and the national supreme courts of the "ordinary" and "administrative" judiciaries with which the European Courts must interact most frequently.[91]

[87] With apologies to purists, I include supreme court, cassation, and high administrative (e.g., Conseil d'Etat) judges in this "supreme court" category.

[88] *See* https://www.echr.coe.int/Pages/home.aspx?p=court/judges&c; https://curia.europa.eu/jcms/jcms/Jo2_7026/en/. The great majority were supreme court, cassation, and high administrative (e.g., Conseil d'Etat) judges, rather than constitutional court judges. *Id.*

[89] ECJ Judges Larsen, Fernlund, Jarukaitis, and Pikamäe are cases in point. *See* https://curia.europa.eu/jcms/jcms/Jo2_7026/en/.

[90] The attentive reader will have noticed that 9 + 3 does not in this case equal 12, but 13. The solution to this riddle is that one of the judges (Alexander Arabajiev) has served successively on both the Bulgarian Supreme Court and Constitutional Court.

[91] There is also a supply side to the tilt toward such judges: there are many more ordinary and administrative than constitutional court judges, which generates a much larger potential applicant pool.

The net result of these professional pathways is the cementing of particularly strong academic-judicial and judicial-judicial links at the transnational level and across the national-supranational divide. Furthermore, the standards and qualifications that have been elaborated over the course of the last twenty years tend, as I suggested in Chapter 3, to promote an increasingly consistent European judicial profile. In particular, the French and English language proficiency requirements, which theoretically function to *lower* linguistic barriers *within* the ECJ and ECtHR, simultaneously function to *raise* such barriers for entry *into* the ECJ and ECtHR. At this point in time, English language proficiency is clearly the less onerous requirement, so much so that it can function fairly well as a professional barrier against particularly inward-looking nationalist judicial candidates: any supranational judicial candidate who cannot get by in English can only be viewed with suspicion. To this threshold standard, however, the French language requirement adds a great deal, given the undeniable fall in the international use of the French language. The French requirement selectively raises the bar for judicial candidates, skewing the applicant pool toward candidates who have demonstrated a tangible commitment to international culture (and to general education).[92]

This anti-parochial or cosmopolitan predisposition is further reinforced, for example, by the 255 Panel's demand that candidates possess a demonstrable "aptitude for working in an international environment in which several legal systems are represented," which is "assessed in terms of ability to comprehend the broad categories and principles of the legal systems of the Member States of the European Union … as well as ability to appreciate the issues that may arise from applying Union law there."[93] This requirement, like the demand on the PACE's "Model curriculum vitae for candidates seeking election to the [ECtHR]" that the candidate list "Activities and experience in the field of human rights,"[94] undoubtedly tilts the applicant pool toward internationalist candidates with a grounding in comparative and international law. It makes perfect sense, therefore, that a majority of all contemporary high European judges—some twenty-seven of forty-seven judges at ECtHR and twenty of thirty-nine at the ECJ—have earned Masters/ LLM degrees from law faculties situated in countries foreign to their own.[95]

Given this increasingly detailed and explicit professional common ground at the intersection of the high academic and judicial fields, it is no great leap to understand the judicial appointments and other reforms that we have studied over the

[92] *See supra* Chapter 3(II)(B).
[93] *Id.*
[94] *See* PACE, Committee on the Election of Judges to the European Court of Human Rights, Procedure for electing judges to the European Court of Human Rights—Information document prepared by the Secretariat, AS/Cdh/Inf (2019) 01 rev (January 23, 2019), at Appendix I, available at http://website-pace.net/documents/1653355/1653736/ProcedureElectionJudges-EN.pdf/e4472144-64bc-4926-928c-47ae9c1ea45e.
[95] *See* https://www.echr.coe.int/Pages/home.aspx?p=court/judges&c; https://curia.europa.eu/jcms/jcms/Jo2_7026/en/.

course of this book as simultaneously molding, reflecting, and supporting the development of a high European judicial identity formation. Indeed, it is precisely this identity formation that shines through former ECtHR and APE Chair Luzius Wildhaber's fury at the slights the APE was receiving (and, frankly, continues to receive) at the hands of Member State governments and assorted Council of Europe institutions.[96] Wildhaber's surprisingly public complaint to the Committee of Ministers demonstrated this emergent and cohesive high judicial identity:

> This experience has left the Panel members with feelings of frustration. These feelings have been exacerbated by a perceived lack of co-operation, or even interest, on the side of the other stakeholders in the election procedure. This explains probably why, at a Panel meeting in October 2012 the members decided to raise these issues with other stakeholders in the election procedure.[97]

Tacitly describing the judicial Panel members as "stakeholders" akin to the other domestic and European political actors involved in the ECtHR judicial appointments procedure, Wildhaber—himself a formidable professor of public international, constitutional, comparative, and administrative law at Basel University, where he eventually served as Rector—can hardly countenance such a breach of institutional, professional, and epistemological boundaries. For Wildhaber and this increasingly coherent academico-judicial class, not only has it become obvious that they should be leading the process of defining and enforcing European judicial qualifications, but it is per se outrageous that professionally incompetent political figures would interfere with their rightfully leading role in applying those professional standards to their prospective peers.

Given this increasingly settled European judicial identity, complete with its attendant professional profile (cosmopolitan legal education, requisite language skills, juridical specialization, publication history, international/European experience, etc.) and conceptual prism (judicial independence and quality, separation of coequal powers, judicial review, judicial self-management through judicial councils, etc.) it only makes sense that the European judicial appointments reform projects that we have been studying over the course of this book have received such staunch academic support. After all, the judicial quality and judicial independence standards that have been so actively promoted within European judicial and academic ranks since the fall of the Berlin Wall reflect precisely the increasingly shared conceptual prism and common professional terrain of this emergent academic/judicial cohort. To put it bluntly, who is better positioned to elaborate and eventually personify those new standards than scholars of European and human rights law and academically inclined and Europhilic high court judges? As a result,

[96] *See supra* Chapter 5(II)–(IV).
[97] *Id.*

it only natural that the academic who published in 2015 the leading volume on European judicial appointments—the Czech law professor Michal Bobek—would now be serving as Advocate General at the ECJ and that the volume would include a chapter by none other than the sitting President of the 255 Panel, Jean-Marc Sauvé.[98]

Nor should it be surprising that the political figures involved in European judicial appointments would have grasped what was gradually occurring; nor that a certain number of them would come to resent and resist it, at times overtly. The tangible effects of these tensions became all too visible in APE Chair Wildhaber's scandalized remonstrances, i.e., the proliferation of instances of domestic and European refusals to play along with the judicial vetting procedures demanded by the APE.[99] But quiet conversations with, for example, leadership figures in the Council of Europe and governmental figures in the Member States also make clear the full extent to which the high European judges and their allies on the new vetting Panels are often regarded as an identifiable cohort of high-handed figures whose sanctimonious proclamations mask self-serving guild interests.

Viewed through this prism, it is all too easy to understand the judicial independence and judicial quality developments as simultaneously a reflection of, and a tool for, this rising academico-judicial elite and its increasingly self-conscious, self-confident, and (sometimes) tactically savvy maneuverings. This professional group has managed in many respects to cut itself free from the executive branch control that had long defined judicial professional and institutional life; and in doing so, it has significantly changed both the conception and the practice of the separation of powers at the intersection of the domestic and European domains. Increasingly, the European judiciary has developed not only its own role definition, but also its own domain and sphere of action, in which its initiates alone can properly partake. In a manner deeply reminiscent of the preliminary reference procedure established by Article 177a of the Treaty of Rome (now Article 267 of the Treaty of Lisbon) and then carefully nurtured by the ECJ, European judges at both the national and supranational levels have been able to engage in judicial-judicial exchanges that not only empower the judiciary to review the acts of the political branches of government,[100] but that also enable the judiciary to do so without having to confront those political branches directly. Almost all the action takes place within the

[98] *See* Bobek (2015). Bobek has been Advocate General at the Court since October, 2015. https://curia.europa.eu/jcms/jcms/rc4_170801/en/; Jean-Marc Sauvé, "Selecting the European Union's Judges: The Practice of the Article 255 Panel," in *id.* at 78.

[99] *See* 2013 Exchange of Views.

[100] For the classic statement of the so-called "judicial empowerment thesis," *see* Joseph Weiler, *The Transformation of Europe*, 100 Yale L.J. 2403, 2426 (1991) at 2426. *See also* Daniel Kelemen & Alec Stone Sweet, *Assessing the Transformation of Europe*, in The Transformation of Europe: Twenty-Five Years On 193, 205 (Marlene Wind & Miguel Poiares Maduro eds., 2017). For nuanced reservations concerning the judicial empowerment thesis, *see* Tommaso Pavone, *Revisiting Judicial Empowerment in the European Union: Limits of Empowerment, Logics of Resistance*, 6 J. Law & Cts 303 (2018).

judicial colleges, in which judges work toward "abstract" rulings of European law that disable national legislative or executive actions without ever directly addressing, never mind contending with, the political institutions that took those measures in the first place.

VIII. Transitional Conclusion

This stunning rise in self-conscious judicial power and its attendant construction of European judicial redoubts can and should be understood in multiple ways. First and foremost, it represents a broad-based institutional response to the challenges posed by the rapid accession of Central and Eastern European Member States to the EU and the Council of Europe after the fall of the Berlin Wall. All European political and judicial players and institutions played key roles in the aggressive elaboration of these seemingly defensive judicial appointments reforms, including everything from the adoption of formal procedural and substantive norms to the establishment of the judicial vetting panels.

That said, the European judiciary, its emergent leadership, and its academic supporters certainly used this anxiety about the arrival of the Eastern barbarians to maximum effect. Leveraging the institutional form of the judicial council and working off classic domestic notions of judicial professional qualification, these judicial players and their academic and professional sympathizers have generated significant procedural, institutional, and conceptual developments. These changes could not reasonably have been foreseen, never mind intended, by the political institutions that originally signed on to these judicial measures both to blunt the threat that the new accession States posed to the European status quo and to support the neoliberal turn and the "law and development" doctrines of the post-'89 period.

Once the judiciary, supported by its academic and professionally specialized allies, came to understand the potential of judicial appointments reform to cement its authority and influence at the intersection (a) of the European national and supranational judicial domains and (b) of the judicial and political branches, institutional identities increasingly coalesced into their current patterns. But the fixing of these judicial identities has not been a professionally localized affair; political actors and institutions now understand quite clearly that judicial self-conceptions have evolved and that the judiciary has acted accordingly, often at their expense. As the high European judiciary has come to conceive of itself as rightfully independent and self-governing and to take it for granted that its prerogatives include the capacity to set and impose judicial policy as a coequal—and in some domains, superior—governmental branch, a steady stream of political actors and institutions at both the domestic and the supranational levels have complained, resisted, and at times openly rebelled. Indeed, the rise of judicial self-consciousness and self-confidence as an independent power has triggered a concomitant reaction not only within the ranks of traditional political institutions, but also within the mainstream media and the public at large. The rise of the European judiciary has thus fed a rise in increasingly overt and even virulent legitimacy challenges. Let us therefore turn to our final chapters, which address these judicial legitimacy issues head on.

13
A Crisis in Legitimacy and Authority

As this book has explained, there are many ways to understand the European judicial appointments reforms of the last twenty years. The book's primary purpose has been to uncover them, to lay them side by side, and to explain how they operate together. As I have stressed, these explanations should not be understood as mutually exclusive. To the contrary, each has its own force and pedigree, its own architects and supporters, and so on; and crucially, all of them are operative and effective at the same time. The power of the judicial appointments debates is precisely their capacity to enlist such a broad range of contrasting perspectives and projects, even when such disparate views appear so fundamentally irreconcilable.

It is crucial to recognize, however, that just because there are so many ways to read and react to the judicial appointments reforms and their associated debates (judicial independence, judicial quality, judicial councils, etc.) does not mean that we cannot reliably identify key procedural, institutional, and conceptual trends and the overall direction in which they have tended to run. We can. As this book has explained, such large-scale developments are important, even if they are by no means uncontroversial. They include a growing sense of the importance of judges; of their legitimate independence from (and increasingly comparable status to) political authority; of their rightful role in controlling key aspects of judicial appointments, promotion, and discipline; and so on. As a comparatist attuned to the classic Civilian (especially French-inspired) understandings of the judicial role, I am keenly aware of just how significant such new perspectives really are.

This chapter focuses on a final theme, which emerges precisely in the context of such large-scale developments in the judicial role: the intimate relationship between the European judicial appointments reforms and the legitimacy of the high European Courts. As we have consistently observed in the European literature on judicial appointments reform, most judicial, institutional, and academic commentators are strongly committed to the propositions (1) that European judicial authority and legitimacy need urgently to be shored up and (2) that this should be accomplished largely through judicial appointments mechanisms, including not only proper judicial selection standards and procedures at the national level, but also proper judicial vetting panels at the European level. The clear assumption is that if judicial quality, competence, and independence were properly assured in the appointments process, then the legitimacy of the European Courts would surely follow suit.[1]

This chapter challenges this dominant assessment and its associated prescriptions. It argues that they represent for the most part a myopic, self-referential, and thus, likely ineffectual professional response to legitimacy problems that are not only of a greater dimension, but also of a different kind.

I. The Orthodox Analysis and Prescription

As this book has shown in some detail, major European judicial figures, institutional players, and academics have generally converged on a common analysis of, and prescription for, the judicial appointments problem. This dominant perspective was on full display in the alarmist letter that European Court of Human Rights (ECtHR) President Jean-Paul Costa sent in 2010 to the Ambassadors of the Council of Europe's Member States, proposing the establishment of a panel of experts to vet judicial appointments to the Strasbourg Court. Costa's letter is worth quoting again at some length:

> In terms of the future of the Court and therefore the Convention system, one of the decisive factors will be the quality of its Judges. Whatever reforms are undertaken, the system will fail if judges do not have the necessary experience and authority.
>
> The quality of the Judges is important not only to guarantee the high standard of the decisions delivered and the jurisprudence developed. It is also essential because, in a subsidiary system where human rights protection falls primarily to the national courts, the European Court as the ultimate arbiter of human rights issues must be composed of persons of sufficient standing and authority to command the respect of national judges, including senior national judges. If this is not the case, the Court itself will suffer from a deficit of authority and the system will lose credibility and effectiveness.
>
> ...
>
> The states clearly have a fundamental role in ensuring that the three candidates whose names are submitted to the Parliamentary Assembly are all suitably qualified so as to offer the Assembly a real choice between candidates of an equivalent standing and to guarantee that, whichever of the candidates is elected, he/she will have a sufficient level of expertise in a relevant field of law (international law, criminal law, administrative law, humanitarian law, etc.). To achieve this means setting up a fair and transparent procedure at national level. This has already been

[1] *See, e.g.*, Michal Bobek ed., Selecting Europe's Judges: A Critical Review of the Appointment Procedures to the European Courts (2015) ["Bobek (2015)"].

> recommended by the Parliamentary Assembly and it is important that this recommendation is fully implemented.
>
> However, this is not enough. That is why I would urge the Committee of Ministers to set up rapidly a panel along the lines proposed by the Wise Persons and the Secretary General. Such a panel, which should be composed of senior figures from a relevant background, would intervene before a list was submitted to the PACE by the contracting party . . .[2]

In this letter, Costa made what we can now recognize as the classic set of thematic and prescriptive links. The judicial appointments process to the ECtHR needed urgently to be reformed via the introduction of a vetting panel at the European level lest the quality, credibility, and thus authority of the Court collapse and the entire ECHR "system . . . fail."

Writing in a more retrospective and congratulatory tone regarding the European Court of Justice's (ECJ) reforms, the President of the 255 Panel, Jean-Marc Sauvé, has drawn even more explicit links between the establishment of the European-level vetting Panel and not only the independence and competence of the judicial candidates, but also the independence, legitimacy, and power of the Court itself. In a speech celebrating the anniversary of the French judicial council (the "Conseil supérieur de la magistrature"), Sauvé thus explained that thanks to the Panel's work to ensure the independence and competence of the judicial candidates, "there has therefore gradually emerged, within the European Union, a veritable 'judicial power,' whose independence and legitimacy have been further reinforced by the creation of the Article 255 Panel."[3] The leading European judicial figures have therefore underlined the seemingly intimate connection between judicial appointments, authority, and legitimacy.

As the work of the Committee of Ministers of the Council of Europe demonstrates so well, committed European institutional actors have subscribed to the same basic point of view. The comprehensive seventy-five-page "Report on the Longer-Term Future of the System of the European Convention on Human Rights," published in late 2015 by the Committee of Ministers' Steering Committee for Human Rights (CDDH), for example, goes to great pains to underline the tight link between the judicial appointments process to the ECtHR, the quality of the Court' judges, and the authority of that Court and of its judgments and case-law.[4] In its

[2] Jean-Paul Costa, Letter from the President of the European Court of Human Rights, addressed to member states' Permanent Representatives (Ambassadors) on June 9, 2010 ["Costa Letter"].

[3] Jean-Marc Sauvé, "Le rôle du comité 255 dans la séparation des pouvoirs au sein de l'Union européenne" 3, intervention lors du colloque pour le 130ème anniversaire du Conseil supérieur de la magistrature le 24 octobre 2013, available at http://www.conseil-etat.fr/fr/discours-et-interventions/la-separation-des-pouvoirs-l-union-europeenne-et-le-comite-255-.html. Sauvé further argued that the development of this full-fledged European judicial power can be seen in the ECJ's emergence as "a veritable supreme court, playing the role of motor of European integration and promoter of fundamental rights." *See id.* at 6.

[4] Steering Committee for Human Rights, Report on the Longer-Term Future of the System.

chapter on "The Authority of the Court," for example, the CDDH devotes an entire section to "The Challenge Regarding the Authority of the [Court's] Case Law"; and in this section, the very first "possible response" to this challenge is addressed precisely toward "The quality of judges" and accordingly to judicial selection.[5] Indeed, assuring the quality of the Court's judges through a proper judicial selection process is sufficiently important that the CDDH addresses not only how this process can be improved within the reformed selection procedures (which now include the Advisory Panel of Experts (APE)), but also produced "a further in-depth analysis" regarding such judicial selection mechanisms,[6] the "Draft Report on the process of selection and election of judges of the [ECtHR]."[7]

The leading academics to address these issues have generally followed the same reasoning. As Michal Bobek states in the Prologue to his leading volume on the European judicial appointments reforms: "A consensus appears to exist on the fact that the expert panels have been put in place in order to guarantee greater professional quality of the judicial appointees, and thusly enhance the legitimacy of both European courts."[8] Although his Czech compatriot David Kosař echoes this assessment ("there is a growing consensus that how judges are selected has an impact on the ECtHR's legitimacy"[9]), he is even more adamant about the urgent need to improve the quality and experience of European judges in order to buttress the legitimacy of their courts. Focusing on the ECtHR, he "argues that the inadequate qualification, experience and stature of some of the Strasbourg judges provide a serious threat to the institutional legitimacy of the ECtHR" and "highlights the importance of electing stellar judges to the Strasbourg bench for maintaining the legitimacy of the ECtHR."[10] To Kosar, "the competence of Strasbourg judges actually lies at the heart of the Court's current difficulties and, in fact, presents the major legitimacy challenge for the ECtHR."[11] Indeed, a single problematic appointment can, he argues, generate serious and long-term legitimacy costs:

> It is important to keep in mind that the election of one sub-optimal judge to the ECtHR has more far-reaching consequences for the Court's legitimacy than one controversial judgment. Most controversial rulings are forgotten after a few years or can be at least moderated by subsequent judgments, but a problematic judge will take part in thousands of decisions. Such a judge thus not only undermines

[5] *Id.* at Chapter III, Section II(A).

[6] *Id* at 6, 41, 44, 48, 71.

[7] *See* Committee of Experts on the System of the European Convention on Human Rights (DH-SYSC), "[Draft] Report on the Process of Selection and Election of Judges of the European Court of Human Rights," DH-SYSC (2017)R4 Addendum (November 2017) ["DH-SYSC, 2017 Report on the Process of Selection and Election of ECtHR Judges"].

[8] Bobek (2015), Prologue at 22.

[9] David Kosař, *Selecting Strasbourg' Judges: A Critique, in* Bobek (2015) at 127 [Kosař (2015)"].

[10] *Id.* at 121, 122.

[11] *Id.* at 124 (footnotes omitted).

> the legitimacy of the ECtHR at the moment of her election, but also becomes the Court's "legitimacy baggage" for nine years.[12]

One could hardly be more explicit about the intimate relationship between judicial quality, authority, and legitimacy.[13]

As should by now be clear, the prevailing orthodoxy within the leading European judicial, institutional, and academic circles has come to place judicial appointments at the epicenter of the legitimacy travails of the European Courts: if only judicial quality, competence, and independence were properly assured by the establishment of appropriate judicial appointments processes, the legitimacy of the European Courts would surely follow suit. This chapter concludes on a note of deep skepticism, offering good reasons to doubt this orthodox diagnosis and prescription.

II. Reasons for Skepticism

A. Çali et al.: Self-Referential Professional Perceptions

In their influential 2013 paper, "The Social Legitimacy of Human Rights Courts: A Social Interpretivist Theory of the Legitimacy of the European Court of Human Rights,"[14] Başak Çali, Anne Koch, and Nicola Bruch offer a complex account of the mechanisms by which domestic political, judicial, and legal elites assess the legitimacy of the ECtHR. Their key finding was that domestic actors do not regard the ECtHR in isolation as a stand-alone institution. Although domestic political, judicial, and legal elites may differ in their ultimate assessments of the ECtHR's legitimacy, they always come to those assessments by relating the Strasbourg Court to domestic institutions. Çali et al. explain:

> The central argument of the article is that the social legitimacy of the European Court of Human Rights is built on a constant comparison between the purposes and performance of domestic institutions and the purposes and performance of the European Court of Human Rights. More specifically, the social legitimacy of the European Court of Human Rights is grounded in what we refer to as the

[12] *Id.* at 161.

[13] *See also* Alberto Alemanno, *How Transparent is Transparent Enough?: Balancing Access to Information Against Privacy in European Judicial Selections*, *in* Bobek (2015) at 205 ("In order to ensure the continuing effectiveness and legitimacy of the European Courts, the panels' mission is to guarantee that proposed judicial candidates are of the highest standards.")

[14] Başak Çali, Anne Koch, & Nicola Bruch, *The Social Legitimacy of Human Rights Courts: A Social Interpretivist Theory of the Legitimacy of the European Court of Human Rights*, 35 Hum. R.Q. 955 (2013) ["Çali et al. (2013)"].

> logic of a *fair compromise*: What domestic actors think they lose by according legitimacy to the European Court of Human Rights must be balanced by what they perceive they will gain. Three factors organize how domestic actors view legitimacy concerns as part of a loss or a gain framing: a) perception of domestic human rights conditions, b) commitment to human rights and international law as cosmopolitan ideals, and c) commitment to domestic institutions.[15]

In other words, the legitimacy assessment of the ECtHR is always a relative appraisal. By definition, that assessment is therefore actively informed by the observer's assessment of something else, namely, of the domestic situation.

These findings carry significant import for our analysis. As the Çali study makes quite clear, the primary variables in the domestic assessment of the ECtHR lie primarily in the sphere of *domestic* self-perceptions and commitments. The authors reiterate:

> Based on our ground up analysis, we identify three factors that ... shape the way in which actors view the legitimacy sources they encounter in their social interactions with the Court... These factors are present among elites in any given country:
> (1) the perceived human rights situation in a given country,
> (2) the commitment to common human rights standards and international law as cosmopolitan ideals, and
> (3) the commitment to domestic institutions.[16]

As a result, "the social legitimacy of human rights courts cannot be viewed in isolation from the domestic social setting."

Even more, the perception of that domestic setting drives the perception of the Strasbourg Court: "A negative perception of the domestic human rights situation increases the relative value of the European Court of Human Rights (and vice versa) as a legitimate institution."[17] As a necessary correlative,

> The importance attached to domestic institutions takes away from the value assigned to the European Court of Human Rights in improving the domestic human rights situation and presents actors with a dilemma to reconcile their aspirations to improve protection of human rights internationally and their concerns to guard and protect their own institutions, be it parliamentary democracy or rule of law through domestic courts and law.[18]

[15] *Id.* at 957.
[16] *Id.* at 976.
[17] *Id.*
[18] *Id.*

On the one hand, such findings should not be terribly surprising. After all, as between two people from different countries, one of whom believes he lives in a country that suffers from persistent human rights abuses and the other of whom does not, it is surely reasonable to expect that the first would be more invested in the legitimacy of an international human rights court that might come to the aid of his people than would be the second, who would see no need for such external intercession in the first place. Indeed, it is surely to be expected—as the third factor in the Çali analysis suggests—that the more the second person is attached and committed to domestic institutions, the less legitimate she would perceive an interventionist human rights court to be.

On the other hand, these seemingly straightforward findings do carry important implications. If domestic actors typically view the legitimacy of the ECtHR through the lens of (a) their perception of their national human rights situation and (b) their own commitment to domestic institutions, then their assessment of the legitimacy of the ECtHR is being driven in significant measure by factors that are largely independent of that Court in the first place.[19] As Çali et al. state, "domestic decision makers who perceive that the human rights situation in their country does not suffer from serious shortcomings regard the ECtHR as superfluous domestically."[20] As a result, "a politician from the United Kingdom who believes that parliamentary sovereignty is vital to the democratic culture and that the United Kingdom is faring well in terms of domestic human rights protections" is likely to come to a "more reluctant assessment" of the legitimacy of the ECtHR and of its interventions than would lawyers, judges, or politicians who would view their own domestic situations and institutions differently. In other words, the domestic assessment of the ECtHR is largely a function of domestic factors over which the ECtHR has relatively little influence.

This first implication carries a second: there are probably limits to what the ECtHR (or, for that matter, the ECJ) can easily do to fundamentally restructure domestic legitimacy assessments. This obviously does not mean it cannot do anything. But if Çali et al. are to be taken seriously, then the legitimacy frame is sufficiently set by domestic factors that the European Court has relatively little room to maneuver.

What this conclusion really means in practical terms is hard to divine. At one level, it could simply mean that in scenarios in which domestic actors are especially proud of their national institutions and confident of their national human rights situation (read: in the British scenario), the ECtHR has to be especially careful

[19] I intentionally use qualified language in this sentence because it is difficult, as constructivists would stress, to parse cleanly between the domestic and international dimensions of such perceptions. In particular, the ECtHR may well play a pedagogical role that could (and likely should) influence domestic understandings of the human rights situation in a given country; and this interaction could help, in turn, to establish the terms of the ongoing human rights debate.

[20] Çali et al. (2013) at 978.

not to behave in a manner that risks compromising its precarious legitimacy. But even under this minimalist reading of the Çali findings, it would be difficult to argue that European judicial appointments reform could do much more than help to avoid some hypersensitive domestic tripwires: it would be naïve to expect that appointments reform could fundamentally alter the legitimacy framework itself. Given that this legitimacy framing is largely self-referential (e.g., is largely a function of how the British see themselves), one should not expect that the ECtHR or the Council of Europe as a whole—never mind European judicial appointments reform all by itself—could generate large-scale effects on the domestic perceptions of the ECtHR's legitimacy. Could judicial appointments issues produce legitimacy effects on the margins? Sure. But could they fundamentally rework the very architecture of how the ECtHR is perceived in the European Member States? Probably not.

A final word about the thought-provoking Çali study. I have so far focused on only two of the three factors that the authors identified as "shap[ing] the way in which [domestic] actors view the legitimacy [of] the Court": "(1) the perceived human rights situation in a given country, . . . and (3) the commitment to domestic institutions." This still leaves "(2) the [domestic] commitment to common human rights standards and international law as cosmopolitan ideals."[21] As we shall see, this second factor—which is patently different in kind from the other two—holds particular importance for our analysis of the relationship between European judicial appointments and the legitimacy of the high European Courts. Before we can fruitfully address such cosmopolitanism, however, it will be useful to turn our attention toward the British example raised by the Çali legitimacy study.

B. British Eurosceptics and the Tabloid Press

As I write in 2018 and 2019, the centrality of the ECJ to the ongoing Brexit negotiations is utterly inescapable. British Prime Minister Theresa May long asserted that ending the jurisdiction of the ECJ was a "red line" in all Brexit negotiations. As she declared in ringing tones in her May 2016 speech to the Tory Conference:

> But let's state one thing loud and clear: we are not leaving the European Union only to give up control of immigration all over again. And we are not leaving only to return to the jurisdiction of the European Court of Justice. That's not going to happen.
>
> We are leaving to become, once more, a fully sovereign and independent country—and the deal is going to have to work for Britain.[22]

[21] *See id.* at 976.

[22] http://www.independent.co.uk/news/uk/politics/theresa-may-speech-tory-conference-2016-in-full-transcript-a7346171.html.

Although there has been a great deal of debate about what the resulting red line exactly means, and about whether Prime Minister May (and later, Boris Johnson) has been blurring this red line when negotiating over Brexit terms with her EU counterparts, one should not lose sight of the underlying fact: the ECJ has somehow become a central subject of heated—and public—political debate. Indeed, as Theresa May's quote demonstrates so clearly, the Court has risen to a position of such prominence that it now figures on the ultra shortlist of most pressing British political issues, joining such a pantheon of flashpoints as immigration, the Irish border, the rights of EU nationals living in the UK, and so on.

Given the current omnipresence of the European Courts (and these days especially, of the ECJ) as a focus of criticism in British domestic politics and in the British tabloid press (such as the *Daily Mail*, *The Sun*, the *Daily Express*, and so on), it is hard to remember that the European Courts long were quasi-invisible actors in the European political arena. The ECtHR was a virtual non-entity for decades.[23] And the ECJ was a largely stealth European operator, handing down judgments of constitutional dimension since the 1960s, but whose presence and import escaped, for all intent and purposes, all but a small circle of knowledgeable juridical, political, and administrative cadres. Indeed, deep into the 1980s and arguably into the 1990s, much of EU legal scholarship consisted precisely of recognizing and highlighting (and, with rare exceptions,[24] celebrating) the Court's achievements.[25] To recall those days is therefore to call attention to just how astonishing it is for the ECJ to have reached such a level of public prominence, especially in the British press today. But how did this current state of affairs come to pass?

1. Ignorance/misinformation about the European Courts

The first recurrent explanation for the dramatic rise of the European Courts as public bones of contention is ignorance, or more precisely, alleged ignorance. The basic idea is that British Eurosceptic politicians, publics, and press are simply misinformed about the nature and function of the ECJ and EtCHR. Such misinformation leads to misunderstandings and, ultimately, to misguided hostility.

Pro-European commentators beat this drum relentlessly. In an unremarkable yet highly representative example, David Allen Green ponders in the *Financial Times* why the ECJ's jurisdiction has become such a line in the sand for the UK in its Brexit negotiations. He writes:

[23] The ECtHR authored all of thirty-six judgments in its first twenty plus years of existence. MARK W. JANIS, RICHARD S. KAY, & ANTHONY W. BRADLEY, EUROPEAN HUMAN RIGHTS LAW: TEXT AND MATERIALS 69–70 (2nd edn., 2000).

[24] *See, e.g.*, HJALTE RASMUSSEN, ON LAW AND POLICY IN THE EUROPEAN COURT OF JUSTICE. A COMPARATIVE STUDY IN JUDICIAL POLICYMAKING (1986) ["Rasmussen (1986)"].

[25] *See, e.g.*, Joseph Weiler, *The Transformation of Europe*, 100 YALE L.J. 2403 (1991) ["Weiler (1991)"]; KAREN ALTER, ESTABLISHING THE SUPREMACY OF EUROPEAN LAW: THE MAKING OF AN INTERNATIONAL RULE OF LAW IN EUROPE (2003) ["Alter (2003)"]; RENAUD DEHOUSSE, THE POLITICS OF JUDICIAL INTEGRATION (1998).

> So, why was such a precise and consequential promise [to end the ECJ's jurisdiction] made? There are at least four possible explanations. The first is that Mrs. May, as a former home secretary, simply transferred her well-documented dislike of the European Court of Human Rights to the similarly named European Court of Justice. (The former is not an organ of the EU and has a separate jurisdiction.)[26]

This clever passage effectively suggests that Theresa May was sufficiently ignorant to confuse the ECtHR for the "similarly named" ECJ: note well the devilish little parenthetical explanation helpfully offered to the uninformed reader (or, perhaps, to the similarly uninformed Prime Minister!): "The former is not an organ of the EU and has a separate jurisdiction." Mrs. May's ignorance apparently led her reflexively to "transfer" her long-standing antipathy from one European Court to the other.

Sir David Edward, who served for a dozen years as the British Judge on the ECJ, was even more blunt about Mrs. May's alleged ignorance and even more condescendingly pedantic in his explanation of EU law:

> "It just shows how ignorant she is. She said it again today . . .," Sir David said, referring to Prime Minister May's insistence that Britain will fully leave the ECJ's jurisdiction when it leaves the EU in March 2019.
>
> "To end UK jurisdiction is simply to say we are not going to obey EU law anymore. Well, this is fine, as long as British business chooses to operate entirely inside the UK."
>
> He added: "If a business manufacturing goods in the UK wants to export goods to the EU, as hundreds of them do, then those goods must comply with EU standards. . . . In that sense, the EU law will continue to apply in the sense that people will have to obey it. We cannot escape the jurisdiction of the ECJ."[27]

As if this were not enough, Judge Edward went on to expand the scope of his critique. The problem is not only that Mrs. May does not grasp the limited practical effects of withdrawing from the formal jurisdiction of the ECJ, but also that she does not seem to understand the nature of the Court's jurisdiction in the first place:

> However, for Sir David, it is not just May's unrealistic promises regarding the ECJ that have left him frustrated, but signs that both she and the government don't fully understand its purpose and remit. "The ECJ does not have 'direct jurisdiction' in or over the UK," the former ECJ judge tells [*Business Insider*].

[26] David Allen Green, "Brexit: Why Did the ECJ Become a UK 'Red Line'?," available at https://www.ft.com/content/32cd1e87-c7d1-3026-86fc-bce5229711d1.

[27] Adam Payne, "Former ECJ Judge: Theresa May's Pledge to End All ECJ Jurisdiction 'Shows Just How Ignorant She Is," available at http://www.businessinsider.com/former-ecj-judge-mays-pledge-to-end-ecj-rule-shows-how-ignorant-she-is-2017-8.

> "What it has is the jurisdiction to answer questions regarding the interpretation and application of EU law. In so far as the UK is bound by EU law, then the ECJ interpretation is binding on the UK. Correspondingly, UK courts that seek to know what the correct law is can put the question to the ECJ. The ECJ doesn't have any other jurisdiction in the UK other than to answer questions put to it by UK courts."
>
> He continues: "They [ministers] use expressions like the ECJ can 'enforce' EU law or can 'direct' the UK—but it can't do any such thing. All it can do is say what the law is. The great thing about EU law is it doesn't have any police and enforcement is entirely by consent."
>
> ...
>
> "It's just ignorant," he adds. "The idea that the ECJ is a body like the US Supreme Court that can strike down legislation of states is just false."[28]

Judge Edward's contempt for Mrs. May's ignorance, misunderstandings, and resulting policy blunders could hardly be more evident. As in the David Allen Green example, the current British fixation on the ECJ is, on this view, a product of ignorance and/or misinformation about the Court, its mission, and its powers.

2. The ECJ's legitimacy shortage

The second recurrent (and often related) explanation for the dramatic rise of the European Courts as public bones of contention is a crisis of legitimacy; and this legitimacy crisis, argue the proponents of this view, is closely tied to precisely the type of judicial appointments, judicial quality, and judicial independence issues addressed by the ongoing European judicial appointments reforms. Thus, as ECtHR President Costa anxiously wrote in 2010, the Strasbourg "system will fail if judges do not have the necessary experience and authority."[29] And as the Czech academic David Kosař has strenuously argued, "the inadequate qualification, experience and stature of some of the Strasbourg judges are a serious threat to the institutional legitimacy of the ECtHR."[30] Indeed, "the competence of Strasbourg judges actually lies at the heart of the Court's current difficulties and, in fact, presents the major legitimacy challenge for the ECtHR";[31] thus, "The very legitimacy of the Strasbourg Court is at stake."[32]

[28] *Id.* It is worth noting that condescending refutations such as the one offered above by Judge Edward are not only ineffective, but also patently misleading, even if technically correct. It is formalistic legal sophistry to argue that the ECJ cannot enforce EU law against the Member States (in Judge Edward's words, "the ECJ does not have 'direct jurisdiction' in or over the UK"). If an ECJ interpretation of EU law empowers the Commission to levy fines against a Member State, or worse, exposes that Member State to liability at the hands of private parties in the national courts, it is silly to stress that this represents no more than "answer[ing] questions about the interpretation and application of EU law."

[29] *See* Costa Letter.

[30] Kosař (2015) at 121.

[31] *Id.* at 124 (footnotes omitted).

[32] *Id.* at 160.

Although the Çali study discussed above offers only tenuous support for the alarmist proposition that judicial appointments shortcomings threaten a large-scale collapse of European judicial legitimacy,[33] there is no question but that the British tabloid press routinely challenges the legitimacy of the ECJ and ECtHR (and/or report enthusiastically on British politicians who do) and that these legitimacy challenges do periodically address European judicial quality, independence, and appointments issues.

Perhaps the best example of this genre of tabloid critique appeared in a 2013 *Daily Mail* article that went under the melodramatic (if ultimately uninspired) title "Human Right to Make a Killing: Damning Dossier Reveals Taxpayers' Bill for European Court Payouts to Murderers, Terrorists and Traitors."[34] Under this uproarious headline, the *Daily Mail* decried the galling injustice that the British government and taxpayers had been forced by the ECtHR to shell out millions (the quoted figure was £4.4 million) as a result of losing "a staggering 202 European human rights cases" brought by a long list of "Murderers, Terrorists and Traitors," of which the poster child was none other than the menacingly bearded figure of Abu Qatada.[35]

The *Daily Mail* article was based on figures obtained by the rebellious Tory MP Philip Davies,[36] who has certainly made no secret of his rabidly anti-European stance or of his staunchly anti-rights positions.[37] The article quoted Davies:

> To me, it's just an absolutely scandalous waste of money. I'm not aware of my decent law-abiding constituents running off to the European Court of Human Rights. It is a charter for illegal immigrants and criminals. We're in a situation where we've got pseudo judges who are making decisions about this country. These cases highlight what an absolute racket it has become. The sooner we scrap

[33] *See supra* Chapter 13 II(A). *See also* R. Daniel Keleman, *Selection, Appointment and Legitimacy: A Political Perspective*, *in* Bobek (2015) 244, at 246–51.

[34] http://www.dailymail.co.uk/news/article-2449256/Human-right-make-killing-Damning-dossier-reveals-taxpayers-European-court-payouts-murderers-terrorists-traitors.html#ixzz570KcIxit.

[35] *See id.* In a particularly high profile judgment, the ECtHR had placed restrictions on the UK's deportation of terror suspect Abu Qatada for trial in Jordan, lest he be subject to torture. *See* Othman (Abu Qatada) v. The United Kingdom (2012) 55 E.H.R.R. 1 (Section IV, ECHR). This provoked the ire of the British Home Secretary, then none other than Theresa May, who not only relentlessly attacked the Strasbourg Court, but who eventually went so far as to lobby for the UK to withdraw altogether from the ECHR, despite the fact that the EU requires all Member States to be signatories to the ECHR and that May actually supported continued British membership in the EU. This complication eventually led to the British government's assurance that it would remain party to the ECHR at least until after Brexit. *See* https://www.theguardian.com/world/2013/jul/08/theresa-may-human-rights-abu-qatada.

[36] For data that illustrates how Davies stands on the extreme right wing of the Conservative Party, see http://www.publicwhip.org.uk/mp.php?mpn=Philip_Davies&mpc=Shipley&house=commons (quantifying how often Davies votes against the majority position of his party).

[37] Davies launched the "Better Off Out" ("BOO"!) campaign in 2006, which advocates for Brexit. http://news.bbc.co.uk/2/hi/uk_news/politics/6209386.stm.

> the Human Rights Act and leave the European Convention on Human Rights the better.[38]

Davies' full comments included a further swipe toward Strasbourg:

> Personally, I would like to see us withdraw from [the European Convention on Human Right] too, to be perfectly honest, because the European Court of Human Rights is no more than a joke. It is full of judges, many of whom are not even legally qualified—they are not actually real judges; they are pseudo-judges—who are political appointees from the member states who have been sent to make political decisions, not legal decisions.[39]

As can readily be seen, these comments overtly make the connection to ECtHR judicial appointments, independence, and quality. The ECtHR "is full of judges, many of whom are not even legally qualified—they are not actually real judges." Indeed, the lack of qualifications of these "pseudo-judges" is not accidental: instead of being appropriately independent "real judges" sent to Strasbourg to render "legal decisions," they are "political appointees from the member states who have been sent to make political decisions." The legitimacy of the Court, it seems, is deeply threatened by the lack of quality and independence of its own judges.

C. Challenging the Orthodox Account

It should by now be evident that the ongoing European judicial appointments reforms (including, inter alia, their judicial quality and independence offshoots) are by no means directed solely at addressing the substance of European judicial shortcomings. They also consist of promotional campaigns both to correct alleged ignorance and misinformation about the European Courts and, relatedly, to bolster these courts' ostensibly faltering legitimacy.

The British tabloid examples we have been briefly discussing provide a particularly good case in point. In the wake of the *Daily Mail*/Philip Davies critiques,[40] the longtime Registrar of the ECtHR, Erik Fribergh, took the remarkable step of issuing a public refutation of the British tabloids' substantive claims. In a

[38] http://www.dailymail.co.uk/news/article-2449256/Human-right-make-killing-Damning-dossier-reveals-taxpayers-European-court-payouts-murderers-terrorists-traitors.html#ixzz570KcIxit.

[39] https://publications.parliament.uk/pa/cm201516/cmhansrd/cm150528/debtext/150528-0003.htm#column_273.

[40] The Sunday Express's version of the story ran under the headline, "Millions Paid Out to Criminal Thanks to the European Court of Human Rights." *See* https://www.express.co.uk/news/uk/435258/Millions-paid-out-to-criminals-thanks-to-the-European-Court-of-Human-Rights.

perplexingly straight-faced rebuttal to the tabloids' overheated Eurosceptic screes, Fribergh ponderously intoned:

> Several British newspapers have this week published articles based on a table produced in Westminster in response to a written parliamentary question. The common theme of the articles is that judgments from the European Court of Human Rights since 1998 have caused the UK government to make substantial payments to successful applicants, the clear suggestion being that this constitutes a massive payout to criminals. The figure cited is £4.4 million.
>
> However, the way in which this has been presented is seriously misleading. First, the figure of £4.4 million includes legal costs as well as compensation. The calculation of the total paid in respect of compensation by the UK since 1998 (as opposed to compensation and costs taken together) is in fact in the region of £1.7 million, less than half the figure of £4.4 million.
>
> The failure to distinguish between compensation and costs creates the impression that applicants were awarded significantly more compensation than they really were and that the sums indicated were for the applicants' sole benefit. For example, one of the articles suggested that Mustafa Abdi "pocketed £7,237", whereas in reality he was awarded €1,500 in compensation. It is also indicated that applicant Douglas Vinter was "awarded £34,500", although he was accorded no compensation whatsoever, the sum cited relating solely to costs and expenses.
>
> A significant proportion of the amounts referred to were therefore paid to lawyers. The particularly high level of legal fees in the U.K. compared with other Council of Europe countries means that in British cases costs normally exceed compensation. One example would be the case of Financial Times and Others v. the UK in which the Financial Times, the Independent, the Guardian, the Times and Reuters were awarded a total of €160,000 in costs, but received no compensation.[41]

Not satisfied with having thus corrected the record on the specifics of the amounts awarded, the Registrar went on to correct the tabloids' mistaken views about the qualifications of the Strasbourg judges:

> Finally, some of the articles cited a familiar refrain that "because they are political appointees many of the Court's judges are not even legal experts". This is simply not the case. Judges are not appointed but elected by the Parliamentary Assembly of the Council of Europe, composed of delegations from national parliaments, including Westminster. A list of three candidates is put forward by the Government, but before the Assembly proceeds to the election the list is vetted

[41] http://humanrightseurope.coe.int/2013/10/court-concern-at-seriously-misleading-uk-news-articles/.

> by an independent international panel of senior judicial figures to ensure that the candidates satisfy the Convention criteria that they must "either possess the qualifications required for appointment to high judicial office or be jurisconsults of recognised competence". In other words they must be shown to be 'legal experts.' The judges on the Court come from different professional legal backgrounds, judges, academics, practitioners, but there are absolutely no grounds for alleging that they are not legal experts.[42]

With this instructive response, Registrar Fribergh helpfully sets matters straight. ECtHR judges are not politically appointed but elected (and are thus not vulnerable to charges of cronyism or lack of independence); and they must be "vetted by an independent international panel of senior judicial figures to ensure that [they are indeed] legal experts." As we can now so clearly see, the establishment of the vetting Panels represents at least in part the knowledgeable European professional's response to judicial legitimacy challenges such as those voiced against the European Courts in the British tabloid press.

As the reader will likely have recognized, however, Registrar Fribergh's public refutation is oddly—though tellingly—tone-deaf. Needless to say, his numbers are likely far more accurate and nuanced than those put forward by the *Daily Mail*, the *Sunday Express*, Philip Davies, and so on. But, to be perfectly honest, so what? Given the provenance and carnivalesque nature of the headlines ("Human Right to Make a Killing: Damning Dossier Reveals Taxpayers' Bill for European Court Payouts to Murderers, Terrorists and Traitors," "Millions Paid Out to Criminal Thanks to the European Court of Human Rights," etc.), would it really surprise anyone to discover that the claims made in such tabloid fare are not entirely reliable? More importantly, does the thrust or impact of the tabloid reports turn on the exact figures in question? For that matter, does it help to defuse the criticism to explain that half or more of the sums paid have gone to cover legal fees? Of course not. What matters are the sensationalist headlines and the underlying notion that the British government and taxpayers have been forced by foreign powers (i.e., European judges) to shell out millions to a rogues' gallery of "Murderers, Terrorists and Traitors." Although Registrar Fribergh was likely perfectly factually correct, one cannot help but marvel, therefore, at the drastic mismatch between the British tabloid critiques and the Registrar's European institutional response.

This disparity is sufficiently important and revealing to warrant further attention. After all, both sides (i.e., (1) the dogged tabloid critiques of European judicial deficiencies and (2) the determined European judicial/institutional efforts to produce judicial quality/independence/appointments reform) stress the legitimacy of the European high Courts (or the lack thereof). But they do so for patently different

[42] http://humanrightseurope.coe.int/2013/10/court-concern-at-seriously-misleading-uk-news-articles/.

reasons: the former in order to discredit and shake free of those courts, the latter in order to improve and promote them. The common focus on legitimacy thus papers over the radical incongruity between the two discourses. On the one hand, as the quotations above already suggest, the Registrar's earnest refutation demonstrates the full extent to which the European insider assumes that judicial appointments reform can address (or has already addressed) the Eurosceptics' misinformed challenges to European judicial legitimacy. But on the other, the Registrar's pedantic refutation appears completely beside the point, failing to address the actual core of those Eurosceptic challenges. Let us therefore plumb this disparity a little further in order to gain some insight into the nature of both the critiques and the responses.

1. Option 1: The European *Courts* are beside the point

As we have seen, European insiders have been all too happy to take the British tabloid press and Eurosceptic politicians to task for their supposed ignorance concerning the European Courts. Theresa May, Boris Johnson, Philip Davies, and the British tabloid press, it seems, simply cannot keep the two European Courts straight, never mind grasp their roles and remits or their composition and appointment mechanisms. The British tabloid press and Eurosceptic politicians are "foolish" and "ignorant," leading to damaging misconceptions and bad policy.[43]

However congenial one may find such self-righteously pedantic "explanations," they are quite telling. At one level, they are blatantly condescending. Whether this condescension is fully and factually warranted is not our primary concern here; but it strains credulity that such major political personages as May and Johnson (and their staffs) could really be quite as ignorant or amateurish as these pseudo explanations would suggest.[44]

[43] *See, e.g.*, Toby Helm and Jamie Howard, "Ex-Legal Chief Attacks Theresa May's 'Foolish' Claim on European Court of Justice," available at https://www.theguardian.com/politics/2017/aug/19/brexit-european-court-of-justice-theresa-may-foolish-attack; Adam Payne, "Former ECJ Judge: Theresa May's Pledge to End All ECJ Jurisdiction 'Shows Just How Ignorant She Is,'" available at http://www.businessinsider.com/former-ecj-judge-mays-pledge-to-end-ecj-rule-shows-how-ignorant-she-is-2017-8.

[44] That said, persistently unflattering professional gossip about the Brexit negotiations certainly shakes one's confidence in the basic competence of the British Civil Service, especially as regards European matters. In a tellingly defensive (if seemingly upbeat) fluff piece, Jeremy Heywood, UK Cabinet Secretary and Head of the Civil Service, wrote:

> We knew from the outset that exiting the EU would make huge demands on the Civil Service and would require all the accumulated professional capability of civil servants. We haven't hesitated to provide new staff and resources to bolster those parts of the Civil Service facing the greatest pressures. We also recognised that, after four decades, the UK lacked some of the specialist skills for tasks that had been centralised within the EU. Most obviously, the UK was short of the specialist trade negotiators we would need when, as confirmed by the European Council, the UK starts to negotiate and sign trade deals during the Implementation Period.

Sir Jeremy Heywood, "The Civil Service, Brexit and Beyond," available at https://quarterly.blog.gov.uk/2018/03/23/the-civil-service-brexit-and-beyond/. Such a passage does little indeed to inspire confidence in the once vaunted British Civil Service!

At another level, however, the condescension demonstrates a specific turn of mind. The pro-European commentators evince a tendency to treat such judicial Euro-skepticism as fundamentally empirically grounded and, judged on those grounds, woefully factually deficient. This perspective therefore appears earnestly substantive: the legitimacy challenges to the ECJ and ECtHR should be taken at face value as critiques of the professional merits of the European judiciary. Under this working assumption, the legitimacy of the ECJ and ECtHR can best be reinforced (1) by directly addressing any professional shortcomings via institutional improvements and (2) by then pointing to the resulting institutional tweaks in order to call out misinformation and to set the record straight.

As a result, almost the entire array of judicial appointments reforms described in this book can be straightforwardly understood as a substantive response to the charge leveled by Philip Davies against the Strasbourg Court: "It is full of judges, many of whom are not even legally qualified—they are not actually real judges; they are pseudo-judges—who are political appointees from the member states who have been sent to make political decisions, not legal decisions."[45] After all, the primary thrust of those reforms has been precisely to make sure that the Luxembourg and Strasbourg judges are "real judges." These reforms—whether instituted by the Treaty of Lisbon, the 255 Panel, the APE, the Parliamentary Assembly (PACE), or the Committee of Ministers—have worked to ensure two basic objectives. First, the judges of the ECJ and ECtHR must be properly qualified: they should therefore demonstrate sufficient professional standing/status, requisite experience, appropriate linguistic skills, etc.[46] And second, these European judges must not be inappropriately political: they must demonstrate sufficient independence from the authorities who select and propose them, these national authorities should in turn be sufficiently independent from the political authorities, and so on.[47] The broad array of European judicial appointments reforms—and the support given to them from European institutions and academics alike—thus give every indication of taking the Davies/tabloid critiques at their word and responding accordingly.

There are several ways to gauge these seemingly earnest European responses. The first is simply to cut to the chase. If the point of these reforms was indeed to put the European judicial institutions and their supporters in the position to give the lie to the ongoing tabloid-style critiques and thereby to shore up the legitimacy of the European high Courts, is there any indication that this approach has actually worked? The unfortunate reality is that one would be hard-pressed to answer that question in the affirmative. After all, although the most visible reforms took place in 2009–10 with the establishment of the two vetting Panels, Parts I through IV demonstrated at some length that these reform efforts have actually been going

[45] *See supra* text accompanying note 978.
[46] *See supra* Parts I and II.
[47] *See id.*

on for some twenty-five years: the ECJ first focused on the connection between judicial appointments and judicial independence in its important 1995 Report in anticipation of the 1996 Intergovernmental Conference; the PACE's Committee on Legal Affairs and Human Rights proposed its Draft Resolution and Report "on the procedure for examining candidatures for the election of judges to the European Court of Human Rights" in 1995 as well;[48] and as we have seen, the reform efforts have continued tenaciously ever since. Yet the bile addressed at both high European Courts has certainly shown no sign of subsiding. If anything, it has only increased, leading to such concrete demands as the Brexit-related "red line" escape from ECJ jurisdiction, the threatened British withdrawal from the European Convention on Human Rights (ECHR), and so on. For all that one might sensibly answer that reforms take time to produce tangible effects and to change perceptions, one might reasonably expect a better rate of return after twenty-five years of concerted effort.

To make the point clearly: the mismatch between the vitriolic tabloid-style critiques of the European Courts and the patronizing empirical corrections/defenses offered by such Court allies as Registrar Fribergh, when combined with the notable failure of twenty-five years of substantive reform efforts to satisfy the critiques, should lead us to consider whether the legitimacy challenges facing the ECJ and ECtHR may have had little to do with those Courts as courts, or with their judges as judges. The judicial appointments, judicial independence, and judicial quality reforms, in other words, may have been something of a red herring. Let me explain.

In his path-breaking 1991 article, "The Transformation of Europe," Joseph Weiler offered a penetrating analysis that can be fruitfully analogized to our object of study. Weiler examined the European legitimacy crisis that fell under the generic term of the "democratic deficit." Over the course of the 1980s, well-meaning EU observers increasingly recognized that the EU (then the European Community) was suffering from a nagging legitimacy crisis; and they argued compellingly that the underlying problem with European legitimacy was that the Community institutions were structurally undemocratic: Community political structures had substituted executive for parliamentary authority by transferring traditional domestic parliamentary powers to domestic executives now operating at the European level (i.e., as the powerful law-making body known as the Council of Ministers). Indeed, the argument continued, the Luxembourg Accord (which effectively permitted national executives to wield unilateral veto power in Council in the name of "very important national interests") compounded this underlying structural problem. The shift in power from parliaments to executives, when combined with the capacity for any given executive to wield unilateral veto power, effectively meant that a lone executive representative could hold the transferred regulatory

[48] PACE Committee on Legal Affairs and Human Rights (Rapporteur: Lord Kirkhill), Report on the procedure for examining candidatures for the election of judges to the European Court of Human Rights 1, Doc 7439, 1403-15/12/95-1-E (1995).

power hostage, singlehandedly frustrating the parliamentary will of the rest of the European people. The vertical shift of power from the national to the European level had therefore concealed a horizontal shift from parliamentary to executive authority, which had only been magnified via the Luxembourg veto. The European commentators' solution—which was utterly irreproachable as a matter of formal democratic theory—was to reverse the parliamentary loss both by increasing the legislative authority of the European Parliament (thereby reversing the loss of parliamentary power at the national level) and by doing away with the Luxembourg Accord and its attendant veto (thereby reversing the unilateral power of national executives operating at the European level).

To these elegant analyses and practical solutions, Joe Weiler had a devastatingly insightful response. Not only were the analyses beside the point, but their supposed solutions were also downright counterproductive. The legitimacy issue was not a problem of formal democratic theory. Indeed, one might add, few European citizens could even list the EU institutions to begin with. The problem was instead a matter of social legitimacy: these citizens did not really understand themselves as European in the first place. As a result, the prospect of further empowering the EU to act (regardless of whether it did so via the European Parliament) was only to aggravate the problem; and such European power became all the more threatening if one also did away with the comforting notion that national executives could as a last resort "protect" their countries by deploying the veto power promised by the Luxembourg Accord.[49] The fundamental problem, in other words, was one of political community, not of political theory: if the European Community could not engender some sense of allegiance and belonging, then any Community empowerment unchecked by visible national safeguards would be experienced as an illegitimate imposition of external political will, regardless of how formally legitimate such European political institutions might actually be.

More than twenty-five years on, it appears that the same basic logic continues to apply, only this time in the judicial context. As in the democratic deficit scenario that Weiler was discussing, there is no doubt whatsoever regarding the formal legitimacy of the European Courts. Both the ECJ and the ECtHR have been established by formally legitimate Treaty means; their judges are appointed via similarly legitimate and legally established mechanisms, and so on. It is a fool's errand, therefore, to attempt to address the much decried legitimacy deficit of the high European Courts by focusing reform efforts on the formal bases of European judicial authority, such as, for example, the judicial appointments process.

Indeed, the fact that the critiques leveled by Eurosceptic politicians such as Philip Davies and/or by tabloid outlets such as the *Daily Mail* make little attempt to be factually or legally accurate represents perhaps the clearest indication of

[49] *See* Weiler (1991) at 2428–30, 2473–74.

the comparative irrelevance of the formal bases of European judicial legitimacy. Do these critiques really hinge, for example, on whether the ECHR actually is "a charter for illegal immigrants and criminals"? Do they truly depend, furthermore, on whether the ECtHR is staffed by judges, "many of whom are not even legally qualified—they are not actually real judges; they are pseudo-judges—who are political appointees from the member states"? Contrary to what Registrar Fribergh's ponderous refutation and former ECJ Judge Sir David Edward's jeering remarks would suggest, these silly claims demonstrate not so much that their purveyors are mistaken or ignorant, but that their factual errors—as factual errors—are fundamentally beside the point.

Two conclusions follow. First, the factual corrections helpfully (i.e., condescendingly) offered up by the pro-European supporters not only fail to address the challenge put forward by European critiques of the tabloid type, but may also fail to grasp its basic nature. Second, and as a result, the procedural and institutional reforms that have been correspondingly introduced to the European judicial appointments processes are unlikely to hit their mark. Even worse, they may well aggravate matters.

The key to grasping the likely futility of the reforms as a means to significantly boost ECJ and ECtHR legitimacy is to take advantage of Weiler's insights regarding the European Community's democratic deficit. On this reading, the core of the legitimacy challenges of the high European Courts does not really lie in those Courts' composition; in their particular modes of judicial selection, appointment, or election; or in the status, experience, or linguistic capacities of their judges. It lies above all in the simple fact that they are European and, of course, in this European-ness being understood to threaten legitimate (read: national) authority, culture, and customs, i.e., the supposed seats of true political and social community.

The ongoing criticisms of the European judiciary accordingly represent the contemporary version of those long leveled against "Brussels." As the Brexit debates and negotiations make all too clear, few indeed are well informed regarding the basics of European governance, never mind the finer points regarding the difference between the jurisdictions, mandates, compositions, judicial terms, and appointments processes of the ECJ and the ECtHR. All that really matters, as in the democratic deficit context that Weiler so penetratingly analyzed, is the vague and familiar sense of alienation and disempowerment that comes from some European institution (it matters not which) "imposing" some kind of judgment or rule on a poor defenseless Member State.

The same basic set of mentalities remains as dishearteningly fresh today as it was when Weiler wrote in the early 1990s. The current tabloid critiques and their political counterparts are thus not truly directed at the European Courts *as courts*. Nor are the "pseudo-judge" critiques truly directed at European judges *as judges*. The critiques are not a matter of political or legal theory; nor are they about legal professionalism. They are about Europe and the threat it represents to domestic authority, culture, and customs, i.e., to what continues to be experienced as rooted political community. To get lost in specific claims regarding this or that European institution is at best to miss the forest for the trees.

Once we understand this, we can see that focusing on judicial appointments allows well-meaning and professionally knowledgeable European supporters to adopt a comfortably condescending approach that in no way challenges their own deep commitments. It allows them to engage in such empty endeavors as defending the EU against charges of overweening institutional behavior by doing little more than debunking the critiques' factual errors. Regardless of how justified these corrections may indeed be on the facts, there is no reason to believe that they will be any more effective at quelling the overwrought legitimacy challenges of today than such corrections have been in the past: no one could reasonably argue, for example, that the persistent critiques of the Commission were ever effectively rebutted by debunking the tenacious myths that "Brussels" was dead-set on banning curved cucumbers, standardizing coffin and condom dimensions, and the like.[50] Why would today's ponderous explanations regarding the qualifications of ECJ and ECtHR judges do any better than yesterday's approach to the cucumber scandals?

In short, today's judicial reforms have little chance of addressing the type of deep-seated angst that the tabloid critiques represent. They offer instead a poker-faced evasion that shifts the debate into a register that is comfortably recognizable to high-grade functionaries of the European institutions and their associated academic commentators. Once displaced to that register, the debates can focus on professional qualifications, linguistic proficiency, institutional and procedural reform, and the like: worthy subjects of reform to be sure, but ones highly unlikely to have a meaningful effect on nationalist anxieties of an altogether different sort. These are instead the debates of professionals, by professionals, for professionals.

Indeed, today's (comparatively minor and obscure) judicial appointment reforms would appear significantly less likely to respond effectively to these legitimacy critiques than were the (comparatively important and visible) democratic deficit reforms of yesteryear. And this is not encouraging, given that the structural reforms instituted to alleviate the Community's democratic deficit (i.e., the empowerment of the European Parliament coupled with the fall of the Luxembourg veto) appear to have done little indeed to enlist or construct popular attachment to Europe as a representative political entity. To put it bluntly: does anyone really believe that anti-ECJ or anti-ECtHR sentiment will be resolved when the public is assured that all European judges now have sufficient experience working "in an

[50] The European Commission still maintains an online index of such "Euromyths." *See* http://blogs.ec.europa.eu/ECintheUK/euromyths-a-z-index.

international environment," never mind that they possess sufficiently eminent academic standing and speak sufficiently good French?[51]

Indeed, there is good reason to worry that the judicial appointments reforms might not only fail to improve, but may actually aggravate, the European Courts' shortage of social legitimacy. To grasp the danger, we need only recognize that the ongoing judicial appointment reforms are not really pitched toward addressing the "social legitimacy" gap on which capitalizes the populist British tabloid press. They are, instead, primarily directed toward relatively narrow professional audiences: they address national high court judges and administrative officials who might chafe under European judicial pronouncements, academic observers who might comment on them, and so on. As ECtHR President Costa declared in 2010 when proposing the creation of the APE:

> The quality of the [ECtHR] Judges is ... essential because, in a subsidiary system where human rights protection falls primarily to the national courts, the European Court as the ultimate arbiter of human rights issues must be composed of persons of sufficient standing and authority to command the respect of national judges, including senior national judges. If this is not the case, the Court itself will suffer from a deficit of authority and the system will lose credibility and effectiveness.[52]

The judicial appointments, independence and quality reforms are above all directed toward knowledgeable institutional actors, because they are precisely the ones most likely to care about the professional status and capacities of the European judges.

The problem is twofold. The first, as we have already seen, is that such professionally oriented measures are unlikely to do much to boost the social legitimacy of the European Courts within the general public. But the flip side of that coin is arguably worse: what if the reform measures nonetheless succeeded in shoring up the "authority" of the European Courts before their primary audience, i.e., the national high courts? Such an outcome, far from improving European social legitimacy, might actually damage it further.

Weiler grasped the problem in the context of European democratic deficit. Empowering the European Parliament and ditching the Luxembourg veto would liberate the EU to act more assertively in the name of the European general interest. This supposed improvement actually represented a threat. The whole point of the democratic deficit critiques, he maintained, was that they revealed the extent to

[51] For the criteria established by the EU's 255 Panel, *see* Article 255 Panel, Activity Report of the Panel provided for by Article 255 of the Treaty on the Functioning of the European Union, First Report of February 17, 2011 (No. 6509/11) at 8–11.

[52] Costa letter. *See also* Kosař (2015).

which the European general public continued to experience political community in national—rather than European—terms. To empower Europe to act more decisively was therefore to further threaten traditional sites of democratic belonging, far more than to legitimate new ones. This would aggravate, rather than remedy, the EU's social legitimacy problems.

The same probably holds true today in the judicial context. Even if European judicial appointments reform (understood widely to include issues of judicial independence, judicial quality, judicial councils, etc.) really did increase the authority of the ECJ and ECtHR, and domestic courts accordingly followed European judicial pronouncements even more enthusiastically than they already do, it is far from obvious that this would generate an overall increase in European judicial legitimacy. That is, there is no particular reason to assume that a localized increase in the formal legitimacy of the European Courts within domestic professional circles would translate into an overall increase in their social legitimacy before the general public (and especially before those elements of the general public who distrust all things European in the first place). After all, why would greater deference by the UK Supreme Court to ECJ and ECtHR judgments placate, rather than aggravate, the ire of Theresa May or Boris Johnson, never mind of Philip Davies or the *Daily Mail*? Indeed, to draw the parallel to Weiler's analysis, is there any reason to believe that the general public distinguishes between the legislative or judicial sources of European regulatory power? The answer to such questions, sadly enough, is probably not.

2. Option 2: The critiques really *are* about the European Courts ...

The analysis we have just completed suggests that the legitimacy challenges facing the ECJ and ECtHR have had little to do with those Courts as courts, or with their judges as judges. They are instead about Europe *tout court* and about the threat that Europe represents to domestic authority, culture, and customs, i.e., to what continues to be experienced as rooted political community. On this view, there is nothing specifically *judicial* about the critiques; the populist claims about a supposed lack of European judicial qualifications or independence are merely pretextual: the real legitimacy challenge to the ECJ and the ECtHR is quite simply that these Courts are clearly not national and therefore that they threaten what legitimately is.

I believe such an analysis to be fundamentally correct. To take the populist critiques at their word and to address their factual claims on the merits is thus to go willingly down a rabbit hole that offers no productive exit or reward. Predictably, however, that rabbit hole may well appeal to knowledgeable professionals: after all, it not only offers the possibility to engage in a familiar set of technical debates (about how to foster judicial independence, how to reform institutional and procedural design, etc.), but also offers a productive field for engaging in assorted professional projects and broader institutional politics. But aside from catering to such professional and institutional proclivities, to invest straightforwardly in debunking those pretextual critiques is really to miss their point. And to respond to them by promoting the professional competence of the sitting European bench is likely as futile as it would have been to answer the anti-Brussels tirades of yore by touting the professional competence of high-ranking DG staff. Today's critiques are no more about the courts than the cucumber critiques were about cucumbers.

That said, I also believe that this conclusion can be somewhat misleading in its own right. Or, to be more precise, it is sufficiently incomplete as to mask certain important insights about the significance of the current judicial debates. The key at this point in our analysis is simply to recognize that the populist critiques, for all of their nominal attention to judicial quality and independence, are effectively treating the European high Courts as if they were functionally interchangeable with any other intrusive European administrative and legislative institution, i.e., as if they were major policy players. But here is the catch: in both the Continental Civilian and the British Common Law traditions, this is no small matter.

For years, academic specialists in European law and politics have emphasized the central role played by the ECJ in the construction of Europe. For the most part, the canonical references on such matters, such as Weiler, Karen Alter, Alec Stone Sweet, and the like, have done so in a generally laudatory manner, although some exceptions, such as Hjalte Rasmussen, could be heard from time to time.[53] What matters for our purposes is not so much the positive or negative valence of such analyses, but rather their need to drive the point home (often in a political science environment and/or in a Civilian context) that the ECJ was indeed a major—and, at times, perhaps *the* major—institutional protagonist in European constitutional developments. The current state of the debates makes abundantly clear that everyone—not just high-grade European legal and political theorists, but European institutional actors and even populist politicians and the tabloid press—has come to understand that the high European Courts are indeed major political players in the construction and operation of Europe and that they therefore need to be treated as such.

In other words, it is true that the current fights over the Court for the most part represent but a variation on the old critiques of the Commission and are thus not really about the Court *qua* court. But the mere fact that the ECJ would now be considered comparable to the Commission is in itself a significant development: it suggests that the Court is in fact increasingly understood as a front-line policy-making institution, regardless of whether that understanding jives with traditional conceptions of the judicial role. As a result, the critiques *are* about the Court, but *qua* political institution; and this really is an important development concerning the nature of the Court *qua* court.

[53] *See* Weiler (1991); Alter (2003); ALEC STONE SWEET, GOVERNING WITH JUDGES: CONSTITUTIONAL POLITICS IN EUROPE (2000). *But see* Rasmussen (1986).

The difficulty provoked by this new perspective on the European Courts, of course, is that if we are really to think of them as important policy-making or political institutions, then classic issues of representation—and thus of political communities—come clearly to the fore. This is not an altogether novel problem. After all, both the ECJ and the ECtHR are comprised of exactly as many judges as Member States; and this rule of one judge per country obviously expresses a distinctly representational logic, however implicit and inchoate it may be.[54]

The reason I bothered to recount the pre-history of the ECJ in Chapter 2 was precisely to stress this utterly crucial point: even before the ECJ was established, indeed *before the ECJ was even conceptualized as a court*, it was envisaged as an institutional mechanism to protect national interests by counterbalancing the centralizing supranational essence of the High Authority (later, the Commission). The discussions over the creation of the Court are what actually generated the creation of the Council; one might almost—*almost*—say, therefore, that the Court was the Council before the Council was. This pre-history demonstrates quite clearly the flexibility and sophistication of the early designers of the Community system. For them, particular institutional forms were decidedly malleable and thus potentially interchangeable: interests could be protected by a political institution (the Council of Ministers) or by a quasi-judicial one (the ECJ) or both. In some sense, then, the current debates are but the delayed working out of the implications of this early insight.

It is not, however, as if the intervening sixty years have elapsed without considering anew the central issue of the representative nature of the European high Courts. On the institutional level, the extended fights over the expansion of the General Court are clear evidence that judicial representation issues have been alive and well: the Member States ardently opposed increasing the size of its membership in some manner that did not guarantee that each Member State would choose the same number of judges, and they were so persistent in their resistance that the only acceptable solution was to agree to double the size of the Court altogether.[55]

But the idea of judicial representation has also received more academic treatment. For this, it is useful to return once again to Joseph Weiler, whose 2001 chapter, "Epilogue: The Judicial Après Nice," squarely addressed the need to incorporate national judicial perspectives and to respect national judicial sensibilities in the European judicial decision-making process. Thus, for example, Weiler argued that the ECJ should fundamentally change the style in which it composes its judicial decisions:

[54] Antoine Vauchez cites to Maurice Lagrange for "the principle of equality between countries (one judge per country)." *See* ANTOINE VAUCHEZ, BROKERING EUROPE: EURO-LAWYERS AND THE MAKING OF A TRANSNATIONAL POLITY 47 (2015), *quoting* Maurice Lagrange, *La CJCE du Plan Schuman à l'Union européenne, in* MÉLANGES FERNAND DEHOUSSE 127, 129 (1979).

[55] *See supra* Chapter 12(I).

> [A]s regards the style of judgments, I think the Court should abandon the cryptic, Cartesian style which still characterizes many of its decisions and move to the more discursive, analytic and conversational style associated more with the common law world—though practiced by others as well, notably the German Constitutional court. As noted above, especially in its Constitutional jurisprudence, it is crucial that the Court display in its judgments that national sensibilities were fully considered and taken into account. And it must amply explain and reason its decisions if they are to be not only authoritarian but also authoritative. The Cartesian style with its pretense of logical legal reasoning and inevitability of results is not conducive to a good conversation with national courts. In the same vein I would argue for the introduction of separate and dissenting opinions. One of the virtues of separate and dissenting opinions is that they force the majority opinion to be reasoned in an altogether more profound and communicative fashion. The dissent often produces the paradoxical effect of legitimating the majority because it becomes evident that alternative views were considered even if ultimately rejected.[56]

As this passage demonstrates, Weiler's analysis and proposal are perched precariously between two tendencies. On the one hand, Weiler sees clearly that the Court must manage national—not to say nationalist—"sensitivities." Thus, it should adopt a "more discursive, analytic and conversational style" because "it is crucial that the Court display in its judgments that national sensibilities were fully considered and taken into account."[57] Even at that relatively early date (2001–02), Weiler saw clearly that the legitimacy problem before the Court was fundamentally a matter of social, legal, and political identity.

On the other hand, the passage put forward a solution that now appears almost charmingly naïve. Weiler suggested that longer and more overtly reasoned judgments (combined with separate and dissenting opinions) might produce "a good conversation with national courts" that would demonstrate a receptivity to "national sensibilities," which would ultimately boost the legitimacy of the Court's decisions. Unfortunately, this quasi-deliberative approach, however appealing it may be on intellectual grounds, has proven patently insufficient for generating European judicial legitimacy in practice. After all, the ECtHR deploys exactly this kind of judicial decision-writing style, with "more discursive, analytic and conversational" judgments, "separate and dissenting opinions," and the like. But would anyone reasonably suggest that the national courts hold the legitimacy of its decisions in higher regard than that of the ECJ? The answer is a resounding no.

[56] Joseph Weiler, *Epilogue: The Judicial Après-Nice*, *in* The European Court of Justice 215, 225 (Gráinne de Búrca & J.H.H. Weiler eds., 2002) (citations omitted) ["Weiler (2002)"].

[57] *Id.*

There are of course many reasons for the relative status of the Luxembourg and Strasbourg Courts, including such complex issues as substantive jurisdiction, geographic diversity, professional profiles, and more, all of which complicate any assessment of the causes and effects of judicial legitimacy at the European level. But one thing is for certain: as the ECtHR example clearly demonstrates, the form of European judicial decisions is by no means sufficient, in and of itself, to generate the kind of legitimacy that Weiler envisions.

Weiler understood this. He therefore took his proposal significantly further. Sensitive as he was to national judicial sensibilities, he proposed that in sufficiently delicate cases (such as preliminary references originating from national supreme courts), the sitting ECJ panel should include a judge from the court making the reference. He wrote:

> I would also suggest that when a reference were made from the highest courts of the Member States to the Court of Justice, to underscore the importance of the matter and the national interest in the case and to ensure the fullest possible consideration of all national sensibilities, the deciding Panel should always include one judge of the national Court making the reference, though not from the actual group of judges deciding the case—in other words a national ad-hoc judge from the highest court of the Member State in those cases where the highest court makes a reference or appeal to the European High Court. One should not gasp. The notion of ad-hoc judges is not novel and faced with an ever more complicated relationship between the ECJ and national jurisdictions some such provisions merit consideration.[58]

Weiler thus fully grasped the need to bridge the national–supranational divide; and he therefore proposed a particularly direct, if seemingly drastic, mechanism for doing so: physically incorporating a member of the national supreme court within the body of the European Court.

Weiler's impulse may at first appear extreme; but the logic is excellent. And the key to this logic is representation. Given the patently major consequences of European high Court judgments—judgments that are of such magnitude that they can only be considered to be of constitutional, never mind routinely political, import—the deciding Court needs to be in some way representative of the affected political community. Hence Weiler's bold suggestion that a member of the national supreme court making the reference be sent on an ad hoc basis to Luxembourg to sit on the ECJ panel deciding the case.

And yet, for all of the professed radicalism of this proposal, it remains far too timid. The first clue should—like the suggestion that the ECJ adopt a more

[58] *Id.* at 224.

discursive style of judgment with the possibility of separate judicial decisions—be rather obvious: ECtHR procedure already demands that the deciding panel include the ECtHR judge of the country whose behavior is being challenged at bar. And once again, would anyone suggest that this—any more than discursive judgments and separate judicial opinions—has raised the legitimacy of the ECtHR and its decisions above the levels attained by the ECJ and its impersonally Cartesian judgments? To pose the question is to answer it.

One might nonetheless offer an important rejoinder: Weiler's suggestion proposes not simply to guarantee—as in Strasbourg—that a British or Czech judge sit in any British or Czech case, but that this judge be a member of the British or Czech supreme court that actually referred the case. This represents a meaningful distinction; but it raises potential problems. At a first level, it clearly raises judicial independence issues. Can one really assume that a particular national supreme court judge (for argument's sake, from Italy), sent to Luxembourg specifically to help rule in a case originating from his or her home institution (e.g., the Italian Corte di Cassazione in Rome), would both be and appear to be sufficiently independent to play an important role in a case that may effectively involve second-guessing a prior ruling of the Corte di Cassazione or a regulatory judgment made by the Italian legislative or executive branches of government?[59]

Imagine, to pick an emblematic example, if the *Francovich* case had been referred by a panel of Corte di Cassazione rather than by the lower Italian courts.[60] One could not but feel sympathy for the particular Cassazione magistrate who would have been assigned to board the plane to Luxembourg where s/he would have had to take part in the momentous decision about whether to expose national governments (and in this case, the Italian State) to potentially colossal liability for political failures to implement European law properly.

In such circumstances, would this lone Italian judge, sent fleetingly to Luxembourg (certainly to the knowledge of all) as the representative of his/her national supreme court, really be and appear to be an independent judge? The answer is not altogether obvious. In addition to hinging on the particular judge and case in question, it probably also depends on what type of representation that judge is expected to perform. As we suggested in the last chapter, such judicial representation might range from a more benign explanatory role (i.e. offering the European judicial colleagues knowledge of, and insight into, the actual operation of the national system) to a more vigorous ambassadorial role (i.e., actively promoting the perspective and interests of the home system).[61] Needless to say,

[59] Knowledgeable observers will also recognize that Cassazione could make plain its preferred ECJ ruling even without having issued a prior ruling: well-crafted questions in a preliminary reference can convey the inclinations of the referring court quite clearly. And this is to say nothing of Weiler's suggestion that national courts making such references should explicitly state how they propose the reference should be answered. *See id.*

[60] *See* Francovich v. Italy, Joined Cases C-6/90 & C-9/90, [1991] E.C.R. I-5357.

[61] *See supra* Chapter 12(II)(A).

the more the model moves toward the latter (ambassadorial) conception of representation, the less the judge and the court appear to be engaging in independent judicial decision-making on the basis of law: this is, after all, the gist of the Philip Davies critique that the ECtHR is composed of "pseudo-judges—who are political appointees from the member states who have been sent to make political decisions, not legal decisions."[62] And yet, sending a national supreme court judge fleetingly to Luxembourg to sit on a particular national case would appear likely to point the judge in precisely that direction: the national system is not only where she spends her daily professional life, it is also where her professional future is likely to lie. The last thing that national judge would need for career purposes would be to be forever known as the Italian judge who went off to Luxembourg and sat with the ECJ in the *Francovich* case, especially if she did not succeed in profoundly influencing the result ...

In short, the tension between representation and independence should be relatively evident. Of course, it not particularly clear how this tension might play out in particular circumstances. We can, for example, easily imagine scenarios in which the national judge's conceptual, deontological, and institutional commitments might drive her to adopt a stance that operates to the ostensible detriment of the national system, especially if that system is internally divided (as it often is). It is not unusual, for example, for the interests of the judicial branch to be at odds with the revealed preferences of the national government. But even in such specific scenarios, the national judge could hardly be described as especially "independent."

Even if we leave such independence questions to the side, furthermore, the representational issues raise practical and theoretical difficulties all by themselves. The first has to do with Weiler's assumption that seconding a national supreme court judge would boost the legitimacy of the ECJ and its judgments. But why would this be so? Given that the ECJ and the ECtHR already possess a judge chosen from each Member State, and that the ECtHR already guarantees that this national judge must sit in every case brought against that State, what would the further judicial enhancement add to the equation? Would that alone really be sufficient to generate a comforting sense of belonging, or at least of representation and respect? One possible answer is that the presence of the seconded supreme court judge might affect the content of the European judgment in the case at bar. Perhaps, for example, *Francovich* would have been decided differently had a Cassazione judge sat with the ECJ. But as suggested above, it is hard to believe that the effect of adding such a judge would have been all that dramatic. For starters, the *Francovich* Court already possessed an influential Italian Judge, G. Frederico Mancini, who, although originally a law professor at the University of Bologna, was sufficiently well placed within Italian legal, judicial, and governmental circles to have sat on the Italian

[62] *See supra* text accompanying note 978.

High Council of the Judiciary prior to his appointment to Luxembourg.[63] And as if this specific example were not enough, one need only recognize that fully a third of current member of the ECJ have served on national high courts (constitutional courts, supreme courts, etc.), not to mention all of those (like Mancini) who have served as high ranking officers in national ministries, and so on. The ECJ does not therefore possess much in the way of gaps in expertise or experience that an ad hoc domestic judge might somehow fill.

Another possible answer might be that there is something representationally special about a national supreme court judge. But this too seems unlikely. After all, Member States are always more or less free to select and propose supreme court judges for European judicial office. Indeed, they very often do. This being so, why would seconded supreme court judges be any more representative or legitimacy-enhancing than the supreme court judges already selected by the national judicial selection procedures to sit Luxembourg?

Yet another potential answer might be that the seconded judge would be more intimately familiar with the stakes of the litigation for the domestic legal, political, or constitutional orders than former supreme court judges. But this is not terribly convincing either: how difficult would it really be, to return to our *Francovich* example, for a former Corte di Cassazione judge (or, for that matter, a British Law Lord) sitting in Luxembourg to divine the consequences in play? Surely a jurist qualified to sit on the Corte di Cassazione or the British Supreme Court in the first place, and especially one specifically selected from there to sit on the ECJ, would be fully capable of recognizing the significance of the case at bar.

The next possible answer, however, points in a somewhat different direction. The issue may not be a matter of technical proficiency at all, or even a matter of systemic and prudential awareness, but simply a matter of institutional identity and allegiance, and if one pushes the analysis a little further, of national identity and allegiance. The value added in Weiler's proposal might be that the seconded judge would be *currently* serving on the national supreme court, not that s/he might once have done so. What this would mean, as a practical matter, is that the sitting ECJ panel would have to address—directly and in person—a sitting member of the national high court that had referred the matter to Luxembourg. This interpersonal negotiation would offer the guarantee that the institutional perspective of the national supreme court would truly be given due consideration by the European Court.

This potential upside, for all its potential virtues, is also quite telling. On a first level, it demonstrates the full extent to which Weiler's proposal is ultimately rather modest. The proposal offers the prospect of what is really an inter-institutional exchange: the ad hoc national supreme court judge is not so much a *national*

[63] See https://curia.europa.eu/jcms/jcms/Jo2_7014/en/.

representative (one judge from each country already sits on each of the European Courts) as the *supreme court's* representative. The proposal, in other words, is primarily directed at fostering judicial—as opposed to national—comity and good will. It is above all about *institutional* identity, legitimacy, and allegiance, not about national identity, legitimacy, and allegiance.

There is no small irony that even Joseph Weiler, the great "big picture" thinker of Europe and its discontents, would present as radical ("One should not gasp . . .") a solution pitched at such a modestly inter-institutional level. This is not to suggest that an institutionally directed proposal could not generate meaningful systemic effects. But as the Weiler of "The Transformation of Europe" would have insisted, merely generating desirable institutional consequences has little to do with generating a corresponding—and far more important—increase in fundamental social legitimacy.

Indeed, the inadequacy of the seemingly daring *Après-Nice* solution as a means to boost the social legitimacy of the European Courts should be relatively obvious. Does anyone really believe that members of the general public, never mind populist politicians or the tabloid press, are sufficiently aware of the composition of specific ECJ or ECtHR panels to feel meaningfully comforted by the addition of an ad hoc judge seconded from the national supreme court? Members of the domestic supreme court might feel a little better about the ensuing European judgment. But members of the domestic general public? This seems doubtful.

One could, of course, stress the importance that the seconded judge really be a sitting *national judge*, not merely a *national* who sits as a *judge* at the ECJ or ECtHR. All the upside would reside, therefore, in precisely the fact that the supreme court judge would have to get on the plane to travel to Luxembourg, rather than live there. But such a perspective only further underlines just how much the European judicial legitimacy issue is ultimately a function of straightforward national and European identity issues: it suggests that the supreme court judge would be duly invested in the national side of the judicial interaction, rather than be compromised through exposure to, and socialization by, the European institutions.

This perspective is rather compelling. But it does raise two fundamental issues. First, if the virtue of the seconded judge is precisely that s/he is a good representative of the national legal order, then this clearly reopens the question of judicial independence: would such a judge not effectively be an ambassador of—not to say a spokesperson or advocate for—the Member State? And second, and maybe even more practically important: is there really any reason to believe that the general public would suddenly feel a new level of comfort with, never mind connection to, the European Court as a result of adding such a national representative, *even if she were expected to play a zealously ambassadorial/representative role*? After all, the Council of the European Union—Europe's dominant legislative organ—is the very definition of an intergovernmentalist institution, composed as it is of ministerial level representatives of the Member States. But the mere fact that each country sends its own cabinet ministers from its capital to Brussels to represent its interests in Council has hardly stood in the way of the Council being experienced as a menacing European institution whose acts threaten the sovereignty and integrity of the Member States. Indeed, this was Weiler's point when, in "The Transformation of Europe," he defended the rationale behind the Luxembourg Accord. For all that the Council was in fact an assemblage of national ministers—i.e., the very definition of national political representatives—its actions were nonetheless experienced as "European"; and because social legitimacy still resided in the national communities, the Luxembourg veto offered an immensely valuable—if transactionally expensive—emotional security blanket: at least, in the very last instance, a country could say "no!" to any Council measure sufficiently threatening to domestic interests to provoke its veto.

In short, given that the general public failed to feel connected to a European political institution composed entirely of highly visible national ministers, why would it suddenly feel connected to a European Court that would include a faceless seconded national judge? And as Weiler suggested in the democracy deficit context, if the proposal for ad hoc judges did successfully boost the credibility and legitimacy of the ECJ and its rulings *among national supreme courts*, might this not aggravate, rather than improve, the Court's social legitimacy problems? It might increase the reach and authority of European judicial power into the domestic sphere and thereby diminish an important source of domestic control on that power: national judicial resistance. Given the enduring lack of European social legitimacy, this 1-2 punch—however practically effective and theoretically justified it may be—would likely be experienced in certain quarters as threatening the proper source of social legitimacy: national community. Once again, what is truly at stake is political, social, and cultural identity, not institutional and procedural design.

Perhaps the best way to visualize the ongoing dominance of the representational and identity-based features of the European legitimacy problem is to engage in a simple thought experiment. What if the Chief Justice of each Member State's most prominent court (the supreme or constitutional court, as the case may be) were empowered to sit *ex officio* in Luxembourg (or, for that matter, in Strasbourg)? Would that solve the European judicial legitimacy problem?

In some sense, yes. Gone, one would hope, would be most of the carping about judicial quality, experience, and so on. But even there, one should not expect too much. Given the persistence of national chauvinism, it would be naïve to think that Eurosceptics—and especially those from long-standing European Member States—would not continue to express suspicion, if not disdain, for jurists hailing primarily from recently acceded States from the East. To expect the *Daily Mail* and Tory MP Philip Davies suddenly to drop their critiques of the ECtHR because it would now include the Chairman of the Bulgarian Supreme Court of Cassation (or the Chairman of the Bulgarian Constitutional Court) would surely be unrealistic. But that is only part of the problem.

Probably more important—though deeply related—is the perpetually vexing issue of identity and belonging. In her September 2017 speech at the "Thinking Europe Forward" Conference, Federica Mogherini (the former Italian Minister of Foreign Affairs who now serves as the EU's Foreign Minister[64]) raised the issue in a succinct manner:

> But, indeed, when you see capitals saying Brussels decided it, it is not a building in Brussels that decides. It is Heads of State and Government, parliamentarians, citizens with their votes taking decisions together. Brussels is the capital of the European Union, but is not someone from Mars taking decisions—it is us coming together.[65]

If, as Mogherini correctly suggests, national foreign ministers, labor ministers, transport ministers, and environmental ministers meeting in Brussels as the Council continue to be transmogrified into a threateningly "Martian"/ "European" institution, then why would domestic judges not suffer the same fate? At least governmental ministers are relatively recognizable figures; yet even they are experienced as extraterrestrial European overlords. Would this not be all the more true of relatively anonymous judges who, especially in Civilian jurisdictions, are extremely rarely known to begin with?

Indeed, even knowledgeable governmental actors take the all too predictable tack of blaming the European institutions when they are confronted with communal European decisions that run counter to their domestic preferences. The judicial appointments developments we have been studying are no exception to this routine feature of European political life. How long did it take, for example, for assorted Member States governments of the Council of Europe—including France—to start throwing temper tantrums when the APE opposed their problematic judicial candidates? No time at all. And one would have a very difficult time gathering a more eminent group of national high court judges than the members of the APE and 255 Panel. This being the case, why would one expect that either the general public or interested governmental actors would suddenly think of an ECJ or ECtHR comprised entirely of national supreme court chief justices as "their" judges on "their" courts, rather than as "European" judges on "European" courts? Regrettably, the answer is probably the same as it was for the European institutions in the democratic deficit context of the 1990s: they likely would not.

This thought experiment demonstrates that the underlying legitimacy issue is not really about courts *qua* courts. It is about the courts *qua* political actors, subject to the same basic representation and power issues as those that characterize other

[64] Formally the "High Representative of the Union for Foreign Affairs and Security Policy."

[65] https://eeas.europa.eu/headquarters/headQuarters-homepage/33162/federica-mogherinis-speech-conference-thinking-europe-forward-occasion-25th-anniversary-treaty_ka.

political/policy players. This does of course represent—and it is worth stressing this once again—a rather momentous shift in how Europeans Civilians and British Common Lawyers have historically thought about courts. But this insight points nonetheless toward the importance of entertaining more explicitly socio-political means to increase the broad-based legitimacy of the European Courts, rather than remaining confined to the narrowly institutional, procedural, and professional mechanisms that have long dominated the European judicial appointments and judicial independence debates. Without some sort of deeper socio-political connection for the European Courts, the intensification of European judicial effectiveness on the domestic level is likely, to use Weiler's terms, to be experienced as more "authoritarian" than "authoritative."[66]

The European judicial bodies and their institutional supporters (such as the Steering Committee for Human Rights of the Council of Europe's Committee of Ministers) have done little if anything to address such fundamental European legitimacy problems directly. In that sense, all of their judicial appointments, judicial independence, judicial quality, and judicial council reforms are largely beside the point, except insofar as they tinker around the edges of intra- and inter-judicial relations (which, it is true, is not altogether unimportant, insofar as it goes).

In another sense, however, these interminable reform efforts do in fact address such classic political legitimacy issues; but they do so by working studiously to displace them. That is, the institutional response to the European judicial legitimacy challenges has been to try to routinize the ECJ and ECtHR by recasting them as ordinary (i.e., non-international and non-constitutional) courts, to present them as largely legal/technical in nature, and accordingly to call for a standard, professionalized judicial appointments process, complete with an operative judicial council checking up on the quality and professional profiles of the European judicial candidates.

The European judicial and institutional response thus seeks to answer the legitimacy challenge by shifting the ground altogether to seemingly apolitical and non-representative bases. Such a professionalizing response, forcefully and for the most part successfully put forward precisely by those most closely invested in such professionalism (the judges themselves, high-grade Committee of Ministers specialists, notable (and potentially judicial) academics, and so on), is an understandable and arguably plausible—though also a highly predictable and self-serving—exercise.

The problem, however, is that that such a professionalizing "judicializing" response is also rather myopic, even if taken more or less on its own terms. Above all, it mistakes form for substance. It behaves as if copying a few basic features of a domestic legal order—such as a judicial council applying minimum norms of

[66] Weiler (2002) at 225.

judicial quality and independence—could suffice to construct judicial legitimacy on the European level. As should be obvious to all, however, the mere reproduction on the European level of assorted elements French judicial procedure (including Advocates General and Reporting Judges) and of French judicial decision-writing (terse, collegial, and univocal judgments and longer, signed, Advocate General Opinions, for example) have not performed the legitimation trick. So why would the mere technical professionalism of the judiciary or the mere existence of a judicial council or vetting panel do much better? These features are but the manifestations and symbols of something much larger: the lush claims to legitimate representation offered by something as historically, institutionally, and ideologically ingrained as national judicial systems.

For all that one can—indeed, for all that one must—contest such uncritical and self-congratulatory national claims to representation, there is no denying their power. True, socio-political developments at both the domestic and the supranational levels increasingly pose challenges to these national claims. But it would be foolish to imagine that one might effectively reproduce, never mind bypass, their remaining social legitimacy by mimicking at the European level a few of the procedural and institutional features that characterize some of the national judicial orders. Without deeper ideological, institutional, and cultural structures, there simply is not much of a there there.

Writing some fifteen years ago about the French judicial system, and trying to do so in as empathetic a manner as possible, I nonetheless stressed the increasingly evident mismatch between the Republic's ideology of a unitary French people or general interest and the reality of French social, economic, cultural, and political diversity. Increasing consciousness of that diversity, I argued, necessarily undercut the standing of institutions whose legitimacy hinged on the supposedly unitary character of the French people and on the meritocratic and republican nature of the French State.[67] The "*gilets jaunes*" protests of 2018–2019 put this legitimacy crisis on full public display. And for political and institutional insiders, the actions of the French State may demonstrate it even more profoundly; President Emmanuel Macron reportedly plans the unthinkable: to close the École national d'administration (ENA) itself.

Although such legitimacy challenges therefore continue to deepen alarmingly (if appropriately) in France, they pale in comparison to those that characterize Europe. As a result, any European attempt to bootstrap social legitimacy by merely taking on some of the traditional professional and institutional trappings of domestic judicial orders can only be a fool's errand. This is not to say that that the institution of such measures cannot produce some benefits for the European Courts: given their massive caseloads, their complex and important remits, and

[67] Mitchel Lasser, Judicial Deliberations: A Comparative Analysis of Judicial Transparency and Legitimacy 333–37 (2004).

their delicate inter-institutional interactions, any improvement in the professional standing and capacities of their judges cannot help but be welcome. Any such improvement can only help to ensure, if only in their interactions with domestic judicial interlocutors, that these European judges will be taken a little more seriously as competent and sensitive judicial colleges.

But such professional inter- and intra-judicial adjustments—including even the more "daring" proposals once put forward by Weiler—merely fiddle around the edges of the large-scale legitimacy issues surrounding the European Courts. Taken at face value, such reforms are but intra-professional modifications whose broader impact can only be limited. Worse: if these reforms are meant to address far-reaching legitimacy issues confronting the flagship European Courts, they divert attention from the fundamental representational dilemmas that continue to hound all European political institutions, a category that now appears by all indications to include the ECJ and the ECtHR.

As this book has shown, it is no accident that the European judicial appointments reforms (including the associated reforms regarding judicial independence, judicial quality, judicial councils, and so on) emerged precisely in the 1990s. The fall of the Berlin Wall and the rapidly ensuing mass accession of new Member States from the former Soviet Bloc posed existential challenges to nascent European identity. Yet the European juridical response was limited to overtly professional, procedural, and institutional measures. Resolutely committed to this specialists' approach, high-grade European judges, academics, and institutional jurists have played that professional card for all it is worth, leveraging it against recalcitrant governments, judicial and professional inferiors, and European political institutions alike.

The problem is that the ideological edifice on which this response is built consists of a technocratic professional model whose credibility barely holds water anymore, even with the general European public. While everyone can surely agree that judicial incompetence is to be avoided, no amount of judicial quality assurance appears sufficient—on its own—to legitimate the European judicial exercise of large-scale and broad-ranging policy-making power. As such disparate figures as Joseph Weiler and Hjalte Rasmussen were already maintaining some thirty years ago, the political and constitutional power wielded by the European Courts is patently enormous.[68] Today, even the leaders of the European judiciary do not hesitate to confirm this reality, and to do so overtly. In 2017, for example, John Murray, the retired Chief Justice of Ireland and former judge of the ECJ then serving as the President of the APE, published the following in his "Exchange of Views" with the Council of Europe:

68 *See* Rasmussen (1986); Weiler (1991).

> It is important that [ECtHR judges] have experience of such high level because, as I have said before, judges are called upon to interpret the Convention in a way that can impact on major social and political issues at national level. First there is the law and then there is its interpretation by judges, and then the interpretation is the law. That is the modern reality. The time of Montesquieu, the era when the judge was the so-called mouthpiece of the law, is long gone. So the calibre of judges refers to people who can make judgments on sensitive issues like the status of the embryo or whether you can trade in embryos for research purposes or the right to suicide and so on. A Court must be capable of dealing with these sensitive issues and where the boundary of Convention obligations and national sovereignty needs to be drawn.[69]

European Courts, in short, are major constitutional players, never mind major political and policy-making institutions (albeit of a distinctive type). Today, not even populist hate mongers and the tabloid press fail to grasp this basic reality.[70] Montesquieu is dead.

The ongoing European judicial debates and reforms nonetheless dodge the challenges that come with this new state of affairs. They seek refuge in a familiar model of judicial regulation that evokes the well-trod professional and institutional structures of domestic jurisdictions, but that generate little faith or adherence when severed from the traditional (if fraying) domestic bases of their ideological, sociological, political, and merely habitual allegiance. Jumping on the opportunity afforded by the large-scale accession of Eastern Bloc countries in the post-1989 era, high-grade European judges, academics, and institutional jurists have capitalized on the associated anxieties to wrest a good measure of autonomy and control from the domestic political actors who traditionally dominated them. Whether these political actors function at the national level (e.g., as national executive branch officers) or at the supranational level (e.g., as such European institutions as the PACE), they now operate in a far more constrained field of action: not only must they jump through the long series of procedural and institutional hoops that have been imposed on European judicial appointments, but they must also deal with the "scandalous" ideological framework that has emerged from, and gets policed by, the European judicial appointments debates.

But none of this professional and institutional jockeying, none of this procedural proliferation, and none of this conceptual reworking does much of anything to address the deep and underlying representational anxiety that now hovers around the European Courts. Surely Justice Murray is correct when he insists that only judges

[69] Steering Committee for Human Rights, Committee of Experts on the System of the European Convention on Human Rights (DH-SYSC), Exchange of Views with Mr. John Murray, President of the Advisory Panel of Experts on Candidates for Election to the European Court of Human Rights (March 1, 2017), DH-SYSC-I(2017)016, May 4, 2017.

[70] *See supra* Chapter 13II(B).

of sufficient "calibre" can hope to "deal[] with these sensitive [fundamental rights] issues and where the boundary of Convention obligations and national sovereignty needs to be drawn."[71] But by the same token, even if we could agree on exactly what such "calibre" of European judge actually consists, no amount of it would now suffice to put the general public, never mind self-interested national executive branch actors, or populist politicians, or the tabloid press at ease. While judicial competence, experience, and quality (however defined) surely matter a great deal, especially for the purposes of inter-judicial comity, they do not solve the representational puzzle. By any measure, Vassilios Skouris, Jean-Paul Costa, and Luzius Wildhaber (the retired presidents of the ECJ and ECtHR who oversaw the creation of the 255 Panel and the APE) were judges of singularly high "calibre." Does anyone really think that the British tabloid press, populist political parties, or even mainstream British pro-Leave supporters would be satisfied with European Courts composed entirely of their judicial clones, even if appointed or elected through pristine institutional procedures? To ask the question is to answer it.

[71] *See id.*

14
Conclusion: Disentangling Three Types of Judicial Legitimacy

This book has offered a thorough examination of the seemingly mundane topic of judicial appointments reform as a means to get a window onto the deep preoccupations of what might be termed "institutional Europe." It has presented, in essence, a quasi-ethnography from deep within the professional ranks of the European judiciary and its primary institutional and professional contacts. This detailed work has, I hope, given the reader privileged access to the dominant self-perceptions of these institutional actors and of their close professional interlocutors. The goal throughout has been to help us grasp and come to terms with this self-perception, which both creates and demonstrates these actors' imagined relation to the outside world. As we have seen, that self-perception has gone through dramatic changes that reflect a major reworking of the European judiciary's place in the separation of powers.

As the book has shown, this professional, institutional, political, ideological, and ultimately constitutional transformation of the judiciary's role definition did not occur overnight. It has resulted from decades of concerted reform efforts that have crossed professional, institutional, and ideological boundaries. This book has described in detail the ongoing investment in such reform projects, which have served many goals and many masters, ranging from established Member State governments made nervous by the rapid accession of former Eastern Bloc countries, to institutionally anchored actors attached to European institutional prerogatives, to academic observers and critics committed both to Europe and to their own professional status (including their own potential judicial futures), to judges from new accession States more attached to their professional credentials and budding European identities than to the whims of their own national governments, to new professional and institutional formations that have congealed through these debates and that have sought to leverage the reforms for institutional, professional, and ideological purposes.

When all of this was put in motion, it eventually yielded a rather complex, if ultimately fairly coherent, alignment of perspectives and projects. This led to a series of reform efforts that eventually transcended not only national boundaries, but also the boundary between the national and the European: these ongoing projects and their institutional and conceptual justifications have been leveraged in all directions to promote reforms at the national level as much as at the European one. This is certainly not to argue that the interests and identities of the assorted actors, interests, and perspectives are always inherently or consistently aligned. As the self-interested resistance of established Member State governments have periodically and dramatically demonstrated (the tantrum thrown by the French Sarkozy government in Strasbourg comes immediately to mind[1]), this is clearly not so. Nonetheless, the intertwined judicial appointments, judicial independence, judicial quality, and judicial council reforms offer a particularly advantageous window from which to observe not only the internal dynamics that make Europe go (or perhaps more accurately, stop and go), but also the general direction in which most of the reforms seem to have been going.

In order to decode and make sense of these reforms and their dynamics, this book has deployed a varied and somewhat eclectic methodological approach. Refusing to be hemmed in by the classic methodological cleavages that have divided International Relations theory, it has layered together intergovernmentalist, neo-functionalist/neo-institutionalist, and constructivist approaches to the subject matter at hand. An intergovernmentalist perspective allowed us to grasp the deep-rooted concern of the established European Member States to protect themselves and the European *acquis* against potential disruption threatened by Eastern enlargement. By combining this intergovernmental perspective with a tactical understanding of the European judicial independence and judicial quality reforms, we were able to understand how the established Member States were able to insure themselves against European judicial, political, and constitutional instability without sacrificing too much of their traditional powers over judicial appointments.

Neo-functionalist and neo-institutionalist theory then put us in a position to grasp how the institutions and actors most directly tasked to manage these judicial reforms took matters into their own hands, leveraging them to their institutional and professional advantage. Judges at both the European and domestic levels, never mind the Panels of judicial experts they have successfully pushed to establish, have taken the bull by the horns to assert ever more thorough control over the definition and management of the judiciary's professional norms and institutional affairs. Effectively grabbing the initiative, the European judicial Panels quickly availed themselves of the power to define publicly and in detail the attributes required for European judicial office and the procedures with which the political branches of government would now have to comply when dealing with judicial appointments, training, promotion, discipline, and so on.

Finally, constructivist theory enabled us to grasp the full extent to which these reform movements increasingly provoked and reflected a large-scale

[1] *See supra* Chapter 10(V).

transformation of the conceptual framework that had long governed European judicial affairs. The judiciary (whether European or domestic) was coming increasingly to be described and understood as a truly "coequal" branch of government: for it to operate properly, the logic now ran, the judiciary must be made institutionally and procedurally independent of the political branches and be fully empowered to make large-scale political and constitutional policy judgments via its paradigmatic rights analysis. Scandal theory helped us to grasp how this new conception of the judiciary gradually took hold, challenging longheld governmental prerogatives under the guise of upholding self-evident and pre-existing truisms about the proper relationship between the judicial and political branches of government. The very definition of the judicial role had thus been radically transformed, and with it the dominant European understandings of the separation of powers in a proper liberal democratic order. The fundamental identity of the European judiciary had been radically (re-)constructed in the process.

By focusing on the seemingly mundane question of judicial appointments reform, we have therefore been able to acquire a privileged perspective on something much more fundamental: the gradual transformation of core European constitutional assumptions. Each methodological perspective focused our attention on different institutions and players, foregrounded different problems and themes, and offered different insights into the conundrum of why such a seemingly humdrum and long dormant issue as European judicial appointments could suddenly arouse such reformist zeal, then sustain this zeal for so long and on so many fronts, ranging from judicial appointments per se, to judicial independence, to judicial quality, to judicial authority, to judicial legitimacy, and so on.

What remains an open question is the effect of all these reforms on the legitimacy challenges they aim so doggedly to address. In closing, then, I would like to linger for a final time on this issue of judicial legitimacy. For the sake of simplicity, I suggest splitting the category into three distinct (though surely overlapping) variations: judicial legitimacy vis-à-vis legal professionals, vis-à-vis the public, and vis-à-vis democratic theory. This simple heuristic device should allow us to conclude by viewing a little more clearly the potential and the limitations of the European judicial reforms we have been examining in this book.

As a practical matter, the great majority of the European judicial reforms have effectively been oriented in the first direction, i.e., toward generating enhanced judicial legitimacy vis-à-vis legal professionals. The stress on judicial quality (including all of its assumed components, such as seniority, experience, international legal education, academic publications, linguistic capacities, and so on), the focus on merit-based appointment by institutions composed predominantly of judicial professionals working with pre-established norms, the minimization (or, at least, the constraining) of political and especially governmental prerogatives in the judicial appointments process, etc., all function as a mechanism to generate buy-in from the European Courts' primary interlocutors: the Member State courts in general and the national supreme and constitutional courts in particular.

However much Mikael Madsen may legitimately argue that the reforms *should* be directed in significant measure toward gaining the confidence of national governmental actors, one would be hard-pressed to argue that this has been their primary thrust. Indeed, it would be all too easy to argue that the tenor of the reforms runs precisely counter to such governmental sensitivities: after all, most of the reforms push to remove governmental prerogatives in the appointments arena. But as this book has hopefully made clear, the minimization of political influence in the appointments process represents different things to different governments. In the post-1989 accession period, Western European governmental actors joined their judges in pushing actively for just such a result, even though it would nominally reduce governmental prerogatives: a professionally oriented positivist approach to judging offered protection to the European *status quo ante*. That said, the tradition-based exceptions built into the reforms demonstrate quite clearly that the established European Member States were keen to have their cake and eat it too: why not maintain as much of their appointments prerogatives as possible while removing as much as possible from the new accession States from the East? In a sufficiently diverse political environment, the judicial professionalism gambit could operate simultaneously to empower Western European governments and to disempower Central and Eastern European ones.

Over time, the lukewarm support of Western European political actors for the judicial appointments and judicial independence reforms offers the clearest indication that those reforms ultimately gave priority to enhancing European judicial legitimacy vis-à-vis legal professionals. In the end, it was more important to the European expert vetting Panels, for example, to demonstrate the quality of European judicial candidates to their primary professional interlocutors (i.e., the domestic courts and interested academic observers) than to maintain cordial diplomatic relations with the national governments whose judicial candidates they were assessing. Indeed, it is precisely this tension between the Panels' professional commitments and their diplomatic relations that has fostered the kinds of resistance we observed in Chapter 5 and that generated the types of scandals we examined in Chapters 10 and 11.

On this professional legitimacy front, there is a plausible argument to be made that an increase in the professional standing of the European Courts' judges could improve the standing of the European Courts themselves, at least in the eyes of their professional colleagues: the high domestic courts, professional institutional actors (such as the staff of the Committee of Ministers in Strasbourg), and knowledgeable academic observers. This might increase the perceived legitimacy of the European Courts, leading—to speak in the persistently alarmist language of the supporters of European judicial institutions[2]—to a potential increase in the "authority" of the Courts and of their jurisprudence.

[2] *See, e.g.*, Jean-Paul Costa, Letter from the President of the European Court of Human Rights, addressed to member states' Permanent Representatives (Ambassadors) on June 9, 2010 and Steering

As I explained in the last chapter, however, I think there are good reasons to question the likelihood of success of even this targeted professional legitimacy project. First, there is little empirical support for the proposition that there exists large-scale and concerted resistance by the Member State courts (or by the Member State governments, for that matter) to European judicial rulings, especially if one focuses on those countries where the attitude toward Europe is not fundamentally confrontational to begin with. Indeed, as I argued when discussing the Çali study,[3] what little empirical data we have suggests that suspicion of the European Courts—including of the more reputationally precarious European Court of Human Rights (ECtHR) that was the focus of that study—is not only relatively limited and localized, but also hinges more on the perception of national conditions than on the perception of the professional merits of the European judiciary itself.[4]

Second, to the extent that such suspicion of the European Courts does in fact exist (precisely because local conditions are perceived to be good enough to obviate the need for European judicial intervention), it is unrealistic to imagine that fiddling with European judicial appointments reforms would do very much to move the needle: the underlying problem is not with the specifics of the European Courts, but with Member State self-perception. Finally, to the extent that the suspicion is due to actual hostility toward European institutions and projects, then tinkering with something as obscure as judicial appointments procedure is unlikely to accomplish much at all. In short, even on the professional legitimacy front—likely the most effective target of the reforms—it is implausible to suggest that very many people would be moved all that much, regardless of how well designed the reforms might be.

Of course, there is no compelling reason to think that the reforms would really *hurt* the credibility, standing, and "authority" of the European Courts. And true, the reforms may somewhat improve judicial quality (however defined) and judicial independence (ditto), especially in those Member States whose governments are not in a position to manage—not to say "game"—the appointments system effectively (i.e., smaller European Member States of more recent vintage). And this may help on the margins to improve the smooth operation of the European Courts. But it is a long way from such a relatively modest outcome to the grand projects proclaimed in the debates and reforms concerning judicial appointments, judicial independence, judicial quality, judicial councils, and so on. Whether such modest

Committee for Human Rights, CDDH Report on the Longer-Term Future of the System of the European Convention on Human Rights, CDDH(2015)R84 Addendum I, available at http://www.coe.int/t/dghl/standardsetting/cddh/reformechr/CDDH(2015)R84_Addendum%20I_EN-Final.pdf.

[3] *See supra* Chapter 13(II)(A).

[4] *See* Başak Çali, Anne Koch, & Nicola Bruch, *The Social Legitimacy of Human Rights Courts: A Social Interpretivist Theory of the Legitimacy of the European Court of Human Rights*, 35 HUM. R.Q. 955, 957 (2013).

returns outweigh the costs of twenty-five years of concerted reform efforts is of course very difficult to say. But the answer would surely vary depending on what one would include in the calculus. Would one include only the legitimacy gains for the European Courts vis-à-vis legal professionals? Or might one include other factors, such as the legitimacy effects of shaming particular Member State governments or classes of Member State governments, or advancing certain institutional and/or professional interests, or helping to define and defend a sphere of juridical expertise vs. the political, and so on? Although including any such factors into the analysis might well change the bottom line calculus, this should not obscure the reality that the reforms offer only modest prospects for producing significant gains on the judicial legitimacy front, even for the limited purposes of boosting European judicial legitimacy vis-à-vis legal professionals.

The prospects are far worse for the second category of judicial legitimacy, i.e., boosting European judicial legitimacy vis-à-vis the public. This attempt to improve what Weiler terms the "social legitimacy" of the European Courts is where the reforms really fall flat. Needless to say, the question of popular/social legitimacy has been the *bête noire* of Europe for decades. It is not only supremely difficult to address, but even to identify. How would one really go about recognizing the social legitimacy of Europe, never mind of European institutions—such as the European Court of Justice (ECJ), the ECtHR, or the General Court—that the European public has little or no meaningful knowledge about in the first place?[5] And what about the social legitimacy effects of procedural reforms to judicial institutions that the public is unlikely to ever learn about at all, except perhaps by the highly attenuated if long-term "trickle down" effect of professional opinion?

Rather than harp on this problem, suffice it to say that for all of the anxiety that European judicial reformers have demonstrated regarding the urgent need to shore up the standing and authority of the European Courts and of their jurisprudence, they have shown little inclination to theorize or explain the connection between the capacity of the European Courts to command the allegiance of the Member State courts and their capacity to elicit the support of the European general public. Indeed, one would be hard-pressed to identify when the European judicial reform debates even distinguish between the two: the debates typically proceed as if professional deference from the national courts and the social legitimacy of the European Courts before the general public were effectively the same.

This conflation is to some extent understandable. Though undoubtedly difficult to measure, one can at least get a sense of the extent to which different national courts are prepared to work with, leverage, or resist the European Courts

[5] Perhaps counter-intuitively, the Eurobarometer polls—though relatively blunt instruments—consistently show that overall public trust in the EU significantly exceeds trust in national governments and parliaments. *See* European Commission, *Standard Eurobarometer 91, Public Opinion in the European Union, First Results* 5 (Spring 2019). Needless to say, such trust varies over time and from country to country. *Id.* at 6.

and their jurisprudence.[6] But the same cannot be said concerning the legitimacy of the European Courts vis-à-vis the public, which is surely far trickier to grasp, especially given the general level of public ignorance concerning the European institutions.[7] Regardless of how one might try in principle to address such thorny epistemological, methodological, and theoretical connections, it is all too clear that the judicial appointments debates and reforms have made little or no attempt to do so. In a manner that strikes me as all too typical of otherwise well-meaning European institutional actors, these professionals behave as if their particular professional, institutional, procedural, conceptual, and other concerns self-evidently connect to popular/social concerns.

This all too easy elision between—or conflation of—the particular field of action of professional European insiders and the general social world demonstrates a distinctively self-centered professional myopia (not to say narcissism); and it betrays what now strikes me as a characteristic combination of insecurity and self-importance that engenders its own form of European institutional dysfunction. When I say dysfunction, I do not mean something as simple as the endless tensions, rivalries, and conflicts between the assorted governmental, institutional and professional perspectives, projects, and interests that characterize interactions at the European level. I believe such complexities are more appropriately understood as routine European institutional dynamics and politics, which one cannot reasonably expect (or desire) to be more organized, unified, or unidirectional. Indeed, I hope that this book has done a good job of demonstrating precisely this kind of multifaceted institutional, juridical, political, conceptual, and constitutional complexity in operation.

By dysfunction, I mean instead the recognizable tendency of European institutional actors and their immediate academic observers to behave as if they can tackle daunting political and identity issues (in this case, questions of European judicial legitimacy and even of European legitimacy in general) by engaging in

[6] There are of course endless examples of each of these national judicial approaches, ranging from the famous instances of resistance by the German, Polish, and Italian constitutional courts to the well-known—if less spectacular—instances of national supreme courts leveraging their support of the European Courts for domestic political and institutional purposes, to countless instances of ordinary national courts routinely following established European jurisprudence. *See, e.g.*, MITCHEL LASSER, JUDICIAL TRANSFORMATIONS: THE RIGHTS REVOLUTION IN THE COURTS OF EUROPE (2009).

[7] It is unfortunately all too easy to find revealing tidbits on this front, such as the fact that in late 2015, only 8% of British MPs—never mind the general public—could properly identify the country holding the presidency of the Council of Europe at the time. *See* Ipsos MORI Survey of MPs on the European Union (February 1, 2016), available at https://www.ipsos.com/ipsos-mori/en-uk/survey-mps-european-union and https://www.ipsos.com/sites/default/files/migrations/en-uk/files/Assets/Docs/Polls/mps-survey-european-union-2016-tables.pdf. As for the general public's understanding of European institutions, barely more than half of Britons interviewed in 2018 recognized that the European Commission was not in fact the name of the European Parliament or that the European Council was not the EU's highest court. *See* Noah Carla, Lindsay Richards, and Anthony Heath, *Leave and Remain Voters' Knowledge of the EU After the Referendum of 2016*, 57 ELECTORAL STUDIES 90, 92 (2019). And that was after years of high intensity, Brexit-induced education.

primarily procedural—and ultimately rather modest—institutional reform. I have conflicting reactions to this highly self-referential perspective and to the praxis it engenders. On the one hand, how can one not be sympathetic to attempts at institutional, professional, and ethical self-improvement, never mind to the specific goals of improving the educational, linguistic, and professional level of the European and domestic judiciaries, strengthening their independence from increasingly inward-looking and often increasingly authoritarian national governments, and enhancing the legitimacy of Europe and its institutions?

On the other hand, it is hard not to be struck by the *chutzpah* of the enterprise. For those Member State government actors and European institutional players knowledgeable and forward looking enough to launch such a reform project as a means to insure the European *acquis* against threats from the new accession States from the East, it was a bold political maneuver masquerading as merely professional and technocratic reform.

But for those lawyers and judges interested in more institutionally oriented projects, it has been an audacious venture in its own right. It has hinged on a strikingly self-important understanding of the role and capacities of the judiciary in contemporary Europe. Who would have imagined that jurists trained overwhelmingly in the Civilian tradition would have thought that judicial institutions might carry sufficient weight to be a pressing matter of concern to the European public at large, never mind that the legitimacy of the European judiciary might play an important role in the construction of overall European legitimacy? For the reasons I have laid out above, I believe that such judicial projects, however well-intentioned they may be as a professional and institutional matter, not only reveal a tellingly overblown and self-centered European judicial self-perception, but are also highly unlikely to be an effective mechanism for generating meaningful social legitimacy before the general public.

That said, it is important to recognize that this self-aggrandizing judicial self-portrait, complete with the European judicial reforms that it has promoted, also represents a bold venture in political and ideological construction. In other words, it also functions on a level that is at least partially distinct from the attempt to generate judicial legitimacy vis-à-vis legal professionals or vis-à-vis the general public: it reflects a concerted project to reconstruct judicial legitimacy vis-à-vis democratic theory.

This book supplemented its intergovernmentalist and neo-functionalist/neo-institutionalist approaches with a constructivist perspective precisely in order to get at this conceptual/ideological feature of the judicial appointments debates. It turned specifically to scandal theory as a means to reveal the dynamic process by which particular actors at particular times in particular contexts came to elaborate and promote particular conceptions of the judicial role and of its proper place in the separation of powers. Scandal theory helped us to identify this important conceptual shift toward understanding the judiciary as an independent and coequal branch of government. By doing so, it put us in a position to recognize that this emerging political theory regarding the proper place of the judiciary in a liberal democratic order did *not* in fact represent some pre-existing norm that was widely shared throughout the Civilian or Common Law jurisdictions of Europe. To the contrary, its emergence was almost as much of a novelty in the long-standing Member States of Northern and Western Europe as it was in the newly acceded Member States of Central and Eastern Europe.

This new theoretical conception was advanced in the emerging panoply of interwoven reform debates on issues ranging from judicial appointments to judicial independence to judicial quality to judicial councils and so on. But it was also greatly aided by the "scandalous" revelations made by advocates increasingly committed to these judicial reforms, including such academic and professional commentators as Jean-François Flauss and Norbert Engel and such leading judicial figures as Luzius Wildhaber (the inaugural president of the Advisory Panel of Experts (APE)). These advocates—along with institutionally empowered actors such as President Jean-Marc Sauvé and Lord Mance of the 255 Panel—gradually elaborated a universalizing vision of the judicial role according to which judges must necessarily play a leading role in any legitimate democratic order. Moving resolutely away from the traditionally limited role played by the judiciary in Civilian jurisdictions (as well as from the traditional British refusal to permit judicial review of Parliament) and working increasingly to impose a hands-off principle on governments in their dealings with the judiciary (including in judicial appointments processes traditionally dominated by the executive branch), these advocates were actually formulating an innovative account of the place of the judiciary in the European national and supranational constitutional orders.

As scandal theory so helpfully suggests, one should not take at face value these advocates' claims to be merely enforcing self-evident and long-settled democratic principles. Indeed, even the Germans, who had elaborated their highly influential neo-Kelsenian model of constitutional court decision-making in the post-War period, had made sure to establish and then to maintain firm political control over their judicial appointments both to the Federal Constitutional Court and to the European Courts. As a result, we can now see clearly that the European reformers have been just that: reformers. They have been advocating for judicial developments on the basis of democratic theory arguments, *not* on the basis of actual historical practice. As a result, they have faced recalcitrant governments who have been understandably loath to renounce their traditional prerogatives. Increasingly frustrated with this enduring and ever mutating resistance, the reformers have pushed resolutely for ever more detailed and formalized procedural, institutional, and substantive norms to govern the issues of European judicial appointments, independence, and quality, thereby elaborating an ever more comprehensive theoretical vision of the judicial role. As scandal theory and constructivist theory would strongly suggest, not only does the very resistance of those governments demonstrate the contested nature of the norms and projects involved, but it was also the very interaction between these congealing factions that helped to motivate and to shape the emerging theoretical construction and its supposed procedural, institutional, political, conceptual, and constitutional implications.

Although it is difficult to measure the success of this emerging theoretical construction as a means of boosting the legitimacy of European judicial authority vis-à-vis legal professionals or vis-à-vis the public, there exists good reason for doubt. Less clear, however, is the success of this self-aggrandizing judicial self-portrait, complete with its accompanying judicial reforms, as a project to reconstruct European judicial legitimacy vis-à-vis democratic theory. After all, how might one go about trying to measure such success independently of some audience, be it legal professionals, political figures or institutions, or particular segments of civil society?

To analyze the democratic theory question in depth would require a whole other book. Allow me in closing to offer two quick skeptical thoughts about whether the European reforms undertaken under the rubric of judicial appointments, judicial independence, and judicial quality really are required—as the European reformers have suggested—to justify and legitimize the exercise of judicial authority in any liberal democratic constitutional system worthy of the name. The first follows from the recognition that the judicial reforms do not merely represent the transposition of existing Western European constitutional traditions onto the new Member States from Central and Eastern Europe. The reforms represent changes to Sweden as well as to the Slovak Republic. Unless one is willing to argue that liberal democracy has yet to exist in Europe (including in Western and Northern Europe), or only came into being in the last twenty plus years (i.e., during the period of the judicial reforms), it is hard to state with confidence that the reforms were truly required for the purposes of instituting proper liberal democratic constitutional orders. Indeed, given the increasingly shaky state of liberal democracy from the UK to France to Germany to Spain and beyond over the last twenty years, one would be hard pressed to argue that the reforms constitute a major development in liberal democratic theory or demonstrate a significant improvement in the praxis of European liberal democracy.

It is not a great answer to reply that the reforms were instituted as a necessary measure to combat the rising illiberal authoritarianism in countries such as Hungary and Poland and to create a firewall against the further spread of their examples. True, the reforms may indeed help somewhat to limit the capacity of such governments to appoint judicial cronies; and one would certainly hope that such would be the case. But as we have seen, the reforms clearly predate the rise to power of Fidesz, PiS, and their ilk. It would be misleadingly anachronistic to argue otherwise. In short, it is hard to argue that the historical record demonstrates that the judicial reforms instituted over the last twenty plus years are either inherent in, necessary for, or a guarantee of, liberal democracy.

The second skeptical thought turns on the puzzlingly bifurcated—if not necessarily conflicting—nature of the European judicial reforms. On the one hand, they demonstrate a new and impressively self-aggrandizing conception of the judicial role and of its place both in the liberal constitutional order and in the public imagination. This newly self-important understanding undergirds all of the reform efforts, providing almost all of the justification needed for the judiciary and its members to break free of the professional and institutional constraints that national governments could traditionally exert upon them, especially at the international/supranational level. On the other hand, they promote for the most part a resolutely old-fashioned professional portrait of judicial quality that harkens back to tried and true technocratic models of national judicial authority. As we have seen, this has led to the endless procedural and other reforms that, especially in Strasbourg, have emerged from the protracted game of cat and mouse between the Strasbourg professionals and the recalcitrant national governments.

Now that we have reached the end of this book, the tension between this piously technocratic and positivist image of judicial legitimacy and the grandly self-important image of liberal judicial legitimacy should be clear to see. At least the 255 Panel has made some attempt to recognize and address the difficulty of fitting the two images together by stressing not only a core of basic professional and linguistic qualifications, but also a more self-reflective component to its interview process, in which candidates are asked to demonstrate a thoughtful posture concerning the complex relationship between the national and European legal orders. Thus,

> the panel seeks to determine the breadth and solidity of the candidates' knowledge of the major judicial issues, the challenges involved in the rule of law, and the key aspects of the Union's legal system and EU law, as well as the candidates' ability to reflect on the application of this law by Member States' legal systems, and on the relationships between these systems and European law.[8]

But this represents a relatively minor exception in the judicial reform debates, literature, and norms. The APE and the Strasbourg institutions, and even the great majority of the academic and professional literature, have, in contrast, done little to try to link their laundry list of required professional qualifications to their more ambitious theoretical claims regarding the role of the judiciary in the checks and balances, separation of powers, and rule of law schemes demanded by a contemporary liberal democratic political order.

[8] Article 255 Panel, Activity report of the panel provided for by Article 255 of the Treaty on the Functioning of the European Union, First Report of February 17, 2011 (No. 6509/11) at 9.

As a result, the reforms and the debates probably do relatively little to enhance European judicial legitimacy, especially in the context of the now decades-long process of increasing judicial power over, and independence from, the political branches of government. That failure is most glaring with regards to the attempt to increase judicial legitimacy vis-à-vis the general public. The prospects are somewhat less grim, however, for promoting judicial legitimacy vis-à-vis professional audiences or democratic theory. True, there is little sign of some dramatic crisis in the legitimacy of the European judiciary vis-à-vis its primary professional interlocutors to begin with. But there is also no reason to believe that the increasingly detailed list of linguistic, educational, and other professional qualifications demanded of European judicial candidates cannot marginally improve the legal professionalism of the European judiciary, even if there is no clear indication that this would markedly improve its professional standing and legitimacy, never mind increase its political sensitivity and acumen.

Most difficult to assess are the prospects of boosting judicial legitimacy vis-à-vis democratic theory. On the one hand, there is little in the historical record to suggest that liberal democracy truly hinges on the types of judicial reforms that have been instituted over the last twenty-five years. Sadly, European liberal democracy hardly seems healthier now than it did in 1995 or 2000, when the ECJ and the Ole Due Report first started recommending practical reforms to the European judicial appointments process, such as the establishment of a blue-ribbon panel of experts to vet candidates proposed to sit in Luxembourg.[9]

On the other hand, we may unfortunately need to acknowledge that the most urgent judicial reform task today is not to improve judicial legitimacy in liberal democracies so much as to do so in increasingly illiberal ones, whether in Europe or the Americas (including the United States). In doing so, we probably need to recognize that the two have become ever more difficult to disentangle. But let's face it: this patently important task of judicial reform is a rear-guard action far more than an inspiring work of democratic theory. The problem with the European judicial appointments and other reforms is that they began well before these increasingly authoritarian developments became patently manifest. As a result, it is difficult to shake the impression that, in the final analysis, the great majority of the reforms consist largely of intra-institutional jockeying and professional self-involvement rather than a forthright acknowledgment of, and solution to, the problem now at hand.

This book has described what has been, in effect, a *sotto voce* reworking of the constitutional relationships between the judiciary and the political branches of Europe in the wake of the large-scale accession of new Member States of the former Eastern Bloc after the fall of the Berlin Wall. To justify these constitutional reforms

[9] *See supra* Chapter 2(II) and (III).

today will require that we squarely address judicial legitimacy not so much vis-à-vis legal professionals and vis-à-vis democratic theory, as judicial legitimacy vis-à-vis the general public. The judicial appointments and other reforms will therefore need to be openly debated on the turf most ardently claimed by populist and illiberal forces: the popular imagination.

Bibliography

Emanuel Adler, *Seizing the Middle Ground: Constructivism in World Politics*, 3 EUR. J. INT. RELAT. 319 (1997).

Advisory Panel of Experts on Candidates for Election as Judge to the European Court of Human Rights, Proposals made by the Panel in its submission to the CDDH in May 2013, in Final Activity Report for the Committee of Ministers.

Advisory Panel of Experts on Candidates for Election as Judge of the ECHR, Final Activity Report for the attention of the Committee of Ministers, Advisory Panel(2013)12EN (December 11, 2013).

Advisory Panel of Experts on Candidates for Election as Judge to the European Court of Human Rights, Second Activity Report for the attention of the Committee of Ministers, Advisory Panel(2016)1 (February 25, 2016).

Alberto Alemanno, "How Transparent is Transparent Enough?: Balancing Access to Information Against Privacy in European Judicial Selections," in MICHAL BOBEK (ed.), SELECTING EUROPE'S JUDGES: A CRITICAL REVIEW OF THE APPOINTMENT PROCEDURES TO THE EUROPEAN COURTS 202 (Oxford: Oxford University Press, 2015).

KAREN ALTER, ESTABLISHING THE SUPREMACY OF EUROPEAN LAW: THE MAKING OF AN INTERNATIONAL RULE OF LAW IN EUROPE (Oxford: Oxford University Press, 2003).

Louis Althusser, "Ideology and the Ideological State Apparatuses," in LENIN AND PHILOSOPHY 127 (Ben Brewster, trans. New York: Monthly Review Press, 1971).

ELIZABETH S. ANKER, FICTIONS OF DIGNITY: EMBODYING HUMAN RIGHTS IN WORLD LITERATURE (Ithaca and London: Cornell University Press, 2012).

Article 255 Panel, Activity Report of the Panel provided for by Article 255 of the Treaty on the Functioning of the European Union, First Report of February 17, 2011 (No. 6509/11); Second Report of January 22, 2013 (No. 5091/13); Third Report of December 13, 2013 (No. SN 1118/2014); Fourth Report of February 10, 2017; Fifth Report of February 22, 2018 ["Activity Report"].

Catherine Barnard and Elenor Sharpston, *The Changing Face of Article 177 References*, 34 COMMON MKT. L. REV. 1113 (1997).

Ed Bates, "The Birth of the European Convention on Human Rights—And the European Court of Human Rights," in JONAS CHRISTOFFERSEN and MIKAEL RASK MADSEN (eds.), THE EUROPEAN COURT OF HUMAN RIGHTS BETWEEN LAW AND POLITICS 17 (Oxford: Oxford University Press, 2011).

IRÈNE BELLIER and THOMAS M. WILSON (eds.), AN ANTHROPOLOGY OF THE EUROPEAN UNION: BUILDING, IMAGINING AND EXPERIENCING THE NEW EUROPE (New York: NYU Press, 2000).

Daniel Berkowitz, Katharina Pistor, and Jean-Francois Richard, *Economic Development, Legality and the Transplant Effect*, 47 EUR. ECON. REV. 165 (2003).

Alexander Bickel, *The Supreme Court, 1960 Term—Forward: The Passive Virtues*, 75 HARV. L. REV. 1940 (1961).

Damien de Blic and Cyril Lemieux, *The Scandal as Test: Elements of a Pragmatic Sociology*, 71 POLITIX 9 (2005).

Peter Bloom, The Ethics of Neoliberalism: The Business of Making Capitalism Moral (New York: Routledge, 2017).

Taylor C. Boas and Jordan Gans-Morse, *Neoliberalism: From New Liberal Philosophy to Anti-Liberal Slogan*, 44 Studs. in Comp. Int'l Dev. 137 (2009).

Michal Bobek (ed.), Selecting Europe's Judges: A Critical Review of the Appointment Procedures to the European Courts (Oxford: Oxford University Press, 2015).

Michal Bobek, "Epilogue: Searching for the European Hercules," in Michal Bobek (ed.), Selecting Europe's Judges: A Critical Review of the Appointment Procedures to the European Courts 279 (Oxford: Oxford University Press, 2015).

Anne Boerger-De Smedt, *La Cour de justice dans les négociations du traité de Paris instituant la CECA*, 14(2) J. of Eur. Integration Hist. 7 (2008).

Luc Boltanski, Distant Suffering. Morality, Media and Politics (G. Burchell, trans. Cambridge: Cambridge University Press, 1999).

Donald Boudreaux and A.C. Pritchard, *Reassessing the Role of the Independent Judiciary in Enforcing Interest-Group Bargains*, 5 Constit. Pol. Economy 1 (1994).

Pierre Bourdieu, La noblesse d'etat: grandes ecoles et esprit de corps (Paris: Les Editions de Minuit, 1989).

Wendy Brown, Undoing the Demos: Neoliberalism's Stealth Revolution (New York: Zone Books, 2015).

Stephen Burbank, *The Architecture of Judicial Independence*, 72 S.Cal. Rev. 315 (1999).

Stephen Burbank, *What Do We Mean by "Judicial Independence"?*, 64 Oh. St. L. Rev. 323 (2003).

Stephen B. Burbank and Barry Friedman (eds.), Judicial Independence at the Crossroads: An Interdisciplinary Approach (Thousand Oaks, London, and New Delhi: Sage Publications: 2002).

Stephen Burbank and Barry Friedman, "Reconsidering Judicial Independence," in Stephen B. Burbank and Barry Friedman (eds.), Judicial Independence at the Crossroads: An Interdisciplinary Approach 9 (Thousand Oaks, London, and New Delhi: Sage Publications, 2002).

Başak Çali, Anne Koch, and Nicola Bruch, *The Social Legitimacy of Human Rights Courts: A Social Interpretivist Theory of the Legitimacy of the European Court of Human Rights*, 35 Hum. R.Q. 955 (2013).

James Caporaso and Alec Stone Sweet, "Conclusion: Institutional Logics of European Integration," in Alec Stone Sweet, Wayne Sandholtz, and Neil Fligstein (eds.), The Institutionalization of Europe 221 (Oxford: Oxford University Press, 2001).

Noah Carla, Lindsay Richards, and Anthony Heath, *Leave and Remain Voters' Knowledge of the EU After the Referendum of 2016*, 57 Electoral Studies 90 (2019).

Elisabeth Claverie, "L'affaire du Chevalier de la Barre: La naissance d'une forme politique," in Philippe Roussin (ed.), Critique et affaires de blasphème à l'époque des Lumières (Paris: Honoré Champion, 1998).

Antonin Cohen, "The European Court of Justice in the Emergent European Field of Power: Transnational Judicial Institutions and National Career Paths," in Yves Dezalay and Bryant G. Garth (eds.), Lawyers and the Construction of Transnational Justice 239 (Oxfordshire and New York: Routledge 2012).

Paul Colomy, *Neofunctionalism and Neoinstitutionalism: Human Agency and Interest in Institutional Change*, 13 Sociological Forum 265 (1998).

Comité des Ministres, *Communication Addendum*, Doc. 10099, in 2004 Session Ordinaire (deuxième partie) [of the PACE], Documents de séance, 26–30 avril 2004 at 225, available at https://books.google.com/books?id=AoiSVp9n5HQC&p-

g=PA225&lpg=PA225&dq=maruste+hion+pisuke+2004&source=bl&ots=lO6YTCK-wIt&sig=LaSmdVO0sisSZtNZ3UZwqPPdF30&hl=en&sa=X&ved=0ahU-KEwjptuaSkf3MAhWENz4KHZIqAI8Q6AEIKDAC#v=onepage&q=maruste%20hion%20pisuke%202004&f=false.

Committee of Experts on the System of the European Convention on Human Rights (DH-SYSC), "[Draft] Report on the Process of Selection and Election of Judges of the European Court of Human Rights," DH-SYSC (2017)R4 Addendum (November 2017).

Committee on Legal Affairs and Human Rights (Rapporteur: Wohlwend), Report on National Procedures for the Selection of Candidates for the European Court of Human Rights, PACE document

12391 (October 6, 2010) Appendix, available at http://assembly.coe.int/nw/xml/XRef/X2H-Xref-ViewPDF.asp?FileID=12764&lang=en.

Committee on Legal Affairs and Human Rights, Work of the Committee on Legal Affairs and Human Rights (AS/Jur): an overview, Information document prepared by the Secretariat, AS/Jur/Inf (2014) 01.

Committee of Ministers, Recommendation Rec R (94)12 on Independence, Efficiency and Role of Judges (October 13, 1994).

Committee of Ministers, Establishment of an Advisory Panel of Experts on Candidates for Election as Judge to the European Court of Human Rights—Implementation, CM/Del/Dec(2010)1101/1.7E (2010).

Committee of Ministers, Resolution CM/Res(2010)26 on the Establishment of an Advisory Panel of Experts on Candidates for Election as Judge to the European Court of Human Rights (November 10, 2010).

Committee of Ministers, Recommendation CM/Rec(2010)12 on Judges: Independence, Efficiency and Responsibilities (November 17, 2010).

Committee of Ministers' Deputies, Guidelines of the Committee of Ministers on the Selection of Candidates for the Post of Judge at the European Court of Human Rights, CM(2012)40 final (March 29, 2012).

Committee of Ministers' Deputies, Guidelines of the Committee of Ministers on the Selection of Candidates for the Post of Judge at the European Court of Human Rights—Explanatory Memorandum, CM(2012)40 addendum final (March 29, 2012).

Committee of Ministers, Resolution CM/Res(2014)44 amending Resolution CM/Res(2010)26 on the Establishment of an Advisory Panel of Experts on Candidates for Election as Judge to the European Court of Human Rights (November 26, 2014).

The Constitution of Sweden: The Fundamental Laws and the Riksdag Act (with an Introduction by Magnus Isberg) 21, Chapter 11 (Stockholm: Sveriges Riksdag, 2016).

Consultative Council of European Judges, "Opinion No. 1 on Standards Concerning the Independence of the Judiciary and the Irremovability of Judges," CCJE (2001) OP No. 1, available at https://rm.coe.int/1680747830.

Consultative Council of European Judges, "Opinion No. 10 on the Council of the Judiciary at the Service of Society," CCJE (2007) OP No. 10.

Consultative Council of European Judges, "Magna Carta of Judges (Fundamental Principles)," CCJE (2010) 3 final (November 17, 2010).

Robert Cooter, "The Rule of State Law and the Rule-of-Law State: Economic Analysis of the Legal Foundations of Development," in Annual World Bank Conference on Development Economics 1996 191 (Washington D.C.: The World Bank, 1997).

Jean-Paul Costa, Letter from the President of the European Court of Human Rights, addressed to member states' Permanent Representatives (Ambassadors) on June 9, 2010 ["Costa Letter"].

Council Decision 2017/2262 of December 4, 2017, appointing the members of the panel provided for in Article 255 of the Treaty on the Functioning of the European Union, available at https://eur-lex.europa.eu/legal-content/EN/TXT/?uri=CELEX%3A32017D2262.

Council of Europe, The European Charter on the Statute for Judges, DAJ/DOC (98)23, available at https://rm.coe.int/16807473ef.

Council of Europe, "Explanatory Report to Protocol No. 11 to the Convention for the Protection of Human Rights and Fundamental Freedoms, restructuring the control machinery established thereby," available at https://rm.coe.int/CoERMPublicCommonSearchServices/DisplayDCTMContent?documentId=09000016800cb5e9.

Council of Europe: Parliamentary Assembly, Official Report of Debates: 2004 Ordinary Session (Second Part), Thirteenth Sitting, Wednesday April 28, 2004 at 3 p.m..

Court of Justice and Court of First Instance, "The Future of the Judicial System of the European Union (Proposals and Reflections)," republished in ALAN DASHWOOD and ANGUS JOHNSTON (eds.), THE FUTURE OF THE JUDICIAL SYSTEM OF THE EUROPEAN UNION 111 (Oxford, UK; Portland, OR: Hart Publishing, 2001).

MIRJAN DAMAŠKA, THE FACES OF JUSTICE AND STATE AUTHORITY: A COMPARATIVE APPROACH TO THE LEGAL PROCESS (New Haven and London: Yale University Press, 1986).

Eric de Dampierre, *Thèmes pour l'étude du scandale*, ANNALES. ÉCONOMIES, SOCIÉTÉS, CIVILISATIONS, 9e année, N. 3, 328 (1954).

RENAUD DEHOUSSE, THE POLITICS OF JUDICIAL INTEGRATION (Basingstoke: MacMillan, 1998).

HERNANDO DE SOTO, THE OTHER PATH (New York: Harper and Row, 1989).

Henri de Wael, "Not Quite the Bed that Procrustes Built : Dissecting the System for Selecting Judges at the Court of Justice of the European Union," in MICHAL BOBEK (ed.), SELECTING EUROPE'S JUDGES: A CRITICAL REVIEW OF THE APPOINTMENT PROCEDURES TO THE EUROPEAN COURTS 24 (Oxford: Oxford University Press, 2015).

Bruno de Witte, "Direct Effect, Supremacy, and the Nature of Legal Order," in PAUL CRAIG and GRAINNE DE BURCA (eds.), THE EVOLUTION OF EU LAW (Oxford: Oxford University Press, 1999).

Simeon Djankov, Rafael La Porta, Florencio Lopez-di-Silanes, and Andrei Shleifer, *The Regulation of Entry*, 117 QUARTERLY JOURNAL OF ECONOMICS 1 (2002).

Simeon Djankov, Rafael La Porta, Florencio Lopez-di-Silanes, and Andrei Shleifer, *Courts*, 118 QUARTERLY JOURNAL OF ECONOMICS 453 (2003).

Discussion Circle on the Court of Justice, Final Report, CONV 636/03, available at http://european-convention.europa.eu/pdf/reg/en/03/cv00/cv00636.en03.pdf.

ANDRÉ DONNER, THE ROLE OF THE LAWYER IN THE EUROPEAN COMMUNITIES (Chicago: Northwestern University Press, 1968).

Andrew Drzemczewski, *The European Human Rights Convention: Protocol No. 11 Entry Into Force and First Year of Application*, DOCUMENTAÇÃO E DIREITO COMPARADO, nos 79/80 1999, available at http://www.gddc.pt/actividade-editorial/pdfs-publicacoes/7980-a.pdf.

Andrew Drzemczewski, *The Parliamentary Assembly's Committee on the Election of Judges to the European Court of Human Rights*, 35 HRLJ 269 (2015).

Andrew Drzemczewski, *Human Rights in Europe: An Insider's Views* EHRLR 134 [2017].

Andrew Drzemczewski, "Election of Judges to the ECtHR," in HÉLÈNE RUIZ-FABRI (ed.), MAX PLANCK ENCYCLOPEDIA OF INTERNATIONAL PROCEDURAL LAW (Oxford: Oxford University Press, 2019), https://opil.ouplaw.com/view/10.1093/law-mpeipro/e3367.013.3367/law-mpeipro-e3367.

Tomas Dumbrovsky, Bilyana Petkova, and Marijn van der Sluis, *Judicial Appointments: The Article 255 TFEU Advisory Panel and Selection Procedures in the Member States*, 51 CM L. REV. 455 (2014).

GÉRARD DUMÉNIL and DOMINIQUE LÉVY, CAPITAL RESURGENT: ROOTS OF THE NEOLIBERAL REVOLUTION (Derek Jeffords trans. Cambridge: Harvard University Press, 2004).

RONALD DWORKIN, LAW'S EMPIRE (Cambridge: Harvard University Press, 1986).

RICHARD EKINS, THE NATURE OF LEGISLATIVE INTENT (Oxford: Oxford University Press, 2012).

N.P. Engel, *More Transparency and Governmental Loyalty for Maintaining Professional Quality in the Election of Judges to the European Court of Human Rights*, 32 HUMAN RIGHTS L.J. 448 (2008).

Lee Epstein, Jack Knight, and Olga Shvetsova, "Selecting Selection Systems," in STEPHEN B. BURBANK and BARRY FRIEDMAN (eds.), JUDICIAL INDEPENDENCE AT THE CROSSROADS: AN INTERDISCIPLINARY APPROACH 191 (Thousand Oaks, London, and New Delhi: Sage Publications, 2002).

Europe1, "Election à la CEDH: La France retire sa liste," (April 11, 2011), available at http://www.europe1.fr/international/election-a-la-cedh-la-france-retire-sa-liste-494725.

European Charter on the Statute for Judges, DAJ/DOC (98) 23 (1998).

European Commission, *Standard Eurobarometer 91, Public Opinion in the European Union, First Results* 5 (Spring 2019).

European Commission, "Euromyths," http://blogs.ec.europa.eu/ECintheUK/euromyths-a-z-index.

European Court of Human Rights, *Advisory opinion on certain legal questions concerning the lists of candidates submitted with a view to the election of judges to the European Court of Human Rights*, February 12, 2008, available at http://hudoc.echr.coe.int/app/conversion/pdf/?library=ECHR&id=003-2268009-2419060&filename=003-2268009-2419060.pdf.

EUROPEAN COURT OF HUMAN RIGHTS DIRECTORATE OF THE JURISCONSULT, PRACTICAL GUIDE ON ADMISSIBILITY CRITERIA (3rd ed. 2014), available at http://www.echr.coe.int/Documents/Admissibility_guide_ENG.pdf.

XLVI EUROPEAN YEARBOOK 1998 (The Hague, Boston, and London: Martinus Nijhoff:, 1998).

DAVID FEDMAN (ed.), ENGLISH PUBLIC LAW (Oxford: Oxford University Press, 2009).

John Ferejohn, *Constitutional Review in the Global Context*, 6 N.Y.U. J. LEGIS. & PUB. POL'Y 49 (2002–03).

Jean-François Flauss, *Radioscopie de l'élection de la nouvelle Cour européenne des droits de l'homme*, 35 REV. TRIM. D. H. 437 (1998) ["*Radioscopie*"].

Jean-François Flauss, *Le Renouvellement triennial de la Cour européenne des droit de l'homme*, 47 REV. TR. D. H. 693 (2001) ["*Le Renouvellement triennial*"]

Jean-François Flauss, *Brèves observations sur le second renouvellement triennal de la Cour européenne des droits de l'homme*, 61 REV. TR. D. H. 5 (2005) ["*Brèves observations*"].

Jean-François Flauss, *Les élections de juges à la Cour européenne des droits de l'homme (2005–2008)*, 75 REV. TR. D. H. 5 (2008).

Neil Fligstein, and Alec Stone Sweet, "Constructing Markets and Polities: An Institutionalist Account of European Integration," 107 Am. J. Sociology 1206 (2002).

Matthew Gabel, Michael Malecki, Clifford Carrubba, and Joshua Fjestul, *The Politics of Decision-Making in the European Court of Justice: The System of Chambers and Distribution of Cases for Decision*, Meetings of the European Consortium for Political

Research, Marburg, Germany (September, 2003), available at http://www.uky.edu/~mjgabe1/GabelMarburg.pdf.

Fruzsina Gárdos-Orosz, *Preliminary Reference and the Hungarian Constitutional Court: A Context of Non-Reference*, 16 German L.J. 1569 (2015).

Nuno Garoupa and Tom Ginsberg, *The Comparative Law and Economics of Judicial Councils*, 27 Berk. J. Int'l L. 53 (2009).

Nuno Garoupa and Tom Ginsberg, *Guarding the Guardians: Judicial Councils and Judicial Independence*, 57 Am. J. Comp. L. 103 (2009).

Nuno Garoupa and Tom Ginsburg, *Building Reputation in Constitutional Courts*, 28 Ariz. J. Int'l & Comp. L. 539 (2011).

Alain Garrigou, *Le boss, la machine et le scandale. La chute de la maison Médecin*, 5 Politix (no. 17) 7, 16 (1992).

Giornalettismo, "Si libera un posto al Parlamento francese? Sarkozy ci mette un amico suo" (March 16, 2011), at http://www.giornalettismo.com/archives/117940/si-libera-un-posto-al-parlamento-francese-sarkozy-ci-mette-un-amico-suo/.

Max Gluckman, *Gossip and Scandal*, 4(3) Current Anthropology 30 (1963).

Martin Golding, *Transitional Regimes and the Rule of Law*, Ratio Juris 9 (1996).

Heather Grabbe, "What Hope for Solidarity in the Enlarged European Union?," in Krzysztof Michalski, (ed.), What Holds Europe Together? Conditions of European Solidarity 42 (Budapest and New York: Central European University Press, 2006).

David Allen Green, "Brexit: Why did the ECJ become a UK 'Red Line'?" available at https://www.ft.com/content/32cd1e87-c7d1-3026-86fc-bce5229711d1.

Kent Greenawalt, Statutory and Common Law Interpretation (New York: Oxford University Press, 2013).

Ernst Haas, The Uniting of Europe: Political, Social, and Economic Forces, 1950–1957 (Notre Dame: University of Notre Dame Press, 3rd ed. 2004).

Michaela Hailbronner, *Rethinking the Rise of the German Constitutional Court: From anti-Nazism to Value Formalism*, 12 I•Con 626 (2014), available at https://academic.oup.com/icon/article/12/3/626/763768.

Sudhir Hazareesingh, Political Traditions in Modern France (New York: Oxford University Press, 1994).

John Hedigan, "The Election of Judges to the European Court of Human Rights," in Marcelo Kohen (ed.), Promoting Justice, Human Rights and Conflict Resolution Through International Law: Liber amicorum Lucius Caflisch 238 (Leyden: Brill, 2007).

Liz Heffernan, "A European Certiorari Revisited," in Mads Adenas and John Usher (eds.), The Treaty of Nice and Beyond: Enlargement and Constitutional Reform 355 (Oxford, UK; Portland, OR: Hart Publishing, 2003).

Toby Helm and Jamie Howard, "Ex-Legal Chief Attacks Theresa May's 'Foolish' Claim on European Court of Justice," available at https://www.theguardian.com/politics/2017/aug/19/brexit-european-court-of-justice-theresa-may-foolish-attack.

Sir Jeremy Heywood, "The Civil Service, Brexit and Beyond," available at https://quarterly.blog.gov.uk/2018/03/23/the-civil-service-brexit-and-beyond/.

High Level Conference on the Future of the European Court of Human Rights, Interlaken Declaration of February 19, 2010, available at http://www.coe.int/t/dgi/hr-natimplement/Source/interlaken_declaration_en.pdf.

Alicia Hinarejos, "Introduction: The ECJ as a Federal Constitutional Court," in Judicial Control in the European Union: Reforming Jurisdiction in the Intergovernmental Pillars 1 (Oxford: Oxford University Press, 2009).

Ran Hirschl, Towards Juristocracy: The Origins and Consequences of the New Constitutionalism (Cambridge: Harvard University Press, 2004).

Ran Hirschl, *The Political Origins of the New Constitutionalism*, 11 Ind. J. Glob. Studs. 71 (2004).

Gil Carlos Rodríguez Iglesias, President of the Court of Justice of the European Communities, Oral presentation to the "discussion circle" on the Court of Justice on February 17, 2003, CONV 572/03, available at http://european-convention.europa.eu/pdf/reg/en/03/cv00/cv00572.en03.pdf.

Interights (Dr. Jutta Limbach, Chair), *Judicial Independence: Law and Practice of Appointments to the European Court of Human Rights* (May 2003), available at http://www.corteidh.or.cr/tablas/32795.pdf.

Ipsos MORI Survey of MPs on the European Union (February 1, 2016), available at https://www.ipsos.com/ipsos-mori/en-uk/survey-mps-european-union and https://www.ipsos.com/sites/default/files/migrations/en-uk/files/Assets/Docs/Polls/mps-survey-european-union-2016-tables.pdf.

Mark W. Janis, Richard S. Kay, and Anthony W. Bradley, European Human Rights Law: Text and Materials (Oxford and New York: Oxford University Press, 2nd edn., 2000).

Franck Johannès, "Petite manœuvre pour placer un ami," Le Monde, March 14, 2011, available at http://libertes.blog.lemonde.fr/2011/03/14/petite-manoeuvre-de-lelysee-pour-placer-un-ami/.

Peter J. Katzenstein (eds.), The Culture of National Security: Norms and Identity in World Politics (New York: Columbia University Press, 1996).

R. Daniel Keleman, "Selection, Appointment and Legitimacy: A Political Perspective," in Michal Bobek (ed.), Selecting Europe's Judges: A Critical Review of the Appointment Procedures to the European Courts 244 (Oxford: Oxford University Press, 2015).

Daniel Kelemen and Alec Stone Sweet, "Assessing the Transformation of Europe," in Marlene Wind and Miguel Poiares Maduro (eds.), The Transformation of Europe: Twenty-Five Years On 193 (New York: Cambridge University Press, 2017).

Y.S. Klerk and L. van Poelgeest, *Ratificatie* à contre coeur: *de reserves van de Nederlandse regering jegens het Europese Verdrag voor de Rechten van de Mens en het individueel klachtrecht*, Rechtsgeleerd Magazijn Athemis 220 (1991).

Donald P. Kommers, Judicial Politics in West Germany: A Study of the Federal Constitutional Court (Beverly Hills and London: Sage Publications, 1976).

Lewis Kornhauser, "Is Judicial Independence a Useful Concept," in Stephen B. Burbank and Barry Friedman (eds.), Judicial Independence at the Crossroads: An Interdisciplinary Approach 45 (Thousand Oaks, London, and New Delhi: Sage Publications, 2002).

David Kosař, *Selecting Strasbourg' Judges: A Critique*, in Selecting Europe's Judges: A Critical Review of the Appointment Procedures to the European Courts 120 (Michal Bobek ed.,2015).

Neil Kritz (ed.), Transitional Justice: How Emerging Democracies Reckon with Former Regimes, Vols. I–III (Washington D.C.: U.S. Institute of Peace Press,1995).

Magda Krzyzanowska-Mierzewska, "The Reception Process in Poland and Slovakia," in Helen Keller and Alec Stone Sweet, A Europe of Rights: The Impact of the ECHR on National Legal Systems 531 (Oxford: Oxford University Press, 2008).

Maurice Lagrange, "La CJCE du Plan Schuman à l'Union européenne," in Mélanges Fernand Dehousse 127 (Paris: Nathan et Labor, 1979).

William Landes and Richard Posner, *The Independent Judiciary in an Interest-Group Perspective*, 18 J. LAW & ECON. 875 (1975).

MITCHEL LASSER, JUDICIAL DELIBERATIONS: A COMPARATIVE ANALYSIS OF JUDICIAL TRANSPARENCY AND LEGITIMACY (Oxford: Oxford University Press, 2004) ["JUDICIAL DELIBERATIONS"].

MITCHEL LASSER, JUDICIAL TRANSFORMATIONS: THE RIGHTS REVOLUTION IN THE COURTS OF EUROPE (Oxford: Oxford University Press, 2009) ["JUDICIAL TRANSFORMATIONS"].

Bruno Latour, *Why Has Critique Run Out of Steam? From Matters of Fact to Matters of Concern*, 30 CRITICAL INQUIRY 225 (2004).

Koen Lemmens, "(S)electing Judges for Strasbourg: A (Dis)appointing Process?," in MICHAL BOBEK (ed.), SELECTING EUROPE'S JUDGES: A CRITICAL REVIEW OF THE APPOINTMENT PROCEDURES TO THE EUROPEAN COURTS 95 (Oxford: Oxford University Press, 2015).

Le Parisien, "Juge à la CEDH: la France devra présenter une nouvelle liste de candidats" (April 11, 2011), available at http://www.leparisien.fr/strasbourg-67000/juge-a-la-cedh-la-france-devra-presenter-une-nouvelle-liste-de-candidats-11-04-2011-1403429.php#xtref=https%3A%2F%2Fwww.google.com%2F.

Corinne Lepage, "Copinage en Sarkozie: la double honte de la France à Strasbourg," available at http://rue89.nouvelobs.com/blog/corinne-lepage/2011/03/24/copinage-en-sarkozie-la-double-honte-de-la-france-a-strasbourg-196747.

René le Senne, "Le Scandal," in L'EXISTENCE 127 (Paris: Gallimard, 1945).

Edward Hirsch Levi, *Some Aspects of Separation of Powers*, 76 COLUM. L. REV. 371 (1976).

Jutta Limbach et al., "Judicial Independence: Law and Practice of Appointments to the European Court of Human Rights" (London: Interights, 2003), available at http://www.interights.org/jud-ind-en/index.html ["Interights Report"].

John Logue, "Conclusion," in ANDREI MARKOVITS and MARK SILVERSTEIN (eds.), THE POLITICS OF SCANDAL: POWER AND PROCESS IN LIBERAL DEMOCRACIES 254 (New York and London: Holmes & Meier, 1988).

Theodore Lowi, "Forward," in ANDREI MARKOVITS and MARK SILVERSTEIN (eds.), THE POLITICS OF SCANDAL: POWER AND PROCESS IN LIBERAL DEMOCRACIES vii (New York and London: Holmes and Meier, 1988).

Piers Ludlow, "Value, Flexibility and Openness. The Treaty of Rome's Success in Historical Perspective," in JULIO BAQUERO CRUZ and CARLOS CLOSA MONTERO (eds.), EUROPEAN INTEGRATION IN HISTORICAL PERSPECTIVE FROM ROME TO BERLIN: 1957–2007 (Brussels: Peter Lang, 2009).

Mikael Rask Madsen, "The Legitimization Strategies of International Judges: The Case of the European Court of Human Rights," in MICHAL BOBEK (ed.), SELECTING EUROPE'S JUDGES: A CRITICAL REVIEW OF THE APPOINTMENT PROCEDURES TO THE EUROPEAN COURTS 259 (Oxford: Oxford University Press, 2015).

Jiří Malenovský, *L'indépendance des juges internationaux*, 349 Recueil des cours de l'Académie de droit international de la Haye 187 (Leiden and Boston: Martinus Nijhoff, 2011).

Lord Mance, "The Composition of the European Court of Justice" (The text of a talk given to the United Kingdom Association for European Law, October 19, 2011) , available at https://www.supremecourt.uk/docs/speech_111019.pdf.

ANDREI MARKOVITS and MARK SILVERSTEIN (eds.), THE POLITICS OF SCANDAL: POWER AND PROCESS IN LIBERAL DEMOCRACIES (New York and London: Holmes and Meier, 1988).

Andrei Markovits and Mark Silverstein, "Introduction: Power and Process in Liberal Democracies," in MARKOVITS AND SILVERSTEIN, (eds.), THE POLITICS of Scandal: Power and Process in Liberal Democracies 1 (New York and London: Holmes and Meier, 1988).

Theresa May, "Britain after Brexit: A Vision of a Global Britain," available at http://www.independent.co.uk/news/uk/politics/theresa-may-speech-tory-conference-2016-in-full-transcript-a7346171.html.

Meeting Report of Drafting Group I on the Follow-Up to the CDDH Report on the Longer-Term Future of the Convention (DH-SYSC-I), 2nd meeting, October 19–21, 2016, DH-SYSC-I (2016)R2.

Robert Merton, "Manifest and Latent Functions," republished in Social Theory and Social Structure 73 (New York: Free Press, 1968).

Krzysztof Michalski (ed.), What Holds Europe Together? Conditions of European Solidarity (Budapest, New York: Central European University Press, 2006).

Andrew Moravcsik, *Liberalism and International Relations Theory*, Harvard University CFIA Working Paper No. 92–6 (1992).

Andrew Moravcsik, *Preferences and Power in the European Community: A Liberal Intergovernmentalist Approach*, 31 J. Com. Mkt. Studies 473 (1993).

Fernand Muûls, Note concernant le projet de traité relatif au charbon et à l'acier, 16.11.1950, AMAElB, Dos.gen. CECA 5216.

Rainier Nickel, "The German Federal Constitutional Court: Present State, Future Challenges," in Andrew Le Sueur (ed.), Building the UK's New Supreme Court: National and Comparative Perspectives 175 (New York: Oxford University Press, 2004).

David M. O'Brien and Yasuo Ohkoshi, "Stifling Judicial Independence from Within: The Japanese Judiciary," in Peter H. Russell and David M. O'Brien (eds.), Judicial Independence in the Age of Democracy: Critical Perspectives from around the World 37 (Charlottesville and London: University of Virginia Press, 2001).

Open Society Justice Initiative, Strengthening from Within: Law and Practice in the Selection of Human Rights Judges and Commissioners (New York: Open Society Foundations, 2017).

PACE, Recommendation 1194 (1992) on Reform of the control mechanism of the European Convention on Human Rights.

PACE, Recommendation 1429 (1999) on National procedures for nominating judges to the ECHR.

PACE, Recommendation 1649 (2004) on Candidates for the ECHR.

PACE, Resolution 1432 (2005) on Procedure for elections held by the Parliamentary Assembly other than those of its President and Vice-Presidents.

PACE, Resolution 1646 (2009) on the Nomination of Candidates and Election of Judges to the European Court of Human Rights.

PACE, Resolution 2278 (2019) on Modification of various provisions of the Assembly's Rules of Procedure.

PACE, Election of judges to the European Court of Human Rights, List and curricula vitae of candidates submitted by the Governments of France, Norway and Switzerland, Doc. 12527 (February 25, 2011).

PACE, 2012 Ordinary Session (Third part), Report, Twenty-first Sitting, Tuesday June 26, 2012 at 10 a.m., Document AS (2012) CR 21, available at http://assembly.coe.int/Documents/Records/2012/E/1206261000E.htm.

PACE, Election of Judges to the ECHR: List and curricula vitae of candidates submitted by the Governments of Bosnia and Herzegovina, Croatia, the Czech Republic, the Netherlands, Poland, the Russian Federation, Sweden and the United Kingdom, Doc.

12936 (May 22, 2012), available at http://assembly.coe.int/Documents/WorkingDocs/2012/COE.PACE.WD.COM.12936.2012.EN.pdf.

PACE, Committee on the Election of Judges to the European Court of Human Rights, Procedure for electing judges to the European Court of Human Rights—Information document prepared by the Secretariat, AS/Cdh/Inf (2019) 01 rev (January 23, 2019), available at http://website-pace.net/documents/1653355/1653736/ProcedureElectionJudges-EN.pdf/e4472144-64bc-4926-928c-47ae9c1ea45e.

PACE Committee on Legal Affairs and Human Rights (Rapporteur: Lord Kirkhill), Report on the procedure for examining candidatures for the election of judges to the European Court of Human Rights 1, Doc 7439, 1403-15/12/95-1-E (1995). ["PACE Report for Examining ECtHR Judicial Candidatures"].

PACE Committee on Legal Affairs and Human Rights (Rapporteur: Wohlwend), Report on National procedures for nominating candidates for election to the European Court of Human Rights 3, Doc. 8505 (September 8, 1999). ["1999 Report on National Procedures for Nominating Candidates"].

PACE Committee on Legal Affairs and Human Rights (Rapporteur: McNamara), Report on Candidates for the European Court of Human Rights 1, Doc. 9963 (October 7, 2003).

PACE Committee on Legal Affairs and Human Rights (Rapporteur: Christopher Chope), Report on the Nomination of Candidates and Election of Judges to the European Court of Human Rights, Doc. 11767, Explanatory Memorandum (December 1, 2008).

PACE Committee on Legal Affairs and Human Rights, Report on National procedures for the selection of candidates for the European Court of Human Rights, Doc. 12391 (October 7, 2010) ["2010 PACE Report on National Procedures for Selecting Candidates"].

PACE Committee on Rules and Procedure (Rapporteur: Rudolf Vis), Report on Procedure for Elections Held by the Parliamentary Assembly other than those of its President and Vice-President, Doc. 10385 (December 21, 2004).

Le Parisien, "Juge à la CEDH: la France devra présenter une nouvelle liste de candidats" (April 11, 2011), available at http://www.leparisien.fr/strasbourg-67000/juge-a-la-cedh-la-france-devra-presenter-une-nouvelle-liste-de-candidats-11-04-2011-1403429.php#xtref=https%3A%2F%2Fwww.google.com%2F.

Tommaso Pavone, *Revisiting Judicial Empowerment in the European Union: Limits of Empowerment, Logics of Resistance*, 6 J. Law & Cts 303 (2018).

Adam Payne, "Former ECJ Judge: Theresa May's Pledge to End All ECJ Jurisdiction 'Shows Just How Ignorant She Is,'" available at http://www.businessinsider.com/former-ecj-judge-mays-pledge-to-end-ecj-rule-shows-how-ignorant-she-is-2017-8.

Jane Perlez, *A Bulgarian is Shot and Motives are Many*, NY Times, November 3, 1996, available at http://www.nytimes.com/1996/11/03/world/a-bulgarian-is-slain-and-motives-are-many.html.

Pierre Pescatore, in Institut für das Recht der Europäischen Gemeinschaften, Zehn Jahre Rechtsprechung des Gerichtshofs der Europäischen Gemeinschaften 614 (Cologne: C. Heymanns, 1965).

Pierre Pescatore, *Les travaux du "groupe juridique" dans les négociations des traités de Rome*, 2 Revue d'histoire luxembourgeoise 34 (1982).

J. Mark Ramseyer, *The Puzzling (In)Dependence of Courts: A Comparative Approach*, 23 J. Legal Stud. 721 (1994).

J. Mark Ramseyer and Eric Rasmusen, *Why Are Japanese Judges So Conservative in Politically Charged Cases?*, 95 Am. Pol. Sci, Rev. 331 (2001).

Andrzej Rapaczynski, "The Rule of Law in Theoretical and Comparative Perspective," in Roger Michener (ed.), The Balance of Freedom: Political Economy, Law, and Learning 81 (St. Paul: Paragon House, 1995).

Hjalte Rasmussen, On Law and Policy in the European Court of Justice. A Comparative Study in Judicial Policymaking (Dordrecht: Nijhoff, 1986).

Report of the Court of Justice on certain aspects of the application of the Treaty on European Union, published in the Court's 1995 Annual Report 19, available at https://www.cvce.eu/content/publication/2003/4/2/3644862f-2e8f-4170-9616-e573a41b61c5/publishable_en.pdf.

Report of the Evaluation Group to the Committee of Ministers on the European Court of Human Rights, EG Court(2001)1 September 27, 2001, available at https://wcd.coe.int/ViewDoc.jsp?id=226195&Lang=fr#P1176_114799.

Report of the Group of Wise Persons to the Committee of Ministers, CM(2006)203.

Report by the Working Party on the Future of the European Communities' Court System (January 2000) ["Ole Due Report"], available at ec.europa.eu/dgs/legal_service/pdfdue_en.pdf.

Paul Reuter, *La conception du pouvoir politique dans le Plan Schuman*, 1 Revue française de Science politique 256, 274 (1951).

Philippe Roussin (ed.), Critique et affaires de blasphème à l'époque des Lumières (Paris: Honoré Champion, 1998).

John G. Ruggie, *What Makes the World Hang Together? Neo-utilitarianism and the Social Constructivist Challenge*, 52 Int. Org. 855 (1998).

Peter H. Russell, "Toward a General Theory of Judicial Independence" in Peter H. Russell and David M. O'Brien (eds.), Judicial Independence in the Age of Democracy: Critical Perspectives from around the World 1 (Charlottesville and London: University of Virginia Press, 2001).

Peter H. Russell, "Conclusion: A General Theory of Judicial Independence Revisited," in Adam Dodek and Lorne Sossin (eds.), Judicial Independence in Context 599 (Toronto: Irwin Law, 2010).

Peter H. Russell and David M. O'Brien (eds.), Judicial Independence in the Age of Democracy: Critical Perspectives from around the World (Charlottesville and London: University of Virginia Press, 2001).

Wojciech Sadurski, "Solange, chapter 3": Constitutional Courts in Central Europe—Democracy—European Union, EUI Working Paper LAW No. 2006/40, available at http://cadmus.eui.eu/bitstream/handle/1814/6420/LAW-2006-40.pdf?sequence=1&isAllowed=y.

Wayne Sandholtz and Alec Stone Sweet (eds.), European Integration and Supranational Governance (Oxford: Oxford University Press, 1998).

Wayne Sandholtz, Alec Stone Sweet, and Neil Fligstein (eds.) The Institutionalization of Europe (Oxford: Oxford University Press, 2001).

Jean-Marc Sauvé, "Le rôle du comité 255 dans la séparation des pouvoirs au sein de l'Union européenne", intervention lors du colloque pour le 130ème anniversaire du Conseil supérieur de la magistrature le 24 octobre 2013, available at http://www.conseil-etat.fr/fr/discours-et-interventions/la-separation-des-pouvoirs-l-union-europeenne-et-le-comite-255-.html [« Le rôle du comité 255 »].

Jean-Marc Sauvé, "The Future of the European Union Courts; Increased Workload: Organisation, Appointment and Training of Judges," Conference organized by the Council of Bars and Law Societies of Europe, Monday April 28, 2014, available at http://www.conseil- etat.fr/content/download/4032/12124/version/1/file/28_04_2014_discours_president_sauve_en.pdf ["The future of the European Union courts"].

Jean-Marc Sauvé, "Selecting the European Union's Judges: The Practice of the Article 255 Panel," in MICHAL BOBEK (ed.), SELECTING EUROPE'S JUDGES: A CRITICAL REVIEW OF THE APPOINTMENT PROCEDURES TO THE EUROPEAN COURTS 78 (Oxford: Oxford University Press, 2015).

ANTONIN SCALIA and BRYAN GARNER, READING LAW: THE INTERPRETATION OF LEGAL TEXTS (St. Paul, MN: West, 2012).

Kim Lane Scheppele, "Declarations of Independence: Judicial Responses to Political Pressure," in STEPHEN B. BURBANK and BARRY FRIEDMAN (eds.), JUDICIAL INDEPENDENCE AT THE CROSSROADS: AN INTERDISCIPLINARY APPROACH 227 (Sage Publications: Thousand Oaks, London, New Delhi, 2002).

Henry G. Schermers, Protocol 11 to the European Convention on Human Rights, available at https://europainstitut.de/fileadmin/schriften/317.pdf.

Secretary General of the Assembly, "Procedure for the election of judges to the European Court of Human Rights," SG-AS (2019) 05 ["Sawicki Memo"].

Secretary General of the Council of Europe, Letter to the President of the Parliamentary Assembly (September 16, 2004), Doc. 10263, Election of a judge to the European Court of Human Rights with respect to Slovakia, available at http://assembly.coe.int/nw/xml/XRef/X2H-Xref-ViewHTML.asp?FileID=10634&lang=EN.

Secretary General of the Council of Europe, Contribution to the Preparation of the Interlaken Ministerial Conference, SG/Inf(2009)20 December 18, 2009.

Martin Shapiro, "The European Court of Justice," in PETER H. RUSSELL AND DAVID M. O'BRIEN (eds.)JUDICIAL INDEPENDENCE IN THE AGE OF DEMOCRACY: CRITICAL PERSPECTIVES FROM AROUND THE WORLD 273 ((Charlottesville and London: University of Virginia Press, 2001).

Stephen J. Silvia and Aaron Beers Sampson, *Acquis Communautaire and European Exceptionalism: A Genealogy*, ACES Working Paper, July 1, 2003, available at https://www.researchgate.net/profile/Stephen_Silvia/publication/29998554_Acquis_Communautaire_and_European_Exceptionalism_A_Geneaology_ACES_Working_Paper_20031_July_2003/links/0a85e52fa5a459100c000000/Acquis-Communautaire-and-European-Exceptionalism-A-Geneaology-ACES-Working-Paper-20031-July-2003.pdf.

A.W.B. SIMPSON, HUMAN RIGHTS AND THE END OF EMPIRE (Oxford: Oxford University Press, 2001).

Vassilio Skouris, Recommendation relating to the operating rules of the panel provided for in Article 255 TFEU, Brussels, January 11, 2010, 5195/10, JUR 5 INST 2 COUR 1.

Vassilio Skouris, Recommendation concerning the composition of the panel provided for in Article 255 TFEU, Brussels, February 2, 2010, 5932/10 JUR 57 INST 26 COUR 13.

Antoine Spohr, "Cour européenne des droits de l'homme: les trois candidats français ajournés," (April 12, 2011), available at https://blogs.mediapart.fr/aspohr/blog/120411/cour-europeenne-des-droits-de-lhomme-les-trois-candidats-francais-ajournes.

SIMON SPRINGER, KEAN BIRCH, and JULIE MACLEAVY (eds.), THE HANDBOOK OF NEOLIBERALISM (New York: Routledge, 2016).

Steering Committee for Human Rights, Ministers' Deputies Exchange of Views with Mr. Luzius Wildhaber, Chairman of the Advisory Panel of Experts on Candidates for Election to the European Court of Human Rights (April 4, 2012), in DH-GDR (2013)005, February 5 2013 ["2012 Exchange of Views"].

Steering Committee for Human Rights, Ministers' Deputies Exchange of Views with Mr. Luzius Wildhaber, Chairman of the Advisory Panel of Experts on Candidates for Election to the European Court of Human Rights (January 30, 2013), in DH-GDR (2013)005, February 5, 2013 ["2013 Exchange of Views"].

Steering Committee for Human Rights, Committee of Experts on the System of the European Convention on Human Rights (DH-SYSC), Exchange of Views with Mr. John Murray, President of the Advisory Panel of Experts on Candidates for Election to the European Court of Human Rights (March 1, 2017), in DH-SYSC-I(2017)016, May 4, 2017 ["2017 Exchange of Views"].

Steering Committee for Human Rights, CDDH Report on the Review of the Functioning of the Advisory Panel of Experts on Candidates for Election as Judge to the European Court of Human Rights, ["CDDH 2013 Report"] CDDH(2013)R79 Addendum II (November 29, 2013).

Steering Committee for Human Rights, CDDH Report on the Longer-Term Future of the System of the European Convention on Human Rights, CDDH(2015)R84 Addendum I, available at http://www.coe.int/t/dghl/standardsetting/cddh/reformechr/CDDH(2015)R84_Addendum%20I_EN-Final.pdf ["Report on the Longer-Term Future of the System"].

Steering Committee for Human Rights, Terms of reference of the CDDH and its subordinate bodies for the biennium 2016–2017, as adopted by the Committee of Ministers at their 1241st meeting (November 24–26, 2015), available at www.coe.int/t/dghl/standardsetting/cddh/Mandats CDDH 2016-2017_EN.asp.

Steering Committee for Human Rights, Committee of Experts on the System of the ECHR, [Draft] Report on the process of selection and election of judges of the [ECtHR], DH-SYSC(2017)R4 Addendum (November 10, 2017) ["2017 Report on the process of selection and election of ECtHR judges"].

Ezra N. Suleiman, Politics, Power, and Bureaucracy in France: The Administrative Elite (Princeton, NJ: Princeton University Press, 1974).

Alec Stone Sweet, "The Third Chamber Model: A Review and Defense," in The Birth of Judicial Politics in France: The Constitutional Council in Comparative Perspective 209 (Oxford, New York: Oxford University Press, 1992).

Alec Stone Sweet, Governing with Judges: Constitutional Politics in Europe (Oxford: Oxford University Press, 2000) ["Governing with Judges"].

Alec Stone Sweet, "Constitutional Courts" in Michel Rosenfeld and András Sajó (eds.), The Oxford Handbook of Comparative Constitutional Law 816 (Oxford: Oxford University Press, 2012).

Alec Stone Sweet, Wayne Sandholtz, and Neil Fligstein (eds.), The Institutionalization of Europe (Oxford: Oxford University Press, 2001).

John Thompson, Political Scandal: Power and Visibility in the Media Age (Cambridge: Polity Press, 2000).

Georg Vanberg, The Politics of Constitutional Review in Germany (Cambridge: Cambridge University Press, 2005).

Georg Vanberg, "Establishing and Maintaining Judicial Independence," in Keith E. Whittington, R. Daniel Kelemen, and Gregory A. Caldeira (eds.), The Oxford Handbook of Law and Politics 99 (Oxford: Oxford University Press, 2008).

Georges Vandersanden, "The Real Test—How to Contribute to a Better Justice: The Experience of the Civil Service Tribunal," in Michal Bobek (ed.), Selecting Europe's Judges: A Critical Review of the Appointment Procedures to the European Courts 86 (Oxford: Oxford University Press, 2015).

ANTOINE VAUCHEZ, BROKERING EUROPE: EURO-LAWYERS AND THE MAKING OF A TRANSNATIONAL POLITY (Cambridge: Cambridge University Press, 2015) ["BROKERING EUROPE"].

Venice Commission (European Commission for Democracy Through Law), "Report on the Independence of the Judiciary—Part I: The Independence of Judges," CDL-AD(2010)004.

Bo Vesterdorf, President of the Court of First Instance of the European Communities, Oral presentation to the "Discussion Circle" on the Court of Justice on February 24, 2003, CONV 575/03, available at http://european-convention.europa.eu/pdf/reg/en/03/cv00/cv00575.en03.pdf.

Bo Vesterdorf, *A Constitutional Court for the EU*, 4 I•CON 607 (2006), available at https://academic.oup.com/icon/article/4/4/607/640268.

Bo Vesterdorf, *La nomination des juges de la Cour de Justice de l'Union européenne*, 47(3) CAHIERS DE DROIT EUROPÉEN 610 (2012).

Stefan Voigt, "Positive Constitutional Economics: A Survey," in CHARLES ROWLEY (ed.), CONSTITUTIONAL POLITICAL ECONOMY IN A PUBLIC CHOICE PERSPECTIVE 11 (Dordrecht: Kluwer, 1997).

Joseph Weiler, *The Transformation of Europe*, 100 YALE L.J. 2403 (1991).

JOSEPH WEILER, THE CONSTITUTION OF EUROPE: DO THE NEW CLOTHES HAVE AN EMPEROR? (Cambridge: Cambridge University Press, 1999).

Joseph Weiler, "Epilogue: The Judicial Après-Nice," in GRÁINNE DE BÚRCA and J.H.H. WEILER (eds.), THE EUROPEAN COURT OF JUSTICE 215 (Oxford: Oxford University Press, 2002).

Alexander Wendt, *Anarchy is What States Make of It*, 46 INT. ORG. 391 (1992).

ALFRED NORTH WHITEHEAD, ALFRED NORTH WHITEHEAD, THE CONCEPT OF NATURE: TARNER LECTURES DELIVERED IN TRINITY COLLEGE, NOVEMBER 1919 (Cambridge: Cambridge University Press, 1920).

MARLENE WIND and MIGUEL POIARES MADURO (eds.), THE TRANSFORMATION OF EUROPE: TWENTY-FIVE YEARS ON (New York: Cambridge University Press, 2017).

WORLD BANK, DOING BUSINESS IN 2004: UNDERSTANDING REGULATION (Washington, DC: World Bank, 2004).

Leo Zwaak, "The Reform of the Supervisory Mechanism under the European Convention on Human Rights: Does it Really Matter?," in MIELLE BULTERMAN, AART HENDRIKS, and JACQUELINE SMITH (eds.), TO BAEHR IN OUR MINDS: ESSAYS ON HUMAN RIGHTS FROM THE HEART OF THE NETHERLANDS 195 (Utrecht: SIM, 1998).

Index

For the benefit of digital users, indexed terms that span two pages (e.g., 52–53) may, on occasion, appear on only one of those pages.